HISTORY OF THE BRITISH ARMY INFANTRY COLLAR BADGE

COLIN CHURCHILL

THE NAVAL & MILITARY PRESS
Unit 10, Ridgewood Industrial Park,
Uckfield, East Sussex TN22 5QE
WWW.NAVAL-MILITARY-PRESS.CO.UK

© 2002 Colin Churchill
This edition © The Naval & Military Press Ltd 2002

First published in 2001 by
The Naval & Military Press Ltd
Unit 10, Ridgewood Industrial Park,
Uckfield, East Sussex TN22 5QE
www.naval-military-press.com

All rights reserved. No part of this book may be reproduced, stored in a retrieval system, or transmitted in any form or by any means without the prior written permission of the publisher, nor be otherwise circulated in any form of binding or cover other than that in which it is published and without a similar condition being imposed on the subsequent publisher.

Designed and produced by Well House Publishing

Printed and bound by Antony Rowe Ltd, Eastbourne

Foreword

Following the publication of my book *British Army Collar Badges, 1881 to the Present* in 1986, which was never meant to be other than a beginner's guide, and which is now out of print, it has become increasingly apparent that a far more detailed work is required for this much neglected subject.

This book is intended to fill this gap and as far as possible to become the standard reference book on the subject, containing both detailed descriptions and variations of each badge worn, with dates when it was worn and on which uniform; with mention of metals and also reasons why a particular design was chosen with explanations of battle honours and mottoes.

Dates and details of Submissions, Approvals, Authorisations, Army Orders, Sealings and depositing at the Army Clothing Department etc. have been quoted, as well as relevant correspondence between the War Office, regiments and manufacturers.

Colin Churchill

Collar badge backings and items worn as both a cap and a collar badge have been covered in the text. The written word is supported by over 2000 actual size photographs and line drawings (not drawn exactly to scale and, as some have been noted from sketches, the accuracy of all details cannot be guaranteed) covering some 800 units. These have been numbered so that each item can, in the future, be recognised and referred to by merely quoting these numbers.

I have tried to standardise the many varied terms used to describe a collar badge, and my aim has been to contain in one book all the information required by a collector/researcher of the British Army Infantry collar badge. Therefore information is included on the evolution and construction of the item, and the uniform it was worn on; additionally the wider field includes sources of information, identification, the preservation and display of the badges, and finally the pitfalls for the unwary.

In brief, I have tried to produce the kind of work I would like to have had available when I first started my collar badge research!

To assist in identification, items have also been included which are often mistaken for British Army collar badges, not only Commonwealth and foreign items but also civilian organisations such as police, fire, ambulance and other civic services. Similarly, such items as beret badges, helmet plate centres, waist belt devices, sweetheart brooches, Old Comrade Associations lapel badges, and cap badges with parts missing, all of which can easily be confused with a regimental collar badge.

Lack of space has made it impossible to illustrate all examples of 'facing pairs' of collar badges, but in the instances of the badges being rare, particularly those prior to 1881, then such pairs have been illustrated.

The same problem has also meant that I am unable to include separate chapters on items such as feather plumes, tigers, castles, dragons and roses, all areas that cause identification problems. To compensate, such collar badges are described in detail and supported by photographs.

Some specialist collectors include in their collections, variations according to the number and position of the fastening lugs on the reverse of the badge. These only vary according to the manufacturer and in view of the additional text that would have been involved in covering this aspect, this topic is not covered in this book.

My first collar badge book only covered items post-1881, and few collectors would disagree that the most difficult period, both for information and collecting, is pre-1881, not only for the regiments of the Line, but also Militia and Volunteers.

A list of pre-1881 Infantry of the Line badges appeared in 1951, supported by photographs and line drawings in 1952. These have largely been the only source of information hitherto. Many years of original research has shown that both the list and the photographs contain many mistakes and the re-issue of both, albeit in good faith, has merely compounded the original errors. However, even now some questions remain unanswered.

Another difficult period for precise information is the early 1950s which covers not only the replacing of the King's crown for the Queen's crown, but also the introduction of anodised aluminium collar badges for other ranks, as well as Officers' No. 1 Dress replacing Service Dress. One often needs to know, for example, whether there was a King's crown anodised for a certain regiment, or did that regiment go direct to a Queen's crown anodised from a King's crown metal? Similarly was there a Queen's crown bronze collar badge in between a bronze King's crown and a silver/gilt Queen's crown? These points are covered in the text.

For so comprehensive a study it has not been possible to cover every single infantry unit in this one book, and it is my intention to publish a second volume covering such units together with Cavalry, Yeomanry, Arms, Services, Women's Forces and sundries.

Obviously over such a long period covered in this book, there will be omissions and it is my hope that, by publishing, new information will be forthcoming that can be included in any re-print.

Naturally, I would not have been able to complete this work without the help from many organisations and individuals all of whom have given freely of both their time and their knowledge. I am indebted to them and included their names in a separate list of acknowledgements.

Happy Collecting!

Acknowledgements

I am very grateful for the help, assistance and advice I have received from militaria collectors who have freely given of their knowledge, photographs and loan of collar badges in order for me to complete this book.

I would especially like to mention the following:

Army Museums Ogilby Trust, especially Colonel P. S. Walton and
  Major M. A. Tamplin T.D.
The Imperial War Museum, especially M. J. R. Allen Esq.
The National Army Museum, especially I. G. Robertson Esq. M.A., F.M.A.,
  P. B. Boyden Esq., Ph.D. M.A., and Mrs. J. L. C. Smurthwaite B.A.
The Ministry of Defence
The Ministry of Defence Whitehall Library, especially Mrs. J. Blacklaw.
The Directorate of Quality Assurance, especially R. N. Stock Esq.,
  P. Kavanagh Esq., M. Bourton Esq.

D. N. Anderson Esq., T. Ashley Esq., J. W. Atkin Esq., A. Barrowcliffe Esq., D. Barrett Esq., the late G. Bartlett Esq., R. Batten Esq., Major R. W. Bennett B.Sc., R. J. S. Betts Esq., D. Brown Esq., P. Brydon Esq., W. Y. Carman Esq., F.S.A., F.R.Hist.S., Field Marshal Sir John Chapple, G.C.B., C.B.E., M.A., F.Z.S., F.R.G.S., Major K.D. Clarke, Major T. Craze, R.C. Cornish Esq., J. Denton Esq., E. Dickinson Esq., D. Dodds Esq., Lt Col C. D. Darrock, G. Frost Esq., the late J. W. F. Gaylor Esq., B. Golding Esq., R. Flood Esq., the late Peter Fuller Esq., R. Handley Esq., Lt Col R. E. L. Hodges, Lt. Cmdr K. B. Hook R.D., R.N., (retd), D. E. Ivall Esq., H. L. King Esq., N. E. H. Litchfield Esq., Major D. D. A. Linaker, D. Mills Esq., the late Lieut Bryn Owen R.N. (Retd), the late G. Archer Parfitt Esq., E. Platt Esq., D. Reeves Esq., D. A. Rutter Esq., the late Mrs. L. Ryan, Lt Col J. D. Sainsbury, R. Sampson Esq., D. Seeney Esq., J. Steele Esq., the late A. C. Sweetnam Esq., P. Taylor Esq., S. Thomas Esq., A. Tonge Esq., D. Twomey Esq., J. Tyler Esq., Col D. R. Wood, J. G. Woodroff Esq., Lt Col R. J. Wyatt M.B.E., T.D.

I am especially grateful to Pauline for her years of typing and computer expertise and also to K. Dixon Pickup Esq. whose suggestions, help, support and encouragement, as well as his expertise and general editing, have so helped me to complete this book.

Abbreviations

a/a	Anodised–Anodised aluminium
A.A.	Anti Aircraft
A.A.G.	Assistant Adjutant General
Bn/Bns	Battalion/Battalions
Bde	brigade
b/m	bi-metal
b/b	blackened brass
bze	bronze
C.I.C.	Commander-in-Chief
C.O.	Commanding Officer
Dress Regs.	Dress Regulations
g/m	gilding metal
H.A.A.	Heavy Anti-Aircraft
K/C	King's Crown
L.A.A.	Light Anti-Aircraft
NCO	Non Commissioned Officer
o/r's	other ranks
Q.C./Q.E.C.	Queen Elizabeth Crown
Q.V.C.	Queen Victoria Crown
r/f	rank and file
Regt.	Regiment
R.V.C.	Rifle Volunteer Corps
R.A.	Royal Artillery
R.E.	Royal Engineers
SL	Searchlight
S/T	Shoulder Title
sil/gilt	silver/gilt
TA	Territorial Army
TF	Territorial Force
Vol/Vols	Volunteer/Volunteers
VB	Volunteer Battalion
VRC	Volunteer Rifle Corps
V.T.C.	Volunteer Training Corps
W.O.	Warrant Officer
w/m	white metal

Glossary of Terms Used

Circle A continuous circular band bearing a motto or title inscription.
(See Fig. 1991)

Strap As for a circle but with a buckle. (See Fig. 56)

Garter When a strap bears the motto of the Most Noble Order of the Garter, 'Honi Soit Qui Mal Y Pense'. This Order was established by King Edward III in 1348 and is the premier Order of chivalry in Great Britain. (See Fig. 185)

Voiding Where part of the badge has been pierced or cut out. It can be anywhere on the item, often in the centre to emphasise the design and sometimes with a coloured cloth or enamel backing to further enhance it.

Non-voided or solid Where only the outline of the badge has been cut out, leaving the item in a solid form.

Index

A

Aberdeen RVC 1st, 2, 3, 4	272
Alexandra Princess of Wales's Own (Yorkshire Regt)	92
Alleyns School Cadet Force	324
Argyllshire RVC, 1st	295
Argyll & Sutherland Highlanders (Princess Louise's)	291
Armagh Light Infantry Militia	286
Army Cyclists	331
Artists Rifles, The Rifle Brigade (Prince Consort's Own)	326
Ayrshire RVC, 1st & 2nd	100

B

Banffshire RVC, 1st	272
Bedfordshire Regt	82 & 327
Bedfordshire Regt (TA)	85
Bedfordshire & Hertfordshire Regt	82
Bedfordshire & Hertfordshire Regt (TA)	85 & 327
Bedfordshire Light Infantry Militia	84
Bedfordshire RVC, 1st	85
Bedfordshire Volunteer Regt	85
Bermuda VRC	258
Berkshire RVC, 1st	215
Berwickshire RVC, 1st	19 & 114
Black Watch (Royal Highland Regt)	186
Border Regt	150
Bradford College Rifle Corps	216
Brecknockshire RVC, 1st	110
Brighton College Cadet Corps	159
Buckinghamshire RVC, 1st & 2nd (Eton College)	192
Buckinghamshire Volunteer Defence Force	192
Bucks VDC	192
Buffs (Royal East Kent Regt)	26

C

Cambridgeshire ACF	313
Cambridgeshire Home Guard	313
Cambridgeshire Militia	68
Cambridgeshire Regt	69 & 313
Cambridgeshire RVC, 1st (Cambridge, Essex & Huntingdonshire)	69

2nd and 3rd (Cambridge University)	69
Cameronians (Scottish Rifles)	116
Cape Town Highlanders	272
Carlow Rifles Militia	234
Cavan Militia	286
Charterhouse School	25
Cheshire Home Guard	103
Cheshire Regt	101
Cheshire RVC, 1st, 2nd (The Earl of Chester's), 3rd, 4th (Cheshire & Derbyshire) and 5th	103
Church Lads Brigade	233
Cinque Ports RVC, 1st (Cinque Ports & Sussex)	157
City of Edinburgh Rifle Vol. Brigade	19
City of Norwich Vols	57
Clackmannanshire & Kinross RVC	295
Clare Militia	300
Connaught Rangers	288
Cornwall RVC, 1st and 2nd	144
Cornwall VTC	145
Cranleigh School	25
Cumberland RVC, 1st	153

D

Denbighshire RVC, 1st	107
Derbyshire Militia, 1st & 2nd (Chatsworth Rifles)	201
Derbyshire RVC, 1st, 2nd, 3rd	201
& 23rd (Glossop)	103
Devon & Dorset Regt	65 & 176
Devonshire Regt	61
Devonshire RVC, 1st (Exeter & South Devon)	63
2nd (Prince of Wales's), 3rd, 4th, 5th, & 9th	63 to 65
Dorsetshire Grammar School OTC	176
Dorset Militia	175
Dorsetshire Home Guard	176
Dorsetshire Regt	171
Dorsetshire RVC, 1st – 11th	176
Douglas RVC, 1st and 2nd	52
Dublin County Light Infantry Militia	304
Duke of Cumberland's Sharpshooters	316
Duke of Edinburgh's (Wiltshire Regt)	238
Duke of Edinburgh's Royal Regt (Berkshire and Wiltshire)	216 & 240
Duke of Lancaster's Own Royal Lancashire Militia, 3rd	206
Duke of Wellington's Regt (West Riding)	146
Duke of York's Royal Military School	81
Dumbartonshire RVC, 1st	295
Dumfrieshire RVC, 1st	115
Dumfries, Roxburgh, Kircudbright & Selkirk (Scottish Borderers) Militia	100
Durban Light Infantry	259
Durham Fusiliers Militia	258

Durham Light Infantry	256
Durham RVC, 1st (Durham & North Riding or York), 2nd, 3rd (Sunderland), 4th & 5th	258

E

East Anglian Regt, 1st (Royal Norfolk & Suffolk)	57 & 69
2nd (Duchess of Gloucester's Own Royal Lincolnshire & Nottinghamshire)	60 & 212
3rd	85 & 198
East Anglian Brigade	57 & 89
Eastbourne College Cadet Corps	159
East Devon Militia, 1st	62
East Kent Militia	28
East Lancashire Regt	134
(East Linton) Corps, Haddington RV, 5th	19
East Norfolk Militia, 2nd	56
East Surrey Regt	138 & 324
East York Militia	80
East Yorkshire Regt (Duke of York's Own)	79
Eastern Regt of Essex Militia	197
Edinburgh (or Queens) Regt of Light Infantry Militia	19
Elgin RVC, 1st	268
Ellesmere College Cadet Corps	227
Essex Regt	195
Essex Rifles Militia	197
Essex RVC, 1st, 2nd, 3rd & 4th	197
Essex & Suffolk Cyclists	198
Eton College VRC, 2nd	192

F

Fermanagh Light Infantry Infantry Militia	122
Fifeshire RVC, 1st	189
First Surrey Regt of Volunteers	323
Flintshire & Carnarvonshire RVC, 1st	107
Forester Brigade	89
Forfarshire RVC	188
1st (Dundee)	188
2nd (Forfarshire or Angus)	188
3rd (Dundee Highland)	188
10th (Dundee Highland)	188

G

Galloway RVC	115
Galway Militia	290
Giggleswick School CCF	149
Glamorganshire Militia	183
Glamorganshire RVC, 1st, 2nd & 3rd	184
Glasgow Highlanders, The HLI	265

Glasgow High School Cadet Corps	117
Gloucestershire Regt	124
Gloucestershire RVC, 1st (City of Bristol), 2nd	126
Godalming School	25
Gordon Highlanders	270
Green Howards (Alexandra, Princess of Wales's Own Yorkshire Regt)	92
Green Jackets (43 & 52), 1st	193
Green Jackets (The KRRC) 2nd	233
Green Jackets (The Rifle Brigade) 3rd	309
Gresham School	57
Guildford Royal Grammar School	25

H

Haddingtonshire RVC, 1st	19
Hamilton Light Infantry, Canada	72
Hampshire Militia	162
Hampshire RVC, 1st, 2nd, 3rd, 4th & 19th (Bournemouth)	163 & 164
Harrow School Cadets	232
Hauraki Regt, 6th, New Zealand	133
Herefordshire Light Infantry	329
Herefordshire RVC, 1st–8th	329
Herefordshire, 1st (Hereford & Radnor) RVC	329
Herefordshire, 1st (Hereford & Radnor) VRC	329
Hertfordshire Militia	84
Hertfordshire Regt	327
Hertfordshire RVC, 1st & 2nd	84
Hertfordshire 1st–7th, 9th–11th & 14th	327
Hertfordshire Volunteer Regt	328
Highland Borderers Light Infantry Militia	294
Highland Light Infantry	261
Highland Light Infantry Militia	276
Highland Volunteers, 51st	273
Highlanders (Seaforth, Gordons & Camerons)	274
Hong Kong Police	216
Huntingdonshire Cyclists	211
Huntingdonshire Rifles Militia	234

I

Inns of Court OTC	326
Inns of Court Reserve Corps	326
Inns of Court RVC, 14th & 23rd	307
Inns of Court Reserve Corps	326
Inns of Court Volunteers	326
Inns of Court & City Yeomanry	326
Inverness, Banff, Elgin & Nairn Militia	276
Inverness-shire (Inverness Highland) RVC, 1st	276
Isle of Man RVC, 1st & 2nd (Douglas)	52
Isle of Wight RVC, 1st	165

K

Kent Cyclists	219 & 331
Kent RVC, 1st	219
Kent RVC, 2nd (East Kent) & 5th (Weald of Kent)	28
Kent RVC, 3rd (West Kent)	219 & 322
Kent RVC, 4th & 26th (Royal Arsenal)	322
Kent RVC, 7th, 8th, 13th, 18th, 21st, 25th, 27th, 28th, 32nd & 34th	322
Kent Volunteer Fencibles	28 & 219
Kerry Militia	300
Kildare Rifles Militia	304
Kilkenny Fusiliers Militia	91
Kincardineshire & Aberdeen or Deeside Highland RVC	272
King Edward VI School, Chelmsford CCF	198
King's Own Borderers	112
King's County Royal Rifles Militia	298
King's Own Light Infantry Regt of Militia	307
King's Own Royal Border Regt	31 & 154
King's Own Royal Regt (Lancaster)	29
King's Own Scottish Borderers	112
King's Own 1st Staffordshire Militia	169
King's Own 2nd Staffordshire Light Infantry Militia	248
King's Own 3rd Staffordshire Rifles Militia	248
King's Own Yorkshire Light Infantry	221
King's Regt (Liverpool)	46
King's Regt (Manchester & Liverpool)	53 & 244
King's Royal Rifle Corps	233
King's Shropshire & Herefordshire Light Infantry	330
King's Shropshire Light Infantry	224

L

Lancing College Cadet Corps	159
Lanarkshire RVC	
1st (Glasgow 1st Western), 2nd & 3rd	117 & 118
4th (Glasgow 1st Northern) & 7th	118
5th (Glasgow 2nd Northern), 6th, 8th (The Blythsword), 9th & 10th (Glasgow Highland)	263 & 264
Lancashire Fusiliers	95
Lancashire Regt (POW's Vols)	137 & 180
Lancashire RVC	
1st, 5th, 13th, 15th, 18th (Liverpool Irish)	49, 50 & 51
19th (Liverpool Press Guard)	50
39th, 63rd, 64th, 71st, 80th & 86th	50 & 51
2nd & 3rd	136
4th & 7th	244
8th & 12th	96
9th, 21st, 47th, 48th & 49th	180
10th	31
11th & 14th	50 & 206
Lancashire Volunteers	135
Leeds Grammar School CCF	149

Leeds Pals	78
Leeds Rifles	77
Leicestershire Militia	88
Leicestershire Regt	87
Leicestershire RVC, 1st	88
Leitram Militia	307
Leitram Rifles	307
Light Infantry	145, 223, 227 & 259
Lincolnshire Regt	58
Lincolnshire RVC, 1st & 2nd	60
Liverpool Vols	53
Liverpool Regt	46
Liverpool Rifle Volunteer Brigade	50
Liverpool University OTC	49
London Regts	See below
London Irish Rifles, The Royal Ulster Rifles	321
London RVC, 1st (City of London VRB)	314
London RVC, 2nd	315
London RVC, 3rd	236 & 315
London VRC, 1st (City of London VRC)	314
London Scottish (Gordon Highlanders) TA	273 & 319
Londonderry Light Infantry Militia	122
Lothian Regt	17
Lowland Volunteers, 52nd	
'A' (Royal Scots)	17 & 18
'B' (The Royal Scots Fusiliers)	100
'C' (KOSB)	113
'D' (Cameronians, Scottish Rifles)	118
'E' (HLI)	265
Loyal Regt (North Lancashire)	204
THE LONDON REGIMENTS	
1–4 (City of London) Battalion, (Royal Fusiliers)	314
5 (City of London) Battalion, (London Rifle Brigade)	314
6 (City of London) Battalion, (City of London Rifles)	315
7 (City of London) Battalion	315
7 (City of London) Battalion, (Post Office Rifles)	316
8 (City of London) Battalion, (Post Office Rifles)	316
9 (County of London) Battalion, (Queen Victoria's Rifles)	316
10 (County of London) Battalion, (Paddington Rifles)	317
10 (County of London) Battalion, (Hackney)	317
11 (County of London) Battalion, (Finsbury Rifles)	317
12 (County of London) Battalion, (Rangers)	317
13 (County of London) Battalion, (Kensington)	318
14 (County of London) Battalion, (London Scottish)	307 & 319
15 (County of London) Battalion, (POW's Own Civil Service Rifles)	235
16 (County of London) Battalion, (Queen's Westminster Rifles)	235 & 320
17 (County of London) Battalion, (Poplar & Stepney Rifles)	321
18 (County of London) Battalion, (London Irish Rifles)	321
19 (County of London) Battalion, (St Pancras)	322
20 (County of London) Battalion, (Blackheath & Woolwich)	322
21 (County of London) Battalion, (1st Surrey Rifles)	323
22 (County of London) Battalion, (The Queen's)	324
23 (County of London) Battalion	324
24 (County of London) Battalion, (The Queen's)	325

25 (County of London) Battalion, (Cyclist)	325
28 (County of London) Battalion, (Artists' Rifles)	325

M

Macquari Regt, N. S. Wales	72
Malvern College OTC	133
Manchester Regt	241
Manchester Regt TA (Ardwick and Ashton) (T)	244
Manchester RVC, 1st, 2nd & 3rd	244
Middlesex Cadets	232
Middlesex Light Infantry Militia, 5th	230
Middlesex Regt (Duke of Cambridge's Own)	228
MIDDLESEX RVC	
1st (Victorian Rifles)	234 & 316
1st (Victoria & St George's Rifles)	316
2nd (South Middlesex)	234
3rd	230
4th (West London)	235 & 318
5th	45
6th (St George's)	234 & 316
7th (London Scottish)	307 & 319
8th	231
9th	45
10th	45
11th (St George's)	45 & 316
12th	235 & 319
13th	235
14th (Inns of Court)	326
15th	308 & 319
15th (The Custom & Docks)	307
16th (London Irish)	308 & 321
17th	322
18th	317
19th	316
20th (Artists)	308 & 325
21st (Civil Service)	235 & 317 & 319
22nd (Queen's Westminster Rifles)	45 & 235
23rd	45 & 326
23rd (Inns of Court)	45 & 307
24th (Post Office)	305 & 316
25th	235 & 319
26th (Cyclists)	236 & 325
28th (London Irish)	308 & 321
29th (North Middlesex)	322
36th	317
37th (St Giles' & St George's, Bloomsbury)	316
38th (Artists)	308 & 325
39th	317
40th (Central London Regiment)	317
49th	308 & 316
50th (Bank of England)	235 & 320
Middlesex (South West Middlesex), 8th VRC	231
Middlesex Volunteer Regt	231
Midland Brigade	89 & 199
Midlothian and Peebles RVC, 2nd	19

INDEX

Midlothian RVC, 3rd (Penicuik)	19
Monaghan Militia	286
Monmouthshire Regt	311
Monmouthshire RVC, 1st, 2nd & 3rd	110 & 311

N

Newcastle-on-Tyne RVC, 1st	35
Norfolk Regt	54
Norfolk RVC, 1st (City of Norwich), 2nd, 3rd & 4th	56
Norfolk Volunteer Regt	57
North Cork Rifles Militia	234
North Durham Militia, 2nd	258
North Hampshire Militia	162
North Irish Brigade	279 & 280
North Mayo Fusiliers Militia	290
North Staffordshire Regt (The POW's)	246
North Tipperary Light Infantry Militia, 2nd	91
North York Rifles	93
Northern Cyclists	37 & 331
Northampton & Rutland Militia	210
Northamptonshire Regt	208
Northamptonshire RVC, 1st	211
Northamptonshire VTC	212
Northumberland Fusiliers	32
Northumberland Light Infantry Militia	35
Northumberland RVC, 1st (Northumberland & Berwick-on-Tweed) & 2nd	35
Northumberland Volunteers	259
Nottinghamshire Militia	201
Nottinghamshire RVC, 1st (Robin Hoods) & 2nd	202

O

Oakham School, Rutland	89
Oxfordshire Light Infantry	190
Oxfordshire Militia	191
Oxfordshire RVC, 1st (Oxford University) & 2nd	191
Oxfordshire & Buckinghamshire Light Infantry	191

P

Pembrokeshire RVC, 1st (Pembroke, Carmarthen & Haverfordshire)	184
(Penicuik) Midlothian RVC	19
Perthshire Militia	188
Perthshire RVC, 1st (Perthshire) & 2nd (Perthshire Highland)	188
Prince Albert's (Somersetshire Light Infantry)	70
POW's Leinster Regt (Royal Canadians)	297
POW's, Royal Regt of Longford Light Infantry Militia	307
POW's Own Donegal Militia	123

POW's Own Royal Regt of Renfrew Militia	294
POW's Own Regt of Yorkshire	78 & 81
POW's Own (West Yorkshire Regt)	75
POW's Volunteers South Lancashire Regt)	177
Princess Louise's Kensington Regt, Middlesex Regt	318
Princess of Wales's Own (Yorkshire Regt)	92
Princess of Wales's Royal Regt (Queen's & Royal Hampshire)	166

Q

22 (Queen's) R.V.C.	320
Queen Victoria's Rifles, KRRC	317
Queen's Edinburgh Rifles Battalions	19
Queen's Lancashire Regiment	137 & 207
Queen's Own Buffs, The Royal Kent Regt	28 & 219
Queen's Own Cameron Highlanders	275
Queen's Own Highlanders (Seaforth & Camerons)	269 & 277
Queen's Own Royal Dublin City Militia	304
Queen's Own Royal Tower Hamlets Light Infantry Militia	306
Queen's Own Royal West Kent Regt	217
Queen's Regt	159 & 232
Queen's Royal Regt (West Surrey)	21
Queen's Royal Rifles	316
Queen's Royal Surrey Regt	25 & 141
Queen's (Royal West Surrey Regt)	21
Queen's Westminsters KRRC	321

R

Radnorshire RVC, 1st & 2nd	329
Rangers, KRRC	318
REGIMENTS OF FOOT	
1st (The Royal Scots)	17
2nd (Queen's Royal)	21
3rd (East Kent - The Buffs)	26
4th (The King's Own Royal)	29
5th (Northumberland Fusiliers)	32
6th (Royal 1st Warwickshire)	38
7th (Royal Fusiliers)	42
8th (The King's)	46
9th (East Norfolk)	54
10th (North Lincoln)	58
11th (North Devonshire)	61
12th (East Suffolk)	66
13th (1st Somersetshire) (Prince Albert's Light Infantry)	70
14th (Buckinghamshire – POW's Own)	75
15th (York, East Riding)	79
16th (Bedfordshire)	82
17th (Leicestershire)	87
18th (The Royal Irish)	90
19th (1st York, North Riding – POW's Own)	92
20th (East Devonshire)	95
21st (Royal Scots Fusiliers)	98

Regiment	Page
22nd (Cheshire)	101
23rd (Royal Welsh Fusiliers)	105
24th (2nd Warwickshire)	108
25th (The King's Own Borderers)	112
26th (Cameronians)	116
27th (Inniskilling)	119
28th (North Gloucestershire)	124
29th (Worcestershire)	128
30th (Cambridgeshire)	134
31st (Huntingdonshire)	138
32nd (Cornwall Light Infantry)	142
33rd (Duke of Wellington's)	146
34th (Cumberland)	150
35th (Royal Sussex)	155
36th (Herefordshire)	128
37th (North Hampshire)	160
38th (1st Staffordshire)	167
39th (Dorsetshire)	171
40th (2nd Somertsetshire)	177
41st (The Welsh)	181
42nd Royal Highland (The Black Watch)	186
43rd (Monmouthshire Light Infantry)	190
44th (East Essex)	194
45th (Nottinghamshire-Sherwood Foresters)	199
46th (South Devonshire)	142
47th (Lancashire)	204
48th (Northamptonshire)	208
49th (Hertfordshire – Princess Charlotte of Wales's)	213
50th (The Queen's Own)	217
51st (2nd Yorkshire, West Riding) or King's Own Light Infantry	220
52nd (Oxfordshire Light Infantry)	190
53rd (Shropshire)	224
54th (West Norfolk)	171
55th (Westmoreland)	150
56th (West Essex)	194
57th (West Middlesex)	228
58th (Rutlandshire)	208
59th (2nd Nottinghamshire)	134
60th (The King's Royal Rifle Corps)	233
61st (South Gloucestershire)	124
62nd (The Wiltshire)	237
63rd (West Suffolk)	241
64th (2nd Staffordshire)	245
65th (2nd Yorkshire, North Riding)	250
66th (Berkshire)	213
67th (South Hampshire)	160
68th (Durham Light Infantry)	256
69th (South Lincolnshire)	181
70th (Surrey)	138
71st (Highland Light Infantry)	260
72nd (Duke of Albany's Own Highlanders)	266
73rd (Pertshire)	186
74th (Highlanders)	260
75th (Stirlingshire)	270
76th	146
77th (East Middlesex – The Duke of Cambridge's Own)	228
78th (Highlanders) - (Ross-Shire Buffs)	266
79th (Queen's Own Cameron Highlanders)	275
80th (Staffordshire Volunteers)	167

81st (Loyal Lincoln Volunteers)	204
82nd (Prince of Wales's Volunteers)	177
83rd (County of Dublin)	279
84th (York & Lancaster)	250
85th (Bucks Volunteers) (King's Light Infantry)	224
86th (Royal County Down)	278
87th (Royal Irish Fusiliers)	281
88th (Connaught Rangers)	288
89th Princess Victoria's)	281
90th (Perthshire Volunteers – Light Infantry)	116
91st (Princess Louise's Argyllshire Highlanders)	291
92nd (Gordon Highlanders)	270
93rd (Sutherland Highlanders)	291
94th	288
95th (Derbyshire)	199
96th	241
97th (The Earl of Ulster)	217
98th (The Prince of Wales')	245
99th (The Duke of Edinburgh's)	237
100th (Prince of Wales's Royal Canadians)	297
101st (Royal Bengal Fusiliers)	299
102nd (Royal Madras Fusiliers)	302
103rd (Royal Bombay Fusiliers)	302
104th (Bengal Fusiliers)	299
105th (Madras Light Infantry)	220
106th (Bombay Light Infantry)	256
107th (Bengal Infantry)	155
108th (Madras Infantry)	119
109th (Bombay Infantry)	297
Reigate Grammar School	25
Renfrewshire RVC, 1st, 2nd & 3rd	295
Rifle Brigade	306
17th (Rosebery) Battalion, Royal Scots	20
Ross, Caithness, Sutherland & Cromarty (Highland) Rifle Militia	268
Rosscommon Militia	290
Ross-shire (Ross Highland) RVC, 1st	268
Roseburgh & Selkirk (The Border) VRC	114
Royal Aberdeenshire Highlanders Militia	272
Royal Anglian Regt	
Royal Norfolk Regt	57
Royal Lincolnshire Regt	60
Beds & Herts Regt	86
Royal Leicestershire Regt	89
Northamptonshire Regt	211
Royal Antrim Rifles Militia	280
Royal Ayrshire & Wigtown Rifles (The Prince Regent's Own)	100
ROYAL ARTILLERY	
7th Brigade, South Irish Division	300
52nd S. L. Regt, (Queen's Edinburgh, The Royal Scots)	19
60th (City of London) A.A. Brigade	314
61st (Finsbury Rifles) A.A. Brigade	317
203rd (TS) Battalion, 101st Field Regt	36
211th (South Wales) Light AD Battery, RA (V) of 104th Light AD Regt	312
350th (The Robin Hood Foresters) Heavy Regt	203
439th (Tyne) Regt, RA (Tyneside Scottish)	36
565th Battery RA (TA)	318

567th (M) LAA/SL Regt, RA (City of London)	316
577th (The Robin Hoods Sherwood Foresters LAA/JL Regt)	203
603rd (M) H.A.A. Regt	311
624th & 625th LAA Regt (Royal Fusiliers)	314
626th H.A.A. Regt RA (TA)	51
629th (The Cambridgeshire Regt) LAA Regt RA (TA)	313
629th The Cambridgeshire Regt) Parachute Light Regt, RA (TA)	313
637th (H) A.A. Regt RA	312
648th H.A.A. Regt	317
'R' (King's Liverpool Scottish) Battery West Lancashire Regt RA (TA)	49
670th L.A.A. Regt (TA)	36
Royal Berkshire Militia	215
Royal Berkshire Regt (Princess Charlotte of Wales's)	214
Royal Berkshire Territorials	216
Royal Brecknock Rifle Corps	109
Royal Bucks (King's Own) Militia	191
Royal Carnarvon Rifle Corps	107
Royal Cheshire Light Infantry Militia, 1st	102
Royal Cheshire Militia, 2nd	102
Royal Cornwall Rangers, Duke of Cornwall's Own Rifles	144
ROYAL CORPS OF SIGNALS	
41st (Princess Louises's Kensingtons)	318
41st Princess Louises's Kensington) Signals Squadron (Vols) of the 31st (Greater London) Signal Regt (Vols)	318
47th (2nd London) Div. Signals	325
Signals Reporting Regt (Princess Louise's Kensington Regt)	318
Royal Cumberland Militia	152
Royal Denbigh & Merioneth Rifles	106
Royal Dublin Fusiliers	303
Royal East Middlsex Militia	230
Royal Elthorne or 5th Middlesex Light Infantry Militia	230
ROYAL ENGINEERS	
31st (City of London Rifles) A-A Battalion	315
32nd (7th City of London) A-A Battalion	316
33rd (St Pancras) A-A Battalion	322
34th (The Queen's Own Royal West Kent) A-A Battalion	323
35th (First Surrey Rifles) A-A Battalion	323
38th (The King's Rifles) A-A Battalion	50
40th A-A Battalion	324
350th (The Robin Hood Foresters) Field Squadron of 49th (West Riding) District	203
1st North Midland Field Company	169
Royal Flint Rifles Militia	234
Royal Fusiliers (City of London Regiment)	42
Royal Glamorgan Light Infantry Militia	183
Royal Gloucester, Berkshire & Wiltshire Regiment	127
Royal Green Jackets	
Oxford & Bucks Light Infantry	193
KRRC	233
Rifle Brigade	309
Royal Guernsey Light Infantry Militia	163
Royal Hampshire Regiment	160
Royal Herefordshire Militia	226
Royal Highland Fusiliers	100 & 265

Royal Inniskilling Fusiliers	119
Royal Irish Fusiliers (Princess Victoria's)	282
Royal Irish Rangers	123, 280, 286 & 287
Royal Irish Regiment	90
Royal Irish Reserve Regiment	280
Royal Irish Rifles	278
Royal Jersey Militia	162
Royal Lanark Militia, 1st	263
Royal Lanark Militia, 2nd	117
Royal Lancashire Militia	
1st (Duke of Lancaster's Own)	30
2nd (Duke of Lancaster's Own Rifles)	49
3rd	206
4th (Duke of Lancaster's Own) Light Infantry	180
5th	136
6th	244
7th	96
Royal Leicestershire Regiment	87
Royal Limerick County Militia (Fusiliers)	300
Royal Lincolnshire Regiment	58
Royal London Militia	43
Royal Louth Rifles Militia	280
Royal Meath Militia	298
Royal Milita of Island of Jersey	162
Royal Montgomery Rifles	110
Royal Munster Fusiliers	299
Royal Norfolk Regiment	54
Royal Norfolk Territorials	57
Royal North Down Rifles Militia	280
Royal North Gloucestershire Militia	126
Royal North Lincolnshire Militia	59
Royal Northumberland Fusiliers	32
Royal Perthshire Rifle Regiment of Militia	188
Royal Queen's County Rifles Militia	298
Royal Radnor Rifles	109
Royal Regiment of Fusiliers	37, 41, 45 & 97
Royal Regiment of Wales	111, 185 & 312
Royal Rifle Regiment of Middlesex Militia, 2nd	234
Royal Scots (The Royal Regiment)	17
Royal Scots (Lothian Regiment)	17
Royal Scots Fusiliers	98
Royal Sherwood Foresters or Nottingham Regiment of Militia	201
Royal South Downs Light Infantry Militia	280
Royal South Gloucestershire Light Infantry Militia	126
Royal South Lincolnshire Militia	59
Royal South Middlesex Militia, 4th	44
Royal South Wales Borderers Militia (Royal Radnor & Brecknock Rifles)	109
Royal Surrey Militia	
1st	140
2nd	23
3rd	140

INDEX

Royal Sussex Light Infantry Militia	157
Royal Sussex Regiment	155
ROYAL TANK CORPS/ ROYAL TANK REGIMENT	
40th (The King's) Royal Tank Regiment	50
42nd (7th (23rd London) Battalion) The East Surrey Regt Bn, RTC	325
Royal Tower Hamlets Militia, 1st & 2nd	306 & 307
Royal Tyrone Militia	122
Royal Ulster Rifles	278
Royal Warwickshire Regiment	38
Royal Welch Fusiliers	105
Royal West Kent (Queen's Own)	217
Royal Westminster Middlesex (Light Infantry) Militia, 3rd	44
Royal Westmoreland Light Infantry Militia	152
Royal Wiltshire Militia	239

S

Scots Guards	273
Scottish Borderers Regiment of Militia	100 & 114
Seaforth Highlanders (Ross-shire Buffs, The Duke of Albany's)	266
Sherborne School Cadet Corps	116
Sherwood Foresters (Nottingham and Derbyshire Regiment)	199
Shropshire Militia	226
Shropshire RVC, 1st & 2nd	226
Somerset Light Infantry (Prince Albert's)	70
Somerset & Cornwall Light Infantry	74 & 145
Somersetshire Light Infantry Militia, 1st & 2nd	73
Somersetshire RVC, 1st, 2nd & 3rd	73
South Africa Irish Regiment	322
South Cork Light Infantry Militia	300
South Devon Militia, 2nd	62
South Durham Militia	258
South Hampshire Light Infantry Militia	162
South Lancashire Regiment (POW's Volunteers)	178
South London VTC	332
South Mayo Rifles Militia	290
South Staffordshire Regiment	167
South Wales' Borderers	108
St Pancras Volunteers	322
Stafford VTC	169
Staffordshire Home Guard	249
Staffordshire Regiment (The POW's)	170 & 249
Staffordshire RVC, 1st, 2nd (Staffordshire Rangers), 3rd, 4th & 5th	169 & 248
Staffordshire VTC	169
Stirlingshire RVC, 1st	295
Suffolk Regiment	66
Suffolk RVC, 1st & 6th (West Suffolk)	68
Suffolk & Cambridgeshire Regiment, TA	66 & 313
Surrey RVC, 1st (South London)	140 & 323
2nd, 4th	23

3rd, 5th	140
6th	23 & 324
7th	141
8th	15 & 324
10th, 23rd	23 & 324
19th	325
26th	324
Surrey RVC, 1st & 2nd	157
Sutherland (The Sutherland Highlanders) RVC, 1st	268

T

Tangier Regiment	21
Territorial Force 1908	310
Tower Hamlets Light Infantry Militia	307
Tower Hamlets RV Brigade, 1st	45
Tower Hamlets RVC, 2nd	309
Tower Hamlets RVC, 3rd, 7th, 10th	309 & 321
Tower Hamlets Rifles, The Rifle Brigade (Prince Consort's Own)	321
Transvaal Scottish Volunteers	20
Tyneside Irish	36
Tyneside Scottish	36

V

Volunteer Force 1914/19	332

W

Warwickshire Militia, 1st & 2nd	41
Warwickshire RVC, 1st (Birmingham)	41
Warwickshire RVC, 2nd	41
Warwickshire Volunteer Regiment	41
Welch Home Guard	185
Welch Regiment	181
Wellington West Coast Rifles Regiment, 7th	149
Welsh Volunteers	312
Wessex Brigade	125
West Essex Militia, 1st	197
West Kent Light Infantry Militia	219
West Lancashire Regiment	134
West Norfolk Militia, 1st	55
West Riding Volunteers	255
West Suffolk Militia	68
West York Light Infantry Militia, 2nd	77
West York Light Infantry Militia, 3rd	253
West York Militia, 4th	77
West York Militia, 5th	93
West York Militia, 6th	148
West York Rifles Militia, 1sts	223

INDEX

West York RVC	223
West Yorkshire Home Guard	76
West Yorkshire Regiment	75
Westmeath Militia	307
Westmeath Rifles	307
Westmoreland RVC, 1st	153
Wexford Militia	91
Whitgift School Cadet Corps	25
Wiltshire Regiment (Duke of Edinburgh's)	238
Wiltshire VRC, 1st	239
Worcestershire Home Guard	133
Worcestershire Militia, 1st & 2nd	131
Worcestershire Regiment	128
Worcestershire RVC, 1st & 2nd	132
Worcestershire & Sherwood Foresters Regiment	133 & 203

Y

2nd York Militia	112
York Regiment (King's Own Borderers)	112
York & Lancaster Regiment	251
Yorkshire Brigade	255
Yorkshire, East Riding RVC, 1st, 2nd & 3rd	80
Yorkshire, North Riding, RVC, 1st & 2nd	93
Yorkshire Volunteers	254
Yorkshire, West Riding RVC	
1st, 3rd & 7th	77
2nd (Hallamshire) & 8th	253 & 254
4th, 6th & 9th	148

History of the British Army Infantry Collar Badge

Definition
The word 'badge' is defined in the Oxford Dictionary as 'a distinctive mark or symbol etc.' and is, in heraldic terms, 'a mark of ownership or allegiance - a distinctive symbol marking possession'.

It is an all embracing word for a sign, symbol or device, and in the military sense is used to describe an ornament or device worn on the uniform of an unit, to distinguish it from another.

A British Infantry Army collar badge is therefore, quite simply, a distinctive insignia worn on the collar of an uniform to assist identification.

Uniforms, dress and clothing regulations
In order to trace the history of the collar badge, it is necessary to have some knowledge of the uniforms on which they were worn, by both Officers and other ranks. These include, Full Dress, Undress, Service Dress and Mess Dress. It is also useful to have some idea of the source of regulations covering the wearing of collar badges. Militia, Volunteer and Territorial uniforms generally followed the patterns worn by the Regular forces.

In the second half of the seventeenth century, soldiers began to wear uniforms and at that time the Colonels 'owned' the Regiments and therefore their personal emblems were usually displayed on the appointments of the Regiment.

In 1751, a Royal Warrant ended the wearing of the Colonel's emblems and replaced them with proper Regimental 'devices', and uniforms became more standardised. This Warrant was the first of a long series of Royal Warrants and precise instructions, the first issue of Dress Regulations appearing in 1822.

Apart from badges of rank which, for a time were also worn on the collar, 'devices' or 'ornaments' were worn in the 1800's, as recorded by prints, paintings etc.

In 1830, soldiers' white fatigue jackets disappeared, being replaced by a red shell jacket with Regimental facings. Some even wore collar badges, the earliest record found.

There is pictorial evidence of soldiers of the 5th Regiment of Foot in 1836 and of the 87th Regiment of Foot in 1844 wearing grenades on their collars. Similarly in 1852 a soldier of the 78th Regiment of Foot is wearing a Thistle on his collar, and in the same year a Lion is being worn on the collar of a soldier of the 4th Regiment of Foot.

In 1855, the introduction of the first infantry tunic, unlike the coatee, was the same basic cut for all ranks. From this date, Officers wore their badges of rank on either side of the collar opening, where they remained until an Army Order of October 1880, when they were removed to broad twisted gold shoulder cords. Though the Officers of some units did wear collar badges ahead of their rank badges, Officers could now wear collar badges generally.

In 1871, Regimental infantry buttons, which identified each Regiment, were replaced by a General Service button, simply bearing the Royal Coat of Arms. Perhaps to compensate for this loss, collar badges were introduced to further identify the wearer's Regiment.

An extract from File PC/Infantry General/No. 111 dated 16th July 1872 states, "Badges for Collar of Tunics Infantry. Regiments with special badges should wear their special badges on their collars. Fusiliers, in like manner-Grenades; Light Infantry-Bugles, Corps with no special device-Crowns."

A further memorandum dated 2nd October 1872 addressed to Fusilier Regiments states, "Several Regiments providing their own badges have been permitted to wear embroidered grenades, provided no expense is incurred by the Public." This was signed by Colonel Arthur Herbert, AAG Horse Guards.

That the Authorities were very 'money conscious' can also be seen from an Army Circular, C1 118 - Clothing, dated September 1873, which contains the following, "The metal crown, or other device which may be authorised to be worn on the collar, and the metal numerals or initials worn on the shoulder straps of tunics or frocks of such Corps as are entitled to them, will not be replaced until worn out."

The Circular goes on to say that, "these articles will, with ordinary wear, last the term of a soldier's service. A full supply having been issued, or authorised to be provided, for the current year, none will be sanctioned for the clothing for 1874/75, excepting for such garments as will be issued to recruits and others who have not been previously supplied." Finally "Commanding Officers will in future make their own arrangements for the provision of the numerals and devices, and they will receive instructions as to the amounts which will be allowed for such purpose, as are to be charged against the public, upon their making application to the Director of Clothing, Grosvenor Road, London SW."

However, the provision of these 'devices' was amended by an Army Circular, C153, dated April 1876 which stated:

"1. Steps are being taken to arrange for the supply, under a Departmental Contract, to Regiments and Corps direct.
2. It is intended that this contract shall come into force on 1st April 1877, but before that date further instructions on the subject will be promulgated.
3. Commanding officers will therefore be careful not to make provision under C1 155 Army Circular 1872 and C1 Army Circular 1873 for more numerals or badges than can be used by 31st March 1877."

The 'device' as used in the 1874 Dress Regulations is replaced by the 'badge' in the 1881 Edition. These Dress Regulations do not mention collar badges under each Regiment, but references are made to them as under the following paragraphs:-

573. Cap and collar badges to be given up by men of the 1st Class Army Reserve on re-transfer, and will be issued to recruits.

578. Cap and collar badges will be retained in the Militia.

610. Cap and collar badges to be given up by men of the Militia Reserve on re-transfer and will be re-issued to recruits.

101. 2 sets of metal collar badges (one for the frock and one for the tunic) will be allowed to each recruit in Regiments and Corps permitted to wear such badges.

102. Metal crowns issued as collar badges will not be supplied to Regiments and Corps which have special collar badges.

104. Highland Regiments will be allowed metal collar badges for both tunic and frock when both garments are in issue at Foreign Stations.

Following the sweeping changes and reforms in 1881 by Edward Cardwell, Secretary of State for War in the 1860's and 1870's, including the abolition of numbered Regiments, and by an Army Order dated 1st July 1881, the consequent amalgamation by pairs of the old Regiments to form new ones under territorial designations, a complete change of badges made the former collar badges obsolete, although several continued to be worn for some time.

At the same time, new helmet plates were introduced with a space in the centre to be filled by a device which would identify the Regiment. In many instances the collar badge pattern was used for this purpose.

During this time of change, most Regiments opted for collar badges displaying the main Regimental device that was already shown on the head-dress badge. However, a few Regiments took the opportunity to display a secondary device, as for example The King's Regiment (Liverpool), who adopted the Lancashire Rose. (Subsequently changed to the White Horse of Hanover in 1895). The Essex Regiment had two collar badges, one depicting the Seaxes from the County Coat of Arms, the other, the Eagle. Other Regiments simply changed the metal of their previous collar badges.

County Militia Regiments seem to have had badges on their clothing from about the end of the eighteenth century or early part of the nineteenth century, and some of the collar badges adopted by the Regular Battalions in 1881, were based upon those of their newly allied Militia Battalions.

At the end of the 1883, Dress Regulations, is a long schedule headed, "Badges of Territorial Regiments." In this, a regulation states, "The badges authorised to be worn on the collars of tunics may be worn on the collars of shell jackets." Also that, "No badges will be worn on the collars of patrol jackets."

Dress Regulations covered the wearing of collar badges by Officers, and the corresponding authority for Other ranks were contained in Clothing Regulations.

In 1887, these Clothing Regulations stated in Part 1, Section II paragraph 112 that, "Two sets of metal collar badges and numerals or initials (one for the frock and one for the tunic) will be allowed to each recruit in Regiments or Corps permitted to wear such badges."

The 1891 Dress Regulations record a scarlet patrol jacket being re-introduced for Officers on which collar badges would be worn.

In 1894, when the side cap was adopted, the Glengarry badge was found to be too large and for a few years the collar badge or a special badge was worn on this cap. By 1898 special badges had been designed and issued.

The 1894 Clothing Regulations gave precise instructions as to where the collar badge should be worn. "Metal Collar badges will be fixed mid-way between top and bottom of the collar, and 2 inches from the centre of the badge to the end of the collar."

In the Dress Regulations for the Army 1900, General Instruction No. 550, covering Full Dress for Infantry of the Line (exclusive of Highland and other Scottish Regiments) states that the tunic will be of scarlet cloth with cloth collar and cuffs of the colour of the Regimental facings. The collar ornamented with ⅝ inch lace along the top and gold Russian braid at the bottom, badges as in Appendix 1. (which lists in Section II the badges to be worn on the collars of Tunics and Frocks and may be worn on the collars of Mess jackets. It also states in Section IV that all badges are in metal, unless otherwise stated and in Section V that collar badges are to be 1¼ inch in height unless otherwise laid down.)

General Instruction 567 covers the Scarlet Frock, stating that the collar shall be that of the Regimental colour and that, "collar badges of similar pattern to those worn on the tunic but with metal substituted for embroidery". General Instruction 578 covers Mess Dress, which again says that the collar shall be that of the colour of the Regimental facings and, "In Regiments which wear Mess Jackets with a roll collar, the collar badges may be worn on the collar 5 inches from the seam of the shoulder."

General Instruction 580 lists, "The undermentioned Regiments wear Mess Dress of Authorised Regimental Patterns."

Listed separately, are Light Infantry (exclusive of the Highland Light Infantry), Fusiliers (exclusive of the Royal Scots Fusiliers), Highland and Scottish Regiments, The Royal Scots, Highland Light Infantry, The King's Own Scottish Borderers, Royal Scots Fusiliers, The Scottish Rifles, King's Royal Rifle Corps, the Royal Irish Rifles and The Rifle Brigade.

Also listed separately, are the Foot Guards, and General Instruction 508, referring to the Tunic states, "Scarlet cloth, blue cloth collar and cuffs; the collar embroidered in front and round the top; at each end, the badge of the Regiment embroidered in silver."

"The Grenadier Guards have a grenade at each end of the collar."

The Coldstream Guards have a Star of the Order of the Garter at the end of the collar,"

The Scots Guards have a thistle at the end of the collar."

On the Mess Dress Jacket, the collar rolled; Regimental badge on the collar 5 inches from seam of shoulder.

General Instruction 803/6 covers Militia Battalions where it states that, "Uniform (and horse furniture) as for the Line Battalions of the Territorial Regiments of which they form part, with exceptions." (No specific reference to collar badges.)

By Army Order No. 10, in January 1902, the former other ranks undress uniform was abolished and replaced for all occasions, except those requiring Full Dress, by a khaki Service Dress. It had a low turned down collar and collar badges were not worn.

A broadly similar Khaki Service Dress, but of finer material, was introduced for Officers at the same time as the men's. From 1908 all Officers abandoned the turned down collar, and instead, had an open top turnback collar, showing the khaki shirt and tie, thus providing for collar badges to be worn on the lapel. In most Line Regiments the caps and collar badges were of bronze metal. The 1902 Edition of Dress Regulations covers the wearing of collar badges on the recently introduced Officers Service Dress.

Besides their Full Service Dress, Officers still had an Undress uniform, which saw a return to the mid nineteenth century in the shape of a double breasted blue frock coat. Gilt, silver or the combination of both metals collar badges were worn on the stand-up collar along with gilt buttons.

In addition, Officers also had Mess Dress, developed in the previous century from the custom of wearing the shell jacket with open collar at mess. Collar badges were worn.

In tropical climates, a khaki drill version of the new Service Dress was issued, and on which metal collar badges were worn. All-white uniforms were also worn.

The 1904 Dress Regulations refer to collar badges to be placed with the centre of the badge 2 inches from the opening of the collar of the tunic or frock coat, adding, "They will be the same size on all garments." Authorised exceptions are listed in an Appendix.

For Mess jackets, "Collar Badges may be worn on the collar 5 inches from the seam of the shoulder."

Instruction No. 746 states, "Militia Officers wear the letter 'M' in gilding metal at the point of the collar, below the collar badges."

In 1908, the old Volunteer Force and the Yeomanry were reorganised and became the "Territorial Force" with the special purpose of Home Defence.

In the 1911 Edition of Dress Regulations it is confirmed that collar badges in bronze can be worn on the Service Dress jackets.

Clothing regulations for 1914 record, "Collar badges will not be worn on khaki frocks or Service Dress jackets".

By an Army Order 298 issued October 1917, all units of the Territorial Force were granted permission to wear the same pattern badges as those of the Regular Army units to which they belonged.

After World War One, Full Dress, although not abolished, was not re-issued to the bulk of the Army, being confined to the Brigade of Guards, Officers attending levees, and bands, corps of drums, and buglers and pipers on special occasions.

In 1921, the Territorial Force became the Territorial Army. In the 1920's Service Dress was considerably smartened up, including the wearing of collar badges by other ranks, a distinction previously the privilege of Officers only.

The 1926 Clothing Regulations stated that metal collar badges would not be worn on garments other than tunics and Service Dress supplied for ceremonial parades and walking out.

The 1928 (provisional) Dress Regulations direct that collar badges, when worn on the Mess jacket, will be placed ¾ inch below any medals worn.

The Dress Regulations of 1934 stated that when serving abroad, collar badges as for the Service Dress jacket, could be worn on the Khaki-drill jacket (General Instruction 775). In this Edition it clearly sets out instructions regarding uniforms worn by Officers, and which badge could be worn on each. These regulations lasted up to World War II, when, in May 1940, The War office published the first of a number of instructions dealing with the subject of dress for all ranks of the Army. Apart from additions and amendments these remained the same until well after the War was over.

In 1938, the War Office signalled the end of the tunic era by approving a uniform resembling a suit of workmen's overalls - battledress. This included a blouse on which collar badges were not to be worn.

Officers wore battle dress similar to that of the other ranks, but collar badges and ties were permitted. Battledress was to be universal for all ranks and all Regiments, and began to be issued in 1939.

Full Dress naturally disappeared during World War II, but was re-introduced in 1948 for the Brigade of Guards, when performing public duties.

As stocks of battledress built up, so the old Service Dress disappeared, although Officers still wore it when not on parade with their men.

As a form of war time economy, Officers of Regiments raised during the 1939 - 1945 period were not required to wear collar badges on their Service Dress jackets. Although the design of the badges was promulgated, the badges were not supposed to have been available until after the War was over. From a study of photographs it is evident that this ruling was not always adhered to.

Several events took place in the Military world in 1947. National Service returned and lasted until 1960. During this period, battledress was considerably improved with the collar of the blouse being opened up to show the shirt and tie. Collar badges were therefore re-adopted by most Infantry Regiments.

Also in 1947 it was felt that, following the War, a special uniform for Ceremonial occasions was required, and this was to be known as No.1 Dress. For most Line Regiments this consisted of a jacket with a stand-up collar. Regimental distinctions were preserved by collar badges being worn.

The Officers' chief uniform remained battledress, to which No. 1 Dress was added. Service Dress and later Mess Dress were allowed on an optional basis. Silver/gilt collar badges were usually worn on the No.1 Dress.

An all white version of No.1 Dress, in drill material was approved for ceremonial duties in hot climates, to be known as No.3 Dress. Collar badges were to be worn, "of a Regimental pattern.".

In the post war reorganisation of the British Army, all Battalions were organised into Training Brigade Groups in 1947, each Battalion representing its Regiment. Following the 1957 White Paper, Infantry of the Line were grouped into 14 Brigades.

During this period, Brigade cap badges were worn, but with Regimental collar badges to preserve identity. At this time many new designs were introduced, as well as some Regiments who had not previously worn collar badges, now doing so.

The 1953 Clothing Regulations states, "Collar badges will be worn on No.1 Dress and No.3 Dress by all other ranks when this dress is issued". It also states, "Collar badges may be worn on battledress by all ranks. They will be supplied at public expense and cannot be provided by the R.A.O.C. on repayment except where collar badges have been specially authorised as a Regimental embellishment."

During 1961 and 1962, battledress was replaced by a new No.2 Dress to be worn by both Officers and other ranks.

The 1963 Clothing Regulations record that collar badges will be worn with No.1, No.2, and No.3 Dress by other ranks of all Regiments and Corps, except the Brigade of Guards and The Royal Green Jackets.

Dress Regulations for Officers of the Army 1969, like previous Editions give detailed instructions for the wearing or not wearing of collar badges on each uniform worn at that time.

They were instructed to be worn, "With the centre of the badge 2 inches from the opening of the collar of the No.1 and No.3 Dress jackets". When authorised they will be worn above the steps of the collar on No.2, No.4, and No.5 Dress jackets, the positioning being left to the discretion of Colonels or Colonels Commandant of Regiments or Corps."

No. 4 Dress, another warm weather uniform was similar to No.2 Dress but in stone coloured polyester and woven worsted.

No.5 Dress was battledress, and the instruction relates to the collar of the battledress blouse.

Pamphlet No.5 of Dress Regulations for Officers of the Army 1973, deals with, Infantry of the Line, and there are separate sections for, The Scottish Division, The Queen's Division, The King's Division, (Excluding the Royal Irish Rangers), The Royal Irish Rangers, The Prince of Wales's Division, The Light Division and The Parachute Regiment.

Again, precise instructions are given for each item of uniform dress, including as to whether collar badges should or should not be worn. At the end of the Regulations, Table 6 gives a description of the collar badges for each Regiment.

These Dress Regulations were superseded by Pamphlet No.5 dated 1986. Dress Regulations have been issued at subsequent intervals to cover changes in formations, uniform and anything that concerns the various forms of Dress.

Clothing Regulations were later replaced by Material Regulations for the Army, pamphlets issued by the Ministry of Defence. These continued to give precise instructions regarding collar badges, not only where they should be worn etc., but also covering other aspects, such as proposed designs. For example in Material Regulations for the Army Volume 3, Pamphlet No. 15 issue in August 1975, Instruction 501 states:-

"Proposed designs of collar badges are to be forwarded by the Colonel or Colonel Commandant of the Regiment to the Army Dress Committee, which will obtain colour drawings as necessary for approval, by the Committee, the Army Board, and the approval of the Sovereign. Approved designs are not to be modified without the agreement of the Committee and the Army Board, and the approval of the Sovereign."

There are also instructions regarding the manufacture of collar badges, how the non tarnishable finish is obtained (to the anodised badges), and cleaning. They point out that although the finish is hard, excessive scratching and rubbing, will, in due course, remove it exposing the aluminium beneath. The use of any abrasive including metal polish or brushing is forbidden, and all that is required is an occasional wipe over with a damp cloth.

In this particular Pamphlet, the Army Dress Committee gives general instructions regarding what can be worn on uniform for No. 1 Dress to No. 14 Dress, in particular it states that collar badges are to be worn with No.1, No.2, and No.3 Dress by soldiers of all Regiments and Corps, except by the Household Division and the Black Watch (The Royal Highlanders). This latter Regiment will wear collar badges with No.1 and No.3 Dress only.

It goes on to say that all collar badges are to be fitted with a short shank of flat metal pierced with an aperture to allow the badge to be fixed by a back plate and pin. Where possible, the single shank is to be fitted on vertically behind the badge; the method of fixing the collar badge avoids leaving unsightly holes when changing badges.

The pamphlet also contains Instruction No.405, regarding the wearing of collar badge backings and how they are to be obtained,.

These Pamphlets continued to be periodically issued.

Metals and materials

Almost every page of Regimental text in this book refers to a metal and/or cloth/embroidered material collar badges, so it would therefore be helpful to describe them in some detail.

- **BRASS**. Collar badges similar to those worn today were authorised for Infantry Regiments of Foot on 16th July 1872, the majority being made in "yellow brass," with brass lugs as fittings. Brass is a yellow coloured alloy consisting of two parts copper and one part zinc which, when polished gives a pleasing yellow/gold lustre. "Yellow brass" describes an item where the final finish is more yellow than golden.
- **WHITE METAL**. Some pre 1881 collar badges were made in white metal. These are exactly as described, white metal with the appearance of silver when new. Made of an alloy of copper, zinc, and nickel, sometimes referred to as nickel-silver. Abbreviated as w/m.

By an Authority, Pattern 1184 dated 25th August 1904 it was decided to, "Amend all badges described as white metal to German Silver." (g/s)

GILDING METAL. Following the sweeping changes brought about by the 1881 Cardwell reforms, new sets of collar badges were required for the new Regiments and the brass ones with brass lugs were replaced by ones made in gilding metal (g/m), with copper lugs.

Gilding metal, so called through being able to be easily gilded, is defined in the 1900 Dress Regulations as, "eight parts of copper to one of zinc." A brass alloy therefore, but now containing a higher proportion of copper than zinc to those previously made.

BI-METAL. Yellow brass, brass, gilding metal, and white metal are generally associated with collar badges worn by other ranks as are those made in a combination of two metals, brass/gilding metal, and white metal. Known as bi-metal (b/m).

ANODISED ALUMINIUM. In 1952, collar badges made in anodised aluminium were introduced, sometimes referred to as "staybrights". This was not only because they were cheaper to manufacture, but also there was no need to remove them from the tunics as they did not require cleaning, thus obviating wear and tear on clothing. The collar badges were so coated to make them look like the original metal, g/m, w/m, b/m. Abbreviated to a/a.

OFFICERS. Officers metal collar badges below the rank of Substantive Colonel, were made in superior metal to those worn by other ranks. They varied from bronze, silver, gilt, and silver/gilt, sometimes with enamels.

BRONZE. Some other ranks collar badges, usually die-struck in a base metal are sometimes artificially coloured to give a bronze appearance, often carried out privately by an Officer, possibly serving overseas and unable to obtain the correct bronze collar badges at the time.

However, when bronze (bze) collar badges are mentioned, they normally refer to those officially made specifically for wear by Officers on their Service Dress. (sometimes referred to as OSD Bronze). The more copper that is added to brass the more the colour became bronze and this can vary from reddish brown right through to dark brown, almost black.

Most bronze collar badges have a flat solid reverse and the collector should check to see whether, when offered a World War One die-struck "brass economy" collar badge, the item is as stated to be, and not a solid back bronze item that has been polished back to brass.

SILVER & SILVER PLATED. A few Officers collar badges, especially the early ones, are found in Hall Marked silver (HM sil), the marks giving both the identity of the Assay Office and the year of manufacture.

These badges and those marked STERLING SILVER are made entirely from the correct amount of silver and the mixture of copper that constitutes 'sterling' (many centuries ago 'easterling', from the eastern Germanic peoples who settled with their silversmithing trade in this country).

Most collar badges are not so made and are often found marked 'S' or 'P' on the reverse, these and others found unmarked indicate that they are of a base metal that has been plated with silver by electrical deposition.

Silver and silver plated collar badges were often worn by Volunteer officers.

GILT. Worn by Officers, WO's and senior NCO's, often on the scarlet frock coat, usually of a copper based composition, subsequently gold plated.

SILVER-GILT. A bi-metal Officers collar badge is one that includes both silver and gilt (sil/gilt). They were often worn on the scarlet frock and No. 1 Dress when it replaced Service Dress.

SILVER-GILT & ENAMEL. Coloured vitreous enamels were sometimes added to Officers' collar badges, making very attractive items. (sil/gilt/enamel).

EMBROIDERED. Was the term used in Dress Regulations to describe those beautiful collar badges in gold and silver metal thread, often referred to as 'bullion', usually on a coloured backing. Details such as animals' eyes, noses and teeth were often picked out in coloured silks.

General

Often, other rank's collar badges are made in corresponding metals to those worn by their Officers, i.e. when the Officers wore collar badges in silver, then the other ranks would be in white metal; and similarly when the Officers wore them in gilt, then the other ranks would be in gilding metal.

By an Authority dated 22nd May 1901, it was decreed that, "Volunteers may wear Territorial badges in white metal and silver but without honours in those cases where the badges have honours attached. Other ranks of Militia usually wore white metal collar badges as did most Scottish Regiments. However there are always exceptions and some Militia, Volunteer and most Cyclist units wore them blackened, as did Rifle Regiments, when worn.

Crowns

Crowns have always been worn by Kings and Queens of Great Britain as an emblem of sovereignty, so it is hardly surprising that they have featured prominently on British Army collar badges.

Naturally they have varied over the years and so give a rough guide as to when they were worn, and one sees the description QVC (Queen Victoria's Crown), KC (King's Crown), and QC or QEC (Queen's Crown) appearing in dealers' lists and sale catalogues.

However, it must be borne in mind that, useful as this information is, when used in relation to the shape of the arches of a crown, these descriptions can be meaningless and misleading.

Other publications may cover crowns prior to 1874 but it was in that year that the Crown was introduced by the Army as a collar badge for those Regiments that had no specific badge of their own. This was referred to in Army Orders as an Imperial crown. In brass, this was Pattern 9386 sealed 30th June 1874, with a single central brass fixing lug, referred to in the text as, "A flat topped Imperial crown" (see Fig. 333).

This was a variant of St. Edward's Crown and is thought by some to have been inspired by the Star of India Crown.

Other Victorian variants include a pattern introduced in 1879 with two additional lateral arches giving the appearance of 'ears', see (Fig.884), and one that endured until c.1900 with the arches rectilinear rather than curved.

The death of Queen Victoria on 22nd January 1901 brought about a departure from the traditional form of St. Edward's Crown, and upon the accession of Edward VII was referred to as the Tudor Crown. The pattern was approved May 1901. No variant is known and it retained its form throughout the reigns of four Kings, leading to the delusion that any crown with semi-circular arches was a 'King's Crown'! Upon the death of King George VI in 1952, and the accession of Queen Elizabeth II a return was made to the more traditional form of St. Edward's crown, as a result this has become known as the "Queen's Crown'.

It might be thought that only Royal Regiments would be permitted to embody a Crown in their collar badge, but this is not the case (e.g. The Sherwood Foresters and The Durham Light Infantry); conversely, not all Royal Regiments include the Crown in their collar badges

Coronets, Cyphers, and other Royal Emblems

Coronets, these being simpler diadems worn by Princes, Princesses, and by the various degrees of the nobility.

Cyphers, letters or initials linked in cursive style, also feature, both those of the reigning Monarch borne by many Royal Regiments and those of other members of the Royal Family past and present.

Other emblems connected with Royalty often appear on collar badges, the most popular being the Prince of Wales's crest, the three ostrich plumes, coronet and motto. It is carried by Regiments which carry 'The Prince of Wales's' in their title structure, as well as The Welch Regiment and other old Welch Regiments of Militia.

Honours and Awards

Regimental collar badges, like Regimental titles, very often epitomize a considerable amount of history, and the inclusion of Battle Honours in commemoration of brave deeds is a development from the original purpose of identification.

Many Regiments, having fought shoulder to shoulder on the same battlefield share the same battle honours or award. Such an instance is the Sphinx, superscribed "Egypt", this war honour being granted by Horse Guards Circular 170 dated 6th July 1802, to those Regiments which took part in the expedition to Egypt in 1801 under Sir Ralph Abercromby.

"Gibraltar" and the fortress's Castle and Key emblems often feature on the collar badges of those Regiments that took part in the defence of this vital base under General Elliot (later Lord Heathfield) from 1779-1783. The honour "Gibraltar" was granted by Horse Guards letter 14th April 1784, but the badges of Castle, Key and motto, "Montis Insignia Calpe" were not authorised until 1835-36, The Key is an allusion to the fact that the Rock is the "Key to the Mediterranean."

Many Regiments have close associations with counties, cities, towns and families, and these are reflected in their collar badges. Heraldic recognition by adapting symbolic creatures of land and air is a very ancient practice. Animals and birds feature prominently on British Army Infantry collar badges, including both the Royal Tiger and the Elephant awarded to commemorate a Regiment's long and arduous service in India. Others include, eagles, horses (The famous White Horse of Hanover appears in various attitudes), lions, stags, antelopes, the Paschal Lamb, cats, and even a boar's head.

Mythological dragons also appear in many forms and hues, the green dragon of the Buffs, the red pen-dragon of Wales, and the highly stylised Chinese dragons.

Some Regiments have made use of old heraldic 'canting,' for example the **hart** that appears on the collar badges of The **Hert**fordshire Regiment

When animals and birds are represented, they usually face inwards towards the collar opening.

Other devices often seen on Infantry collar badges are, stars, wreaths, bugles and bugle horns. In the case of the latter, these are worn with the mouthpiece of the instrument at the collar opening, as if being blown by the wearer. They are generally associated with Rifle and Light Infantry Regiments, brought about by such troops being required to move quickly; the conveyance of orders via the bugle being easier than that of the traditional drum.

Several collar badges, together with similar devices in the headdress badge, were responsible for the time-honoured 'nick-names' by which the Regiments have become known. With a combination of the Paschal Lamb of the Queen's Royal Regiment (West Surrey) and the name of one of its early Colonels, Kirke, the Regiment was familiarly referred to as "Kirke's Lambs."

"Lions" was the sobriquet of the King's Own Royal Regiment (Lancaster) derived from its Royal Lion badge.

The King's (Liverpool Regiment) were popular as, "The King's Hanoverian White Horses," whilst the Royal Leicestershire Regiment and the Royal Hampshire Regiment have long been known as the "Tigers" or "Royal Tigers," all being references to their badges, including the collar badge.

Identification, Verification and Sources of Information

Identification of an item will doubtless, from time to time, cause problems for the collar badge collector. Hopefully this book will cover all but a few Infantry collar badges, but it is still worthwhile joining one of the many societies concerned with the collection and study of Military insignia, both nationally and locally. This will enable one to attend meetings when other collectors of a like mind can be found. Much valuable information can be found in the Societies' journals and special publications, and if all else fails, the problem item can be illustrated in the magazine of such a society, when hopefully it will be identified.

A word of warning! Treat with caution the 'know-all' who has an answer to every item put forward at meetings for identification. Certainly, listen to what they have to say - they may even be correct on the odd occasion, but do enquire of their source and how they can verify what has been said. Often there is silence.

Information on collar badges is not easy to find, but there are sources that help, though it should be emphasised that one source is usually not sufficient to establish beyond doubt, a positive identification.

Obviously, an actual uniform with collar badges attached provides an ideal source of information, but so often the tunic or jacket of the uniform has had the collar badges removed. Even when one is fortunate enough to find a uniform with collar badges there are still pitfalls.

Although the tunic/jacket may be authentic, this does not necessarily mean that the collar badges are also authentic. Incorrect patterns could well have been added later, "to complete the uniform." Also beware of tunics that have been 'modified' for wear at tattoos, fancy-dress parties, or theatrical productions.

Illustrations provide another source of information. Many paintings and prints of a military nature appeared in the nineteenth century, some accurate, others not so. Precise detail, the very ingredient looked for by the researcher/collector, was sometime sacrificed for the overall impression. It should also be remembered that very often the finer details , such as collar badges, were painted in after the subject had left the studio.

By the time of the Crimean War the camera had improved to such an extent that they show very clearly what was being worn on the collar. However, my own experience is that most photographs of that period were of Officers who wore badges of rank on their collars until late 1880. What photographs there were of other ranks usually showed the soldiers 'sporting' a beard that completely covered the collar, thus obscuring any view of a collar badge!

Although accurately recording an individual uniform it must be remembered that, "the camera is a silent observer". By this is meant that what is recorded by the camera does not in itself constitute either a regulation or an established custom. As an example, it has been known for a soldier about to be photographed in a studio, to remove his headdress and then, to identify his Regiment, to place either his hat badge or shoulder title on the collar! Admirable for the photograph but a minefield for the later historians, researchers and collectors trying to establish exactly what was worn on the collar at a particular time. Additionally, a black and white or sepia photograph cannot definitely establish the metal of any collar badge shown.

Official documents or regulations are other sources of information, but suffer from scarcity for early items, and lack of detailed information for later ones. Dress Regulations only cover what collar badges are required to be worn, but it should be remembered that an authorisation to wear a badge, in no way indicates the date when, or even, if such a badge was worn. Additionally regulations were sometimes brought in, to sanction the wearing of a collar badge, that had been in use by the Regiment for some considerable time.

Illustrations of military collar badges appear from time to time in magazines and books, as for example, 'The Boys Own Paper'. In 1896 the magazine, 'The Regiments,' published a list of Regimental collar badges. Tailors' and manufacturers' records can also be most useful in obtaining information, but are not necessarily conclusive on their own. Messrs. Gaunts were for many years the principle suppliers of collar badges to the Army.

Regimental museums can be helpful, but they do not always have either the qualified staff, or the available time to answer collar badge queries. In addition it should be remembered that just because an uniform on display carries collar badges, it is not necessarily authentic or original and may have been added to at a later date, albeit with the best of intentions. I am reminded of seeing at one Regimental museum an obviously authentic uniform of the Royal Marine Light Infantry, who were merged and lost their identity in 1923. Fitted to this tunic were anodised aluminium buttons of the Royal Marines, introduced for wear only in the 1950s!

"Sealed patterns" are an excellent source of official information, as they contain, not only the actual approved collar badge, but also the date of sealing, the Authorisation details as well as on which uniform the badge should be worn.

The pattern is sealed with wax by an Official source, the Board of Ordnance, The War Office or the Ministry of Defence. The 1928 Dress Regulations state that sealed patterns were deposited at The War Office 'for reference and guidance.' They add that duplicates of the sealed pattern badges were in possession of Officers commanding Regiments, Battalions and Infantry depots. For an example see Figs.577 and 578 which relate to a facing pair of collar badges for the frock collar of the Lancashire Fusiliers, sealed 20th February 1901. Sealed patterns are used partly to maintain standards, and are sent to manufacturers as a guide. Consequently there are a number of sealed patterns relating to the same collar badge, sealed at different times.

These are standard patterns, but there is only one Master Pattern. Even standard patterns are very difficult to find as over the years many have been lost or mislaid or destroyed through lack of storage space.

One interesting memorandum records, 'Notice of Alteration in Patterns - By a decision 22nd December 1874 under Authority PC (Establishment) 2174 - in future, patterns of the Militia will not be sealed by the Assistant Adjutant General of Clothing but by the Inspector General of the Auxiliary and Reserve Forces.'

It is worth remembering that, particularly in later years, some collar badges were taken into use before the pattern was sealed.

As can be seen, there are many sources from which to obtain collar badge information, but all have defects and should not be relied upon in isolation. Usually it requires more than one source to establish reliable facts.

Although Army Orders record the actual date a collar badge is authorised to be worn, and a sealed pattern the actual date the item is sealed and ready to be worn, this does not of course establish when, or even if, the item was worn. When a new collar badge had been submitted, approved, authorised, and finally sealed and manufactured, it was quite common for the first issue of the badge to be sent to the Regiment, with an instruction to the Colonel, that to save expense, "They are not to be issued until stocks of the present badge have been exhausted." This was sometimes accompanied by an estimate that present stocks were expected to last a certain number of years. So it could be several years before an authorised collar badge was actually worn, especially if the Regiment was serving overseas at that time.

There are many instances of such items never being worn at all. It is quite easy to see how this can happen, as for example a new K/C anodised aluminium collar badge, to replace one in metal deposited at the Regiment with the usual, 'Present stocks to be exhausted before issue' directive. The Monarch dies and new Q/C collar badges are approved, sealed and issued to the Regiment. So although officially authorised and sealed, this particular example would never have been worn. In these instances the K/C collar badges would be either returned to and destroyed by the War office or other appropriate Authority, or the Regiment itself would be directed to destroy them.

Human nature being what it is, it has been known for the person responsible for destroying the badges, to retain one or two examples for their own use, and when these surface, perhaps many years after the person concerned has died, it can cause all sorts of complications.

Conversely, there are many instances where collar badges have been worn although never officially approved or authorised, and naturally therefore never sealed. Then of course there are trial patterns, submitted by a Regiment but not approved. The problem of dating and usage is further complicated by the considerable licence engaged in by Colonels of Regiments, who often totally disregarded Dress Regulations and Army orders, and privately had made collar badges of their own design. An example being The Dorsetshire Regiment, where 'male' Sphinx collar badges were made for one Battalion to distinguish it from the official 'female' Sphinx worn by the other Battalion. (For full details, see under The Dorsetshire Regiment.)

With a Battalion of a Regiment serving overseas, it often took years before such a practice was officially noticed and rectified. Naturally as such practices were entirely unofficial, it is difficult to exactly date the wearing of such items.

'Old Sweats' too, complicate usage and dating by often continuing to wear their original collar badges long after they have been officially replaced; it is common to see photographs of such old soldiers still wearing their metal K/C collar badges, whilst new recruits wear the correct Q/C anodised versions.

In conclusion, a final word of warning. Usually one can be fairly certain of the metal used in the making of a collar badge, but it should be borne in mind that metal can alter 'colour' due to many circumstances, *inter alia* moisture, heat and sunlight.

The Hobby

Collar badges have always been sought by collectors, in the main to complete a set of cap badges, shoulder titles and buttons to a particular unit. Recently however, more and more Collectors are forming collections purely made up of collar badges. This is hardly surprising as they are delightful pieces of history, often miniatures of the cap badges and at present much cheaper to buy. They are relatively easy to find and most dealers include a section of their lists, devoted entirely to collar badges. Military fairs and exhibitions are another good source, and they can also be found in antique, curio, and bric-a-brac shops. Here they can often be purchased for pence rather than pounds. Some of the early collar badges are, of course, 'antique' by definition. Militaria auctioneers usually include a number of collar badge lots in their sales.

A Militaria Society, both national and local, will put one in touch with other collar badge Collectors and a good 'swap session' usually takes place during meetings.

A collection can be all embracing, confined to one arm such as Infantry, or one can specialise in one particular Regiment or group of Regiments. A family or residential tie can be an influence. Some Collectors are interested in every type of collar badge, whilst others only collect old metal versions, eschewing the modern anodised aluminium. Again other people are only interested in the attractive embroidered items.

Having decided on what one will collect, then the decision has to be made as to whether one should collect a single example or a pair. There are those Collectors who feel that one example is sufficient, whilst others are of the opinion, that as they were worn in pairs, then they should be collected as such. Some Collectors effect a compromise when the pair are the same, but obtaining both when they are a facing pair.

From experience, I know how difficult it can be to complete the facing pair, there always seem to be plenty on offer of the one you have, but never the one you require!

Dealers and Collectors Descriptive Terms

Newcomers to the hobby are faced with many different descriptions of collar badges that appear on dealers' lists:- 'mirror pairs,' 'matching pairs, 'facing pairs,' worn on the right collar, 'as worn,' 'facing left,' 'facing right,' 'as viewed' etc. etc.

Mirror and matching pairs are one and the same - a facing pair that exactly match in every detail, apart from the fact that they face in opposite directions! This would imply that a simple 'facing pair' did not match, but most collectors use the phrase, 'facing pair' to mean that they are the same, but if there is a really marked difference, then this fact will be recorded.

It is necessary to standardise terms so that everyone knows exactly what is meant, and I believe the easiest to understand is the simple, 'Facing left,' and 'Facing right.' This means when looked at when the item is displayed. For an example of a collar badge, 'Facing left,' see Fig.50 and Fig.49 for one, 'Facing right.'

Another term that requires clarification is that used to describe the fitting on the back of the badge.

Early Clothing and Dress Regulations deal purely with the positioning of the badge on the collar. In the 1966 Clothing Regulations the fastening is dealt with in minute detail. Originally the fittings were normally two in number, but three and even four are not uncommon, as confirmed by the official extract, 'Collar badges are normally fitted with a standard single horizontal shank, except for those of exceptional design, for which additional support is necessary.' These 'shanks' are variously known as, 'rings,' 'loops,' 'eyes,' etc., the term I have adopted for use in this book is the ubiquitous word, 'lugs.'

Although I have seen collar badges with a 'slider' fastener, this is exceptional and usually confined to headdress badges of the post 1910 period, and of the earlier period of paggri badges.

'Tangs,' which is the term often used to refer to the fixings on Officers' cap badges, have on very rare occasions been used as a fixing on a collar badge, but these are also exceptional and can really be disregarded.

One other term sometimes seen on a dealer's list is, 'lapel badge,' this usually indicates an item worn on a uniform which has a turned down collar and open top, usually Officers' Service and mess dress. I choose not to use this term in such circumstances, preferring to keep to the general 'collar badge', leaving 'lapel badge' to describe those items, both military and civilian which are worn singly on the lapel. However, when Dress Regulations have so described an item, this is recorded as such.

Cost

Whether to collect one or a pair of collar badges could of course be partly decided by the cost involved. It is not my intention to include any sort of price list or guide with this book, but obviously it plays a very important part in any hobby and cannot be ignored.

With today's prices it is certainly interesting, though somewhat galling, to look back through early price lists. In, 'New Regulations for Uniform, Laces, Badges etc. to be worn by the British Army (Infantry of the Line and Militia.), compiled from The General Order issued by His Royal Highness, The Duke of Cambridge, Commander-in-Chief, 11th April 1881, there is included a price list recording Royal Marines Light Infantry collar badges for the tunic at 7/6d (37p) per pair and similar for the mess vest at 5/6d (27p) per pair. Collar grenades for the Royal Marine Artillery were also listed at 7/6d (37p) per pair. These were officers badges, quite expensive when one considers what 10/- (50p) could buy in those far off days.

The Vocabulary of Clothing 1923, lists soldiers collar badges (metal, with pin) at 3d (1p) per pair.

One has to say that costs have risen considerably since then! The cost of any one particular collar badge depends on several factors. Firstly, the condition, which can range from 'Mint' or 'Pristine' right through to 'Scuffed' or 'badly worn'. Secondly, supply and demand, and thirdly, scarcity or even rarity. All these play a very important part in arriving at a price, but perhaps the most important aspect is just how badly a collector wants an item; and it is when more than one collector decides that he is willing to pay 'over the odds' in order to say complete his collection, that prices really rise.

The pre 1881 Line Infantry and County Militia collar badges are both scarce and expensive. These rarities apart, the early post 1881 Cavalry and Yeomanry collar badges are on the whole the most expensive, followed by Line Infantry, with those of Arms and Services being the least expensive. Elite forces and Guards items always seem to be expensive, and Volunteer items costing more than their Regular counterparts.

Soldiers collar badges in gilding metal, white metal and bi-metal normally cost less than those in bronze, silver, gilt, and silver-gilt as worn by Officers. There are always exceptions, say in the case of a very short lived Unit or very few personnel.

Certainly, collar badges have been quite inexpensive when compared to headdress badges, but of late they have increased in price, with a pair of rare collar badges equalling the cost of the relevant headdress badge.

Display

There is no right or wrong way to display one's collection of collar badges, and a Collector should display them in whatever way suits their individual taste.

One *cri de couer* that I would make is that should the Collector display them at an exhibition, any judge or panel of judges would be much more impressed if there were full and comprehensive labelling of the items.

Before the final display, collar badges can be placed on pieces of thick card with spaces for those items still to be obtained.

Some Collectors are content with this medium, whilst others make their final display in a frame. Mounted on a thick card or even plywood, if a large number of badges are to be displayed, this can then be covered with coloured material such as beize, velvet or hessian, perhaps a tartan for Scottish items. The whole effect is most attractive.

Metal collar badges can be secured at the back by the use of the regulation split pin. Cloth or embroidered badges can be stitched in position, or for the less nimble, a product such as 'Blu-tack,' this, rather than double-sided tapes which usually destroys the old paper backing of embroidered badges, should the badges require dismounting. The acidic content of some modern adhesives can also be destructive.

The frame itself can take many forms but must be strong enough to support the collective weight of the collar badges, and perhaps a glazed front.

Cleaning

Once again there are divided opinions - some Collectors preferring to display their badges 'as found,' and it must be said that some metals do develop a most attractive bloom or patina over the years. Metal polishes are both abrasive and erosive in action, and constant polishing can remove some of the detail of the design. Certainly many badges have been damaged, sometimes beyond redemption by wrong methods of cleaning.

Other collectors point out that the British Army is renowned for its 'spit and polish' and as collar badges would have to be polished before passing inspection, then they should be so polished in one's collection.

It would take a separate treatise to record all the many ways badges can be cleaned, and most collectors have their own 'pet' methods, often closely guarded, especially if they compete against other Collectors. Suffice to say that if one does decide to clean the badges, the following are tried and tested methods which do work.

- **BRASS/GILDING METAL.** Clean thoroughly by immersing the badge in a solution of one part sulphuric acid to twenty parts water. After one hour, remove any deposit with a wire brush and wash off in warm water, dry, and polish with an approved metal cleaner. As an alternative, mix together a cup of water, a cup of flour, a cup of vinegar, two teaspoons of citric acid powder and two teaspoons of salt. Brush the compound on thickly and thoroughly, rinse and dry.
- **WHITE METAL.** The same as for brass and gilding metal badges but in a separate solution.
- **BI-METAL.** The same as for brass/gilding metal.
- **BLACKENED BRASS.** The blackening can be restored by several methods, the easiest by spraying the badge with a matt-finish black aerosol car spray. It generally takes four or five applications allowing each coat to dry thoroughly. Some such badges have polished highlights, and great care should be taken with such items. In my opinion, restoration of such items is best left to the expert badge repairers. For normal polishing an application of black shoe polish followed by a light brushing should suffice.
- **SILVER.** Oxidises or tarnishes fairly quickly, requiring almost constant attention and being a soft metal needs gentle treatment. (Do not use any

form of wire brush!) A light clean with cotton wool soaked in pure lemon juice, followed by a polish with an approved silver cleaner should be sufficient.

- **BRONZE**. If polished, the bronze patina will be eroded exposing a brass or copper surface. Application of dark brown shoe polish followed by a light brushing will help to restore some of the toning. If you acquire some badly polished specimens, then these can be restored at a bronze sculptor's foundry.
- **GILT**. These fine badges should not be polished otherwise the gold plating will be removed, exposing the brass or copper base metal, and thus ruining the badge entirely. Usually a wash in warm soapy water will be sufficient, but if the item is particularly dirty or stained, immerse in a solution of one part ammonia and twenty parts water, wash off in cold water and dry thoroughly with a soft cloth. The original richness will then be restored. Such badges completely stripped of their gilding, can be regilded, but the modern restrictions on mercury gilding result in a finish that does not compare with the pre 1914 product.
- **ENAMELS**. A light agitation with a soft tooth brush that has been in warm water and concentrated washing-up liquid, is about the most that can be accomplished. The vitreous enamel is a form of glass, and therefore great care must be taken not to damage the enamelled areas. Fortunately, correct restoration of damaged specimens is now possible, at quite a reasonable cost.
- **EMBROIDERED/BULLION**. A dry cleaner spray can be used, but in my own experience the results are hardly worthwhile, and a light brush to remove dust is about all that can safely be done without harming the badge.
- **VERDIGRIS**. This a green or greenish blue deposit that forms on brass and copper as a rust. It detracts from the appearance of the badge and should be removed as quickly as possible. This can normally be achieved by using pure lemon juice, but if well established may require a solvent that can be obtained from bicycle and motor factor shops.

General

Cleaning, polishing, restoring all need great care to prevent spoiling the item, so if uncertain, do take expert advice, and if still in doubt ... don't!

Some Collectors, to preserve their efforts and displays, spray their badges with a clear retail varnish. Apart from being difficult to remove, all these varnishes are of a migratory nature, and the badges become dull and discoloured. There are two solutions, the badges can be framed and glazed ensuring total sealing of the edges. Secondly, and this suits those Collectors who prefer their badges to be accessible, museum lacquers, which are vitally inert lacquers and can be obtained on a wholesale basis. 'Frigelene' for silver, and 'Ercalene' for brass, gilding metal and white metal. The badge should be completely immersed in the product, removed with tweezers, by the fasteners, stood on the fasteners, and allowed to dry (5 minutes). The normal film of varnish is not discernible, and the badge need never be cleaned again.

Re-strikes, Reproductions, Copies and Spurious Badges

Re-struck badges have been with us for a long time, but seem to have increased over recent years. 'Re-pro' and 'Re-strike' mean different things to different people, so I will record my own interpretation of these oft-used words.

- **RE-STRIKE**. Is any badge made from the original die(s) after the die(s) have become obsolete. Regimental Museums, amongst others have had badges made, from the original die(s), to sell to the general public in order to raise funds. If, as is usually the case, the Regiment has long been disbanded or merged, then personally I cannot regard them as a genuine badge. My definition of genuine being, a badge that was made and worn officially whilst the unit was in existence.

Usually no intention to deceive is intended when these items are re-struck.

REPRODUCTIONS and COPIES. These are usually made with one purpose in mind - to deceive the Collector into thinking they have purchased a genuine badge, whereas the item is a reproduction or copy. The perpetrator making a large profit for themselves through the sale, having priced it as for an original item.

SPURIOUS ITEMS. A spurious item is one which has been made in either the incorrect metals or design or even both. Also one that has been 'made -up' by an individual and never worn by a Regiment or Unit.

These 'repro' items have yet to penetrate the collar badge market in any numbers so far, although I have of late seen some Cavalry collar badges so made. For the experienced Collector these are not too difficult to spot, but newer Collectors should seek advice before purchasing. Do be most suspicious of the dealer who issues frequent lists, all containing scarce and rare collar badges. Many of these have been artificially aged to make them appear genuine. A genuine badge should be crisp or worn, never that blurred, smudgy appearance. Caveat emptor indeed!

MAKERS NAMES. Some collar badges, usually those of Officer quality, have the manufacturer's name on the reverse, often in the form of a small tablet. Naturally this helps to establish the authenticity of the item, but it has been known for unscrupulous persons to attach a genuine maker's tablet to the reverse of a fake item!

CAST COLLAR BADGES. Since the 1970's cast collar badges have appeared, having emanated from abroad. These are generally cheap and their appearance leaves much to be desired. None of them are authentic, but should not be confused with those cast collar badges usually made in India, for a Regiment serving overseas. Sand cast and made by local craftsmen, they were bought and worn by soldiers of many Infantry Regiments.

EMBROIDERED. Nothing can compare with the beautiful hand made embroidered/bullion collar badges, especially those worn prior to 1914. Over the years since that time, not only has the standard of product dropped, but the price has increased, and their cost is now almost prohibitive.

The Royal Scots (The Royal Regiment)

Pre 1881
The 1st or The Royal Scots Regiment of Foot
In 1872, the premier Regiment of the Line, not wishing to wear the brass crown authorised to be worn as a collar badge by Regiments of the Line, received permission to adopt a special badge. The one chosen was a tall narrow thistle with leaves either side, the left as viewed, attached to the thistle head, and with the end of the stem curving either to the left or right according to the side worn.

Made in brass, the Pattern No.9310 was sealed on 16th July 1873, and worn by rank and file in facing pairs on the collar of the full dress tunic and frock, at an angle and with the stem of the thistle curving towards the collar opening. (Fig.1). In 1873, the Regiment received further permission to wear the crown, rejected as a collar badge, above the '1' on the shoulder strap of the NCOs and privates.

After the Officers rank badges were removed to the shoulder in 1880, they wore thistles of a similar design but in embroidered wire thread.

Post 1881
In 1881, came the Territorial system which abolished the numerical titles. On 1st July 1881, the Regiment was renamed, *The Lothian Regiment*, but later in the year this was altered to, *The Royal Scots (Lothian Regiment)*, finally in 1920 to *The Royal Scots (The Royal Regiment)*. They adopted the dress sanctioned for Lowland Regiments, this included new collar badges for wear on the doublet. This new badge for rank and file, Pattern No.9876, sealed on 8th December 1881, was a thistle above a scroll inscribed, 'ROYAL SCOTS.' In gilding metal and worn in facing pairs, again with the end of the stem curving towards the collar opening. (Fig.2). Minor variations exist such as voiding and non-voiding above the title scroll, but these are merely manufacturing quirks. Renewal of the standard pattern, 'Was demanded in November 1897 to be cut from new dies.' The resulting Pattern, No.9876a was sealed on 6th April 1898. There was no change in the general design. This was the pattern used as a guide for the eventual gold anodised version. (Fig.3)

The gilding metal pattern is also known in both white metal and 'silver' anodised, both worn by pipers. The first white metal badge was a 'chunky' item with 2 lug fittings. (Fig.4). This badge was replaced, again in white metal in 1954, when on the 26th March, Pattern No.16187 was sealed, 'For the 7th/9th Battalions,' under Authority 39/154/4025 (Order 17). These were flatter and had a single lug fitting. (Fig.5). Like the ones they replaced, they too were 'For wear by pipers and pipe-majors,' and it was this pattern that was used as a guide for the eventual pattern in silver anodised, Pattern No.18580 sealed in 1961. (Fig.6). A renewal Pattern, No.19202 was sealed 7th May 1964 under Authority 54/INF/8773, again for use by pipe-majors and pipers of the 'A' (Royal Scots) Company, 1st Battalion *Lowland Volunteers*, No.1 (8th/9th) Battalions, Royal Scots Company, and No.1 Company, 2nd Battalion *The Lowland Volunteers*.

The 1976 Edition of the Catalogue of Ordnance Stores lists gold anodised for all except pipers and pipe majors - silver anodised, for them. Confirmed by the 1978 Edition with, 'Gold anodised aluminum for other ranks, Scottish No.1 Dress in Archer green handed design.' Also confirmed in later Editions.

The other ranks pattern is also known in chrome, in gilt, worn by Warrant Officers, and in silver, worn by some pipe-majors. The gilt and silver versions are

Fig.1

Fig.2

Fig.3

Fig.4

Fig.5

Fig.6

HISTORY OF THE BRITISH ARMY INFANTRY COLLAR BADGE

believed to have been worn in the early post 1881 period, and the one in chrome in the mid 1950's.

In 1881, Officers of the Regiment adopted as their collar badge, 'The Thistle in gold embroidery, on a blue cloth ground.' These were worn in facing pairs, horizontally, with the stalk nearer the opening of the collar. (Fig.7). In 1894, the new pattern of mess jacket with roll collar was introduced into the Regiment, and a small embroidered Star of the Order of the Thistle was worn on the lapels, (Fig.8), this replacing the thistle which had previously been worn on the stand up collar of the old mess jacket. (Fig.9).

Towards the end of 1901 and the beginning of 1902, the plain blue double breasted frock coat replaced the scarlet patrols, and the 1902 Dress Regulations records for collar badges, 'On the mess jacket and frock coat, as for forage cap but smaller.' The collar badge referred to was the Star of the Order of the Thistle in silver plate; on the star a raised circle inscribed with the Motto of the Order, 'NEMO ME IMPUNE LACESSIT' (No one provokes me with impunity) in gilt; within the circle on a ground of green enamel, the Thistle in gilt. (Fig.10). The same design, but in bronze, was worn on the collar of the Service Dress, also introduced in 1902, The collar badge for mess jackets, Service Dress, and renewal for No.1 Dress was sealed on 20th November 1903.

The badge worn on the mess jacket and blue patrol jacket varied considerably from a similar badge portrayed on the buckle of the full dress waist belt, the latter being identical to the badge worn by the Officers of the Scots Guards. This discrepency was relayed to the War Office by the Colonel-in-Chief of the Regiment on 8th September 1930, culminating in a letter from the War Office dated 16th April 1931, notifying the Regiment that an amended pattern was to be sealed. This new pattern was in bronze and also in silver, gilt and enamel. (Fig.11)

Many variations exist from almost circular to a lozenge shape, and there are both voided and non-voided centres. Some are made in one piece, others in two, whilst those in bronze vary from light brown through to very dark brown, almost black. Some centres are only slightly raised above the star, whilst others are in high relief. Both the size and design of the thistle vary. (Figs.12,13,14 for three early bronze variations). Besides the bronze and silver/gilt and enamel versions, the pattern also exists in bi-metal, a gilding metal centre with the remainder in white metal. These were worn by Warrant Officers and Sergeants in the 1920's, (Fig.15). Warrant Officers Class 2 wore them in all gilt, (Fig.16 later pattern). The Officers pattern has been noted in chrome, though the dress and period usage are unknown.

There has been no great changes of pattern for the Officers badges throughout the Regiment's history, and although a new pattern was cut on 20th July 1961 for wear by Officers of the 8th/9th Battalions, The Royal Scots TA, the badge remained the same for wear on the No.1 Dress, Service Dress, and Mess Dress.

In 1982, Officers and Warrant Officers of A (Royal Scots) Company, 1st Battalion, *Lowland Volunteers*, and No.1 (8th/9th Battalions Royal Scots) Company, 2nd Battalion, *The Lowland Volunteers*, wore collar badges in nickel silver, gilt and enamel on the Mess Dress jacket. Pattern No.30481, sealed 20th October 1983, No.2 Dress in gilding-metal with a bronze finish, the Star and Motto of the Order of the Thistle, Pattern No.30133, sealed 10th December 1981. No.1 Dress, the Thistle in gold embroidery on a blue cloth ground, worn horizontally in pairs. The 1986 Dress Regulations confirm these patterns.

Fig.7

Fig.8

Fig.9

Fig.10

Fig.11

Fig.12    *Fig.13*    *Fig.14*

Militia
The Edinburgh (or Queen's) Regiment of Light Infantry Militia

A Gaunt pattern book in the National Army Museum records that this Regiment wore a knotted ribboned bugle as their collar badge. In white-metal for other ranks (Fig.17), and in silver for Officers, annotated,' For shell jacket collar ornament R & L.' (Right and Left facing). (Fig.18). On 1st July 1881 the Regiment became the 3rd Battalion, The Royal Scots.

Rifle Volunteer Corps, Volunteer, Territorial Force & Territorial Army Battalions
City of Edinburgh Rifle Volunteer Brigade

Like most Rifle Regiments, the City of Ediburgh Rifle Volunteer Brigade wore no collar badges, and when in 1881 they formed part of the Royal Scots as the 1st Volunteer Battalion (later expanded to 2nd & 3rd Battalions), they adopted the collar badge worn by the Regular Battalions.

Only in 1908, when they became the 4th & 5th (Queen's Edinburgh Rifles) Battalions, Territorial Force, did they adopt their own pattern of collar badge. It was a smaller version of the glengarry badge - The Star of the Order of the Thistle with a K/C above the Motto circle and a bugle horn below. The bugles do not face. Other ranks wore them in white-metal (Fig.19), Officers in bronze for wear on the recently adopted Service Dress. Two sizes are recorded, (Figs.20, 21). They also appear in both silver/gilt, (Fig.22) and silver/gilt/enamel, for full dress. The latter was also used as a pouch badge. These were worn until 1921 when the two Battalions were amalgamated to become the 4th/5th Battalion. (Queen's Edinburgh). They gradually adopted the collar badges of the Regular Battalions. They were transferred to the Royal Artillery, 22nd July 1940 as *52 SL Regiment RA (Queen's Edinburgh, The Royal Scots.)*

5th (East Linton) Corps, Haddington Rifle Volunteers

This Corps was consolidated 13th April 1880 as the *1st Haddington R.V. Corps*, and up to that time had worn as a collar badge, a strung/ribboned bugle with figure 'V' between the strings, (Line drawing No. 23). Similar in design to the larger headdress badge. The Corps became the 6th Vol. Battalion, The Royal Scots, 1st July 1881 and redesignated in April 1888 as the 7th Vol. Battalion. From 1904 to 1908 they wore as a collar badge a smaller version of the Regular Battalions other ranks glengarry badge, but in white metal. (Fig.24). In 1908 they amalgamated with the 6th Vol. Battalion to form the 8th Battalion (TF) The Royal Scots. They then adopted the parent Battalions' other ranks collar badges, up to further amalgamation with the 6th (TF) Battalion in 1920, and subsequent conversion to a Royal Artillery unit.

1st Berwickshire Rifle Volunteer Corps

Consolidated in 1880 as the *1st Berwickshire Rifle Volunteer Corps*, they were allied to the Royal Scots in 1881 as one of its allotted Volunteer Battalions, but retaining its 1880 title. In 1887 it was transferred to the King's Own Scottish Borderers. Both Officers and men wore the same collar badge, a similar Thistle to that worn by the parent Battalions (other ranks), but in place of the 'Royal Scots' on the scroll appeared, '1st BERWICK R.V.' (Fig.25). Drawings of the approved badge were placed in the pattern room at Horse Guards 23rd May 1884 and appear under reference V/1/BERWICK/303, dated 12th September 1884.

3rd (Penicuik) Midlothian Rifle Volunteer Corps

Formed 22nd May 1860, the Corps wore as their collar badge in the late 1870's, the figure of a demi-huntsman with a whip in one hand and blowing a horn with the other. (Line drawing No. 26). This represents the Crest of the Clerks of Penicuik and concerns the singular tenure by which the family hold the lands. 'That when the Sovereign shall come to hunt on the Boroughmuir near

Fig.15

Fig.16

Fig.17

Fig.18

Fig.19

Fig.20

Fig.21

HISTORY OF THE BRITISH ARMY INFANTRY COLLAR BADGE

Edinburgh, the proprietor must sit on the Buckstone and wind three blasts upon a horn.'

The Corps was consolidated in 1880 as the *2nd Midlothian and Peebles Rifle Volunteer Corps* and redesignated as the 6th Vol. Battalion, The Royal Scots in 1888., amalgamated with the 7th Vol. Battalion in 1908 to become the 8th Battalion (TF) The Royal Scots, with head-quarters at Haddington. Joined the 6th (TF) Battalion in 1920 and converted to a Royal Artillery unit.

10th (Cyclist) Battalion (TF)

Formed from the 8th Vol. Battalion in 1908, both Officers and other ranks wore the same badges as those used by their counterparts in the Regular Battalions, but with a distinctive blackened finish. (Figs.27, 28 respectively).

17th (Rosebery) Battalion

Raised 1st May 1915. An enamel badge in the form of a primrose was given to all ranks of this Service Battalion upon raising, by the Earl of Rosebery. On the uppermost petal was inscribed, '17th BATN.', on the next two, 'R' and 'S', and across the two petals, 'ROSEBERY' (Line drawing No.29). The Earl of Rosebery's family name is Primrose. The badge was worn as a collar badge on one side of the collar only. The Battalion was disbanded 2nd May 1919.

Other Items

One collar badge that is sometimes confused with those of the Royal Scots is a thistle spray, not unlike that worn by the Regiment, but over a scroll inscribed, 'ALBANAM BUADH'. (Fig.30). It is, however, a collar badge of the *Transvaal Scottish Volunteers*. Another item of similar design but with the scroll reading, 'CABER FEIDH,' and in white metal. (Fig.31) This motto, 'Antlers of the Deer' is generally associated with the Seaforth Highlanders, but is not restricted to them. As the 9th Vol. Battalion, The Royal Scots were the only 'Highlanders' associated with the Regiment (1900-08), it was possibly worn by them.

General

Those collar badges involving the Thistle were worn with the stem of the flower facing towards the collar opening.

It was announced 23rd July 1991 that under Options for Change, The Royal Scots were to merge with The King's Own Scottish Borderers. On 3rd February 1993, this decision was rescinded.

Fig.22

Fig.23

Fig.24

Fig.25

Fig.26

Fig.27

Fig.28

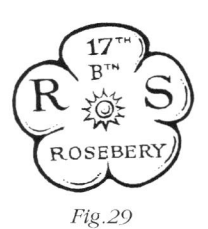

Fig.29

Fig.30

Fig.31

The Queen's Royal Regiment (West Surrey)

Pre 1881
The 2nd (Queen's Royal) Regiment of Foot

Although collar badges were authorised to be worn by an Army Order, 30th June 1874, those of the 2nd Foot were not sealed until 26th July 1877. It was generally agreed that the proposed other ranks collar badge would be a Paschal Lamb, but there were several different views as to exactly how the Lamb should appear. Eventually a trial pattern in brass was struck, with the Lamb standing on 'ground'. (Fig.32). It was not adopted and it must be assumed that the heraldic purists won the day by having the eventual pattern showing the Lamb standing on a torse. (Figs.33 & 34 illustrate a facing pair). Pattern No.9575, sealed, as stated, 26th July 1877. Haloed and with the left front leg 'crooking' a staff which extends upward from the torse to behind the shoulder and above and behind the head. At the top flies a swallow tailed banner emblazoned with a cross.

In brass and with the halo and area between the raised front leg and staff unvoided, they were worn in facing pairs. The left facing one is almost identical to the top part of the other ranks glengarry of the period.

From 1880, Officers of the Regiment wore similar design badges but in embroidered metal thread and silk. (Fig.35).

There have been many theories regarding the usage of a Paschal Lamb as a Regimental device, but the origin and adoption remain obscure. The two most likely are the Regiments raising in 1661 as The Tangier Regiment or Queen's Own Regiment of Foot, the Queen being Catherine of Braganza, wife of Charles II. Part of her dowry was the North African enclave of Tangier, and the Regiment was required to defend and consolidate the settlement against the Moors, a Christian emblem therefore was perhaps appropriate. Secondly the lamb may have been a personal badge of the House of Braganza, though no heraldic connection has been definitely established. Indeed, the original lamb that appeared on the colours and appointments was not a Paschal Lamb, having a bushy tail and without the staff and banner. In the 'Regulations for Clothing and Colours, 1747,' it is referred to as 'a Lamb being their ancient badge.' Only in 1830 did the Officers first introduce a Paschal Lamb onto their shoulder belt plate.

Post 1881

On 1st July 1881, the Regiment became *The Queen's (Royal West Surrey Regiment)*, but it was not until 20th January 1882 that a new pattern collar badge No.9980 in gilding-metal was sealed to replace the pre 1881 type.

The pattern adopted was very similar to that of the previous one, the main difference being the placing of the Lamb on a tablet inscribed 'QUEEN'S' in place

Fig.32

Fig.33

Fig.34

Fig.35

Fig.36

Fig.39  *Fig.38*  *Fig.37*

of the torse. Different dies show voided and unvoided areas between the raised leg and staff. One unusual feature was that both ends of the scroll, curved back behind the animal's feet, ending in a fish tail shape similar to the banner. (Fig.36). On 14th December 1897, authorisation was recorded for the standard pattern to be renewed and cut from new dies. This was Pattern No.9980a and in gilding-metal as before; the opportunity was taken to slightly alter the design of the Lamb, and to place it on a more substantial tablet. Where previously, with ones facing to the right a front leg was above the apostrophe on the tablet, it now stood on the 'N' of 'QUEEN'S'. (Figs.37 & 38 for variations).

During this early period, Dress Regulations describe the Officers collar badge for tunic collars as 'The Paschal Lamb in frosted gilt metal,' (Fig.39). On a torse and similar in design to the other ranks collar badge pre 1881, the Lamb was larger, the halo was voided and the staff had a cruciform finial. Officers also wore embroidered badges, the Lamb, ground, halo, and staff in gold thread, the banner in silver, and the cross on the banner, plus the Lamb's eye, nose and mouth picked out in red silks. (Figs.40 & 41).

In 1894, the Regiment received notification from the Army Authorities, dated 19th April and stating that when their stock of collar badges, estimated to last a further three years, was used up, a new collar badge was to be introduced. This was to have the definite article placed in front of 'QUEEN'S'. This was followed by a further instruction 30th November 1896 under reference ACD/patt/8189, after which sketches for the proposed badge were forwarded for approval on 25th October 1897. As well as the title addition, the badge differed from the earlier one in two respects. There was a change in the shape of the Lamb and the tablet was replaced with a white metal scroll. The badge, Pattern No.4682 was sealed 22nd July 1898 and worn until 1920. There were the usual minor variations. (Figs.42 & 43).

Officers wore similar badges but in silver/gilt for wear on the tunic, mess jacket and frock coat. New dies were cut 4th February 1904, recorded in Dress Regulations as 'The Paschal Lamb in frosted gilt or gilding metal. In silver a scroll inscribed The Queen's.' (Fig.44). On the introduction of Service Dress for Officers in 1902, bronze collar badges were worn on the jacket in facing pairs, described in the 1902 Dress Regulations, 'As for tunic collar, with scroll as for forage cap.' One pattern had the same length of scroll as that worn by the soldiers, but others had much longer forage cap length scrolls (Figs.45 & 46). The same pattern is also found polished and worn on the khaki drill jacket. These larger ones usually having the extra support of three lug fittings.

An other ranks pattern in gilt and omitting the apostrophe was worn by Warrant Officers (Fig.47).

The 1911 Dress Regulations records, 'For the mess jacket, the badge in gold, silver and crimson embroidery, without a scroll.' There are also embroidered badges with the scroll (Fig.48).

For some time, the Dress Committee had been aware that the collar badge worn on the right side differed from the orthodox pattern. They observed that the pole could not be borne on the 'off' shoulder of the Lamb and 'meticulous accuracy must give way to symmetry in appearance'. The pole should therefore be placed on the 'hidden' shoulder and the corresponding leg raised. When on 1st January

Fig.40

Fig.41

Fig.42

Fig.43

Fig.44

Fig.45

Fig.46

Fig.47

THE QUEEN'S ROYAL REGIMENT (WEST SURREY)

1921 the title of the Regiment was changed to *The Queen's Royal Regiment (West Surrey)*, they took the opportunity to introduce new collar badges which were strictly in accordance with drawings from the College of Arms. These were based on Army Order 509 of 1920. This new badge (Fig.49) shows that, in addition to the changes already mentioned, the Lamb became more upright, the swallow tailed banner was replaced by a square flag and the title scroll was abondoned in favour of a torse.

This was Pattern No.3990 sealed 5th June 1924 under reference P1160/OP4682. These were worn until 1952, when a renewal pattern was cut from new dies. Pattern No.3990a and sealed 2nd May 1952 under Authority 54/Officers/4051. Very similar but with a central single lug fitting, (Fig.50) This was the pattern used as a guide for the later version in gold anodised. Facing to the left it was used for wear in the beret (slider fastener). Noted also in chrome and said to have been used, unofficially, by the Regimental Police in the mid 1950's.

Dress Regulations describe the Officers tunic badge as 'The Paschal Lamb in frosted gilt or gilding metal, in pairs.' Design as for other ranks. Made in bronze for wear on the Service Dress (Figs.51 & 52) for variations. For the mess jacket the description reads, 'The badge is in gold, silver and crimson embroidery, on blue cloth.' (Figs.53, 54, 55) show three varieties.

Militia
2nd Royal Surrey Militia

The other ranks collar badge in white-metal, Pattern No.7584 for wear on the tunic was sealed on 28th April 1876 under Ref. PC/2SM/206. It was an eight pointed rayed star of Garter style, but with the title '2nd ROYAL SURREY MILITIA' inscribed on the strap. (Fig.56). Legend has it that the badge was awarded to the Regiment by the Duke of York, as a mark of his pleasure on their smart appearance, at a review at Ashford, Kent, in 1803. The badges are non facing.

The Regiment became the *3rd Battalion The Queen's (Royal West Surrey Regiment)* 1st July 1881. A Gaunt pattern book of the period shows the gilt Paschal Lamb with swallow tailed pennant and standing on a torse as, '3rd Battalion - 2nd Royal Surrey Militia collar badge.' (Fig.57). The other ranks equivalent is of similar design but in brass. It has pointed ends to the banner and is the only other ranks Paschal Lamb collar badge on a torse prior to 1881 that has the halo voided. (Figs.58 & 59, a facing pair).

Rifle Volunteer Corps, Volunteer, Territorial Force & Territorial Army Battalions

On 1st July 1881, the *2nd, 4th, 6th, and 8th Surrey Rifle Volunteer Corps* became Volunteer Battalions of the Regiment and on 1st March 1883 were redesignated 1st, 2nd, 3rd, and 4th Volunteer Battalions respectively.

Up to 1897, they wore the same other ranks pattern collar badge as the Regular Battalions, but in white-metal.

A new design, in keeping with the one adopted by the Regular Battalions in 1897, was submitted by Messrs. Samuel Bros., contractors, London, 'in German

Fig.48

Fig.49

Fig.50

Fig.51

Fig.52

Fig.55 *Fig.54* *Fig.53*

HISTORY OF THE BRITISH ARMY INFANTRY COLLAR BADGE

Fig.56

Fig.57

Fig.58

Fig.59

silver,' on behalf of the 3rd. Vol. Battalion in 1894. This was approved by Horse Guards, 10th October 1894 under Authority V/6 Surrey/360, but not worn until supplies of the previous pattern had been exhausted. Worn by all the Vol. Battalions.

There were the usual minor variations in shape and size of the Lamb, and voiding and non voiding in the raised front leg area. (Figs.60 & 61).

Officers wore similar badges to those of the Regulars, but in silver embroidery and also in silver. Many variations are found, not only with the usual voiding or non voiding, but in the shape of the halo, and the shape of the finial cross. The fixing of the banner to both the animal and the staff vary as do the banners themselves, some with a small cross, others with the cross occupying the whole banner. (Figs.62 & 63). The pattern is also known in white-metal, and conversely the other ranks pattern is known in silver (Fig.64).

The above applied to the 1st, 3rd, and 4th Vol. Battalions, but the 2nd Vol. Battalion, to emphasize their former Rifle connection, wore the badges with a blackened finish, both in the early pattern and the later one. This applied to all ranks.

In keeping with the Regular Battalions, the Vol. Battalions changed the pattern in 1898, wearing the same design but in white-metal. (Fig.65). The Officers also adopted the corresponding pattern, but in silver (Fig.66). The 2nd Vol. Battalion continued the practice of the blackened finish. When Service Dress was introduced in 1902, Officers of the Vol. Battalions wore the same bronze collar badge as the Regulars. The letter 'T' was sometimes placed below the collar badge, and photographs of the 1914-1918 period clearly show this. (Fig.67).

The Officers of the 1st Vol. Battalion wore for a short time a distinctive bronze collar badge. A smaller Paschal Lamb standing on a torse in place of the scroll. (Fig.68). They are also known with a blackened finish, perhaps worn by the 2nd Vol. Battalion (Fig.69).

In 1908, the Vol. Battalions were reorganised into Territorial Force Battalions continuing to wear the same pattern of collar badge. In 1920 they adopted the square flag and torse pattern of the Regulars, and in 1922 they were redesignated Territorial Army Battalions.

Fig.60    *Fig.61*    *Fig.62*    *Fig.63*

Fig.64    *Fig.65*    *Fig.66*

24

THE QUEEN'S ROYAL REGIMENT (WEST SURREY)

As stated, the badges of the Regular units were in use, but some badges exist which suggests that there were some attempts to continue with a 'Volunteer' distinction. The Officers post 1920 pattern is known in silver (Fig.70), and in a blackened form, presumably worn by the 5th Battalion (Fig.71).

The other ranks followed the Regulars in wearing their badges in gilding-metal and the subsequent gold anodised (Fig.72).

Schools

Several schools in Surrey adopted the Paschal Lamb for their OTC badges, using both the swallow tailed banner and the square flag patterns. Charterhouse (Figs.73 & 74), Cranleigh, Reigate Grammar School, Royal Grammar School, Guildford, and Godalming. Whitgift School Cadet Corps was formed in 1875 and attached to the 2nd Surrey Rifle Volunteers and the ensuing 1st Vol. Battalion. A photograph of the Corps in 1901 shows the CO, Lieut. A.T. Smith, wearing the parent Regiment's collar badge, but the NCOs are wearing badges of circular formation, details of which are not discernible.

General

The shape and size of the Paschal Lamb has varied considerably over the years, so too has the banner/flag and staff finial. They were worn in facing pairs with the lamb facing inwards towards the collar opening.

On 14th October 1959, The Queen's Royal Regiment (West Surrey) amalgamated with The East Surrey Regiment to become *The Queen's Royal Surrey Regiment*.

Fig.67

Fig.68

Fig.69

Fig.70

Fig.71

Fig.72

Fig.73

Fig.74

The Buffs (Royal East Kent Regiment)

Fig. 75

Fig. 76

Fig. 77

Fig. 78

Fig. 79

Pre 1881
The 3rd (East Kent) Regiment of Foot (The Buffs)

In 1874, approval was received by the Regiment for the NCOs and men to wear the Dragon on the collars of the tunics, as from the 1st March. The Pattern, No.9540, in brass, was sealed 19th May 1875. Heraldically it was a 'dragon passant' standing upon a torse. Details show it to be of elongated form with the wings back and closed, the tail is 'S' shaped culminating in an arrowhead form, which points away from the body of the beast. A front leg is raised and points downward. There are minor variations such as thickness of the body and voiding, part voiding and non voiding of the area behind the neck. (Figs.75 & 76 show a facing pair with solid neck areas). Senior NCOs wore a partly voided pattern in white metal. (Fig.77)

Officers wore the Dragon collar badge in both silver and in embroidered thread from c1880.

In 1878, the 2nd Battalion, then in South Africa, received a new pattern kersey tunic with brass Dragon collar badges, and it was this tunic that the Battalion wore during the Zulu War.

Although new collar badges were called for after the 1881 reforms, photographs show this pattern of badge still in use in 1885.

Post 1881

In 1881, the Regiment became *The Buffs (East Kent Regiment)* and, following a decision made 22nd December 1881, received an Order which included the abolition of the Dragon as a collar badge. The White Horse of Kent rampant and with scroll below inscribed 'INVICTA', the Horse in white-metal and the scroll in gilding-metal, was to take its place.

Drawings of the new badge were submitted by Messrs. Smith & Wright, Birmingham, Pattern No.9978 sealed 20th January 1882, having been revised by Colonel Blundell, A.A.G. Horse Guards. A later Pattern No.10237, was sealed 4th August 1882. The badge was first taken into use by the 2nd Battalion, then stationed in Hong Kong, 26th November 1882. (Fig.78).

A Gaunt pattern book shows the Officers pattern to be quite different, in silver only, the Horse is now passant. (Fig.79). A proposed other ranks bi-metal version of this pattern was not adopted.

It is extraordinary to note that at some stage before the badge was finally approved, it was the intention to make the White Horse in gilding metal!

Although there is no written or photographic proof as yet, it would seem that the White Horse had already been borne upon the drums as early as 1866.

On 23rd May 1894, H.R.H. The Duke of Cambridge, C-in-C, approved that the Dragon badge be again worn as the collar badge of the Regiment and invited submissions showing the design and size required. These must already have been to hand, as it was on the 31st May that the drawings were approved and the sketches 'abstracted for future guidance.'

The new badge, Pattern No.4054 in gilding-metal, was sealed 14th August 1894, and differed greatly from the dragon worn by the 3rd Foot. The Dragon was far less elongated, its wings were open and upright and it was standing on ground. The tail remained 'S' shaped and with arrowhead finial. The raised leg still pointed downward. (Fig.80)

The College of Heralds registers the badge of the Buffs as a 'Dragon proper on

THE BUFFS (ROYAL EAST KENT REGIMENT)

a mount, vert,' but the circumstances regarding the introduction of the Dragon as a Regimental device remains obscure. It seems probable that it was granted to the Regiment in 1707 because of the good services, and that a Royal badge was allowed on the grounds that the Regiment was in Royal ownership. The particular device of the Dragon was probably chosen as connecting the Regiment with Queen Elizabeth I in whose reign it traces its origin. Recorded in the 1747 Clothing regulations as 'The Green Dragon' and referred to as 'The ancient badge of the Regiment' in the Royal Warrant of 1751.

In 1896, a new Field Service cap badge was introduced but the collar badge remained the same. However, on 13th September 1898 a new pattern, again in gilding metal was sealed. Pattern No.4054a, annotated, 'The position of the wings of the Dragon altered to follow the design of the new Field Service cap badge.' The body of the Dragon remained much the same, apart from the wings, which were now closed, still on ground and with one leg raised, but now pointing upward. The four point comb on the Dragon's neck was reduced to three points. (Figs.81 & 82 show two variations). Before the introduction of the anodised version, they were made with a single lug fitting. Worn until 1956, there had been no change of pattern when the Regiment was redesignated, *The Buffs (Royal East Kent Regiment)* 3rd June 1935.

The gold anodised version was introduced in 1956, Pattern No.4054a being used as a guide. Sealed 9th October 1956. Worn until amalgamation in 1961.

For Officers, the period Dress Regulations describe the tunic collar badge as, 'In silver, the White Horse of Kent on a gilt scroll inscribed INVICTA.' (Fig.83). After the re-adoption of the Dragon badge, the Dress Regulations 1894 state that on the collar of the tunic shall be worn, 'The Dragon, in silver.' later also for the frock coat and mess jacket. This was the upright and open wing pattern, worn until 1898. (Fig.84). Over the many years since the final pattern change in 1898, they have varied in size and design. The early ones in H.M. silver, unmarked silver, and the later silver plated types clearly illustrate these variances, (Figs.85, 86, 87, 88). That shown in (Fig.87) is strcitly a silvered other ranks pattern and possibly was so treated when the Regiment was overseas and the official Officers badges were unobtainable.

For Officers Service Dress introduced in 1902, Dress Regulations record for the collar badge, in bronze, 'As for tunic collar with scroll as for forage cap.' These were sealed in 1903 (Fig.89). They were found to be too large for the collar and the size was reduced. Two variants of this successive type are known, medium size (Fig.90) and small size (Fig.91). There are many photographs taken during and after WWI showing both sizes in use by the Officers on their khaki drill

Fig.80

Fig.81

Fig.82

Fig.83

Fig.84

Fig.85

Fig.86

Fig.87

Fig.88

Fig.89

Fig.90

Fig.91

HISTORY OF THE BRITISH ARMY INFANTRY COLLAR BADGE

uniform, and some polished down to the base metal. (Figs.92 & 93).

A bronzed other ranks pattern is also recorded (Fig.94) usage unknown.

A gilt K/C version is known, gilded by the Regiment for wear at the 1937 Coronation.

Militia
East Kent Militia

Other ranks wore white-metal collar badges sealed 4th March 1876, 'for tunic and frock collars.' These were the White Horse of Kent on a distinctive ovoid base inscribed "INVICTA", 23mms high x 25mms in width. (Line drawing Fig.95). Worn in facing pairs with the Horse facing inwards towards the collar opening. From c1880 Officers wore the same pattern but in silver. On 1st July 1881 they became the 3rd Battalion The Buffs (East Kent Regiment).

Rifle Volunteer Corps, Volunteer, Territorial Force & Territorial Army Battalions.

The 2nd Kent (East Kent) RVC and the *5th Kent (Weald of Kent) RVC* became Volunteer Battalions of the Regiment 1st July 1881, redesignated the 1st and 2nd Vol. Battalions respectively 1st May 1883, and becoming the 4th and 5th (TF) Battalions 1st April 1908.

There is nothing to indicate that these Battalions wore anything other than the collar badges of the Regular Battalions, this practice continuing right up to conversion to Territorial Army status. The Officers sealed pattern 9th October 1961 confirms them as being in silver and the gold anodised other ranks Pattern No.18581 was sealed 26th September 1961.

There are items however that could be attributed to the Volunteer/TF Battalion periods. One is the large bronze collar badge introduced in 1902, in blackened form which was often adopted by Vol. Battalions as a reminder of their formal Rifle status. (Fig.96). The others relate to the later medium and small versions of the badge. These appear in silver plate and could well have been 'adapted' to differentiate between the Regular and Volunteer units. (Figs.97 & 98).

Kent Volunteer Fencibles

This WWI unit wore as their collar badge a white-metal White Horse of Kent on an oval background, above was a scroll inscribed "K.V.F." and below a scroll inscribed "INVICTA". A small version of the cap badge, they were worn in facing pairs with the Horse facing inwards towards the collar opening. (Fig.99). They later became the *Kent Volunteer Regiment* and finally the 1st - 4th Volunteer Battalions, The Buffs. Disbanded 1919.

General

All collar badges of the Regiment, Horses and Dragons were worn in facing pairs, with the animal facing inwards towards the collar opening.

On 1st March 1961, the Regiment was amalgamated with The Queen's Own Royal West Kent Regiment to form *The Queen's Own Buffs, The Royal Kent Regiment*.

Fig.92

Fig.93

Fig.94

Fig.95

Fig.96

Fig.97

Fig.98

Fig.99

The King's Own Royal Regiment (Lancaster)

Pre 1881
The 4th (The King's Own Royal) Regiment of Foot

Having received permission for a special pattern collar badge, Pattern No.9270 was sealed 8th May 1872 and was confined to usage by the other ranks. The badge was a large Lion of England, passant guardant, without ground or torse. A front paw raised and pointing upwards, the tail curling up over the back and towards the head. In brass and with two brass lugs. (Figs.100 & 101, a facing pair).

On 20th July 1872, under ref. 1/POB, the Regiment received authority for 'Lions to be worn on the collars of Officers tunics and serge frocks.' These were embroidered versions of the other ranks pattern; photographs clearly show them being worn nearest the collar opening, with the rank badges behind. When rank badges were removed to the shoulder in 1879, the collar badges remained as before. (Fig.102). The 4th Regiment of Foot was one of only a few regiments to wear the collar badge as well as the rank badge at the same time. (Plate 1, Lieut. E.J. Lugard, c.1875 - see page 37).

The Lion of England, the ancient and time honoured badge of the Regiment, is purported to have been awarded to them by William of Orange in recognition of their devotion to him and to his cause, after his landing at Torbay in November 1688.

Post 1881

In 1881, the Regiment became *The King's Own (Royal Lancaster Regiment)* and an interim statement 30th September 1881 confirmed 'collar badges to be the same as at present - a Lion.' However on 8th December 1881 a new collar badge in gilding-metal for wear on the tunic and frock Pattern No. 9877 was sealed, ' to replace Pattern No.9270.' This was quite a different Lion, though still passant guardant, much smaller, on ground, and with the tail curling and ending above the rear leg practically identical to the central part of the new other ranks helmet plate. (Fig.103). The Officers equivalent was in gilt but confined to wear on the patrol jacket (Fig.104). The Gaunt rubbings and patterns records a 'new pattern collar badge in silver deposited at the War Office 11th October 1882 from scratched bright dies.' Thought to have been for wear on the mess jacket. The badge for the Officers tunic was in gold embroidery but with a gilt metal mask-like face, extraordinarily the front paws are both down and the pairs of legs are close together. (Fig.105).

On 24th September 1889, the Officer Commanding the Regiment asked for a change in the pattern of collar badge, and on 17th December a sample was extracted. On 18th February 1890 a new pattern, No.2381 was sealed 'in lieu of Pattern No.9877.' This was a return to the type worn by the Regiment in 1872, but now in gilding metal and fitted with copper lugs. (Fig.106).

In 1894, the glengarry cap was abolished and a field service cap of blue cloth introduced, the badge for the cap being the same as the left hand collar badge. In 1896, the badge to be worn by all ranks on the white helmets was to be the same as the collar badge and fastened into the pugaree.

Renewal of the standard pattern in gilding-metal was 'demanded' 18th April 1898, this to be cut from a new die. Sealed 26th September 1899, this was Pattern No.2381a. 'for tunics and frocks to replace Pattern No.2381.' This was the pattern used as a guide for the later gold anodised version.

On 1st January 1921, the Regiment was redesignated *The King's Own Royal*

Fig.100

Fig.101

Fig.102

Fig.103

Fig.104

Fig.105

HISTORY OF THE BRITISH ARMY INFANTRY COLLAR BADGE

Fig.106

Fig.107

Fig.108

Fig.109

Fig.110

Fig.111

Fig.112

Regiment (Lancaster), but there was no change in the collar badge. Over the years, dies were renewed but there were only very minor variations, and other ranks wore the same badge right through to the 1959 amalgamation. The last pattern in gilding-metal having a single lug fixing. A chrome version with the single lug was thought to have been worn by the Regimental Police in the mid/late 1950's (Fig.107).

Dress Regulations from the early 1880's up to the 1934 Edition have described the Officers collar badge for tunic, frock coat, and mess dress as simply 'The Lion in silver.' (Figs.108, 109, 110) show variations. These were also worn on blue patrols, tropical uniforms and great coats.

Similar, but in gilt metal, were worn by Warrant Officers. In 1896 smaller Lions, in silver, were introduced for wear on the mess jacket, and again in gilt for the Warrant Officers, (Figs.111). After the embroidered types already discussed, a different pattern and design was adopted (Fig.112).

The Regiment first wore the 1902 Service Dress in 1903, this incorporated a new pattern of collar badge, described in the 1902 Dress Regulations, 'As for forage cap but in pairs.' This was the large Lion of England over the letters, 'THE KING'S OWN'. The letters conjoined by a central horizontal bar. In facing pairs, several variations are recorded, not only the shape and size of the Lion, but also on which letter its back paw rests. (Figs.113 & 114). The pattern is also known in polished form and was worn by the Officers on their khaki drill uniform. The same pattern, but in gilt, was worn by the Warrant Officers; there is no known other ranks equivalent to this pattern collar badge.

On 3rd September 1936, Colonel Barrett, CB, CMG, CBE, DSO. Colonel of the Regiment wrote to the Under Secretary of State for War, requesting changes in the sealed pattern of Officers Service Dress collar badges - namely that the lettering, The King's Own, be removed for the following reasons:

    i) That the lettering was already on the cap.
    ii) That it made the collar badge an exceptionally large size.
    iii) It was not considered necessary and was not worn by the other ranks.
    iv) The Regimental badge is the Lion of England.

On the 7th October, a letter was sent to Major The Hon. A.Harding, CB, CVO, MC at Buckingham Palace, advising him of the proposed modification and confirming that the Army Council was prepared to accede to the Regiment's request, subject to approval by H.M. The King. Approval was given 8th October 1936 with instructions to 'suitably amend Dress Regulations 1934 in due course.' Ref. 54/INF/7502.

A further letter was written to the Colonel of the Regiment telling him that the mess jacket collar badge was a deviation from Army Regulations and asking him why he had not also reported this in his previous correspondence. His answer, 3rd February 1937 was simply that, 'There is no one in the Regiment who imagined that it was irregular.' He went on to say that the badge was being worn when he joined the Regiment in 1898, and as far as he was aware the tunic badge had never been worn on the mess jackets. There are no further letters to record the outcome!

So the free standing Lion was introduced for wear on the Service Dress and worn up to the 1959 amalgamations (Fig.115, as worn with a red cloth backing).

Militia
1st Royal Lancashire Militia (Duke of Lancaster's Own)

The Army Clothing Department Pattern Room Journals record 'White metal collar badges for tunic and frock, sealed 14th July 1876.' An entry dated 14th May 1878 states, 'Collar badges to be the same pattern as worn by the 4th West York Militia, pattern 7509.' This was the Rose in white metal. (Fig.116).

The Officers of this Militia Regiment were certainly one of the first, if not the first, to wear collar badges. On an Officer's coatee c.1848-1855 in the Preston Museum, can be seen gold bullion and silk Red Rose collar badges. These are placed centrally on the double panels of silver collar lace,

THE KING'S OWN ROYAL REGIMENT (LANCASTER)

approximately 1½ inches back from the collar opening. Further confirmation of this practice is illustrated in Plate.2 (see page 115). This is a Captain's double breasted tunic of the 1855-1856 period. The gold metal thread and crimson silk Red Roses are 1½ inch in diameter and are placed nearest to the collar opening. The Captain's rank badges of a crown and a star are confirmed by the lack of Field Rank lace on the cuff. It is a fair assumption that these badges were carried forward onto the 1856 and 1869 patterns of tunic. Perhaps the inspiration for the Officers of the 4th Foot who adopted this practice in 1872. The 1st Royal Lancashire Militia became the 3rd Battalion The King's Own (Royal Lancaster Regiment) July 1881.

Fig.113

Rifle Volunteer Corps, Volunteer, Territorial Force & Territorial Army Battalions
10th Lancashire Rifle Volunteer Corps

Under General Order 14th February 1883, this Corps was redesignated as the 1st Volunteer Battalion of the King's Own (Royal Lancaster Regiment). In 1900 a 2nd Volunteer Battalion was formed.

Fig.114

The Gaunt rubbings and pattern books show the collar badge of the Volunteer Battalion to be similar to those worn by the Regulars from 1881-1890. The date is given, '24/8/88', Volunteer Officers wore silver embroidered badges on the tunic and mess jacket of relevant size. (Figs.117 & 118). Again, with the metal mask-like face and the non-raised paw of the tunic badge.

For the other ranks a new pattern was submitted by Messrs. Hobsons, and this was approved by Horse Guards 20th August 1888, under Ref V/10 LANCS/653-658. This was the large Lion of England, but in white-metal. Again there was a silver embroidered version for the Officers, the equivalent of the gold embroidered type shown in Fig.112.

Fig.115

In 1908, the 1st and 2nd Vol. Battalions became the 4th and 5th (TF) Battalions respectively, gradually adopting the collar badges of the Line Battalions. Some Officers however retained their individuality by blackening their Service Dress collar badges. Badges for the 4th/5th Battalion (TA) were sealed 1st October 1956, silver plate for Officers No.1 and No.3 Dress, in bronze for Officers Service Dress.

Anodised collar badges are recorded in both 'silver' and 'gold' (Figs.119), and also a small one in silver anodised (Fig.120). Whether this last one was ever worn is doubtful, probably being worn by the post 1959 King's Own Royal Border Regiment.

Fig.116

Other Items

A small badge in gilt metal shows the Lion standing on a solid tablet inscribed, "THE KINGS OWN", (no apostrophe). Not unlike a 'sweetheart' brooch, it does not have the usual pin fastening for such an item, but the two lug fixings normally associated with collar badges. Unidentified. (Fig.121)

Fig.119

General

The Lion of England badges worn by the Regiment were worn in facing pairs with the Lion facing towards the collar opening. On 1st October 1959, the Regiment merged with The Border Regiment to become *The King's Own Royal Border Regiment*.

Fig.120

Fig.117

Fig.118

Fig.121

The Royal Northumberland Fusiliers

Fig.122

Fig.123

Fig.124

Fig.125

Fig.126

Pre 1881
The 5th (Northumberland) (Fusiliers) Regiment of Foot

A plain brass universal Fusilier grenade badge was authorised by Horse Guards letter 21st May 1872, for wear on the collar by other ranks of the 1st Battalion, and by a similar letter 2nd September 1872 for the 2nd Battalion. (Fig.122). These to be worn horizontally in facing pairs, with the ball of the grenade nearest the collar opening.

In 1873, red kersey frocks were authorised for wear by the men in lieu of their shell jackets, and these collar badges were then brought into use. The Pattern, No.9281 sealed 2nd October 1872 was received at the depot 21st April 1874 and worn until 1895. They were also used as a cap badge from 1893 -1895 and as part of the shoulder titles c.1874-c.1920. By an Army Order 14th February 1905 it was decreed that 'all Fusilier regiments are to wear the Royal Artillery collar grenade, Pattern No.9933, with metal shoulder titles, on the shoulder straps of drab jackets and greatcoats.'

An embroidered white worsted grenade was worn horizontally on full dress tunics and frocks from c.1872-c.1895.

Although 1873 was the first time other ranks had worn metal grenades on their collars, they had, from 1836, worn brass grenades on the skirts of the coatee, and grenades of white worsted cloth on the collars; both authorised by Horse Guards letter 27th March 1838, these being worn until c.1855.

The 1872 brass collar badge, but with the addition in white metal of St. George slaying the Dragon, was reputedly worn by senior NCOs from c.1872-c.1895.

The first collar badges for Officers were introduced in 1836 and authorised by the 1838 Horse Guards letter. These were large embroidered gold wire grenades with plain ball, worn on the coatee and shell jacket up to 1855. From c.1869 and up to 1898 grenades of the same composition but approximately 60mm long were worn horizontally on the stand-up collars of the mess jacket.

On the full dress tunic c.1875-1881 they wore embroidered gold wire grenades with St. George and the Dragon in gilt on the ball. Worn horizontally. During the same period they also wore a seven flamed grenade in gilt with St. George and the Dragon above the numeral 'V' in silver mounted on the ball. Worn vertically on undress uniforms. Volunteer Officers wore similar but in silver plates from c.1886.

There is no record of when St.George slaying the Dragon was first adopted by the Regiment but the Royal Warrant of 1751 described it as 'The ancient badge of the Regiment.' The 'Quo Fata Vocant' (Where fate calls us) motto, was authorised in addition to its ancient badge 31st March 1831.

Post 1881

In 1881, the Regiment was redesignated *The Northumberland Fusiliers*, and on 30th September it was decreed, 'the collar badges to be the same as at present for other ranks - a grenade,' but on 11th January 1882 a new grenade in gilding-metal, Pattern No.9933 was sealed, 'in lieu of original pattern.' This grenade with copper lugs was similar to the earlier one other than the metal changes. (Fig.123)

It is assumed that a similar grenade in white-metal was worn by the men of the 2nd and 3rd Volunteer Battalions from c.1895.

A new field service cap and facing collar badges in gilding-metal were approved 24th November 1894, notified to the Regiment by Horse Guards letter

No.61002/4713, 21st December 1894. Pattern No.10334. There was much correspondence regarding these new badges for collar and cap (Pattern No.42766, sealed 14th March 1895). Initially it was intended to reduce the size of the glengarry cap grenade for the new field service cap and the collars, but by 30th May 1895 it was decided that one badge was not suitable for both cap and collar. The Officer Commanding the 1st Battalion was asked to obtain the concurrence of both the 2nd Battalion and the depot for a change of pattern. Presumably this must have been obtained, as on 2nd August 1895 a new collar badge was approved and a sample prepared for sealing. Pattern No.4338a was finally sealed 3rd September 1895, 'in lieu of the Royal Artillery grenade.'

Fig.127

The badge in gilding-metal was a horizontal grenade with St. George and the Dragon appearing within a motto strap, QUO FATA VOCANT, on the ball. For wear by other ranks on the full dress tunic and undress jacket. (Fig.124). Worn until 1939.

The same badge, but in blackened gilding-metal, is thought to have been worn by the men of the 1st Vol. Battalion from 1897-1908, and in white-metal by the soldiers of the 2nd and 3rd Vol. Battalions during the same period. Both on the full dress and undress garments. Also worn on the blue serge uniform by the TF Battalions 1908-1914. These badges were also worn in the vertical position.

Fig.128

In 1935, the Regiment received the additional title 'Royal'. Accordingly a new type of badge, Pattern No.11090 (Cat. No.CB0573), was authorised and sealed 3rd May 1937, under reference 54/INF/7307, this to replace Pattern No.4338a. This was an upright grenade in gilding-metal with St. George and the Dragon within a motto circle in white-metal. Worn until c.1952/53 when it was replaced by a similar but horizontal grenade. Worn on the No.1 and No.3 Dress jackets. (Fig.125). Use of these badges ceased in the Regular battalions in 1962., but continued in the TA units. On 23rd April 1965 the badge in gold and silver anodised was sealed. Pattern No.19702. Made by Messrs. Dowler, it is interesting to note that on the sealed pattern studied, St. George and the Dragon face right on both examples. A similar grenade, but vertical, was worn on the No.2 Dress jacket and on the mess waiters livery jacket c.1956-c.1963. (Fig.126). It is doubtful if these were officially authorised

Fig.129

Gold and silver anodised grenades with St. George and the Dragon within a motto circle were sealed 9th October 1956 under reference 54/INF/8779 for wear vertically on No.2 Dress soldiers jackets of D Company (TA), but whether they were ever worn is not known.

Fig.130

From 1962-1968, the men wore Fusilier Brigade pattern vertical collar badges in gold and silver anodised on the Service Dress jackets. (Fig.127)

From 1881, the Officers wore a vertical seven flamed gilt grenade with St. George and the Dragon in silver, on undress jackets, and also a gold embroidered grenade with silver metal St. George, worn horizontally on the full dress tunic and mess jacket. Worn also on the blue frock coat after its introduction in 1900. This pattern was sealed 8th May 1900 and worn until 1914 (Figs.128 & 129 for varying patterns).

Some have an extra flame on the grenade and known to have been worn by the Sergeants of the 3rd Battalion in 1903, as a cap badge.

Officers of the 2nd and 3rd Vol. Battalions wore on the full dress c.1896-1914 the same pattern badges, but with silver embroidered grenades and gilt metal St. George and the Dragon mounts.

From 1896 until 1914, Regular Officers wore a seven point flamed grenade in gilt metal with silver plated St. George and the Dragon within a motto strap. Worn horizontally on the patrol jacket and similar on the white collar of the scarlet patrol jacket. The same badge was worn by the Bandmasters c.1905-1906 on the full dress tunic.

Fig.131

Officers of the 2nd and 3rd Vol. Battalions wore similar badges but in silver plate, on the patrol jackets from 1896-c.1908. Some with different flame structures and in white metal were also worn during this period.

HISTORY OF THE BRITISH ARMY INFANTRY COLLAR BADGE

The following types were worn on Service Dress during the period 1896-1919:
i) Bronze metal imitation embroidered grenades with St. George and the Dragon also in bronze. Worn horizontally on the Service Dress jacket. (Fig.130)
ii) Similar but vertical (Figs.131 & 132).
iii) As for ii) but with St. George and the Dragon within a motto strap, worn vertically. (Fig.133). According to annotations in a Gaunt Pattern book, these were worn by the 16th (Newcastle) Service Battalion, 1914-1919.
iv) As for ii) but with the grenade in gilt metal and St. George and the Dragon in silver plate. These are not thought to be authentic Service Dress badges, but possibly for wear on a tropical jacket. Some of these were worn at an angle on the deep turn down collar of the early service Dress jacket.

From 1898-1914, both Volunteer and Territorial Officers wore vertical silver bullion grenades, with St. George and the Dragon in gilt, on the mess dress jackets. A similar grenade exists but in gold embroidery and a brass mount, usage and dates unknown.

From 1898-1963, Regular Officers wore vertical gold embroidered grenades with the mount in silver, on the gosling green roll collars of the mess jacket. They vary in size (Figs.134 & 135). Officers of the 2nd and 3rd Volunteer Battalions wore similar but with silver embroidered grenades c.1898-1914.

Regular Officers wore similar collar badges to Fig.135, but worn horizontally on the No.1 and No.3 Dress jackets, c.1951-1963. TA Battalion Officers wore these badges concurrently and beyond this period. (Fig.136).

There were also gilt metal grenades in imitation embroidery with St. George and the Dragon in silver. These were worn vertically on the tropical mess dress jacket. The pattern was authorised by War Office letter 8th July 1898, sealed 9th February 1903, and successively 13th January 1904 and 22nd February 1961.

From 1902-c.1938, bronze grenades with bronze mounts were worn with St. George and the Dragon within a circle inscribed "NORTHUMBERLAND FUSILIERS". These were of quite a different shape having nineteen point fan-like flames. These were also worn on the Service Dress, vertically. Recorded both in facing pairs and with St. George facing left only. (Figs.137 & 138 showing minor variations.)

By 1913, Regular Officers had ceased wearing this pattern of badge but they continued to be worn by some Territorial Officers until 1938.

From c.1908-1924, Officers of the 4th, 5th, and 6th (TF) Battalions wore this pattern of grenade in bronze, but with the addition of a battle honour scroll inscribed, "SOUTH AFRICA 1900-02". This was attached to the base of the grenade. (Fig.139). A War Office letter 5th July 1924 decreed that there should be only one list of battle honours for all Battalions of each Regiment, and it was probably because of this Directive that the badge ceased to be worn officially after 1924. Photographic evidence indicates that they were still being worn as late as 1934. It has been suggested that these badges were made up privately by those Officers who had served in the Boer War.

From 1939-c.1945, vertical grenades in bronze (44mm x 26mm) with St. George and the Dragon facing left within a motto circle were worn. It is interesting to

Fig.132

Fig.133

Fig.134

Fig.135

Fig.136

Fig.137

Fig.138

note that successive copies of Dress Regulations, 1902, 1911, and 1934, when mentioning bronze collar badges for Service Dress, do not authorise facing pairs. In fact the 1904 Edition states, 'Not to be worn in pairs.'

Regular Officers wore, from 1951-1963, emboidered gold grenades with silver mounts on the No.1 and No.3 Dress jackets. Worn afterwards by the Territorial Officers. Worn horizontally. Additionally, during the period 1953-1966, Officers wore a grenade in gilt metal, 44mm x 26mm, the ball mounted in silver with the design of St. George and the Dragon within a motto circle. Worn horizontally on No.1 and No.3 Dress jackets. (Fig.140). This is the Officers equivalent to the mens' pattern (Fig.125).

From 1962-1968, Officers wore the Fusilier Brigade pattern collar badge, a gilt grenade with Q/C, the ball mounted with St. George and the Dragon within a laurel wreath, in silver plate. Ordered to be worn from 1st September 1962, vertically on the Service Dress jacket. (Fig.141). A gold embroidered and silver plate version was worn vertically on the mess dress jacket. (Fig.142)

The same badge, worn horizontally, was used for the No.1 Dress jacket (Fig.143). Both types were sealed 15th March 1965.

Militia
The Northumberland Light Infantry Militia

The Army Clothing Department Pattern Room Journals record 28th January 1876, 'white metal collar badges for tunic and frock, sealed.' These badges were of a distinctive and attractive pattern. A bugle horn suspended from a looped, buckled strap on which is inscribed in three separate sections, NOR THUM BERLAND, the 'R' and the 'T' are partially obscured by the 'knotting' of the strap. The numerals XXVII are on another part of the strap, these represent the county precedence of the Regiment. (Fig.144). Worn in facing pairs with the mouthpiece nearest the collar opening.

Also worn by the Officers in silver and silver plate, sometimes with the letter 'M' below the badge..

From 1904, Officers of the 3rd (Militia) Battalion wore gilt metal imitation embroidered grenades with St. George and the Dragon in silver plate. Worn horizontally on the patrol jacket. The Regiment became the 3rd Battalion, The Northumberland Fusiliers in July 1881.

Rifle Volunteer Corps, Volunteer, Territorial Force & Territorial Army Battalions.

Consolidated in 1880, the *1st Northumberland (Northumberland and Berwick-on-Tweed) Rifle Volunteer Corps*, the *2nd Northumberland Rifle Volunteers*, and the *1st Newcastle-on-Tyne Rifle Volunteer Corps* were nominated as Volunteer battalion in 1881. Redesignated as the 1st, 2nd, and 3rd Volunteer Battalions respectively in 1883.

There is no evidence to suggest that the Rifle Volunteer units wore collar badges. The 1st Vol. Battalion did not wear collar badges as far as is known, and

Fig.139

Fig.140

Fig.141

Fig.142

Fig.143

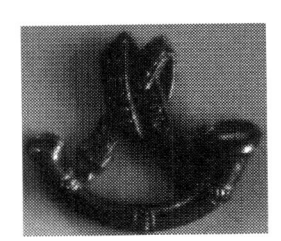

Fig.144

Fig.145

Fig.146

Fig.147

Fig.148

Fig.149

those of the 2nd and 3rd Vol. Battalions have been discussed in the previous text.

In 1908, these three Battalions were redesignated as the 4th, 5th and 6th (TF) Battalions respectively, again their badges have been discussed.

WWI Service Battalions

20th, 21st, 22nd, 23rd Service Battalions. The 1st, 2nd, 3rd, 4th Tyneside Scottish. Most of the Service, Reserve and Garrison Battalions of the WWI era wore the collar badges of their parent Regiments, one exception being the Tyneside Scottish Battalions of the Northumberland Fusiliers, who evolved their own design, a demi-lion rampant emerging from a tower and holding a pennant bearing the Cross of St. Andrew. This device is part of the Arms of Newcastle, Scottish residents having had a long affinity with the town, indeed there was a kilted Highland company in the Rifle Volunteers of 1861.

The only collar badges known to have been worn during WWI are those in bronze, worn by Officers on the Service Dress. (Fig.145)

Those that appear in white metal and silver are almost certainly of modern manufacture and were worn by the pipers of the Tyneside Scottish Pipe Band after WWII. Officers of the 203 (TS) Battery, 101 Field Regiment RA, TA also wore the same badge, the pipe band being part of that unit.

Again, in gilt and slightly larger than the others and in gilding-metal (Fig.146) are almost certainly from a pattern sealed in 1956. Also in gold anodised Pattern No.19471, sealed 15th March 1965 under Authority A/54/Misc/7593, for wear by *439 (Tyne) Regiment RA (Tyneside Scottish)*.

Also worn by *670 LAA Regiment RA (TA)* who up to 1947 were the Tyneside Scottish. Their collar badges in gilding-metal were sealed 18th May 1953, Pattern No.15731. Worn in facing pairs with the lion facing outwards from the collar openings. Photographic evidence indicates that they were also worn facing inwards.

The 14th, 17th, 18th, and 19th Service Battalions (Tyneside Pioneers)

These units wore the universal crossed rifle and pick collar badges in facing pairs, in gilding-metal for the men and bronze for Officers. (Figs.147 & 148 respectively). The other ranks badge was Pattern No.8365, sealed in 1915 and marked 'obsolete 25/4/21/' under Authority ACD/43896.

24th, 25th, 26th, 27th Service Battalions (The Tyneside Irish)

During the Great War, these four Battalions and two Reserve Battalions were known as the Tyneside Irish. There is very little information concerning their insignia, and no authorisation can be found for the wearing of special pattern collar badges, either for Officers or men.

There are posed studio photographs of soldiers wearing on their collars, the distinctive crowned Harp and title scroll badge that formed part of their shoulder title. Similarly the Harp by itself. There are also photographs of Warrant Officers, Sergeants, Pipe Majors and Pipers wearing small crowned Harp badges on their collars. (Fig.149). These same items appear on the photograph of Private Sykes when he received the Victoria Cross from HM King George V. Bandsmen are said to have worn a different shaped harp.

To confuse the issue still further, there are many photographs of the Battalions where no collar badges are being worn at all - either by the Officers or the men.

The Northern Cyclist Battalion

THE ROYAL NORTHUMBERLAND FUSILIERS

It was proposed that an 8th (Cyclist) Battalion be part of the Northumberland Fusiliers in 1908, but shortly after its formation the unit became the Northern Cyclist Battalion.

Because of this rather tenuous connection, they are listed under the Northumberland Fusiliers along with illustrations of their collar badges.. These were twelve spoked cycle wheels, superimposed on crossed rifles and surmounted by the K/C. Worn in gilding-metal by the men and in bronze by the Officers. (Figs.150 & 151) respectively.

Other Badges

In bronze and sometimes mistaken for a collar badge (Fig.152) is a sweetheart brooch. Secondly a very small grenade with nine flames and the numeral 'V' on the ball. (Fig.153) There are only three known examples of this item, one of which is in the Regimental museum. Whether it was ever worn as a collar badge cannot be confirmed. It has been suggested that it might have been worn by NCOs above their rank chevrons, but again this is unconfirmed.

General

All the grenade collar badges with St. George and the Dragon worn by the Regiment were worn in facing pairs (except where stated) with St. George facing towards the collar opening. The flames on the narrow grenades varied from 7 to 9 in number.

On 23rd April 1968, The Royal Northumberland Fusiliers was redesignated the *1st Battalion, The Royal Regiment of Fusiliers.*

Fig.150

Fig.151

Fig.152

Fig.153

*Plate 1
Lt E. J. Lugard, 4th Foot,
c. 1875. See page 29.*

The Royal Warwickshire Regiment

Pre 1881
The 6th (Royal First Warwickshire) Regiment of Foot

By Authority PC/INFY GEN/111, 16th July 1872, the collar badge adopted for wear by the other ranks of the Regiment was an Antelope embellished with a coronet around its neck, and attached to which was a chain, this looped round the body, dropped down between the rear legs to a torse on which the animal stood. (Figs.154 & 155 a facing pair.) The Pattern No.9304 was sealed 1st May 1873. The badge was in brass.

After 1880, the Officers wore similar badges but in embroidered metal thread, again in facing pairs.

The origin of the Antelope as a Regimental device is obscure, but legend has it that when the Regiment was serving in Spain and involved in the defeat of the combined Spanish and French at Saragossa in 1710, they captured a standard bearing the Antelope as its device. In recognition of their prowess Queen Anne gave permission for the Regiment to adopt it as their badge.

Certainly the Antelope is recorded as the Regiment's 'Ancient badge' in the 1747 Clothing Regulations. Confirmed in the Royal Warrant of 1751.

Post 1881

When the Regiment became *The Royal Warwickshire Regiment* 1st July 1881, it was decided to replace the Antelope collar badge with that of the county Militia Regiment, 'The Bear and Ragged Staff.' The origins of this badge are lost in antiquity but certainly it was the badge of the ancient Earls of Warwick, the Beauchamps and the Nevilles. Still borne as a second crest by the present Earls and used by Warwickshire County Council as their principle charge. Variously shown with the Bear standant or sejant, the latter position was used when the Regiment opted for this new collar badge. (Fig.156). Pattern No.9850 was introduced into the Regiment, 'in lieu of Pattern No.9304', 29th September 1881. In gilding-metal for the other ranks and in silver for the Officers, recorded in the 1883 Dress regulations as "In silver, the Bear and Ragged Staff: the Bear muzzled and chained." (Fig.157)

The other ranks of the two Volunteer Battalions wore from 1883-1890, similar collar badges but in white-metal (Fig.158). There appears to be no official reference to the Volunteer Officers at this time, but as collar badges of this pattern are known in gilt, it seems logical to assume that with the usual metal 'colour' change from that of the Regulars, that these would pertain to those Officers. (Fig.159).

The sitting (sejant) Bear was never popular with the Regiment and it came as no surprise when in 1890 it was replaced by the heraldic alternative, a Bear

Fig.154

Fig.155

Fig.156

Fig.157

Fig.158

Fig.159

Fig.160

Fig.161

standant. Adorned with a collar from which the chain again encircled the animal, but this time partly behind the body, reaching down behind its rear hind leg to a torse. The other hind leg now touched the Staff in addition to the front legs. (Figs.160 & 161) show two variations. This too was in gilding-metal for other ranks and silver for Officers. Described in the 1894 Dress Regulations, 'In silver, the Bear and Ragged Staff: the Bear muzzled and chained.' - for wear on the tunic collar. (Figs.162 & 163) show early and later patterns.

As for the first pattern, other ranks of the Volunteer Battalions wore the same but in white-metal, but an extant other ranks tunic of the 2nd Vol. Battalion worn c1890-1902 has gilding-metal collars. They would appear to have been on the tunic for some considerable time. As mentioned in the introductory text, this feature does not necessarily mean that the uniform's badges are correct, but worthy of note.

Both patterns of Bear appear in chromed metal, never worn by the Regiment, they are usually Police, Ambulance or other civil bodies. (Fig.164).

Yet another change occurred in 1894 when it was decided to replace the Bear collar badge with that of the Antelope. Samples for both the field service cap and the collar badge were received 15th November 1894, and finally approved 24th December 1894. 'Antelope as in centre of old pattern cap badge P972.' This is believed to be Pattern No.9850a.

In white-metal for other ranks this Antelope, 'ducally chained and gorged' was of an entirely different pattern from that worn prior to 1881. The beast now stood on ground, was of squat appearance and had its right fore-leg raised. Not worn in facing pairs. (Fig.165) shows a trial pattern, (Fig.166), an actual specimen.

As it was directed that these badges were only to be brought into use, 'when present stocks are exhausted', and a further pattern was introduced in 1896, it is perhaps doubtful as to whether they were ever worn - if they were, then only for a very short period.

On 10th June 1896, specifications were 'demanded' for an improved design of collar badge, to be the same shape as the new field cap badge. 'To take the place of the wrong shape of those previously demanded.' This new Pattern No.9850b was sealed 7th October 1896 under Ref. ADC/Patt./8279. It was the same design as the one worn prior to 1881 but in white metal. This for wear by the other ranks. Figs.167 & 168 show two variations including the angle of the segments on the torse. When the Regiment was redesignated as Fusiliers in May 1963, the same badge was worn in silver anodised form. This was Pattern No.18482 sealed 23rd February 1961 under Authority 54/INF/8782. Manufactured by Messrs. Smith & Wright. Worn also by the 7th (TA) Battalion being sealed 29th November 1960 and further sealed 14th November 1961. The Band is also said to have worn the anodised badge as part of their shoulder insignia. (Fig.169).

As traditionally the Volunteer Battalions of a Regiment wore badges in opposite metal 'colours', a problem arose when the Line Battalions opted for a white-metal badge in 1896. There is no known equivalent to the white-metal antelope for the 1894-96 period and indeed there is some doubt as to what the volunteers wore on their collars from 1896-1908, but it is believed that they were the same as those worn by the Line Battalions.

It is known that the other ranks of the 1st Vol. Battalion c1900 wore the white-

Fig.162

Fig.163

Fig.164

Fig.165

Fig.166

Fig.167

Fig.168

Fig.169

Fig.170

metal antelope collar badge as a cap badge, as did the boys of the Rugby School Cadet Corps.

From 1896, Officers wore similar pattern Antelope collar badges but in silver and gilt metal. The 1900 Dress Regulations state, 'In frosted silver, the Antelope with gilt or gilding metal collar and chain for wear on the tunic and scarlet frock.'

This was confirmed in the 1902 and 1904 Editions but adding 'and the mess jacket.' The 1911 Edition further clarifying, 'in pairs.' Confirmed in the 1934 Edition, 'for wear on collar of tunic and mess jacket.' Also worn on the later appropriate uniforms.

As can be seen, the basic pattern has remained constant, but minor variations help to pinpoint different periods of use.

Those of the 1896 era have a separate ornate and moveable coronet with a separate moveable chain that can be draped around the animal. (Fig.170). Worn only for a short time these were replaced by a type with a plain but still moveable coronet and chain. The chain looped over and behind the body, reappearing at the top of the back legs, looping behind one rear leg, and coming to rest between the rear legs, on the torse. The Antelope had slightly shorter horns. Some examples have three lug fasteners. Worn until c.1914. Fig.171 illustrates the smaller Antelope with plainer and smaller coronet. Fig.172 shows a larger Antelope and with heraldically an incorrect torse, continual lines. Minor variations are also recorded but c.1934 a noticeable change took place. The torse error was amended, the coronet still separate and again ornate; a cable like 'chain' replaced the earlier linked pattern, and taking a quite different direction. Dropping down from the coronet behind both front legs, it looped behind and over the animal's body to rest against the right hind leg. With longer horns this type was worn until 1963. (Fig.173)

A similar pattern for wear on the No.1 Dress by Officers of the 7th (TA) Battalion was sealed 29th November 1960 and again 14th November 1961. The coronet and chain were now fixed to the animal. (Fig.174)

Upon elevation to Fusilier status in May 1963, the Officers continued to wear the Antelope collar badge on Nos.1 & 3 Dress.

With the introduction of Service Dress for Officers in 1902, a new collar badge was required, described in the 1902 Dress Regulations, 'As for tunic collar with scroll as for forage cap, in bronze.'

Again there are variations, the attitude of the Antelope, voiding and non-voiding between chain/legs/body. Some with the chain reaching down to between the rear legs (Fig.175). Others with the chain coming to rest between front and rear legs. (Fig.176). There are also many minor variations of the torse, angles and sections. (Fig.177) vis-a-vis (Figs.175, 176). The major difference however is that on those worn prior to c.1934 the coronet and linked chain are loose, whereas those since have the fixed cable and coronet.

Later worn by the 7th (TA) Battalion on No.2 Dress. Sealed at the same time as the silver and gilt and anodised patterns.

The same badge, but polished down to the base metal, was worn by Officers on the khaki drill during the mid 1930s.

THE ROYAL WARWICKSHIRE REGIMENT

Militia
1st Warwickshire Militia
The Journals of the Army Clothing Department Pattern Room record under Ref.PC/1WM/146. 'White metal collar badges Patt.7588 for wear on the tunic and frock collars, sealed 11/5/76. The Antelope.'

2nd Warwickshire Militia
The same source records under Ref/PC/2WM/183. 'white metal badges Patt.8925, sealed 9/2/77. The Antelope.' Officers of both regiments wore the Antelope collar badge in all silver, the plain coronet and chain are separate. The direction of the chain varied. (Figs.178 & 179) The Antelope did not feature on any other badges of either Regiment, nor did it have any family or civic connection. A remarkable anticipatory choice. The two Regiments became the 3rd and 4th Battalions, The Royal Warwickshire Regiment, July 1881.

Rifle Volunteer Corps, Volunteer, Territorial Force & Territorial Battalions
1st Warwickshire (Birmingham) Rifle Volunteer Corps
Formed in and around Birmingham 1859/60, the Volunteers wore a distinctive white-metal collar badge of an upright acorn with two oak leaves either side and joined at the base, the whole on a broad torse. Date of adoption is unrecorded but c1874-83 is a reasonable assumption. (Fig.180). The Officers gilt and silver version is illustrated in the Gaunt Pattern books, annotated. 'G & S pairs, 2 shanks, 1st Warwickshire Rifle Volunteers.'

Nominated as a Volunteer Battalion of the Royal Warwickshire Regiment in 1881, the Corps became the 1st Volunteer Battalion in 1883, and upon the creation of the Territorial Force in 1908 became the 5th and 6th Battalions.

2nd Warwickshire Rifle Volunteer Corps
With head-quarters at Coventry this consolidated Battalion was nominated in 1881 and became the 2nd Volunteer Battalion, The Royal Warwickshire Regiment in 1883. It is believed that they wore a quite distinctive, 'Bear and Ragged Staff' collar badge. In blackened brass it differed greatly from those worn by the Regular Battalions, both in size and shape. (Fig.181) shows the animal to be mid-way between the sejant and standant positions. The Officers badge was in gilt metal, (Fig.182). In 1908, they became the 7th (TF) Battalion.

Warwickshire Volunteer Regiment.
Part of the VTC movement formed in 1914, the Officers of the Regiment wore a distinctive collar badge. In bronze, the Bear and Ragged Staff upon a torse, below which is a tri-part scroll inscribed, THE – WARWICKSHIRE – VOLTR REGT. (Fig.183). Worn in facing pairs. The other ranks equivalent was in blackened gilding-metal and was without the scroll. (Fig.184)

General
All the Antelope and Bear and Ragged Staff collar badges, except for the 1881-1890 period, were worn in facing pairs with the animal facing towards the collar opening.

On 23rd April 1968, The Royal Warwickshire Fusiliers became the *2nd Battalion, The Royal Regiment of Fusiliers.*

Fig.178

Fig.179

Fig.180

Fig.181

Fig.182

Fig.183

Fig.184

The Royal Fusiliers (City of London Regiment)

Fig.185

Fig.186

Fig.187

Fig.188

Pre 1881
The 7th (or Royal Fusiliers)

By an Order, 2nd October 1872, those Fusilier Regiments that were providing their own collar badges were permitted to wear embroidered grenades, provided no expense was incurred to the public. This applied to the 7th, and their worsted embroidered grenade collar badges were sealed 18th October 1872, Pattern No.9284.

A special brass fused grenade Pattern No.9542 was sealed 17th May 1875, 'in lieu of Pattern No.9284, worsted embroidered grenade.' This had seven point flames, and on the ball the 'Rose within the Garter and Crown over it.' Additionally the United Red and White Rose had the Arabic numeral '7' superimposed on the centre. Two types are recorded, one with a large '7' (Fig.185 for 5mm size), whereas that in (Fig.186) is 2.5mm. This badge was also worn in gilt by senior NCOs.

The 1874 Dress Regulations directed Fusilier Officers to wear a grenade in gold embroidery, at the end of the collar of their tunics, in front of their badges of rank.

Probably one of the reasons the Regiment was granted the Royal and Ancient badges of Rose, Crown, and garter, was that pieces of Ordnance were cast with Royal badges upon them until the reign of Queen Anne - the badges would therefore be appropriate to a Regiment originally raised for the protection of the Ordnance. At some time during the period 1685-1751 it was known as 'Our Ordnance Regiment.' The 7th was also the first Regiment ever designated as 'Fusiliers'. The fusil, a flint lock weapon lighter than the musket being their particular armament.

Post 1881

On 1st July 1881, the Regiment became *The Royal Fusiliers (City of London Regiment)* and an interim statement of 30th September from the AAG at Horse Guards confirmed the Regiment could continue wearing the same collar badges. It was not until 21st March 1882 that a new Pattern No.10145 in gilding-metal was sealed, 'to replace the brass pattern 9542 of the 7th Regt of Foot.'

Apart from the standard change of metal the only difference in design was the removal of the '7' from the centre of the Rose. Two sizes are recorded (Figs.187 & 188). The same badge in white-metal was worn by the other ranks of the Volunteer Battalions, and in silver by Volunteer Officers (Fig.189). Further, the same pattern but in bi-metal, gilding-metal grenade and white-metal rose was worn by the Militia Battalions.

On 4th July 1894, the Officer Commanding asked 'if the proposed new cap badge was approved, would it also be accepted for wear as a collar badge?' This was granted and badges for the field service cap and the collar were received 15th November 1894 and finally approved 24th December 1894. The mens' gilding-metal collar badge was renewed in 1898 with Pattern No.10145a being sealed 21st March 1898, 'in lieu of Patt. 10145'. It would appear that this same badge fitted with a slider fastener was worn on the Broderick cap 1898-1905.

Although an Officers pattern bearing a K/C was introduced in 1904, it was many years later that the other ranks equivalent officially came into use. The Journals of the Army Clothing Department recording on 17th April 1914, 'Patt. 8047 again in gilding-metal replaced patt. 10145a with Tudor crown on lower part of flames.' (Fig.190). There is a smaller flatter pattern (Fig.191) which appears in gilding-metal, and bronze and gilt all fitted with lugs. A similar one with brooch pin fastening is a sweetheart's brooch. Another K/C variant has the grenade in gilding-metal and the rose in white-metal, 2.5cm in height and said to have been worn on the blue walking out dress c.1951.

The K/C patterns were followed by bi-metal ones with the relevant Q/C c.1953. A much smaller bi-metal Q/C badge, Pattern No.17062 was sealed 30th January 1956. This was declared obsolete 30th December 1965, but had been the guide for the gold/silver anodised version (Fig.192). The anodised pattern was sealed for wear by the 8th (TA) Battalion, 9th October 1956.

The 1883 Dress Regulations records the Officers collar badge as, 'A grenade in gold embroidery.' The 1888 Edition adds, 'with the White Rose in silver on the ball' for wear on the tunic collar. The 1891 and 1894 Editions are the same but the 1900 Edition omits the word 'gold'. (Fig.193). This was also worn on the field service cap.

The 1902 Dress Regulations direct, for wear on the tunic and frock coat, 'A grenade in silver embroidery with the White Rose in gilt metal on the ball.' (A slight contradiction in terms!). (Figs.194 & 195). On the mess jacket a small grenade in gold embroidery with the White Rose in silver metal on the ball. (Fig.196). For the recently introduced Service dress, 'As for forage cap in bronze.' Approved by the War Office 3rd June 1904. (Fig.197). The 'Royals' were the only Fusilier Regiment to make a change in the colour of the embroidery for the Regular Battalion Officers. The 1911 and 1934 Dress Regulations maintain the 1902 directions. The K/C bronze grenades were replaced with Q/C versions c1953, and a small bronze upright grenade 28mm in height was sealed 26th January 1956 for wear on the mess jacket (Home Service) by Officers of the 8th (TA) Battalion. There are also smaller upright grenades in bronze with only the rose on the ball (Fig.198). The same pattern occurs in gilt, silver/gilt, gilding-metal and white-metal, some struck in one piece, others with the rose separate. All purport to have been worn on khaki drill.

There are a number of upright collar badges in silver/gilt, the earliest being with a QVC - the grenade, crown and garter in gilt and the rose in silver, below the Garter, also in silver the White Horse of Hanover facing to the left (Fig.199). This was followed by K/C and Q/C patterns (Fig.200 & 201). The Q/C pattern was sealed 26th January 1956 for wear on the Nos. 1 & 3 Dress by the 8th (TA) Battalion. For the Officers of the same unit a much smaller upright grenade in silver/gilt for wear on the tropical white mess dress was also sealed 26th January 1956. (Fig.202). The White Horse of Hanover along with the motto "Nec Aspera Terrent" was directed to be worn on the flap of the Grenadiers' cap in the Regulations for Clothing and Colours, 1747.

The badge worn on the scarlet frock in the late 1890s was a horizontal gilt metal imitation embroidery grenade with a silver rose. (Fig.203). A later simpler pattern is shown in (Fig.204).

Militia
Royal London Militia
Collar badges in white-metal, Pattern No.7470, for wear on the tunic and frock

Fig.189

Fig.190

Fig.191

Fig.192

Fig.193

Fig.194

Fig.195

Fig.196

HISTORY OF THE BRITISH ARMY INFANTRY COLLAR BADGE

collars were sealed 30th June 1875 under Ref. PC/London Militia/159. So far it has not been possible to confirm a description of the badges for the other ranks, but two embroidered items, one much larger than the other, purport to be from the tunic and forage cap of a Regimental Officer c.1878. The collar badge is illustrated in (Fig.205). The Lion is in gold metal thread, with red silk crown and mouth, black silk is used to delineate the eyes and whiskers. The circular strap of gold embroidery has a background of blue velvet, upon the strap also in gold thread is the 'DOMINE DIRIGE NOS' (The Lord Direct Us). Within the strap the Arms of the City of London, the cross in red velvet outlined in gold thread on a silver thread base; the sword picked out in gold thread and red silk. The Arms and Motto date back to c.1359.

The Regiment became the 4th Battalion, The Royal Fusiliers, July 1881; upon the formation of two extra Line Battalions 1898-1900, it was redesignated the 6th battalion in 1898 and finally the 7th Battalion in 1908. The Regiment had the privilege of marching through the City of London with Colours flying, bands playing, and bayonets fixed, a privilege inherited from the old Trained Bands of the City.

Photographs of Officers of the 6th Battalion often show them wearing two collar badges. The one nearest the collar opening is the normal Royal Fusiliers grenade, worn horizontally on the full dress tunic, in gold embroidery with silver rose up to c1902. The second collar badge worn behind the grenade was of crowned embroidered circular format displaying the Motto and Arms of the City of London. With QVC and gold thread until 1902, thereafter K/C and silver thread. (Line drawing Fig.206). The same badge in bronze and K/C only, was worn behind the bronze upright grenade badge on the 'stand and fall' collar of the post 1902 Service Dress. (Plate No.4). One photograph of the period shows the additional 'M' worn below the grenade. A triple collar badge display being rare if not unique.

3rd or Royal Westminster Middlesex (Light Infantry) Militia

On 25th June 1878, it was decreed that the collar badge of this Militia Regiment be 'assimilated to that of the Royal South Gloucester Militia, Pattern No. 8935.' This was the standard bugle horn in white-metal (Fig.207). Worn by the other ranks with the Officers equivalent in silver/silver plate (Fig.208).

The Regiment became the 3rd Battalion The Royal Fusiliers in 1881, redesignated the 5th Battlion in 1898 upon the expansion of the Line Battalions.

4th or Royal South Middlesex Militia

The Army Pattern Room Journals record, 'White metal collar badges for tunic and frock sealed 21/2/1878.' This was an eight pointed star upon which, within a blank circular strap, appeared the county arms of a shield bearing three seaxes. (Fig.209). The Regiment became the 5th Battalion, The Royal Fusiliers in 1881, redesignated the 7th Battalion in 1898.

Fig.197

Fig.198

Fig.199

Fig.200

Fig.201

Fig.202

Fig.203

Fig.204

Fig.205

THE ROYAL FUSILIERS (CITY OF LONDON REGIMENT)

Rifle Volunteer Corps, Volunteer, Territorial Force & Territorial Battalions

The 5th, 9th and 22nd Middlesex Rifle Volunteers were allotted to the Royal Fusiliers as Volunteer Battalions in 1881, but were all transferred to The King's Royal Rifle Corps 1882/83.

The 10th Middlesex Rifle Volunteers were transferred from the same Corps in 1883, and became the 1st Volunteer Battalion, The Royal Fusiliers. *The 23rd Middlesex Rifle Volunteers* became the 2nd Volunteer Battalion in 1883, but not until 1890 did the *11th Middlesex Rifle Volunteers* become the 3rd Volunteer Battalion. Notes taken at a parade of the 23rd Middlesex Rifle Volunteers in 1888 record that the men were wearing red tunics with blue facings, and wearing white worsted grenades as collar badges.

The 1st or Tower Hamlets Rifle Volunteer Brigade became the 4th Volunteer Battalion only in 1904. As stated earlier the collar badges of the Volunteer Battalions were white-metal or silver versions of their Regular counterparts.

NB. (To achieve uniformity each Middlesex RV unit has been entered under its new parent Regiment of 1881).

Fig.206

Fig.207

WWI Service Battalions
10th Battalion The Royal Fusiliers

While serving in France and forming part of 111th Brigade of 'Kitchener's Army,' NCOs of the 'Shiny Tenth' wore as a distinguishing mark, a small brass '10' on the right lapel of the collar on their Service Dress jackets (Fig.210). Thought to be the only Battalion in the British Army to adopt such a practice.

25th (Frontiersmen Battalion), The Royal Fusiliers

This unit raised in February 1915, wore a distinctive collar badge, a small version of one of their cap badges. It was a grenade with the K/C at the base of the flames, on the ball the numerals '25', below on a tri-part scroll bearing the legend, 'ROYAL/FRONTIERSMEN/FUSILIERS.' (Fig.211). In bronze and worn by the Officers and senior NCOs, the first badges were engraved, the later ones die-struck. The battalion was disbanded 29th June 1918.

Fig.208

Fig.209

38th, 39th, & 40th (Jewish) Battalions, The Royal Fusiliers

The 38th and 39th were raised on 20th and 21st January 1918 respectively. The Third Battalion was initially raised 15th January 1918 as the 42nd Battalion but redesignated as the 40th Battalion 12th July 1918. Their distinctive collar badge, again a smaller version of their cap badge, was the menorah, a seven branched candlestick, beneath was a scroll inscribed in Hebrew, 'KADIMAH' (Eastward). (Fig.212). In bronze and worn only by the Officers, it was approved and sealed under Reference 1277/QMGY/War Office, 3rd October 1918.

Cadets

A Cadet Battalion of The Royal Fusiliers was formed in 1901 and a special collar badge was produced. A grenade, the ball bearing the Arms of the City of London, in gilding-metal for the cadets and gilt for the Officers. (Fig.213).

Fig.210

General

Collar badges of The Royal Fusiliers were worn both vertically and horizontally according to the uniform in use. They do not face.

The Regiment became the *3rd Battlion, The Royal Regiment of Fusiliers*, 23rd April 1968.

Fig.213

Fig.212

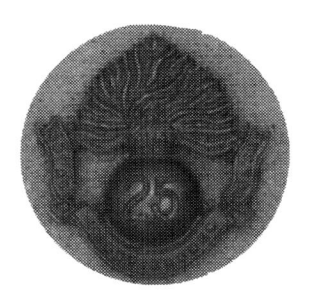

Fig.211

The King's Regiment (Liverpool)

Fig.214

Fig.215

Fig.216

Fig.217

Pre 1881
The 8th (The King's) Regiment

Authorised by an Order PC/Infy.Gen./111, 16th July 1872. Pattern No.9525, sealed 9th December 1874 was the collar badge adopted for other ranks to be worn in facing pairs on the tunic and frock collars. The pattern shows the White Horse of Hanover in prancing attitude, in white-metal, with its hind legs resting on a brass furled scroll inscribed, in Roman lettering, 'KINGS'. There is usually a small brass strengthening bar between the furl of the scroll to the rear legs. (Fig.214). Sergeants wore this badge upon their rank chevrons for many years, certainly as late as 1896.

In recognition of their services during the Jacobite Rising of 1715, and their good conduct on all occasions, King George I was graciously pleased to grant the Regiment the right to wear the White Horse of Hanover as a badge, and to be titled The King's Regiment.

The post 1880 Officers version collar badge has not been confirmed but, as rank badges were not removed until late 1880, it is doubtful if there was an O/R's equivalent.

Post 1881

For a few months after 1st July 1881, the Regiment was designated *The Liverpool Regiment*, but by the end of the year became *The King's (Liverpool Regiment)*.

To further the policy of allying Territorial links between the Line and auxiliary forces, the Red Rose of Lancaster was incorporated into the new collar badges of the Regiment, replacing the White Horse of Hanover. The design for rank and file was the Red Rose of Lancaster above a scroll, inscribed in Roman lettering, 'KING'S. In gilding-metal Pattern No.9880 was sealed 15th December 1881 and worn from 1882. (Fig.215). Similar badges, but in white-metal, were worn by the other ranks of the Volunteer Battalions (Fig.216). The Gaunt Pattern books show a similar badge to the one adopted, but with chevron finial ends to the scroll, creating a tri-part effect. (Line drawing Fig.217). This was submitted by the 4th Vol. Battalion and annotated, 'Not approved 20/11/83'. The 4th and 6th Vol. Battalions was as shown in Fig.216. Submitted by Messrs. Hobson & Sons, approved by the War Office, Horse Guards under Ref. V/15Lancs/1028, letters dated 23rd & 28th June 1888 respectively. The other ranks of the 3rd and 4th Militia Battalions, and those of the 7th (Isle of Man) Volunteer Battalion wore similar badges to Pattern No.9880 but in bi-metal. Slightly larger versions in bi-metal were worn by the Warrant Officers and Sergeants of the Militia Battalions. The badge is also recorded in blackened gilding-metal, possibly worn

Fig.218

Fig.219

Fig.220

THE KING'S REGIMENT (LIVERPOOL)

by the 1st Vol. Battalion or as an alternative by the Militia Battalions, both having strong Rifle connections. In gilt, by the Warrant Officers of the Line Battalions Finally in bronze, precise usage unconfirmed.

For the Line Battalions, the Officers equivalent was a most attractive badge, a copper gilt Rose, the centre and edges remaining in gilt, the petals and sepals were of vitreous red and green enamels respectively. Below, a gilt metal scroll inscribed, in Old English capitals, 'KINGS' (Fig.218). Equally attractive badges but with silver scrolls, edging and centres, were worn by Volunteer Officers. (Figs.219).

Officers of the Militia units wore a delightful mixture of both types! The enamelled and gilt Rose and edge to petals with a silver scroll. (Fig.220).

It is interesting that whereas the Officer's collar badge has Old English lettering with no apostrophe, the other rank's equivalent has Roman lettering and an apostrophe. Variations have a sepal at the top centre of the rose whilst others have it at the bottom centre.

Further research concerning the tri-part scroll of the submitted pattern by the 4th Vol. Battalion via Hobsons of London has shown that after its rejection in 1883, a decision was made 1st August 1885, under Ref. V/15Lancs/903, 'for the scroll to be omitted.'

This short lived triumph was rescinded 21st August 1885 under Ref.905. The pattern for the 2" VB is annotated 13/3/1888.

The Regular Battalions strongly objected to the loss of the White Horse badge, referring disdainfully to the Rose badges as 'cow-pats'. Indeed, the 2nd Battalion in Afghanistan at the time of the change, completely ignored the new pattern, and were still wearing the White Horse badge on their tunic collars in 1894. In April of that year they were 'Ordered' to wear the correct pattern!

The 1st Battalion, under the 'very nose of Authority', were obliged to submit to the new pattern, though leaving no stone unturned to have the Order rescinded. After thirteen years of endeavour they were successful, when the War Office agreed to restore the White Horse.

The change was approved 24th December 1894 for cap and collar badges. Samples demanded 13th June 1895 were to include a scroll inscribed, 'THE KING'S' at the base, in place of the pattern initially submitted which was the White Horse without a scroll (as per the other ranks helmet plate centre). Pattern No.9880a. The new Pattern No.9880b was finally approved 19th November 1895 and contractors alerted to supply them, but it was not until 7th January 1896 that the new pattern was sealed. As usual, the new pattern was not to be issued until present stocks were exhausted. The 1st Battalion then serving in Jamaica achieved this exhaustion quite rapidly; upon receiving the first consignment of the new badges 1st June 1896, it is said that on the same evening, the 'cow-pats' were taken down, placed in a sack, rowed to the centre of Kingston Harbour and heaved overboard. Strict compliance!

The new pattern was again a prancing horse in white-metal over a scroll in gilding-metal inscribed in Roman lettering, 'THE KING'S'. (Fig.221). There are numerous and considerable variations concerning the position and attitude of the Horse. Well nourished and under-fed Horses with variable length manes. The slope of the scrolls and the punctuation of the inscription. An unusually upright

Fig.221

Fig.222

Fig.223

Fig.224

Fig.225

Fig.229  *Fig.228* *Fig.227*  *Fig.226*

47

HISTORY OF THE BRITISH ARMY INFANTRY COLLAR BADGE

Fig.230 *Fig.231* *Fig.232* *Fig.233*

Fig.234

Fig.235

Fig.236

Fig.237

horse with anchored tail is seen in (Fig.222), without the apostrophe (Fig.223) whilst that in (Fig.224) is a throw back to the pre 1881 type, complete with strengthening bar. The same overall pattern but in gilding-metal is thought to have been worn by Warrant Officers on their mess jackets and Service Dress. A smaller pattern, in bi-metal is believed to have been worn by mess waiters.

Officers wore on their full dress tunic and scarlet frock collars, a similar but larger version, the Horse in silver and the scroll in gilt, there were again many minor variations. (Figs.225 & 226) for two such examples. In addition there are silver/gilt versions of the other ranks pattern which were worn unofficially c1900-1914. (Fig.227).

The 1902 Dress Regulations, as well as stipulating that the badge shall be worn on the mess jacket, further directs, 'As for tunic but in bronze,' for the newly introduced Service Dress. Sealed 13th May 1903. The usual variations ensued.(Figs.228 & 229) as examples. As with other Regiments, when polished down, they were worn on the khaki drill. Worn by the Warrant Officers in gilt (Fig.230).

There was also extant during this period a 'hybrid', the post 1926 design of the Horse in white-metal or silver, on a gilding-metal or gilt torse all above a scroll in gilding-metal or gilt inscribed with Roman lettering of the pre 1926 era. 'THE "KINGS". and also "THE KINGS". It is recorded in bi-metal (Fig.231), bronze, gilt and silver/gilt (Fig.232). These are thought to have been worn unofficially c.1900-1914, again by the 1st Battalion

On 23rd June 1888, drawings of collar badges for the 4th Volunteer Battalion were deposited in the Army Pattern Room, later drawings were deposited 12th February 1895 and approval given by Horse Guards under Ref. V/4/8/8. These were the same design as worn by the Line units but in white-metal, worn until 1908. (Fig.233). Both Officers and other ranks wore the Line Battalion's collar badge for a while.

The other ranks of the 1st Volunteer Battalion are known to have worn the same badge, but the Officers wore distinctive patterns. One displayed the Horse standing on a torse above a curved scroll inscribed 'THE KING'S' in Roman lettering. Completely in silver or silver plate also believed to have been worn by senior NCOs. Another was similar but with '1st VB.' between the torse and the scroll. The Horse, '1st VB.' and the torse in silver, the scroll in gilt with silvered lettering. (Fig.234).

The Regiment was redesignated *The King's Regiment (Liverpool)* with effect from 1st January 1921.

In 1926, a new collar badge was introduced, the Horse was larger with a more pronounced mane. The rear legs rested upon a torse but the forelegs, though still in a prancing attitude rested on the end of a new form of title scroll. This was of wavy aspect with furled ends, inscribed, in Old English capitals, 'KING'S.' For other ranks the Horse and its base were in white-metal, with scroll in gilding-metal. (Fig.235). Sealed 9th February 1927, Pattern No.10054. The Officers version in silver and gilt was sealed 20th October 1926. (Figs.236 & 237) show two minor variants. On the Officers' Service Dress the badge was in bronze. (Figs.238 & 239 show variable sizes of horse). That in Fig.238 has been noted in silver and gilt.

The other ranks pattern was worn thereafter until amalgamation. It was used as

48

THE KING'S REGIMENT (LIVERPOOL)

Fig.238 *Fig.239* *Fig.240* *Fig.241*

a guide for the silver and gold anodised type., Pattern No.19355, sealed 18th June 1964. Made by Messrs. Firmins..

As with other Regiments, the bronzed OSD badge was officially polished and worn on the khaki drill uniform.

Militia
2nd Royal Lancashire (Duke of Lancaster's Own Rifles)

Styled and dressed as Rifles from 1854, when a second battalion was raised. The Officers shako plates and other ranks glengarry badge all had a bronze finish, and to date no bronze collar badges have been attributed to them. A pattern of Rose collar badge worn by the Officers has a red velvet backing to the silver Rose. (Fig.240). A facing pair of Officers embroidered corded bugle collar badges worn with the embroidered forage cap badge have been noted. In 1881 the Regiment became the 3rd and 4th Battalions, The King's (Liverpool Regiment). Other ranks then adopted the rose over scroll collar badge similar to pattern 9880 (as illustrated under Fig.215), but in bi-metal. Warrant Officers and Sergeants wore larger versions of the badge. The indications are that, generally, they adopted the badges of the Regular units, but some badges were worn in reverse metal colours, white-metal Rose, gilding-metal scroll. (Fig.241) Officers wore an enamelled and gilt Rose and edge to petals with a silver scroll as illustrated under Fig.220.

Fig.242

Rifle Volunteer Corps, Volunteer, Territorial Force & Territorial Army Battalions
1st Lancashire Rifle Volunteer Corps

This ten company unit became a Volunteer Battalion of the Regiment in 1881, being designated the 1st Volunteer Battalion in 1883.

The white metal other rank collar badges and the special pattern worn by the Officers have been discussed earlier. The unit became the 5th Battalion (TF), The King's (Liverpool Regiment) in 1908, and wishing to revive their former 'Rifles' status, blackened their cap and collar badges. Up to 1916, the Officers badges were worn in conjunction with the standard 'T' badge below. (Fig.242). In September of that year, the Commanding Officer, Lieut-Colonel J. J. Shute introduced a new pattern of 'cap badge.' Simply the black shoulder title 5/KING'S, and on the collar a black 'T' only. Presumably this was the Battalion's contribution to the 1916 Economies!

The battalion was reconstituted in 1920, and in due course wore the post 1926 pattern of badge, again with a blackened finish. (Fig.243).

The chromed Liver birds shown in (Figs.244, 245) are not collar badges, but arm badges worn by the 5th Battalion.

A larger white-metal version (Fig.246) is not a military badge, but pertains to one of Liverpool's civil services.

The Battalion later on wore the silver/gold anodised issues. Pattern No.19355. (Fig.247). This badge was also worn by *Liverpool University OTC* and an obscure TAVR Artillery unit, *'R' (King's Liverpool Scottish) Battery, West Lancashire Regiment RA. (TA).*

Fig.243

Fig.244

Fig.245

49

HISTORY OF THE BRITISH ARMY INFANTRY COLLAR BADGE

Fig.246

Fig.247

Fig.248

Fig.249

Liverpool Rifle Volunteer Brigade, or 5th Lancashire Rifle Volunteer Corps

(Formerly the 5th, 14th, 19th, 39th, 63rd, 64th, 71st & 86th Lancashire R.V.C.'s) Nominated as a Volunteer Battalion in 1881, the Corps did not become the 2nd Volunteer Battalion until 1888. They were redesignated as the 6th Battalion (TF) in April 1908, and by 1909 as the 6th (Rifle) Battalion (TF), The King's (Liverpool Regiment). The Officers, wishing to maintain their strong Rifle Volunteer ties, adopted distinctive cap and collar badges. A strung bugle horn, with the Lancashire Rose displacing the bows of the knot. In blackened brass or gilding-metal, worn in facing pairs with the mouth-piece towards the collar opening. Also known in silver. (Fig.248).

Upon reconstitution in 1920, a smaller pattern was taken into use, in blackened gilding-metal and bronze (Figs.249 & 250). Upon transfer to The Royal Engineers as *38th (The King's Regiment) A.A. Battalion, R.E.* in 1936 and a further transfer in 1940 to The Royal Artillery, these distinctive badges continued to be worn on the collar. The badge is still in current use by various cadet units.

13th Lancashire Rifle Volunteer Corps

Nominated in 1881, the Corps became the 3rd Volunteer Battalion, The King's (Liverpool Regiment) in 1888. The unit was disbanded in 1908.

The 13th Lancashire RVC wore on their collars, small ribboned bugle horns in white-metal for the other ranks and silver for the Officers, (Fig.251). The Gaunt Pattern Books illustrate a Rose collar badge annotated '1888'. It is of identical format to the one that appeared above the numerals '13', in the Officers shako and helmet plates. There is no reference concerning usage etc.

15th Lancashire Rifle Volunteer Corps

Nominated in 1881, the Corps became the 4th Volunteer Battalion under Army Order No. 81 March 1888. Redesignated the 7th (TF) Battalion The King's (Liverpool Regiment) in 1908.

The Gaunt pattern books illustrate a prancing horse on a ground annotated "LANCASHIRE RIFLE VOLS", cap and collar badge 13/3/1885. Facing to the right, this item is known to exist in W/M, silver plate and gilt. The 15th Lancashire RVC had the same horse in the centre of their glengarry badge worn 1880-88. Whether this item was approved is not known.

The Journals, Army Clothing Department, Pattern Room record under 1st August 1885. 'Design of collar badges "AR" for the 15th Lancashire RV has been detached from the above paper and placed in the pattern room. ref V/15 Lancs/903.' This was followed 21st August, 'To note that the scroll with the word "Kings" inscribed to be restored to the collar badge.' The reference to the 'AR' collar badges which are shown hand drawn in scrolled end capitals in not yet understood. The old 15th Corps are shown in the Army Lists as 'Liverpool', but perhaps a more immediate locality such as Aintree may be indicated.

After 1926, Officers wore the new pattern but in silver plate. (Fig.252). Other rank's in white-metal. In 1939 the Battalion was converted to the *40th (The King's) RTR.*

Fig.250

Fig.251

Fig.252

18th (Liverpool Irish) Rifle Volunteer Corps

Raised in 1860 as the *64th Lancashire RVC*. They were renumbered 18th in 1880. The collar badge c.1880-1888 was the QVC crowned Maid and Harp, in white-metal for the men (Fig.253) and silver for the Officers. Authority untraced.

Allotted in 1881, the Corps provided six companies for the 5th (Irish) Volunteer Battalion, The King's (Liverpool Regiment) when redesignated in 1888. The new collar badge in blackened brass displayed the QVC over the Maid and Harp; below an elaborate tri-part scroll with furled ends inscribed, '5th IRISH VB/THE KINGS/L'POOL REGT'. (Fig.254). It may be assumed that the K/C version was current c.1903-1908.

The unit was redesignated as the 8th Battalion (TF) in 1908 and the 8th (Irish) Battalion (TF) by March 1909.

Two patterns of collar badge appear in the Gaunt Pattern Books, firstly a K/C crowned circle inscribed 'QUIS SEPARABIT', within the circle the Maid and Harp. This was not adopted. The pattern chosen was sent to Messrs. Hobsons & Sons 21st December 1908. Of similar design to its predecessor, the K/C over the Maid and Harp, the tri-part scroll now, '8th IRISH BT/THE KINGS/L'POOL REGT.' (Fig.255). In blackened brass and bronze and worn in facing pairs on Service Dress, the Maid facing towards the collar opening. Worn until disbandment in 1922. The crown, harp strings and areas between the scrolls are normally voided. They are also recorded in white-metal usually die-cast and without any voiding. (Fig.256). The Officers wore in facing pairs and of blackened silver plate, badges similar to that worn in the forage cap of The Royal Irish Rifles; the K/C Maid and Harp over a furled scroll, 'QUIS SEPARABIT' (Fig.257). In 1939, they were reformed as a duplicate to the 5th Battalion, Officers wearing in facing pairs on their Service Dress, bronze Horses/scroll as illustrated in Figs.238, 239. In 1947 they became 626 H.A.A Regiment, R.A. (TA).

19th (Liverpool Press Guard) Rifle Volunteer Corps.

Raised as the *80th Lancashire Rifle Volunteer Corps* in 1860/61 under the command of Lieut-Colonel George M'Corquodale. He had hoped that the Corps would be Artillery Volunteers but without success; nevertheless a white-metal grenade did feature in the centre of the shako and helmet plates. There is no evidence as yet that grenades were worn as collar badges. M'Corquodale was still the Hon. Colonel when the Corps were redesignated 19th in 1880. It has been suggested that the same white-metal badges as illustrated in Fig.253 were worn.

Nominated in 1881 they became the 6th Volunteer Battalion, The King's (Liverpool Regiment) in 1888.

Drawings were deposited at the Army Clothing Pattern Room 23rd June 1888 on behalf of the 6th Vol. Battalion, 'For NCOs and Men.' These being the same as those of the Regular Battalions but in white-metal. Approval was granted 8th April 1895 for the adoption of a new pattern field service cap, the badge to be the White Horse of Hanover. Approval was also given for the same badge to be worn on the collar. The Gaunt Pattern Books illustrate these badges. The White Horse on ground with fore legs raised, facing to the left. Annotated, 'FS cap, 6 VB L'pool Regt, approved Horse Guards, WO, 6/4/95.' Another Pattern Book shows the

Fig.253

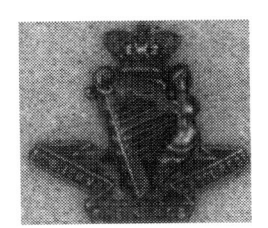

Fig.254

Fig.255

Fig.256

Fig.257

Fig.259   *Fig.258*

HISTORY OF THE BRITISH ARMY INFANTRY COLLAR BADGE

Fig.260

Fig.261

Fig.262

Fig.263

Fig.264

same horse but this time facing right. Annotated, 'Cap and collar badge, 13/3/95.' No metal is quoted but other records show them to be in white-metal for the men, (Fig.258) and in silver plate for the Officers (Fig.259). The same badge in gilt was worn by the Warrant Officers. (Fig.260). These badges should not be confused with a similar pattern worn by the 3rd Hussars (Fig.261). The Officers adopted a further distinctive collar badge, as it is in bronze it perhaps dates from c1898-1908. The White Horse above a torse, below a furled scroll inscribed, 'THE "KINGS", between the scroll and the torse, '6th V.B'. The fore legs and the tail are not anchored to the title scroll. (Fig.262).

Redesignated in 1908 as the 9th (TF) Battalion, they wore the usual pre 1926 pattern badges of the parent units. Photographs confirm that a bronze 'T' was sometimes worn by Officers, below the bronze collar badges. The Battalion was disembodied in 1919. Reconstituted as a unit of The Royal Engineers in 1920.

1st Isle of Man Rifle Volunteer Corps

In 1880, the only remaining Volunteer Rifle Corps on the Island was the *2nd Douglas*, being redesignated 1st later that year. Allotted in 1881 the Corps became the 7th (Isleof Man) Volunteer Battalion, The King's (Liverpool Regiment), 1st March 1888. In 1908 they remained outside the Territorial system, continuing to serve under the old Volunteer system. Two further companies were formed in November 1914, but the whole unit was disbanded in 1920. Other ranks adopted the same collar badges as the 3rd and 4th Militia Battalions (see under Militia section for details).

8th (Scottish) Volunteer Battalion

The Scottish residents of Liverpool had not been able to maintain a Rifle Volunteer with Scottish distinctions at the commencement of the second Volunteer Movement in 1859. This was put right when they raised no less than eight companies in 1900, many of whom saw service in the Boer War. They were given Volunteer Battalion status in October 1900.

Their collar badges were of the pattern used by the other volunteers, but the title scroll read, '8th V.B. THE KING'S'. In white-metal for the other ranks, (Fig.263), and bronze for the Officers Service Dress (Fig.264). It is also known in silver plate for the Officers full dress doublet. Officers also wore this type on the mess jacket, but the indications are that the badges were somewhat larger.

Reorganised as the 10th (Scottish) (TF) Battalion, The King's (Liverpool Regiment) in 1908, new badges became necessary. The same white-metal other ranks badge was used but with 'SCOTTISH' replacing the old Volunteer distinction. The Officers badges in silver were similar to those worn by the Regular units but the scrolls were inscribed, in Roman lettering, 'SCOTTISH' (Figs.265 & 266) depict a facing pair. Bronze versions were used on the Officers Service Dress. In February 1920 the Battalion was redesignated, 10th (Liverpool Scottish) Battalion, and as such was transferred to the Queen's Own Cameron Highlanders. The other ranks now wore the collar badges of their new parent Battalions, but

Fig.265    *Fig.266*

THE KING'S REGIMENT (LIVERPOOL)

the Officers maintained their loyal Liverpool ties by adopting a silver plated badge similar to that worn by the other ranks after 1908. (Fig.267). Note that the horse's tail is attached to the scroll.

WWI Service Battalions
11th (S) Battalion (Pioneers)
Raised 23rd August 1914 as Infantry and converted to Pioneers, 1st January 1915 and, as with other Infantry units of this nature, the universal crossed rifle and pick collar badges were used. Gilding metal for the men and bronze for the Officers. (Fig.147). Disbanded 18th June 1918.

17th, 18th, 19th and 20th Service Battalions
These famous Battalions, known collectively as the 'Liverpool Pals', typified the great patriotic spirit that pervaded throughout the country upon the outbreak of war in 1914. Raised at a public meeting chaired by the 17th Earl of Derby during the early weeks of the War, he gave to each recruit who joined before 16th October 1914, a hall-marked silver badge. This was in the form of the ancient crest of the Stanleys, 'On a chapeau gules, turned up ermine, an eagle, wings extended, or, preying on a child proper, swaddled gules, in a cradle laced or.' Approval granted by H.M. King George V (14th October 1914). Subsequent issues were in gilding-metal and bronze; in addition to being worn in the cap, the Officers wore them in bronze on the collar. Non facing. (Fig.268). The Battalions were disbanded in 1918.

The Earl of Derby, in addition to being a local landowner of great magnitude was a powerful member of the Government. Appointed Official Director for Recruiting in 1915, he became Under Secretary of State for War July 1916, Secretary of State for War in the National Ministry, December 1916, and President of the Army Council 1918.

Unidentified
A prancing horse on ground above a scroll inscribed, in Roman lettering, 'THE KING'S'. In blackened brass. (Fig.269). Similar but with different shaped scroll, tail and fore-leg attitudes in gilt (Fig.270). Both these types are known in a variety of metals, blackened brass, gilding-metal, white-metal, and gilt. Some with the usual two lug fitting, others with brooch pin fastener. It has been suggested that they are sporran badges worn by the 8th (Scottish) Volunteer Battalion, c.1900-1908.

Fig.271 illustrates a complete 'hybrid.' A shortened torse supports the White Horse, above a pattern of gilt scroll that appeared on the Rose pattern Officers collar badge of 1881-1895. There are no recorded details of this badge, and it is suggested, that it is an interim trial pattern, c.1895, submitted but not approved.

General
There are so many variations to the collar badges worn by the Regiment, that it has only been possible to illustrate the more obvious types. Many of the other varieties have no real currency significance, and are merely manufacturing interpretations.

All the horse badges were worn in facing pairs, with the animal facing inward towards the collar opening.

The Regiment, less its Territorials, was amalgamated with The Manchester Regiment to form *The King's Regiment (Manchester & Liverpool)*, 1st September 1958.

Fig.267

Fig.268

Fig.269

Fig.270

Fig.271

HISTORY OF THE BRITISH ARMY INFANTRY COLLAR BADGE

The Royal Norfolk Regiment

Fig.272

Pre 1881
The 9th (East Norfolk) Regiment of Foot

Authorised by an Order PC/Infy Gen/111, 16th July 1872, the Regiment adopted their time honoured badge of Britannia as their first collar badge. Portrayed in the familiar seated position and without headdress, she carries a seven leaf sprig of olive in one hand and cradles the trident with her other arm. Resting against the latter forearm is an oval shield bearing the Arms of the Great Union. In front of the shield a Globe. At her feet lies a partially obscured Lion of England. All upon ground. Pattern No.9278, sealed 31st August 1872, for wear by the other ranks. (Fig.272). The badge 32mm in height was found to be too large for the collar, and a smaller type 26mm in height was submitted by the Regiment; approved and sealed 29th October 1872. Recorded by the Army Clothing Department, 4th November 1872. (Figs.273 & 274) show a facing pair. No pattern number has been traced, but upon deduction it must have been 9285, 9286 or 9287. Both patterns were in brass.

Fig.273

Tradition asserts that the badge of Britannia was awarded to the Regiment by Queen Anne in 1707, for gallantry at the battle of Almanza, but there is no documentary evidence to support this. Further claims include involvement by the 1st Battalion in the siege of Saragossa, 1707-1710, though records indicate that the Regiment took no part in these operations. A further claim concerns the bravery shown by the 2nd Battalion in North America, 1776-1777.

Fig.274

What is certain, is that the Regiment received a letter from Horse Guards, 30th July 1799 stating that, 'His Majesty has been pleased to confirm to the 9th Regiment of Foot, the distinction and privilege of bearing the figure of Britannia as the badge of the Regiment.'

Post 1881

The Regiment became simply, *The Norfolk Regiment*, 1st July 1881. A letter from Horse Guards, 30th September 1881 had confirmed Britannia as the collar badge, but on 20th January 1882 a new Pattern No. 9966 in gilding-metal was sealed. A seated Britannia again but of radically different form, smaller and her head adorned with a Romanesque helmet, her tunic or shift of more elaborate design. The hand holding the olive sprig (five leaves) is now at rest on her knee. Both the Lion and Globe are omitted. The trident is shorter, and the semi lying attitude of the figure is almost sensual. (Figs.275 & 276) show voided and solid variants, and on the latter a larger head and helmet. The lowering of the arm and the shortening of the trident may have been to protect the badge from damage on these weak extremities, or to make the representation more in keeping with the figure that appeared on some of the late seventeenth century coinage.

Fig.275

Fig.276

Fig.277

Fig.278

54

The badge facing to the left was also worn in the field service cap up to the introduction of a new cap badge in October 1897.

Perhaps the rather slovenly attitude of the figure was the reason for the appearance of a new badge in 1898. Cut from new dies and numbered 9966a, the badge was sealed 21st March 1898. (Fig.277) shows a return to the larger upright figure; the hand is again raised, the olive sprig bears seven leaves, and the trident is lengthened.

The figure is more fully dressed. (Fig.278) shows a different design with the upper part of the figure further embattled by the addition of chain mail. Recorded with a chromed finish (Fig.279) and thought to have been used by the band at some time.

The Regiment was raised to Royal status in 1935 and new badges were designed. Pattern No.11084 was sealed 21st April 1937, Ref.54/Inf/1308. In gilding-metal for the men. Larger than the last version, the helmet has been redesigned, the chain mail omitted, and the trident lengthened yet again. The olive leaves, 8 in number, are now closed. (Fig.280). This was followed by a single lug version. A final type, Pattern No.14294 was sealed and taken into use 10th January 1950. In gilding-metal and reduced in size, this pattern was used as the guide for the gold anodised successor. (Fig.281).

The Officers collar badges generally followed the mens as regards patterns and periods of currency, but (Figs.282,283,284,285,286) all in gilt metal, illustrate a variety of shapes, sizes and other minor details. The 1883 Dress Regulations record the badge as, 'The figure of Britannia in gilt metal.' For wear on the tunic and frock; confirmed in subsequent issues with the 1900 Edition adding, 'On the mess jacket in gold embroidery.'

For wear on the new Service Dress the 1902 Edition states, 'As for tunic collar with a scroll inscribed "The Norfolk Regt".' In bronze, the pattern varied over the years, not only in the size of the figure, but in voiding and non-voiding between the figure and the title scroll. (Fig.287) displays an early issue with red cloth backing, and a seven leafed olive sprig. (Fig.288) a five leaf olive sprig, and (Fig.289) with no voiding between the figure and the scroll. Officially polished down to the base metal for wear on the khaki drill. A curious hybrid is shown in (Fig.290), the pre 1937 figure but without the scroll. Upon elevation to a Royal Regiment, new badges for the Officers were sealed 12th January 1937, Ref 54/Inf/7308, in gilt, (Fig.291), and a larger bronze version (Fig.292).

In January 1949, H.M. King George VI, Colonel-in-Chief, approved new collar badges for the Regiment under Authority WO letter 54/ Officers/4025 Ord.17a, 10th February 1949. In silver plate the figure of Britannia in pairs. (Fig.293). A still later and smaller version, was sealed 9th October 1956. (Fig.294). All the post 1937 types indicate that the olive sprig has eight leaves.

Militia
1st or West Norfolk Militia
Collar badges in white-metal, Pattern No.7496 for wear on tunic and frock collars were sealed 31st December 1875, Ref PC/1st W.Norfolk Militia/65. This is sadly only recorded as 'a star'. It probably took the form of the mens' glengarry badge, 1874-1881. This was an eight pointed star on which was a strap inscribed, 'FIRST NORFOLK', within the strap, a castle.

In 1881, the Regiment became the 3rd Battalion, The Norfolk Regiment.

Fig.279

Fig.280

Fig.281

Fig.282

Fig.283

Fig.286

Fig.285

Fig.284

HISTORY OF THE BRITISH ARMY INFANTRY COLLAR BADGE

2nd or East Norfolk Militia

Pattern No.7485, sealed 9th November 1875 under Ref PC/E Norfolk Militia/85, show badges in white-metal for wear on the collars of the tunic and frock. In silver for the Officers. The common badge of both county Militia regiments was the Arms of the City of Norwich. A facing pair are shown. (Figs.295 & 296).

In 1881, the Regiment became the 4th Battalion, The Norfolk Regiment. Both Battalions after 1881 adopted the badges of the Regular Battalions.

Fig.287

Rifle Volunteer Corps, Volunteer, Territorial Force & Territorial Army Battalions

In 1881, the *1st Norfolk (City of Norwich), 2nd, 3rd, and 4th Norfolk Rifle Volunteer Corps* were nominated as Volunteer Battalions. In 1883 they were accordingly redesignated, 1st, 2nd, 3rd, and 4th Volunteer Battalions respectively. There is no evidence that the county Rifle Volunteer Corps wore collar badges.

In 1908, the 1st & 4th Vol. Battalions became the 4th (TF) Battalion, and the 2nd & 3rd Vol. Battalions merged to become the 5th (TF) Battalion

From 1881, the Officers adopted similar collar badges to those worn by the Regular units but in silver/silver plate. Britannia with hand raised and olive sprig of five leaves. (Figs.297 & 298). The pattern is shown in the Gaunt Pattern Books, annotated, 'Officers FP of collar badges, Aug. 25 1881.' The same design, but in white-metal is annotated, 'For privates, 28/3/1887.' (Figs.299 & 300) show two variations. These were worn until 1898 when the larger Britannia was introduced. Again in white-metal for the men, (Fig.301) shows the 'chain mail' on the upper part of the body. The silver Officers example, (Fig.302) shows the fully draped figure.

Fig.288

Photographs show the early pattern still in use many years after 1898.

The descendant TA Battalions adopted the same collar badge as the Regular units and a sealed pattern 10th October 1956 annotated, '"A" Coy 4 TA Battalion.' shows the same badge in both gilt and silver plate, as per the Regular Battalion. The other ranks badge is in gold anodised, Pattern No.14294. (Fig.303). A further anodised Pattern No.19244 was sealed 3rd February 1964, Ref.54/Inf/8847. Similar, but in silver plate, were also sealed, for wear by the Officers on Nos.1 & 3 Dress. Photographs show Officers of the 5th Battalion (TF) sometimes wore a 'T' below their collar badge.

Fig.289

Fig.290

Fig.291

Fig.292

Fig.293

Fig.294

Fig.295

Fig.296

Fig.297

Fig.298

56

THE ROYAL NORFOLK REGIMENT

These badges continued in use after the 1959 amalgamation of the parent Regiment, both by the *Royal Norfolk Territorials*, formed 1967, and also by *'A' (Norfolk) Coy of the 6th (Volunteer) Battalion Royal Anglian Regiment*.

6th (Cyclist) Battalion (TF), The Norfolk Regiment

Raised at Norwich 1st April 1908 from the cyclist companies of the 1st and 4th Volunteer Battalions. Transferred to the Royal Engineers 1920. No official documentation for special collar badges for this unit has been discovered, but Britannia collar badges in blackened metal do exist, and it is probable that these were so worn. A popular expedient with many other cyclist units of this period. (Figs.304 & 305) illustrate two Officers badges with the blackened finish.

VTC

Two of the WWI VTC units adopted special pattern collar badges to compliment the cap badge. *The City of Norwich Volunteers* simply utilised the Arms of the City, 'Gules, a three towered Castle argent, below a Lion passant guardant or.' Below this a tripart scroll inscribed, CITY OF/NORWICH/VOLUNTEERS. (Fig.306). In bronze.

The Norfolk Volunteer Regiment

The other ranks of this unit wore, in white-metal a K/C over the capital letters 'NVR'. (Fig.307).

Cadets

Gresham's School, Holt, Norfolk. The OTC wore at some time the Britannia badge, but with a scroll beneath inscribed, 'O.T.C. Gresham School.' (Fig.308) Olive sprig broken off.

General

All the Regiment's Britannia badges were worn in facing pairs with Britannia facing inwards towards the collar opening. As has been shown she has endured many changes of posture, clothing, equipment and attendants.

The Regiment became part of the East Anglian Brigade in 1958 and on 29th August 1959 merged with The Suffolk Regiment, to form the *1st Battalion East Anglian Regiment (Royal Norfolk & Suffolk)*.

Fig.299

Fig.300

Fig.301

Fig.302

Fig.305

Fig.304

Fig.303

Fig.308

Fig.307

Fig.306

The Royal Lincolnshire Regiment

Fig.309

Fig.310

Fig.311

Fig.312

Fig.313

Pre 1881
The 10th (North Lincoln) Regiment of Foot

By an Order dated 16th July 1872, the Regiment adopted for the mens' collar badge the Sphinx and Egypt device in brass. A 'male' type with frontal mantling only. The tail rising up over the body towards the head. Below a tablet inscribed in Roman lettering, "EGYPT". (Figs.309 & 310) show a facing pair. Pattern No.9327 sealed 29th May 1874. The design of the Sphinx closely followed that displayed on the mens' glengarry badge 1874-1879. In the latter year by an Order, 30th July, the collar badge was assimilated with that being worn by the 24th (2nd Warwickshire) Regiment. Pattern No.9567. This type, again in brass, was of the 'female' variety, the mantle extending down the back, and the tail rising up to become part of the profile of the badge, and pointing away from the head. (Fig.311). This again coincided with the type of Sphinx on the new pattern of glengarry badge, 1879-1881. Worn in facing pairs.

The Sphinx commemorates the Regiment's service in Egypt in 1801. Authorised to the Regiment 6th July 1802.

Though embroidered versions for the Officers 1880-1881 were probably in use, evidence in any medium has yet to be discovered.

Post 1881

The Regiment became simply, *The Lincolnshire Regiment*, 1st July 1881. An interim statement from Horse Guards, 30th September confirmed the collar badge, 'to be the same as at present worn.' By 22nd December, however, a decision was taken for a new collar badge to be introduced, 'in white metal and gilding metal.' This from a design submitted by Messrs. Smith & Wright, Birmingham, and revised by Bt. Colonel R.Blundell-Hollingshead-Blundell, AAG, Horse Guards.

This decision for a bi-metal badge must have been rescinded as on 20th January 1882 a new badge in white-metal was sealed, Pattern No.9969, 'to replace patt 9567 of the 10th.' (Fig.312). The male Sphinx was restored but larger than before, the tablet and inscription correspondingly enlarged. The tail now reverted to the direction of the first pattern.

The badge was renewed in 1898, and the opportunity was taken to improve the design. The format was that being used by the South Wales Borderers, formerly the 24th Foot. Pattern No.9969a, sealed 21st March 1898. (Fig.313). This was almost indentical to the initial badge of the old 10th, but in white-metal. The pattern is perhaps the one most associated with the Regiment.

Worn until 1948, it is not surprising that there are many minor variations concerning the size, delineation of the outline, and even the sexual aspect of the Sphinx. (Figs.314, 315, 316).

Fig.314  *Fig.315*  *Fig.316*  *Fig.317*

Warrant Officers and some other senior NCOs wore the same pattern, initially in silver, later in silver plate. A curious blackened gilding-metal variety was probably worn by a cyclist section c.1883-1908. (Fig.317).

By Army Order 167/1946, 'The King was graciously pleased to approve that the Lincolnshire Regiment shall in future, enjoy the distinction of "Royal".' As a result approval was given for a new design of collar badge. For the men this was to be the same male Sphinx over a tablet inscribed Egypt, all in white-metal, but now to be placed above a scroll in gilding-metal inscribed "*ROYAL LINCOLNSHIRE REGIMENT*". (Fig.318). Pattern No.13941, sealed 17th March 1948. Initially fitted with three lugs for better support, this was later reduced to one, with backing plate. This rather cumbersome badge was a smaller version of the new cap badge, worn until 1960.

For Officers, the early Dress Regulations describe the collar badge for wear on the tunic and frock as, 'On a silver eight pointed star, a circle in gilt metal, inscribed, Lincolnshire Regiment. Within the circle on a ground of blue velvet, the Sphinx over EGYPT in silver.' (Fig.319). Later issues replaced the velvet with vitreous blue enamel. (Fig.320)

The 1902 Edition adds, 'Mess jacket,' and to cover the introduction of Service Dress, 'The Sphinx over Egypt, with a scroll below inscribed Lincolnshire.' In bronze. (Fig.321). This pattern sealed 13th May 1903. The same badge in gilding-metal was worn on the khaki drill. These badges were worn until 1946 when the Regiment received its elevation. The star pattern badge, still with the blue enamel centre, now included the prefix 'ROYAL' around the circle, (Figs.322 & 323) show two minor variants. This badge was worn on all uniforms, and ones with the Sphinx facing left were also worn on the Officers headdress. Usually these are distinguishable by having longer lugs.

There appears to be no documentary details regarding the change from blue velvet to blue enamel as a centre backing, but the velvet ones, as with the corresponding Officers forage cap badge, are around pre 1892 in date.

Militia
Royal North Lincolnshire Militia
The Journals in the Pattern Room record, 'Collar badges in white metal, patt 7576 for wear on the tunic and frock collars, sealed 1/4/1876 under Authority PC/N.Lincs. Militia/127.' Another source states, 'Shield.' This could be the same shield as in the centre of the mens' glengarry badge, 1874-1881. A shield bearing the charges from the 1st and 4th quarters of the Arms of the Earls of Lindsey, (Bertie).'Argent, three battering rams barwise, in pale proper, armed and garnished azure.' (Line Drawing Fig.324).

The Regiment became the 3rd Battalion, The Lincolnshire Regiment, July 1881.

Royal South Lincolnshire Militia
Pattern No.7592 sealed 19th May 1876, Authority PC/SLM/92 shows distinctive white-metal collar badges. (Line Drawing Fig.325). The family Crest of the Earls Brownlow (Cust). 'A lion's head erased sable, gorged with a collar paly wavy of six, argent and azure.' The badge also featured in the mens' glengarry badge of the period, 1874-1881. The Cust family had a long association with the Regiment.

The Regiment became the 4th Battalion, The Lincolnshire Regiment, July 1881.

Fig.318

Fig.319

Fig.320

Fig.321

Fig.322

Fig.325

Fig.324

Fig.323

HISTORY OF THE BRITISH ARMY INFANTRY COLLAR BADGE

Rifle Volunteer Corps, Volunteer, Territorial Force & Territorial Army Battalions

1st & 2nd Lincolnshire Rifle Volunteer Corps, two consolidated Battalions, nominated in 1881, became the 1st & 2nd Volunteer Battalions, The Lincolnshire Regiment, in May 1883.

They wore the same white-metal collar badges as the Regular units. Records show that drawings were deposited in the Patttern Room for the 2nd Vol. Battalion, 12th April 1889. They were submitted by Messrs. Samuel Bros, Ludgate Hill, London. Approved by Horse Guards 19th March 1889 under Authority V/2 Lincolns/737. Formal permission was given to the 1st Vol. Battalion 8th January 1894 to wear the same collar badge as the Line Battalions.

The Volunteer Officers wore the same design as the Regulars but of an all silver composition with blue velvet centre. (Fig.326). A quite different format is shown in (Fig.327), fretted lettering, star and Sphinx of different designs.

The 3rd Volunteer Battalion, was raised 20th June 1900, the personnel wearing the same collar badges as the 1st & 2nd Volunteer Battalions.

In 1908, all three Volunteer Battalions were dispersed on a location basis, to form the 4th & 5th (TF) Battalions The other ranks were now required to wear their cap and white-metal collar badges devoid of battle honours. (Fig.328). The Officers suffered likewise, a bronze Service Dress example, and one polished to the base metal for use on khaki drill being shown in (Figs.329 & 330). This was a curious decision as the personnel of the 'Volunteer' period, 1883-1908 had been permitted to wear the honours as well as the badges. In 1922 having discovered that the 'Terriers" died in much the same way as the Regulars during 1914-1918, the Authorities graciously allowed all Battalions of a Regiment to wear the same badges. The Territorial Officers star pattern badges for the tunic and mess jacket also had these blank plinths below the Sphinx. Photographs often show a bronze T being worn below bronze collar badges.

The 'Royal' 13941 pattern was used as a guide for the later gold and silver anodised badges. They were not issued to or worn by the Regular Battalion, but were sealed 8th October 1956 for wear by other ranks of *'A' (Royal Lincolnshire) Coy. 7th (Vol.) Battalion, The Royal Anglian Regiment*. Pattern No.13941a. (Fig.331). Superceded by Pattern No. 20812, sealed 12th July 1973, War Office Regulations Ord.17b, for wear by soldiers of *5th (Vol.) Battalion, The Royal Anglian Regiment*.

General

All Sphinx badges worn by the Regiment, both Officers and other ranks, were worn in facing pairs, with the Sphinx facing inward towards the collar opening. Variations occur, especially in the Officers badges, where the size and shape of the Sphinx differ both in the Sphinx/EGYPT/title and star patterns.

The scarce and attractive 'Lincoln Imp' badge in brass or gilding-metal is not a collar badge, but was worn as an arm badge around WWII by the Regular units. (Fig.332)

In 1958, the Regiment joined the East Anglian Brigade and in 1960, it merged with The Northamptonshire Regiment, forming the *2nd Battalion, East Anglian Regiment (Duchess of Gloucester's Own Royal Lincolnshire and Northamptonshire)*.

Fig.326

Fig.327

Fig.328

Fig.329

Fig.330

Fig.331

Fig.332

The Devonshire Regiment

Pre-1881
The 11th (North Devon) Regiment of Foot

By Authorisation PC/Inf.Gen./111, 16th July 1872, the Regiment wore the Imperial crown in brass, as their collar badge. Worn 1874-1878 by the other ranks. (Fig.333). (Plate No.6) illustrates the badge in use, being worn by Sergeant-Major Gambrill, c.1877.

The Regiment decided that a more precise distinction was necessary, Pattern No.9656 being sealed 9th August 1878. An eight pointed star, the top most point displaced by a QVC. On the star, a strap inscribed "NORTH DEVON", within the voided centre, '11'. (Fig.334). In brass, this complemented the last pattern mens' glengarry badge, worn until 1882.

No Officers badges for the 1880-1881 period have been identified.

Post 1881

In 1881, the Regiment was designated *The Devonshire Regiment*, and after the usual interim period, new badges were issued. Pattern No.10104, sealed 8th February 1882. In gilding-metal the Castle of Exeter superimposed upon an eight pointed star (Fig.335). This badge was not popular and a decision was taken 29th September 1884 to approve a new design. A lead impression was abstracted, sealed and sent to the Army Pattern Room as a guide. It was emphasised that the new badge was not to be issued until existing stocks had been used up. On 10th February 1885 it was estimated that there were, at that time, sufficient stock to last a further two years.

In gilding-metal, the new badge Pattern No.910, sealed 16th April 1886, was, in shape, almost identical to the pre 1881 type. Exeter Castle displaced the numerals, and the legend altered to read, "THE DEVONSHIRE REGIMENT" (Fig.336). On 24th May 1888, the C.O. of the 1st Battalion was asked to send a few collar badges struck from the die in his possession for comparison with the sealed pattern. As a result Pattern No.910a was cut from new dies and sealed 26th Septermber 1899. The opportunity was taken to alter the shape of the star, less pointed rays, resulting in a more squat appearance (Fig.337). In gilding-metal and worn until 1902, when it was replaced with one bearing a K/C, still in gilding-metal, Pattern No.910b, sealed 28th May 1902 (Fig.338). The pre 1902 type is also recorded with a blackened finish, possibly for a cyclist unit. By an Order 11th May 1904 future collar badges were to be of 'diamond-cut' pattern, but it was not thought necessary to make any alterations to existing patterns.

A new Q/C pattern was necessary following the death of HM King George VI in 1952, but it was not until 12th November 1955 that Pattern No.17010, in gilding-

Fig.333

Fig.334

Fig.335

Fig.336

Fig.337

Fig.338

Fig.341

Fig.340

Fig.339

metal, was sealed under Authority 54/Gen/586. Worn up to amalgamation in 1958 (Fig.339).

From 1886, all the other ranks' patterns had unvoided centres.

The 1883 Dress Regulations describe the Officers badge for tunic and frock collars. 'In gilt metal on a silver eight pointed star, a circle surmounted by the crown. On the circle, "The Devonshire Regiment." Within, in silver, the Castle of Exeter with scroll inscribed, "SEMPER FIDELIS" on a ground of blue velvet.' (Fig.340). Types with gilt metal replacing the blue velvet are known, but the usage is unrecorded. Also noted are similar in gilt with cloth centre, but with white-metal instead of silver. After 1902, patterns with the K/C ensued. (Fig.341). At about this time the impractical blue velvet was replaced with blue enamel (Fig.342).The more squat type was also current, (Fig.343). Worn until 1955 when the corresponding Q/C pattern retained the same star outline. (Fig.344). Worn up to amalgamation in 1958.

The 1902 Service Dress pattern was to be, 'as for forage cap.' In bronze. (Fig.345). Replaced by the post 1955 Q/C pattern (Fig.346). Voided centres for both.

Militia
1st or East Devon Militia

Collar badges in white-metal for the other ranks tunic and frock collars were sealed 10th January 1876. They took the form of the three towered Exeter Castle (Fig.347). These rare badges should not be confused with those worn by the Devonshire police. Same format but in chromed metal. (Fig.348).

Another item stated to have been a Militia collar badge has been noted in white-metal and brass, a large bugle horn with the numeral '1' over 'RDM' within the curl. (Fig.349). The Regiment was never a Royal one, and the badge is not connected with any Devonshire Regiment.

The Regiment became the 4th Battalion, The Devonshire Regiment, July 1881.

2nd or South Devon Militia

It is highly likely that the men's collar badge c.1876-1881 was a rampant white metal Lion (Fig.350). Certainly this had been the motif borne on all the shoulder belt, shako, and helmet plates of the Regiment, c.1800-1881. It also featured on the mens' glengarry badge, 1874-1881. An ancient badge of the Earls of Devon (Redvers, later Courtenay), it occupies the 2nd and 3rd quarters of their Arms, 'Or, a rampant Lion azure.'

The Regiment became the 3rd Battalion, The Devonshire Regiment, July 1881.

Fig.342

Fig.343

Fig.344

Fig.345

Fig.346

Fig.347

Fig.348

Fig.349

Fig.350

THE DEVONSHIRE REGIMENT

Rifle Volunteer Corps, Volunteer, Territorial Force & Territorial Army Battalions

The Devonshire Rifle Volunteers enjoyed the premier precedence position in the United Kingdom, by virtue of their premier Corps, *1st (Exeter & South Devon)*. The commission dates of the first Officers being 1852/3. The unit had appeared in the Army Lists from 1854. A unit of battalion strength, they were nominated in 1881, and were redesignated, *1st (Exeter & South Devon) Volunteer Battalion, The Devonshire Regiment*, 1st November 1885.

There is no evidence that any personnel of this Rifle Volunteer Corps wore collar badges.

In 1908, the 1st Vol. Battalion merged with the 3rd Vol. Battalion, to form the 4th (TF) Battalion The other ranks wore a blackened version of the Regular collar badge (Fig.351). The more elaborate Officers pattern was also blackend, some have been traced with a dark brown (originally black?) cloth backing. (Fig.352)

2nd Devonshire Rifle Volunteers (Prince of Wales's)

This consolidated battalion (1880) of the former 2nd Administrative Battalion, were allotted in 1881, becoming the 2nd (PRINCE OF WALES'S) Volunteer Battalion, The Devonshire Regiment, 1st November 1885. As the Royal title and Prince of Wales's crest appears on the helmet plates, c.1880-1885, it is reasonable to assume that the recorded collar badges came into use c1880. The blackened brass pattern, with the motto scrolls tight to the coronet, c.1880-1885 (Fig.353), the later white-metal type with wide spread scrolls (Fig.354). The battalion continued to dress as Rifles after 1885, the Officers wearing the POW badge in silver plate (Fig.355). H.R.H. Prince Alfred of Edinburgh, K.G. was a Lieutenant in the Corps and a photograph of 1895 clearly shows these silver collar badges.

Post 1902 photographs show large POW feathers collar badges in bronze being worn on the Service Dress. (Fig.356). In 1908, the 2nd Vol. Battalion along with the 5th Vol. Battalion became the 5th (Prince of Wales's) Battalion (TF). They continued to wear the same collar badges but in gilding-metal for the men (Fig.357) a reversion to the 'tight' scrolls. But c.1918, a wider scroll type reappeared (Fig.358). Officers continued to wear the badge in silver plate and the smaller bronze type on their Service Dress. (Fig.359). The pattern with 'tight' scrolls and blackened was worn on the mess jacket.

Fig.351

Fig.352

Fig.353

Fig.354

Fig.357

Fig.358

Fig.359

Fig.355

Fig.360

Fig.361

Fig.362

Fig.356

3rd Devonshire Rifle Volunteer Corps

Allotted in 1881 and designated as 3rd Volunteer Battalion, The Devonshire Regiment, 1st November 1885. No collar badges have been traced prior to 1885. From then until 1902 the other ranks wore similar badges to the Regular units but in white-metal (Fig.360). The K/C pattern followed, c.1902-1908 (Fig.361). Both types with unvoided centres. Officers, c.1885-1902 wore similar star badges to those worn by the Regulars, but the circle was inscribed, "DEVONSHIRE 3RD VOLR BATTN". The K/C pattern followed in 1902. Both badges in silver plate.

Fig.363

4th Devonshire Rifle Volunteer Corps

This consolidated Battalion became the 4th Volunteer Battalion, The Devonshire Regiment, 1st November 1885. From c.1885 the men wore the standard badge in white-metal, but the Officers adopted a particular pattern, in silver only, based on that of the Regular units; the circle was inscribed, "DEVONSHIRE REGT 4TH VOL BATT". Worn with the QVC to 1902 (Fig.362) and thereafter until 1908 with K/C (Fig.363). In both types the Castle had a backing of blue velvet. The battalion became the 6th (TF) Battalion in 1908, with the other ranks continuing to wear the K/C white-metal badges. It is thought that the Officers correspondingly wore an all silver plate version of the Regulars type with blue velvet and blue enamel backings. (Figs.364, 365 and 366). The normal large bronze badges were worn on the Service Dress, often with a separate 'T' below.

Fig.364

5th Devonshire Rifle Volunteer Corps

The former 5th Administrative Battalion was consolidated in 1880, initially numbered 9th, retitled 5th by June of that year. Nominated in 1881, the Corps became the 5th (THE HAY TOR) Volunteer Battalion, The Devonshire Regiment, 1st November 1885. A photograph taken c.1885 shows other ranks of this battalion wearing white-metal Imperial crown collar badges. (Fig.367). After 1885 the battalion chose a distinctive collar badge, an eight pointed diamond cut star on which was mounted a crowned circle. This was inscribed, 5 (THE HAY TOR) VB DEVONSHIRE REGT. Within the circle a rampant lion. In white-metal and with an unvoided centre for the men; the Officers slightly larger pattern in silver plate, had a blue velvet centre backing to the lion. (Fig.368). Similar were later worn with a K/C. The lion badge also appeared in the pre 1902 headdress badges of the battalion, but was dropped in favour of the Castle and Motto centre of the other Battalions, in the K/C helmet plate. Whether the collar badges also changed is uncertain.

Fig.365

Fig.366

7th (Cyclist) Battalion (TF)

Formed in 1908 at Exeter from the cyclist sections of the 1st and 5th Volunteer Battalions. It is believed that they adopted blackened collar badges of the standard pattern, (Figs.351 & 369) show other ranks and Officers respectively. The unit was converted to Artillery in 1920.

As with other Territorial units, the badges of the Regular Battalions were gradually adopted, and a sealed pattern, 19th October 1956 shows the Officers silver/gilt/enamel Q/C badge, 'For Nos.1 & 3 Dress.' The bronze Q/C type for Service Dress.

Fig.367

Fig.368

Fig.369

Fig.370

THE DEVONSHIRE REGIMENT

The men wore the Q/C gilding-metal collar badge, Pattern No.17010, and this was used as a guide for the later version in gold anodised. Pattern No.19210, sealed 30th December 1963, Authority 54/Inf/8848. (Fig.370).

General

As can be seen from the illustrations, the shape of the star has varied considerably, but the squat pattern appears to have been the more popular or 'correct' one.

The Volunteer Battalions badges have been difficult to research, as they varied not only from those of the Regular units, but also within the different Volunteer units. Some questions are still unanswered. The following badges cannot yet be definitely attributed. (Figs.371 & 372) are in all silver apart from the blue velvet centre backing. By process of elimination, these most probably pertain to the 1st (Exeter & South Devon) Vol. Battalion, as it would have been unusual for the Officers at least, not to have worn collar badges.

Fig.373 displays an Officer's pattern badge with QVC, but with a solid centre and in white-metal, two features normally associated with other ranks badges. Certainly an odd amalgam, the usual suggestions of use by senior NCOs of the Vol. Battalions, has been propounded. An all white-metal pattern with K/C and voided centre is also known.

A much smaller badge with K/C is in all silver and unvoided centre (Fig.374). Mess jacket use is a possibility. The first three items are inscribed, "THE DEVONSHIRE REGIMENT", while the latter has the abbreviated, REGT. They all have the usual two lug fasteners.

The Regiment, (less territorials) was amalgamated with The Dorset Regiment (less territorials) to form the *The Devonshire and Dorset Regiment*, 17th May 1958.

Fig.371

Fig.372

Fig.373

Fig.374

Royal Fusliers

HISTORY OF THE BRITISH ARMY INFANTRY COLLAR BADGE

The Suffolk Regiment

Fig.375

Fig.376

Fig.377

Fig.378

Fig.379

Fig.380

Pre 1881
The 12th (East Suffolk) Regiment of Foot

The first collar badge for the men was the brass Imperial crown (Fig.333), authorised 16th July 1872, PC/Infy Gen/111. In 1875, a more distinctive badge was approved. This was the triple towered Castle of Gibraltar, with a vertical Key atop the central tower. This singular position of the Key occurred on the last pre 1855 Officers shoulder belt plate. Each tower shows a single look-out, whereas the central wall has three. Below the middle of these three is an archway with a partly raised portcullis and steps leading down to a curved ground. (Fig.375). Pattern No.9535, sealed 18th March 1875, in brass for wear by the other ranks on their tunic and frock collars. The badge was almost identical to the top of the mens' glengarry badge, 1874-1881. It is also recorded in silver plate for wear by Senior NCOs. (Fig.376). After 1880, the Officers wore exactly the same design but in embroidered gold thread, sadly on the illustrated example the Key has been lost (Fig.377). This design is shown in the Gaunt pattern books.

Post 1881

On becoming *The Suffolk Regiment*, 1st July 1881, the Regiment received the standard Horse Guards letter 30th September confirming usage of the existing collar badge, but on 29th December 1881, a new badge in gilding-metal was sealed. Pattern No.9907, 'in lieu of brass patt.9535.' A quite different Castle and Key distribution. Only a twin towered Castle and the Key lying horizontally at the base of the archway. The archway was increased in height and edged with eleven stones. The portcullis fully down. Each tower had two look-outs, and the whole edifice rested on uneven ground. The towers had slightly rounded tops, and the handle of the Key was of irregular outline. In gilding-metal the Keys were not facing (Fig.378). This badge was also worn on the field service cap being replaced by the more familiar pattern badge in 1897.

A variant displays thirteen stones around the archway and the handle of the Key is of plainer outline. (Fig.379). This is the type more commonly found.

The War Office notified the Regiment 30th January 1900 that the Castle and Key of Gibraltar was represented by a different design in each Regiment to which the distinction had been granted. Enclosed was an illustration of the correct representation, that used on the Seal of Gibraltar granted 1502, and subsequently upon its coinage.

It would seem that the Regiment had prior knowledge, as renewal of their standard collar badge had been demanded, to be cut from new dies, 27th November 1897. A new Pattern No.9907a was sealed 6th April 1898. In gilding-metal it had the correct triple towered Castle, but otherwise was as before. (Fig.380). This pattern was practically ignored by the Regiment, who after a short time, reverted to the twin towered type. A further triple towered pattern was introduced in 1931, under Authority 54/Infy/6632. The Key vertical again but depending from a torse on which the Castle now stood. The archway was similar to that of the pre 1881 type, and again the portcullis was displayed partially raised. All the look-outs were omitted. The towers were in low relief giving the badge a flat appearance. Pattern No.10459, sealed 11th February 1931. (Fig.381).

This pattern was used as a guide for the ensuing gold anodised version, but there is no evidence that it was ever used by the Regular Battalion. They were worn by the soldiers of *'B' and 'C' Coys., The Suffolk and Cambridgeshire*

THE SUFFOLK REGIMENT

Regiment (Territorials) from 1961. Pattern No.19269, sealed 1964. (Fig.382).

The Officers embroidered badges after 1881 changed very little save for the Key which now appeared in the archway of the Castle; there were the inevitable minor varieties that occur with hand made badges. (Figs.383,384,385). Dress Regulations laconically state, 'The Castle and Key in gold embroidery.'

The 1902 Edition of Dress Regulations makes mention of the new bronze badge for the Service Dress, 'As for forage cap but in bronze.' The newly designed triple towered Castle and Key with scroll above inscribed "GIBRALTAR", all within a circle inscribed, "MONTIS INSIGNIA CALPE", surmounted with the K/C. The whole within a wreath of oak, at the base a tri-part scroll inscribed, "THE/SUFFOLK/REGT". (Fig.386). A sealed pattern in the Regimental Museum displays the post 1953 Q/C. (Fig.387)

Under Ref 55/Gen/188, 13th May 1903, new embroidered collar badges were sealed for wear on the tunic, frock coat and mess dress. (The 1904 Dress Regulations record only one badge, the sealed pattern card shows a separate collar badge for the mess jacket.) The new badge featured the triple towered Castle with vertical Key below, all within a wreath surmounted by a K/C. In gold metal thread, with red and green silk embroidery to the crown, and black silk embroidery on the turrets and archway of the Castle. The whole with a yellow cloth backing. (Fig.388). This replaced the earlier twin towered Castle pattern (Fig.389). The 1911 Dress Regulations appear to clarify the matter, 'In gold embroidery, the Castle and Key within a laurel wreath, surmounted by a crown. For wear on the tunic, mess jacket and frock coat'. The 1934 Edition however finally establishes the two types of collar badge. 'In gold embroidery, on yellow cloth, the Castle and Key, For the mess jacket the Castle is within a laurel wreath surmounted by a crown'. There must be therefore a triple towered Castle and Key only embroidered badge for the tunic and the frock coat, before the abolition of the latter.

To confuse the issue still further, a photograph of Bandmaster W. Froud, 2nd Battalion, c.1913, shows him to be wearing twin towered Castle and (horizontal?) Key silver metal collar badges. (Plate 7.)

A gilt metal collar badge was introduced c.1946, and worn on all Officers uniforms except mess dress. (Fig.390). A later identical pattern was sealed 22nd November 1956, 'For No.1 Dress.' A slightly larger variety is recorded polished to the base metal for wear in the tropical Service Dress. (Fig.391)

Since 1881, an unofficial pattern of collar badge was worn variously on tropical mess dress and No.3 Dress. A crowned circle inscribed "GIBRALTAR", at the base of the circle XII, within, the Castle and Key; the whole lodged within laurel wreaths. In gilt and silver. The QVC early issues show a twin towered Castle with vertical Key above the castellations. (Fig.392). This was followed by the short lived twin towered Castle with K/C. (Fig.393), and the triple towered version with Key below (Fig.394). This one is also recorded in all silver plate (Fig.395). The badge finally gained official recognition, for a Q/C pattern was sealed, 22nd November 1956, 'For wear on tropical mess dress.'

An oddity that has so far remained a mystery is a small version of the K/C silver cap badge (Fig.396). Hall marked with dates usually c.1910-1918, and with the

Fig.381

Fig.382

Fig.383

Fig.384

Fig.385

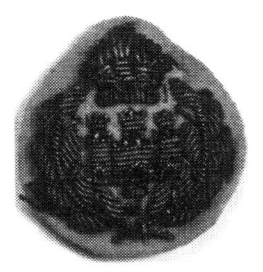

Fig.388

Fig.387

Fig.386

HISTORY OF THE BRITISH ARMY INFANTRY COLLAR BADGE

Fig.389

marks of Messrs. Carrington & Co. London. The usual panaceas of 'sweethearts' and 'side hat' have been suggested.

Militia
West Suffolk Militia

New glengarry and collar badges in white-metal were issued to the Regiment 21st April 1876, these badges and the Officers embroidered forage cap and later helmet plate, all featured a twin towered castle, flags flying from the rounded towers. Below a tri-part scroll inscribed, "WEST/SUFFOLK/MILITIA." 20mm x 45mm. (Line Drawing, Fig.397). The use of this castle is somewhat of a mystery, the only established reference to such a castle being used is in Fox-Davies and Crookes, 'The Book of Public Arms.' 1894. At that time, the common seal of the East Suffolk County Council was, - A castle domed, and on each dome a pennon, and above the battlements upon a wreath is a lion rampant. Perhaps it had formed the old overall county seal. The Regiment became the 3rd Battalion, The Suffolk Regiment, 1881.

Fig.390

Cambridgeshire Militia

The Journals of the Pattern Room record under Ref. PC/Cambridge Militia/147. 'White metal collar badges, pattern 7486 for wear on tunic and frock collar, sealed 18/11/75.' These were, 'Castle, flag and key.' A curious description this, for the long established badge of the Regiment was the crest from the Arms of the City of Cambridge. Though described as a 'bridge' (a fortified bridge), it appears as a domed triple towered castle, with flags flying. The Regiment became the 4th Battalion, The Suffolk Regiment in 1881.

Fig.391

Rifle Volunteer Corps, Volunteer, Territorial Force & Territorial Army Battalions

1st Suffolk Rifle Volunteer Corps, nominated in 1881, became the 1st Volunteer Battalion in 1887, becoming the 4th (TF) Battalion in 1908. There is no evidence that the 1st Suffolk RVC wore collar badges. One of their component Corps the 10th Eye formed in 1860 certainly wore distinctive shako, pouch belt and pouch badges. These featured the human eye which formed part of the crest of the borough (The Arms granted 1592). It has been suggested that the badge shown in (Fig.398) was their collar badge. However this badge almost certainly relates to the South African Cape Police, the lugs are of typical 'round' colonial shape, and the format is unlike any of the other known badges of the Eye RVC. The Volunteer Battalion personnel wore corresponding badges to the Regulars but in silver embroidery and white-metal.

Fig.392

A bronze K/C Officer's Service Dress cap/collar badge similar to Fig.386 has been noted but without the "Gibralter" above the castle, possible worn by the 4th (TF) Battalion, circa 1918.

6th Suffolk (West Suffolk) Rifle Volunteer Corps

Upon consolidation in 1880, the battalion declined to be the 2nd Battalion Suffolk RVC, retaining the number of their most senior company, 6th Stowmarket (later Sudbury). Following nomination they became the 2nd Volunteer Battalion in

Fig.393

Fig.394  *Fig.395*  *Fig.396*  *Fig.397*

THE SUFFOLK REGIMENT

1887. The other ranks wore the twin towered Castle, (Fig.399) followed by the triple towered version, both in white-metal. Officers wore similar but in silver plate (Fig.400) illustrates the twin towered pattern. In 1908, the unit became the 5th (TF) Battalion.

Photographs circa 1915 show a bronze 'T' being worn below the bronze collar badge (Fig.386) by Territorial Battalion Officers.

1st Cambridgeshire (Cambridge, Essex and Huntingdonshire) Rifle Volunteer Corps

This conglomerate Corps became a Volunteer battalion of the Suffolk Regiment in 1881, and was redesignated 3rd (Cambridgeshire) Volunteer Battalion, December 1887. In 1908, they became the Cambridgeshire Battalion, The Suffolk Regiment, and in 1909, 1st Battalion The Cambridgeshire Regiment. (See under separate section.)

As the Regulars continued to wear the twin towered collar badge long after the supposed introduction of the triple towered pattern, the Volunteers, not to be outdone, went as far as breaking the middle tower off the new pattern. One assumes that the Regulars wishing to retain the old pattern, for once adhered to the rule, 'Until present stocks are exhausted.'

Other rank's firstly wore the 2 tower pattern collar badge (Fig.401) then the 3 tower pattern (Fig.402) both in white-metal. Neither had the usual horizontal key at the base of the castle and these were often referred to as "collar badges with the ghost key". Officers wore similar, again with no key, in silver plate - slightly smaller and neater (Fig.403).

2nd Cambridgeshire Rifle Volunteer Corps

Formerly the *3rd Cambridgeshire (Cambridge University) RVC*. Nominated in 1881 and redesignated December 1887 as the 4th (Cambridge University) Volunteer Battalion. In 1908 the unit became the Cambridge University Contingent of the Senior Division O.T.C. To date no evidence has been forthcoming concerning any collar badges worn either before or during the Volunteer Battalion periods.

Cyclists
6th (Cyclist) Battalion

Raised in 1910 and disembodied 13th March 1919. The cyclists wore the Regulars standard collar badge but with a blackened finish.

WWI Service Battalions
9th (Service Battalion)

Raised 22nd September 1914; the Battalion went to France as part of 'Kitchener's Army', and photographs show them wearing brass shoulder titles on the collars of their blue emergency uniforms (Fig.404). These were not collar badges as such, despite being worn on the collar. Uniforms were so difficult to obtain in the early days of the War that any uniform was used, often as it is believed in this case, those of postmen, which were without shoulder straps. These soldiers, therefore, had shoulder titles but nowhere to attach them so for identification purposes, placed them on their collars. The unit was disbanded 16th February 1918.

General

Over the years, the Key has appeared on the Regiment's collar badges, vertically and horizontally. The vertical one has faced to the left and right, but always facing the same way on any one pattern.

The Regiment adopted the East Anglian Brigade badges in 1958, merging with The Royal Norfolk Regiment, 29th August 1959 to form the *1st East Anglian Regiment*.

Fig.398

Fig.399

Fig.400

Fig.401

Fig.402

Fig.403

Fig.404

The Somerset Light Infantry (Prince Albert's)

Fig.405

Fig.406

Fig.407

Fig.408

Fig.411

Fig.412

Fig.409

Fig.410

Pre 1881
The 13th (1st Somersetshire) (Prince Albert's Regiment of Light Infantry)

The first collar badge of the Regiment was Pattern No.9312, sealed 28th July 1873. A mural crown over a strung bugle horn corded and tassled, in white metal. (Figs.405 & 406). These were worn for just over a year, being replaced by similar but in brass and with the addition of a scroll inscribed "JELLALABAD" placed above the crown. Pattern No.9511, sealed 29th September 1874 for wear by other ranks on the full dress tunic and scarlet kersey frock field service jacket. (Figs.407, 408).

Officers wore the same pattern but in embroidery c.1880-1881. (Figs.409, 410) show two slight variants.

As with all later bugle patterns they were worn in facing pairs, the mouthpiece facing inward towards the collar opening.

The mural crown representing the ramparts of the fortress of Jellalabad was given to the Regiment 20th August 1842 together with the honour "Jellalabad", to commemorate the gallant defence of the fort by the Regiment in April 1842 during the First Afghan War. According to history, the mural crown was first awarded as a badge to Roman troops who successfully scaled the walls of a besieged fortress. The bugle horn was adopted in 1822 when the 13th Foot were elevated to Light Infantry.

In the S.A.H.R. Journal Volume XXII, No.89, in an article by E.J.Martin Esq., 'The Universal Helmet Plate 1878-1914', it states that the helmet plate centre (Fig.411), 'was formerly worn as a collar badge'. No documentary or photographic evidence has been located that confirms this statement.

Post 1881

In 1881, the Regiment was redesignated *The Prince Albert's (Somersetshire Light Infantry)* with the ensuing requirement for new badges. One suggested design was of a bugle horn above a scroll inscribed, 'Prince Albert's Lt. Infy.' The AAG at Horse Guards ruled against this. The pre 1881 pattern was retained but now in gilding-metal with copper lugs. Pattern No.9879, sealed 15th December 1881. (Fig.412). Photographs show them being worn on the scarlet, white and khaki drill clothing, 1891-1908, by the 1st Battalion in India. The pattern was renewed 6th April 1898, new dies being made and the resultant Pattern No.9879a replacing 9879. No change in design.

A minor title change occurred in 1912, *Prince Albert's (Somerset Light Infantry)* but this did not effect the collar badge. The final change took place 1st January

THE SOMERSET LIGHT INFANTRY (PRINCE ALBERT'S)

1921 when the Regiment became, *The Somerset Light Infantry (Prince Albert's)*. A new pattern of collar badge was sought and this was authorised 13th June 1924. Pattern No.3996 in gilding-metal, content wise the badge remained as before but the badge became more elongated, there were ends to the scroll and more space between the crown and scroll. All the features became narrower and finally the treble loops of the bugle cords appeared below the crown. (Fig.413)

A third pattern change occurred 20th May 1930 when by Authority 54/Inf/6317 Pattern No.10400 replaced 3996. Still in gilding-metal but with the addition of 'PA' (Prince Albert) within the strings of the bugle horn. The tassles of the strings being 'drawn up' to accommodate this feature. (Fig.414). A slight variant, cast, and of Indian manufacture has been noted (Fig.415). Again an example in chromed finish is thought to have been worn for the Allied Victory Parade after WWII.

In 1948, a further design was considered and finally sealed 14th March 1950, Pattern No.14335. In white-metal and displaying further changes in the shape of the scroll and the space between the scroll and the crown. The badge again of slightly squatter shape. (Fig.416). Initially issued with the usual two lug fittings, later issues occur with the single lug and back plate system. This pattern was used as a guide for the silver anodised version, and although manufactured it is doubtful if they were ever worn due to the amalgamation of the Regiment in 1959. The sealed pattern 9th October 1956 contains a facing pair of silver anodised collar badges annotated, '1st Battalion TA.'

A distinctive silver anodised version with two lug fixings follows the design of the last gilding-metal type, (Fig.417). The sealed Pattern, 19590, 4th January 1966, shows a single lug variant. (Fig.418)

After 1881, the Officers continued to wear bullion wire badges on their tunics and frock coats, described in the early Dress Regulations as, 'Gold and silver embroidery on a ground of green cloth, a bugle with strings, surmounted by a mural crown embroidered in silver, above the crown in gold embroidery, a scroll inscribed "Jellalabad." ' (Figs.419, 420, 421) show variations.

The 1902 Edition adds the smaller embroidered version for the mess jacket. (Fig.422). That for the new Service Dress, 'As for forage cap but in pairs,' in bronze. (Fig.423). Sealed 2nd June 1904. Since its introduction the size of this badge has gradually reduced, (Fig.424) being introduced c.1915, and a modern version worn up to amalgamation, (Fig.425). A very small type (Fig.426) is cast, made locally in India and worn during one of the Regiment's tours in that country.

Bronze collar badges were also sealed 9th October 1956 for wear by the Officers of, '1st Battalion TA.'

Most regiments have badges that do not appear in any issue of Dress

Fig.413

Fig.414

Fig.415

Fig.416

Fig.420

Fig.419

Fig.417

Fig.421

Fig.422

Fig.418

HISTORY OF THE BRITISH ARMY INFANTRY COLLAR BADGE

Fig.423

Fig.424

Fig.425

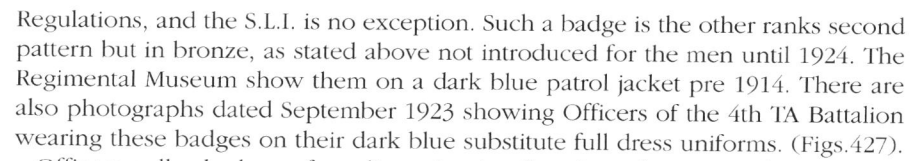

Regulations, and the S.L.I. is no exception. Such a badge is the other ranks second pattern but in bronze, as stated above not introduced for the men until 1924. The Regimental Museum show them on a dark blue patrol jacket pre 1914. There are also photographs dated September 1923 showing Officers of the 4th TA Battalion wearing these badges on their dark blue substitute full dress uniforms. (Figs.427).

Officers collar badges of medium size in silver have been noted, thought to have been worn from 1915 (Fig.428). Much smaller versions in silver were worn by Officers of 1st Battalion TA. on Nos.1 & 3 Dress, sealed 9th October 1956 (Fig.429). Large cap badge size silver badges are reported as having been worn in the collar of the white mess dress with a green cloth backing. Certainly many unofficial badges were worn by Regiments when serving abroad, but so far all the examples noted have faced left and are probably cap badges only (Fig.430).

Other oddities are gilt versions of the first three other ranks patterns. A photograph of the 3rd Reserve Battalion (formerly Militia Battalions) c.1912, shows a party of W.O.s, Sergeants, and soldiers all wearing the first pattern other ranks collar badge, excepting the R.S.M. who is clearly wearing gilt versions. One of the Officers in the same photograph wears the same other ranks pattern but almost certainly in silver and gilt. (Fig.431).The scroll, crown, and tassles are gilt, the bugle and strings in silver. It cannot be established whether these variants were confined solely to the 3rd Reserve Battalion.

The second other ranks pattern in gilt was worn by Warrant Officers. (Fig.432)

The third pattern in gilt is cast and has the appearance of Indian manufacture. The usual corded strings and loops are ribboned, and the ends of the honour scroll are square. (Fig.433). Possibly worn by senior NCOs during service in India. It has also been suggested that they were worn on the bush jacket when the Regiment was in Austria in the late 1940s. The same variant has been noted in bronze, possibly for wear on the khaki drill.

Another variety that is unrecorded in any official source is that shown in (Fig.434). A ribboned bugle horn with XIII within the strings in gilt metal. A photograph of Officers, NCOs and men of 'G' Company 2nd Battalion S.L.I. taken at Devonport in 1894, shows this badge being worn by an Officer on the collar of the frock coat. There is also a Sergeant's mess dress uniform in the Regimental Museum which carries the same badge but in polished brass (These were most probably originally gilt metal). This uniform was worn by Sergeant later Sergeant Major T. Tobias, DCM, 4th Militia Battalion. These badges are similar to those worn by the Canadian, Hamilton Light Infantry, and also the 13th Infantry Battalion, The Maquarie Regiment, New South Wales; both units being allied to the S.L.I.

Fig.426    *Fig.428*    *Fig.429*

Fig.427    *Fig.430*    *Fig.431*    *Fig.432*

THE SOMERSET LIGHT INFANTRY (PRINCE ALBERT'S)

Militia
1st Somersetshire Light Infantry Militia
Collar badges in white-metal Pattern No.7585 were sealed 28th April 1876 under Authority PC/1SM/170 for wear on the tunic and frock collars. A small ribboned bugle horn with tab ends. Of rather delicate manufacture and worn for two years only, in facing pairs. (Fig.435, end broken)

2nd Somersetshire Light Infantry Militia
Collar badges in white-metal, Pattern No.7583, were sealed 28th April 1876 under Authority PC/2SM/153. A similar small ribboned bugle horn. Worn for two years only (Fig.436)

In 1878, it was decided to standardise the various bugle horn badges worn by the several Light Infantry Militia Regiments. Accordingly, both regiments received a copy of the following direction. 'Decision PC/S Down Militia/195, 26th March 1878 - collar badges Pattern Nos. 7585 and 7583 to be obsolete. Assimilated to Pattern No.8935 sealed for Royal South Gloucester Militia.' This was the standard white-metal bugle horn badge. (Fig.207).

In 1881, the two Regiments became the 3rd and 4th Battalions, Prince Albert's Somersetshire Light Infantry.

Rifle Volunteer Corps, Volunteer, Territorial Force & Territorial Army Battalions
The *1st Somersetshire Rifle Volunteer Corps* became a Volunteer Battalion in 1881 and was redesignated the 1st Volunteer Battalion in 1882. As such they adopted a special collar badge, a mural crown on which was superimposed, 1 VB, over a strung bugle horn. A scroll above the crown was inscribed, "SOMERSET". In white-metal the pattern was sealed 17th March 1885 under Ref./V/1 Somerset/333. The castellations of the crown are both voided and unvoided (Figs.437). Officers wore similar but in silver plate.(Fig.438).

The former *2nd Somersetshire Rifle Volunteer Corps* became the 2nd Volunteer Battalion in 1882, and wore equally distinctive collar badges. Again in white-metal with a "SOMERSET" scroll above a mural crown; below a ribboned bugle horn with 2 V B between the strings, the Officers version again in silver plate (Fig.439). These were also worn on the field service cap. The Army Clothing Department Journal, record the pattern being approved by the War Office 22nd May 1893 under Ref V/2/13/80, 'for NCOs and men.'

Officers wore a badge of quite different format. In silver, the mural crown over a strung bugle horn with PA between the strings, above the crown a scroll inscribed "2nd V.B. SOMERSET"; below the bugle horn another scroll inscribed, "SOUTH AFRICA 1900-01". Also worn on the peaked forage cap. (Fig.440). The bronze badge shown in (Fig.441) is also thought to have been worn by the Officers of the 2nd Vol. Battalion after 1902 on the Service Dress. Similar to those worn by the Line Battalions, but with the scroll inscribed "SOMERSET". The same item is known in silver plate and as these are die-stamped, could well have been plated privately, which would indicate that there was an other ranks white-metal equivalent.

The *3rd Somersetshire Rifle Volunteer Corps*, nominated in 1881 became the 3rd Volunteer Battalion in 1882, and also adopted a special pattern of collar badge. In white-metal and of similar size to that of the 1st Vol. Battalion, however the scroll above the crown was inscribed, "SOMERSET VB." and the numeral 3 appeared within the strings of the bugle horn. Also worn in the field service cap. (Fig.442). Same pattern worn by the Officers but in silver plate, and sometimes with the addition of a silver plate V below the badge but on the left side only. After 1902 the same pattern in bronze was worn on the Service Dress. Both other ranks and Officers badges of this battalion are found with a blackened finish, the Officers' having a round top to the 3. (Fig.443) shows the other ranks type.

Photographs of Officers of the 3rd and 4th Battalions c.1903-1908 show a bronze 'M' being worn below their Service Dress collar badge.

Fig.433

Fig.434

Fig.435

Fig.436

Fig.437

Fig.438

Fig.439

HISTORY OF THE BRITISH ARMY INFANTRY COLLAR BADGE

Fig.440

Fig.441

Fig.442

Fig.443

Fig.444

Fig.445

The three Volunteer Battalions were merged in 1908 to form two TF Battalions, 4th and 5th. On the scarlet full dress tunics they now wore white-metal versions of the current Regular pattern, but with the top scroll inscribed "SOUTH AFRICA 1900". Unusual variants are gilding-metal examples worn by the 5th Battalion only, officially 1908-1914 on the full dress tunic and perhaps on the other ranks Service Dress c.1914-1917. (Figs.444, 445). In 1908, the new TF Battalions were given the option of changing their silver/white-metal lace, badges buttons etc. to gold lace etc. Economically many units stayed as they were, the 5th Battalion S.L.I. opted for the change.

In S.A.H.R. Journal Vol.XXII No.86, E.J. Martin Esq. published an article on 'Badges of the Territorial Infantry Battalions 1908-1922.' Referring to the 4th and 5th Battalions S.L.I. he mentions that the cap badge was for the Regular Battalions except that the honour scroll was inscribed, South Africa 1900-01. He further states, 'on the collar badge for the men the scroll was omitted entirely. They were in white metal.' Whilst in agreement with the cap badge information, there is no evidence to support his comment on the collar badge.

There is some evidence that the other ranks wore for a short time the large white-metal cap badge as a collar badge. (Fig.446).

Officers in full dress wore similar bullion badge to the Regulars but with the top honour scroll replaced with "SOUTH AFRICA 1900-01". (Fig.447). Similar badges in bronze with an additional but separate 'T' were worn in the Service Dress (Fig.448).

One final item in this section is that shown in (Fig.449). Though often referred to as a collar badge, 'Volunteer or Miltia,' it is the central mount from the Officers' waist belt clasps.

The 2/4 TF Battalion went to France in 1918, wearing the usual crossed rifle and pick collar badge. (Fig.147).

General

All bugle type collar badges were worn in facing pairs, with the mouthpieces facing inward towards the collar opening.

On 6th October 1959, the Regiment amalgamated with The Duke of Cornwall's Light Infantry to form the *The Somerset and Cornwall Light Infantry*.

Fig.446

Fig.447

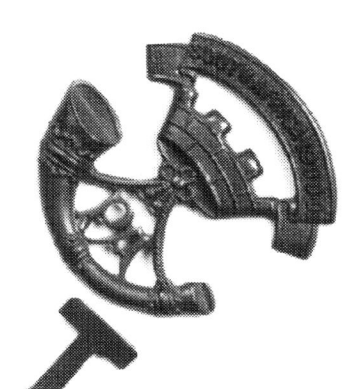

Fig.448

Fig.449

74

The West Yorkshire Regiment (The Prince of Wales's Own)

Pre 1881
The 14th (Buckinghamshire or The Prince of Wales's Own) Regiment of Foot

By a Horse Guards letter December 1874, authority was given for 'The Royal Tiger' to be worn on the collar of the mens tunics, Pattern No.9303 being sealed 25th March 1873. In brass, this was a large free standing animal with one front paw raised and pointing downward. The head facing fully sideways, and the tail curling up over the body, reaching midway along the back and finally curling back upon itself.. Worn in facing pairs with the head facing towards the collar opening. (Fig.450). On 27th September 1877 it was decreed that the pattern was to be assimilated to the pattern being worn by the 75th Regiment, Pattern No. 9519, sealed 3rd November 1874. Again in brass but quite different attitude. The head down in the stalking position but still regarding the viewer, the tail down, and the animal upon a narrow foliage ground. Worn in facing pairs (Figs.451,452).

The Royal Tiger was authorised by a Horse Guards letter 8th November 1838, commemorating the arduous years of constant campaigning in India, 1807-1831.

The second pattern was not popular with the men as it was thought to show a 'cowed' animal, having its tail between its legs.

Officers wore an embroidered version of this second pattern 1880-1881.
At various times, written articles have stated that the 1st Battalion, sometime prior to 1881, wore a White Horse collar badge, this upon a downward curving torse, similar to that worn on the Regiment's pre 1881 glengarry badge. This badge found in facing pairs was worn at one time as part of the shoulder strap insignia, and was not a collar badge.

Fig.450

Fig.451

Fig.452

Post 1881

In July 1881, the 14th were redesignated, *The Prince of Wales's Own (West Yorkshire Regiment)*, and a decision was taken to introduce new pattern collar badges. However for the interim, the tiger badges were retained, a Directive 5th October 1881, Ref. PC/1W York Regt/35 drawing the Regiment's attention to the correct positioning of the badge.

Messrs. Smith & Wright submitted a new design 22nd December 1881, 'in a combination of white and gilding metal.' This design was revised by the A.A.G. Horse Guards, being sealed 20th January 1882. Pattern No.9981, replacing 9519. The pattern was also authorised for the men of the Prince of Wales's Leinster Regiment (Royal Canadians).

The new badge was the Prince of Wales's Crest and Motto, the plumes and scroll in white-metal, the coronet in gilding-metal. (Fig.453). The badge was granted to the Regiment when the then Prince of Wales (later Edward VII) presented new colours and the title 'Prince of Wales's Own' to the 1st Battalion in Lucknow, January 1876. These awards were confirmed in the London Gazette 6th June 1876.

This Pattern 9981a was renewed and cut from new dies 3rd August 1899; no change in the pattern took place when the Regiment was redesignated *The West Yorkshire Regiment (Prince of Wales's Own)* 1st January 1921. It continued in use until amalgamation in 1958 on all forms of dress, latterly with a single lug and plate fastening (Fig.454). The pattern was to have been used as a guide for the

Fig.453

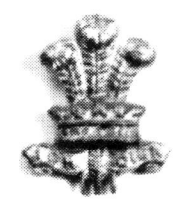

Fig.454

HISTORY OF THE BRITISH ARMY INFANTRY COLLAR BADGE

anodised version, but no details of its manufacture have been discovered.

Officers wore the same badge in silver and gold embroidery on the tunic, frock coat and later the mess jacket. (Fig.455). The 1934 Dress Regulations add, 'on buff cloth', (Fig.456). Additionally, Officers wore the same in silver and gilt on drill order until 1902, and on No.1 Dress mess jacket and patrol jacket from the 1930s onward.

By letter dated 4th July 1894, the Regiment asked the War Office that if the proposed White Horse cap badge was approved, would it also be adopted as a collar badge. The answer was forthcoming when the new cap badge was received 15th November 1894 (approved 24th December 1894) with a codicil, 'the present pattern collar badge No.9981 will continue to be worn.'

It was not until 1902 that the White Horse was used as a collar badge on the new Service Dress, similar to the cap badge, above a scroll inscribed, 'WEST YORKSHIRE.' In bronze they were worn in facing pairs, the horse facing inward towards the collar opening. The horse, ground and scroll all varied slightly in size and outline, some of the collar badges being larger than the cap on occasions. (Figs.457, 458, 459 & 460). The same pattern, polished, was worn on the khkai drill. Old soldiers of the Regiment claim that their Regiment was the only one in the British Army to wear a collar badge, larger than the cap badge as only the small horses were worn in the cap. However, facing pairs of all sizes prove their claim cannot be substantiated. The other ranks pattern is also found in bronze, buts its usage is unknown (Fig.461).

The bronze White Horse badges were worn until 1925 when they were replaced by the Prince of Wales's Crest and Motto in bronze, quite a wide shaped display, (Fig.462), sealed 8th January 1925.

In a questionaire sent to the Regiment after WWI, the O.C. 2nd Battalion stated that Officers of his battalion wore no collar badge; though he was aware that Officers of the other Battalions did wear the White Horse badges.

Officers also wore for a short period the other ranks bi-metal collar badge on their khaki drill, Service Dress and ensuing battle dress. A sealed pattern 16th October 1956, whilst showing the usual Crest and Motto in silver and gilt for wear on the No.3 Dress and tropical mess dress (Fig.463), also shows a distinctive pattern for wear on Officers' No.1 Dress. (Fig.464). A silver/gilt collar badge, Pattern No.16577, sealed 23rd June 1954 under Auth. 9/HG/363 for use by Officers of the Home Guard (Fig.465).

Fig.455

Fig.456

Fig.457

Fig.458

Fig.460

Fig.462

Fig.459

Fig.461  *Fig.463*  *Fig.464*  *Fig.465*

THE WEST YORKSHIRE REGIMENT (THE PRINCE OF WALES'S OWN)

Militia
2nd West York Light Infantry Militia
Collar badges in white-metal for the men were sealed 14th September 1878, 'in lieu of Pattern No.7234.' The replacement collar badge was a rose between the strings of a ribboned bugle horn, the ribbon ends extending to both ends of the bugle horn (Fig.466). It has not been possible to trace details of pattern 7234, except that it was sealed between April and June 1875, although a combination of the rose and bugle horn with crown above is thought to have been worn. (Fig.467).

4th West York Militia
Collar badges in white-metal for the men were sealed 1st March 1876. Pattern No.7509. This was simply the White Rose of York, (Fig.468). Officers wore similar but in silver embroidery, (Fig.469).

These two Regiments became the 3rd and 4th Battalions of the Regiment in 1881, adopting in general the badges of the Regular Battalions. However a pattern taken from the tunic of an Officer of one of the Militia Battalions shows a distinctive format of the Crest and Motto and with a separate gilt 'M' worn below. (Fig.470).

Other Badges
An item of interest is shown in (Fig.471), in white-metal, shape and size as per the centre of the other ranks helmet plate. It is not a collar badge, but the first pattern other ranks cap badge, replaced in 1892 by the more familiar type, large White Horse and title scroll.

One item that has remained unidentified is shown in (Fig.472). A similar horse to that of Fig.471 but on a different ground and with the Prince of Wales's Crest and Motto above. The coronet is in gilt and the remainder in silver. The badge occurs in facing pairs, have normal two lug fittings, and show no signs of having formed part of a larger badge. Most likely Officers collar badges, but on what uniform it was worn or in what period remains unknown. A further 'unknown' is that illustrated in (Fig.473), the Prince of Wales's Crest and Motto in silver and gilt, the numerals XIV in silver. Normal two lug fittings. Suggestions include, Officers full dress c1880-1881, Officers mess jackets at some period, trial pattern not approved. It is fair to assume that the badge does relate to the British 14th/West Yorkshire Regiment.

Rifle Volunteer Corps, Volunteer, Territorial Force & Territorial Army Battalions
The consolidated Battalions *1st, 3rd, and 7th. Yorkshire, West Riding Rifle Volunteer Corps*, became Volunteer Battalions of the Regiment in 1881, being redesignated 1st, 2nd and 3rd Volunteer Battalions 1st December 1887. No collar badges of these former Rifle Volunteers are known or recorded. By a decision taken 13th October 1887, other ranks and Officers were to wear similar collar

Fig.466

Fig.467

Fig.468

Fig.469

Fig.471

Fig.472

Fig.473

Fig.470

Fig.474

Fig.475

Fig.476

Fig.477

badges, the pattern as worn by the Regular Battalions, but in white-metal for the men and silver or silver plate for the Officers. (Fig.474). The men of the 1st Volunteer Battalion did wear this pattern, submitted by Messrs. Samuel Bros, London, and approved by Horse Guards, 9th December 1888, under Auth. V/1 W Yorks/787. However, the 2nd and 3rd Battalions submitted a different display of the badge, more like the Officers version (Fig.475). Approved, 'for NCOs and men.' 3rd March 1888 under Auth V/3 W Yorks/778. Officers wore similar but in silver plate (Fig.476).

In 1908, the 1st and 2nd Volunteer Battalions became the 5th and 6th (TF) Battalions, and the 3rd Volunteer Battalion formed two Battalions, *7th and 8th (Leeds Rifles) (TF) Battalions*. Officers of these two Battalions wore solely a bronze 'T' on the left side only of their Service Dress jackets. (Fig.477). Plate 8 illustrates this quite clearly.

Two of the Kitchener's Army Battalions, *15th and 17th (The Leeds Pals)*, adopted the City of Leeds coat of arms as a cap badge for both other ranks and Officers. Only the Officers wore collar badges, the bronze White Horse and title scroll pattern.

21st Battalion (Wool Textile Pioneeers)

Raised 24th September 1915, the Battalion went to France in June 1916 as another of the Kitchener's Army Battalions, wearing the usual crossed rifle and pick collar badges (See Fig.147).

General

To illustrate just how difficult it is to be precise about what was worn and when, a studied photograph of the Officers of the West Yorkshire Regiment taken in France 1918, shows that most Officers are wearing the large bronze collar badge; however some have separate 'T' below, other have the 'T' only worn on both lapels, while a few have no badge at all.

All tiger and horse collar badges were worn in facing pairs with the animal facing inwards towards the collar opening.

On 25th April 1958, the Regiment (less Territorials) amalgamated with The East Yorkshire Regiment (less Territorials) to form *The Prince of Wales's Own Regiment of Yorkshire*.

The East Yorkshire Regiment (The Duke of York's Own)

Pre 1881
The 15th (York East Riding) Regiment of Foot
By Authority PC/Inf Gen/111, 16th July 1872, other ranks of the Regiment adopted as their collar badge a brass eight pointed rayed star, upon this a laurel wreath and within the voided centre, the numerals '15'. (Fig.478). Pattern No.9322, sealed 11th May 1874. Photographs of Senior NCO's show them in use prior to this. The outline of the star followed that of the second pattern glengarry badge worn up to 1881. There is no evidence so far of an Officers' version 1880-1881.

Post 1881
The Regiment became the *The East Yorkshire Regiment* in 1881 and from a design submitted by Messrs. Smith and Wright and revised by the AAG (Horse Guards), a new badge was decided upon 22nd December 1881 that incorporated the White Rose of York. In addition to this badge being an old badge of the Regiment, though not displayed, it was the badge of the East York Militia, and also the badge granted to Regiments in 1881 that had no distinctive badge. In gilding-metal with a white-metal Rose centre Pattern No.9973 was sealed 20th January 1882. The size and shape of the star and rose varied slightly according to manufacture. (Figs.479, 480). The badge was retained until 1958, though when the badge was renewed and cut from a new die on 14th December 1897, the opportunity was taken to alter the shape of the star. (Fig.481). Pattern No.9973a, sealed 5th April 1898. This pattern was used for the later anodised gold/silver version. A later anodised pattern was manufactured (Fig.482) but it is doubtful if they were ever worn. Warrant Officers and other Senior NCOs wore the other ranks pattern but in all gilt and with a black enamel background to the rose.

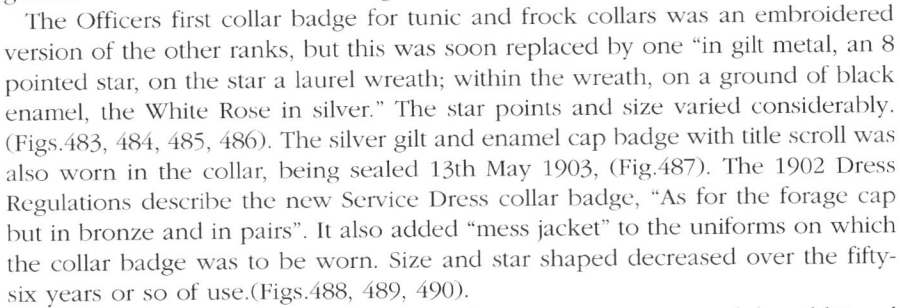

The Officers first collar badge for tunic and frock collars was an embroidered version of the other ranks, but this was soon replaced by one "in gilt metal, an 8 pointed star, on the star a laurel wreath; within the wreath, on a ground of black enamel, the White Rose in silver." The star points and size varied considerably. (Figs.483, 484, 485, 486). The silver gilt and enamel cap badge with title scroll was also worn in the collar, being sealed 13th May 1903, (Fig.487). The 1902 Dress Regulations describe the new Service Dress collar badge, "As for the forage cap but in bronze and in pairs". It also added "mess jacket" to the uniforms on which the collar badge was to be worn. Size and star shaped decreased over the fifty-six years or so of use.(Figs.488, 489, 490).

No change of pattern took place when the Regiment was granted the additional title, '*Duke of York's Own*' on 3rd June 1935.

The Regiment's, 'Details of Officers Dress' c.1931 list four companies as being recognised military tailors for the Regiment, all being in possession of the

Fig.478

Fig.479

Fig.480

Fig.481

Fig.482

Fig.484

Fig.485

Fig.486

Fig.483

HISTORY OF THE BRITISH ARMY INFANTRY COLLAR BADGE

Fig.487

approved patterns, together with a printed extract from Regimental Standing Orders. Listed in these were several references to collar badges.
- Service Dress – Jacket badges - gilt stars on collar lapels, small size (as worn on mess jacket).
- Full Dress Tunic – the centre of the collar star should be 1½ inches from the opening at the throat.
- Mess Dress – Collar badges are placed 5 inches below the shoulder seams.
- Blue Undress – Stand up collar with small gilt collar stars, centre of star 1½ inches from opening at the throat.'

A photograph of Major R. Laird of the 7th Battalion, in 1944, clearly shows him wearing collar badges on his battledress collar.

Militia
East York Militia

Fig.488

Reconstituted 1760 with headquarters at Beverley, the Regiment later acquired the unofficial title, 'The Beverley Buffs.' This was co-opted into the design of the 1878 pattern Officers helmet plate, but not the collar badges. These being the plain White Rose of York in white metal for other ranks and in silver for Officers. Worn from c1876. On 8th March 1878 the pattern was assimilated to that sealed for the 3rd West York Militia, Pattern No.7582 in white metal (sealed 28th April 1876) (Fig.491). The Regiment became the 3rd Battalion in 1881.

There exists a star collar badge in reverse metals (Fig.492). The laurel wreath in gilt, the star and rose in silver on a ground of enamel. It is thought worn by Officers of the 3rd Battalion.

Rifle Volunteer Corps, Volunteer, Territorial Force & Territorial Battalions

Fig.489

Raised 1859-1860 various small Corps were grouped into the *1st Yorkshire, East Riding, Rifle Volunteer Corps*. From c.1878 they are said to have worn a collar badge in white-metal consisting of the White Rose within a circle inscribed, "EAST YORK R.V.C.", surmounted by a QVC. (Line Drawing Fig.493) Messrs. Wilson and Collinson make no mention of such a badge in their history of the East York Volunteer Infantry 1859-1908, nor is there any other source of information concerning this badge. After nomination in 1881, the battalion became the 1st Volunteer Battalion in 1883, permission to wear the badges of the parent Regiment being granted in 1885. An Officer's bronze collar badge has been noted, similar to Fig.489, but with an additional scroll inscribed "1st VOLR BATTN" at the base of the rose.

The former 1st Administrative Battalion became the *3rd, later the 2nd Yorkshire, East Riding, Rifle Volunteer Corps* in 1880. Nominated in 1881 the battalion became the 2nd Volunteer Battalion in 1883.

Fig.490

The 1st Volunteer Battalion became the 4th (TF) Battalion in 1908, but the 2nd Volunteer Battalion was amalgamted with the 2nd Volunteer Battalion, The Yorkshire Regiment, becoming part of the 5th (TF) Battalion of the Regiment. As with many other Regiments, white metal and silver or silver plated versions of the Regulars' collar badges were worn by the Volunteer Battalions c.1885-1908. Senior

Fig.491    *Fig.492*    *Fig.493*    *Fig.494*

THE EAST YORKSHIRE REGIMENT (THE DUKE OF YORK'S OWN)

NCOs wore a larger white-metal star. (Fig.494).

A sealed pattern, 6th November 1956, shows the usual star collar badge in bi-metal for O/Rs and gilt for Officers for "E. York T/A".

The 1st Volunteer Battalion formed a Cyclist Section in 1893 followed by a similar in the 2nd Volunteer Battalion. They wore distinctive collar badges in white metal, a miniature version of the usual collar badge superimposed upon a cycle wheel of twenty-nine spokes. (Line drawing Fig.495). A new 5th (Cyclist) Battalion, The East Yorkshire Regiment was formed in 1908, the nucleus of Officers and NCOs coming from the former 1st V. Battalion In common with other cyclist Battalions blackened metal badges were worn, the pattern being that of the Regular Battalions. (Figs.496, 497). The latter Officers' type has a green enamel rose centre. Worn until the battalion was disembodied in 1919. Later being reformed as part of the Royal Corps of Signals. A photograph of 'H' Coy (Cyclists) 1st Volunteer Battalion in 1902 shows the small distinctive collar badge being worn on the blue field service cap.

The 6th Battalion assumed a pioneer role in January 1915 wearing the usual crossed rifle and pick collar badge (Fig.147).

General

The boys of The Duke of York's Royal Military School wore the same collar badges as the Regiment though not connected with the Regiment in any way.

The badge shown in (Fig.498) is not a collar badge, in gilding-metal it is an arm badge.

On 25th April 1958, the Regiment (less Territorials) amalgamated with The West Yorkshire Regiment to form *The Prince of Wales's Own Regiment of Yorkshire*.

Fig.495

Fig.496

Fig.497

Fig.498

The Bedfordshire and Hertfordshire Regiment

Pre 1881 - The 16th (Bedfordshire) Regiment of Foot

The first other ranks collar badge was Pattern No.9531, sealed 10th February 1875 having been authorised 16th July 1872 by Order. PC/ Inf.Gen/111. In brass the design was taken from the Arms of the Borough of Bedford, "An eagle displayed and with wings inverted looking towards the sinister sable, ducally crowned or, and surmounted upon its breast by a castle of three degrees or". A "chunky" item, (Fig.499) they do not face. No corresponding Officers version has been located for the 1880-1881 period.

Fig.499

Post 1881

In 1881, the Regiment was redesignated The Bedfordshire Regiment. After Smith and Wright's submission and revision a new collar badge, Pattern No.9909 was sealed 29th December 1881 for wear by the other ranks of both Regular Battalions. This took the form of a hart in white-metal with one front leg raised (trippant), all within a ford of gilding-metal. (Fig.500). This was the badge of the former Hertfordshire Militia who had become the 4th Battalion of the Regiment in 1881. A renewal pattern was cut from new dies in 1898 and the opportunity taken to slightly alter the attitude of the hart, the raised leg being lifted clear of a more distinctive ford. Pattern No.9909a, sealed 21st March 1898. (Figs.501, 502 a facing pair). These were worn through the change of title in 1919 and up to 1921.

The Officers pattern was more elaborate, described in the early Dress Regulations, 'In dead gilt metal, a Hart crossing a ford; the water in silver. On a scroll below, 'BEDFORDSHIRE.' (Figs.503, 504 show facing variations). The same pattern in all gilt was worn by the Warrant Officers. With the advent of the 1902 Service Dress a bronze collar badge ensued, following the pattern of the forage cap badge, worn in facing pairs until 1919. (Fig.505). Medium and small variations were worn around WWI (Figs.506, 507). Both these sizes have been noted polished down for wear in the khaki drill. A similar pattern in gilt is thought to have been worn at some time on the mess jacket. (Fig.508).

To acknowledge Hertfordshire's contribution to the Bedforshire Regiment, the title of the Regiment was extended 29th July 1919 to *The Bedfordshire and Hertfordshire Regiment.* (Army Order 269/1919). New badges were required, but it was not until 9th February 1921 that the new other ranks collar badge Pattern No.3455 was sealed under Authority ACD/37280/4.12.20. The chosen design was similar to the Officers' pattern worn up to the title change, a hart in a ford in

Fig.500

Fig.501

Fig.502

Fig.503

Fig.504

Fig.505

THE BEDFORDSHIRE AND HERTFORDSHIRE REGIMENT

white-metal over a gilding-metal scroll inscribed with the new title, 'BEDFORDSHIRE & HERTFORDSHIRE,' (Fig.509). Worn up until 1958 firstly with two lug fasteners, latterly with single lug and fixing plate. In facing pairs and to be used as a guide for any future anodised collar badges. The corresponding badges for Officers are described in the 1934 Dress Regulations as, 'For tunic, in dead gilt or gilding metal, a Hart crossing a ford; the water in silver. On a scroll below, "BEDFORDSHIRE & HERTFORDSHIRE" (In pairs).' (Fig.510). For mess jacket, 'In silver a Maltese cross on a diamond cut eight pointed star. On the cross the Garter with Motto; within the Garter a Hart (pierced) crossing a ford on a ground of blue enamel. Below, a scroll inscribed "BEDFORDSHIRE & HERTFORDSHIRE."' (Fig.511). A similar badge in bronze was adopted for Service Dress. (Fig.512).

The same badge in polished gilding-metal was used for the khaki drill. There is also a much larger cap/collar badge in bronze (Fig.513). An unusual variant is the Officers mess dress pattern but with only the star in silver, the cross, Garter and scroll in gilt, and the blue enamel centre.. Perhaps worn by the redesignated 3rd (Militia) Battalion of 1921 renaissance. (Fig.514). A similar pattern but in white-metal, with blue enamel centre was not worn as a collar badge but made as a special Order by Gaunts to complement a set of medallions.

Fig.506

Fig.507

Fig.510

Fig.509

Fig.508

Fig.511

Fig.512

Fig.513

Fig.514

HISTORY OF THE BRITISH ARMY INFANTRY COLLAR BADGE

Fig.515

Fig.516

Fig.517

Fig.518

Fig.519

Fig.520

Fig.521

Fig.522

Fig.523

Militia
The Bedfordshire Light Infantry Militia.

The white-metal collar badge for wear on the other ranks tunic and frock was sealed 1st June 1878, the Officers in silver plate. (Fig.515). This was a bugle horn. An earlier pattern of coiled bugle horn inscribed "BEDFORDSHIRE' also in white-metal has been associated with the Regiment, but no documentary or photographic evidence is yet available to support this. In July 1881 the Regiment became the 3rd Battalion, The Bedfordshire Regiment.

Hertfordshire Militia

Collar badges in white-metal were sealed for the other ranks 31st May 1876, Authority PC/HM/95, Pattern No.7594. A hart in water but of distinctive design, Officers wore the same in gilt from c1880-1881. (Fig.516). The Regiment became the 4th Battalion in July 1881.

After 1881, Officers of both Militia Battalions wore the same collar badges as the parent units, but in reversed metals. (Fig.517). The hart and water in silver on a gilt scroll.

Rifle Volunteer Corps, Volunteer, Territorial Force & Territorial Army Battalions

The consolidated Corps, *1st and 2nd Hertfordshire Rifle Volunteer Corps* nominated in 1881 became the 1st and 2nd (Hertfordshire) Volunteer Battalions in 1887. Elements of the 2nd Hertfordshire Rifle Volunteer Corps were wearing a white-metal version of (Fig.500) in the early 1870s (also worn on the service cap), upon conversion to Volunteer Battalions the 2nd for a time continued to wear a similar but slightly modified badge in white-metal (Fig.518). Photographs of the men of the 1st show them to be wearing a larger hart collar badge in blackened gilding-metal and of more standing attitude. (Fig.519). Similar but in blackened silver plate was worn worn by the Officers. The 2nd battalion also changed to a more distinctive pattern at some time in the 1880s, a hart standing in a ford the latter having a curved base, again in blackened gilding-metal. (Fig.520). The same badge facing left was worn on the slouch and field service hats; also worn as a cap badge by Berkhamstead School OTC. The same badge in silver was worn by the Officers of the 2nd V.Battalion (Fig.521).

The 1st Bedfordshire Rifle Volunteer Corps, nominated in 1881 were redesignated the 3rd Volunteer Battalion December 1887. They wore, as shown in the Gaunt pattern books, a hart in white-metal, but with both front legs in a ford, annotated, 'For privates in facing pairs, 12/5/87.' (Fig.522). The Officers wore all silver or silver plate versions of the Regular Battalions pattern, (Fig.523) shows a slightly larger variant. Warrant Officers wore the O/R's pattern collar badge but in gilt (Fig.524).

The 4th Volunteer Battalion was raised in Huntingdonshire in 1900. The Gaunt pattern book shows a distinctive collar badge, the hart in a ford, but with a double scroll below, the top one inscribed, '4th (HUNTS) VOLR. BATT. and below, 'BEDFORDSHIRE.' (Line Drawing, Fig.525). The reference in the pattern book is 'H4 8/3/1902.' No metal is quoted but the Officers pattern has been noted as being in silver.

In 1908, the majority of the 1st & 2nd (Hertfordshire) Volunteer Battalions formed a new Territorial Regiment, dealt with under their new title, *The Hertfordshire Regiment*. The 3rd & 4th Volunteer Battalions amalgamated to become the 5th (TF) Battalion, and with the change of parent title in 1919, other ranks and Officers adopted similar collar badges to those of the Line Battalions but in different metals. White metal for the men and silver or silver plate with blue enamel for the Officers.

The Bedfordshire and Hertfordshire Regiment amalgamated with The Essex Regiment in 1958 to form the *3rd East Anglian Regiment (16th/44th)*. The 5th Territorial Battalion reverted to its original designation, 5th Battalion *The Bedforshire Regiment (TA)* and wore as its collar badge the hart in a ford. In silver anodised for the men, pattern No.18212, sealed 1st January 1960, under Authority 54/Inf/18888 (Fig.526); the Officers slight variant in silver plate (Fig.527). In early 1961 a further reorganization resulted in amalgamation with the 1st Battalion The Hertfordshire Regiment (TA). The ensuing unit *The Bedfordshire and Hertfordshire Regiment (TA)* wore new collar badges, a hart kneeling in a ford, the latter with curved base. In silver anodised for the other ranks and silver plate for the Officers (Fig.528). This was Pattern 18807 sealed 14/9/62 under Authority 54/INF/8984.

The Bedfordshire Volunteer Regiment raised as part of the Volunteer Training Corps in 1914, produced two Battalions and was accepted for service in the Volunteer Force in 1916. They were designated as 'Volunteer Battalions' by 1918 but disbanded in 1920. A photograph of 2nd Lieut. R.Cook of the 2nd Battalion shows him wearing Service Dress with Royal Arms collar badges in bronze and a separate 'V' below. (Plate No.9.)

Unidentified

Two badges remain unidentified.
(1) A large hart standing in water on a scroll inscribed Hertfordshire. In yellow brass. (Fig.529)
(2). A similar badge but smaller and with less elaborate scroll. In silver and gilt (Fig.530). This latter item is also recorded in bronze.

Fig.524

Fig.525

Fig.526

Fig.527

Fig.528

Fig.529

Fig.530

When the Territorial Force came into being in 1908, a new battalion was formed, originally to be called the 6th (Hertfordshire) Battalion, The Bedfordshire Regiment. This proved unacceptable as far as Hertfordshire was concerned, and after a year was redesignated The Hertfordshire Battalion, soon to become a Regiment in its own right.

It is quite possible that the above badges relate to this one year period of final 'Bedfordshire' control.

General

All the hart collar badges were worn in facing pairs, with the animal facing inwards towards the collar opening.

On 1st September 1964, in accordance with the formation of the large Regiments, the Regiment was reorganised as the 3rd Battalion, *The Royal Anglian Regiment (16/44 Foot)*, the sub title omitted 1st July 1968.

2nd Lt L. C. Wilson 3rd Battalion. c. 1915

The Royal Leicestershire Regiment

Pre 1881
The 17th (Leicestershire) Regiment of Foot.
The other ranks first collar badge was authorised by Order PC/Infy. General/111, 16th July 1872, being Pattern No.9522, sealed 27th November 1874. In brass, the Royal Tiger passant on a grass ground all within a continuous oval of laurels. (Fig.531). On 25th June 1825, George IV approved the Regiment to bear on its Colours and appointments the Royal Tiger with the word HINDOOSTAN superscribed, as a lasting testimony of their exemplary conduct during their period of service in India 1804-1823.

Post 1881
The Regiment was designated *The Leicestershire Regiment*, July 1881. The existing collar badge was confirmed in September, but in January 1882 a new pattern was sealed, No.9967. Similar to the existing type but now in gilding-metal and with copper lugs on either ends of the laurel wreath, replacing the brass ones that had been on the Tiger. The badge was also worn on the field service cap up to the introduction of a new pattern cap in 1897. On 7th December of that year a new pattern 9967a was sealed, cut from new dies. (ACD/Patts./4026). The design remained constant until 1952, when the Tiger became white-metal, the laurels remaining gilding-metal. (Pattern No.15062) sealed 24th June 1952. Noted with both two lugs and the single. (Fig.532) This pattern was used as a guide for the silver/gold anodised type, Pattern No.18318, sealed 8th June 1960.

An entirely new badge, Pattern No.18318A, sealed 5th December 1962, under Authority 54/Inf/8783 was a larger Tiger passant in gold anodised with a scroll above inscribed, "*HINDOOSTAN*", and a scroll below inscribed, "*ROYAL LEICESTERSHIRE*" in silver anodised aluminum. (Fig.533). The Sealed Pattern is certainly designated 'The Royal Leicestershire Regt.' but whether they were ever issued to the Regular battalion is uncertain. They were worn by the Territorial units of the Regiment.

When the Regiment was in India, native mess servants wore on their jacket collars the intertwined capitals 'L' and 'R' with a K/C above, all in white-metal (Fig.534). A larger version was worn on their puggarees.

Officers wore similar badges to the other ranks on their tunic and frock collars, 'The Royal Tiger in silver within a wreath in gilt metal.' Later extended to the mess jacket. (Fig.535 shows a variant with the front paw raised higher than usual). For the Service Dress introduced in 1902, the same badge with the addition of a bottom scroll inscribed "*LEICESTERSHIRE*" was worn in bronze. (Fig.536). Sealed WO 13th May 1903. The area between the wreath and the scroll varied. (Fig.537 shows an unvoided type). The same badge in gilding-metal was worn in the khaki

Fig.531

Fig.532

Fig.533

Fig.534

Fig.535

Fig.536

Fig.537

drill. A version in white-metal was also reputed to have been worn on an undress uniform. An item sometimes confused with a collar badge is the bronze or enamelled 'sweethearts' brooch. (Fig.538).

By Army Order 167/1946, the Regiment was elevated to Royal status, on 28th November 1946 but new collar badges were not worn until 1951. These followed the design for the anodised other ranks, but in silver and gilt. (Fig.539).

Militia
Leicestershire Militia

Collar badges in white-metal, Pattern No.7580 were sealed 13th April 1876, Authority PC/Leicestershire Militia/198. These were described as, 'Star, Harp and Crown.' (Fig.540). A tiny badge, half an inch in height worn in silver by Officers. The Irish Harp was awarded to the Regiment in 1798 for services in Ireland. It also featured in the other ranks glengarry 1874-81 and the Officers helmet plate 1878-1881.

The Regiment became the 3rd Battalion in 1881. The Harp being perpetuated on the Officers forage cap badge and waist belt plates of all three Battalions.

Rifle Volunteer Corps, Volunteer, Territorial Force & Territorial Army Battalions

The consolidated battalion, *1st Leicestershire Rifle Volunteer Corps*, nominated in 1881 became the 1st Volunteer Battalion in February 1883. No collar badges have been recorded for the county Rifle Volunteers prior to this date. The first collar badge design submitted by the 1st V.Battalion was a dog (possibly a greyhound) with one paw raised, a scroll below inscribed, 'AGE QUOD AGIS' (Do what there is to do). (Line Drawing Fig.541). These were to have been in facing pairs, 'for both Officers and privates.' The design was rejected 5th January 1883. This design reflected no connection with the city or county of Leicester. The only possible association was with the Lieut-Colonel Commandant at this time, Sir Henry St.John Halford. Bart. (4th and last Baronet of the 3rd creation), Wistow Hall, Leciestershire. The ancient arms of the family had been a greyhound passant, though by the late 19th century this had been reduced to a greyhound's head couped, and relegated to the secondary crest of the family. The motto cannot be accorded to any family or civic authority, and was just a typical 19th century industrious exhortation.

The battalion now submitted a new design through Messrs. J & B Pearse & Co., 28, Hart Street, Covent Garden, London.The three lions or leopards of England differenced with the Mark of Cadency of the eldest son of the Sovereign, enclosed with a near circle of laurels. The design was approved, adopted and extracted, 30th January 1885. In white-metal for other ranks (Fig.542). The Officers badge had gilt lions and the remainder in silver. The central area backed with crimson velvet. (Figs.543,544) show a facing pair. The badge without the laurel wreath, white-metal for other ranks and gilt/silver for Officers was for wear in the field service cap. (Fig.545). A curious choice this, resurrecting the fact that the ancient Earldom of Leicester, created by King John in 1206, extinct 1264, for the de Montforts, was merged with the Crown becoming a minor title of the Princes of Wales. Later discharged by Elizabeth I to Robert Dudley. The badge became the centre piece for all badges worn by the 1st Volunteer Battalion until 1902. Why the battalion did not adopt the badges of the parent Battalions is not known.

In 1902, perhaps as a result of the change of Crown and the advent of Service Dress, the battalion did adopt the Royal Tiger as their central device. The bronze badge for the Service Dress bore a bottom scroll inscribed. '1st VB LEICESTERSHIRE.' The same badge in silver was worn on the Officers full dress tunic. The other ranks adopted a white-metal Royal Tiger on ground, similar to that worn by the Gordon Highlanders. The Tiger and Wreath badges both in white-metal and silver plate are known, they were probably taken into use after 1908 when the battalion became the 4th and 5th (TF) Battalions. Certainly the Officers versions in silver plate (Fig.546) were used after the TA's reformations in the 1920s. After the granting of Royal status in 1946, TA personnel duly adopted the new collar badges, c.1951. An all silver plate Officers version has been recorded. (Fig.547). A sealed pattern for, 'R.Leicester Regt 4/5/ TA.' showing a facing pair of Officers bronze collar badges was annotated in pencil, '18/12/61.' A separate 'T' was often worn under Officers collar badges on Service Dress. The Territorials retained their Regimental collar badges after the parent battalion became part of The Royal Anglian Regiment in 1964, with the Officer's equivalent worn by O/R's, but in silver/gold anodised.

Fig.544

WWI Battalions
11th Battalion, (Midland Pioneers)

Raised in 1915 the Battalion went to France the following year serving as the Pioneer Battalion of the 6th Division, wearing the usual crossed rifle and pick collar badge. (Fig.147).

Schools

Oakham School OTC wore a Royal Tiger over a scroll inscribed "OAKHAM SCHOOL OTC", with a scroll above inscribed with laurels. A sealed pattern, approved 27th July 1934 includes, 'Undress - as for Leicestershire Regt.' The same badge but larger was worn in the cap.

Fig.545

Unidentified

A large Royal Tiger on a grass ground in gilt. (Fig.548) Similar to the Tiger on the later forage cap badges they exist in facing pairs. There are no signs of the badge being part of a larger badge. Associations with the 65th, 67th and 75th regiments are also possible.

Fig.546

General

The tiger collar badge worn by the Regiment were worn in facing pairs with the animal facing inwards towards the collar opening. According to which manufacturer was used, the badges vary both in the size and shape of the tiger and some with front paw pointing downward, some pointing upwards.

Voiding and non voiding are to be found between the wreath and the scroll. The wreath is distinct from any other Regiment of the British Army in that it is continuous, with no breaks.

In 1958, the Regiment became part of *The Midland Brigade*, subsequently redesignated *The Forester Brigade*. In 1962, the Regiment became the 4th Battalion of the *East Anglian Brigade*, and on 1st September 1964, the 4th Battalion, *The Royal Anglian Regiment*.

Fig.547

Fig.548

The Royal Irish Regiment

Pre 1881
The 18th (The Royal Irish) Regiment of Foot.

Permission for the wearing of the 'Crown and Harp' on the collar of other ranks tunic and frock was granted 13th May 1872, Pattern No.9277 being sealed 29th August 1872. The Harp had a decorated frame, unvoided strings, but voided between the outer string and frame; surmounted by the QVC. In brass and worn in facing pairs. (Fig.549). Officers wore an embroidered version 1880-1881.

The Harp and Crown were conferred on the Regiment by William III in recognition of the distinguised conduct and gallantry in the seige and assault of Namur in 1695.

Fig.549

Post 1881

On 1st July 1881, the 18th were redesignated *The Royal Irish Regiment* adopting new collar badges in the following year, Pattern No.9983 being sealed 20th January 1882. In gilding-metal and worn in facing pairs, the design was an escutcheon of the Arms of Nassau, 'Azure billettee a lion rampant or.'

Below on a three part scroll was inscribed the motto, 'VIRTUTIS NAMURCENSIS PRAEMIUM.' (The reward of valour at Namur) (Fig.550). A mis-spelt variant shows 'VIRTOTIS' (Fig.551). Both these distinctions were conferred by William III in 1695. It should be noted that the Lion of Nassau on these other ranks collar badges is shown incorrectly, as it bears aloft a sword in the dexter front paw.

In 1890, the Colonel of the Regiment sought permission for the lion on the badge to face the heraldic way only; however, he was notified 13th October 1890 that there was to be no change in the wearing of the lion, and to emphasise the point, 'i.e. lions on shield to face one another, not to face one way as requested by the C.O.'!

Instructions for the collar badge to be reviewed were received 30th November 1896, Ref ACD/patt/8189, but when the Regiment's new field service cap was about to be introduced, it was decided that the collar badge would remain as before. Those facing to the left and previously been worn as a cap badge, would now 'be utilised for use on the collar.'

Without change of design the other ranks collar badge was renewed and cut from new dies, 4th December 1897, Pattern No.9983a. These were worn until the Regiment was disbanded when an official Order 4th August 1922 stated, 'Badges collar 9983a/1897 gilding-metal rendered obsolete.'

The same badge is known in white-metal, and though possibly worn by the post 1881 designated Militia Battalions, it is more probable that they were worn by Sergeants and other senior NCOs on their mess jackets.

The Gaunt pattern books show the intended design for the Officers' collar badges followed the same design as was approved and adopted for the men, but were to be made in silver and gilt metals. However, the design was rejected. For the design adopted, the features remained the same, but the format was different. The Lion is now shown correctly, without a sword, and the shield outline and motto scrolls are simplified. In silver and worn in facing pairs for the tunic and frock coat, later extended to the mess jacket. (Fig.552). Over the forty or so years of use the badge varied considerably, silver or silver plate, sometimes with the Lion applied rather than part of the stamping or casting. Fig.553 displays a more squat Lion. Fig.554, a quite incorrect type showing the Lion on a torse. The same

Fig.550

Fig.551

Fig.552

Fig.553

THE ROYAL IRISH REGIMENT

badge with a gilt Lion is known and has possible Militia battalion connections. Also one in white-metal possibly for wear by the Warrant Officers.

With the advent of Service Dress in 1902, the badge adopted was, 'As for forage cap, in bronze.' This was the Harp and Crown with a three part scroll below inscribed, "THE ROYAL IRISH REGIMENT." (Fig.555)

Militia
Wexford Militia
Collar badges in white-metal for tunic and frock were sealed 18th January 1877. These were QVCs over the Harp, decorated and voided as for the 18th Foot, and sprays of shamrock extending upward from the base of the Harp. (Fig.556). Officers wore similar smaller badges in silver (Fig.557 - part of wreath missing). In 1881 the Regiment became the 3rd Battalion.

2nd or North Tipperary Light Infantry Militia
Documentary or photographic evidence of collar badges for this Regiment have not been traced so far, though a combination of bugle horns and shamrocks is most probable. In 1881 they became the 4th Battalion.

Kilkenny Fusiliers Militia.
White metal grenade collar badges were sealed 25th November 1875, Authority 51/Kilkenny Militia/(Fusiliers)/288. This was Pattern No.7488. (Fig.558). Similar but in silver plate were worn by Officers. A later pattern but of the same design was sealed 20th February 1878. In 1881 the Regiment became the 5th Battalion.

Rifle Volunteers etc.
The Volunteer Movement of 1859 did not take place in Ireland, so there are no Rifle Volunteer Corps, Volunteer Battalions etc.

The 5th Battalion assumed a pioneer role in 1915 going to France in 1918, wearing the usual crossed rifle and pick collar badge (Fig.147).

General
All shield collar badges were worn in facing pairs with the lion facing inwards towards the collar opening.

On the formation of the Irish Free State, The Royal Irish Regiment was disbanded 31st July 1922.

Fig.554

Fig.555

Fig.556

Fig.557

Fig.558

The Green Howards
(Alexandra, Princess of Wales's Own Yorkshire Regiment)

Fig.559

Fig.560

Fig.561

Fig.562

Fig.563

Pre 1881
The 19th (1st York, North Riding) Princess of Wales's Own Regiment of Foot

Officially, the pre 1881 other ranks collar badge was the brass Imperial Crown, authorised 16th November 1872 (Fig.333). Regimental tradition persists with the legend that after the granting of the Princess of Wales's Own title in 1875, they wore a brass coronet. (Fig.559), with the Officers' equivalent in gilt. There is no documentary or photographic evidence to support this claim, and if such badges were worn, then they would have been unofficial. It is possible that the Imperial Crown collar badge, with its flat arches, could conveniently be described after 1875 as a coronet.

Although the brass Imperial Crown was the first official collar badge, the 1st Battalion whilst serving in Canada 1840-50 wore Arabic '19' numerals in their collars.

Post 1881

Photographs show the crown collar badge was still being worn long after the Regiment was redesignated *The Princess of Wales's Own (Yorkshire Regiment)* 1st July 1881. However, a new collar badge was sealed 29th December 1881, in gilding-metal Pattern No.9908, 'in lieu of Imperial crown.' This was the cypher of HRH Alexandra, Princess of Wales, combined with a Danish cross, the Dannebrog, inscribed "1975". (Fig.560). Renewal of this pattern 'was demanded' 27th November 1897, to be cut from new dies. Authorised 14th December, Pattern No.9908a was sealed 5th April 1898. 'To be the new standard pattern.' Similar to the last type but more compact. (Fig.561). These were worn until 1950 (in 1928 the 1st Battalion were directed not to wear collar badges on their blue patrols) when the same badge but in white-metal was introduced. Pattern No.14399, sealed 27th July 1950. Initially issued with the usual two lugs, it was followed by the single lug and plate type. Some of these later issues had voiding between the cypher and cross. The last metal issue was used as a guide for the silver anodised version (Fig.562). This was Pattern No.19199, sealed in the early months of 1964. Unpopular, a further type was submitted for approval, with a neater, slimmer look overall. (Fig.563). Pattern No.19199a, sealed 4th June 1964 under Authority 54/Inf/8787.

The 1883 Dress Regulations describe the Officers first collar badge as.'The Cypher of HRH the Princess of Wales, combined with a cross. The Cypher and Coronet in gold embroidery; the cross in silver.' The 1900 Edition adds 'on a crimson velvet cap' for the Cypher and coronet. The 1902 Edition extends the usage to the mess jacket. According to the Regimental Museum display at Richmond, North Yorkshire, the embroidered collar badges worn 1881-1882 have a separate coronet, and all on a cloth backing. These were followed by ones worn 1882-1889 (Fig.564). 1889-1899, (Fig.565). 1899-1939 (Fig.566). A further pattern in use since 1899 (Fig.567). Some patterns overlapped as a photograph circa 1891 of a 1st Battalion Sergeant-Major shows. On his white collar, embroidered with gold lace, he is wearing the 1882-89 embroidered collar badge.

The 1902 Dress Regulations states for Service Dress, 'The Cypher of HRH the Princess of Wales combined with a cross and surmounted by the Coronet of the Princess. On the centre of the cross the figures 1875 and the word 'Alexandra'.

On a scroll below, "The Princess of Wales's Own Yorkshire Regiment", in bronze.' (Fig.568). This covered the change in title of the Regiment in 1902, when Queen Alexandra became the Regiment's Colonel, and the Dannebrog cross was adopted as the badge of the Regiment. The title now became, *Alexandra, Princess of Wales's Own (Yorkshire Regiment)*. An omission was corrected in the 1911 Dress Regulations with the addition in the wording, 'In the centre of the scroll the White Rose.' This was an old badge of the Regiment, used on the mens' 1874 glengarry badge, and the Officers' 1878 pattern helmet plates. During WWII, the Officers Service Dress badge appeared with a KC instead of the Coronet. (Fig.569). This was not intentional and was put down to, 'Regimental incompetence,' and like most mistakes at that time was blamed on the War! Known affectionately as the 'Eiffel Tower', photographs show it at times being worn horizontally, with the Rose and scroll nearest the collar opening. The badge, polished down to gilding-metal was worn officially on the khaki drill. A pair has been noted where the scrolls and Rose have been carefully removed. Why this was done, and whether they were ever actually used is unknown.

The Regiment underwent a further change of title in 1921, being redesignated, *The Green Howards (Alexandra, Princess of Wales's Own Yorkshire Regiment)*. There were no changes to the collar badges. The 1934 Dress Regulations confirms the Officers collar badges as already described, but in 1951 a silver version of the mens' collar badge was introduced for wear on both Service Dress and No.1 Dress (Fig.570). Superceded in 1979 when Pattern No.30194, sealed 3rd July 1979 was introduced; very slightly smaller and more compact. (Fig.571).

Militia
5th West York Militia
This relatively 'new' Regiment, raised in 1853 rather surprisingly took precedence over the more senior Corps, becoming the 3rd Battalion of the Regiment in 1881. It has been suggested that a White Rose collar badge with or without a crown, or a bugle, was worn by the Corps, but there is no evidence of any sort to support such claims.

North York Rifles
The Regiment dressed as Rifles even before 1800; officially recognised as such in 1853. Not deviating from Rifles traditions, the Regiment did not wear collar badges. They became the 4th Battalion in 1881.

Rifle Volunteer Corps, Volunteer, Territorial Force & Territorial Army Battalions
The consolidated Battalions, *1st & 2nd Yorkshire (North Riding) Rifle Volunteer Corps*, nominated in 1881 became the 1st and 2nd Volunteer Battalions 1st February 1883. No collar badges are recorded prior to 1883 and there is no evidence to indicate that they wore collar badges of a different pattern to those of the Regular units, other than the mens' badges being in white-metal and the

Fig.564

Fig.565

Fig.566

Fig.567

Fig.570

Fig.571

Fig.569

Fig.568

Fig.572

Officers in silver and all silver embroidery. However, records show that a silver rose collar badge was worn on a 1st Volunteer Battalion Officers' ordinary pattern tunic. The collar was white with a bottom black edging. After conversion to TF battalion status in 1908, the badges of the Regular units were adopted. Minor differences such as the backing material to the collar badges in battle dress have been noted; none for the TF/TA units, green cloth for the Regular Battalions.

TF Officers often wore a separate bronze "T" below their collar badges on their Service Dress (see plate 10).

The Regimental Museum state that silver/gilt K/C collar badges were worn by the 4th (mounted) Battalion Circ 1902-1907.

WWI Service Battalions
8th Service Battalion
Raised 22nd September 1914, other ranks did not wear collar badges. Disbanded 12th April 1919.

12th Battalion (Tees-side Pioneers)
Raised 19th February 1915, serving in France during WW1 wearing the usual crossed rifle and pick collar badges. (Fig.147). Reduced to a Cadre 25th April 1918.

General
Both the Officers and the other ranks collar badges have been worn as a cap badge during several periods of the Regiment's service. The collar badge of the 19th (Queen Alexandra's Own Royal) Hussars is sometimes mistaken for a Yorkshire Regiment's, the difference being the date on the cross, 1885. (Fig.572).

The Lancashire Fusiliers

Pre 1881
The 20th (East Devonshire) Regiment of Foot

The Sphinx superscribed Egypt was authorised to be worn by the Regiment 6th July 1802, to commemorate their service in the 1801 campaign. This was the chosen design for the collar badge, when authorised 16th July 1872. A male Sphinx with front mantle and tail extending to midway along its back, on a tablet inscribed "EGYPT" in Roman lettering. In brass and worn in facing pairs, Pattern No.9548 was sealed 8th October 1875 (Fig.573).

In 1879, it was decided to standardise the Sphinx collar badges of those Regiments employing them. The Regiment was directed 'to assimilate with Pattern.9567,' the pattern being worn by the 24th Regiment. Again in brass this was a female Sphinx with mantle extending down the back, and with tail rising up over the back (Fig.574). Officers of the 20th, in anticipation of the change of status, were directed to wear grenades in front of their badges of rank. The nine flame grenade in gold embroidery was embellished on the ball with a silver crowned laurel wreath enclosing the Sphinx and EGYPT tablet (Fig.575). This design was in current use on the mens' glengarry badge and the Officers' tunic button.

Post 1881

On 1st July 1881, the 20th were redesignated *The Lancashire Fusiliers* and by 21st October were authorised to wear the standard brass fusilier grenade Pattern No.9281. (see Fig.122). This was soon superceded by similar badges in gilding-metal, Pattern No.9933, sealed 11th January 1882. For wear on the tunic and frock collars. (See Fig.123). This collar badge was also worn on the field service cap up to the introduction of the new cap in September 1897. The pattern was renewed and cut from fresh dies 7th December 1897, 9933a, but without change in the design. By an Authorisation 14th February 1905, all Fusilier regiments were to wear the same badge with their metal shoulder titles, on the shoulder straps of drab jackets and great coats. A renewal Pattern No.15705, sealed 13th April 1953, in gilding-metal continued the pattern. The gold anodised version was sealed 29th June 1964, Pattern No.19356, under Authority 54/Inf/8792 and worn until amalgamation (Fig.576).

The early Dress Regulations describe the Officers' collar badge as, 'A grenade in gold embroidery,' repeated until 1911 when, 'On the mess jacket the grenade is smaller.' was added. The Dress Regulations make no mention of the number of flames to the grenade, but a sealed pattern 17th April 1906 shows a large horizontal gold bullion grenade (65mm x 30mm). This had a nine flame grenade and plain ball, the smaller mess dress grenade (35mm x 22mm) had only seven flames. The number of flames is interesting because a War Office sealed pattern 20th February 1901 contains a pair of gilt horizontal collar badges for the frock coat which have eight flames, seven main ones and one in front, (Figs.577 & 578). On the sealed pattern these are annotated 'Frock collar badges'. Photographs show them still being worn during WWI.

The bronze collar badge was introduced in 1902 for wear on the new Service Dress, and these had wide flamed grenades, on the ball, the Sphinx over Egypt within a laurel wreath. Below the grenade, a three part scroll inscribed 'The Lancashire Fusiliers' (Fig.579). The laurel wreath is said to have been awarded for

Fig.573

Fig.574

Fig.575

Fig.576

HISTORY OF THE BRITISH ARMY INFANTRY COLLAR BADGE

Fig.577 & 578

service at Minden in 1759. The pattern is also known in blackened gilding-metal said to have been worn during 1914 - 1918.

Two other different patterns of bronze collar badges followed, the first was virtually the same as the 1902 pattern but minus the scroll (Fig.580, 581). The second had the same features but with a quite different shaped grenade and flames (Fig.582). It is difficult to be precise as to the dates these were introduced, but photographs show the first two being worn in 1914 and the latter in 1915. Certainly all three patterns were being worn at the same time during WWI. Photographs show the 1902 pattern still being worn in 1925 but the 1934 Dress Regulations refer only to 'A grenade, on the ball the Sphinx within a laurel wreath'. All three patterns are found struck as one piece items and also with separate Sphinx and wreath fittings, some grenades are domed others flat and there are many different shapes and sizes of the Sphinx. All three patterns are found in polished gilding-metal for wear on the khaki drill jacket.

Silver/gilt collar badges were also worn on the appropriate uniform collars, both vertically and horizontally. Figs.583, 584 show vertical grenades with Sphinx variations and Fig.585 shows a horizontal grenade. A small grenade with ten flames and without a wreath was worn on the mess dress jacket (Fig.586).

Militia
7th Royal Lancashire Militia

There is no record in the Army Clothing Department pattern room journals of any collar badges relating to this Regiment. They became the 3rd Battalion in 1881, dividing into two Battalions in 1891, as the 3rd and 4th. Renumbered 5th and 6th in 1898, only to be renumbered 3rd and 4th in 1908. Officers of the 4th battalion post 1902 wore bronze grenade collar badges with the Sphinx over a blank tablet and the wreath in silver. (Figs.587, 588). A captain's uniform of the 3rd Battalion, in 1918 shows an ordinary grenade collar badge, with a 'M' at the end of the shoulder strap.

Fig.579

Fig.580    *Fig.582*    *Fig.583*

Fig.581    *Fig.584*    *Fig.585*

96

Rifle Volunteer Corps, Volunteer, Territorial Force & Territorial Army Battalions

The 8th and 12th Lancashire Rifle Volunteer Corps became Volunteer Battalions in 1881, redesignated the 1st and 2nd Volunteer Battalions respectively 1st February 1883. Reorganised as the 5th and 6th Territorial Force Battalions, 1st April 1908. Like their Regular counterparts they also wore a grenade collar badge but in white-metal.

Volunteer, and later TF, Officers likewise wore similar collar badges to those worn by the Regular units but with a blank tablet below the Sphinx instead of Egypt. One such collar badge was the bronze Service Dress pattern with title scroll below (Fig.589) Similar, but without the scroll, the last pattern (Fig.590) The blank scroll also extended to the silver/gilt collar badge (Fig.591) for vertical variety and (Fig.592) for the horizontal one.

Photographs of TF Battalion Officers sometimes show them wearing, not the bronze blank scroll collar badge, but one with the Egypt tablet and with a separate bronze 'T' below. TF and TA Battalions gradually adopted the collar badges as worn by the Regular Battalions, but it is interesting to note that a sealed pattern, 9th October 1956 approved under Authority ADO5/ORDY 17 for '5T/A Battalion' shows the usual silver gilt horizontal collar badge with Egypt tablet 'For No. 1 Dress' and an upright bronze collar badge with blank tablet 'For No. 2 Dress'.

General

Like many other Fusilier Regiments, The Lancashire Fusiliers did not adhere to any particular grenade collar badge and they varied, not only in the number of flames, but also to the shape, size and general spread of the flame.

Collar badges were worn in facing pairs with the sphinx facing inwards towards the collar opening.

On 23rd April 1968, the Regiment was redesignated as 4th Battalion *The Royal Regiment of Fusiliers.* Only to be disbanded 1st November 1969.

Fig.586

Fig.587

Fig.588

Fig.589

Fig.590

Fig.591

Fig.592

The Royal Scots Fusiliers

Pre 1881
21st (Royal Scots Fusiliers) Regiment of Foot.

It has been generally accepted that the 21st Regiment and The Royal Scots Fusiliers wore the same collar badges pre and post 1881, except for metals, but research has shown this to be incorrect.

A painting of a Bandsman of the 21st c1856 shows gold grenades on the collar which differ from the official first pattern grenade, but as the painting predates the first official badge by some sixteen years, and allowing for some artist's licence, this is not surprising.

On more sure ground, the first collar badge for the 21st was the universal brass grenade, Pattern No.9281, (see Fig.122). Authorised 16th July 1872, sealed 2nd October 1872. These were worn until 1878. On 6th February a brass Pattern No.9630 was sealed, 'in lieu of Patt.9281.' There is no annotated description for this pattern and its format can only be deduced from post 1881 descriptions. On 22nd December 1881, after the title change, it was confirmed that the new collar was to be in gilding-metal and white-metal, yet on 8th February 1882 a gilding-metal Pattern No.10105 was sealed, 'to replace patt.9630.' This is rather contradictory as the first collar badge for the men after redesignation was in bi-metal, so possibly Pattern No.9630 was also in bi-metal, in fact the description is strictly correct; the actual grenade was in brass, later gilding-metal, but one would have expected, 'and white-metal on the ball.' to have been added.

An actual specimen shows the badge to be a brass multi flamed grenade with a thistle spray in white-metal on the ball, with brass lugs pre 1881; and in gilding-metal with copper lugs post 1881. A distinctive feature to the earlier pattern grenade is the quite marked indent to the point of the flames on the left side. These were worn horizontally. (Fig.593).

It is perhaps significant that the description, 'both gilding-metal and white-metal' were not mentioned until 22nd December 1881. It is probable that an all brass collar badge was worn prior to 1881, especially as several examples are extant. (Fig.594). These are one piece die stampings. They are not later Officers issues lacking the mount or bronze ones rubbed down. They all have the pre 1881 'indent' and brass lugs.

Fusilier Officers were directed in the 1874 Dress Regulations to wear a grenade emblem at the end of their tunic collars, ahead of their badges of rank. Photographs show them being worn as early as 1870. As was so often the case Dress Regulations simply confirmed what was already being done!

There are some interesting memorandae amongst the Gaunt papers including one from Jennens & Co. 22nd January 1876. 'Please tell bearer if the thistle worn on the collar grenades of either Battalion of the 21st are silver?' The recipient, obviously an economist in words, simply wrote 'Wrong' across the question. This necessitated a further memo on the same day repeating the request and adding, 'Was it silver or gilt?' Again the laconic reply 'Gilt', End of correspondence! (Fig.595) shows the gilt thistle on the gold embroidered grenade.

Photographs of the 2nd Battalion in Zululand show the men to be wearing the collar badges horizontally on the undress scarlet serge tunic. Pipers appear to be wearing a white-metal version on their dark blue jackets (Fig.596). In the same photographs Officers can be seen to be wearing embroidered collar badges, some in metal (silver/gilt?), some with what appears to be the mens' pattern, while others wear none at all. This illustrates just how difficult it is to be precise on what

Fig.593

Fig.594

Fig.595

Fig.596

Post 1881

After 1881, the Regiment became *The Royal Scots Fusiliers* and the men wore the badge already described. Renewal of the standard pattern, and from new dies was demanded on 9th February 1898. Sealed 3rd August 1899. Pattern No.10105a. The design was worn until after WWII. The shape and size of the thistle varied slightly. During WWI the same badge was used as part of the shoulder strap badge replacing the standard plain ball grenade. Towards the end of the same conflict the 2nd Battalion brought about the first usage of a collar badge on Home Pattern Service Dress, abolished after the cessation of hostilities.

A photograph taken of the Band in 1939 shows bandsmen wearing their grenade collar badges on a blue ground, the Band Sgt wearing a brass grenade on the high collar whilst the Bandmaster wore similar to the bandsmen, but in gilt. To complete the picture the Drum Major was not wearing collar badges!

A different pattern of grenade badge was sealed 22nd May 1951. Pattern No.14636., a gilding-metal imitation embroidery grenade with a white-metal mount. The flames reduced to five, and the thistle correspondingly larger. (Fig.597). This was worn up to amalgamation. Pipers wore this badge in white-metal (Fig.598); earlier they had worn white worsted grenades.

The 1883 Dress Regulations describe the Officers collar badge for the tunic as, 'A grenade in silver embroidery; on the ball of the grenade the Thistle in silver metal.' (Fig.599) Minor variations exist. That for the scarlet frock was of metal, a silver Thistle on a gilt grenade, the Thistle spray upright (Fig.600). The 1900 Edition adds, 'On the Mess Jacket, gold embroidery, with Thistle in silver.' (Figs.601, 602 & 603). When Service Dress was introduced in 1902, the collar badge was described, 'As for tunic but in bronze.' This was a nine flamed grenade, seven long and two short. (Figs.604, 605). Approved and sealed 15th April 1904. The 1911 Edition makes an amendment substituting 'Doublet' for 'Tunic.' The same badge rubbed down was worn on the khaki drill. Also in bronze and with nine flames is a horizontal grenade Fig.606). A small seven flame version, the base looking more like a Royal Engineers pattern is shown in (Fig.607).

Fig.597

Fig.598

Fig.599

Fig.600

Fig.601

Fig.602

Fig.603

Fig.604

Fig.605

Fig.607

Fig.606

HISTORY OF THE BRITISH ARMY INFANTRY COLLAR BADGE

Fig.608

Fig.609

Fig.610

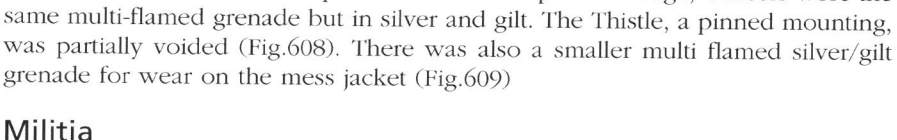

Fig.611

Fig.612

Fig.614

Fig.613

On the introduction of the post WWII fusiliers pattern badge, Officers wore the same multi-flamed grenade but in silver and gilt. The Thistle, a pinned mounting, was partially voided (Fig.608). There was also a smaller multi flamed silver/gilt grenade for wear on the mess jacket (Fig.609)

Militia
Dumfries, Roxburgh, Kirkcudbright, and Selkirk (Scottish Borderers) Militia

Originally raised in 1798, they underwent many title changes becoming, in 1863 *The Scottish Borderers Regiment of Militia*. Collar badges in white-metal were sealed 3rd December 1875. Pattern No.7489. Authority PC/Scottish Borderers Militia/132. Described as, 'The initials SB.' There was no line drawing, and the precise structure of the lettering is unknown. In 1881 they became the 3rd Battalion, but were transferred to the Kings Own Scottish Borderers in 1887.

Royal Ayrshire and Wigton Rifles (The Prince Regent's Own)

As with the majority of Rifles, this Corps did not wear collar badges. In 1881, they became the 4th Battalion, being renumbered 3rd in 1887.

From then, the other ranks wore a larger white-metal grenade with applied white-metal Thistle spray. (Fig.610). Also worn in the glengarry. Officers wore the large embroidered collars with applied silver metal Thistle as per the Regular units, but with gold embroidered grenades. (Fig.611). Whereas Pipers of the other Battalions generally wore worsted grenades, Pipers of the 3rd Battalion wore theirs in white-metal. Whilst in France in 1918, Officers wore the ordinary Fusilier grenade collar badges.

Rifle Volunteer Corps, Volunteer, Territorial Force & Territorial Army Battalions

The consolidated Battalions, 1st and 2nd Ayrshire Rifle Volunteer Corps were nominated in 1881, and were redesignated the 1st and 2nd Volunteer Battalions, in December 1887. Collar badges for the 1st VBn. were approved by Horse Guards 20th April 1885, Authority V/1 Ayr/185. These were similar to those worn by the Regular Battalions but in white-metal. They were worn horizontally. Drawings being deposited 20th April 1888. (Fig.612). Officers wore the same but in silver. Photographs show them in use on the blue serge undress jacket in the 1890s. It is more than probable that the 2nd V.Battalion also wore the same badges.

Sealed patterns show that in 1908 the redesignated 4th and 5th TF Battalions (amalgamated in 1921 to become the 4th/5th (TF) Battalion.) wore the same collar badges as the Regular Battalions. Also used when converted to a TA Battalion, and by 'B' Coy (The Royal Scots Fusiliers) 1st Battalion 52nd Lowland Volunteers, T. & A.V.R. Pattern 14636 was used as the guide for the fusiliers version collar badge in gold and silver anodised. Sealed 24th May 1968, Authority A/78/CLO/22522. (Fig.613). Pipers wore the same but in silver anodised.

Other badges

Sometimes thought to be a collar badge, (Fig.614) is in fact a sporran badge.

General

Like most Fusilier regiments, the R.S.F. did not adhere to any precise patterns as regards the number and shape of the flames on the grenade. They did not face.

On 20th January 1959, the Regiment (less territorials) amalgamated with The Highland Light Infantry to form *The Royal Highland Fusiliers (Princess Margaret's Own Glasgow and Ayrshire Regiment)*.

The Cheshire Regiment

Pre 1881
The 22nd (Cheshire) Regiment of Foot

From 1872, the other ranks of the Regiment wore the brass numerals '22' on their tunic collars (Fig.615). It was not until 13th June 1879 that the first official collar badge was sealed. Pattern No.9680 was a small, eight-pointed rayed star with cross cut decoration. The voided centre bore the numerals '22' encircled by an oak wreath. In brass (Fig.616), they do not face. Officers did not wear collar badges prior to 1881. The design of the collar badges is similar to that on the pre 1881 tunic button. It was still being used as the motif on Regimental stationery as late as the 1920s.

Post 1881

The 22nd were redesignated *The Cheshire Regiment* in July 1881. A new collar badge for other ranks, Pattern No.9982 was sealed 20th January 1882, this was a gilding-metal acorn spray, worn in facing pairs with the stalk of the acorn facing inwards towards the collar opening (Fig.617). Photographs also show them being worn incorrectly. The badge was also worn in the field cap up to the introduction of the new pattern in November 1897. Renewal of the standard pattern was demanded 27th November 1897, Pattern No.9982a cut from new dies being sealed 6th April 1898. The opportunity was taken to slightly modify the design, and although the general shape and size remained the same, the badge was strengthened by attaching more of the oak leaves to the acorn (Fig.618). The same pattern in gilt was worn by the Warrant Officers. This pattern was declared obsolete 13th December 1922.

For Officers, the 1883 Dress Regulations state: 'Acorn with oak-leaves. The leaves and cup in dead gilt metal; the acorn in burnished silver.' Altogether a more elegant display (Fig.619). The badge is also recorded in all gilt for wear on the frock (Fig.620).

For the newly introduced Service Dress, the 1902 Dress Regulations record, 'An eight pointed star with a scroll below inscribed 'Cheshire'; on the star, the acorn with oak leaves.' (Fig.621). In bronze this cap/collar was considered to be ugly, out of proportion, and too large and clumsy to be worn on the collar. Accordingly Officers removed the acorn and oak-leaf section from the badge and wore this on their Service Dress (Fig.622). Officers also wore the other ranks pattern in bronze.. The 1904 Dress Regulations repeated those of 1902, but the 1911 Edition gave official blessing, 'Acorn with oak leaves.'

Fig.615

Fig.616

Fig.617

Fig.618

Fig.619

Fig.620

Fig.621

Fig.622

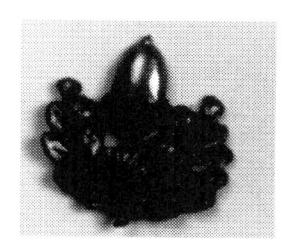

HISTORY OF THE BRITISH ARMY INFANTRY COLLAR BADGE

Fig.623

Fig.624

Fig.625

Fig.626

Fig.627

The choice of an acorn with oak leaves as the Regimental collar badge, was to be expected, it being an emblem long associated with the Regiment. By tradition, it commemorates the Regiments services at the battle of Dettingen, 1743, when Goerge II is purported to have presented an acorn and leaves on the battle field to a detachment of the Grenadier Company. There is no proof that this did occur, and it seems more likely that it comes from the sinister supporter of the Arms of the Dukes of Norfolk, 'a horse argent with an acorn slipped in his mouth.' The 6th Duke was the first Colonel of the Regiment. The Acorn and Oak Leaves were not officially recognised as the Regiment's badge, and therefore not borne on the Colours, until 1921.

A similar but neater version of the Officers collar badge was authorised and sealed for all ranks 13th December 1922. This new Pattern No.3691, for other ranks displayed the oak leaves and cup in gilding-metal and the acorn in white-metal (Fig.623).The pattern for wear on the Service Dress was sealed 24th January 1924, and worn up to c.1952, when they were replaced by similar but in gold and silver anodised (Fig.624). Pattern No.20115, sealed 27th June 1969, Authority 54/Inf/8790. Officers badges, confirmed in the 1934 Dress Regulations, were in silver/gilt for tunic and mess dress (Fig.625), and in bronze for the Service Dress. Also in all gilt and probably worn by the Warrant Officers. Further confirmed in the 1973 Dress Regulations, 'In silver and gilt for No.1 Dress, and in bronze for No.2 Dress.' The Officers embroidered beret badge was also worn in pairs on the mess jacket (Fig.626).

Two star pattern badges were submitted in 1881 and appear in the Gaunt pattern book dated 16th May. No mention is made as to whether they were ever approved or adopted. One is in silver and may have been a trial pattern. Also certainly utilised as the Officers field service cap badge (Fig.627). The other is illustrated under line drawing 628. The 1986 Dress Regulations record: "No 1 and No 2 Dress, an acorn with oak leaves, the leaves and cup of the acorn in dead gilt or gilding-metal, the acorn in burnished silver plate." This is Pattern 30213, sealed 5th June 1985.

More details of other early collar badges, appear in the Unidentified section.

Militia
1st Royal Cheshire Light Infantry Militia

There are no details available clarifying what, if any, collar badges were worn by this Regiment. A combination of a bugle horn and/or the Prince of Wales's Crest and Motto, are most likely. The Prince is also Earl of Chester. In 1881 they became the 3rd Battalion The Cheshire Regiment.

2nd Royal Cheshire Militia

The Regimental Museum state that the Prince of Wales's Crest and Motto were worn as collar badges, presumably in white-metal for other ranks, and silver for Officers. (This is discussed in the Unidentified section). In 1881 they became the 4th Battalion.

After 1881, the Officers wore the badges of the Regular units but in reversed metals, the leaves and cup in silver, the acorn in gilt (Fig.629). A rarer distinction was the post 1902 bronze collar badge with a silver acorn for difference (Fig.630). The other ranks badges have not been recorded in reverse metals.

Fig.628

Fig.629

Fig.630

THE CHESHIRE REGIMENT

Rifle Volunteer Corps, Volunteer, Territorial Force & Territorial Army Battalions

The consolidated Battalions *1st, 3rd, 4th, 5th Cheshire Rifle Volunteer Corps*, nominated in 1881, became the corresponding Volunteer Battalions 1st December 1887. The mens' collar badge was for the Regular units but in white-metal. A silver plated version is known, but in general the Officers wore an all silver version of the Regular Officers pattern. The same badge is recorded in blackened metal, period and unit usage unknown (Fig.631).

The consolidated battalion, *2nd Cheshire Rifle Volunteer Corps*, had been granted the secondary title, 'Earl of Chester's' in 1870. This title was carried forward into the Volunteer Battalion period. The other rank's collar badge was the Prince of Wales's Crest and Motto, in white-metal (Fig.632). Officers wore similar but in silver.

The 4th Cheshire (Cheshire & Derbyshire) Rifle Volunteer Corps, consolidated as such in June 1880, included the *23rd Derbyshire Rifle Volunteers (Glossop)* raised 1876. The badges of the 23rd Derbyshire comprised the Crest and Motto of Lord Howard of Glossop, also, at that time, appropriated for use on the Seal of the Corporation of Glossop. 'On a chapeau gules turned up ermine, a lion statant with the tail extended or'. Below the motto, 'VIRTUS VERITAS LIBERTAS', (Virtue, truth and Freedom). Adopted by the 4th consolidated battalion for wear on the collar. In facing pairs, white-metal for other ranks and silver for Officers. (Line drawing Fig.633).

In 1908, with provision for only four TF Battalions in the area, the 1st, 4th, and 5th Volunteer Battalions became the 4th, 6th, and 7th TF Battalions; the 2nd and 3rd Volunteer Battalions amalgamated to form the 5th (Earl of Chester's) TF Battalion.

The TF Battalions gradually adopted the same collar badges as worn by the Line Battalions.

WWI Service Battalions
12th Service Battalion (Pioneers)

Raised 14th September 1914 and disbanded 28th November 1919. Crossed rifle and pick collar badges were worn (Fig.147).

Cheshire Home Guard

Under Authority 9/HG/363 silver/gilt collar badges were sealed 23rd June 1954 for wear by Officers. This was Pattern 16573 (see Fig.625 for similar).

Cadets

This battalion was formed in 1901 and affiliated to the 4th Battalion, wearing the Regulars' acorn collar badges.

Unidentified

There are three badges which have so far not been positively identified.

1) An eight-rayed star superimposed with the usual acorn and oak leaf motif, known in gilding-metal and bi-metal (Fig.634). The Regimental Museum state these items to be, 'The cap star 1898-1922 but with the long scroll removed.' However, all the items of this type studied show no marks which would indicate that they had ever been attached to anything else. Also there are no signs of where a slider has been attached; furthermore, all the ones examined have the usual two lug collar length fastenings. They would appear to be collar badges/field service cap badges of a fairly early era.

2) An eight-pointed rayed star on which is superimposed the Prince of Wales's Crest and Motto. Recorded in gilding-metal, white-metal, and all silver (Fig.635). The Regimental Museum states that this is the other ranks helmet plate centre, but removed from within the title circlet, and worn independently on the glengarry. This would certainly be correct for such bi-metal examples, which have the white-metal Crest and Motto superimposed, and with one single central h.p.c. type

Fig.631

Fig.632

Fig.633

Fig.634

Fig.635

Fig.636

fitting. However the gilding-metal ones examined are die struck in one piece, with two lug fasteners, and no sign of any central fitting, nor is there any sign of the badges being detached from larger items. Photographs of old collections show these items to be in the collar badge sections. It is the Author's belief that these are collar badges, the gilding-metal for the Regular Battalions c.1881-1883, the white-metal and silver ones for the Volunteer other ranks and Officers, c.1883. Alternatively the latter two could have been worn by the 2nd Royal Cheshire Militia, c.1878-81.

3) The usual eight-pointed rayed star with acorn and leaves in the centre; below the star a scroll inscribed, 'CHESHIRE' (Fig.636). Recorded in gilding-metal and bronze, with two copper lugs. The Regimental Museum state, 'A brooch in its simplified form worn by the "Regimental women" rather than the "Ladies of the Regiment", who wore similar, but embellished with diamonds and enamel, c.1893-1923". Though not wishing to challenge this dyad of social distinction, it is unusual for a brooch to have two lug fasteners which would undoubtably damage a woman's clothing. None of the items examined have any pin brooch fasteners. As already mentioned, the 1902 Service Dress cap/collar badge was not popular as being too large for the collar, and perhaps like many other regiments prior to 1914, reduced the size. It is possible therefore that this is an Officers Service Dress bronze collar badge c.1904-1910. The ones in gilding-metal awaiting bronzing or polished down for khaki drill. It has also been suggested that it was worn on a side hat c.1920.

General

Although the collar badge of the Regiment has virtually remained the same throughout, there have been a large number of different metals and combination of metals. Very few variations in design have been noted, probably due to the same manufacturers being used.

The Regiment remains intact since 1881, surviving even the proposed 1991 amalgamation, rescinded 3rd February 1993.

The Royal Welsh Fusiliers

Pre 1881
The 23rd (Royal Welsh Fusiliers) Regiment of Foot

Although Fusilier regiments were not authorised to wear embroidered grenades on their collars until 2nd October 1872, both fusiliers and bandsmen of the 23rd were wearing white worsted horizontal grenades on their tunic collars in 1871, and possibly as early as 1869. (1868 pattern tunic with pointed cuff.)
Similarly, Officers wore horizontal plain silver bullion grenades nearest the collar opening, ahead of their rank badges, as authorised by the 1874 Dress Regulations (Fig.637).
Fusiliers were permitted to wear brass grenades as from 4th June 1872, and perhaps influenced by the wide flames on their other grenade badges, chose a collar badge with the same distinction (Fig.638).

Fig.637

Fig.638

Post 1881

After redesignation in 1881 as The Royal Welsh Fusiliers, there was much discussion regarding the other ranks collar badge being a grenade with a Dragon on the ball. However this was never agreed to, and the collar badge adopted was the brass universal Fusilier grenade. (Pattern No.9281, sealed 2nd October 1872), later replaced by the same but in gilding-metal. (Pattern No.9933, sealed 11th January 1882, Figs.122, 123).

The Officers Commanding 1st and 2nd Battalions received a Directive from Horse Guards, 16th April 1884. 'To discontinue in the Regiment, the wearing of embroidered grenades, and to adhere to the regulations and wear metal grenades, and also to discontinue wearing piping on the collar of the Kersey Frocks'. It would seem that scant notice was taken of this requirement as on 6th February 1893 the 2nd Battalion were ordered, 'To wear brass grenades instead of worsted'.

The standard pattern grenade was renewed and cut from fresh dies 7th December 1897, Pattern No.9933a, there was no change in the design. On 14th February 1905 all Fusilier regiments were directed to wear the Royal Artillery collar grenade with their metal titles on the shoulder straps of drab jackets and great coats.

There was no change in the collar badge when the Regiment adopted the older spelling of Welch in 1920. The grenade was again renewed when Pattern No.15705 was sealed 13th April 1953. The same badge in gold anodised was later used. (Pattern No.19356, 29th June 1964) Authority 54/Inf/8792 (Fig.576).

As already stated, Officers wore a plain grenade in silver embroidery from 1874, together with their badges of rank until 1880, when the latter were removed to the shoulder. This is confirmed in the 1883 Dress Regulations, continued until the 1902 Edition, when the following is added for wear on the mess jacket, "a grenade in gold embroidery with a Dragon on the ball in silver metal". To be worn vertically. Sealed 14th May 1903. (Fig.639). For the recently introduced Service Dress, 'As for mess dress but in bronze'. Over the years there have been different shapes and sizes of the dragon, according to variable manufacturers. One significant difference has been in the dragon's tail, the early types had a curved tail culminating in a tuft of hair (Fig.640). Later ones had a loop in the tail and ended in an arrow head formation (Figs.641, 642). Also worn in polished gilding-metal on the khaki drill. The same pattern badges were later used on the

Fig.639

Fig.640

HISTORY OF THE BRITISH ARMY INFANTRY COLLAR BADGE

No.2 Dress; Pattern No.30217, sealed 26th March 1979. They were so made that the Dragon can be swivelled round on the ball, so enabling the badge to be worn vertically or horizontally.

The Officers collar badge for the No.1 and No.3 Dress, was a seven flamed horizontal grenade in gold embroidery with a silver plated Dragon on the ball (Fig.643). Similar were sealed 9th October 1956 for wear by Officers of the 4th and 6th/7th TA Battalions.

The upright gold embroidered grenade also differs quite considerably in the design of the Dragon, and like their bronze counterparts, the early ones have a curled tail with tufted end, whilst the later ones have the loop in the tail and arrowhead finial (Fig.644). The later mess dress collar badges in gold embroidery have nine flames with silver plated Dragons, on a red cloth backing for the Warrant Officers, and dark blue cloth for lesser ranks (Fig.645).

Other noted Officer quality grenades include a nine flamed grenade in gilt metal with large silver Dragon (Fig.646); similar but with different outline to the flames and much smaller dragon (Fig.647). Finally, one similar but in all gilt (Fig.648) possibly for wear by the Warrant Officers. All early items, as the Dragon's tail is without a loop.

Militia
Royal Denbigh and Merioneth Rifles

An ornate bugle horn with ribbons and tassels in blackened brass was worn by the Regiment just prior to 1881, when on 1st July they became the 3rd Battalion (Fig.649).

Fig.641

Fig.642

Fig.643

Fig.645

Fig.646

Fig.644

Fig.647

Fig.648

Fig.649

THE ROYAL WELSH FUSILIERS

Royal Carnarvon Rifle Corps

A bronzed collar badge for tunic and frock was sealed 6th November 1876. A ribboned bugle horn (Fig.650). They became the 4th Battalion, Royal Welsh Fusiliers in 1881.

For some time c.1881-1908, Officers of the 3rd and 4th Battalions wore silver embroidered grenades of seven flames mounted with gilt metal Dragons (Fig.651). The 4th Battalion was disbanded in 1908.

Rifle Volunteer Corps, Volunteer, Territorial Force & Territorial Army Battalions

The consolidated Battalion, *1st Denbighshire Rifle Volunteer Corps* nominated in 1881, became the 1st Volunteer Battalion, June 1884. Grenades in white-metal for use by the rank and file were submitted for approval by Messrs. Charles Prater & Co. 16 Bedford Street, Covent Garden. This was received 28th February 1885, Authority V/1 Denbigh/287, the collar badge being received at the Army Pattern Room, 3rd March 1885 (Fig.652).

A large consolidated unit, the *1st Flintshire and Carnarvonshire Rifle Volunteer Corps* nominated in 1881 became the 2nd Volunteer Battalion in 1884. In 1897 part of this battalion formed the 3rd Volunteer Battalion. The 2nd Volunteer Battalion submitted their proposed collar badges 1st May 1887, receiving amended approval from Horse Guards, 24th August 1887. That for Officers states, 'A grenade in gold embroidery' amended in red ink with 'gold' deleted and 'silver' substituted (Fig,653). At the same time authority was given 'For NCOs, Rank and File, on the collar of tunic and serge frock, grenades in silver metal.' One assumes white-metal.

In 1908, the three Volunteer Battalions became the 4th, 5th, 6th (TF) Battalions. The 4th and 5th Battalions adopted the badges of their Regular units, but the 6th Battalion wore no collar badges.

4th (Denbighshire) Batallion took on a pioneer role and photographs show Officers wearing a bronze 'T' below their bronze crossed rifle and pick collar badges (Fig.654).

General

Like all Fusilier regiments, the Royal Welch were not consistent in the number of flames on their grenades. All Dragon badges were worn in facing pairs with the Dragon facing inwards.

Fig.650

Fig.651

Fig.652

Fig.653

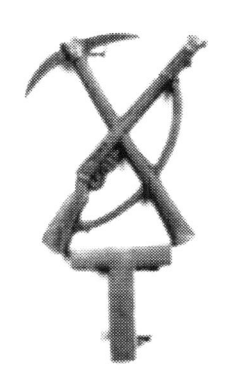

Fig.654

The South Wales Borderers

Pre 1881
The 24th (2nd Warwickshire) Regiment of Foot

Although there are photographic instances, c1872 of soldiers of the Regiment wearing the all in one piece brass numerals '24' on their tunic and greatcoat collars (Fig.655), their first official collar badge, Pattern No.9318 was sealed 24th October 1873. This was a front mantled male Sphinx with tail rising up across the body towards the head, a tablet below inscribed "EGYPT" (Figs.656, 657). In brass and worn until 1877 when it was replaced by Pattern No.9567, sealed 23rd February 1877. Still in brass and of the same general format, but this time a female Sphinx with mantle extending down over the back and with the tail finial pointing away from the head (Fig.658). This was the badge in use during the Zulu War. Clearly shown on the tunic collar of Private W. Jones, one of the Rorke's Drift VC winners. A photograph of Lieut. R.W. Franklin dated 1879 shows him wearing an embroidered Sphinx ahead of his rank badges (Fig.659).

Post 1881

On 30th September 1881, soon after the Regiment had been redesignated *The South Wales Borderers* (the only Regiment to take its title from the county Militia Regiment), the collar badge was 'confirmed as at present.' By 21st March 1882 however, a white-metal collar badge Pattern No.10146 was sealed to replace the brass Pattern No.9567 (Fig.660). This badge was almost identical to its predesessor. In the mid 1880s the War Office seemed obsessed with uniformity and assimilation of patterns, so it came with no surprise when the Regiment was advised 18th August 1886 that their collar badge was to be declared obsolete.

One may recall that in 1879 the other ranks collar badge of the 10th (North Lincoln) Regiment was assimilated to that worn by the 24th Regiment, so it was somewhat ironical that this time the position was reversed with the Lincolnshire Regiment's other ranks white-metal collar badge Pattern No.9969 replacing that worn by the South Wales Borderers.

Renewal of the sealed pattern white-metal badge was called for at the beginning of 1898, and these were cut from new dies and sealed 21st March. This was Pattern No.9969a, again the same as being worn by the Lincolnshire Regiment (Fig.661). The sealed pattern shows the Egypt tablet as having a mottled background, and with a border around the edge. Worn until 1959. The collar badge was certainly made in silver a/a, but it is doubtful as to whether they were ever issued or worn (Fig.662).

Although officially the male Sphinx was worn from 1886, there is evidence that the female version usually associated with the Manchester Regiment was also worn (Fig.663).

The Sphinx superscribed "EGYPT" was authorised 6th July 1802 to commemorate the services of the 24th Regiment in the 1801 Campaign.

The other ranks collar badge worn post 1959 displayed the numerals XXIV within a complete wreath of immortelles (Fig.664). The Pattern, No.18213 in silver a/a was sealed 31st Decmeber 1959 under Authority 54/Inf/8793 and later re-sealed 25th May 1965 under Authority NV82/2154, d/d 23/11/64, for wear by other ranks of the 2nd Battalion The Monmouthshire Regiment (TA). Similar but in superior white-metal, with single lug fitting, are said to have been worn by senior NCOs.

The wreath of immortelles is an unique distinction, authorised 1st December 1880 by direct Order of HM Queen Victoria. To be borne on the pole of the Queen's Colour of both Regular Battalions, it commemorates both the gallantry of Lieutenants Melville and Coghill in saving the Colour after the disaster of Isandlwana 1879, and also of the ensuing heroic defence of Rorke's Drift by 'B' Company of the 2nd Battalion.

The 1883 Dress Regulations record the Officers tunic collar badge as, 'The Sphinx over Egypt in dead gilt metal'. Repeated in ensuing Editions, the 1900 one adding, "or gilding metal" and "for wear on the tunic and scarlet frock". An example has been noted on a Gaunt's sample card (Fig.665). It also appears in the Gaunt Pattern book annotated, 'sealed 1882'. The 1902 Dress Regulations confirms the description but adds 'Mess Jacket'. The Gaunt Pattern books also show two designs of gilt collar badge dated 11th January 1882. The first, a female Sphinx shows a long neck and mantle reaching down to the breasts, the tail rising up over the body and pointing to the rear (Fig.666). A pattern sealed 10th July 1903 and annotated '2nd Battn.', was also a female Sphinx, with rounded head, mantle extending down over part of the back, and tail rising up from the back leg terminating with a tuft above the back (Fig.667).

The 1902 Dress Regulations also covered the bronze collar badges for Service Dress. 'As for tunic with S.W.B. below'. The design of the Sphinx followed that of the first pattern gilt collar badge and was sealed 10th July 1903; also annotated '2nd Battn' (Fig.668). This was worn until 1928 when on 28th February the second pattern was sealed. This time the Sphinx followed the design of the smaller second pattern gilt collar badge, trial pattern die (Fig.669) and specimen (Fig.670), also annotated '2nd Battn.'. Worn until 1955 when a third pattern was sealed 1st September, worn until amalgamation in 1969 (Fig.671).

By 1951, Officers were wearing a male Sphinx over the Egypt tablet in silver plate (Fig.672), confirmed by a later sealed pattern 1st September 1955. Annotated, 'For No.1 Dress'. Marked 'obsolete 21/12/59', it was replaced post 1959, when Officers adopted a silver plate version of the XXIV and immortelles badge for wear on No 1 Dress. Sealed 31st December 1959.

Militia
Royal Brecknock (Rifle Corps)
The lineage background to this Corps is quite complex, but this was the title they enjoyed in 1876, when the Pattern Room Journal records, 'Bronzed collar badges for tunic and frock sealed 4/3/76'. There is no description of the badge. They amalgamated later that year with the *Royal Radnor Rifles* to form the *Royal South*

Fig.664

Fig.665

Fig.666

Fig.667

Fig.668

Fig.672   *Fig.671*   *Fig.670*   *Fig.669*

HISTORY OF THE BRITISH ARMY INFANTRY COLLAR BADGE

Fig.673

Fig.674

Fig.675

Fig.676

Fig.677

Wales Borderers Militia (Royal Radnor and Brecknock Rifles). This Corps is said to have worn as their collar badge, 'A lion as Kings Own Royal Regiment but black'. Such an item is shown in (Fig.673) but no confirmation in any medium has been traced. The Regiment became the 3rd Battalion The South Wales Borderers in July 1881.

Royal Montgomery Rifles
No collar badges have been traced to this Regiment prior to it becoming the 4th Battalion in 1881. It was disbanded 31st July 1908.

Rifle Volunteer Corps, Volunteer, Territorial Force & Territorial Army Battalions

The 1st Brecknockshire Rifle Volunteer Corps nominated in 1881, became the 1st (Brecknockshire) Volunteer Battalion in 1885. A photograph of 'E' Company c.1895 shows a white-metal Dragon being worn on the collar, it has one fore-leg raised and is standing on a narrow ground. The Officers version was in silver plate (Fig.674). It is not certain as to whether this battalion had earlier worn the Sphinx collars described below for the 3rd, 4th and 5th Volunteer Battalions.

In 1908, the South Wales Borderers were allocated one Territorial Battalion, the former 1st V.B. therefore became the The Brecknockshire Battalion. Officers of the unit wore as their collar badge, a Dragon with looped tail standing on ground below which was a scroll inscribed 'BRECKNOCKSHIRE'. Below this and attached to the scroll was the capital 'T' with serifs. Voided between the ground and the scroll, in bronze (Figs.675, 676). A similar but larger version is known, this has a longer scroll and the 'T' is without serifs. All examples noted have faced to the left only, and it is most likely that these are cap badges. Information regarding the badges worn by this battalion is scant, but it is generally accepted that the men wore the same Dragon as the Officers pattern but in gilding-metal and minus the scroll and 'T'. (Fig.677). The battalion amalgamated with the 3rd Battalion, The Monmouthshire Regiment 31st January 1922.

The 1st Monmouthshire Rifle Volunteer Corps, became the 2nd Volunteer Battalion in 1885. On the formation of the Volunteer Battalions the Gaunt pattern books show that Messrs. Pearse & Co., London, submitted a white-metal male Sphinx for approval, this was similar to the one worn by the Regular units; this was not allowed, but the adopted pattern also illustrated in the Gaunt books depicts a full breasted female Sphinx, with rounded head, long neck and mantle and tail finally pointing to the rear. Below, a blank tablet. In white metal (Fig.678). In a camp photograph taken in 1902 the white-metal Dragon badge as worn by the 1st V.B. is now in evidence. Quite when this change took place is not known. In 1908, the battalion became the 1st Battalion, The Monmouthshire Regiment. Their badges are dealt with separately.

The consolidated *2nd Monmouthshire Rifle Volunteer Corps* became the 3rd Volunteer Battalion in 1885. The prescribed white-metal Sphinx collar badges were worn by this battalion. After 1902, silver plated versions of the Service Dress bronze collar badge (Fig.679) do occur, and were possibly worn by the Officers of this and the 4th VBs. In 1908 the battalion became the 2nd Battalion, The Monmouthshire Regiment.

Fig.678

Fig.679

110

THE SOUTH WALES BORDERERS

The consolidated *3rd Monmouthshire Rifle Volunteer Corps* nominated in 1881 became the 4th Volunteer Battalion in 1885. On 17th March 1888 approval was received for the NCOs and men of this battalion for a new white metal collar badge. This was the same female pattern as described above but with the tablet inscribed "EGYPT". Annotated, '4 VB, female Sphinx, Authty V/3/Monmouth/357'. In 1908 the unit became the 3rd Battalion, The Monmouthshire Regiment.

The 5th Volunteer Battalion was raised in 1897 with headquaters at Newtown, Montgomeryshire. In October of that year a similar but not identical pattern of collar badge to that of the 4th VB was submitted for approval, but by a decision taken on the 26th October, "EGYPT" was deleted from the tablet. (Authority V/5/24/34) (Fig.680). In 1908 the battalion became part of the 7th (TF) Battalion, The Royal Welsh Fusiliers.

Fig.680

Service Battalions 1914-1918

The new 5th and 6th Service Battalions both served as Pioneer Battalions. The 6th, while awaiting the usual Pioneer collar badges, wore on their left collar only, a round badge made of tin with '6' over 'SWB' engraved upon it (Line drawing 681). The 5th wore the usual crossed rifle and pick collar badge (Fig.147).

Fig.681

Unidentified

1) A Dragon on ground within a laurel wreath (Fig.682). Recorded in gilding-metal and also white-metal. These items have appeared in photographs of old S.W.B. collections. All the ones examined face to the left. The emblems have long been associated with the Regiment, and the Dragon, of course, with Wales as a whole. A Welsh Militia badge of unrecorded origin is quite possible.
2) A smaller version of the Regimental cap badge in gilding-metal with lugs (Fig.683).
3) An even smaller version in gilding-metal (Fig.684). A sweetheart's badge has been suggested, though the badge is fitted with standard lug fasteners.

Fig.682

General

All Sphinx and Dragon badges were worn in facing pairs, with the beasts facing towards the collar opening. The Regiment is well known for the many variations of Sphinx both male and female. The only noted consistency has been that the bronze badges are always female Sphinxes.

On 11th June 1969, the Regiment amalgamated with The Welsh Regiment to form *The Royal Regiment of Wales (24th/41st Foot)*.

Fig.683

Fig.684

The King's Own Scottish Borderers

Fig.685

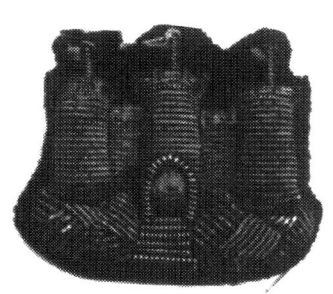

Fig.686

Fig.687

Fig.688

Fig.689

Fig.690

Pre 1881
The 25th (The King's Own Borderers) Regiment of Foot

The first other ranks collar badge of the Regiment was sealed 28th August 1873. This was Pattern No.9316, and as the Regiment was originally the Edinburgh Regiment, it is perhaps not surprising that the design chosen was that of Edinburgh Castle, a badge along with the motto of the City authorised in March 1832. In brass, the Castle is shown having three round topped towers each with a triangular shaped pennant flying to the left as viewed. The two outer towers with two vertical lookouts while the centre one has only one, below this is an archway with portcullis, from this depends hewn steps amid a rocky base.. Each wall between the towers has a square lookout. Worn on the scarlet doublet, the flagged towers do not face (Fig.685). Also known in white metal believed worn by Pipers. Officers removed their rank badges to the shoulder in 1880 and wore as their collar badge large embroidered versions of the other ranks badge. On a ground of gold embroidery with the castle in silver, the battlements, pennants, lookouts and archway picked out in blue silk (Fig.686).

It has been written that prior to the first official collar badge the other ranks wore the brass '25' numerals on their tunic collars. (Fig.687). It has not been possible to confirm this.

Post 1881

In April 1881, under the proposed Territorial reforms, the 25th, to everybody's horror, were to become *The York Regiment (King's Own Borderers)*, the *2nd West York Militia* were nominated as the 3rd Battalion. Though other very harsh changes did take place, this crass decision was rescinded and by July 1881 the Regiment's headquarters were confirmed at Stirling with the title, *The King's Own Borderers*. On 30th September the Regiment received an interim statement from Horse Guards, 'confirming the same collar badge as at present - Edinburgh Castle'. A new collar badge was sealed, however, 8th February 1882, Pattern No.10101, in gilding-metal. This was a similar Edinburgh Castle to its predecessor and can easily be confused. The differences apart from the metal change are as follows; the two square lookouts on the walls have gone, the base is more 'craggy', and the steps leading down have distinctive edges which at first glance make it appear like one long archway. (Figs.688, 689, 690) The last one depicts the top lookouts as mere dots. A photograph of Sgt. Laurie, 10th March 1888 clearly shows the post-1882 badge in use. (Plate 11).

The Regiment was redesignated *The King's Own Scottish Borderers*, 1st May 1887, and by the 5th May a change of collar and other badges was called for. However, the design for the collar badges was not approved, and 'a demand for new drawings for NCOs and men' was made to the O.C. 2nd Battalion, 21st July

1888. (The 1st Battalion being in India). He was also informed that any new pattern would not be supplied until existing stocks were exhausted.

It was not until 3rd June 1889 that the new Pattern, No.1972, was sealed and deposited in the Army Pattern Room. Again Edinburgh Castle, albeit smaller and now with only one lookout in each tower, and with no portcullis in the archway. Also gone was the rocky base, the Castle now resting on Thistle sprays, below which was a three-part scroll inscribed, 'THE KING'S OWN/SCOTTISH BORDERERS'. In gilding-metal and worn with a red cloth backing (Fig.691). Renewal of the pattern was demanded 18th April 1898, the new Pattern No.1972a being sealed 26th September 1899. Still in gilding-metal, the opportunity was taken to slightly modify the design of the Castle which now had a longer archway, and a different display for the Thistles (Fig.692). Both collar badges on the pattern card have flags flying to the left. The same pattern was later worn in gold anodised, introduced 25th January 1961 Pattern No.18477, Authority 54/Inf/8774. This was replaced by Pattern No.18477a, sealed 19th July 1963. This was a neater design and with wider steps leading down from the archway (Fig.693).

The 1978, 1982, and 1987 Catalogues of Clothing and Necessaries all record this badge for 'C' (K.O.S.B.) Coy. 1st Battalion and No.3 (K.O.S.B.) Coy. 2nd Battalion of the *52nd Lowland Volunteers*.

Pipers have always worn different dress and embellishments and those of the K.O.S.B. were no exception. Pipers wearing white-metal versions of the standard other ranks patterns followed by silver anoodised, sealed 2nd November 1961, superceded by Pattern No. 19145 sealed 19th July 1963 under Authority 54/Inf/8774, also in silver anodised. Pipe Majors wore similar but in silver plate. Drum Majors wore embroidered collar badges (Fig.694).

For Officers, the 1891 Dress Regulations records a change in the collar badge for wear on the tunic collar. 'On a dark blue cloth ground, the Castle of Edinburgh in silver embroidery. A flag in blue and crimson embroidery flies from each tower. The Castle rests on thistle leaves etc. in gold embroidery. Beneath the gold embroidery, a scroll, inscribed, "The King's Own Scottish Borderers', on a ground of light blue silk" (Fig.695). Confirmed in subsequent Editions, the 1900 issue adding 'and scarlet frock', the 1902, 'and mess jacket'. A sealed pattern 13th April 1904 is annotated 'Doublet and Mess Jacket'. (Figs.696, 697) show two variations. This is confirmed in the 1911 Edition, though substituting 'Doublet' for 'Tunic'. Being hand-manufactured, the collar badge has varied in both shape and design over the last 100 years or so. Naturally the earlier ones were of better

Fig.691

Fig.692

Fig.693

Fig.694

Fig.695

Fig.696

Fig.697

HISTORY OF THE BRITISH ARMY INFANTRY COLLAR BADGE

Fig.698

Fig.699

Fig.700

Fig.701

quality, and the flags flew to the viewer's left only, but from c.1953 they do face. Figures 698 and 699 show such a pair, sealed 23rd January 1956, for wear on Nos.1 & 3 Dress.

The 1975 Dress Regulations amend the description for wear on No.1 Dress by referring to the flags as flying 'from each of the 3 turrets', and omitting 'The Castle rests on thistle leaves in gold embroidery'.

The 1902 Edition covers the collar badge to be worn on the Service Dress, 'The Castle, with a scroll below, inscribed, 'The King's Own Scottish Borderers', in bronze (Fig.700). In 1913 Army Order 279 introduced a Service Dress jacket with open collar and bronze collar badges were then worn on the lapels. The 1975 Dress regulations, for wear on the No.2 Dress, records, 'Not in pairs'. These were worn until 1978 when a new pattern, No.30142, was sealed 7th July. It displays wider steps and different angle of thistles to the base of the Castle (Fig.701). One of the bronze pattern collar badges has been noted in gilt metal, but the usage or any authority for such a badge cannot be traced.

Militia

As a result of the April 1881 fiasco, no Scottish Militia Regiment was nominated for the old 25th Regiment, and it was not until 1887 that the Lowland conglomerate Corps, brought together in 1863 as the *Scottish Borderers Militia* and allocated to the Royal Scots Fusiliers as their 3rd Battalion, was tranferred as the 3rd Battalion, The King's Own Scottish Borderers. Mention of a possible collar badge for the Scottish Borderers Militia has been recorded under The Royal Scots Fusilier notes. After 1887 Officers of the new 3rd Battalion wore their embroidered tunic collar badges in reverse metal threads, (Fig.702) though not able to illustrate the colour difference does show other minor variations in composition.

Rifle Volunteer Corps, Volunteer, Territorial Force & Territorial Army Battalions
1st Roxburgh and Selkirk (The Border) Volunteer Rifle Corps

Joined the K.O.S.B. in 1887 from The Royal Scots. Though ranked as the 1st Volunteer Battalion, they did not assume that title; the majority of their badges bear the title Border Rifle Volunteers. In keeping with many Rifle Volunteers, collar badges were not worn. In 1908 together with the 2nd Volunteer Battalion they formed the 4th (TF) Battalion.

1st Berwickshire Rifle Volunteer Corps

Again, with The Royal Scots until 1887. Prior to 1881 the consolidated battalion wore as their collar badge, a distinctive Thistle in white-metal for other ranks (Fig.703), and in silver for Officers (Fig.704). Worn at an angle with the stalk

Fig.702

Fig.703

THE KING'S OWN SCOTTISH BORDERERS

facing inwards towards the collar opening. In May 1887 under General Order 61 they became the 2nd (Berwickshire) Volunteer Battalion. As mentioned above they jointly formed the 4th (TF) Battalion in 1908.

The consolidated *1st Dumfriesbire Rifle Volunteer Corps* became the 3rd (Dumfries) Volunteer Battalion of the K.O.S.B. From 1881-1887 they had served as a Volunteer Battalion of the Royal Scots Fusiliers. The Gaunt Pattern Books show the pre-1887 Castle collar badge in white-metal annotated, '3rd VB'. Also in silver for Officers (Fig.705). From 1889 similar badges to the Regular units but in white-metal were worn, the pattern changing in 1899 as per the Regulars., but still in white-metal. The Officers wore similar but in silver plate (Fig.706). The unit formed part of the 5th (TF) Battalion in 1908.

The consolidated unit, *The Galloway Rifle Volunteer Corps*, representing the counties of Wigtown and Kirkcudbright joined the Royal Scots Fusiliers as one of its Volunteer Battalions in 1881. The Corps were transferred to the K.O.S.B. only in 1899, being nominated the 4th Volunteer Battalion, but in fact serving without a title change. In 1908 they jointly formed the 5th (TF) Battalion.

The collar badges of the Regular Battalions were adopted soon after 1908, and continued in use for those surviving units thereafter. A sealed pattern 2nd November 1961 shows gold a/a collar badges for the other ranks, and silver a/a for the pipers. A bronze example for Officers Service Dress. All annotated '4/5 Battalion K.O.S.B. TA'.

Other badge

A gilding-metal item that is sometimes thought to be a collar badge is in fact the centre portion of the short-lived gilding-metal helmet plate centre 1881-1884. It may have been worn as a badge on the field service cap (Fig.707).

General

The design of the Edinburgh Castle has remained much the same on the metal collar badges. Early badges have a short archway while the later ones have a higher one as well as having the thistles at a more acute angle than the early ones. The castle flags do not face on the other ranks' badges, and only after 1953 do they face for the Officers' embroidered badges.

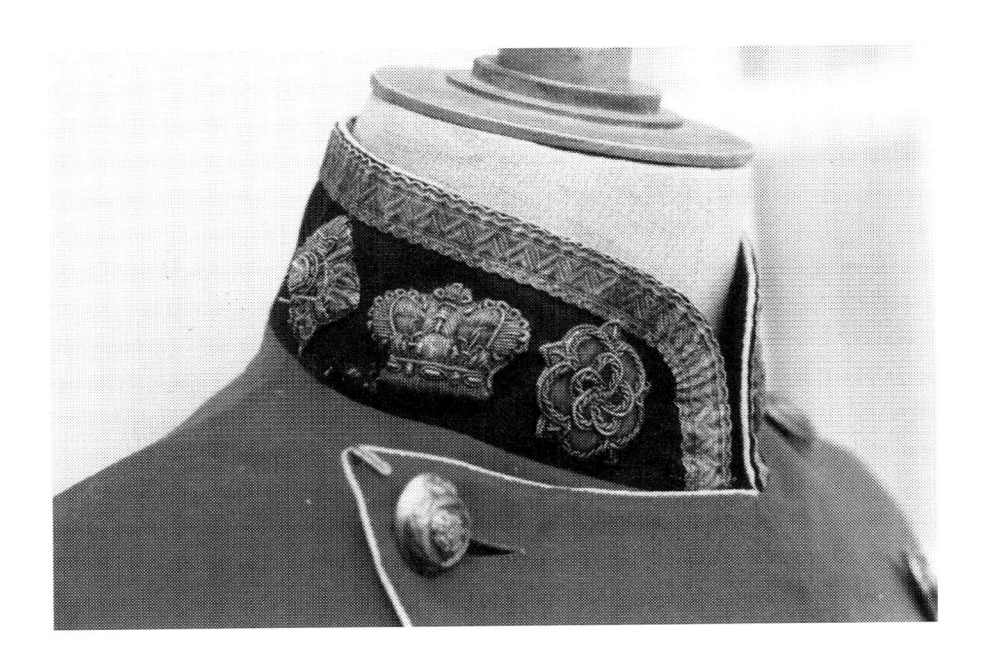

Fig.704

Fig.705

Fig.706

Fig.707

King's Own (Royal Lancaster)

The Cameronians (Scottish Rifles)

Pre 1881
The 26th (Cameronians) Regiment of Foot

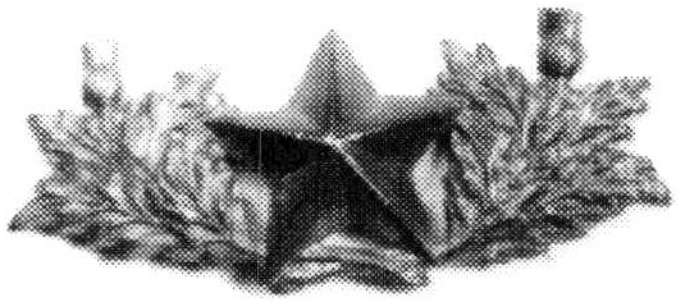

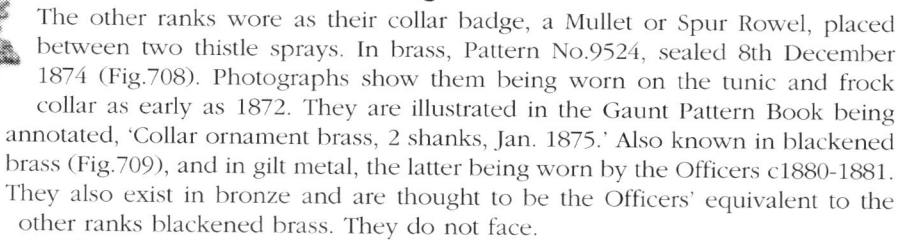

The other ranks wore as their collar badge, a Mullet or Spur Rowel, placed between two thistle sprays. In brass, Pattern No.9524, sealed 8th December 1874 (Fig.708). Photographs show them being worn on the tunic and frock collar as early as 1872. They are illustrated in the Gaunt Pattern Book being annotated, 'Collar ornament brass, 2 shanks, Jan. 1875.' Also known in blackened brass (Fig.709), and in gilt metal, the latter being worn by the Officers c1880-1881. They also exist in bronze and are thought to be the Officers' equivalent to the other ranks blackened brass. They do not face.

The Regiment was raised from the bands of religious dissenters, The Cameronian Guard, c.1688, designated by 1689 as the Earl of Angus's Regiment. The Mullet or star badge certainly occurs in the arms of the old Earls of Angus (Douglas), now merged as a title borne by the Duke of Hamilton and Brandon, and though borne by some branches of the Graham family, it was not used by Thomas Graham, later Lord Lynedoch (extinct 1843) who is credited with having raised the Regiment.

The 90th (Perthshire Volunteers) (Light Infantry)

In 1873, a submission was made to HM The Queen by the Commander-in-Chief, The Duke of Cambridge on behalf of the 90th Regiment, seeking her approval for the Regiment to wear the Arms of the Royal Burgh of Perth on the collars of their tunics. The submission did receive the Royal approval, notified by Horse Guards letter 13th February 1873 to General Eden, Colonel of the Regiment.

The resultant badge followed the ancient Scottish heraldic description fairly closely, 'Gules, ane Holy Lambe regardant, staff and cross argent, with the banner of St. Andrew proper, all within a double tressure counter-flowered of the second, the escutcheon being surmounted on the breast of ane eagle with two neckes displayed or. The Motto in an escroll, 'PRO REGE LEGE ET GREGE'. (For the Crown, the Law and the People). In fact the badge omitted the 'double tressure counter flowered'. Struck in brass, Pattern No.9307 was sealed 14th May 1873 (Fig.710). They are well illustrated in a portrait of a Colour-Sergeant Smith DCM. Officers wore the same badge in silver 1880-1881 (Fig.711). They do not face.

Post 1881

The 26th and 90th Regiments were amalgamated 1st July 1881 to form the 1st and 2nd Battalions respectively of The Cameronians Regiment (Scotch Rifles), but in November of the same year this was amended to The Cameronians (Scottish Rifles). Elevation to Rifles status meant the end of collar badges for all ranks, and in the case of the other ranks this was observed until 1953, when a design based on the background of the old 26th and 90th came into use. In blackened gilding-metal Pattern No.15871 was sealed 8th September 1953, a strung bugle surmounted by the mullet (Fig.712). Also known in white-metal for wear on No.1 Dress, Pattern No. 15871 was sealed 8th September 1953 under Authority 59/54/Officers/4025 (Fig.713). These were replaced under Authority/54/Inf/8775 in 1960 by similar badges but in blackened anodised, Pattern No.18319, sealed 20th June 1960 (Fig.714 worn with a rectangular red cloth backing). Chromed versions are also known to have been in use in the mid-1950s, possibly by Regimental police.

THE CAMERONIANS (SCOTTISH RIFLES)

It is not until 1902 that collar badges for Officers are first mentioned, this covered the wearing of such badges on the new Service Dress. The badge to be the same as worn on the puggaree but in bronze:- 'A thistle wreath, within the wreath, a mullet. On the bottom of the wreath, a bugle with strings' (Fig.715). Approved 13th April 1904 and worn 1904-1908. The puggaree badge was in fact much larger and of different format (Fig.716). In 1908 the pattern later adopted by the other ranks, but larger, was introduced. In bronze (Fig.717). Unpopular, a smaller pattern was introduced in 1909 (Fig.718).

The 1911 Dress Regulations finally give sanction to a collar badge for the Officers' mess jackets, this had been sealed 17th May 1904, 'a silver bugle with strings surmounted by a mullet', (Fig.719). Also noted in blackened silver. A badge that is sometimes thought to be a collar badge is in fact the ornament from the Officers shako corded boss (Fig.720).

Militia
2nd Royal Lanark Militia
Raised in 1854, and forming two battalions in 1877, they became the 3rd and 4th Battalions of the Regiment in 1881. The battalions adopted the dress and appointments of the parent units, but omitting the battle honours from the whistle guard. Officers adopted the post-1902 Service Dress badges of the parent battalions.

Rifle Volunteer Corps, Volunteer, Territorial Force & Territorial Army Battalions
1st Lanarkshire (or Glasgow 1st Western) Rifle Volunteer Corps
The other ranks wore as their first collar badge an ornate bugle horn with the figure '1' in the curl and all surmounted by the QVC. In white-metal (Fig.721). Though nominated as the 1st Volunteer Battalion in 1881, the Corps did not adopt the title. The same badge continued in use until 1908, with the necessary change of crown in 1901-02 (Fig.722). Officers wore similar but in silver and also in bronze for the Service Dress.

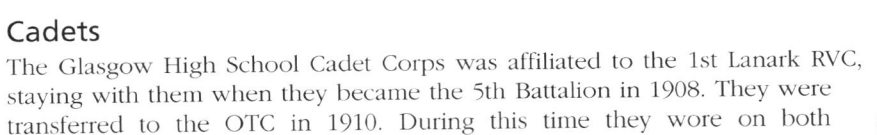

Cadets
The Glasgow High School Cadet Corps was affiliated to the 1st Lanark RVC, staying with them when they became the 5th Battalion in 1908. They were transferred to the OTC in 1910. During this time they wore on both glengarry and collar a very distinctive badge. In white-metal a double

Fig.713

Fig.714

Fig.715

Fig.716

Fig.718  *Fig.719*  *Fig.720*

Fig.721  *Fig.722*  *Fig.717*

117

headed eagle appeared within a strap inscribed "1st LANARKSHIRE RIFLE VOLUNTEERS". Below, a three-part scroll was inscribed, 'CADET/H.S.G./CORPS'. At the top, the Crest from the City Arms, the demi figure of St. Kentigern affronte, vested and mitred, his right hand raised in the act of benediction, and having in his left hand a crozier, all proper (Fig.723).

Fig.723

2nd Lanarkshire Rifle Volunteer Corps
Consolidated in 1880 under this title, the Corps adopted the title *2nd Volunteer Battalion* in 1887. Badges similar to those of the above 1st Lanarkshire RVC are believed to have been worn, but omitting the numeral from the curl. Again in white-metal for the other ranks QVC and KC patterns are recorded (Figs.724, 725). Again Officers wearing the superior metal equivalents.

3rd Lanarkshire Rifle Volunteer Corps
Again nominated in 1881, the battalion did not adopt the 3rd Volunteer Battalion title. The other ranks white-metal collar badge was a smaller version of their glengarry badge. A star, in the centre a strap inscribed "LANARKSHIRE RIFLE VOLUNTEERS", within the strap the figure '3'. The strap being surmounted by a QVC. In silver for Officers.

Fig.724

4th Lanarkshire (Glasgow, 1st Northern) Rifle Volunteer Corps
Became the *4th Volunteer Battalion* in 1887. Officers wore a distinctive collar badge, the mullet over strung bugle with a scroll below inscribed, '4TH VOLR BATTN.' In silver plate and worn in facing pairs (Fig.726).

7th Lanarkshire Rifle Volunteer Corps
This consolidated battalion became the *5th Volunteer Battalion* in 1887. No individual collar badges have been noted. The battalion was disbanded in 1897 for ill discipline.

Fig.725

In 1908, the remaining four units became the 5th, 6th, 7th, 8th (TF) Battalions respectively. Adopting the badges of the parent units at last, the 5th Battalion maintained some individuality by placing the figure '5' within the strings of the bugle horn on their glengarry and sporran badges. It is not impossible that the badge shown in (Fig.727) was their collar badge. It occurs in gilding-metal, bronze and silver/gilt. The Regimental Headquarters maintain that these badges are not collar badges, but have no alternative explanation.

In 1950, the remaining 6th and 7th TA Battalions amalgamated to form 6th/7th Battalion. Later 'D' Coy (The Cameronians) (Scottish Rifles) and No.4 Coy (formed from the remains of the 6th/7th Battalion, became the 1st and 2nd Bns., 52nd Lowland Volunteers. They adopted the blackened gilding-metal collar badge of the parent battalion.

Fig.726

General
All bugle horn and mullet badges were worn in facing pairs, the mouthpiece facing inwards towards the collar opening. The Regiment was disbanded 14th May 1968.

Fig.727

The Royal Inniskilling Fusiliers

Pre 1881
The 27th (Inniskilling) Regiment of Foot
The Castle of Inniskilling with St. George's colours flying in a blue field and the name 'Inniskilling' over it, is mentioned in the Royal Warrant of 1751 as a castle with three turrets. It commemorates the Protestant defence of Enniskillen in 1689, borne on the Colours of the Regiment since the early 18th century.

It was appropriate therefore that this Castle was chosen as the first collar badge of the 27th. Somewhat similar to the design atop the mens' glengarry badge c.1872-81, the two outside towers each show a circular look-out, and the central tower flies the flag of St. George, oddly at the side of the tower. The curtain wall shows three circular look-outs with an archway below. All upon 'ground'. The flags fly both ways and were worn on the tunic and frock with the flag facing inward towards the collar opening (Fig.728). In brass, Pattern No.9296, authorised 16th July 1872, was sealed 13th February 1873.

Fig.728

The 108th (Madras Infantry) Regiment
Though two short-lived 108th Regiments had existed in the 18th century, this Regiment was one of nine Regiments transferred to the British Establishment in 1861-62. Raised in 1854 as The Hon. East India Company's 3rd (Madras European Infantry), redesignated 3rd (Madras) European Infantry Regiment in 1858.

An Army Order 16th July 1872 set out the wearing of 'badges for collars of tunics, infantry', including, 'Regiments with no special device - Crowns'. The 108th therefore adopted the 'Imperial' crown (Fig.333). It is doubtful if these were worn before 1877 as the Regiment did not arrive in England until December 1876.

Fig.729

Post 1881
The two Regiments amalgamated 1st July 1881 to form *The Royal Inniskilling Fusiliers, 1st and 2nd Battalions* respectively. Elevation to Fusilier status necessitated a grenade as a collar badge, and to perpetuate the Territorial affiliation and ancient badge of the 27th, the Castle of Inniskilling was placed upon the ball.

The 1st Battalion were stationed in Hong Kong at the time of the Cardwell Reforms, and it was not until 2nd February 1882 that the new collar badge, Pattern No.10012 was sealed. Both the multi-flamed grenade and the castle were in gilding-metal, the three-towered castle now differed from that worn by the old 27th. The rectangular look-outs had now been reduced to one in each outside tower. The flag now flew from a central position. Worn horizontally on the full dress tunic collar, (Figs.729,730 show the flag flying in both directions). Warrant Officers and senior NCOs worn the same in gilt.

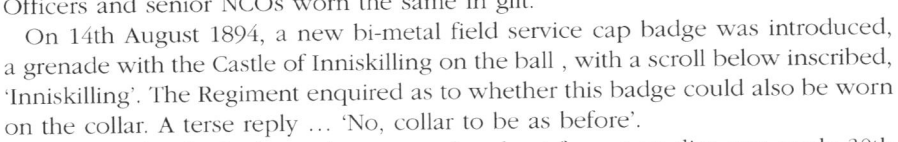

Fig.730

On 14th August 1894, a new bi-metal field service cap badge was introduced, a grenade with the Castle of Inniskilling on the ball, with a scroll below inscribed, 'Inniskilling'. The Regiment enquired as to whether this badge could also be worn on the collar. A terse reply ... 'No, collar to be as before'.

A request for the badge to be renewed and cut from new dies was made 30th November 1896. They were authorised 14th December 1897, Pattern No.10012a, still in all gilding-metal, and no change in design. These were worn until 1927.

Fig.731

During this period Pipers are reputed to have worn a white-metal Castle of Inniskilling, but no evidence is forthcoming to support this.

Fig.732

HISTORY OF THE BRITISH ARMY INFANTRY COLLAR BADGE

In 1927, new bi-metal collar badges were approved, Pattern No.10214 being sealed 7th December 1927. A further horizontal type with a redesigned Castle now in white-metal (Fig.731). A further change took place in 1928, when the badge became a vertical type. In bi-metal, Pattern No.10276 was sealed 19th September 1928 under Authority 54/Inf/5871 (Fig.732). Later issues were fitted with the single lug and plate fixings. This pattern provided the guide for the a/a version, Pattern No.18934 being in gold and silver a/a. Sealed 3rd December 1962, Authority 54/Inf/8795 (Fig.733). A renewal Pattern No.19197 was sealed 11th September 1963. Pipe Majors and Pipers wore similar to the fusiliers but in white-metal, (Fig.734), giving way to silver a/a, Pattern No.18934 being sealed 31st December 1962 (Fig.735). A further issue Pattern No.19913, was sealed for Pipers 9th May 1968. Figures 732 - 735 have all been illustrated as they differ in both the shape of the grenade and the castle. The anodised collar badges do not face.

For Officers, the early Dress Regulations describe the collar badge for wear on the tunic collar as, 'A grenade in gold embroidery; the Castle, in silver on the ball'. A pair taken off the collar of an early 1880s tunic show the old design of the Castle, with the flag flying to the left on both badges. An interesting feature is that the central flame is depicted pointing in different directions (Figs.736, 737). (The Castles have been 'turned', as collars of this size could not physically be worn vertically.) The same badge was worn on the Officers forage cap 1881-c.1898. The 1900 Dress Regulations record similar, but with metal grenades substituted for embroidery, for wear on the scarlet frock (Figs.738, 739). The grenades being nine flamed. Such an item was sealed 11th November 1903. A further embroidered pair, somewhat smaller with eight flames, show the post -1881 design of Castle (Figs.740, 741). The sealed pattern confirms that both flags fly in the same

Fig.733

Fig.734

Fig.735

Fig.736

Fig.737

Fig.738

Fig.739

Fig.740

Fig.741

THE ROYAL INNISKILLING FUSILIERS

direction. A photograph of Colonel C.J. Lloyd Davidson D.S.O., clearly show these grenades in use on a post -1904 full dress tunic (Plate 12). A similar eight flamed grenade but with the new pattern of Castle was sealed by the War Office 26th September 1927 (Fig.742). The sealed pattern card has later been annotated 'Obsolete', sadly this amendment is undated.

There are also silver/gilt badges of the same pattern as the other ranks , and a version in all silver was sealed 11th November 1903 for wear on the mess jacket (Fig.743).

Fig.742

The Colonel of the Regiment, General Sir Travers Clarke wrote to the War Office 19th January 1927 requesting clarification regarding the badges of the Regiment. The reply dated 3rd March 1927 informed him of changes approved by the Army Council. These included the following in respect of collar badges:-

Tunic and Mess Jacket: To be worn as at present authorised but substituting the new Castle design, without the title 'Inniskilling'. The size to be reduced to that of the Service Dress collar badge.

Service Dress: The grenade as at present authorised but substituting the new Castle design on the ball of the grenade and omitting the title 'Inniskilling'.

Fig.743

Several patterns of silver/gilt vertical grenades, some with Inniskilling below the Castle, have also been noted (Figs.744, 745 show early 'flat' and later 'domed' versions). This badge was also the Officers cap badge c.1902-1927 occuring with both blades and lugs. The same badge in bi-metal was worn by the senior NCOs, though again it was the other ranks field service cap badge c.1894-1902 (Fig. 746). The first post -1927 issues in silver/gilt were also 'flat' (Fig.747), followed by 'domed' types with Castle design variations (Figs.748, 749, 750). The silver/gilt types were worn from c.1945 in No.2 Dress, and worn until disbandment.

In 1902, a bronze multi flamed grenade with the Castle on the ball and "INISKILLING" scroll beneath was introduced for wear on Service Dress. Again the early ones were 'flat' (Fig.751), with the later ones 'domed' (Fig.752). The flame structure also varies. Photographs indicate that during WWI the 4th Battalion wore these badges in their caps. These badges polished to gilding-metal were worn in the khaki drill .A very interesting bronze variant has a 'flat' grenade with early Castle design and a wide spread of flames. This could have been a trial pattern (Fig.753).

Fig.744

Fig.745

Fig.747    *Fig.748*    *Fig.749*

Fig.750    *Fig.751*    *Fig.752*    *Fig.753*    *Fig.746*

HISTORY OF THE BRITISH ARMY INFANTRY COLLAR BADGE

After 1927, the bronze grenade was worn without the title scroll (Fig.754), and horizontally (Fig.755).

The design of the embroidered/silver mess dress grenades has also varied (Figs.756, 757 show Castle variants; Fig.756 being of an early pattern.

After WWII, Officers wore on their No.1 and No.3 Dress, the Castle of Inniskilling with a separate "INNISKILLING" scroll above, all in silver. These are in facing pairs (Figs.758, 759). These recall the short-lived cap badge introduced for all ranks c.1926-c.1935.

Militia
Fermanagh Light Infantry Militia

The first other ranks collar badge was a bugle horn with a castle in the non voided curl. The castle has two towers, each with two lookouts and with domed turrets. The curtain wall also has a lookout and archway below, with steps leading down. A flag flies from the curtain wall. In brass and worn from 1875 until 1877, in facing pairs with even the flags doing so (Figs.760, 761). On 5th January 1877 a similar badge but in white-metal was sealed, 'For tunic and frock'. Again in facing pairs and with the area between the castle and 'curl' now voided. The castle represented the Watergate of Enniskillen and was the Common Seal of the town. It had been the badge of the Regiment for some time. An item that may also have been a collar badge of the Regiment is shown (Line drawing Fig.762). In gilding-metal and with two lugs, there is no evidence to substantiate this supposition.

In 1881, the Regiment became the 3rd Battalion, The Royal Inniskilling Fusiliers.

Royal Tyrone Fusiliers Militia

Granted the title Fusiliers in 1855, subsequent white-metal grenade collar badges were sealed 12th May 1876. Under Authority PC/TM/173. Pattern No.7589 (Fig.763). They became the 5th Battlion in 1881 being renumbered 4th May 1882. They did not adhere strictly to Regulations as is illustrated by an Order, 21st January 1889, Horse Guards. 'The Star of St. Patrick on the collar of the Officers mess jacket must be discontinued, the grenade with the Castle of Inniskilling must be worn'.

The Londonderry Light Infantry Militia

Collar badges in white-metal were sealed 10th January 1876. These were similar to the brass collar badges worn by the 27th Foot (Fig.764). The Regiment became the 4th Battalion in 1881. Converted in 1882 to 9th Brigade, North Irish Division RA, later Londonderry RGA (Militia).

Fig.754

Fig.755

Fig.756

Fig.757

Fig.758

Fig.759

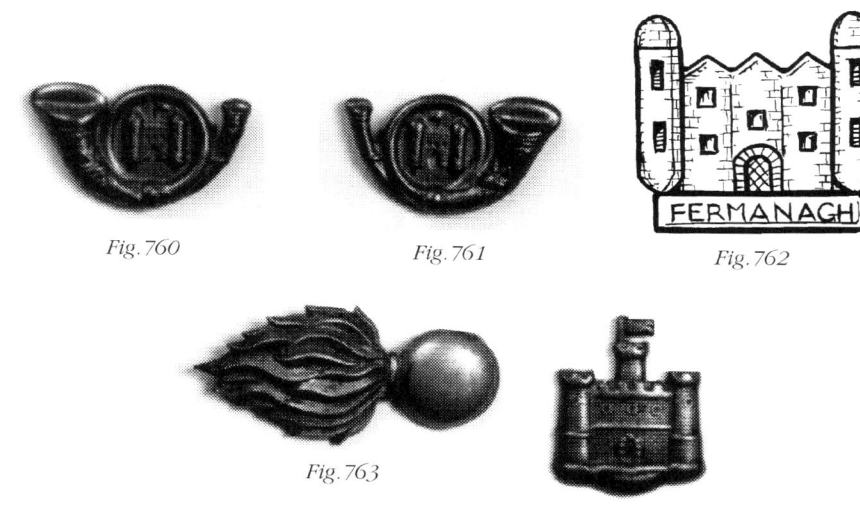

Fig.760

Fig.761

Fig.762

Fig.763

Fig.764

The Prince of Wales's Own Donegal Militia

Raised as such in 1793, the Prince of Wales's crest and motto were in general use by the Regiment when collar badges were sealed 24th May 1877. For other ranks in white-metal the 'ICH DIEN' scrolls were distinctive, being long and almost horizontal (Line drawing Fig.765). The Regiment became the 6th Battalion in 1881, being renumbered 5th in 1882.

Fig.765

Territorial Army

The 5th (Territorial) Battalion was formed in 1947 and wore the same collar badges as the Regular battalions, both Officers, other ranks, and pipers. The Battalion later became 'A' (Royal Inniskilling Fusiliers) Coy, 4th (Vol) Bn., Royal Irish Rangers, North Irish Militia, but continued to wear the same badge

General

Officers' collar badges face both ways as do the other ranks in gilding-metal. All the ones noted in bi-metal and anodised do not face. When facing, they are worn with the flag flying inwards towards the collar opening.

The Regiment amalgamated 1st July 1968 with The Royal Ulster Rifles and The Royal Irish Fusiliers to form The Royal Irish Rangers (27th Inniskilling, 83rd and 87th).

Sgt Major Gambrill of the 1/11th Regiment of Foot, c. 1877

HISTORY OF THE BRITISH ARMY INFANTRY COLLAR BADGE

The Gloucestershire Regiment

Pre 1881
The 28th (North Gloucestershire) Regiment of Foot

On 23rd May 1873 a Major Newry decreed, 'The Sphinx will be worn by the NCOs and men on the collar of the tunic and kersey from this date'. Authority had been received 16th July 1872, but the badge, Pattern No.9306, had only been sealed 1st May 1873. The approved design was a large female Sphinx with long neck, square cut mantle top and with tail rising up over the body the finial facing towards the head; below, a tablet inscribed "EGYPT". In brass. (Figs.766, 767 show a facing pair.)

After the removal of the rank badges to the shoulder in 1880, Officers wore the same but in embroidered metal thread (Fig.768). A similar badge to the mens' pattern but in silver has also been noted (Fig.769).

The 61st (South Gloucestershire) Regiment of Foot

By an Authority 16th July 1872 the Regiment also wore the Sphinx/Egypt badge as their first collar badge, but of a different design to those worn by the 28th. Sealed 16th June 1873, Pattern No.9309 was also a female Sphinx but smaller, with rounded head and tail lying alongside the body. In brass. (The central part of Fig.778 shows the design.) On 15th May 1878, the Regiment was directed to assimilate their collar badges to those worn by the 28th Regiment, and from that date the two Regiments wore the same collar badges, up to amalgamation in 1881.

There is also a different pattern badge in gilt worn by Warrant Officers when the Regiment was in India (Fig.770).

The Sphinx/Egypt badge was awarded to both Regiments for their services in the Egyptian Campaign 1801. Authorised 6th July 1802.

Post 1881

After amalgamation in 1881 the new Regiment, The Gloucestershire Regiment, received confirmation on 21st October to continue wearing Pattern No.9306. However, Messrs. Smith & Wright had submitted a design for a new collar badge, and after some 'revising' by Horse Guards it was decided on 22nd December to adopt the new Sphinx/Egypt badge, 'but in a combination of gilding metal and white metal'. Presumably the tablet would have been in gilding-metal and the Sphinx in white-metal. But, although nothing is recorded, there must have been further 'revision', for when the new pattern with rounded head and different direction of the tail was sealed 22nd February 1882, Pattern No.10128 was in white-metal only (Fig.771).

When the new field service cap was introduced 14th July 1896, the directive was, 'Old pattern as for collar', and it was not until 1898 that a new pattern was requested to be cut from new dies. This was Pattern No.10128a, sealed 21st March 1898. Similar to the one worn pre 1881 with square top mantle (Fig.772).

Fig.766

Fig.767

Fig.768

Fig.769

Fig.770

Fig.771

Fig.772

124

THE GLOUCESTERSHIRE REGIMENT

Curiously, the 'pair' on the sealed pattern card are somewhat different from one another! Since that date the design has altered slightly according to the various manufacturers, long and short necks, rounded and square heads, plain and dimpled grounds to the tablet, and the latter with and without borders. One notable sphinx variant has the flank deeply incised and rather skeletal legs (Fig.773). Latterly they were issued with single lug fastening, and finally in silver anodised aluminum (Fig.774). Whether this final issue was ever worn by the Regular battalion is doubtful as on 12th December 1961 a new design, Pattern No.18526 in silver a/a was sealed. A smaller Sphinx / Egypt was now lodged within a spray of laurel leaves (Fig.775). Authorised by WO letter 54/Inf/8785 (WODG) - 'All ranks to wear collar badges as worn by Officers on their No.1 Dress'.

Blackened gilding-metal collar badges are known and believed to have been worn by cyclists (Fig.776).

The badges shown in (Figs.772/3 & 775) were worn when the Regiment was part of the Wessex Brigade, the former two 1958-1961, the latter 1961 until the end of the Brigade system.

The laurel wreath commemorates the celebrated feat of arms by the 28th at the Battle of Alexandria, 1801.

The 1883 Dress Regulations describe the Officers' collar badge as, 'In dead gilt metal on two twigs of laurel, the Sphinx over Egypt'. This was a female Sphinx with tail lying correctly alongside the body, the laurel twigs of four veined leaves each. The twigs being looped at their junction (Fig.777). A cast collar badge with solid back was made in India. A later pattern shows a different design of female Sphinx, one central vein to the leaves, and with a double tie to the twigs (Fig.778). Also noted is a male Sphinx type with five leaves to each laurel twig (Fig.779). A Regimental photograph taken in 1904 at Lucknow, depicts a group of Officers, including Lieut-Col. Capel Currie, wearing just such a pair of badges on his frock coat.

These gilt collar badges were worn on the full dress tunic up to 1914, on special parades and occasions thereafter, and on the blue substitute full dress and patrol jacket up to the early post WWII period. A much smaller version was introduced for No.1 Dress c.1946 (Fig.780). Worn until 1961.

The 1902 Dress Regulations describe the collar badge for the Service Dress, 'As for tunic collar, with scroll as for forage cap'. In bronze sealed 21st May 1903, a male Sphinx, five veined leaves to each twig (Fig.781). A thinner, male sphinx pattern, die struck rather than die-cast is thought to have been in use during WWI. A later pattern had a female sphinx (Fig.782). There

Fig.773

Fig.774

Fig.775

Fig.776

Fig.777

Fig.778

Fig.779

Fig.780

Fig.781

Fig.782

HISTORY OF THE BRITISH ARMY INFANTRY COLLAR BADGE

Fig. 783

Fig. 784

Fig. 785

Fig. 786

Fig. 787

Fig. 788

were the usual variations in leaves, veins ties etc. Some had berries between the laurel leaves at the top and at the end of the leaves.

All patterns have been noted in polished form and were worn on the khaki drill. Some even had 'official blessing', RHQ quote a period, 27th July 1927 to 30th June 1934. Though all the above have the tail lying correctly alongside the body, one noted variant, in pale bronze, displays a male sphinx with tail rising over the body with the finial facing towards the rear. It has a different design of nine laurel leaves either side and is thought to have been in use in Egypt c.1930 on the KD dress.

All the above bronze collar badges were worn until 1932 when an entirely different new pattern was introduced. This was at the request of the Regiment who wished to wear their existing badges but without the scroll.

Although their request was not officially granted until W.O. letter 19th May 1932 under Authority 54/Inf/6830, photographs show them being worn as early as 1929. Again there were the usual variations, including both male and female sphinxes (Figs.783, 784). A later pattern, No. 30222, was sealed 3rd October 1977 (Fig.785).

From 12th December 1961, the smaller design of other ranks collar badge, but in silver plate, was worn on No. 1 Dress (Fig.786). They are also to be found in a 'greyish' silver plate with one central lug fitting with a hole in the centre. These are made in Pakistan.

For Mess Dress, the 1891 Dress Regulations record the collar badge as, 'The Sphinx over Egypt upon two twigs of laurel in dead gilt'. The 1st Battalion adopted a new design of mess dress in 1897, which they first wore in Calcutta. Collar badges were not worn. The 1900 Edition mentions collar badges for mess dress as being the same as for tunic collar, 'but in embroidery'. These were officially approved in 1899 with silver embroidery on a white backing, amended in the 1911 issue by adding, 'but smaller'. Modern ones worn from c.1980 are in gold thread on a dark blue cloth backing, with the tail of the sphinx rising incorrectly over the body (Fig.787).

Militia
Royal South Gloucestershire Light Infantry Militia
Collar badges in white-metal for wear on the other ranks tunic and frock collars were sealed 1st August 1877, Auth. PC/SGM/170. This was Pattern No.8935, a three-looped ribboned bugle with cords, tassels and ribbon ends (Fig.207). Worn in FPs with the bugle facing outwards from the collar opening. Officers wore similar but in silver plate. The Regiment became the 3rd Battalion in 1881.

Royal North Gloucestershire Militia
Collar badges in white-metal for wear by other ranks were deposited at the Army Clothing Department pattern room 14th July 1879. This was the Royal Crest but with a crown of pre-Restoration design (Fig.788). Officers wore similar but in silver. Worn in facing pairs with the lion facing inwards towards the collar opening. The Regiment became the 4th Battalion in 1881.

After 1881, the Militia Battalions initially opted to maintain their silver lace, accordingly their Sphinx/Egypt badges were in silver or silver plate. A photograph of the 3rd Battalion c.1897, shows the Officers wearing an other ranks pattern of collar badge, presumably in silver. From 1902 a bronze 'M' was worn below the Service Dress collar badge.

Rifle Volunteer Corps, Volunteer, Territorial Force & Territorial Army Battalions
The battalion strength unit 1st Gloucestershire (City of Bristol) Rifle Volunteer Corps, was designated 1st (City of Bristol) Volunteer Battalion in 1883. There is no evidence to indicate that collar badges were worn by the Rifle Volunteers.

THE GLOUCESTERSHIRE REGIMENT

The consolidated battalion 2nd Gloucestershire Rifle Volunteer Corps nominated in 1881 was designated 2nd Volunteer Battalion in 1883. Again there is no evidence of RV collar badges.

The 3rd Volunteer Battalion was raised in Bristol only in 1900. So far there is no evidence that the other ranks of the Volunteer Battalions wore collar badges. When Service Dress was introduced in 1902, Volunteer Officers wore the same bronze collar badges as their Regular counterparts, but with a blank tablet below the sphinx. All the usual variants have been noted, male and female patterns are shown (Figs. 789, 790). Photographs taken in 1906 and 1908 show Volunteer Officers wearing the Regulars' (i.e. with Egypt) badges and with a small silver 'V' below.

When the Active Service Volunteer Company (1900-01) formed from the 1st and 2nd Volunteer Battalions returned to Britain from South Africa, they were wearing the Regulars' white-metal pattern collar badge on their slouch hats. This head-dress was retained for some time for undress wear, with NCOs wearing the same collar badge but with a blackened finish. The other ranks white-metal collar badge was also worn on the slouch hat by mounted Officers of the 1st Battalion during the Boer War; worn above the other ranks shoulder title.

After 1908, other ranks of the 4th & 6th Battalions wore a white-metal female sphinx with rising tail and blank tablet collar badge on their full dress tunics (Fig.791). Other ranks of the 5th Battalion wore similar but in blackened gilding-metal, emphasising their former Rifles status. Officers of the 4th & 6th Battalions wore similar badges to the Regulars, in gilt but with blank tablets (1908-1914) (Fig.792). Officers of the 5th Battalion wore Rifles pattern full dress, and did not wear collar badges.

On Service Dress after 1908, Officers of the 4th & 6th Battalions wore the same badges as before but sometimes with a separate 'T' below (Fig.793). The badges of the 5th Battalion Officers had a blackened finish. Regular battalion collar badges were gradually introduced after WWI, though photographs indicate that some Officers clung to their distinctive designs for a considerable time afterwards.

All Band Sergeants wore the Officers' pattern collar badge.

WWI Battalions
13th (Forest of Dean) Battalion
This pioneer battalion wore the usual crossed rifle and pick collar badges (Fig.147). They formed part of Kitcheners' Army in WW1.

Other badges
Often thought to be a collar badge (Fig.794) in both white-metal and with blackened finish, a female sphinx with blank tablet and South Africa 1900-02 below, was in fact worn by the 2nd Volunteer Battalion c.1903-08 on the field service cap, and on the Officers peaked cap. Often on a circular red cloth backing.

General
As can be seen there are many varieties of Sphinx/Egypt badges, but they were all worn in facing pairs, the Sphinx facing inwards towards the collar opening.

Under the Government's Options for Change policy, 23rd July 1991, it was announced that The Gloucestershire Regiment was to merge with The Duke of Edinburgh's Royal Regiment (Berkshire and Wiltshire). This merger has taken place and the new Regiment is The Royal Gloucestershire Berkshire and Wiltshire Regiment.

Fig.789

Fig.790

Fig.791

Fig.792

Fig.793

Fig.794

The Worcestershire Regiment

Pre 1881
The 29th (Worcestershire) Regiment of Foot

Authorised to wear collar badges by Authority PC/Infy/Gen/111, 16th July 1872, the Regiment adopted the brass Imperial crown as their first collar badge for non-commissioned ranks (Fig.333). First worn in 1873. This was short lived as in the same year a new pattern was authorised, an eight-pointed rayed star, slightly elongated, centrally a Garter Proper enclosing the numerals '29' upon a solid centre. In brass (Fig.795). A further change took place later that year when the centre was voided, thus highlighting the numerals. Additionally, a red cloth backing was worn behind the numerals. Authorised by Horse Guards 12th August 1873 and worn 1874-1882 (Fig.796). The origin of the star is not definite, but it is believed that when Colonel Farrington of the Coldstream Regiment of Foot Guards raised the Regiment in 1694, he introduced the Garter Star to symbolise his link with the two Regiments. Certainly the eight-pointed star was an old badge of the 29th, and the 'Worcester Star' with the same format was adopted as the other ranks' second pattern glengarry badge in 1879.

Though Officers removed their rank badges to the shoulder in 1880 no collar badge was worn prior to 1881.

The 36th (Herefordshire) Regiment of Foot

By the same authority of 1872 the 36th adopted in 1873 the brass Imperial crown for the other ranks first collar badge. Again short lived for a new pattern was adopted later that year. The Royal Crest in brass was worn in facing pairs until 1882. The lion facing inwards towards the collar opening (Figs.797, 798). This was an old badge of the Regiment and was certainly in use on the shoulder belt plates from 1800. No badges for Officers have been noted 1880-1881.

Post 1881

The Regiments came together in 1881 to form the 1st and 2nd Battalions of The Worcestershire Regiment respectively. Both battalions continued to wear their old collar badges until 1882, when a new design, Pattern No.10127, was sealed 22nd February. A crowned lion superimposed upon an eight-pointed rayed star. In gilding-metal (Fig.799). By way of distinction the 2nd Battalion wore a gilding-metal '2' below (Fig.800). The star part of the badge was identical to part of the other ranks helmet plate centre. Perhaps because of its rather ill-balanced appearance, it was later replaced by one approved 12th December 1882. Not sealed until 23rd October 1883, made by Firmins, Pattern No.10314 carried the following caveat, 'The stores of the old pattern are to be issued in the ordinary way'. The first pattern is certainly a rare badge.

The replacement pattern again in gilding-metal was still a squarish shaped star but better balanced. Upon the star the Garter Proper while within an incorrect crowned lion passant guardant (Fig.801). An uncrowned version is known (Fig.802). As neither the 29th nor 36th were entitled to this style of lion badge, another change took place in 1884. In gilding-metal a larger squarer eight pointed star, the Garter Proper as before but with the Lion correctly shown as having all four feet on the ground, but uncrowned. Across the bottom star point a scroll inscribed 'FIRM' (Fig.803). The first time that this distinction appeared on the collar badge, a descendant honour of the 36th; though the origin is obscure two

THE WORCESTERSHIRE REGIMENT

theories prevail. In 1810, the CO of the 36th made a statement that to his certain knowledge, the motto had been borne by the Regiment since 1773. The other is that Lord Stair, the then C-in-C, personally saw the 36th distinguish themselves most conspicuously at the battle of Lauffeld, Flanders, 22nd July 1747, in recognition of which he permitted them to adopt his own family motto, 'FIRM'.

Following a submission from the Regiment 1st October 1890 for the Royal approval and signature, the CO received a reply from Horse Guards, 17th October advising him that HM had approved new pattern badges for the Regiment. One of the principal alterations was the granting of a correctly shaped Garter star. A new standard pattern of collar badge was demanded 25th February 1891, 'in lieu of pattern 10314', and the new Pattern, No.3151 was sealed 15th August 1891. The new elongated star still carried the circular Garter Proper and Lion within but this time with a voided centre. A scroll inscribed 'FIRM' across the bottom of the star. All in gilding-metal (Fig.804). This collar badge, with the lion facing left was worn on the field service cap up to the introduction of a new cap in May 1897.

Renewal of the standard pattern was demanded 18th April 1898, to be cut from new dies. Presumably there was little liaison with the manufacturers because the resulting badge, Pattern No.3151a had a solid centre and crowned Lion (Fig.805). This was quickly rectified with a new voided centre badge with uncrowned Lion, sealed 26th September 1899. These were worn until 1923 with minor variations according to the manufacturer. The main difference was in the size, Fig.805 being 22mm x 25mm, while the example in Figure 806 is 26mm x 32mm.

A new design of cap and collar badges were authorised 20th April 1923, under Authority 54/Inf/5135/P501. The new pattern of collar badge being No.3737 and made in gilding-metal and white-metal. The star in white-metal and the now oval Garter Proper in gilding-metal; the Lion was in a semi-solid centre, once more crowned and this time standing on a tablet inscribed 'FIRM', in white-metal (Fig.807). Latterly issued with the single lug and plate fastener, and with the centre fully voided, (Fig.808). These were used as a guide for the gold/silver anodised version. Although an Order No 6441 dated 22nd December 1954 authorised anodised badges, Pattern No.19243 was not sealed until 3rd February 1964, under Authority 54/Inf/8791, 'to supercede pattern 3737'. The sealed pattern carries a later annotation, 'Worcestershire - 'C' (Derbyshire Foresters) Coy, 'E' (Nottingham and Sherwood Foresters) Coy, and 3rd Vols.' This pattern (Fig.809) follows exactly Pattern No.3737, but there also exists a smaller rejected design (Fig.810). The correct design was worn up until amalgamation in 1970.

Fig.800

Fig.801

Fig.802

Fig.803

Fig.804

Fig.805

Fig.806 *Fig.807* *Fig.808*

Fig.809 *Fig.810*

HISTORY OF THE BRITISH ARMY INFANTRY COLLAR BADGE

Fig.811

Fig.812

Fig.813

Fig.814

Fig.815

For the Officers, the first pattern supplied by Messrs. Cater & Co. on 28th November 1881, described in the 1883 Dress Regulations. 'In silver, on a silver eight pointed star, the Garter pierced with the motto, HONI SOIT QUI MAL Y PENSE; the ground of blue enamel. The Lion in gilt metal within the Garter, on a ground of blue enamel. Below the Garter, a scroll, in gilt metal, inscribed, "FIRM". This collar badge is clearly shown in the Gaunt pattern book annotated 'Oct. 1881'. The star consists of 32 rays, the Lion is uncrowned and standing on a torse, and with the Motto fretted it stands out well against the blue enamel. 'FIRM' is on a tri-part scroll, and the whole effect is most pleasing, a triumph of the badge maker's art. (Figures 811, 812 show a facing pair.) Also worn on the mess jacket. This pattern changed slightly c1883 when frosted silver replaced the blue enamel sections, and the 'FIRM' scroll became curved. (Figure 813 shows a fretted Garter though solid examples are known.) Worn until c.1890, although the 1888 Dress Regulations are already stating, 'on a black velvet ground'. In 1890 the elongated star design was adopted the badge being described in the 1891 Edition, 'On a silver eight pointed star, in gilt metal, the Garter with motto; within the Garter, in silver the Lion pierced on a black velvet ground. Below the garter, in gilt metal, a scroll inscribed, 'FIRM'. These were worn until 1923 and as might be expected over such a period there are many variations, voiding and non-voiding between the scrolls and the Garter, and also in the shape of the star. The earliest examples are to be found with blue enamel backing to the Lion (officially incorrect) (Fig.814). A very odd specimen has the Garter and scroll in bronze (Fig.815). Types having the black velvet backing soon replaced the blue enamel variety.

When the roll collar mess jacket was introduced in 1896, badges similar to those worn on the Officers forage cap 1881-1897 were authorised, an embroidered star with gilt fretted Garter and silver Lion, and a separate embroidered 'FIRM' scroll below.

A curious badge appears in the Gaunt pattern book, and is annotated, '29/36 Worcesters - Officers collar - Hawkes Aug 27 1897'. No metals are quoted but is almost certainly in silver and gilt. The one illustrated (Fig.816) has blue enamel backing to the uncrowned Lion and the usual two lug fasteners. The size is identical to the then recently introduced Officers' forage cap, and although they do appear in facing pairs, there is no extant authority or mention of them in Dress Regulations; be that as it may, the ones noted definitely show signs of wear!

In 1923, a new pattern of collar badge was authorised. This was described in Dress Regulations as , "On an eight pointed elongated silver star of forty-eight rays, the Garter, oval shaped, in gilt or gilding metal. Within the Garter, in silver, on a pierced ground upon a pedestal inscribed 'FIRM", the Lion of the Royal Crest, in pairs'. For tunic and mess dress collar, sealed 20th April 1923. (Fig.817). Although 'the Lion of the Royal Crest' is specifically mentioned, there are some with an uncrowned Lion (Fig.818). Worn as stated and latterly on the No.1 Dress, indeed they were still in use at the time of the 1970 amalgamation.

When full dress was phased out in the 1930s, an all-silver version of the above was also in use. Regimental Dress Regulations record:

D. Mess Dress. Jacket facings of emerald green poplin silk of regimental shade, jacket of scarlet cloth, embroidered shoulder badges of rank and silver collar badges.

Fig.816

Fig.817

Fig.818

Fig.819

E. Undress. Jacket, regulation blue serge patrol jacket, cuffs slit with buttonholes. Silver collar badges.
F. Review Order. Jacket, khaki (Spinners No.1 Stockport). Pair of polished silver collar badges of regimental device, Lions facing inwards.
J. Mess Dress. During hot weather, a white drill mess jacket is worn. The lapels are eyeletted to take silver collar badges.

For the 1902 Service Dress, the Officers collar badge is described as, 'As for tunic collar, with scroll as for forage cap'. In bronze (Fig.819). As with many other Regiments, these were considered too large for the collar and were made smaller and modified well before WWI. Numerous varieties have been recorded concerning size and shape of star, voiding and non-voiding of the centre, and indeed the overall size of the badge. (Figs.820 to 824 illustrate some of these many differences.) Officially polished down and worn in the khaki drill, this pattern extended until 1923.

The bronze star only, was also worn. These were not broken off parts, but are well made complete badges. There appears to be no official authorisation or mention of them in Dress regulations, but a collection of photographs taken in 1906 clearly shows them in use. In 1914 another group picture shows no less a person than the Adjutant of the 2nd Battalion wearing such badges, so the badges must have had the battalion's blessing at least (Figs.825, 826).

In 1923, the shape of the Garter changed from round to oval and "FIRM" was now placed on a tablet beneath the Lion, the title scroll was omitted (Fig.827). This is confirmed in the 1934 Dress Regulations, 'As for tunic'.

One bronze badge that remains a mystery is a 'hybrid', the post-1923 star with oval Garter and "FIRM" beneath the crowned Lion, but on the pre-1923 "WORCESTERSHIRE" scroll (Fig.828). They face both ways and may well have been a trial pattern not subsequently adopted. The pair recorded are indeed in mint condition which does support the trial pattern theory.

Militia
1st and 2nd Worcestershire Militia
The county Militia Regiment formed in 1778, divided into two Regiments in 1874. Though the longstanding insignia of the Regiment was the Tower of Worcester Castle, there are no collar badges recorded for the Regiment in the Army Clothing Department Pattern room, and it is doubtful that any such badges were worn prior to 1881. In that year the two battalions became the 3rd and 4th Battalions

Fig.820

Fig.821

Fig.822

Fig.823

Fig.825

Fig.826

Fig.827

Fig.828

Fig.824

respectively. In 1890, upon the formation of two extra Regular battalions, they were renumbered 5th and 6th Battalions.

It was not uncommon for the Officers of Militia Battalions to wear the Regulars' badges but in reverse metals. Examples indicate that Worcestershire was no exception. However, the first Officers collar badge is believed to be unique, there being no Regular counterpart. A small, eight-pointed star with a scroll inscribed "FIRM" displacing the bottom three star points. Superimposed on the star, a round Garter Proper, and within a crowned Lion on a thin ground with a solid background. The star, Lion and centre in silver, the Garter and scroll in gilt (Fig.829). Worn c.1881-1883. The other ranks are believed to have worn similar but in blackened metal. After 1883, the Officers wore similar to the Regulars but in reverse metals (Fig.830, 831). The other ranks wore similar to the Regulars, but with the star in white-metal and the remainder in gilding-metal (Fig.832). Worn until c.1890. A very similar badge to Figure 829, but with different shaped gilt scroll and with the rest in silver, it is also thought to have Militia connections. The pattern has been noted on a Militia Officers' mess jacket c.1906 (Fig.833).

Rifle Volunteer Corps, Volunteer, Territorial Force & Territorial Army Battalions

The consolidated battalions, 1st and 2nd Worcestershire Rifle Volunteer Corps became the 1st and 2nd Volunteer Battalions, The Worcestershire Regiment in 1883. Collar badges prior to this date were not worn. The other ranks of the 1st Volunteer Battalion wore the same first pattern collar badge as per the Regulars but in white-metal. It appears in the Gaunt Pattern book annotated, 'Collar badge, Private V Bn., Oct 18 1887. S.Bros.' Senior NCOs wore the same badge but in silver plate.

The 2nd Volunteer Battalion carried on wearing Rifles pattern tunics and wore the same collar badge in blackened metal. In 1890, both battalions changed to the new pattern as per the Regulars, but maintaining their respective white-metal and blackened metal distinctions. Worn until 1908. Photographs taken at the turn of the century show cyclists of the 1st VB wearing the white-metal collar badges on their caps, as well as on the collar.

It was unusual for Volunteer Officers with former Rifle connections to wear collar badges, but from 1883 the Officers of both Volunteer battalions wore similar badges to the Regulars, but with the star, Garter, and Lion in silver, and only the scroll in gilt (Fig.834). These were worn until 1890 when they again wore similar to the Regular other ranks pattern but in silver. Worn until 1908, often with a black cloth backing to the voided centre.

In 1908, the two battalions became the 7th and 8th (TF) Battalions respectively, gradually adopting the same badges as the Regular battalions, often with a separate 'T' below their bronze collar badges, on Service Dress.

A questionnaire sent to the Regiment in 1914 was returned stating that the other ranks of the 3rd (Regular) Battalion, 7th and 1st/8th (TF) Battalions did not wear collar badges at that time.

WWI Battalions

14th (Severn Valley Pioneer) Battalion and 17th (Pioneer) Battalion both wore the usual crossed rifle and pick collar badge. Photographs of the 14th Battalion show them being worn with the pick facing inwards.

Fig.829

Fig.830

Fig.831

Fig.832

Fig.833

Fig.834

Fig.835

Home Guard

Pattern No.16578, sealed 8th July 1954 under Authority 9/HG/363, in respect of a silver and gilt collar badge for wear by Officers of the Worcestershire Home Guard (Fig.835).

Schools – Malvern College O.T.C.

Officers of the OTC wore on their Service Dress the bronze collar badges of the Worcestershire Regiment with a bronze 'T' below.

Unidentified

A large star, round Garter and Motto superimposed with crowned Lion on a torse within. Solid centre "FIRM" scroll on bottom point of the star, all in gilt metal (Fig.836). The ones noted show the Lion facing left only, so it is possibly an unrecorded headdress badge. A corresponding other ranks version in brass has been noted (Fig.837).

Other badges

The usual pattern of the other ranks gilding-metal star collar badge worn pre 1923, but with the star and Lion in white-metal and the Garter and scroll in gilding-metal. The FIRM scroll however reads NULLI SECUNDUS, and pertains to the 6th Hauraki Regiment, New Zealand (Fig.838). A later version sees NULLI SECUNDUS replaced by the Maori KIA HAMA (Fig.839). Though there is no affiliation between the Regiments, it is known that a Sergeant of the Worcestershires was sent to new Zealand in 1910 to assist in the reorganisation of the country's military forces.

General

Unlike many other Regiments, quite a lot of material is available regarding the insignia worn by the Regiment; however, some of the information is conflicting both between the Regimental sources and those of the Dress regulations and other official data. Despite the many varieties of size and design, the one consistent factor is that all badges were worn in facing pairs, the Lion facing inwards.

On 28th February 1970, the Regiment amalgamated with The Sherwood Foresters to become *The Worcestershire and Sherwood Foresters Regiment (29th/45th Foot)*.

Fig.836

Fig.837

Fig.838

Fig.839

The East Lancashire Regiment

Pre-1881
The 30th (Cambridgeshire) Regiment of Foot

By an Authority 16th July 1872, the Regiment's first collar badge for the other ranks was a female Sphinx, the tail rising up over the body, resting upon the Roman numerals 'XXX', all over a scroll inscribed "CAMBRIDGE". Pattern No.9315 was sealed 15th August 1873. In brass, they were worn in facing pairs, the Sphinx facing inwards (Figs.840, 841). The badge was similar to the central part of the other ranks current glengarry badge. After 1880, Officers wore the same badge in embroidered metal thread. The Sphinx was awarded to the Regiment for distinguished service at the Battle of Alexandria, 1801. Authorised 6th July 1802.

The 59th (2nd Nottinghamshire) Regiment of Foot

Authorised 16th July 1872 the Regiment adopted the brass Imperial crown as the other ranks' collar badge, which they wore right through to the 1881 amalgamation (Fig.333).

This is officially recorded, but it has been suggested that this badge was replaced by a 'laurel wreath' badge some time before 1881. This was not a special honour but had in the past appeared on some of the Regiment's insignia. Such a badge in brass (Fig.842), is said to have been removed from the tunic collar of a soldier of the 59th. If it was worn, it was not with any written official approval, and bearing in mind the shallow depth of the pre-1881 tunic collar, the soldier must have suffered some laceration to the chin!

Post 1881

Upon amalgamation in July 1881, the new Regiment was initially titled The West Lancashire Regiment. This was soon amended to The East Lancashire Regiment. A new pattern collar badge was sealed 20th January 1882 with the Army Clothing Department pattern room journals recording, 'to replace brass 9315 for 30th; 59th wore the crown'. This does tend to confirm that the 59th did only wear the Imperial crown up to 1881. The new badge, Pattern No.9977 was a double 'Rose of Lancaster' with five outer and five inner petals, all with sepals in between, and a dotted stamen (Fig.843). This pattern was in what can best be described as 'yellow brass'. It was worn on the white collar of the scarlet tunic until 1897, when a renewal of the standard pattern was demanded. Pattern No.9977a was cut from new dies and sealed 7th December 1897. A 'renewal pattern' the only difference was in the colour of the metal, being a somewhat darker gilding metal. The first pattern badge had also been worn on the field cap up to the introduction of the new field cap in October 1897. The 1882 sealed pattern also illustrated how the badge should be worn on the collar, with an outer petal at the top, and a sepal in between two petals at the bottom. The pattern remained constant up to amalgamation in 1958 and naturally over such a long period minor production variances occurred, some 'flatter' than others, some with the centre standing proud, and some with plain centres. Although some centres have worn with wear, others were deliberately polished to give a plain centre, this accomplished by the 'old sweats' to emphasize their long service! Warrant Officers and other senior NCOs are said to have worn the same pattern badge but with the outer petals in white-metal (Fig.844); but written or photographic evidence is lacking. Pattern No.9977a was used as a guide for the later anodised version, and the official

Fig.840

Fig.841

Fig.842

Fig.843

Fig.844

Master sealed pattern actually states, 'To supercede pattern 9977a'. This is Pattern No.19242 sealed 3rd February 1964, under Authority 54/Inf/8858. It is ironical that the badge is upside down! There is also a sealed pattern (not the Master pattern) dated 24th October 1956 headed, 'East Lancashire Regiment T/A' which also relates to the gold anodised rose collar badge. Both have a single lug fastening but differ very slightly in design. Figures 845 and 846 show the 1956 and 1964 sealed patterns. Neither of these patterns was worn by the Line battalion as amalgamation took place prior to issue. The 1978 and 1982 Catalogue of Clothing and Necessaries record the Rose of Lancaster in gold anodised for wear by 'A' (East Lancs) Coy, 2nd Bn, The Lancashire Volunteers.

It is very easy to confuse these collar badges with those worn as part of the shoulder title by the Coldstream Guards, the latter having square lug fasteners, which is the only difference.

The 1883 Dress Regulations describe the Officers collar badge for wear on the tunic collar as, 'The Rose of Lancaster in red and gold embroidery'. The 1902 Edition adds 'For Mess Jackets'. There is a slight change in the 1911 Edition, 'On red velvet in gold embroidery', confirmed in the 1934 Edition. At some time after this date, a small silver Sphinx inscribed Egypt was worn above the Rose, the latter being correspondingly smaller (Fig.847). On occasions the Sphinx only was worn (Fig.848). Worn on Nos. 1 and 3 Dress, the Sphinx facing inwards towards the collar opening. The Sphinx is well illustrated in the Gaunt Pattern book, and the double collar badge is clearly shown in the photograph of Liuet-Colonel C.W. Griffin MC, the last CO of the 1st Battalion, The East Lancashire Regiment (Plate 13).

Also in early use on the scarlet frock was the Rose of Lancaster in gilt, later replaced by a smaller pattern (Figs.849, 850).

The 1902 Dress Regulations describe the collar badge for the Service Dress 'As for tunic collar with scroll as for forage cap, in bronze'. Sealed 1st December 1903. There were more than a few varieties of this badge, particulary regarding the structure of the Rose, the title scroll and their junction points. Some petals were rounded at the edges, others not, and others had no veins on the petals (Figs. 851-854). The same badges but polished down to the gilding-metal were worn on the khaki drill. The badges also appear in all silver plate (Figs. 855-857). So far there is no conclusive evidence as to when these badges were worn or by whom; it is not impossible that the Officers of the 3rd (Militia) Battalion wore them on the full dress tunic at some time between 1881-1908. Also known in gilt, possibly

Fig.845

Fig.846

Fig.847

Fig.850

Fig.851

Fig.852

Fig.848

Fig.853

Fig.854

Fig.849

HISTORY OF THE BRITISH ARMY INFANTRY COLLAR BADGE

worn by WOs. Officers also wore the bronze Rose without the scroll (Fig.858). What may have been a trial pattern for the Regiment is shown in Figure 859, a smaller version of the Service Dress cap badge.

Silver plate facing pairs of Sphinxes inscribed "EGYPT" were also worn in the mess dress (Figs.860, 861), and a small silver plated Rose with green sepals is also thought to have been worn at some time, again on mess dress. (Fig.862)

Militia

Raised in 1853, The 5th Royal Lancashire Militia became the 3rd Battalion in 1881. The other ranks collar badge was sealed 21st November 1876, and took the form of white metal palm fronds, worn in facing pairs (Figs.863, 864). This was part of the design that appeared on the tunic button.

Rifle Volunteer Corps, Volunteer, Territorial Force & Territorial Army Battalions

The consolidated battalion 2nd Lancashire Rifle Volunteer Corps, formerly the 8th Administrative Battalion, though nominated in 1881, did not assume the title of 1st Volunteer Battalion until 1889. The other ranks of the VB wore similar collar badges to the Regular battalions, but in white-metal. The one shown (Fig.865) is a particularly large, early example.

The 2nd Volunteer Battalion was formed from the consolidated 3rd Lancashire Rifle Volunteer Corps, again only assuming the title in 1889. Both VBs were awarded the South Africa 1900-02 honour, and certainly the 2nd VB adopted a special pattern collar badge after 1903, adding the honour scroll to the Rose. Two types are known, both in white-metal. Figure 866 shows the Rose to be upside down, and then corrected (Fig.867). Officers wore similar but in silver plate. For the Officers Service Dress a more elaborate badge evolved, the usual title scroll under the Rose reading, "2 V.B. EAST LANCASHIRE". with an additional scroll below reading, "SOUTH AFRICA 1900-02". A separate bronze 'T' below (Fig.868 Line Drawing).

Fig.855

Fig.856

Fig.857

Fig.858

Fig.859

Fig.860

Fig.861

Fig.862

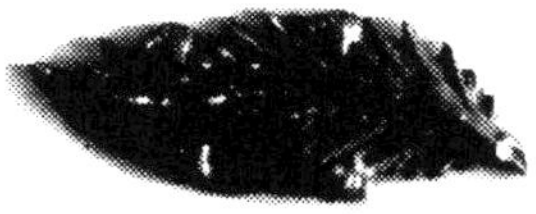

Fig.863

Fig.864

Fig.865

Fig.866

Fig.867

Fig.868

From c.1889, Officers had worn silver Roses in their full dress tunics, (Fig.869 for a large early pattern) but it is not impossible that a silver version of Fig.868 was used after 1903. Again, the silver Rose and East Lancashire scroll badges are possibilities.

In 1908, the two Battalions became the 4th and 5th (TF) Battalions respectively. These units and their successor TA Battalions gradually adopted the badges worn by the parent Battalions. 'A' and 'C' Companies, 4th Battalion wearing the smaller embroidered Rose below silver plated Sphinxes. These were worn on Nos 1 and 3 Dress. They also wore the same bronze Service Dress collar badges. Both types were sealed 24th October 1956.

Fig.869

WWI Service Battalions

11th (Service) Battalion, this unit known as the Accrington Pals Battalion was raised in 1914 and disbanded 20th November 1919; throughout their existence they wore the same collar badges as the Regular units.

General

Although the Rose of Lancaster was used throughout the Regiment's existence, they came in a large variety! Centres, petals and sepals all varying in shape and size, according to the various manufacturers interpretations of what a Rose of Lancaster should look like.

On 1st July 1958, The East Lancashire Regiment amalgamated with The South Lancashire Regiment (The Prince of Wales's Volunteers) to form The Lancashire Regiment (Prince of Wales's Volunteers). This Regiment was on the 25th March 1970 further amalgamated with The Loyal Regiment (North Lancashire) to form The Queen's Lancashire Regiment.

The East Surrey Regiment

Fig.870

Fig.871

Pre 1881
The 31st (Huntingdonshire) Regiment of Foot
Authorised 16th July 1872, Pattern No.9515 was the Regiment's first collar badge, sealed 6th October 1874, for wear by other ranks on the tunic and frock collar. In brass, the Imperial crown lodged within two laurel sprays (Fig.1028). An Officers example (1880-1881) is of the same format but 'darkened', perhaps originally gilt.

The 70th (The Surrey) Regiment of Foot
By the same Authority of 1872, the Regiment were to wear the brass Imperial crown collar badges (Fig.333). It is officially recorded that, 'In accordance with Regimental custom' they were being worn by all ranks on their white stand up collars when the Regiment was in India in 1876. Officers wore their rank badges on their collars until 1881.

Post 1881
The two Regiments came together in 1881 as The East Surrey Regiment, necessitating a new collar badge. The design submitted was a shield on which was the Arms of Guildford: "sable, on a mount vert a castle with two towers embattled, on each tower a spire; from the battlements of the castle, rising ,a tower triple towered or, the whole between two woolpacks in fesse argent, the base barry wavy of the last and azure, and over all in base a lion passant guardant, also or".

This blazon is recorded at the College of Arms, however the Coat of Arms frequently made use of and as it appears upon the Seals of the Town and the County Council of Surrey, differs in several points, agreeing with Burke in his 'General Armory', namely: 'Sable, on a mount vert a castle with two towers embattled, on each tower a spire, surmounted with a ball. From the battlements, between the towers a tower triple-towered all argent, and charged with an escutcheon, quarterly, of France and England; under the battlements of the castle two roses in fesse or, the port proper charged on the centre with a key and portcullised both gold, on the mount before the port a lion couchant guardant. On each side of the castle in fesse, a woolpack of the third paleways, the base of the field water proper.'

As can be seen, the Military sided with the College of Arms in this instance, but put a further charge upon the blazon, a shield bearing the Arms of Kingston-upon-Thames, 'Azure, three salmon naiant proper'. Thus was combined the general location of the new Territorial Regiment , and the precise headquarters of both the Line Regiment and the former 1st and 3rd Royal Surrey Militia Regiments, now allied to The East Surrey Regiment .

Pattern No.10191 was sealed 16th June 1882 and worn until 1894. Though officially in gilding-metal, the first issues were in a rich yellow brass metal (Fig.871). These were followed by the more standard darker gilding-metal. On 19th May 1894, "a new pattern was demanded to sample similar to that worn on the new pattern field service cap for Officers, but in gilding metal". The existing shield pattern badge was reduced in size and superimposed on an eight-pointed rayed star, the top point displaced by a flat topped QVC. Pattern No.4036 was sealed 1st August 1894 under Authority PC/2 E Surrey Regiment/796 (Fig.872). As

THE EAST SURREY REGIMENT

usual, stocks of the old pattern were to be exhausted before the new type could be issued. A pleasing amalgam this, the eight pointed star of both Militia Regiments and the Imperial crown of both Line Regiments.

Worn until 1903 when the KC version became necessary, Pattern No.4036a being sealed 6th April 1903, still in gilding-metal (Fig.873). Most of the KC versions have a voided crown. With the accession of Queen Elizabeth II in 1953, a further change was necessary, Pattern No.16570, sealed 6th December 1954 under Auth 54/Gen/321. Additionally, there was a change in metals, with the star and castle in white-metal and the shield and crown in gilding-metal (Fig.874). Worn until amalgamation in 1959. This would have been the guide for the anodised version, but they were not made. The KC version is known with a chrome finish, thought to have been worn by The Regimental Police in the mid 1950s, but its use was not official.

The Officers of the Regiment wore their first collar badges from mid-1882, recorded in the 1883 Dress Regulations as, 'The Arms of Guildford in silver on a shield in frosted gilt metal with burnished edges' (Fig.875). Strictly this is not correct, as no mention is made of the Arms of Kingston-upon-Thames. The early types were considerably larger than the other ranks version, later ones of a more similar size. Worn until 1894 when they were replaced with ones described as, 'On a bright cut silver star, the Arms of Guildford in silver on a shield in frosted gilt or gilding metal, with burnished edges, surmounted by a gilt or gilding metal crown'. These were to be worn on the tunic and scarlet frock (Fig.876). Note, still no mention of Kingston. This badge appears in the Gaunt Pattern books dated 2nd March 1896. The KC version was sealed 24th September 1903. Two slight variations are shown (Figs.877, 878). Replaced c.1954 with a QC version (Fig.879). Worn until amalgamation in 1959.

The first bronze collar badges for the Officers Service Dress were of forage cap badge size and format, the star and shield with a title scroll inscribed 'EAST SURREY' beneath. Sealed 24th September 1903, variants have voided and non voided crowns (Figs.880, 881). Worn on the stand up collars until 1913, and later on the flat lapels, however a smaller bronze badge was introduced in 1914, a slightly smaller star without the scroll (Figs.882, 883). There are economy examples of other ranks badges with a bronze finish. There is no mention of these in Dress Regulations and they were not worn after 1918.

Fig.872

Fig.873

Fig.874

Fig.875

Fig.876

Fig.878

Fig.879

Fig.880

Fig.881

Fig.882

Fig.883

Fig.877

Militia
1st Royal Surrey Militia

There is no definite record of the collar badges, if any, worn by this Regiment prior to 1881. It is possible that an eight-pointed rayed star, the top displaced by a QVC and with the Arms of Guildford superimposed on the star, all in white-metal, was worn.

3rd Royal Surrey Militia

Collar badges in white-metal were sealed 21st September 1876 for wear on the tunic and frock collars. Simply a QVC (Fig.884). A later pattern, introduction date not recorded, was based on that worn by the 2nd Royal Surrey Militia, a white-metal Garter type star, but with the strap left blank (Fig.885).

These Regiments became the 3rd and 4th Battalions in 1881. The Officers' badges post-1882 were as for the Regular battalions, but in reverse metals, a silver shield with castle etc. in gilt. Worn until 1894 when the crowned type was adopted, still in reverse metals and carried over into the KC period (Fig.886 shows an unusual variation). Most probably the other ranks wore white-metal versions of the Regulars' patterns.

Rifle Volunteer Corps, Volunteer, Territorial Force & Territorial Army Battalions
1st Surrey (South London) Volunteer Rifle Corps

The county's premier Rifle Corps was nominated in 1881 as a volunteer battalion, this unit maintained its title structure right through until 1908, when it became the 21st Battalion, The London Regiment. No collar badges have been recorded for this Corps throughout its existence.

The consolidated 3rd Surrey Rifle Volunteer Corps nominated in 1881 became the 2nd Volunteer Battalion, 1st December 1887. Their first collar badge was a white-metal version of the Regulars' shield only pattern (Fig.887). It appears in the Gaunt Pattern books dated 27th October 1887. Worn until 1894 upon the change of pattern to the crowned star pattern, still in white-metal. An official War Office pattern book shows these collar badges annotated, 'For 2 V B E Surreys' and 'as approved, Horse Guards WO 9th March 1896 under Authy V/2/31/23 from a specimen submitted by J & A Pearce & Co, 28 Floral Street, Covent Garden, London'. Following the change of Monarch a KC white-metal version was worn until 1908.

The Officers wore the corresponding patterns, as worn in the years 1882, 1894, and 1903 but in all silver or silver plate. The battalion became the 5th (TF) Battalion in 1908.

The old 2nd Administrative Battlion was consolidated in 1880 as the 5th Surrey Rifle Volunteer Corps, nominated in 1881, they became the 3rd Volunteer Battalion in 1887. They maintained their former 'Rifles' status by wearing the three patterns of Regulars collar badge with a blackened finish. Examples of all types are well recorded.

The majority of the Officers badges of this battalion bore reminders of the founder areas of the old Rifle Volunteers and of the current recruiting area. The item illustrated (Fig.888), though certainly worn as the Officers' busby boss badge and on the side hat, was possibly the first pattern collar badge, though no definite confirmation is forthcoming. A cross surmounted by a QVC with a blank tablet below. The end of each arm of the cross is inscribed with the name of a town in the area, "KINGSTON", "RICHMOND", "CHERTSEY", and "ESHER". In the centre of the cross, a circle inscribed, "THE EAST SURREY REGT. 3rd VOLUNTEER BATTN." Within this title circle the Arms of Guildford upon an eight-pointed star. In blackened silver plate. In 1908 they became the 6th (TF) Battalion, the unit continued to wear blackened versions of the standard collar badges. A variant of the KC pattern is recorded showing the star in silver, the KC and shield in gilt, and the castle blackened, most probably worn by this battalion at some time 1903-1914 (Fig.889).

Fig.884

Fig.885

Fig.886

Fig.887

Fig.888

Fig.889

Nominated in 1881, the consolidated 7th Surrey Rifle Volunteer Corps became the 4th Volunteer Battalion in 1887. The unit wore the same white-metal collar badges as the 2nd Volunteer Battalion. A photograph taken at Winchester in 1900, shows four NCOs of the Cyclist Section, and whereas three of them wear the crowned star pattern collars the fourth still wears the obsolete shield pattern badges. In 1908 this unit became the 23rd Battalion, The London Regiment.

A sealed pattern, annotated 'E. Surrey T/A', has the silver/gilt star with QC for wear on No.1, No.3 and Service Dress. Another sealed pattern 10th October 1956 has similar but in bi-metal for other ranks.

WWI Service Battalions
12th (Bermondsey) Service Battalion, The East Surrey Regiment

One of many such Service Battalions, this unit was raised 14th May 1915 by the personal effort of John Hart, the Mayor, and the Borough Council of Bermondsey. To mark the connection, War Office approval was received for members of the battalion to wear special collar badges bearing the Arms and Motto of the borough, granted by the College of Heralds in 1901. In gilding-metal for the other ranks and in bronze for the Officers. These and a special cap badge were both supplied and paid for by the Mayor.

Arms – 'Quarterly azure and gules, in chief a lion passant guardant supporting a crozier erect and flanked by two letters B, all gold; in the third quarter a battle axe erect, its haft encircled by a crown, both gold; and in the fourth an ancient three-masted ship of gold, its sails spread and pennons flying'.

Crest – 'On a wreath gold and azure, a lion passant guardant gules charged on the shoulder with a gold letter B and holding erect a gold crozier'.

Motto – 'Prosunt gentibus artes'. (Arts benefit the people.)

An heraldic exception was made with the manufacture of the collar badges, the 'crest' lions were made to face inwards (Figs.890, 891). The battalion was disbanded at Aldershot, 10th June 1919.

Other items

Three items that are sometimes thought to be collar badges do turn up quite regularly and need clarification. Figure 892 shows a large white-metal shield displaying the Arms of Guildford as used on the common Seal of the town. Sadly not a rare Volunteer Rifles or Volunteer battalion variant but an early badge of the Guildford Police. Figures 893 and 894 are in gilding-metal and silver respectively. They are the centres from the other ranks and Officers helmet plates, the former being detached from the title circle.

General

With the exception of those worn by the 12th (Bermondsey) Service Brigade, collar badges of the Regiment do not face.

The Regiment amalgamated with The Queen's Royal Regiment (West Surrey) to form The Queen's Royal Surrey Regiment, 14th October 1959.

Fig.890

Fig.891

Fig.892

Fig.893

Fig.894

The Duke of Cornwall's Light Infantry

Fig.895

Fig.896

Pre-1881
The 32nd (Cornwall) Light Infantry

The Coronet of the Duke of Cornwall (The Prince of Wales), the Arms of the Duchy, a black shield bearing 15 gold bezants, and the County Motto, 'One and All', have long been associated with the military units of the County.

It was curious therefore that the first collar badge authorised 16th July 1872 should display a Guelphic crown over the Arms and Motto. Adopted 30th June 1874 for wear by other ranks on the tunic collar, Pattern No.9526 was sealed 8th December 1874. In brass, there are two varieties, one completely solid the other voided between the Arms and elaborate Motto scroll (Fig.895). Worn until 1882.

There is no evidence that Officers wore collar badges prior to 1881.

The 46th (South Devonshire) Regiment of Foot

By an Authority 16th July 1872, the collar badge adopted for wear by the other ranks was the brass Imperial crown, Pattern No.9386 (Fig.333). Worn until 1882. Officers did not remove their rank badges from their collars until 1880 and did not wear collar badges prior to amalgamation.

Post 1881

The two Regiments were amalgamated July 1881 to form the 1st and 2nd Battalions, The Duke of Cornwall's Light Infantry. On 8th February 1882, a new collar badge Pattern No.10106 was sealed. Like many of the new Regiments, the D.C.L.I. adopted as their first collar badge the same device as worn in the middle of the other ranks' helmet plate centre. In this case a bugle horn with two crossed feathers upon it, superimposed upon the feathers, a castle. All in gilding-metal (Fig.896).

The Light infantry bugle horn had been a badge of the 32nd since their elevation to Light Infantry status in 1858, this a reward for their gallant defence of the Residency at Lucknow during the Indian Mutiny. The castle, sometimes described as 'a turreted archway' displayed two lookouts in each tower with a further five and a port in the central wall. This is said to represent the main gateway to Launceston Castle, Cornwall; an alternative interpretation suggests that it represents the Residency at Lucknow. The two red feathers were featured on insignia worn by the 46th Regiment. They commemorate the fierce actions fought by a special battalion of Light Companies (which included that of the 46th) during the American War of Independence. Singled out for retaliation by the Americans, the 'Light Bobs' responded by dyeing their hat feathers red as a distinguishing badge, to prevent the enemy withholding quarter from other British troops by mistake. This became the badge of these six companies throughout the war. As units were disbanded and broken up, only the Light Company of the 46th retained the distinction. Maintained on their headdress as a red feather, later a ball tuft, the honour was extended by Her Majesty's gracious permission to the whole of the Regiment when flank companies were abolished in 1858.

Though this splendid badge was retained on the helmet plates of both Officers and other ranks, it was very soon to change as a collar badge; on 27th July 1882 an Order was issued, 'In future to be the Arms of the County of Cornwall (as formerly worn by the 1st Bn. 32nd Regiment), Pattern No. 9526 but in gilding metal instead of brass. The badge approved for the Regiment 8th February 1882

THE DUKE OF CORNWALL'S LIGHT INFANTRY

viz. Pattern No.10106, bugle, castle and feather now becomes obsolete accordingly'.

The new pattern was 'demanded accordingly' 7th August 1882 and instructions in a letter 23rd September 1882 also 'enclosed the pattern of Officers' collar badges the design of which should be followed in future issues for NCOs and men'. This signed by the AAG Horse Guards. Further correspondence stated, 'the new pattern is to be put forward to follow the Officers' design but in gilding metal, and the regulation 7th August 1882 for similar badges following the OP9526 to be cancelled'. A pencil note records that the Officers' design was handed to the Pattern Room Keeper at Horse Guards 6th October 1882. (OP stood for Old Pattern.)

Correspondence 7th December 1882 under Ref. 61002/2598 included instructions that the new other rank's collar badge must have 'a coronet as on Officers' badge instead of a crown'. Pattern No.10283 was eventually sealed 1st February 1883. Variants include voided and non-voided scroll to shield types (Fig.897). The badge was further confirmed 27th November 1894 and it was not until 9th February 1898 that a renewal of the standard pattern was demanded, these to be cut from new dies. This was Pattern No.10283a, adopted 22nd April 1898 and sealed 3rd August 1899. Again in gilding-metal with the same overall design but with the top of the shield now straight instead of curved and with a different shaped coronet, wider and flatter than before. Pierced and non-pierced varieties are recorded (Fig.898). Also found in blackened form, possibly worn by Cyclists (Fig.899). A hybrid is known, incorporating the long shield and taller coronet of the second pattern, but with the straight top to the shield of the third pattern (Fig.900). Perhaps a trial pattern.

There is no evidence that the Regular battalions wore the medium-sized white-metal bugle horn and coronet with "CORNWALL" scroll as worn by the Territorial battalions, (Fig.913), but senior NCOs did wear a very small version of this format in white-metal on their patrol jackets c.1930-1932 (Fig.901). Warrant Officers wore the same in silver plate (Fig.902).

The 1883 Dress Regulations describe the Officers' collar badge as: 'In black enamel set in gilt metal, the badge of the County of Cornwall, surmounted by the Coronet, in gilt metal, of the Prince of Wales, as shown on His Royal Highness's Great Seal as Duke of Cornwall. On a scroll the motto One and All, pierced in gilt letters' (Fig.903). As with the other ranks' badge, the design changed in 1899 with the top of the shield losing its curve and the advent of a larger coronet (Fig.904).

The 1900 Edition records the same description apart from adding, 'or gilding metal' after 'gilt', and finishing with, 'On a ground of blue velvet'. This description was continued up to the 1934 Dress Regulations.

As with the other ranks there is a hybrid, curved top to the shield but with the wider larger coronet. Varieties of colour regarding the velvet backing have been noted. Dark blue, light blue, brown and red relate to the curved top patterns, whereas green has been noted for the straight top version. Others have been noted with the backplate (they are made in two parts) enamelled in green, light blue, dark blue, and red.

There is certainly no official explanation for these colour variances, but it is possible that they relate unofficially to the different battalions. If so, it would seem

Fig.897

Fig.898

Fig.899

Fig.900

Fig.901

Fig.902

Fig.903

Fig.904

HISTORY OF THE BRITISH ARMY INFANTRY COLLAR BADGE

Fig.905

Fig.906

Fig.907

Fig.908

likely that the red ones relate to the 2nd Battalion, recalling the feathers of the 46th Regiment. Probably worn as late as 1939.

For the Officers' Service Dress, 1902, collar badges were, 'As for forage cap. A bugle horn with strings surmounted by the Coronet; below the coronet a scroll inscribed "Cornwall". In bronze'. Worn with red cloth backing, in facing pairs (Fig.905). Normally die-cast, but some are found die-struck. Worn in the khaki drill polished down to the base metal (Fig.906). Worn until 1932 when on the 8th October a smaller version was sealed (Fig.907). Worn until the late 1960s by associated School Cadet Officers.

The same pattern in silver or silver plate was later worn on the Nos.1 & 3 Dress (Fig.908). The other ranks' pattern of collar badge is also found bronzed, perhaps worn as an alternative to the very large bugle type, or when supplies of the latter were unavailable (Fig.909).

Militia
Royal Cornwall Rangers, Duke of Cornwall's Own Rifles

As Rifles, it is highly unlikely that any collar badges were worn prior to 1881, when the Regiment became the 3rd Battalion. Blackened versions of the Regular battalions' collar badges have been noted, and it is possible that these were worn by the 3rd Battalion.

Rifle Volunteer Corps, Volunteer, Territorial Force & Territorial Army Battalions

The consolidated 1st Cornwall Rifle Volunteer Corps, nominated in 1881 was designated the 1st Volunteer Battalion in 1885. The unit continued to wear Rifles style uniform and did not wear collar badges. They became the 4th (TF) Battalion in 1908.

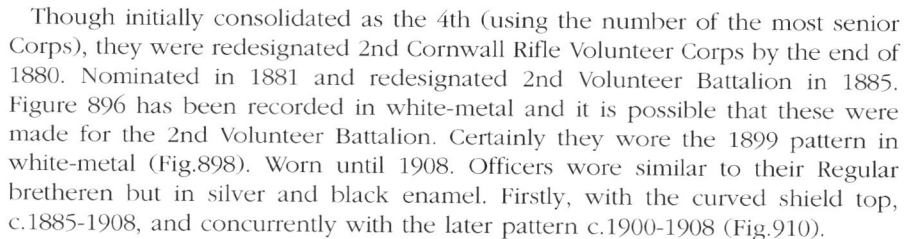

Though initially consolidated as the 4th (using the number of the most senior Corps), they were redesignated 2nd Cornwall Rifle Volunteer Corps by the end of 1880. Nominated in 1881 and redesignated 2nd Volunteer Battalion in 1885. Figure 896 has been recorded in white-metal and it is possible that these were made for the 2nd Volunteer Battalion. Certainly they wore the 1899 pattern in white-metal (Fig.898). Worn until 1908. Officers wore similar to their Regular brethren but in silver and black enamel. Firstly, with the curved shield top, c.1885-1908, and concurrently with the later pattern c.1900-1908 (Fig.910).

This battalion wore from c.1895-1908 a white-metal field service cap badge of a coronet over a ribboned bugle horn. The badges occur in facing pairs, and are believed to have been worn as collar badges in South Africa 1899-1902 (Figs.911, 912). The Regular battalions had worn a gilding-metal version in their field service cap c.1895-1898.

After 1902, Volunteer Officers wore the large bronze collar badges with a separate bronze 'V' below. From 1908, the TF battalions wore the same badges as the Regulars but the 4th Battalion wore a separate 'T' below. After 1932 the samller version was adopted, some with a separate 'T', others with it brazed to the bugle horn.

From 1951, the Territorial other ranks wore a smaller version of the cap badge. Firstly in white-metal, Pattern No.14617, sealed 25th April 1951 (Fig.913), followed

Fig.909    *Fig.910*    *Fig.911*    *Fig.912*

by the silver anodised version. Sealed 10th October 1956. Also worn by associated cadets. The D.C.L.I. (Territorials) wore the same design in silver plate on No.1 and No.3 Dress and similar in bronze on Service Dress.

Finally 'A' Coy, 5th (Volunteer) Battalion and 'C' & 'D' Coys, 6th (Volunteer) Battalion, The Light Infantry wore the same insignia.

WWI Battalions
1/5 and 10th Battalions (Cornwall Pioneers)
Both these Pioneer Battalions wore the usual crossed rifle/pick collar badges but whereas the 1/5 wore theirs with the rifle facing inwards, the 10th adopted the opposite with the picks facing inwards.

Volunteer Training Corps, 1914-1918
Officers were directed under ACI 1936 / 16 to wear a separate bronze 'V' below their Service Dress collar badges. There was no other ranks equivalent.

General
The bezants that appear on the Regiment's collar badges represent Byzantine gold coins arranged 5, 4, 3, 2 and 1 in descending order. The origin of the motto "One and all" is obscure and, although not forming part of the Arms of the Duchy, has been associated with the Regiment from at least the 18th century.

All the bugle collar badges were worn in facing pairs, the mouthpiece facing inwards towards the collar opening. They are sometimes worn with a red cloth backing to commemorate the action at Brandywine in 1777.

On 6th October 1959, the Regiment was amalgamated with The Somerset Light Infantry to become the 1st Battalion, The Somerset and Cornwall Light Infantry. Redesignated 10th July 1968 as 1st Battalion, The Light Infantry.

Fig.913

The Duke of Wellington's Regiment (West Riding)

Fig.914

Fig.915

Fig.916

Pre 1881
The 33rd (The Duke of Wellington's) Regiment

In 1806, Sir Arthur Wellesley, the future Duke of Wellington became Colonel of The Regiment he had commanded at the storming of Seringapatam in 1799; the 33rd (1st Yorkshire West Riding) Regiment of Foot, a position he held until 1813. Following his death in 1852 and in recognition of his distinguished service, H.M. The Queen directed that as from 18th June 1853 (Waterloo Day) the Regiment would be known as, The 33rd (The Duke of Wellington's) Regiment. The Crest and Motto of the Duke was also authorised as a badge. He had been offered this distinction during his life time, but had requested that it be granted only after his demise.

The other ranks collar badge, Pattern No.9288 was sealed 30th November 1872. In brass, it featured the Crest of the Duke of Wellington, 'Out of a ducal coronet, a demi-lion rampant gules, holding a forked pennon, of the last, flowing to the sinister, one third per pale from the staff, argent, charged with the Cross of St. George'. One of the smallest pre territorial collar badges, it was similar to the top of the other ranks glengarry badge 1874-1881. Despite being a family badge it was worn in facing pairs, the Lion facing inwards (Fig.914). The Crest and Motto were adopted by the Officers only on their forage cap, c1857-1881, and their helmet plate 1878/79-1881. No corresponding collar badges 1880-1881 have been traced.

A badge commonly thought to have been worn by the 33rd is that shown in Fig.915. In facing pairs they have been noted in gilding-metal, white-metal, gilt and silver, and face only to the left. It is certainly identical to the centre of the other ranks' helmet plate 1881-1914 (gilding-metal), but there is no evidence that it was worn on the collar pre or post 1881. A more likely attribution is the 5th (Wellington Rifles) New Zealand, whose badge was the Crest only of the Dukes of Wellington. Despite seeing a torn out section of a sample/pattern card annotated, 'West Riding Regiment, 1896, facing to the left', there is no evidence of such a pattern in the Army Clothing Department pattern room journals. A similar badge sealed 6th August 1920, was for side hat ornament. A similar badge in silver embroidery has been noted on a Volunteer Officer's side hat, c1898-1908.

The 76th Regiment of Foot

The collar badge worn by the other ranks of the Regiment prior to 1881 was an Elephant with Howdah, cloth and girth strap. In brass with brass lugs, authorised to be worn 30th June 1876. Pattern No.9605 was sealed 2nd November 1877, for wear on the tunic collar in facing pairs, the Elephant upon a thick grassy ground, with its trunk not anchored to the ground (Fig.916). Officers wore an embroidered version 1880-1881.

The Elephant and Howdah were conferred on the Regiment 17th January 1807 in recognition of their distinguished service in India 1788-1806, and in particular the campaigns of 1803-04.

Post 1881

The two Regiments merged in 1881 to form The Duke of Wellington's (West Riding Regiment); in 1920 this was amended to The Duke of Wellington's Regiment (West Riding). It was decided that the first collar badge for the combined Regiment would continue to be the Elephant and Howdah, confirmed

THE DUKE OF WELLINGTON'S REGIMENT (WEST RIDING)

21st October 1881. This badge Pattern No.9972 was sealed 20th January 1882, the Pattern Room journal records, 'to replace 9288 of the 33rd, and 9605 of the 76th'. (This certainly confirms that the 33rd wore the small crest badge through to 1881). The badge in gilding-metal was cut from new dies. The trunk was now in contact with a narrower ground.

When a new forage cap was introduced in 1894, the O.C. enquired as to whether the new cap badge could also be worn on the collar. Approval for the new cap badge was received 24th December 1894 but with the addition, 'Present collar badge for collar'.

The standard pattern was cut from new dies and sealed 3rd August 1899 this being Pattern No.9972a. No significant changes took place throughout the badge's currency, 1882-1958, though inevitably minute manufacturers' varieties occurred, size of Elephant, its ears, width of trunk etc. Similar differences applied to the Howdah and cloth. Figures 917 and 918 illustrate some of these minutiae. The later issues with single lug fitting.

Following on from the Government's White Paper, July 1957 (Command 230), the 'Dukes' became part of The Yorkshire Brigade, wearing a new Brigade cap badge, a crowned White Rose over a scroll "YORKSHIRE". To distinguish themselves from other Regiments in the Brigade, the Regiment chose a new collar badge; this was virtually their former cap badge shorn of its title scroll, the Crest and Motto of the Iron Duke, 'VIRTUTIS FORTUNA COMES', (Fortune is the companion of honour). Though specimens have been noted in white-metal (Fig.919) and gilding-metal the 1st Battalion wore only the silver anodised version, Pattern No.17634, sealed 24th March 1958 (Fig.920). Authority 54/Officers/4025. Worn until 1965 when a renewal anodised pattern was cut from new dies 16th July, Pattern No.17634a. Minute differences have been noted: a different shaped coronet, less voiding and a slight lowering of the staff bearing the pennon (Fig.921). Officers wore similar to the other ranks pattern but in silver plate, some with a 'frosted' appearance (Fig.922). Also noted in gilt.

With the breaking up of the Brigade system in 1969, permission was sought and granted for the Regiment to resume the use of their former badges. The old cap badge was issued in November 1969 in Hong Kong and worn for the first time at the Governor General's Parade. It was worn with the old Brigade collar badges. The gold anodised Elephant collar badge, Pattern No.202333 was sealed 8th June 1970, with Pattern No.9972a being used as a guide (Fig.923). This pattern was also worn by all senior NCOs with a shaped red cloth backing on No.11 Dress. Other ranks are supposed to wear a circular backing on No.3 Dress. Though the Regimental Journal, August 1969 stated that there would be considerable delay in the issue of the new badge as there was a two-year stock of the old pattern, it is known that the gold anodised Elephant was back in use by mid-1970!

The 1883 Dress Regulations describe the Officers collar badge for wear on the tunic collar as, 'The Elephant in dead gilt metal with Howdah in silver'. Format as per the other ranks. First sealed in 1882, and worn on the shell jacket and scarlet frock. Again sealed 18th May 1903 with no change in design, and apart from the Brigade period worn on the appropriate uniform thereafter. A later sealing recorded was Pattern No. 30205, 22nd September 1983, with pin and clutch fastening. They appear on the relative catalogue, 'For No.2, 3, 4, Dress handed design'. During the Brigade system the Officers wore silver plate versions of the

Fig.917

Fig.918

Fig.919

Fig.920

Fig.922   *Fig.923*   *Fig.921*

HISTORY OF THE BRITISH ARMY INFANTRY COLLAR BADGE

other ranks' pattern.

With the introduction of Service Dress in 1902, the collar badge in bronze was described as, 'As for the tunic collar with scroll as for forage cap'. This scroll was inscribed "THE WEST RIDING". (Figs.924, 925 show slight variations.) When first worn on the high collar they were worn at an angle. Of interest, is illustrated a bronze collar badge showing the holes ready for cutting (Fig.926). During WWII they appeared in what the Regimental Museum describe as 'Wartime ersatz metals, colours varying from almost black to a dull orange'. This pattern was also officially polished and worn in the khaki drill. The Elephant without the scroll, still in bronze, was also worn on the Service Dress just prior to WWII (Fig.927). The 1986 Dress Regulations record the Elephant and Howdah silvered on a scarlet cloth backing for wear on No.11 Dress. This Pattern No.30434 was sealed 22nd September 1983 (Fig.928).

Collar badges for the mess jacket are first mentioned in the 1900 Dress Regulations, 'The Duke of Wellington's crest in gold embroidery. The flag in silver, within a gold edging. The Cross scarlet'. This badge sealed 4th July 1899 is a very pleasing item with the lion's eye and tongue in scarlet. The backing of ribbed crimson silk is of rectangular outline. The modern version is stitched straight into the jacket rather than mounted on the crimson silk.

Though not officially sanctioned it is known through the study of an extant jacket, that the 2nd Battalion wore embroidered Elephants on the mess jacket at some time c.1881-1900. (Fig.929 shows one variant.)

With the advent of a tropical mess dress for use in the Sergeants' Mess, c.1900, white metal Elephant collars were taken into use, and when relevant are still in use.

Militia
6th West York Militia

Raised in 1853, the Regiment divided into two battalions in 1879, becoming the 3rd and 4th Battalions of the 'Dukes' in 1881. White metal collar badges, Pattern No.8922 were sealed 1st February 1877 under Authority PC/6 WYM/185. This was a rose with five outer petals and five inner, turned over at the edge and with sepals in between. The rose centre is dimpled and is in relief. Worn until 1881 (Fig.930).

After 1881, according to the Regimental History, Officers and men continued to appear in the pre 1881 uniforms until well into the decade. It would appear that Officers in particular continued with silver lace, the old sky blue facings and Militia badges; the changes to the Regular battalions' badges only occurring as new Officers arrived. Certainly collar badges in silver plate with gilt Howdahs have been recorded and these could pertain equally to the Militia Battalions and the Volunteer Battalions (Fig.931).

Rifle Volunteer Corps, Volunteer, Territorial Force & Territorial Army Battalions

The strong Halifax Corps, 4th Yorkshire, West Riding Rifle Volunteer Corps, nominated in 1881 became the 1st Volunteer Battalion in 1883. Similarly, the consolidated battalions 6th and 9th Yorkshire, West Riding Rifle Volunteer Corps (Huddersfield and Skipton) became the 2nd and 3rd Volunteer

Fig.924

Fig.925

Fig.926

Fig.927

Fig.928    *Fig.929*    *Fig.930*    *Fig.931*

THE DUKE OF WELLINGTON'S REGIMENT (WEST RIDING)

Battalions also in 1883. No collar badges have been associated with these Corps prior to conversion. A white-metal version of the Regular units pattern was submitted by the 1st Volunteer Battalion for approval in 1885. This was received 9th April with the additional note, 'Also to be worn by the 2nd and 3rd VBs'. An all silver plate version for Officers has also been noted.

In 1908, the 1st VB became the 4th (TF) Battalion, the 2nd VB formed the 5th and 7th (TF) Battalions, and the 3rd VB the 6th (TF) Battalion. The badges of the Regular units were gradually adopted, a 'T' being worn below the bronze collar badges of the Officers; they wore a similar embroidered 'T' below the mess jacket crest collar badge.

Fig.932

Cadets
Upon the formation of the CCF after WWII, Giggleswick School and Leeds Grammar School eventually became affiliated to the Regiment and badged accordingly.

Home Guard
Under Authority 9/HG/363, a silver/gilt elephant collar badge pattern 16574 was sealed 23rd June 1954 for Home Guard units badged to the Duke of Wellington's Regiment (Fig.932).

Fig.933

Other badges
One item sometimes confused with the Regiment's insignia is a collar badge in gilding-metal of the Duke's Crest over a motto scroll inscribed 'AGER IN ARMIS' (Strong in Arms), this pertains to the 7th (Wellington West Coast Rifles) Regiment. New Zealand (Fig.933).

Another item which has all the appearnace of the genuine article displays the Elephant and Howdah over a scroll inscribed '2nd Volunteer Battn.' In silver plate the badge is totally spurious and was made privately in 1992. For whatever reason one can only guess (Fig.934).

Fig.934

General
All collar badges, both crests and elephants, were worn in facing pairs with the animals facing inwards. Minor variations abound, especially with the elephant badges where the howdahs, ears, overall size and ground can be distinctive.

The Border Regiment

Pre 1881
The 34th (Cumberland) Regiment of Foot

The other ranks of the Regiment wore as their collar badge, an oval shaped open topped laurel wreath; the leaves interspersed with berries, the sprays tied at the base (Fig.935). In brass, Pattern No.9305 was authorised 16th July 1872 and sealed 1st May 1873, worn up to amalgamation in 1881 and beyond with photographs showing them still in use by some soldiers as late as 1884; when the Battalion was in Burma - well away from Official eyes!

Traditionally, the laurel wreath was awarded to the Regiment for their part in covering the retreat of the Army at Fontenoy in 1745, a rare case of a Corps being awarded an honour for a tactical withdrawal. The badge was sometimes referred to as 'A Fontenoy wreath'.

The 55th (Westmoreland) Regiment of Foot

Pattern No.9325, was sealed 18th May 1874 (Authorised 16th July 1872). In brass, the design was a long bodied free standing 'Dragon of China'. With two tails and one front paw raised. (Figs.936, 937 show a facing pair.) Gilt items are known, possibly worn by senior NCOs. Similar gold embroidered Dragons for wear by the Officers 1880-1881 are known, via photographs and actual specimens.

The Regiment served in the First China Wars 1840-42 and to commemorate their distinguished service were awarded the Dragon superscribed China, 12th January 1843. To be borne on their Colours and appointments.

Post 1881

The Regiments amalgamated in 1881 to form The Border Regiment; on 22nd October the AAG, Horse Guards verbally decreed that the new Regiment would wear as their collar badge, 'A Dragon in a Wreath - a different pattern from the Welsh Regiment'. The choice pleased everyone and Pattern No.10013, 'to replace 9305 of the 34th and 9325 of the 55th' was sealed 2nd February 1882, made in gilding metal.

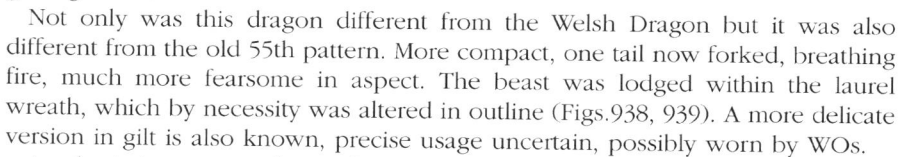

Not only was this dragon different from the Welsh Dragon but it was also different from the old 55th pattern. More compact, one tail now forked, breathing fire, much more fearsome in aspect. The beast was lodged within the laurel wreath, which by necessity was altered in outline (Figs.938, 939). A more delicate version in gilt is also known, precise usage uncertain, possibly worn by WOs.

A submission was made 22nd July 1884 by the Colonel of the Regiment, 'That the collar badge as now being worn (a sealed pattern was enclosed) does not adequately exhibit the correct laurel wreath'. Following on from this, General Sir H.C. Daubenny GCB was requested 20th January 1885, 'to supply a sketch of the item as proposed by the CO's of the 1st and 2nd Battalions.' The sketch was approved 11th February and a new pattern demanded, 'In one piece instead of two as at present, gilt for Officers, yellow metal for other ranks - to be in pairs, one for each side'. The resultant badge Pattern No.312 was sealed 1st May 1885 with the instruction, 'Present stock to be used up first unless it is agreed to issue for military purposes only'.

This badge restored the wreath to its correct shape, still open at the top, and partly enclosing a round convex ground on which was the Dragon with 'CHINA' inscribed above. This Dragon was of an emaciated appearance, still free standing but now balancing on one rear and one front foot, the other two being raised; it was also reduced to one tail. (Figs.940, 941 show slight variations in the Dragon's display.)

Worn until 1895 when yet another pattern was introduced, entirely different and described as, 'Old pattern cap badge, reduced for collar and cap'. Pattern No.312b 'to replace pattern 312', approved 22nd November 1894, sealed 9th April 1895. (There is no reference to any Pattern No.312a, or any trace of a drawing or submission bearing this number). In white metal the badge was of ornate design, upon the laurel wreath was imposed a Maltese Cross, in the centre of the cross a circle inscribed, 'ARROYO DOS MOLINOS 1811', within the circle, the top half inscribed 'CHINA', and the Dragon in the voided bottom half. Below the Cross and Wreath a tri-part scroll inscribed 'THE BORDER REGT.' A scarlet cloth backing was worn behind the lower voided central area.

The Maltese Cross, though not officially authorised until 22nd July 1881, had featured on many badges of the old 34th. The arms of the cross contained eleven battle honours, from the top clockwise, "PYRENEES, NIVELLE, NIVE" (34th), then "PENINSULA, ORTHES", (34th) "ALMA" (55th), then "LUCKNOW" (34th), "SEVASTOPOL" (34th & 55th), "INKERMAN" (55th),' and finally "ALBUHERA, VITTORIA" (34th).

The honour 'Arroyo dos Molinos 1811' was awarded to the 34th for their gallantry at this Peninsula War engagement. Marked by the wearing of red and white plumes later ball tufts in their headdress, this distinction was lost when red and white was permitted for all Infantry other than Rifles and Light Infantry, but revived on the Officers helmet plate of the 34th in 1878 when a red and white enamel centre appeared by the numerals; carried forward on the 1881 pattern plates and later forage cap badges (Fig.942).

This pattern was worn until 1906, when a similar pattern but including the new honour, "RELIEF OF LADYSMITH" was introduced. Again in white metal Pattern No.312c was sealed 24th January 1906, Authority ACD Patts/1428 & 1386, with the instruction, 'Each badge to be fitted with a piece of scarlet cloth No.3'. With more voiding between the cross and title scroll, the main difference was in the battle honour distribution. From the top and clockwise the badge now showed, "PENINSULA, ALBUHERA, VITTORIA, PYRENEES", then "RELIEF OF LADYSMITH, SOUTH AFRICA 1899-1902", thirdly "NIVE, NIVELLE, ORTHES", finally "LUCKNOW, SEVASTOPOL, INKERMAN, ALMA" (Fig.943). Worn until 1959, latterly with a single lug and plate fastener.

The early Dress Regulations describe the Officers collar badge as, 'A laurel wreath in silver; within the wreath in gilt metal, the Dragon of China; above the Dragon, a scroll in gilt metal, inscribed "China." Ground of half white half red enamel.' This very handsome badge was confirmed in the 1888 Dress Regulations but was altered by the time the 1891 Edition appeared, 'In gilt metal, a laurel wreath; within the wreath on a burnished convex ground, badge as on the button. (Fig.944). (In the 3rd and 4th Battalions the word "China" is omitted') This replaced the beautiful but perhaps fragile vitreous enamelled centre backing of the earlier type. Similar to the then current other ranks pattern but voided between the convex centre and laurels, and of course in superior metals. Worn until 1895 when the cross pattern badge was introduced. Described in the 1900 Edition as, 'In silver, a laurel wreath; on the wreath a Maltese Cross with a lion between each division. On the divisions of the Cross, the battles of the Regiment. On the centre of the Cross, a raised circle inscribed "Arroyo dos Molinos 1811". Within the circle, on a ground of red enamel, the Dragon of China in silver and "China" on a silver ground. Below the wreath a scroll inscribed "The Border Regiment"' (Fig.945). Also worn on the scarlet frock and later on the mess jacket. The battle honour distribution was identical to the other ranks and changed likewise in 1906 (Fig.946). These were worn up to amalgamation in 1959.

The Service Dress collar badge of 1902 was described thus, 'As for forage cap, in bronze'. Which itself was described, 'As for collar badge on an eight pointed diamond cut star, surmounted by a crown.' This was of course a KC; two variations have been recorded, differing by the battle honour distribution. Fig.947

Fig.940

Fig.941

Fig.942

Fig.943

Fig.944

Fig.945

HISTORY OF THE BRITISH ARMY INFANTRY COLLAR BADGE

Fig.946

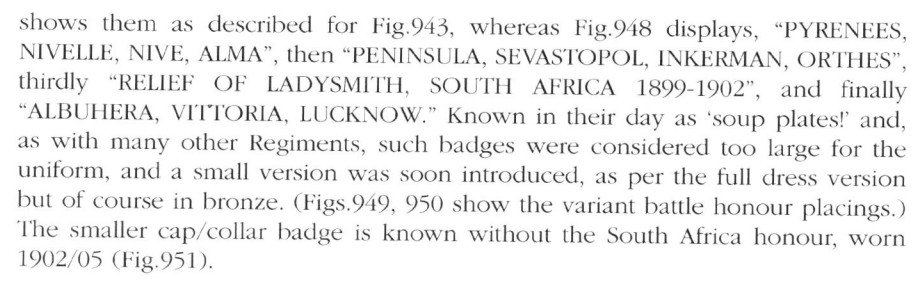

shows them as described for Fig.943, whereas Fig.948 displays, "PYRENEES, NIVELLE, NIVE, ALMA", then "PENINSULA, SEVASTOPOL, INKERMAN, ORTHES", thirdly "RELIEF OF LADYSMITH, SOUTH AFRICA 1899-1902", and finally "ALBUHERA, VITTORIA, LUCKNOW." Known in their day as 'soup plates!' and, as with many other Regiments, such badges were considered too large for the uniform, and a small version was soon introduced, as per the full dress version but of course in bronze. (Figs.949, 950 show the variant battle honour placings.) The smaller cap/collar badge is known without the South Africa honour, worn 1902/05 (Fig.951).

Militia
Royal Cumberland Militia

Reconstituted in 1760 and becoming 'Royal' in 1804 the Regiment became the 3rd Battalion in 1881. There is no record in the Army Clothing Department Pattern Room Journals of any collar badge for the Regiment, and so far there is no material evidence of any such badges.

Royal Westmoreland Light Infantry Militia

Becoming 'Royal' in 1804 and Light Infantry in 1854, the Regiment became the 4th Battalion in 1881. (The second 'E' in Westmoreland was not in use until c.1870). Under Authority PC/WM/150, 1st April 1879, it was decreed that the collar badges to be worn by the other ranks would be the same white metal bugle horns, Pattern No.8935, as worn by the Royal South Gloucester Militia (Fig.207). Though indeed identical, their own Pattern No.7193 was sealed 17th April 1879.

Fig.947

Officers wore the same in silver plate. Worn with the mouthpiece facing inwards towards the collar opening.

After 1881, the first entry in the Pattern Room Journals regarding their collar badges is dated 25th June 1885. 'Provision of special patterns for the Militia Bns.', followed 30th July 1886 by, 'Militia Bns. noted demand for collar badges can go forward and when a supply is wanted, contractors will be required to submit a pattern from design and description that will be given'. The supply was required, the contractors supplied with a description, the collar badge was designed and approved, Pattern No.1336 being sealed 22nd December 1887. In gilding-metal this was similar to those worn by the Regular units but without 'CHINA' above the Dragon. (Figs.952, 953 show two variants.) Officers wore similar, in gilt metal, voided between the centre and wreath (Fig.954). Curiously, by an Order 7th August 1888, the Permanent Staff of the

Fig.948

Fig.949

Fig.950

Fig.951

Fig.952

Fig.953

152

3rd & 4th Battalions 'were required to wear Line collar badges,' but it is believed that to comply but retain their Militia status, they in fact wore a silver plated version (Fig.955).

A new pattern collar badge for these battalions was discussed in 1894, and on 24th May 1895 it was decreed that the new badge would be similar to that of the Line battalions but without 'China' above the Dragon in the centre of the badge, and with no battle honours on the arms of the cross. In addition, in place of the central honour 'Arroyo dos Molinos 1811' would be the Garter Motto. The Garter Proper was an old badge of the Royal Westmoreland Militia. In white metal for other ranks, the bottom half of the centre was voided and backed by scarlet cloth. This was Pattern No. P1336b, sealed 22nd October 1895 (Fig.956). The Officers wore similar but in silver plate and with red and white enamel centres. Worn until 1908. The 4th Militia Battalion was disbanded in 1908.

Rifle Volunteer Corps, Volunteer, Territorial Force & Territorial Army Battalions

Nominated in 1881, the consolidated battalion 1st Cumberland Rifle Volunteer Corps, became the 1st Volunteer Battalion in 1887. The other ranks collar badge in white metal was similar to that of the Regular units but without 'China'. As a result the badge displayed a larger Dragon with larger 'fire' (Figs.957, 958 show two variants). Officers wore similar but in silver plate and with the usual voiding twixt the wreath and centre (Fig.959). These badges appear in the Gaunt Pattern books as, 'Collar ornaments H & Co. 22/2/87'.

The consolidated battalion 1st Westmoreland Rifle Volunteer Corps became the 2nd Volunteer Battalion also in 1887 (Gen.Order 181). Other ranks wore a distinctive white metal collar badge, the pattern adopted by the Militia Battalions in 1895 (Fig.956), but below the usual title scroll, an additional one inscribed, '2nd VOLR. BATTN' (Fig.960). Officers wore the same but in silver plate and enamels; also recorded in bronze for use on the Service Dress, 1902-1908.

In 1900, five companies were detached from the 1st Volunteer Battalion, and with the addition of three newly raised companies formed the 3rd Volunteer Battalion. As far as is known they wore the same collar badges as the 1st Volunteer Battalion.

In 1908, the 1st and 2nd Volunteer Battalions amalgamated to form the 4th (Cumberland and Westmoreland) TF Battalion. Again a distinctive badge was worn. The other ranks white metal pattern displayed the Maltese Cross with a solid centre and circle, '4th' in the centre and the circle inscribed, 'SOUTH AFRICA 1900-02'. Around the bottom half of the badge a long ornate scroll inscribed, 'BORDER-CUMBERLAND & WESTMORELAND REGIMENT' (Fig.961). The Officers Service Dress pattern was similar but in bronze (Fig.962). There is most probably an Officers' full dress version in silver plate.

The 3rd Volunteer Battalion became the 5th (Cumberland) TF Battalion in 1908, and both other ranks and Officers wore similar collar badges in white metal and bronze to those worn by the 4th Battalion, but with the corresponding '5th' in the centre, the central South Africa honour, and the bottom scroll inscribed, 'BORDER-CUMBERLAND-REGIMENT'. Officers of this battalion later wore on their Service Dress jackets a mid sized bronze badge, of star, cross and KC design.

Fig.954

Fig.955

Fig.956

Fig.957

Fig.958

Fig.960 *Fig.961* *Fig.962* *Fig.959*

HISTORY OF THE BRITISH ARMY INFANTRY COLLAR BADGE

Fig.963

Fig.964

Fig.965

In the solid centre of the cross the Dragon only, within a circle inscribed "SOUTH AFRICA 1901-02". No battle honours on the arms of the cross, and title scroll, "THE-BORDER-REGT." below (Fig.963).

A similar bronze badge but with the Garter Proper in the centre is believed to have been worn by the 4th. Battalion. These distinctive badges continued in use probably up to 1939. After the amalgamation of the 1st Battalion in 1959, the Regular type collar badges continued to be worn by the surviving TA units, Pattern No.312c being used as a guide for a silver anodised version. This was Pattern No.19325, sealed 16th September 1964, Authority A/54/Inf/8845; again to be worn with a scarlet cloth backing. Worn by soldiers of the 4th (T) Bn. The Border Regiment (Fig.964). The Officers continuing to wear the silver plate and enamel version.

WWI Battalions

The 9th (Pioneer) Battalion wore the usual crossed rifle and pick collar badges (Fig.147). The 11th (Lonsdale) Battalion was raised by the famous 'Yellow Earl', Hugh Cecil Lowther, the fifth Earl of Lonsdale. His family crest was adopted as a cap badge by all ranks and as a collar badge in bronze by the Officers. A dragon passant argent standing upon a scroll inscribed, 'Eleventh Battalion' this depended into a flowing finials inscribed, 'Border Regiment' (Fig.965). The Battalion was disbanded 31st July 1918.

General

As can be seen, a wide variety of badges was worn by the various elements of the Regiment. All badges featuring central Dragons were in facing pairs (except the 11th Lonsdales), with the animals facing inwards towards the collar opening.

The Regiment amalgamated with The King's Own Royal Regiment (Lancaster) to form The King's Own Royal Border Regiment, 1st October 1959.

The Royal Sussex Regiment

Pre 1881
The 35th (Sussex) Regiment of Foot
By an Authority 16th July 1872, the other ranks of the Regiment adopted the brass Imperial crown as their collar badge, worn until 1882 (Fig.333)

The 107th (Bengal Infantry) Regiment
The collar badge for the other ranks was Pattern No.9308, sealed 7th May 1873. This was a cross pattee with single inner delineation, dimpled on the outer sections and smooth within. In the voided centre, the numerals '107' within a plain strap, itself within a laurel circle. In brass and worn until 1882 (Fig.966).

Fig.966

Post 1881
Upon the linking of the two Regiments in 1881 to form The Royal Sussex Regiment, the usual discussions took place concerning the new collar badges, each Regiment wishing to retain some distinctive aspect. It should also be remembered that the badge or badges of the county Militia Regiment(s) were also involved and in many instances adopted into some of the new Regiments' badges. The composition of the collar badge for The Royal Sussex Regiment was quite involved but was an achievement. The background cross had a double ancestry. First, it was said to commemorate the taking of Malta by the 35th in 1800 and certainly featured on the Officers' shoulder belt plates, c.1832-1855. Second, it was a badge used by the old H.E.I.C.'s 3rd Bengal European Light Infantry Regiment, and has been seen on the transferred 107th Foot. The Cross was placed over the Plume, an ancient badge of the 35th. Adopted in 1759, but not officially authorised until 30th June 1880. It was immediately brought into use as part of the embroidered Officers' forage cap badge, but had not been in use on any of the other badges of the Regiment prior to that Authority. It commemorates the services of the 35th at the Battle of Quebec, when they are said to have taken the white plumes from the caps of the defeated soldiers of the Royal Roussillon Grenadiers. Upon the Cross was placed the laurels of the 107th (these had also featured in earlier badges of the 35th), and within the laurels the Cross of St. George and the Garter Proper, the ancient badge of the Royal Sussex Light Infantry Militia. Though in gilding metal the first issues were more brass like in appearance. Pattern No.10102 was sealed 8th February 1882 (Fig.967).

Fig.967

A renewal of the standard pattern was demanded to be cut from new dies in 1897, Pattern No.10102a being sealed 14th December 1897, Authority UK/CIC/208. There was no significant change, perhaps neater (Fig.968), and the pattern was resealed 17th January 1938. Some issues have been noted with a 'flatter' centre section. The badge was later used as a guide for the gold anodised version, introduced c1954 and worn until 1960 (Fig.969).

Fig.968

A later Pattern, No.18394 but in silver anodised was sealed 16th November 1960, Authority 54/Inf/8776, differing considerably in size and with a longer Plume (Fig.970). These badges were worn when the Regiment formed part of the Home Counties Brigade, and were worn up to amalgamation in 1966.

In 1958, when news reached the 1st Battalion regarding their inclusion in the Home Counties Brigade and thereby losing their regimental cap badge, a deputation of Private soldiers asked the Commanding Officer if they could wear their cap badge as a collar badge. Permission was granted, the slider fasteners

Fig.969

HISTORY OF THE BRITISH ARMY INFANTRY COLLAR BADGE

were removed from the cap badges, lugs affixed, and the badges were worn in the battle dress lapels until 1960 when (Fig.970) was introduced. The cap badge, white metal with a gilding metal scroll is shown in (Fig.971).

After 1881, the Officers wore on the full dress tunic, 'A Maltese cross, in gilt metal, on a feather in silver; on the cross a wreath in silver and green (enamel); on the wreath a raised circle in blue enamel set with silver. Within the circle the Cross of St. George in red enamel, set with silver, on a silver ground,' (Figs.972, 973, 974 show variations). This description was extended for wear on the frock in the 1900 Dress Regulations, and slightly amended. After 'gilt' was added 'or gilding metal' and enamel after 'green'; further, replacing, 'on the wreath a raised circle' with 'on the wreath the Garter and Motto'. Very beautiful badges and reflective of the badge maker's art. Also known in all gilt apart from the coloured enamels, and thought to have been worn by Warrant Officers.

The 1900 Dress Regulations also gave deatils of the badge to be worn on the mess jacket. 'The feather in silver embroidery with the stem gilt. On the feather the Star of the Order of the Garter in gold embroidery. The centre of the Star as above.' (i.e. as for tunic and frock collar). Sealed 1st December 1903. Attractive badges, they were worn in facing pairs with the top fall of the feather pointing outwards from the jacket collar (Figs.975, 976).

The Officers badges were confirmed in the 1934 Dress Regulations, and when No.1 Dress was introduced c.1951, the collar badge, although of the same general design was now, 'In silver plate the Maltese cross on a Plume, on the cross a wreath in silver plate and green enamel, within the wreath the Garter and Motto in blue enamel set with silver plate; within the Garter the Cross of St. George in red enamel on a ground of silver plate (Figs.977, 978).

With the advent of the Brigade System, the Officers adopted a superior version of the other ranks collar badges (Fig.970). In silver plate and enamels it was worn until amalgamation in 1966 (Fig.979).

Fig.970

Fig.971

Fig.972

Fig.973

Fig.974

Fig.975

Fig.976

Fig.977

Fig.978

Fig.979

Fig.980

THE ROYAL SUSSEX REGIMENT

When Service Dress was introduced in 1902, the collar badge to be worn was thus, 'As for forage cap, in bronze.' The forage cap badge was identical to the other ranks shown in Fig.971. Sealed 23rd July 1903, (Fig.980). Although not recorded in Dress Regulations a bronzed other ranks pattern was also worn by the Officers on their Service Dress (Fig.981).

Militia
Royal Sussex Light Infantry Militia

Raised in 1778, elevated to Light Infantry status in 1835 and made Royal in 1846, the Regiment formed the 3rd and 4th Battalions in 1881. Amalgamated in 1890 as the 3rd Battalion. Collar badges in white metal for wear on the tunic and frock were sealed 5th December 1878, Pattern No.7189, under Authority PC / SM / 335. This was the Star of the Order of the Garter (Fig.982). The Garter Star had long been in use, the shoulder belt plate of c.1810 displayed it above a scroll inscribed 'Sussex'. This collar badge was worn for a very short time, as by an Order 4th May 1879 the Regiment was directed that its collar badge 'To be assimilated to the 2nd Royal Surrey Militia, pattern 7584 but to have the words on the Garter, "Royal Sussex Lt. Infy. Militia"' Also in white metal (Fig.983). Worn until 1881.

After c.1882, Officers wore collar badges in accordance with the pattern described for the Regular units, but in reversed metals, a silver Cross with a gilt Plume (Fig.984).

Rifle Volunteer Corps, Volunteer, Territorial Force & Territorial Army Battalions

The Battalion strong 1st Sussex Rifle Volunteer Corps based at Brighton was nominated in 1881, becoming the 1st Volunteer Battalion in 1887.

The very widely spread 1st Administrative Battalion was consolidated in 1880 as the 2nd Sussex Rifle Volunteer Corps. The badge shown in (Fig.985) is stated to be that worn by this consolidated Corps, in white metal a shield bearing the Arms as used by the County Justices of the Peace, 'azure, six martlets or, three, two and one'. They were, after 1889, co-opted into the Arms of the County councils of East and West Sussex. Officers of the Corps reputedly wore the same badge in silver. So far there is no conclusive evidence that such badges were used.

The Corps adopted the 2nd Volunteer Battalion title in 1887. The other ranks of the 1st VB. wore white metal versions of the Regular units pattern. Officers badges were in silver and enamels. The same pattern white metal badge and corresponding Officers but replacing the Garter and Motto with a plain circle, is thought to have been worn by the 2nd Volunteer Battalion (Fig.986, broken at the base). Again to date there is no firm basis for such conjecture.

On 1st April 1908 the 2nd VB was designated the 4th (TF) Battalion, but the 1st VB was transferred as part of the Home Counties Brigade, Royal Field Artillery. The Officers refused to comply with this directive and were placed on the unattached list until August 1912, when they were redesignated as 6th (Cyclist) Battalion (TF). The Officers and other ranks wore their respective collar badges blackened. The unit was disbanded at Brighton 29th December 1919.

Various elements of the 1st Administrative Battalion, Cinque Ports Rifle Volunteers were consolidated 13th April 1880 to form 1st Cinque Ports (Cinque Ports and Sussex) Rifle Volunteers. nominated as the 3rd Volunteer Battalion in 1881 but did not take up the title, maintaining their 'Rifles' status until 1908. They wore a special pattern collar badge, designed by the senior Captain, H.S. Johnson, who commanded 'A' and 'F' Coys at Headquarters. The Maltese Cross and Plume of the Regulars' badge was retained, but the central area became a plain disc upon which was placed a shield bearing the Arms of the Cinque Ports. 'Party per pale gules and azure, three demi-lions passant guardant in pale or, conjoined to the hulks of as many ships argent'. The Gaunt Pattern books record the approved design, annotated, 'Samuel 9/11/98'. It was introduced in 1899 for other ranks in white-metal until 1908, (Fig.987), when upon reorganisation as the 5th (Cinque

Fig.981

Fig.982

Fig.983

Fig.984

Fig.985

Fig.986

HISTORY OF THE BRITISH ARMY INFANTRY COLLAR BADGE

Fig.987

Fig.988

Fig.989

Fig.990

Ports) Bn. TF, The Royal Sussex Regiment, it was issued in gilding-metal. Even after 1908, the white-metal badge was still being worn in full dress as a reminder of the Volunteer tradition. The cap badge, shoulder titles and buttons were also in white-metal.

The Officers' badges also introduced in 1899 displayed a silver Cross and Plume with red and blue enamels backing silver demi-lions and hulks (Fig.988). Also noted with gilt central charges. An all-silver version is also recorded which may be a senior NCO's version or an Officers undress variety (Fig.989). From 1902 Officers wore the cap badge (as for the collar but with a scroll below inscribed, 'Cinque Ports') in bronze as a collar badge on the Service Dress, regulations allowing them to be worn with a separate 'T' below (Fig.990). Photographs show Officers wearing the collar badge only, the 'T' only, and the Regular units' badge, all very confusing when the object is to try to establish what was worn at any one time. One example of the Cinque Ports pattern in bronze but without the title scroll is known. this was worn by the late Sir Winston Churchill KG etc., in his capacity as Lord Warden of the Cinque Ports, and when he wore the uniform as Colonel in Chief of the Regiment. It is known that he wore these collar badges when attending both the Yalta and Potsdam Conferences.

In 1903, the Officers grey mess dress was replaced by one resembling that of the parent Regiment, save for the facings which were in 'Cinque Ports blue' material. The lapel badges were embroidered in bullion wire and silks in their correct heraldic colours, worn in facing pairs with the fall of the plume facing outwards from the collar opening (Figs.991, 992). Larger versions shown (Figs.993, 994), may pertain to the 1899-1903 period.

This battalion maintained their individual badges long after other 'Terrier' units had abondoned theirs. When the badges of the 4th/5th (CP) Bn. were standardised as those for the Royal Sussex Regiment in 1951, Officers of the battalion were permitted to continue wearing their existing badges on No.1 Dress.

No collar badges were worn when serving in France with the 1st Division in 1915, but on transfer to the 48th (South Midland) Division as their Pioneer battalion wore the usual crossed rifle and pick collar badges.Photographs of Officers in Service Dress taken in 1917 show them wearing the Cinque Ports bronze collar badges with the bronze pioneer emblem below.

WWI Service Battalions
8th (Service) Battalion

Raised 18th November 1914 as Infantry and converted to Pioneers 4th February 1915 and disbanded 20th June 1919. During their pioneer role they wore the usual crossed rifle/pick collar badges, with the rifles facing inwards towards the collar opening. This is shown in Plate 14, a lighthearted photograph taken near Arras in 1917.

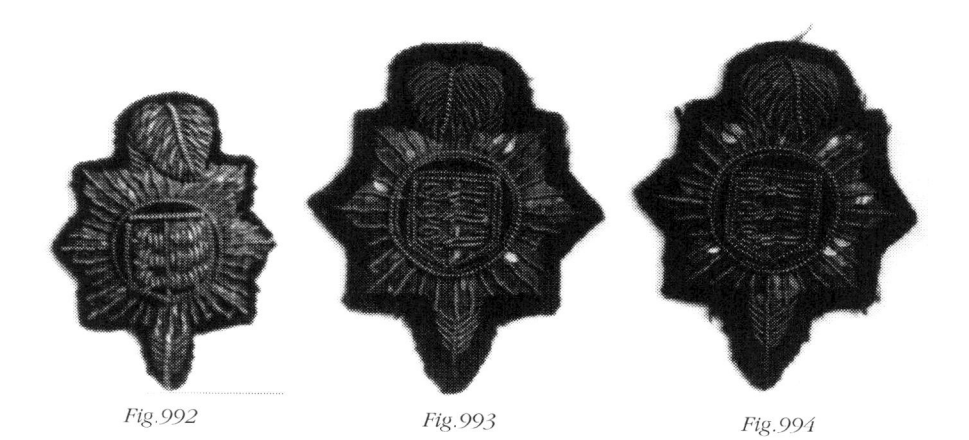

Fig.991   *Fig.992*   *Fig.993*   *Fig.994*

Cadets
Eastbourne College Cadet Corps
Established in 1896, attached to the Royal Sussex Regiment with both Officers and cadets wearing the same collar badges as worn by the Regiment but in white metal.

Brighton College Cadet Corps
Attached to the 1st Volunteer Battalion, Officers and cadets wearing the badges of this Corps.

Lancing College Cadet Corps
Attached and badged as per the 2nd Volunteer Battalion.

General
As can be seen, the collar badges of The Royal Sussex Regiment remained very constant throughout the eighty years of currency. There were the inevitable minor variations regarding metals, centres and plume lengths. Apart from where stated they did not face.

The Regiment became the 3rd Battalion, The Queen's Regiment, 31st December 1966.

Bandmaster W. Froud, 2nd Battalion The Suffolk Regiment, 1895-1913

The Royal Hampshire Regiment

Fig.995

Pre 1881
The 37th (North Hampshire) Regiment of Foot

The collar badge adopted for wear by the other ranks was Pattern No.9543, sealed 31st May 1875, Authority 16th July 1872. In brass, the design was a QVC lodged within an open topped laurel wreath, the sprays of nine leaves either side interspersed with berries (Fig.995). Laurels had featured on earlier badges of the 37th.

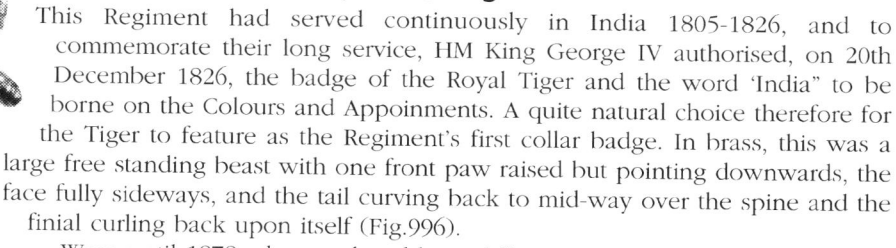

Fig.996

The 67th (South Hampshire) Regiment of Foot

This Regiment had served continuously in India 1805-1826, and to commemorate their long service, HM King George IV authorised, on 20th December 1826, the badge of the Royal Tiger and the word 'India" to be borne on the Colours and Appoinments. A quite natural choice therefore for the Tiger to feature as the Regiment's first collar badge. In brass, this was a large free standing beast with one front paw raised but pointing downwards, the face fully sideways, and the tail curving back to mid-way over the spine and the finial curling back upon itself (Fig.996).

Worn until 1878 when replaced by a different pattern Royal Tiger, a leaner animal, the raised paw straight out and the other three resting on a torse; the head not fully frontal and the tail less adavnced along the spine (Fig.997). In brass, Pattern No.9655, sealed 9th August 1878. Both patterns worn in facing pairs, the Tiger facing inwards. The second pattern is known in metal thread embroidery, worn by the Officers late 1880-1881.

Fig.997

Post 1881

When the two Regiments were amalgamated in 1881 to form The Hampshire Regiment, new badges were required, the Royal Tiger of the 67th became the principle charge in the headdress badges, the 37th and the Hampshire Militia being represented in the collar badge. (Fig.998) shows the design of Pattern No.10123, the Hampshire Rose lodged within an elongated laurel wreath, voided all round, the Rose having five outer and inner petals turned over at the edges and with sepals between the outer petals only. The Rose being slightly proud of the laurels. The Rose in gilding metal and the laurel wreath in white metal, it was sealed 22nd February 1882.

Fig.998

The double red Rose had been bestowed on the Trained Bands of Hampshire in the reign of King Henry V, to commemorate their service to him at Agincourt, 1415.

The 1st Battalion accepted the badge and wore them until 1899 after a new pattern was demanded, 9th February 1898. This Pattern No. 10123a was cut from new dies and sealed 3rd August; still in the two metals, there was no significant change but the resultant badge was slightly neater and smaller all round (Fig.999). The 2nd Battalion, apparently not pleased with the first post 1881 pattern, managed to introduce and wear their own badge. A Royal Tiger, again considerably smaller than the second pre 1881 type and standing on ground. In gilding-metal they are not recorded in the official Pattern Room journals and were quite without authority. Dating is difficult, but it is believed they were worn up to c.1897 (Fig.1000).

Fig.999

Fig.1000

At first glance this Tiger can easily be confused with the Regiment's first field

THE ROYAL HAMPSHIRE REGIMENT

service cap badge (Fig.1001); smaller again and more rounded ground, it is found only facing to the viewer's left, whereas the collar badges face both ways, the Tiger facing inwards towards the collar opening.

The 2nd Battalion, obliged to wear the official pattern c.1897, responded by having it made in gilding metal only (Fig.1002), adopting the post 1899 pattern in due course, but still in all gilding metal. How long this variance continued is not recorded but the late 1920s would seem to be the first time that both battalions wore the bi-metal collar badge.

The Regiment received 'Royal' status in 1946, but continued to wear the same collar badge up to 1949 when the die was renewed under Authority 54/Misc/5751. Although a new Pattern No. 14048 was given with the sealing, 26th January 1949, there was no change in design. This was the pattern used as a guide for the gold anodised version (Fig.1003). Pattern No.18584 being sealed 6th October 1961 (Authority 54/Inf/8786). The slight variant shown in (Fig.1004) was worn up to the Regiment's amalgamation.

The gold anodised version was also used by the soldiers of 'A' Coy (4th/5th Royal Hampshire) The Royal Hampshire and Isle of Wight Territorials.

A chromed version of the standard other ranks collar badge exists, thought to have been worn by the Regimental Police during the 1950's.

The 1883 Dress Regulations simply describe the Officers collar badge as 'The Hampshire Rose in gold and red and green embroidery'. The 1900 Edition adds for the scarlet frock, 'Collar badge of similar pattern but with metal substituted for embroidery' (Fig.1005). The last mention of embroidered collar badges was in the 1934 Edition, 'For tunic collar and mess jacket'. This was the pattern sealed 24th September 1907 (Fig.1006).

The 1951 Edition states, 'Within a laurel wreath the Rose in gilt and red enamel'. One such pattern was sealed 12th January 1956 (Fig.1007). Repeated in subsequent Editions until 1986 which confirms it, 'For No.1 Dress', adding, 'No.2 Dress, not worn.' This was Pattern No.30232, sealed 13th February 1980 (Fig.1008).

For the 1902 Service Dress adopted by the Regiment in 1903, the collar badge was to be the same as worn on the forage cap, but in bronze, 'An eight pointed star, on the star the Garter and crown, within the Garter, the Rose. On the lower part of the star, a scroll inscribed "Hampshire"'. (Figs.1009, 1010 show slight variation in the star formation.) The above official extract was adopted and adhered to by the 1st Battalion.

Fig.1001

Fig.1002

Fig.1003

Fig.1004

Fig.1005

Fig.1006

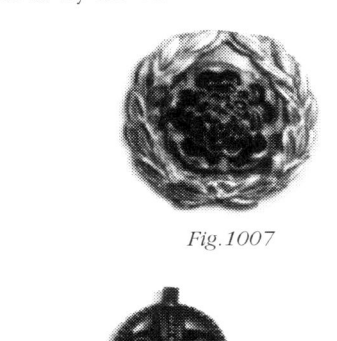

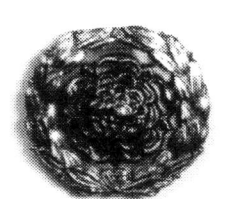

Fig.1007

Fig.1008

Fig.1009

Fig.1010

HISTORY OF THE BRITISH ARMY INFANTRY COLLAR BADGE

Fig.1011

Fig.1012

Fig.1013

Fig.1014

Fig.1015

The 2nd Battalion's Officers were already the subject of a variable sealed pattern for the full dress collar badge. Dated 14th October 1903 and headed, '2nd Bn. 61002/Inf/906 for wear on tunic, frock coat and mess jacket'. Though displaying the same embroidered Rose as for the 1st Battalion, the metal thread parts are silver. The red silk section is also more a purple/red though this may be due to fading over the years. The same sealed pattern card also shows the bronze cap/collar already described for the 1st Battalion; however it is doubtful if the 2nd Battalion adhered to this pattern immediately as there are bronze versions of their other ranks Tiger collar badge (Fig.1011).

When the cap/collar badge was worn, the 1st Battalion wore theirs in a light tan colour whereas the 2nd Battalion wore theirs almost black. This battalion did not wear collar badges on the Service Dress during WWI, and the 1st Battalion ceased wearing theirs shortly after the cessation of hostilities.

The gilt/ enamel pattern is also found in bronze (Fig.1012), though there is no official sanction for these badges, it is understood that they were worn on the khaki drill while overseas.

Another recorded bronze collar badge is a smaller version of the cap badge (Fig.1013). The only recorded use of them is on a photograph which shows them being worn on the lapels of the Battle Dress tunic. The picture, believed to have been taken shortly after WWII shows the men drawn up as if awaiting inspection. A reliable source has stated that these badges were not made specifically for the WWII Victory Parade, a practice carried out by some Regiments.

The other ranks pattern collar badge is also known in gilt, perhaps for wear in the khaki drill; and also in bronze, usage and period unknown.

Militia
The Hampshire Militia

The Regiment was formed in 1852 when the North Hampshire and South Hampshire Light Infantry Militia Regiments were amalgamated, the Light Infantry status not being maintained. The other ranks pattern collar badge in white metal, No.6939 was sealed 12th March 1875, under Authority 51/Hants/356. The description is, 'Star and Rose'. Though an example has not yet been located it might have been the display as per the tunic button 1855-1881, a crowned eight pointed star bearing the Garter Motto and a Rose within.

Upon becoming the 3rd Battalion, The Hampshire Regiment in 1881, Officers wore, for a short time, a collar badge depicting an enamelled Rose within a silver wreath (Fig.1014).

Royal Militia of the Island of Jersey

When the Channel Islands were evacuated in 1940, the Royal Jersey Militia became the 11th Battalion, The Hampshire Regiment. They continued to wear their own collar badges, a shield with three lions-leoparde superimposed upon a saltire and surmounted by a crown. In gilding metal for other ranks, and initially with a QVC (Fig.1015). The Gaunt Pattern books show them with the date 22nd January 1895, but they were in fact not sealed until 1898 being Pattern No.1724; renewed in 1899 as Pattern No.1724a. In 1940 they were of course bearing a KC (Fig.1016). This, Pattern No.1724b was sealed 25th June 1902. Approved 20th May 1901 to be worn on the new pattern forage cap, 'Left hand collar badge only and

Fig.1016    *Fig.1017*    *Fig.1018*    *Fig.1019*

THE ROYAL HAMPSHIRE REGIMENT

to be fitted with a vertical shank'. Officers wore the same pattern in bronze for the Service Dress jacket, approved and sealed at the War Office 30th December 1904. Also in gilt for use on the scarlet frock (Fig.1017), and in embroidery for full dress and mess dress (Figs.1018, 1019). Worn in facing pairs with the lions facing inwards.

An earlier white metal QVC version, Pattern No.3417 had been sealed 16th November 1880 along with, 'Those for 1st Class Staff Sgts. and bandsmen to be plated'. Pattern No.3418 sealed 26th November 1880.

Royal Guernsey Militia (Light Infantry)

Though this Regiment was not linked to the Hampshire Regiment it would appear appropriate, territorially, to record their badges at this juncture. By 1896 the infantry elements of the Island, 1st (East) Regiment, 2nd (North) and 3rd (South) were all designated as Light Infantry.

The first recorded badges in white metal, Pattern No.3416 were sealed 15th July 1880, with instruction that the badges for, '1st class Sgts. to be plated'. The format of this pattern is not described. Pattern No.1723 sealed in 1888 and resealed in 1889 under Pattern No.1723a, in gilding metal, bugle with crown above. (Fig.1020 shows the QVC type, Fig.1021 the KC). The latter was a cap/collar badge, Pattern No.6110, sealed 23rd November 1904. In silver for Officers they were worn in facing pairs with the bell ends facing inwards.

Near concurrent or successor patterns were quite different. (Figs.1022, 1023) show a facing pair, the earlier one in brass, the later in gilding-metal. An elongated lion-leoparde passant guardant. Officers wore similar in bronze for the Service Dress, sealed 7th December 1904 (Fig.1024). Also noted in silver plate and in gold bullion wire, mouth and eyes in red silk, sealed at the War Office 7th December 1904, 'For wear on tunic, frock coat and mess jacket'. (2nd Battalion, Fig.1025). A similar badge was sealed for the Officers of the 1st Battalion 12th January 1905 (Fig.1026).

Rifle Volunteer Corps, Volunteer, Territorial Force & Territorial Army Battalions

The collar badges worn by the consolidated battalion, 1st Hampshire Rifle Volunteer Corps, c.1880-1885 were simple strung and ribboned bugle horns, in silver plate for the Officers and white-metal for the men (Fig.207). Nominated in 1881, they became by General Order 91, 18th August 1885, the 1st Volunteer Battalion. The collar badge then adopted was similar to those of the parent units, but in white-metal. Shown in the Gaunt Pattern Books dated 3rd February 1886. Also shown is the badge for the Officers, the same pattern as used by the Regular unit Officers. The more squat other rank's pattern was adopted c.1899, again in white-metal.

The consolidated unit, 2nd Hampshire Rifle Volunteer Corps adopted Tiger collar badges quite early on, (Fig.1027) shows the free standing type, in white-metal for the men and silver for the Officers. After redesignation as the 2nd Volunteer Battalion the Tigers continued in use until 1894, when the white-metal Rose and wreath pattern was adopted. This is shown in the official

Fig.1020

Fig.1021

Fig.1022

Fig.1023

Fig.1024

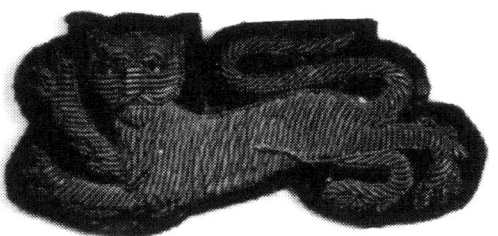

Fig.1025

Fig.1027

Fig.1026

HISTORY OF THE BRITISH ARMY INFANTRY COLLAR BADGE

Fig.1028

Fig.1029

Fig.1030

Fig.1031

Fig.1032

volunteer pattern book under Horse Guards Authority, V/2 Hants/1005, 28th July 1894.

When, on 1st April 1908, the 1st and 2nd Volunteer Battalions became the 4th and 5th (TF) Battalions respectively, both units adopted the collar badges worn by the 1st Battalion. The Cyclist Companies of the 4th (TF) Battalion wore blackened collar badges, (Rose and wreath) (Fig.1028).

The consolidated 3rd Hampshire Rifle Volunteer Corps, nominated in 1881 became the 3rd Volunteer Battalion in 1885. Redesignated 3rd (Duke of Connaught's Own) Volunteer Battalion, when HRH The Duke of Connaught was made Honorary Colonel of the Battalion. Upon the formation of the TF in 1908 they became the 6th (Duke of Connaught's Own) Battalion.

They wore a distinctive collar badge, the Hampshire Rose within a strap inscribed, 'Duke of Connaught's Own', the whole within a laurel wreath open at the top and with the Duke's coronet resting on the open ends. The other ranks in white-metal (Fig.1029), (much later replaced by one in silver anodised). Officers wore similar but larger and in bronze on their Service Dress. The title strap being voided along with the areas between the coronet and laurels (Fig.1030). One recorded variant has a smaller coronet and a solid centre (Fig.1031). On their full dress tunics the Officers wore the same pattern but in silver, a blue enamel background to the title strap, and red, white and green enamel additiond to the Rose (Fig.1032). Two other patterns are known, both without the laurel wreath, one in silver with the enamels as described above. The other in white-metal and enamels.

The other ranks white-metal badges were also worn by 388 A/T Regiment. RA, TA, being Pattern No.15190, sealed 6th August 1952, under Authority 54/Officers/4051. Additionally worn by 'B' Coy (Duke of Connaught's) 6th Royal Hampshire RA, The Hampshire and Isle of Wight Territorials.

With foundations as the 19th Hampshire Rifle Volunteer Corps (Bournemouth), and redesignated the 4th Hampshire Rifle Volunteer Corps in 1880, the Corps became the 4th Volunteer Battalion in 1885. The earlier Corps had used the 'dog guage' badge on its appointments from their birth, and this was utilised as the collar badge c1880-1908, in white-metal for other ranks (Fig.1033); silver for Officers and in bronze for use on the Service Dress (Fig.1034).Also known in gilt, believed to have been worn by WOs. The pattern is illustrated in the Gaunt books annotated, 'Pearce & Co 20/9/85'. Upon redesignation in 1908 as the 7th (TF) Battalion, the other ranks badge was worn in gilding-metal.

The dog guage which resembles a stirrup has nothing to do with horse riding but is a metal guage once used to measure the size of dogs in the New Forest. Any dog that could pass through the guage had to have the three middle claws of its front legs removed, thus to prevent it running fast enough to catch the Royal deer.

Later, the 5th/7th Battalion wore the same badge but with a Rose in the centre c.1928-1932, in gilding-metal, bronze, and silver (Fig.1035). These were later replaced with the Regular units' Rose and wreath pattern.

A larger gold anodised dog guage badge was later worn by 'E' Coy (7th Royal Hampshire) The Hampshire and Isle of Wight Territorials (Fig.1036).

A curious plasticised rubber version was also worn by a New Forest detachment of the Army Cadet Force (Fig.1037).

Fig.1033    *Fig.1034*    *Fig.1035*    *Fig.1036*

THE ROYAL HAMPSHIRE REGIMENT

1st Isle of Wight Rifle Volunteer Corps

This scattered small Corps were grouped and consolidated 13th April 1880 under the above title, nominated in 1881, and being redesignated 5th (Isle of Wight, Princess Beatrice's) Volunteer Battalion, 18th August 1885. Re-organised as the 8th (Princess Beatrice's Isle of Wight Rifles) (TF) Battalion, 1st April 1908.

They wore distinctive collar badges, the centrepiece representing Carisbrooke Castle. The other ranks badges showed the castle enclosed in a laurel wreath, closed at the top. Below the wreath a scroll inscribed, 'PRINCESS BEATRICE'S I OF W.' There was voiding between the wreath and the castle, and the wreath and the scroll. In white-metal (Fig.1038). Also in gilding-metal and worn with a dark green cloth backing (Fig.1039). A similar one is recorded with a blackened finish.

Officers wore a smaller version of their cap badge. This was the castle within a circle inscribed, 'ISLE OF WIGHT RIFLES', within a laurel wreath, open at the top and between the ends, a scroll inscribed, 'SOUTH AFRICA 1900-01'; the whole topped by a KC. Below the circle and superimposed on the base of the wreath, a scroll inscribed, 'PRINCESS BEATRICE'S'. The centre was voided. In bronze or blackend finish and worn on the Service Dress only, usually with a separate 'T' below (Fig.1040). A silver 'T' was worn on the black rolled collar of the green mess jacket.

HRH The Princess Beatrice, Queen Victoria's youngest daughter was Honorary Colonel of the Battalion 11th May 1937 until her death 26th October 1944. She was also Governor of the Isle of Wight and Carisbrooke Castle.

Cyclists
9th (Cyclist) Battalion
Raised November 1911, disembodied 5th February 1920.

1st/9th (Cyclist) Battalion (1914-1920) India and Siberia
2nd/9th (Cyclist) Battalion (1914-1919) Home Defence

These Battalions wore distinctive collar badges. The Hampshire Rose superimposed on a bicycle wheel, the other ranks in gilding-metal with either 12 or 30 spokes (Figs.1041, 1042). Officers wore similar with 30 spokes, in bronze on their Service Dress and sometimes with a bronze 'T' affixed at the base. Also worn on the khaki drill in India 1914-1919. The Officers 12 spoke version was a cap badge.

Buttonhole badges were also worn, but a similar item in gilt with red, white and blue enamels, and fitted with correct lug fasteners, is said to have been made privately and worn by the OC the Cyclist Battalion. (Fig.1043).

WWI Service Battalions
11th (Service) Battalion
Raised 9th September 1914 at Winchester as Infantry and converted to Pioneers 3rd December 1914 wearing the usual crossed rifle and pick collar badges (Fig.147). Photographs show the picks faced inwards. Disbanded 6th June 1919.

Fig.1037

Fig.1038

Fig.1039

Fig.1040

Fig.1041

Fig.1042

Fig.1043

Fig.1044

Unconfirmed badge

An embroidered collar badge showing the Hampshire Rose surmounted by a QC and with a 'Hampshire' scroll below, is reputed to have been worn by senior NCOs on their mess jackets. The Regimental Museum staff are quite adamant that these badges were never worn (Fig.1044).

General

Researching the many types of badges worn by the Regiment and its associates has proved to be difficult. Whereas it is normal practice for the Volunteer Battalions to wear variable badges from the Regular units, it is not so common for the two Regular Battalions to also wear different insignia. On the whole the 1st Battalion accepted and adopted new directives quite quickly, whereas the 2nd Battalion were reluctant to do so, ignoring Dress Regulations, and finally, for a time wore individual badges with a degree of Official blessing.

The shape and pattern of the Royal Tiger has varied considerably, but an official document 12th October 1925 signed by the Garter King at Arms, and Inpector General of Colours does portray the correct version. This has the beast facing fully towards the viewer, its tail curving back to mid-way above its back and then curving backwards and upwards. It is standing on ground with one front leg raised, the paw at a further upward angle finishing level with its eyes.

The Royal Hampshire Regiment survived an earlier amalgamation threat with the Gloucestershire Regiment in 1969, but under the Options for Change cuts 23rd July 1991, were on 9th September 1992, merged with The Queen's Regiment to become The Princess of Wales's Royal Regiment (Queen's and Royal Hampshire).

The South Staffordshire Regiment

Pre 1881
The 38th (1st Staffordshire) Regiment of Foot
The other ranks collar badge was Pattern No.9502, sealed 19th August 1874, 'for wear on the tunic and frock'. The Stafford Knot in brass with brass lugs was worn officially until 30th July 1879 (Fig.1045). There was then an assimilation of patterns to that worn by the 80th (Staffordshire Volunteers) Regiment, the slightly larger version, Pattern No.9523. Officers wore an embroidered version from late 1880 (Fig.1046).

Though the adoption of the 'Knot Simpliceter', the ancient badge of the Stafford Family probably dates back to 1782, when the 38th were given their first Territorial title, the first record of the badge on appointments is on the Officers shoulder belt plates c1795. It featured on successive plates and shako plates.

The 80th (Staffordshire Volunteers) Regiment of Foot
The re-raised 80th Regiment of 1793 were given the above title and adopted the 'Knot' onto their appointments immediately. The badge appearing on shoulder belt and shako plates. The 1874 Dress Regulations authorises the use of the badge in addition to the numerals on the Officers forage cap. As has been noted above the Regiment's first collar badge was Pattern No.9523, sealed 8th December 1874. In brass with brass lugs (Fig.1047). This badge appears on many photographs of NCO's and men during the South African Campaign of 1879. The same badge appears on the full dress photograph of Colour Sergeant Anthony Booth who won the VC for bravery at Ntumbe Drift, March 1879.

According to Official records, Pattern No.9523 was worn up to the 1881 amalgamation but it is thought that after 1879, when the 38th were to wear the same badge, the Regiment unofficially wore a distinctive brass female Sphinx over a tablet inscribed "EGYPT" (Fig.1048). This distinction had been bestowed on the Regiment 6th July 1802, for their distinguished services in the Egyptian Campaign. Officers wore an embroidered version of the Stafford Knot, 1880-1881 (Fig.1049). Additionally an embroidered pair of Sphinxes/Egypt collar badges reputedly taken from the tunic of an Officer of the 80th are shown (Figs.1050, 1051). They were worn with the Sphinx facing inwards.

Post 1881
When the two regiments were amalgamated in July 1881 to form the 1st and 2nd Battalions, The South Staffordshire Regiment, the 38th were stationed in Malta, the 80th in Ireland; both Battalions therefore continued to wear their existing

Fig.1045

Fig.1046

Fig.1047

Fig.1048

Fig.1050

Fig.1051

Fig.1049

HISTORY OF THE BRITISH ARMY INFANTRY COLLAR BADGE

Fig.1052

Fig.1053

Fig.1054

Fig.1055

Fig.1056

Fig.1057

Fig.1058

Fig.1059

collar badges for some time.

Understandably in this case, both Battalions agreed on adopting the 'Knot' as the collar badge. Pattern No.9523 was confirmed as the badge for both units 21st October 1881, but a new Pattern No.9881 was sealed 15th December 1881. Similar to the old type but in gilding-metal with copper lugs (Fig.1052). A new forage cap was introduced 20th December 1894 and for a time this collar badge was also used as the cap ornament.

Renewal of the standard pattern was demanded to be cut from new dies 27th November 1897, and the resultant Pattern No.9881a was sealed 6th April 1898. There was no change in design.

These badges were worn by soldiers of the 2nd Battalion on their foreign service white and khaki uniforms, but no collar badges were worn by either Officers or men of the 1st Battalion on their khaki uniforms during the South African War 1899-1902. After WWI, the 1st Battalion did wear them on their khaki drill during service in India.

From 1935, collar badges were worn with a piece of Brown Holland material backing, this was a distinction awarded by HM King George V in commemoration of fifty-seven years continuous service of the old 38th in the West Indies, 1707-1764. It is reputed that due to lack of supplies the troops had to mend their clothing with ticking (Holland) from old sacking. The distinction was extended to the 2nd Battalion who for a time wore a smaller pattern of the 'Knot' (Fig.1053). The 'brown' is in fact more of a buff colour. Initially the backing was oval shaped and overlapped the 'Knot', but gradually it has decreased in size and has been noted cut to the outline size of the badge, particularly in examples to the 2nd Battalion (possibly because the honour had been awarded to the old 38th).

Though officially no badges were to be worn on battle dress during WWII, there are many photographic instances of the opposite.

In early 1949, new collar badges in white metal were introduced for wear on the new battle dress with open collar. This was Pattern No.14033, sealed 6th December 1948. Worn until amalgamation (Fig.1054)

The early Dress Regulations describe the Officers tunic badge as, 'The Staffordshire Knot in gold embroidery'. Strictly this is incorrect as it should be the 'Stafford Knot', this error was perpetuated until 1934. The badge was approved 17th September 1881, and is illustrated in the Gaunt Pattern books under the date 23rd November 1881. Later used on the scarlet frock and the blue frock coat, on white cloth backing for the tunic and scarlet frock and on blue cloth for the frock coat (Figs.1055, 1056). After 1935 with an additional backing of the Brown Holland (Fig.1057). Initially collar badges were not worn on the blue frock but when a new pattern was introduced in 1902 they were adopted. The 1900 Dress Regulations direct for the scarlet frock, 'Collar badges of similar pattern to those worn on the tunic but with metal substituted for embroidery. In gilt (Fig.1058).

The collar badges for mess dress, first mentioned in the 1911 Edition, were similar to those worn on the full dress tunic but smaller (Fig.1059). In 1935 the colour of the facings and the mess waistcoat were changed, and the embroidered badges gave way to gilt substitutes (Fig.1060); worn until 1949 when they were replaced with silver metal imitation embroidery versions (Fig.1061).

The badge introduced for wear with Service Dress in 1902 was as for the forage cap in bronze, a KC over the 'Knot' with a scroll below inscribed, "SOUTH STAFFORDSHIRE" (Fig.1062). Considered to be too large, photographs of Officers c.1917-18 show them wearing bronze 'Knots' only. A questionnaire returned just after the end of WWI by the 1st Battalion revealed that in 1918 their Officers were wearing the 'Knot' only (Fig.1063), whereas the 2nd Battalion were still using the large cap/collar badge. Though a note on the return of the latter Battalion indicates that they wore the 'Knot' only when abroad. Generally the 1st Battalion appear to have worn larger standard size 'Knot' only, bronze badges, whereas the 2nd Battalion persisted with the smaller type (Fig.1064). The 1934 Dress Regulations continued to describe the Service Dress badge, 'as for forage cap' but the single 'Knots' were worn by some Officers on battle dress during WWII, and on Service Dress until 1949; after 1935 whith the Brown Holland material backing.

Around 1924-1925, Officers of the 2nd Battalion wore silver Knot collar badges even extending these to the khaki Service Dress. In 1935, Officers of the 1st Battalion wore similar badges on their blue patrols. Bronze collar badges were given up in 1949 and the silver metal imitation embroidered badge was adopted (Fig.1065). The Regimental Sergeant Major wore collar badges of gold embroidery on the Brown Holland cloth (Fig.1066).

Militia
(The King's Own) 1st Staffordshire Militia

The Regiment adopted the Stafford Knot in white-metal for wear in the tunic collar. The badge being sealed 13th May 1878. Size as for the 80th Foot. The Regiment had divided into two Battalions in 1874. In 1881 the Regiment became the 3rd and 4th Battalions, The South Staffordshire Regiment, but serving as a double Battalion. They were divided 1st August 1900.

Rifle Volunteer Corps, Volunteer, Territorial Force & Territorial Army Battalions

The consolidated Battalions, 2nd and 5th Staffordshire Rifle Volunteer Corps, nominated in 1881, were exchanged for the 1st, 3rd and 4th Staffordshire Rifle Volunteer Corps in 1882. These three units becoming the 1st, 2nd and 3rd Volunteer Battalions in 1883. No collar badges have been noted for use prior to these changes. The subsequent collar badges were white-metal versions of the Regulars pattern. The design for the men of the 1st VB was submitted 14th June 1883 and authorised under Authority V/1 Stafford/282, while similar approval for the 2nd VB was received 13th January 1885, and for the 3rd VB, 28th March 1885 under Authority V/4 Stafford/223. They were identical. The Officers wore silver embroidered badges. Upon conversion to the Territorial Force in 1908, most elements of the 1st VB became part of the 1st North Midland Field Company, Royal Engineers. What remained, merged with the 2nd VB and became the 5th Battalion, the 3rd VB becoming the 6th Battalion. The badges of the parent units were gradually adopted, though separate 'T' badges were worn below the cap/collar bronze Service Dress badges.

A sealed pattern 7th November 1956 pertaining to the 5th Battalion (TA), shows a medium sized silver metal imitation embroidery Knot with Brown Holland material backing for Officers, and in white-metal for the men. Pattern No. 14033 was used as a guide for the silver anodised collar badge, Pattern No.19230, sealed 23rd January 1964, under Authority 54/Inf/8523.

Volunteer Training Corps (1914-1918)

When the various Staffordshire VTC were integrated into the Army as a Volunteer

Fig.1060

Fig.1061

Fig.1062

Fig.1063

Fig.1064

Fig.1065

Fig.1066

Fig.1067

force, Officers wore a small bronze 'V' below their collar badges on Service Dress.

WWI Service Battalions
9th (Service) Battalion

Raised 3rd October 1914 as Infantry and converted to Pioneers 21st April 1915 wearing the usual crossed rifle and pick collar badges (Fig.147). Disbanded 8th April 1919.

Another badge

An item sometimes thought to pertain to the Staffordshire Rifle Volunteers is shown (Fig.1067). A QVC over the Knot in white-metal, the badge applies to the Staffordshire Yeomanry.

General

Although unquestionably the 'Knot' is worn with the end uppermost, the direction of the rope in its formation of the loops has been noted in opposite directions. The Author is of the opinion that these are not manufacturers' variations but an attempt to make the badges in facing pairs; certainly pre 1881 examples do 'face' and many post 1881 are likewise. Both versions would fulfill the desire of the ancient member of the Stafford family - to hang three people similtaneously with one piece of rope!

The Regiment amalgamated with The North Staffordshire Regiment (The Prince of Wales's) 31st January 1959 to form The Staffordshire Regiment (The Prince of Wales's).

The Dorset Regiment

Pre 1881
The 39th (Dorsetshire) Regiment of Foot

By an Authority PC/Infy/Genrl/111 dated 16th July 1872, the Regiment received permission to wear the brass Imperial crown as the first other ranks collar badge. Worn from 1874-1878 (Fig.333).

The shell jacket of a Colour Sergeant shows that when he was discharged in 1877, large brass '39' numeral badges were being worn on both sides of the collar (Fig.1068).

The honour 'Gibraltar' was awarded to the 39th (then the East Middlesex Regiment, becoming Dorsetshire in 1807) for their part in the heroic defence of the Rock 1779-1783. The honour was authorised 14th April 1784, but the Castle and Key distinctions obviously taken into use at about the same time, were removed by the Inspector of Colours in 1807 and not authorised until 17th November 1835. After this date they featured very much in the insignia of the Regiment.

In 1877, the War Office suggested that, 'The Castle and Key' be worn as a collar badge and a design was submitted from India dated 29th October; the War Office giving approval by letter 27th December. This badge Pattern No.9634, sealed 14th February 1878 was in brass with brass lugs. A wide horizontal twin towered Castle of Gibraltar, each tower with a lookout in the top section, the curtain wall having two lookouts and a closed archway. Above, a turret with a flag flying to the right. Below the Castle, a tri-part scroll inscribed 'PRIMUS IN INDIS'. The Key facing right depends from the archway to the centre section of the scroll (Fig.1069).

After 1880, Officers wore an embroidered version of this badge. The badges were not worn in facing pairs.

"Primus in Indis" was an unique honour, awarded to the 39th for their bravery at the Battle of Plassey in 1757, their outstanding service during the campaign of 1754-1757, and the fact that they were the first Regiment of the Line to serve in India.

The Regiment to hold the title 'Dorsetshire' for the first time was the 35th, 1782-1805.

The 54th (West Norfolk) Regiment of Foot

The Sphinx with Egypt, authorised 6th July 1802, was awarded to all Regiments who took part in the Egyptian Campaign 1800-1802; the 54th later received an unique distinction, the Sphinx superscribed 'Marabout'. Both Battalions of the Regiment were in Egypt, the 1st Battalion particularly distinguishing itself in the capture of the Marabout fort at the entrance to the harbour at Alexandria. The honour 'Marabout' was awarded 18th Decmeber 1841. Some sources indicate that this was the restoration date, the honour being awarded in 1802, but this is not so.

The Officers of the 54th were some of the earliest to adopt the practice of wearing collar badges in addition to their rank badges. Prior to their return from Gibraltar in 1856, Officers were wearing gold thread embroidered Sphinx/EGYPT badges, (Fig.1070), soon after their return they wore similar, but with "MARABOUT" replacing Egypt (Fig.1071). Although this practice was objected to on the grounds that it was not in accord with current Dress Regulations (1857), the Regiment successfully appealed, quoting the original Horse Guards letter 20th January 1842. The 1857 Dress Regulations certainly authorise the wearing of the

Fig.1068

Fig.1069

Fig.1070

Fig.1071

HISTORY OF THE BRITISH ARMY INFANTRY COLLAR BADGE

Sphinx/Marabout badge above the numerals '54' in the Officers forage cap. This badge is illustrated (Fig.1072) to show the similarity in design between the Sphinx and that of the collar badge (Fig.1071).

Records in the National Army Museum indicate that in 1860, Officers of the 54th wore a collar badge, 'in gold / enamel'. These are also featured in the Gaunt Pattern books with the same date. The illustration shows a female Sphinx with rounded head, mantle extending down over the back, and with the tail rising up over the back and pointing towards the head. The tablet below inscribed "MARABOUT". The Sphinx, edging of the tablet and letters in gilt, background to the tablet dark green enamel. Surely one of the earliest metal collar badges, and a fine example of the badge maker's art (Fig.1073).

By an Authority 16th July 1872, approval was given for the NCOs and men to wear a Sphinx/Marabout collar badge. In brass, Pattern No.9501 was not sealed until 6th August 1874. (Figs.1074, 1075 show a facing pair). As the Regiment spent most of the 1870's in India, not returning to this country until 1886, some of the brass collar badges were of local 'sand-cast' manufacture, and vary considerably in size (Fig.1076).

Fig.1072

Fig.1073

Fig.1074

Fig.1075

Post 1881

The two Regiments amalgamated in 1881 to form the 1st and 2nd Battalions, The Dorsetshire Regiment. The AAG Horse Guards (22nd October) verbally confirmed that the new collar badge, 'would be the present pattern of the 54th Foot, pattern 9501'. Using this pattern as a guide, a new Pattern No.10016 was sealed 2nd February 1882, the badge now being in white metal. This pattern is illustrated in the Gaunt Pattern books annotated, "German silver in pairs – ground, line horizontally – 1881" (Fig.1077).

When the collar badge was actually taken into use is not known, but a description of 'the 2nd Battalion arriving at Portsmouth' from Aden at the end of 1886 records one man still wearing his old pre 1881 glengarry hat badge, and many of the men still wearing their brass 54th collar badges. Some soldiers, however, were wearing the correct collar badge, as borne out by a letter sent by the OC 1st Battalion enquiring as to the correct position of the new collar badge worn on the Serge Frock. 'As the 1st Bn. wear theirs 1½ inches from the opening and ⅓ inch above the lower edge of the collar, whereas the 2nd Bn. wear theirs 1 inch from the opening and touching the seams of the collar.' A decision was made 26th February 1884 as follows, 'There being no instructions on the subject, collar badges are to be fitted as at present fitted in the Home Bn (Viz 1st Bn.)'

On such momentous decisions the British Army was built!

However, this was not the end of the matter as the GOC Aldershot was advised 4th April 1884 that there was now a need for a proper regulation covering the position, it was felt that the best position would be as already advised to the Dorsetshire Regiment, but before any final decision was taken circular letters were being sent. These were sent to the OCs 1st Bn. Somerset Light Infantry, 1st Bn. The Duke of Cornwall's Light Infantry, 1st Bn. South Wales Borderers, 1st Bn. Northamptonshire Regiment (in N. Ireland), 2nd Battalion Gordon Highlanders, and 2nd Battalion Argyll & Sutherland Highlanders (in N. Ireland), 'to ascertain whether any better position can be assigned'.

The first pattern collar badge was also worn by the 2nd Battalion on the field

Fig.1076

Fig.1077

172

cap (facing to the left) prior to the introduction of a new field service cap in August 1897. There is no evidence that it was worn by the 1st Battalion.

A call for the renewal of the pattern to be cut from new dies was made 30th November 1896. Pattern No.10016a was sealed 4th March 1897 under Authority ACD/patt/8189. There was no change in design even after the Regiment was redesignated The Dorset Regiment in 1951, and the same badge was worn right through to amalgamation in 1958, the latter issues with single lug and plate fasteners. There were remarkably few manufacturers' variants, an example with slightly smaller lettering is shown (Fig.1078). The later issues with the Sphinx having a different face had more of a greyish silver finish (Fig.1079). After amalgamation, the Regimental Museum had some specially made for resale in their shop, and these followed the pattern last worn by the Regiment.

Although never officially approved, other ranks collar badges were given a chrome finish by the Regimental Armourer and were worn by the Regimental Police in the mid 1950's together with chromed cap badges, buttons and shoulder titles.

The standard collar badge was worn in Korea 1954-1955 with a square of green cloth backing. Noted also with a blackened finish and probably worn by a Cyclist Section c.1885-1914. Silver plated versions of the other ranks collars occur, but are not the subject of any written authority.

After the link up in 1881, Officers of the 39th and 54th continued to wear their old embroidered badges for a few months, but eventually a gold embroidered Sphinx over the Marabout tablet was introduced. These are recorded in the Gaunt Pattern books, 22nd November 1881. Some of the earliest examples have a red backing and others a yellow. (Figs.1080, 1081 show an early period facing pair.) The same source also illustrates a female Sphinx annotated, 'Silver Sphinx, gilt and green enamel plinth, 1881'. Described in the 1883 Dress Regulations as, 'The Sphinx in silver, on a gilt tablet. On the tablet "Marabout" in gilt letters on a ground of green enamel.' These were worn on the tunic, frock coat, and from 1904 on the mess jacket. They continued to be worn on the appropriate uniforms up to 1958. The embroidered badges therefore were very short lived.

All were full breasted female Sphinxes of which there were many minor variations. Fig.1082 shows a large Sphinx, male face, double line round edge of mantle, and with the front feet ending beneath the breasts. Pronouncedly tall lettering on the tablet. A variant is similar but with more squat lettering. That in (Fig.1083) shows a different form of Sphinx and with the front legs extending to the near edge of the plinth. Other examples show varying combinations of these features, including examples with a slightly smaller 'O' in Marabout (Fig.1084). The colour of the enamel varies, on the early ones the correct dark green to almost lime green on the later examples (from c.1908 onward). Construction varies, some having a solid back section and others a die struck reverse. Generally it would appear that those examples with the retracted front feet and more masculine faces were made by Messrs. Firmins, the others by Messrs. Gaunt.

A sealed pattern 13th October 1903 was noted but regretably the collar badges were missing.

The last War Office sealed pattern noted was on 13th October 1956 under Authority 54/Officers/4025, being annotated, 'For No.1 Dress'.

Fig.1078

Fig.1079

Fig.1080

Fig.1081

Fig.1082

Fig.1084

Fig.1083

HISTORY OF THE BRITISH ARMY INFANTRY COLLAR BADGE

Fig.1085

Fig.1086

Fig.1087

Fig.1088

When Service Dress was introduced in 1902, Officers wore similar collar badges but in bronze. All the variations listed above apply to these as well, along with the usual finished colour differences (Figs.1085, 1086 for two such examples, 1086 being the one sealed by the War Office 3rd October 1956).

The above collar badges were worn by the 2nd Battalion who appear to have immediately adopted and abided by the written orders. Not so the 1st Battalion who disliked the female Sphinx, in particular one early post 1881 CO is purported to have stated, 'No female will reign over my Castle'. This referring to the Officers' forage cap badge. His views also extended to the collar badges because he had his own pattern made up for use by the Officers. A male Sphinx with no visible tail, and with an asp on top of the mantle, a variant also used by the Gordon Highlanders. Believed to have been made by Messrs. Gaunt there are no known variations in the silver/gilt/enamel pattern. (Fig.1087). Being unofficial there is no record as to how long they were worn, but it appears they were worn on the blue patrols up to 1947, and on the No.1 Dress up to 4th September 1948 when the 1st and 2nd Battalions were amalgamated. The badge in bronze was worn on the Service Dress, here variations have been noted as Messrs. Gaunt and Messrs. Jennens examples have been recorded. All variants have the asp on the mantle. (Figs. 1088, 1089 show two examples.) When Service Dress was introduced, the impossible task of providing these badges immediately was resolved by the Battalion's armoureres removing the tails from the female pattern! (Fig.1090, 1091 show two minor variants.) It is recorded that the bronze male Sphinx collar badges were worn up to the end of WWI when they were ordered to wear the correct pattern. If this is correct it is difficult to understand why the 1st Battalion were allowed to continue wearing the full dress version.

Photographs of Officers of the Dorsetshire Regiment, serving with the Royal Flying Corps, show bronze female sphinx/Marabout collar badges being worn, with the usual RFC cap badge.

Both female and male patterns were rubbed down to gilding-metal and worn by the Warrant Officers and other senior NCOs.

Although there is no authority via Dress Regulations, photographs and actual uniforms indicate that the bronze cap badge with blades removed and lugs fitted were worn on the lapels of the Officers Service Dress. The cap badge is described in Dress regulationas as, 'A laurel wreath with a scroll inscribed 'Dorsetshire', the wreath and scroll forming a circle. Within the circle, The Castle and Key. Above the Castle, the Sphinx resting on a tablet inscribed, 'Marabout'. Below the Castle a scroll with the words, 'Primus in Indis'. There are two variations, one with the Castle resting on a narrow bar (Fig.1092), and another with the Castle resting on more definite ground (Fig.1093).

Fig.1089

Fig.1091

Fig.1090

Fig.1092

Fig.1093

THE DORSET REGIMENT

One bronze item about which no information has been forthcoming is that shown in Fig.1094. A male 'Lincolnshire' Sphinx over the Marabout tablet. It must pertain to the Regiment, as Marabout is an honour unique to the Regiment. Most probably post 1902, and being 'male' may well pertain to the 1st Battalion. Two other such items have been noted, both with considerable service wear, indicating that they were not trial pieces.

Both the 2nd Battalion, with their female pattern, and the 1st Battalion, with their male version, wore collar badges in silver and silver plate on their red patrols c.1897-1890 (Figs.1095, 1096).

Illustrated in (Fig.1097) is one of a facing pair of collar badges in green silk embroidery on a dark green backing. They may well apply to the "Dorsets" but so far there is no recorded or photographic evidence. Possibly worn unofficially in the late 1930s.

Embroidered Sphinx/Marabout collar badges were worn on mess jackets (Fig.1098,1099), period uncertain though most probably before the sanction of the metal ones in the early 1900s.

Militia
Dorsetshire Militia

Reconstituted in 1759 under the Colonelcy of The Hon. George Pitt (created Lord Rivers of Strathfieldsaye in 1776). The Regiment became the 3rd Battalion, The Dorsetshire Regiment in 1881. An interesting entry in the Journals of the Army Pattern Room records, 'By a decision under PM/Dorset Militia/363, 10th August 1881, Dorset Militia (3rd Bn. The Dorsetshire Regiment) it is noted that sample badges for tunic and frock collars were approved for design only on 15th February 1876 under PC/DM/149. The Commanding Officer was informed that the collar badge then in possession might be retained for use, but when new dies are required, the badge must be reduced to the proper dimensions. Three badges were to be sent for standard patterns but have yet to be received (25th August 1881).'

The design under discussion was the crest of the late Lord Rivers (peerage extinct 1828), 'A stork proper', this was embellished by placing a Baron's coronet above the stork. The Pattern Room Journal notes, 'One of the badges, half a pair extracted from PC/Dorset Militia/149 and retained as a sample in the Pattern Room in design only. The other half pair being left in the paper (15th August 1881).'

The design can be seen in the Gaunt Pattern books dated 16th March 1878. This coincides with the use of the badge as the Officers helmet plate centre 1878-1881. It was not in use prior to this date. The late Major H.G. Parkyn in his notes on the badges of English Militia Regiments (SAHR Journal No.60, Winter 1936), states that the crest was worn as a collar badge on Officers' mess jackets prior to WWI. This is borne out by an extant example of such a jacket, the badges in silver and gold metal thread embroidery are a facing pair. The stork on a torse is surmounted by the Baron's coronet, further surmounted by a KC - this decorated with green and red silks; the whole on a green backing and stitched onto the green lapels of

Fig.1094

Fig.1095

Fig.1096

Fig.1097

Fig.1098

Fig.1099

Fig.1101

Fig.1100

175

HISTORY OF THE BRITISH ARMY INFANTRY COLLAR BADGE

Fig.1102

Fig.1103

Fig.1104

Fig.1105

Fig.1106

the jacket (Figs.1100, 1101). No examples of the mens' white-metal collar badges c.1876-1881 have been traced so far.

Regular pattern Officers collar badges but in reverse metals are well recorded and may well have been used by the Officers after 1881.

Rifle Volunteer Corps, Volunteer, Territorial Force & Territorial Army Battalions

Raised 1859 onward as the 1st to 11th Dorset Rifle Volunteers and finally consolidated 1st June 1880 as the 1st Dorsetshire Rifle Volunteer Corps, the Corps did not wear collar badges. Nominated in 1881, they became the 1st Volunteer Battalion 1st December 1887. Under this title the undress hat badges are sometimes mistaken for collar badges (Figs.1102, 1103 show the Officers and other ranks badges respectively). Both with a red cloth backing the title reads '1 VB DORSET REGT', and the central device shows the old County Rifle Volunteer precedence number '16', above this a cap of maintenance with flames issuing from the top of it. There is no civic background to this device, but as Roman fasces were also used on other badges of the Dorsetshire Rifle Volunteers, they perhaps recall the stand against oppression made by the Tolpuddle Martyrs. The badges appear in varied metals but all are headdress badges. The other ranks of the 1st Volunteer Battalion wore the same collar badge as the Regulars. The Officers wearing an all silver and green enamel version of the female pattern (Figs.1104, 1105).

Upon reorganisation as the 4th (TF) Battalion in 1908, the other ranks continued to wear the standard pattern and Officers gradually changing to silver/gilt/enamel pattern. The bronze Officers Service Dress collar badge was however worn with a blank tablet.

When the 1st Battalion merged with the Devonshire Regiment in 1958, the 4th Battalion TA continued to wear the old insignia. In 1963 the other ranks white-metal, Pattern No.10016a collar badge was used as a guide for a silver anodised version. This was Pattern No.19605 sealed 27th November under Authority 54/Inf/8854 (Fig.1106). Made with a solid back and one central fitting it is not known if they were ever worn or indeed issued. The unit later formed part of 'B' Coy, The Dorset Territorials in 1967, but no collar badges were worn.

Schools
Sherborne School Cadet Corps

Attached to the 1st Volunteer Battalion, the Corps wore the standard pattern collar badges.

Dorchester Grammar School O.T.C.

No collar badges worn.

Home Guard

Although "badged" to the Dorsetshire Regiment, no collar badges were worn.

General

The Regiments, 39th, 54th, and The Dorsetshire have been difficult to research, particularly as the 1st Battalion wore unofficial badges. The Regiment did make an effort in 1934 to establish the correct pattern of Sphinx, and a reply from The College of Arms, 22nd March confirmed that the Sphinx granted for the 1801 Egyptian Campaign was, 'Female with tail erect.' It is officially recorded that, 'All Battalions of the Dorsetshire Regiment wear the same collar badge.' This is unusual as most Volunteer and Militia Battalions were not allowed to bear battle honours on their insignia. All sphinx collar badges were worn in FPs with the Sphinx facing inwards towards the collar opening.

On 17th May 1958, the Regiment amalgamated with The Devonshire Regiment to become The Devonshire and Dorset Regiment (both less Territorials).

The South Lancashire Regiment
(The Prince of Wales's Volunteers)

Pre 1881
The 40th (2nd Somersetshire) Regiment of Foot

By an Authority of 16th July 1872, Pattern No.9532, sealed 8th February 1875, became the first other ranks collar badge for wear on the tunic and frock collars. A female Sphinx with "EGYPT" tablet below, lodged within and upon a 'flat' ovoid of laurels; on the top of the laurel a QVC which depends onto the mantle of the Sphinx. In brass, with brass lugs, the badges were worn in facing pairs with the Sphinxes facing inwards (Figs.1107, 1108 show a facing pair). The Sphinx/Egypt commemorate the Regiment's service in Egypt when the flank companies of the 1st/40th Regiment displayed outstanding gallantry at Aboukir and Alexandria. Awarded 6th July 1802.

The Sphinx is of the female or Grecian variety as opposed to the male or Egyptian Sphinx, this being confirmed as correct by a letter 22nd March 1934 from the Garter King at Arms and Inspector of Regimental Colours.

Fig.1107

Fig.1108

The 82nd (Prince of Wales's Volunteers) Regiment of Foot

Pattern No.9298 sealed 13th February 1873, was the badge authorised 16th July 1872. A large brass Prince of Wales's Crest and Motto (Fig.1109). This badge was worn until 1881 when there was a slight change in outline and the metal changed to white-metal (Fig.1110). It has not been possible to ascertain the precise date of introduction, but the badge was short lived for after amalgamation in July 1881, new collar badges were sealed in the December following.

The Officers wore c.1880 to late 1881, a beautifully embroidered version in silver and gold thread and blue silk backing to the Motto scroll (Fig.1111).

The 82nd, when formed for the third time in 1793, consisted entirely of volunteers and their Colonel, General Charles Leigh, an Officer in the Household of the Prince of Wales, obtained for the Regiment, the title, The Prince of Wales's Volunteers.

Fig.1109

Post 1881

The two Regiments merged in July 1881 to form The Prince of Wales's Volunteers (South Lancashire Regiment). Consultation between the Officers resulted in the retention of the Prince of Wales's Crest and Motto for the new

Fig.1110

Fig.1111

Fig.1112

Fig.1113

Fig.1114

Fig.1115

collar badge, but now with a long scroll enveloping over half of the badge, inscribed, "PRINCE OF WALES VOLUNTEERS". The design was submitted by Messrs. Smith and Wright, Birmingham, on behalf of the Regiment. It was not initially accepted, being revised by the AAG Horse Guards, who also directed that the new badge would be in white-metal and gilding-metal. The final design was Pattern No.9910, sealed 29th December 1881, the Feathers and Motto in white-metal and the Coronet and title scroll in gilding-metal (Fig.1112). This badge was also worn on the field cap up to the introduction of a new field service cap in December 1897. The opportunity was then taken to cut a renewal of the standard pattern from new dies. The resultant Pattern, No.9910a being sealed 14th September 1899. No change in design.

In 1920, the Regiment was redesignated The Prince of Wales's Volunteers (South Lancashire), and after prolonged discussion the decision was taken to amend the spelling on the collar badge to match that of the Regiment's title, i.e. 'WALES'S'. This resulted in Pattern No.3716, sealed 20th February 1923, under Authority 2037/QMG7/1923 (Fig.1113).

The Regiment was again redesignated in 1938, The South Lancashire Regiment (The Prince of Wales's Volunteers); though no doubt fresh designs were submitted for approval, WWII soon intervened and the minutiae of badge design became rather secondary. As a result, the precise time at which the new collar badge (Fig.1114) was introduced is not known; the scroll, still of the same outline was now inscribed, 'SOUTH LANCASHIRE REGIMENT'.

A further larger design, Pattern No.14613, sealed 16th March 1951, was assimilated to the current Officers pattern, the larger tri-part scroll reading, 'THE SOUTH LANCASHIRE REGIMENT' (Fig.1115). All the ones noted have the single central lug fastener. This was used as a guide for the silver/gold anodised version, and though probably never worn by the 1st Battalion, was worn by the TA units.

The 1883 Dress Regulations describe the Officers collar badge as, 'The Prince of Wales's Plume, in gold and silver embroidery, on a blue cloth ground, the scroll in blue silk with the motto in silver embroidery'. Sealed late 1881, early 1882 (Fig.1116). Being hand made, there have been minor variations in size and outline (Figs.1117, 1118). They were also worn on No.1 Dress and the mess dress jacket. For the scarlet frock the badge was in silver and gilt metals, various patterns are recorded, firstly the other ranks equivalent with 'WALES' spelling, worn until 1923 (Fig.1119), followed by similar but with 'WALES'S' (Fig 1120). Some of the first pattern have been noted with gilt Motto scrolls. The larger pattern with tri-part scroll is also found with both spellings (Figs.1121, 1122). Finally, with change of

Fig.1116

Fig.1118

Fig.1119

Fig.1117

Fig.1120

Fig.1121

Fig.1122

THE SOUTH LANCASHIRE REGIMENT

title scrolls, 'THE SOUTH LANCASHIRE REGIMENT" as per (Fig.1115). Worn up to amalgamation.

Yet another pattern is also recorded in silver/gilt, more delicate separated plumes and a fuller rounder scroll. Both spellings occur, 'WALES' and 'WALES'S'. These were worn by the Warrant Officers (Figs.1123,1124). A badge of similar design in all gilding-metal with 'WALES' spelling was also worn by these Officers, on early mess dress and later on Service Dress (Fig 1125).

The badge for the Officers' 1902 Service Dress was described as, 'As for forage, but in bronze'. Thus, 'The Sphinx over Egypt. Above the Sphinx the Prince of Wales's Plume, Motto and Coronet. On either side a spray of laurel; betweenthe top ends of the spray a scroll inscribed, "South Lancashire"; between the bottom ends another scroll inscribed, "Prince of Wales's Vols." This description has omitted the metals as the Service Dress badges were, of course, bronze. Sealed by the War Office 30th September 1903 (Fig.1126). They were made in facing pairs with the Sphinx facing inwards.

A letter to the Regiment from the War Office, 20th June 1934, under Authority 54/Officers/3140 reads; 'I am commanded by the Army Council to inform you that it has come to their notice that in many units the dress of both Officers and men do not conform in all respects with that laid down in Regulations. A number of irregularities referred to appear to be associated with Regimental history or are customs of long standing. If your unit desires to have any such items of dress regularised, applications should be submitted to the W.O. with your recommendations and supported by a statement of the reasons to continue the departure from Regulations'.

A reply dated 9th July 1934 from Major General A. Solly-Flood CB, CMG, DSO. Colonel of the Regiment was sent from Peninsula Barracks, Warrington to the Under Secretary of State, W.O., SW1. as follows; 'Whilst on an official visit to the Regimental Depot my attention has been drawn to a W.O. letter, 54/Officers/2997, 5th January 1933, and to the box of sealed patterns of Officers' devices amended 2nd January 1934. The bronze dress collar badge, in pairs with Sphinx facing inwards has not to my recollection of over 40 years aquaintance with the Regiment ever been worn as a collar badge. My statement is supported by many old photographs held in the Regimental Museum here, and the opinion of the oldest members of the Regiment. The badge in question is most unsuitable as a collar badge. I enclose a specimen of that which has invariably been worn, and request that action may kindly be taken to have this regularised as the sealed pattern, for use by all Battalions of the Regiment, and the card of Officers devices amended accordingly.'

Unfortunately, his eloquence was not matched by his staff's competence, as the badge was not sent. A further letter, 11th July, apologised for the omission and also stated, 'The same size and pattern (in silver gilt and gold scrolls) is worn by Officers on blue undress uniforms.'

The bronze badge submitted was the type with the 'WALES' spelling (Fig. 1127). There is also a slightly smaller type with the less full scroll (Fig 1128). There is no extant record of the outcome of these exchanges, but as the later patterns, 'WALES'S' and 'THE SOUTH LANCASHIRE REGIMENT' are well recorded, it must have been favourable.

In a questionnaire returned by the Regiment after WWI, it is recorded that no

Fig.1123

Fig.1124

Fig.1125

Fig.1126

Fig.1127   *Fig.1128*

collar badge was worn on Service Dress by the 1st Battalion during the 1914-1918 War, and to the question as to whether any special or different collar badge was worn by Officers, the answer from the 2nd Battalion was, 'No, same badge for all ranks'.

Dress Regulations for the Regiment, 19th January 1955 direct under Section 24. "Collar badges - The Feathers with scroll under, in bronze or gilt and silver (according to dress) to be 1⅕ inches wide and in height."

Militia
4th Royal Lancashire (Duke of Lancaster's Own) Light Infantry Militia

This Regiment raised in 1853 became the 3rd Battalion in 1881. A list of collar badges worn in 1881 records records for the 4th Royal Lancashire, 'Bugle, crown and Rose, these in white metal were sealed 2nd November 1875. Pattern books show the collar badge under the date 'Feb.1877'. (Line drawing, Fig.1129) shows a delicate crowned bugle horn with double Rose within, the badge of a more horizontal appearance than most bugle horn badges.

Fig.1129

Fig.1130

Fig.1131

Rifle Volunteer Corps, Volunteer, Territorial Force & Territorial Army Battalions

The 9th and 49th Lancashire Rifle Volunteers were merged in 1880 as the 9th Corps, nominated in 1881, they became the 1st Volunteer Battalion in 1886. Similarly the 47th and 48th Lancashire Rifle Volunteers were allied in 1880 to form the 21st Corps, nominated in 1881 and becoming the 2nd Volunteer Battalion in 1886.

It was not until 1888 that drawings of the intended collar badge for wear by the 1st VB were submitted for approval by Messrs. Hobson & Son, London, on behalf of the Battalion. The pattern, identical to that worn by the Regular units but in white-metal, was approved 5th March 1888 for 'Rank and file' under Authority V/9 Lancashire/423. These were also worn by the 2nd VB. Officers of both Battalions wore an all silver version of the Regular Officers' silver/gilt metal frock badge. Both badges had the 'WALES' spelling.

In 1908, the two Battalions became the 4th and 5th (TF) Battalions respectively and gradually adopted the collar badges of the Regular units. There were exceptions as ever, Officers of the 4th Battalion are reputed to have worn their Service Dress collar badges with the tablet below the Sphinx left blank (Fig.1130). Officers of the 5th Battalion wore the same but with a blackened finish to the badge.

A sealed pattern 10th October 1956 (54/Officers/4025) shows the last pattern bronze collar badge, 'For No.1 & 3 Dress', and in silver/gold anodised for the men (Fig.1131).

WWI Battalions

The 11th (St Helen's Pioneer) Battalion raised 1st September 1914 and converted to Pioneers 13th October 1918. They wore the usual crossed rifle and pick collar badges (Fig.147). Disbanded 30th June 1919.

General

The Regiment amalgamated 1st July 1958 with The East Lancashire Regiment to become The Lancashire Regiment (Prince of Wales's Volunteers).

The Welsh Regiment

Pre 1881
The 41st (The Welsh) Regiment of Foot
Regulations directed that the first other ranks collar badge would be the Prince of Wales's, Crest and Motto. In brass, this was Pattern No.9516, sealed 14th October 1874 (Fig.1132). Photographs in the Regimental Museum show them being worn by a Drum Major c.1875, and by the Band in Natal, May 1881. The Prince of Wales's Crest and Motto were authorised 19th December 1831, along with a Welch motto, 'GWELL ANGAU NA CHYWILYDD' (Death rather than dishonour). The origins for this adoption are uncertain, it is the motto of a leading Monmouthshire family, the Marckworths of Glen Usk. The Lieutenant Colonel of the 41st at the time, himself a Welchman is thought to have petitioned for the motto, a suitably martial one, when applying for the 41st to become a Welch Regiment. No doubt the Mackworths were also approached for permission to use their family motto.

Fig.1132

The 69th (South Lincolnshire) Regiment of Foot
The first other ranks collar badge was Pattern No.9527, sealed 11th December 1874. This was a circle inscribed "SOUTH LINCOLN", in the centre a plain raised disc, the whole within a berried laurel wreath, open at the top. Resting upon the title circle a flat topped Imperial crown, (noted as solid and voided). In brass with brass lugs (Fig.1138). It is recorded that in 1880, a tunic of a Sergeant Major had, 'Collar lace round top, and braid at bottom (like Officers), the collar red but with a pointed green patch approx. 2½ inches long at each end of the collar, and collar badge (the centre is domed) in gilt'. It is interesting that the sketch with this description shows a more standard high arched QVC.

Fig.1133

Post 1881
The two far flung Regiments were merged in 1881 as *The Welsh Regiment*. On 22nd October the AAG Horse Guards verbally agreed that the collar badge for the new Regiment would be, 'The Dragon in wreath' and adding 'But of a different pattern from that of the Border Regiment'. However on 12th November the following statement was issued. 'Welsh Regiment - Wreath around Dragon for the collar is an error; wreath should be removed (also for helmet plate centre and glengarry badges)'. The Regimental Museum are adamant that no such collar badge was ever worn and in view of the short time between the two statements this could be correct. However, an item which fits the description does exist, in white metal and with the Dragon facing to the right (Fig.1134). In mint condition this could be one of a few trial pieces struck, but whether it is the intended collar badge for the Welsh Regiment is not known. There is a suggestion that it was to be worn by a Volunteer Battalion of the South Wales Borderers, probably the Brecknockshire Battalion. Its flat style is more akin to the pre 1881 low collared tunic and could be an unidentified Welsh Militia collar badge. It is interesting that the dragon has no loop in its tail.

Fig.1134

A new collar badge in gilding-metal Pattern No.9976 was sealed 20th January 1882, a Dragon with upright wings, standing upon a grassy ground, one front foot raised (Fig.1135). The standard pattern was renewed and cut from new dies 7th December 1897, this being Pattern No.9976a, no change in design. These first patterns were also worn on the field cap up to the introduction of a new field service cap in April 1898. The Red Dragon of Wales was the badge of the allied Militia Regiment, the Royal Glamorgan Light Infantry. Photographs taken during

Fig.1135

HISTORY OF THE BRITISH ARMY INFANTRY COLLAR BADGE

Fig.1136

Fig.1137

Fig.1138

Fig.1139

Fig.1140

this period indicate that the collar badge was only worn on the full dress tunic.

In 1908, there was considerable activity regarding the Regiment's insignia including amendments of certain descriptions to accord with the correct heraldic terms.

The OC 1st Battalion made a submission on 30th April, 'That the Plumes of the Prince of Wales may be substituted for the Dragon as a collar badge'. A reply from the Colonel, ADDC, 5th May said, 'The proposal cannot be considered unless all Battalions of the Regiment are unanimous in desiring the change'. In reply to this a letter of the 29th August informed the Authorities that there were, 'Strong claims for change, 1,2,3, Battalions all being in favour'.

Further correspondence included the reminder that there was nothing on record to indicate how the change to a Dragon had come about, as it was not one of the Regimental badges. As all Battalions were in favour of the change (the badge was already in use, being the centre ornament of both the Officers and other ranks helmet plates), the submission was approved by letter to the Regiment, 2nd September 1908, ' A sound case and change should take place; the wastage of existing badges would represent about £30.'

The new badge, Pattern No.6905 was sealed 19th November 1908, under Authority ACD/ Welch /456, and introduced 11th July 1909 for wear on full dress and khaki Service Dress (for all climates). The badges were manufactured by Messrs. Jennens. In white-metal the Prince of Wales's Crest and Motto were placed over a scroll inscribed with the Regimental motto, 'GWELL ANGAU NA CHYWILYDD' (Figs.1136, 1137 show two slight variations. Photographs of other ranks 1909-c.1939 show collar badges being worn only on full dress up to 1922, and only from around that date do they appear on the khaki Service Dress. No collar badges were worn during WWI.

Worn up to c.1937, when, with the advent of battle dress, they were discontinued, no collar badges being worn by other ranks during WWII, with at least one noted exception; a picture of the 1st Battalion's Band taken at the Depot c.1944 shows the bandsmen wearing the pre 1937 khaki Service Dress complete with collar badges, a practice continued until 1947.

After WWII, the general practice of all ranks wearing the same pattern collar badge was adopted by 1949. The Welch Regiment now reverted to a Dragon for the new common badge, the metals of course varying in quality. Pattern No.14046 being sealed 20th January 1949. In white-metal and fitted initially with two lugs, and later with the single central fitting. The design varies somewhat, (Fig.1138) shows a return to the pre 1909 style, whereas (Fig.1139) displays the slimmer later format. This latter one was worn by the other ranks for the street lining party at the 1953 Coronation, on the then recently introduced blue No.1 Dress tunic. A chrome version of the badge also exists. The pattern was used as the guide for the silver anodised version, Pattern No.19085 being sealed 23rd May 1963, (54/Inf/8794). Worn up to amalgamation in 1969, unpopular, the men were able to invoke the old dictat, 'Until existing stocks are exhausted'. to the letter!

The 1883 Dress Regulations describe the Officers collar badge as, 'The Welsh Dragon in gilt metal'. Of similar design to that of the other ranks, and noted on photographs of 1882, the badge sufficed for many orders of dress, full dress, frock coat, undress blue frock, and both patterns of mess dress. Additionally worn on the white tropical dress and khaki drill. The same badge was worn by the RSM on full dress.

For the 1902 Service Dress, the collar badge prescribed was as for the forage cap but in bronze. The Prince of Wales's plumes as for centre of helmet plate; a scroll below inscribed, 'The Welch'. Sealed 30th September 1903 (Fig.1140). A post 1920 pattern with title scroll, 'THE WELCH' has been noted (Fig.1141), but as far is known was never officially worn on the collar. Bronze versions of the 1909 pattern were soon issued (Figs.1142, 1143 show two variants). A silver version (Fig.1144) was worn on full dress, but the gilt Dragon was retained for mess dress etc. The Dragon badge in bronze was also worn on Service Dress. The early pattern has the dragon with long ears, the later ones with short ears (Figs.1145, 1146). During WWI, Officers of the 1st and 2nd Battalions wore this

THE WELSH REGIMENT

badge, but Officers of the Service Battalions wore the bronze Plumes and Regimental Motto badges. In WWII, Officers wore the Dragon in gilding metal or bronze. The Plumes and Motto badges officially polished down to the base metal were worn in the khaki drill. The same badge has been noted in silver with a gilt Motto scroll, usage unknown, possibly worn by the senior NCOs.

There are two similar but smaller badges in bi-metal, one with both Motto scrolls in gilding-metal with remainder in white-metal, the other also displays the Coronet in gilding-metal. Two superior metal versions exist, one all gilt, one silver and gilt. One is shown in (Fig.1147), the Plumes have more pointed turn-overs, are more fully divided than on the collar badge, and these characteristics are present on all varieties. They are not collar badges but tropical helmet ornaments, and were worn by the Officers and Band of the 2nd Battalion in India c1906.

On the collar badges and the helmet plate centres, the spelling of the Regimental Motto sometimes reads, 'GWELL ANGAU NEU CHYWILYDD'. It particularly occurs on all these tropical helmet ornaments.

Major General D.P. Dickinson, Colonel of the Regiment, wrote to the Under Secretary of State at the War Office, 4th January 1946, stating: 'Officers and other ranks of The Welch Regiment, before the War, wore different collar badges (as regards design), with Service Dress uniform - Officers, the Welch Dragon in bronze, other ranks - POW's Plumes with words Gwell Angau Na Chywilydd on scroll below, in white metal. It is desirous that Officers and other ranks should wear the same badge - The Welch Dragon should be the collar badge, silver for Officers, white metal for other ranks. Permission sought.'

A decision was deferred because of the expense incurred - this with a note, 'set of cap and collar badges in silver/gilt £2.10/- (£2.50p) in excess of similar articles in bronze'.

But on 28th June 1948 the following note was issued, 'The present authorised design of collar badge is, Officers, the POW's plumes with scroll below inscribed 'THE WELCH', and for other ranks the POW's plumes with scroll below inscribed, "GWELL ANGAU NA CHYWILYDD". In view of the gradual introduction of No.1 Dress it is desired to introduce a modified collar badge, i.e. The Welch Dragon for all ranks instead of two different designs as now, for Officers and other ranks.'

The final proposal 15th January 1949 was for the Welch Dragon in pairs, Officers, silver plated, other ranks white metal and gilding metal. 'Subject to approval by The King'. This was received 20th January with patterns to be made by Messrs.Gaunts, but the other ranks badge was amended to white metal only. The 1934 Dress Regulations description of the Officers badge would be amended. (Fig.1148) is in silver plate (Authority 54/Inf/8459).

Militia

The Glamorganshire Militia was raised in 1760, receiving 'Royal' status in 1804 and 'Light Infantry' elevation in 1812. The Regiment became the 3rd Battalion, The Welsh Regiment in 1881. There is no evidence that collar badges were worn prior to 1881. Photographs of Officers and their extant uniforms indicate that silver Dragon badges were worn c.1882-1908. Similar ones in white-metal were probably worn by the other ranks.

Fig.1141

Fig.1142

Fig.1143

Fig.1144

Fig.1146

Fig.1147

Fig.1148

Fig.1145

HISTORY OF THE BRITISH ARMY INFANTRY COLLAR BADGE

Fig.1149

Fig.1150

Fig.1151

Fig.1152

Fig.1153

Fig.1154

Rifle Volunteer Corps, Volunteer, Territorial Force, Territorial Army Battalions

The consolidated Battalion, 1st Pembrokeshire (Pembroke, Carmarthen, and Haverfordwest) Rifle Volunteer Corps, nominated in 1881 was redesignated 1st (Pembroke) Volunteer Battalion in December 1887. The Pattern Books record a Dragon pattern collar badge submitted by the contractors, Messrs. Samuel Bros, London, on behalf of the 1st VB, and approved by Horse Guards 19th June 1990, 'For NCO's and men.' This was a smaller Dragon than that worn by the Regular units, the wings are swept back, a pattern more associated with the Monmouthshire units (Fig.1149) In blackened gilding metal, probably for wear with a black full dress tunic. The unit became the 4th (TF) Battalion in 1908. It is believed similar but in white-metal was worn at some stage.

The consolidated Battalion 1st Glamorganshire Rifle Volunteer Corps nominated in 1881 became the 2nd (Glamorgan) Volunteer Battalion December 1887. Blackened or white metal Dragon collar badges were most probably worn by the other ranks, the large version being worn at some period (Fig.1150). The Officers initially wore the Regular units' collar badge in silver plate, but c.1890 adopted the smaller Dragon in silver or silver plate. In 1908, the unit underwent a major change of role becoming the 7th (Cyclist) Battalion (TF). Embodied in 1914 the unit was disembodied in 1919, Reconstructed in 1920 but amalgamated with the 6th Battalion by the end of the year. The small Dragon badge in gilding-metal (Fig.1151) was adopted as the collar badge, changing to a blackened version (Fig.1152) upon the introduction of a Rifles dark green tunic (worn by most Cyclist units) c.1912.

The 2nd Administrative Battalion Glamorganshire Rifle Volunteers, was consolidated in 1880 as the 2nd Glamorganshire Rifle Volunteer Corps, nominated in 1881, and becoming the 3rd (Glamorgan) Volunteer Battalion in December 1887. The Pattern Books show the same collar badge as worn by the 1st VB but in white-metal, the entry states, 'Officers and privates Jan. 18th 1888' (Fig.1153). Drawings show them in use by a Colour Sergeant c.1896 on the full dress and undress tunics. Officers badges were in silver plate. They became the 5th (TF) Battalion in 1908.

The large independent Corps, 3rd Glamorgan Rifle Volunteers though nominated as the 4th Volunteer Battalion, did not assume the title and were redesignated in December 1891 as the 3rd Glamorganshire Volunteer Rifle Corps. They wore a distinctive squat prince of Wales's plumes and Motto collar badge in white-metal for other ranks and silver plate for Officers (Fig.1154). Reorganised as the 6th (TF) Battalion in 1908. The Officers thereafter wore the large bronze cap/collar badge with separate 'T' below on the Service Dress, until c.1917 when they changed to the Plumes and Regimental Motto type in bronze, still with the separate 'T'.

The badges of the parent units were gradually adopted for the TF later TA Battalions. A sealed pattern 'For 5/6 TA Bn' dated 20th November 1961 shows the large silver plated Dragon, 'For No.1 & 3 Dress' and a similar in gilt 'For Service Dress'.

WWI Battalions
11th (Cardiff Pals) (Cardiff Commercial) Battalion

A small shield inscribed 'Cardiff Pals Battalion, 11th Welsh Regt', and bearing centrally the Prince of Wales's Plumes Motto and Regimental Motto has been mistaken for a collar badge. They were specially designed by the Editor of The Pals Magazine and advertised at 1/- (5p) each (Postage 2d extra) to raise funds for the Battalion's Gift Scheme. Originally with pin-back fitting, some have subsequently been fitted with lug fasteners. This Battalion wore the Regular units' collar badge.

16th (City of Cardiff) Battalion

Often mistakenly referred to as the 'Cardiff Pals'. When raised in 1914 it was

THE WELSH REGIMENT

intended that this 'City' Battalion would wear on their caps and collars, the Arms of the City of Cardiff. In effect it was only worn on the collar by the first 1000 recruits. Made in 'yellow' gilding metal (Fig.1155). A large badge it contains two mottoes "DEFFROMAE'N DYDD" (Awake! it is day) and "Y DDRAIG GOCH DDYRY GYCHWYN" (The Red Dragon shall lead). See Plate 16 for both cap and collar badge being worn.

Pioneer Battalions
The 8th (Service) Battalion raised 25th August 1914, converted to Pioneers in January 1915 and disbanded 23rd August 1919. The 19th (Service) Battalion (Glamorgan Pioneers) were raised 10th October 1914 and the 23rd (Service Battalion) Welsh Pioneers were raised 30th September 1915. The 8th wore the usual crossed rifle and pick collar badges (Fig.147) but although it is thought both the 19th and 23rd did likewise, it has not been possible to confirm.

Home Guard
Sealed pattern 16576, 23rd June 1954 shows the gilt Dragon for use by Welch Home Guard units. Authority 9/HG/363 (Fig.1156).

General
Dragon collar badges were worn in facing pairs with the Dragon inward towards the collar opening.

On 11th June 1969, the Regiment amalgamated with The South Wales Borderers to become *The Royal Regiment of Wales (24th/41st Foot)*.

Fig.1155

Fig.1156

Lt A. R. Welsh, 4th Battalion Alexandra (Princess of Wales' Own) Yorkshire Regiment

The Black Watch (Royal Highland Regiment)

Pre 1881
The 42nd Royal Highland (The Black Watch) Regiment of Foot

The first authorised collar badge, 16th July 1872 was the brass Imperial crown (Fig.333). Introduced around 1874 with photographs taken in 1875 showing them in general use. Worn until 1878 when the Regiment introduced a more distinctive badge, Pattern No.9626 being sealed 18th January. In brass, St Andrew stands on a grassy ground in front of a rough hewn Cross, only one hand supports the Cross, the other outstretched. Voided between the feet and the bottom of the cross, they were worn up to 1882 (Fig.1157). There is another brass St. Andrew but standing behind the Cross that may have been worn before 1881 but there is no record as such in the Pattern Room Journals. Additionally the badge would appear somewhat tall for the pre-1881 tunic collar (Fig.1158).

Fig.1157

Fig.1158

The 73rd (Perthshire) Regiment.

Appropriately, the first collar badge for the Regiment was a display of the Arms used by the County, a double headed spread eagle, on its breast a shield bearing the Paschal Lamb. Below, a three part scroll inscribed, 'PRO REGE, LEGE ET GREGE'. (For King, Law and the People). This was Pattern No.9520, in brass, sealed 11th November 1874 (Fig.1159). Worn until 1879 when by an order 17th June, the badge was assimilated to that of the 90th Regiment (Fig.710). They do not face.

Fig.1159

Post 1881

The two regiments were amalgamated in 1881 as The Black Watch (Royal Highlanders). An interim statement issued 30th September by Horse Guards, confirmed that the new collar badge would be as formerly worn by the 42nd, 'St.Andrew and Cross'. However, a new design in white metal, Pattern No.9971 was sealed 20th January 1882, 'To replace Pattern No.9626 of the 42nd and 9307 of the 73rd.' Photographs taken in 1882 show them being worn on the dark blue collar of the scarlet serge undress tunic. The standard pattern was authorised to be renewed 30th November 1889, Authority ACD/patt/8189 & patt 9971a, cut from new dies and sealed 14th December 1897 (Fig.1160) shows an early example, and (Figs.1161, 1162) later versions. This last type was used as the guide for the silver anodised version which was sealed 16th January 1963 (Authority 54/Inf/8798), (Fig.1163). This is the type being later worn on Nos.1 & 3 Dress. Unlike most other Infantry Regiments they were not worn on No.2 Dress. The badge is also recorded with a chrome finish and these were worn by the Band on their white drill uniforms in Palestine in the 1930s (Fig.1164).

Fig.1160

Fig.1161    *Fig.1162*    *Fig.1163*    *Fig.1164*

THE BLACK WATCH

To clarify matters for collectors, badges that are sometimes thought to be collar badges are shown (Figs.1165, 1166 and 1167). In white metal and silver anodised they are sporran badges.

The 1883 Dress Regulations describe the Officers collar badge as simply, 'St. Andrew and Cross, in silver'. Confirmed up to and including the 1902 Edition which also records, 'On mess jacket, no badge'. This was repeated in the 1904 Edition but omitted from the 1911 Edition which only mentions, 'On collar of doublet'. This appears in later Dress Regulations.

The Gaunt Pattern book shows the collar badge, 'As supplied to Hawkes & Co. Nov. 1881', as very similar to that worn prior to 1881 by the Officers of the 3rd Forfarshire (Dundee Highland) Rifle Volunteers, see Fig.1182, though the base is more of a grassy mound and St. Andrew has bare legs from the knee downwards. Later patterns show the Saint in more conventional pose, standing behind the Cross and holding same with both hands. As one might expect over a period of a over 100 years there are many minor varieties both in size and design. (Fig.1168) shows a very distinctive early pattern in silver, the same metal being used in (Figs. 1428, 1429). Later silver plate types in (Figs.1171, 1172). A later one worn with a red leather backing is Pattern No.30483, sealed 18th April 1984 (Fig.1173).

For the Service Dress of 1902, the badge as described in Dress Regulations is, 'As for doublet, in bronze'. These too varied considerably (Figs.1174-1178). A questionnaire returned by the Regiment after WWI records that Officers of the Regular Battalions did not wear collar badges during the war period, but Officers of the Territorial Battalions did wear the large bronze version.

There was no change in the design of the collar badges when the Regiment was redesignated in 1934, The Black Watch (Royal Highland Regiment).

Fig.1165

Fig.1166

Fig.1167

Fig.1170

Fig.1171

Fig.1172

Fig.1168

Fig.1173

Fig.1174

Fig.1175

Fig.1176

Fig.1177

Fig.1178

Fig.1169

187

HISTORY OF THE BRITISH ARMY INFANTRY COLLAR BADGE

Fig.1179

Fig.1180

Fig.1181

Fig.1182

Fig.1183

Militia

Raised in 1798 as the Perthshire Militia, and being granted Royal status in 1804, the Regiment was redesignated in 1854 as The Royal Perthshire Rifle Regiment of Militia. It is recorded that the collar badge worn prior to 1881 was the Arms of Perth in white-metal (Fig.1179); Officers wore the same badge in silver. They do not face. In 1881 the Regiment became the 3rd Battalion, The Black Watch.

Rifle Volunteer Corps, Volunteer, Territorial Force & Territorial Army Battalions

The Battalion strength unit 1st Forfarshire Rifle Volunteer Corps nominated in 1881 wore collar badges similar to those of the Regular Battalions, a small St. Andrew and Cross in white-metal for the men and the large silver type for the Officers. These are shown in the Gaunt Pattern Books. By General Order 181, 1st December 1887 the unit was designated as the 1st (Dundee) Volunteer Battalion, later changed to (City of Dundee) 2nd February 1889. The Corps now adopted an additional collar badge, placed behind St. Andrew and the Cross, and representing their Dundee origins, being the sole charge from the Arms of the Royal Burgh, 'Azure, a pott of growing lillies argent'. In white-metal for other ranks (Fig.1180, 1181) and in silver for Officers. The dual badges were worn up until 1908 when the Corps became the 4th (TF) Battalion. They do not face.

The 1st Administrative Battalion Forfarshire Rifle Volunteer Corps was consolidated in 1880 as the 2nd Forfar (Forfarshire or Angus) Rifle Volunteer Corps. Nominated in 1881 and assuming the uniform of the Black Watch in 1882 (31st October), they were redesignated the 2nd (Angus) Volunteer Battalion 1st December 1887. Though precise information is not available, photographs indicate that the Battalion wore the same badges as the parent units.

The six company strong 10th Forfarshire (Dundee Highland) RVC was renumbered in 1880 as 3rd Forfarshire (Dundee Highland) Rifle Volunteer Corps. Officers wore a distinctive collar badge during this time, St. Andrew standing in front of the Cross with only one arm holding the Cross. In silver (Fig.1182). Nominated in 1881 and redesignated in 1887 as 3rd (Dundee Highland) Volunteer Battalion. They also, adopted double collar badges, the 'Pott of Lillies Growing argent' was placed behind St. Andrew and the Cross; on this occasion they were in gilding-metal for the men and gilt for the Officers, the latter in two sizes (Figs.1183, 1184) small, and the larger ones (Figs 1185, 1186). They do not face.

In 1908, this unit and the 2nd VB amalgamated to form the 5th (TF) Battalion.

The consolidated 1st Perthshire Rifle Volunteer Corps were redesignated as the 4th (Perthshire) Volunteer Battalion in 1887, as such and until 1908 they wore in white-metal for the men and silver for the Officers, the double headed eagle badge from the Arms of Perth (Fig. 1187). They do not face. In 1908, the unit became the 6th (TF) Battalion.

The consolidated 2nd Perthshire (Perthshire Highland) Rifle Volunteer Corps after the usual nomination, was redesignated in 1887 as 5th (Perthshire Highland) Volunteer Battalion. In 1883, the Battalion had adopted dark grey doublets with scarlet cuff and collar but it would appear that collar badges were not worn. In 1908 the Battalion was converted to a cyclist unit, The Highland Cyclist Battalion;

Fig.1184  *Fig.1185*  *Fig.1186*  *Fig.1187*

188

up until 1914 collar badges were rarely worn but those of the Regular units were worn on occasions usually with a blackened finish.

Notes and sketches made by an observer at Blair Atholl in 1915 when the Battalion was in training, record a distinctive cap badge, the men wearing trews, but with their kilts and sporrans strapped to their bicycle carriers. The observer further records that on the tunic collars were badges, 'bigger than half of the cap badge'. The accompanying sketch shows the item illustrated in (Fig.1188). The Star of the Order of the Thistle but with St. Andrew and the Cross in the centre, unit title scrolls top and bottom. Officers wore blackened collar badges (Fig 1189). The Battalion was disembodied 3rd December 1919.

The consolidated 1st Fifeshire Rifle Volunteer Corps became the 6th (Fifeshire) Volunteer Battalion in 1887. From 1881 the Battalion adopted as a collar badge the device used on the common seal of the County Council of Fife, this represents the Crest of His Grace the Duke of Fife. 'A horse in full gallop, argent, covered with a mantling, gules, bestrewed with escutcheons, or, each charged with a lion rampant of the second (gules). On his back a knight in complete armour, with his sword drawn proper. On his sinister arm a shield charged as the escutcheons. On the helmet a wreath of the colours, thereon a demi-lion rampant gules.' The Battalion further adopted His Grace's principal motto, 'VIRTUTE ET OPERA' (By virtue and deeds). Fifeshire had no armorial bearings at this time.

Worn in white-metal by the men there are several variations both in size and design. Some with the end of the knight's sword ending between the first and second words on the scroll, others ending between the 'E' and 'T' of "ET".

(Figs.1190, 1191 show a variable facing pair). The officer's badges were in silver or silver plate, bronze for the 1902 Service Dress and silver/gilt. All these collar badges were worn in facing pairs with the horse facing inwards towards the collar opening. However, whereas the lion on the Knight's shield faces only to the left on the other rank's badges, they face both ways on all those worn by officers. (see Figs.1192 and 1193 for items in silver and silver/gilt showing the shield lion facing both ways). In 1908 the Corps became the 7th (TF) Battalion. All Battalions gradually adopted the badges of the regular units.

General

As has been noted, the badge of St. Andrew and his Cross has been worn for over a hundred years, there are many, many minor variations in dress attitude, size etc. Not only are there many shapes and sizes of St. Andrew himself but there are wide variations in the amount of hair on his head, his dress - his robe loosely opened at the neck, a 'V' neck and with tight collar fitting, the garment itself sometimes reaching down so that just his feet are visible other times finishing just below his knee. Even the sleeves vary from being open at the wrist and hanging down, to being tight and closed. There are many differences in the type of ground on which he stands, sometimes standing in front of the cross but more usually behind with the position of his hands too numerous to list. The cross itself has many variations, some held almost head high, some reaching down to the ground whilst others end just below the knee.

Everyone it seems has a different idea of what St. Andrew should look like! A collar badge well liked by the Regiment and a well known soubriquet is 'Wee Andie wi' his bed boards'.

Fig.1188

Fig.1189

Fig.1190

Fig.1191

Fig.1192

Fig.1193

The Oxfordshire and Buckinghamshire Light Infantry

Fig.1194

Fig.1195

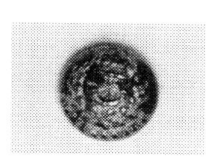

Fig.1196

Fig.1197

Fig.1198

Fig.1199

Pre 1881
43rd (Monmouthshire Light Infantry) Regiment of Foot
52nd (Oxfordshire Light Infantry) Regiment of Foot

There have been many descriptions of the collar badges worn by the other ranks of both the 43rd and 52nd - 'small bugle', 'large bugle horn', 'smaller than that worn by the 68th, more decorated than that of the 68th', 'corded', 'ribboned' etc, etc. Authority was received 16th July 1872 under Order PC/Inf Gen/111 for Light Infantry Regiments to wear a bugle as a collar badge should they so wish. Both Regiments declined the option and neither wore any collar badge, bugle or otherwise prior to 1881.

There is no evidence to date of the Officers of the 43rd wearing collar badges prior to 1881, but for the 52nd it would appear that the 'gorget button and loop' with numbered button, of course, was in use c.1880-81.

Post 1881

The Regiments amalgamated in 1881 to form the 1st and 2nd Battalions, The Oxfordshire Light Infantry. 'It was desired' 21st October 1881 that 'the collar ornament is to be the bugle Pattern 9299'. This was in brass and had been sealed 15th February 1873 (Fig.1194). These were ribboned and with the tassel ends hanging down each side from the bow. On 2nd February 1882 the new universal pattern in gilding/metal, Pattern No.10011 was sealed (Fig.1195). Apart from the metal, the principle change was to the bugle strings which were now corded.

However, on 3rd October 1883, the following Order was issued under Authority 61002/2526, 'Oxford Light Infantry - collar badge may be dispensed with in the Line Battalions'.

On 14th July 1893 under Order PC/Gen/1639 it was directed that 'collar badges (left side) be worn upon the field service cap by Infantry - exception, Oxford LI'.

The universal bugle pattern was renewed 14th December 1897, being cut from new dies, this being Pattern No.10011a. This was the pattern that, on 10th February 1905, all Light Infantry Regiments were directed to wear with their metal titles on the shoulder straps of their drab jackets and greatcoats.

The early Dress Regulations describe the Officers tunic collar badge as 'Edgeless button; on the button within a laurel wreath, a bugle with strings; above the bugle, a crown; below the wreath "Oxfordshire". A piece of gold Russia braid 2½ inches long, attached to the button'.

This description was repeated in later Editions which added, 'For frock coat and mess jacket'. Altered in the 1911 Edition to read, 'Plain edged buttons as on Mess Dress. A loop of gold Russia cord. 2½ inches long attached to the button, connecting it with the front edge of collar of tunic. On the frock coat the cord is dark blue. No badge on the Mess jacket'. (By this time the button would have been inscribed, 'Oxfordshire & Buckinghamshire'). The last two sentences are omitted from the 1934 Dress Regulations. The button was later worn on a loop of rifle green cord. These buttons are known in silver, gilt and bronze, with both the QVC and KC over "OXFORDSHIRE", (Figs.1196, 1197) and the K/C over "OXFORDSHIRE & BUCKINGHAMSHIRE". (Figs.1198, 1199).

The QVC was worn from 1881 to the change of crown in 1902, although the KC button patterns were not sealed by the War Office until 31st March 1904, 'for tunic & frock collars'. The next change came in 1908 when Buckinghamshire was added to the Regiment's title to become The Oxfordshire and Buckinghamshire Light Infantry.

It is recorded that the Officers silver button with Q/C and loop was sent to the War Office under reference 54/Inf/8748 when the Regiment formed part of The Green Jackets Brigade in 1958.

When Service Dress was introduced in 1902, Dress Regulations directed the collar badge to be, 'A bugle and strings'. This was a large bugle badge with corded loops and strings, and with a knot in the centre of the loops. (Fig.1200). Although this description was confirmed in the 1904 Edition, the badge was worn for a short time only, and in the 1911 Edition the description had been replaced with a bronze button and drab cord. (Fig.1201). The bronze collar badge was officially polished and worn on the khaki drill. The button and cord collar badges were also worn by Warrant Officers.

Fig.1200

Fig.1201

Militia
Royal Bucks (King's Own) Militia

Collar badges in white metal were sealed for wear by other ranks on the tunic and frock collars 1st November 1878 under Authority PC/Bucks Mil/268, this being Pattern 7187. Although an actual specimen has not been noted, information indicates that the badge features the crowned Lion of England with one front paw raised and standing on a deep ground. This was certainly the device used in the centre of the Officer's shako and helmet plate and also on their forage cap badge. (Fig.1202). Officers would have worn similar but in silver, c.1880-81. The Regiment became the 3rd Battalion, The Oxfordshire Light Infantry in 1881.

Fig.1202

Oxfordshire Militia

Raised in 1778, the Regiment became the 4th Battalion, The Oxfordshire Light Infantry in 1881. In 1908 upon the disbandment of the 3rd Battalion, they became the 3rd Battalion, The Oxfordshire and Buckinghamshire Light Infantry. Though the arms of Oxford and later the Ox featured considerably on the shoulder belt, shako and helmet plates of the Oxfordshire Militia, there is no evidence to date that the Regiment wore collar badges prior to 1881. By an Order 4th March 1889 under Authority PM/4OXLI/515 the wearing of collar badges by the Militia Battalions of the Regiment was to be discontinued. What they had been wearing and whether they were then to adopt the button and cord collar device is not known. Certainly an uniform of a Militia Officer c.1898 bears the silver button and cord.

Fig.1203

Rifle Volunteer Corps, Volunteer, Territorial Force & Territorial Army Battalions
1st Oxfordshire (Oxford University) Rifle Volunteer Corps

Raised 8th August 1859, designated July 1881 as a Volunteer Battalion and becoming the 1st in 1908 they became part of the Senior Division of the Officer Training Corps.

A Cadet Corps was formed 3rd May 1873 and affiliated to the Battalion, but was later disbanded. The Corps wore attractive collar badges - the Prince of Wales's plumes, coronet and motto above a strung bugle, and with two scrolls attached to the tops of the plumes, these conjoin with the Ich Dien scrolls and are inscribed 'OU - RV'. Worn in silver (Fig.1203). Another version shows the Prince of Wales's crest perched rather precariously on a bugle, also in silver, (Figs.1204, 1205 show a facing pair). Worn with the mouthpiece facing inwards towards the collar opening.

The Prince of Wales became Colonel-in-Chief in 1869.

Fig.1204

Fig.1205

2nd Oxfordshire Rifle Volunteer Corps

Consolidated as such in March 1873, formerly the 1st Administrative Battalion. Designated in July 1881, and becoming the 2nd Volunteer Battalion in December 1887. In 1908 the unit became the 4th (TF) Battalion, The Oxfordshire &

Fig.1206

Buckinghamshire Light Infantry. Photographs show white metal corded bugles being worn on the white collars of their scarlet tunics. (Fig.1206). Officers wore the silver button and cord device.

1st Buckinghamshire Rifle Volunteer Corps

Consolidated as such from the former 1st Administrative Battalion in April 1876. They wore as their collar badge the principle device of their other insignia, the White Swan from the Arms of the town of Buckingham, which was also the badge of the (Stafford) Dukes of Buckingham, by descent from the ancient family of de Bohun. The Swan has a gold coronet around its neck and a chain of the same metal turned over its back. "Party per pale sable, and gules a swan with wings expanded and inverted argent, ducally gorged or." Worn from 1876 by the other ranks in blackened gilded metal (Fig.1207) and by the Officers in silver (Fig.1208).

The unit was nominated a Volunteer Battalion in 1881 and although subsequently entitled the 3rd VB, in fact retained its Rifle status until 1st April 1908; upon transfer to the Territorial Force they became The Buckinghamshire Battalion.

2nd Buckinghamshire Rifle Volunteer Corps

In 1878, the Eton College detachment of the 1st Buckinghamshire R.V.C. became the 2nd Buckinghamshire (Eton College) Rifle Volunteer Corps. Redesignated in December 1887 as the 4th (Eton College) Volunteer Battalion, but reverting to the 2nd (Eton College) Volunteer Rifle Corps in 1902 and eventually forming part of the OTC in 1908. They wore their own Swan type collar badges with scroll below inscribed "ETON COLLEGE OTC", in blackened gilding metal (Fig.1209).

WW1 Volunteer Defence Corps

A swan with base inscribed 'BUCKS.V.D.C. 1914' in bronze was probably worn as a lapel badge and/or in the collar by the Officers. (Fig.1210).

The Staffords derived the Swan badge from the Bohuns by the marriage of Edmund, Earl of Stafford (d.1403) with Anne, daughter of Thomas of Woodstock, Duke of Gloucester and Earl of Buckingham, who had married Eleanor, co-heiress of the Bohun Earls of Hereford and Northampton. (Eleanor's sister, Mary, married Henry IV who, with his son Henry V, also used the Swan of Bohun as a badge). The Bohuns had derived the swan from the Mandevilles, who may have adopted it in token of their descent from Fitzswanne.

Bugler's Arm Badge

One item that is sometimes thought to be a collar badge of the Regiment is an attractive oval item in green enamel with burnished gilt rim, upon this is mounted a bugle horn in white and brown enamel. With a two lug fastening device, all available evidence indicates that this is a Regimental bugler's arm badge, most probably post WWII (Fig.1211).

Service Battalions

During the 1914-18 War, Service Battalions of the Regiment wore corded bugle collar badges, in blackened gilded metal (Fig.1212). The 8th Service Battalion raised 14th October 1914 were converted to Pioneers 25th January 1915 wearing the usual crossed rifle and pick collar badges (Fig.147). Disbanded 21st November 1919.

General

There have been many theories put forward as to why the other ranks of the Regiment, did not wear collar badges of any description some not even worthy of comment.

When the 43rd and 52nd amalgamated in 1881, it was suggested by the Authorities that the collar badge for the new Regiment should be either a bugle or the English Rose. The bugle, associated with Light Infantry regiments, was not acceptable to either the 43rd or the 52nd as being the senior Light Infantry Regiments in the British Army, has always considered that this fact was too well known to require advertisement. The English Rose meant nothing to either Regiment. The Regiment's own suggestion was the head of the county Ox, a good link with the old Oxford Militia.

Sanction was received about this time for Officers to wear as their collar ornament the 'gorget button and loop', this already having been worn by Officers of the 52nd prior to 1881, as noted earlier. These items evolve from the time (pre 1830) when gorgets were worn and were in their final era suspended from the buttons at the end of the lace panels on the 3 inch stand up collar of the full dress coatee. Its descendent 'collar badge' was displayed correctly with the button at the end of the loop furthest from the collar opening.

Soldiers of the Regiment have always received a lot of banter from other Regiments for having no collar badges, and for a few years soldiers of the 1st Battalion, whilst in India during the 1880s, unofficially wore the 'gorget button and loop' on the collars of their khaki jackets.

Bugles, when worn, were in facing pairs with the mouthpiece facing inwards.

The Regiment was redesignated The Oxfordshire and Buckinghamshire Light Infantry on 16th October 1908. They became the 1st Green Jackets (43rd &52nd) 1st April 1958 in accordance with the 'Large Regiment' formations, and were redesignated the 1st Battalion The Royal Green Jackets (43rd & 52dn) 1st January 1966; the sub title was omitted from 1st July 1968.

Aldershot Third Brigade 1881 – 56th Foot

The Essex Regiment

Pre 1881
44th (East Essex) Regiment of Foot

The collar badge introduced in 1874 for wear by the other ranks on their tunic collars was the standard brass Imperial crown, authorised by PC/Inf Gen/111, 16th July 1872 (Fig.333). Photographs show them being worn by the band in 1878 and by 'I' Company in 1879, who, incidentally, were still wearing the Balmoral or 'pork-pie' hat numerals on their glengarry hats.

Sometime prior to 1879, they also wore, unofficially it would seem, a Sphinx over Egypt tablet collar badge, an honour awarded to the Regiment in recognition of its service in Egypt in 1801, authorised 6th July 1802. The Authorities were well aware that this collar badge was in use, and in order to generally standardise the various collar badges of this design, issued a directive 8th January 1879 apropos the 44th. 'The collar badge (Sphinx) to be assimilated to that of the 96th Foot, pattern 9530'. Up to this time the Sphinx worn by the 44th had been of the female variety with tail rising above its back to end with the tuft facing forward. From its rounded head, the mantle extended downwards ending over the back (Figs.1213, 1214 show a facing pair).

The Sphinx as worn by the 96th was quite different, still female but a longer, less upright variety with a square head and different shaped mantle (Figs.1215, 1216 show a facing pair). Worn until 1882. Both types were in brass and worn with the Sphinx facing inwards towards the collar opening.

Officers, c.1880-81 wore an embroidered version (Fig.1217). The other ranks pattern in gilt was most probably worn by the Warrant Officers and other Senior NCOs.

56th (West Essex) Regiment of Foot

A general lack of information has made it difficult to be precise regarding collar badges for this Regiment prior to 1881, but research indicates that there were no less than five different types; three for other ranks and two for Officers.

The first other ranks collar badge was Pattern 9538, 'a brass castle', sealed 20th April 1875. This was a small two tower castle with a central turret from which flew a flag. There were voided look-outs in both the top and bottom sections of each tower, and a voided archway with a partially raised portcullis. There was also a look-out in the central turret. below the castle a horizontal Key (Fig.1218). Although the Key always faces one way, the flags do fly in both directions and were worn with the flags facing inwards towards the collar opening.

A similar badge had been worn by the 58th (Rutland) Regiment since 1874, and it is possible therefore that to avoid confusion, the 56th introduced, unofficially, a larger Castle collar badge; photographs show these being worn right up to the 1881 amalgamation. Again in brass and maintaining the same design, almost identical to the Castle on one of their pre 1881 glengarry cap badges, though on the latter the Key was on the Castle. See photograph 17 for a group of Pioneers at Aldershot, just prior to the 1881 amalgamations.

The third pattern, in brass, was of a similar Castle, midway in size between the first two, and with the same flag, look-outs and archway, but this time with the portcullis fully down; the archway and look-outs are unvoided. The Key however now depends vertically below the Castle, and a scroll at the top is inscribed 'POMPADOURS' (Fig.1219). It is not known whether they were worn in facing

Fig.1213

Fig.1214

Fig.1215

Fig.1216

Fig.1217

Fig.1218

pairs, the only ones recorded all show the flag flying to the viewer's right. 'Pompadours' was a nickname of the Regiment traditionally earned when the crimson facings were changed in 1764, and the then Colonel chose blue, but this was refused, being the preserve of Royal Regiments only. He then opted for purple, a favourite colour of Madame de Pompadour, a mistress of King Louis XV of France. An alternative explanation is not so romantic but perhaps more factual; the original deep crimson colour of the facings were known in the tailoring trade as 'Pompadour'.

The Regiment is known to have had three different patterns of other ranks glengarry cap badges between 1874 and 1881, so it may well have been that the collar badge variants were concurrent with the head-dress badges. Unfortunately it is not known precisely when, or indeed in what order these three glengarry badges were worn, the dating of the collar badges therefore is equally uncertain.

The honour "Gibraltar" was conferred on the 56th for its part in the defence of the Rock 1779-83, authorised 14th April 1784, the insignia of the Castle & Key though mentioned at the time were not permitted for display until after 1830. In the Regimental Museum there is an uniform pertaining to an officer in the 56th, the scarlet tunic of 1868-81 pattern has purple velvet facings and upon the collar ahead of the embroidered rank insignia are embroidered castle collar badges. In gold thread and of the pattern worn by the other ranks, complete with two towers, look-outs, archway, etc. above the Castle, a blue velvet scroll inscribed 'MORO' in gold metal thread; below the ground on which the Castle stands, a vertical key above a blue velvet scroll inscribed 'GIBRALTAR', again in gold metal thread. (Fig.1220). c.1879-80. Another Officers item, again embroidered, has the usual Castle with flag and horizontal key below a scroll inscribed 'POMPADOURS'. (Line Drawing 1221). Probably worn on the 'officers' glengarry cap as well.

Post 1881

On the 1st July 1881, the two Regiments amalgamated to become the 1st and 2nd Battalions respectively of The Essex Regiment, but surprisingly no element of the former Regiment's collar badges was embodied in the ensuing collar badges for the new Regiment. The new badge for the other ranks incorporated the assumed County arms of Essex, 'Gules, three seaxes fessways proper'. These had been used by the 56th Regiment on one of their glengarry badges and by the Essex Rifles Militia up to 1881. Identical to those claimed by Middlesex and long in use by various Essex authorities, these arms were not granted to the Essex County Council until 1932. The collar badge, in gilding-metal was Pattern No.10103 being sealed 8th February 1882. The same badge was used on the field service cap c.1894-97. A renewal was demanded 9th February 1899, Pattern No.10103a being sealed 3rd August 1899, with no change in design. There are slight variations, mainly the size and shape of the seaxes, the smaller types are probably the early issues. These were worn on the various dress uniforms until 1948 and on Service Dress from 1920. (Figs.1222, 1223). They are also recorded in bi-metal, with white metal seaxes on a gilding-metal shield, possibly worn by the senior NCOs.

A French Imperial Eagle pattern collar badge was worn on the blue patrol jacket from 1898 until that jacket's abolition. It was re-introduced for wear on all uniforms from 1947. The first pattern worn until 1902 was in gilding metal, the Eagle perched upon a plinth has high rounded outstretched wings and a laurel

Fig.1219

Fig.1220

Fig.1221

Fig.1222

Fig.1223

Fig.1225

Fig.1224

HISTORY OF THE BRITISH ARMY INFANTRY COLLAR BADGE

wreath upon its breast (Fig.1224). The following pattern (Fig.1225) again in gilding metal has lower outstretched wings and the laurel wreath is omitted. These were still being worn regularly by senior NCOs during the 1920s, and photographs indicate usage as late as 1928. The later types, Pattern No.16172 being sealed 24th February 1954 under Authority 54/officers/4025 also in gilding metal displayed a much larger Eagle, (Fig.1226). Worn up to amalgamation in 1958. A much smaller Eagle in gold anodised was later worn on the No. 1 Dress by the Territorials, and just possibly by the Regular Battalion just prior to amalgamation. (Fig.1227). The Eagle badge was conferred on the old 44th in 1902 to commemorate the capture of the Regimental Eagle of the 62me Regiment de Ligne at the Battle of Salamanca.

Curiously, some of the detachments present at the Coronation in 1953 were wearing the old shield of arms collar badges - presumably due to a shortage of correct Eagle badges.

For Officers, early Dress Regulations describe the collar badge for tunic collars as, "The County Badge. The shield in gilt metal; the blades of the seaxes in silver. 2nd & 3rd Battalions, the badge is in embroidery with the seaxes wholly in silver." (Fig.1228). All metal. (Fig.1229) embroidered.

The 1900 Edition does not specify any particular Battalion with the description, "The County Badge. The shield in gilt or gilding metal; the blades of the seaxes in silver". Also for wear on the scarlet frock. Directions are also appended for the collar badge to be worn on the mess jacket, "An Eagle on a plain tablet in gilt or gilding metal". (Fig.1230). These instructions are repeated in subsequent Editions up to and including the 1934 version. Photographs taken in 1896 show a group of Officers of the 1st Battalion wearing blue serge jackets with no collar badges in evidence, but similar photographs taken in 1898 show Officers in the same dress but now wearing large gilt Eagle collar badges. (Fig.1231). Similar badges were worn on Service Dress post 1949. For a short time, Officers wore collar badges with silver and gilt seaxes on a red enamelled shield (the correct heraldic colour).

When Service Dress was introduced in 1902, the collar badge instruction states, "As for tunic collar with scroll as for forage cap". In bronze, the scroll inscribed 'THE ESSEX REGT' varies as does the size of the shield. (Figs.1232, 1233, 1234 for variations). Another interesting type has what appears to be the ends of a wreath

Fig.1226

Fig.1227

Fig.1228

Fig.1229

Fig.1230

Fig.1231

Fig.1232

Fig.1233

Fig.1234

Fig.1235

below the title scroll, similar indeed to the base of the cap badge (Fig.1235). The bronze badges were sealed by the War Office 18th May 1905, Authority 61002/Inf/416. The same sealed pattern is marked "obsolete May 1949 - collar badge for No. 1 Dress under Authority 54/officers/4025". Photographs of groups of Officers of the 2nd Battalion taken in 1902 show some of the Officers wearing the bronze cap badge in both collars.

Photographs taken 1917-18, show polished versions being worn and from c.1920 worn by the Drum-Major and Band Sergeants on both Service Dress and Full Dress scarlet tunics.

Also recorded is the other ranks pattern in bronze, usage uncertain. In gilt, the other ranks pattern is thought to have been worn by the Warrant Officers and Staff on their scarlet tunics 1881-1914.

Fig.1236

Militia
Eastern Regiment of Essex Militia

The former Eastern Regiment of Essex Militia was converted to Rifles in 1853 under the title Essex Rifles Militia. They became the 3rd Battalion, The Essex Regiment in July 1881. No collar badges are recorded prior to 1881. A drawing of a proposed collar badge was officially deposited 17th May 1895, but the drawing is no longer extant. Photographs taken of the Officers at Felixstowe in 1908 and again at Colchester in 1909 clearly show that some are wearing the bronze cap badge in both collars. Often worn blackened.

1st or West Essex Militia

Augmented in 1759, the title did not change until they became the 4th Battalion, The Essex Regiment in 1881. The unit was disbanded in 1908. Officers wore on their Service Dress collars the bronze cap badge with the sphinx facing both ways; the sphinx facing inwards towards the collar opening (Fig.1236).

The Officers of both Militia Battalions wore on their scarlet tunics the shield and arms collar badge but with metals reversed, gilt seaxes on a silver shield.

It is assumed that the other ranks of the Militia Battalions wore the same gilding-metal shield and arms badges as the Regular units, but some have been recorded with a blackened finish, and these may pertain to the 3rd Battalion, being a former Rifles unit.

Fig.1237

Rifle Volunteer Corps, Volunteer, Territorial Force & Territorial Army Battalions
The 1st and 2nd Essex Rifle Volunteer Corps

Consolidated in 1880 and nominated in July 1881, being redesignated the 1st and 2nd Volunteer Battalions, The Essex Regiment in February 1883. They became the 4th and 5th (TF) Battalions in 1908. During the period 1883-1908 the other ranks wore no collar badges on their tunics. The Officers possibly wore the other ranks pattern badge but in silver plate. On their Service Dress the Officers wore, in bronze, a similar badge to the Regular units but the three part title scroll was inscribed either 1VB or 2VB - ESSEX - REGT. Worn c.1902-08.

Fig.1238

The 3rd and 4th Essex Rifle Volunteer Corps

Nominated in 1881 and redesignated the 3rd and 4th Volunteer Battalions, The Essex Regiment in February 1883, they became the 6th and 7th (TF) Battalions in 1908. On their tunics the other ranks of the 3rd and 4th VBs eventually wore the same badge as their Regular counterparts but in white-metal, the 3rd VB from 1896 and the 4th VB from 1902. Officers of both VBs probably wore the same silver plate collar badge as worn by the 1st and 2nd VBs, whilst on their Service Dress c1902-08 they wore the standard bronze shield and title scroll badge but prefixed with either 3VB or 4VB. (Fig. 1237 shows that of the 3rd VB). On the Mess Dress, small silver Eagle badges were worn on a coloured circular backing (Fig.1238) and larger Eagle badges on other uniforms (Fig.1239).

After 1908, all units gradually adopted the badges of the Regular Battalions.

Fig.1239

Fig.1240

After amalgamation in 1958, the Essex Territorial units continued wearing their insignia until 1965, when the other ranks pattern 16172 was used as a guide for a version in gold anodised. This was Pattern No.19223 sealed 8th February 1965 (Fig.1240).

The sealed pattern for 'C' Company, 6th (Vol) Battalion, The Royal Anglian Regiment formed from the ashes of The Essex Regiment Territorials, previously the 4th/5th Battalion, shows the larger Eagle collar badge in gold a/a for wear by soldiers, (at regimental expense). Officers wore the same size badge but in gilt metal, 'For No.1 and No.3 Dress' with the smaller Eagle in gilt, 'For Mess Dress'.

Essex and Suffolk Cyclist Battalion

Raised 1st April 1908 and transferred to the Essex Regiment in 1911 as the 8th (Cyclist) Battalion. From 1908 they had worn their own distinctive cap and collar badges. The Arms of the County of Essex above a Castle of the Suffolk Regiment, the whole within a KC berried laurel wreath, a scroll at the base was inscribed, 'ESSEX & SUFFOLK CYCLIST BATTN'. In gilding-metal for other ranks. (Fig.1241). These were worn on the other ranks' blue 'full dress'. Photographs taken in 1913 however now show a mixture of Shield/Arms and Eagle collar badges. Officers wore similar badges but in bronze. (Fig.1242).

Cadets

King Edward VI School, Chelmsford CCF. Since 1938 the Corps of Drums have worn uniforms with the Shield/Arms gilding-metal collar badges.

TF Cadets

This unit wore from c.1908-23, a collar badge of the usual Shield/Arms type, but all within a wreath. In gilding-metal and bronze 13mm x 12.7mm. (Line drawing Fig.1243).

General

All Eagle and Sphinx collar badges face both ways and were worn with the creatures facing inwards towards the collar opening. Generally, the Shield/Arms type did not face, but exceptions are some of the embroidered ones, which do have the seaxes facing both ways and worn with the hand grips furthest from the collar opening. Some silver and gilt examples also exist with this departure.

On 2nd June 1958, the Regiment was amalgamated with The Bedfordshire and Hertfordshire Regiment to form the 3rd East Anglian Regiment (16th/44th Foot).

The Sherwood Foresters
(Nottinghamshire and Derbyshire Regiment)

Pre 1881
45th (Nottinghamshire Sherwood Foresters) Regiment of Foot
95th (Derbyshire) Regiment of Foot

By the General Order 16th July 1872, the other ranks of both these Regiments were authorised to wear the brass Imperial crown on the collars of their tunics; these were worn until 1882. (Fig.333). No collar badges for Officers of either Regiment have been noted prior to 1881.

Post 1881

On 1st July 1881, the Regiments combined to form the 1st and 2nd Battalions respectively of The Sherwood Foresters (Derbyshire) Regiment. As both Regiments had formerly worn the Imperial crown collar badge, a completely new design was called for. The background to any such discussion was not a happy one, the very senior 45th losing the 'County' part of its title to the very junior 95th (raised in 1824), a matter not finally resolved until 1903. However, the other ranks pattern collar badge, Pattern No.9964 was sealed 20th January 1882. In gilding-metal this was a Maltese cross with QVC. Each limb of the cross having a thin plain outer edge with ball finials. Superimposed on the cross a circular wreath of oak leaves with a scroll either side inscribed, 'SHERWOOD' and 'FORESTERS' respectively. Within the wreath a stag couchant facing to the left. Across the bottom limb of the cross a scroll inscribed, 'DERBYSHIRE'. They did not face - the stag always facing to the left (Fig.1244).

This collar badge was also worn on the field service cap up to the introduction of the new pattern in 1897. A new standard pattern was demanded 9th February 1898, this being Pattern No.9964a, cut from new dies and sealed 3rd August 1899. There was no significant change in the design save for slightly smaller scrolls (Fig.1245). After the death of Queen Victoria, the crown was changed to the design known as 'Tudor', although the title of the Regiment was not changed until 1902, no other ranks collar badge was issued with the KC and 'DERBYSHIRE' scroll. After much bitterness, the title of the Regiment was changed to 'The Sherwood Foresters (Nottinghamshire and Derbyshire) Regiment'. Pattern No.5877 was sealed 25th May 1903 under Authority ACD/Notts/883. In gilding-metal the same general design was observed but the bottom scroll now read 'NOTTS & DERBY'. On this pattern and all ensuing other ranks patterns the stags faced both ways. (Fig.1246). Slightly larger badges with larger crown were worn by senior NCOs on their mess jackets. (Fig.1247). Pattern No.5877 was worn until 1955 when replaced with a QC. In gilding-metal, Pattern No.16634 was sealed 1st February under Authority 54/Gen/321. (Fig.1248), worn latterly with a single lug fixing.

In 1958, the Regiment formed part of The Midland Brigade, soon to be renamed The Forester Brigade. Though a new brigade cap badge was brought into use, the Regiment retained its old pattern collar badges. In May 1963, upon the break up of this Brigade, the Regiment joined The Mercian Brigade. In 1961, using Pattern No.16634 as a guide, the Regiment introduced a gold anodised version, this was Pattern No.18513, sealed 1st May under Authority 54/Inf/8699. (Fig.1249). These were worn up to amalgamation in 1970.

The structure of the collar badge was quite interesting. The Maltese cross background perhaps echoed the old 95th or Rifle Regiment, 1803-16, which

Fig.1244

Fig.1245

Fig.1246

Fig.1247

Fig.1248

HISTORY OF THE BRITISH ARMY INFANTRY COLLAR BADGE

Fig.1249

Fig.1250

Fig.1251

Fig.1252

Fig.1253

became The Rifle Brigade in that year; certainly this pattern of cross featured on all the pouch belt plates of the Rifle Brigade from 1821 onwards. The last pattern shoulder belt plate of the 95th Derbyshire Regiment, 1840-55 featured the Star of the Grand Cross of the Order of the Bath, more latterly a cross with '95' in the centre had been the glengarry cap badge, c.1874-81.

The central section was taken from the recently adopted badge of The Royal Sherwood Foresters Militia. Perhaps foreseeing that the Arms of the City of Nottingham would not be acceptable to the 95th upon amalgamation, the County Militia hastily changed the centre ornament for the new 1878 pattern helmet plate to 'Azure, a stag lodged', surrounding the title circlet was a wreath of oak leaves. A stag lodged or couchant was also adopted as the mens' collar badge. At best the only Nottinghamshire connection was ancient stag hunting in Sherwood Forest!

At this time neither Derbyshire nor Derby had any official armorial bearings. The arms attributed to Derby were 'Argent, on a mount vert, a stag lodged all within park-pales and a gate, all proper'. The ancient Seal of the town simply represents the stag as lodged in a wood. Clearly therefore, the stag centre section was from the Nottinghamshire side, but was subsequently acceptable to the Derby element.

For Officers, the early Dress Regulations describe the Officers tunic collar badge as, "A Maltese cross surmounted by the Crown, in silver. Wreath and scrolls in gilt metal, as for buttons. Within the wreath, a Stag lodged, in silver on a ground of blue enamel". The scrolls on the buttons are described as, "A half scroll on the left division of the cross, inscribed 'Sherwood'; another on the right division, inscribed 'Foresters'. On the lower division, a scroll inscribed 'Derbyshire'." By contrast the Officers badges were worn in facing pairs. (Fig.1250). A variation has a slightly larger crown and furled ends to the bottom scroll. (Fig.1251). The above was confirmed in the 1900 Dress Regulations which also added, "for wear on the scarlet frock". The 1902 Edition adds, "for wear on Mess Jacket", but amended the description of the bottom scroll to "Notts & Derby". In the interim months between the death of Queen Victoria and the change of unit title, all Officers badges, from the helmet plates to the buttons, were made, sold and worn with KC and "DERBYSHIRE" bottom scroll. (Fig.1252). The KC with "NOTTS & DERBY" bottom scroll was sealed 26th September 1903. There were many minor varieties, (Figs.1253, 1254) for two early versions (Fig.1255) for later type with solid crown. A larger pattern with larger crown was worn on the Mess jacket. (Fig.1256). These were worn until 1955 when the QC types were introduced. (Fig.1257).

For the 1902 Service Dress, the description is, "As for tunic collar, with scroll as for forage cap, Notts & Derby, in bronze". This pattern was sealed 26th September 1903. As for the full dress badges, KC with "DERBYSHIRE" bottom scroll bronze cap and collar badges were used. (Fig.1258). Three variants of the Notts & Derby scroll pattern. (Figs.1259, 1260, 1261). These badges all had voided centres, noted in the 1911 Edition for the first time, 'centre pierced'.

Although the 2nd Battalion continued wearing these bronze collar badges, the 1st Battalion, by 1914 were wearing the badge without the bottom scroll (Fig.1262). A bronzed other ranks pattern with a solid centre was also in use, (Fig.1263). For a while a slightly larger overall badge, in bronze, was worn on the Mess jacket by Officers of the 1st Battalion (Fig.1264). In 1955 the QC bronze

Fig.1254  *Fig.1255*  *Fig.1256*  *Fig.1257*

version was introduced (Fig.1265). Collar badges in gilt with both QVC and KC are recorded, worn by the Warrant Officers (Figs.1266, 1267).

Curiosity
A bronzed other ranks pattern with QVC and "DERBYSHIRE" scroll, usage unknown (Fig.1268). Possibly a trial pattern.

Militia
2nd Derbyshire Militia (The Chatsworth Rifles)
Raised only in 1853, this unit was the virtual property of the Dukes of Devonshire. Their family arms dominated all aspects of the Regiment's insignia, shako, helmet and pouch belt plates; the Ducal coronet replaced St Edward's crown, and the 1835 Silver lace etc. Order for the Militia was completely ignored, as all their badges were in gilt metal! No collar badges were recorded prior to 1881. The 45th and Nottinghamshire suffered further indignity when this junior Militia Regiment took the premier place in 1881, becoming the *3rd Battalion, The Sherwood Foresters (Derbyshire) Regiment*. In 1891 the 5th Militia Battalion was absorbed into this unit. Blackened standard pattern collar badges were worn by both other ranks and Officers, c.1883 onwards.

Royal Sherwood Foresters or Nottinghamshire Regiment of Militia
Raised in 1775 as the *Nottinghamshire Militia* redesignated with the above title in 1813. The ancient Arms of Nottingham, recorded and confirmed by the Heralds' Visitation in 1614, are, 'Gules, two staves raguly couped one in pale, surmounted by the other in fesse vert, between two ducal coronets in chief or, the bottom part of the staff in pale enfiled with a like ducal coronet'. These arms begin to appear on the badges of the Regiment c.1850 on a second pattern of the 1844 Alvert shako plate, and so on until the advent of the 1878 helmet plate, when, as mentioned earlier, the Regiment drop these ancient marks and adopt the 'Stag lodged' device. This extended to the mens' collar badge, in white-metal and for wear on the tunic and frock collars, the pattern was sealed 17th May 1877, a Stag lodged or couchant, worn in facing pairs with the beast facing inwards towards the collar opening. Officers later wore the same badge in silver plate. (Fig.1269). The Regiment became the 4th Battalion, Sherwood Foresters (Derbyshire) Regiment in 1881.

Fig.1258

Fig.1259

Fig.1260

Fig.1263

Fig.1264

Fig.1265

Fig.1261

Fig.1266

Fig.1267

Fig.1268

Fig.1262

1st Derbyshire Militia

Raised in 1778 as Derbyshire Militia and redesignated as 1st in 1855. The Regiment became the *5th Battalion, The Sherwood Foresters (Derbyshire) Regiment* in 1881. It merged with the 3rd Battalion in 1891. The ancient badges of the Regiment featured a crown over a Rose, (Shako and shoulder belt plates). These devices disappeared c.1855 and were replaced by the simple 'VR' cipher. There is no record in the Army Clothing Department Pattern Room journals of any collar badge patterns.

Fig.1269

Rifle Volunteer Corps, Volunteer, Territorial Force & Territorial Army Battalions
1st Derbyshire Rifle Volunteer Corps

This consolidated battalion, nominated in 1881 became the 1st Volunteer Battalion in April 1887. Reorganised as the 5th (TF) Battalion in 1908.

3rd Derbyshire Rifle Volunteer Corps

Consolidated 16th March 1880, the unit was renumbered *2nd Derbyshire Rifle Volunteers* 15th June 1880. Nominated July 1881 and redesignated the 2nd Volunteer Battalion in April 1887. The unit became the 6th (TF) Battalion in April 1908.

Fig.1270

2nd Nottinghamshire Rifle Volunteers

The consolidated battalion of the former 1st Administrative Battalion. A nominal Volunteer battalion in July 1881 the unit was redesignated the *4th (Nottinghamshire) Volunteer Battalion* in April 1887.

The other ranks of the above three Battalions gradually adopted white-metal versions of the Regular units pattern after 1887. QVC with "DERBYSHIRE" bottom scrolls types have similar minor variations as regards size and scrolls. The pattern was submitted by Messrs. Hobson & Sons, London on behalf of the 2nd VB and approved together with the Officers version, by Horse Guards 21st April 1887 under Authority V/2 Derby/249. Unlike the Regular units' badges these QVC other ranks badges did face both ways. (Fig.1270 Stag facing right) No KC other ranks Derbyshire collar badges appear to exist for the VBs, so the final pattern was the KC with "NOTTS & DERBY" bottom scroll.

Fig.1271

The Officers versions were very handsome badges being all silver with blue enamel centres, initially with QVC (Fig.1271) followed by KC with "DERBYSHIRE" scroll and finally KC with "NOTTS & DERBY" scroll. They adopted the standard pattern Service Dress bronze badges in 1902.

Upon conversion to the Territorial Force in 1908 all ranks gradually adopted the relevant Regular unit types.

The sealed pattern for both the Nottinghamshire (T) Battalion and the Derbyshire (T) Battalion of the Sherwood Foresters show the gold anodised collar badges annotated, 'At Regimental expense'.

The Sherwood Foresters (TA) (45 & 95) (Notts & Derby Regt) 5/8 Battalions (TA) also wore the same QC collar badge, sealed 10th October 1956, under Authority 54/Inf/8784; Officers in silver gilt and enamel 'for No.1 & No.3 Dress' and in bronze 'For Service Dress'

1st Nottinghamshire (Robin Hoods) Rifle Volunteer Corps

This prestigious Volunteer unit was raised in Nottingham 15th November 1859. They won a vast number of prizes during the period of the second Volunteer movement, and were famous throughout the land as 'The Robin Hoods'. Though nominated as the 3rd Volunteer Battalion, this battalion strength unit did not adopt the title and remained the 1st Notts. RVC right through to 1908, when they became the 7th (Robin Hood) Battalion. Breaking with their strong Rifles background, the Corps now adopted collar badges. These were smaller versions of the cap badge; a laurel wreath surmounted by a crown, within the wreath the Cross of the Order of the Bath, in the centre of which a circle, inscribed, 'THE

ROBIN HOODS'. Within the title circle a crowned strung bugle horn. The two lateral divisions of the Cross inscribed 'SOUTH' & 'AFRICA' the bottom division inscribed '1900-02'.

They are recorded in gilding-metal. and white-metal (Fig.1272, 1273,) both types worn by the other ranks. For the senior NCO's the badge was in blackened white metal with polished highlights (Fig.1274), and for the Officers in silver plate. (Fig.1275) All with KC.

After the reformation of the Territorial Army in 1920, several changes of title and role occurred, and in 1949 the unit was redesignated *577 (The Robin Hoods, Sherwood Foresters) LAA/JL Regiment*. During this period their collar badge was the white-metal KC pattern already discussed, but now with single lug fitting. This being pattern No. 14725, sealed 21st September 1951. Further changes evolved in 1953 and again in 1955 when, on 10th March they became *350 (The Robin Hood Foresters) Heavy Regiment*. The white-metal collar badge now carried the QC, Pattern No. 17396, sealed 27th March 1957. (Fig.1276). This pattern was used as the guide for the later silver anodised version, (Fig.1277).

Further changes on 1st May 1961 resulted in the unit becoming *350 (The Robin Hood Foresters) Field Squadron of 49 (West Riding District, Royal Engineers*. Under Authority 54/Misc/7139, 17th February 1961, they were to wear the Royal Engineers grenade with Ubique scroll; in gold anodised for the men and bronze for the Officers, (Figs.1278, 1279). Local legend has it that this Directive was 'gently ignored' and the old collar badges continued in use.

WWI 12th SERVICE Battalion
Raised at Derby 1st October 1914 and converted to Pioneers 7th April 1915. Until disbandment at Heytesury 14th June 1919 they wore the standard cross pick and rifle collar badges. (Fig.147).

General
The collar badges have remained much the same throughout with only minor variations. Other ranks' badges have solid centres, whereas the Officers' and Warrant Officers' are voided. With the exception of the gilding-metal other ranks badges for the Regular Battalions 1881-1901, wherein the Stag faced to the left only, all other collar badges face both ways with the Stag facing inwards towards the collar opening.

On 28th February 1970, The Regiment amalgamated with The Worcestershire Regiment to become *The Worcestershire and Sherwood Foresters Regiment (29th/45th Foot)*.

Fig.1272

Fig.1273

Fig.1274

Fig.1275

Fig.1277 *Fig.1278* *Fig.1279* *Fig.1276*

The Loyal Regiment (North Lancashire)

Fig.1280

Fig.1281

Fig.1282

Pre 1881
47th (Lancashire) Regiment of Foot

The Royal Crest of England - the Crest of the Duchy of Lancaster was worn on some of the earliest appointments by Officers and this was the device used as their other ranks first collar badges introduced in 1874.

This Pattern 9328, a distinctive design in brass and sealed on 4th June. (Fig.1280). Army Records show a Directive was issued 6th April 1878 that "For the present, the 47th Regt of Foot be allowed to wear the collar badge with the Lions all facing one way... not in pairs".

Officers wore the same, but embroidered, when they removed their rank badges from their collars in late 1880.

81st (Loyal Lincoln Volunteers) Regiment of Foot

The following Regimental Order was announced by the 81st Regiment of Foot on 2nd March 1874 - "The distinctive button hitherto worn by the Regiment bearing the words 'Maida', 'Corunna' having been abolished in consequence of the adoption of an universal pattern button for all Line Regiments, H.R.H. the Field Marshall C in C approves of a distinctive collar badge being worn by the Regiment; the design being the Lincoln shield, surmounting a scroll with the words 'Maida', 'Corunna'".

This collar badge, in brass, was Pattern 9504 "for other ranks tunic and frock collars", sealed 19th August 1874. (Fig.1281). They did not face.

The "Lincoln Shield" of the 81st was the heraldic silver shield of its birthplace, the City of Lincoln, and bore the Red Cross of St. George and the gold fleur-de-lis thereon.

"Maida" was the Regiment's first battle honour awarded for their gallantry against a superior body of French soldiers at Maida in Southern Italy in July 1806. This was the first time British troops had fought and defeated Napoleon's troops in Europe. Authorised 2nd February 1807.

The battle honour "Corunna" was authorised for the 2nd Battn. 20th February 1812 in recognition of the part they played at the Battle of Corunna, Spain, in January 1809 during the retreat of Sir John Moore's Army. Not a victory in the fullest sense of the word but a good military achievement. Authorised for the whole Regiment 18/7/1816.

Post 1881

The two Regiments amalgamated in 1881 to become respectively, the 1st and 2nd Battns, *The Loyal North Lancashire Regiment*.

The other ranks collar badge was the "Lincoln Shield" of the old 81st in gilding-metal, Pattern No 9974, sealed 20th January 1882. "to replace brass Patterns 9504 of the 81st and 9328 of the 47th" (Fig.1282).

A new field service cap badge "Lion, crown and rose" was finally approved 24th December 1894, but after discussion it was decided that this would be for the cap only and "present collar badge for collar".

Renewal of the standard pattern was demanded 9th February 1898 and the resulting pattern 9974a was cut from new dies and sealed 3rd August 1899. No change in design, and worn until 1961.

Certainly, these were the collar badges worn by the 2nd Battn. but it is believed

THE LOYAL REGIMENT (NORTH LANCASHIRE)

that a completely different design was worn for a short while by the 1st Battn.

This was similar but slightly smaller than the device in the centre of the Helmet Plate Centre as worn by the other ranks of the Regiment from 1881. With a two lug fitting this was the Royal Crest over the Lancaster rose, all in gilding-metal (Fig.1283). They do not face and were worn until circa 1883/4

It seems probable that, like many other Regiments after the 1881 amalgamations, Officers of one former Regiment felt aggrieved that insignia of the new Regiment appeared to favour that of the other former Regiment

The new collar badge in this case was virtually that of the old 81st minus the scrolls. The old 47th, the senior of the two Regiments, felt somewhat chastened and consequently adopted the centre of the Helmet Plate as their collar badge. it is not impossible that the centre was cut out from the Helmet Plate and this would explain the lack of documentation regarding their badge.

The red rose of Lancaster was an old badge of the 47th, first displayed on the shoulder belt plates Circ 1818.

The title of the Regiment changed 1st January 1921 to *The Loyal Regiment (North Lancashire)*, but there was no change in the other ranks collar badge. No collar badges had been worn during the 1914/1918 war period and it was not until 1924 that other ranks, for the first time since khaki became the Service Dress of the Army, wore the gilding-metal 'Lincoln Shield".

The Brigade system was introduced in 1957 and when the Regiment joined part of The Lancastrian Brigade, they wore from 1958, the Brigade cap badge together with their own Regimental collar badge.

A new collar badge was introduced in 1961, the Royal Crest above a rose with a long scroll inscribed "THE LOYAL REGIMENT". Voided between the bottom of the Queen's crown, the rose and the scroll. The Royal Crest in silver anodised and the remainder in gold anodised, they faced both ways. This was Pattern 18497 sealed 23rd March 1961 under Authority 54/Inf/8778. (Fig.1284). The sealed pattern shows the rose in gold anodised but many were later painted red (Fig.1285). Worn up to amalgamation in 1970.

Early Dress Regulations describe the Officers tunic collar badge as "In embroidery, the Arms of the City of Lincoln. The ground of the shield in silver, the Cross of St. George in red silk on the shield; the fleur-de-lis in gold on the cross". (Fig.1286). Repeated in the 1900 and 1902 Editions but in the latter "for tunic and frock coat" and the additional "on mess jacket - centre of helmet plate", described under that section as "In silver, the Royal Crest. Below the crest, the Rose of Lancaster in silver gilt and red and green enamel".

The rose has five outer and five inner petals all turned down at the edges and all with sepals in between each petal and with a raised centre. The K/C rests squarely on the top outer petal (Fig.1287 and 1288 for two variations). An interesting smaller item has the Royal Crest in gilt and could possibly have been worn by Officers of the Militia battalions (Fig.1289). They were worn on the mess jacket introduced in 1897 with white roll collar and with rank badges worn on the shoulder-straps.

The description for both tunic and mess jacket were repeated in the 1904, 1911, 1912 and 1934 Dress Regulations but when the title of the Regt changed 1st January 1921 to *The Loyal Regiment (North Lancashire*, the rose underwent a

Fig.1283

Fig.1284

Fig.1285

Fig.1286

Fig.1288 *Fig.1289* *Fig.1287*

HISTORY OF THE BRITISH ARMY INFANTRY COLLAR BADGE

Fig.1290

change. Still with the five outer petals, turned down at the edges and with sepals in between each petal, but no longer with the five inner petals, now replaced by five separate sepals. The centre was now flat. The greatest change was that the rose was turned and now with a sepal uppermost and on which the crown balanced precariously. (Fig.1290). When these were first worn is not known but when the change of title was made it was specifically laid down that "in Order to avoid undue expense, the necessary changes in the uniform and on the appointments, should only be made gradually and not before the existing stocks are exhausted".

As already described, the Regiment joined part of The Lancastrian Brigade in 1957 wearing the Regimental collar badges and it was not until 1961 that the new Officers collar badge was introduced under Authority 54/Inf/8778 and sealed 23rd March. As already described for the soldiers badge but in silver, gilt and red and green enamel (Fig.1291). Designated for Nos.1, 2 and 3 Dress. They faced both ways with the lion facing inwards towards the collar opening. Shown on the same sealed pattern is the badge for wear on the mess jacket - the same design as for the one worn post 1921 but now with a Q/C (Fig.1292). Also recorded, but with red enamel replaced by white enamel (Fig.1293) they do not face.

The 1902 Dress Regulations describes the collar badge for the new Service Dress "as for tunic collar, with scroll for forage cap", in bronze. The scroll was inscribed "Loyal North Lancashire" (Fig.1294). The 1911 Edition slightly modifies the description with "as for tunic but smaller, with scroll as for forage cap".

Fig.1291

With the change in the Regimental title in 1921 came the corresponding change in the bronze collar badge - same general design but now, on the scroll, the new title "The Loyal Regiment" (see Figs.1295 and 1296 for two variations). The 1934 Dress Regulations confirmed the alteration.

The same badges were officially polished to gilding-metal and worn on the khaki drill uniforms.

Militia
3rd Duke of Lancaster's Own Royal Lancashire Militia

On 1st July 1881, the 1st and 2nd Battalions became, respectively, the 3rd and 4th (Militia) Battalions, *The Loyal North Lancashire Regiment*, adopting the collar badges as worn by the Regular Battalions They amalgamated in 1896 becoming the 3rd Battalion

Fig.1292

Prior to 1881, the collar badges are described as "Lion and Crown" in white-metal. It has not been possible to confirm whether this was similar to the collar badge worn by the old 47th, in brass, (Fig.1297, which is in white-metal) or whether it was similar to the one worn by the Royal North Gloucestershire Militia (Fig.788).

Rifle Volunteer Corps, Volunteer, Territorial Force & Territorial Army Battalions

On the reorganisation of the Army and the introduction of the Territorial system on 1st July 1881, the *11th and 14th Lancashire R.V.C.'s* became, respectively, the 1st and 2nd V.B.'s The Loyal North Lancashire Regiment.

Fig.1293

Drawings of the proposed other ranks collar badge for the 2nd V.B. were

Fig.1294  *Fig.1295*  *Fig.1296*  *Fig.1297*

THE LOYAL REGIMENT (NORTH LANCASHIRE)

submitted for approval by manufacturers Hobson & Sons, Little Windmill Street, London on 15th September 1883. These were similar to those worn by the Regular Battalions, but in white-metal, and were approved "For rank and file" on 6th October 1883, under Authority V/14/Lancashire/102. The same design was approved for the 1st V.B. 23rd April 1888.

Volunteer Officers wore similar embroidered collar badges to those worn by the Line Battalion Officers, in all silver embroidery or with metals reversed and with silver enamel only (Fig.1298).

After 1902, the mess jacket collar badge with Crest and Rose was worn.

As a reward for their services during the war in South Africa, both the 1st and 2nd V.B.'s were authorised to bear the battle honour "South Africa, 1900 - 02", on their appointments. This included the bronze collar badge worn on Service Dress (Fig.1299).

On 1st April 1908, the 1st and 2nd V/B.s, became, respectively, the 4th and 5th Territorial Battalions of the Regiment and some Officers wore a bronze 'T' below their bronze collar badges. Gradually the Territorial Battalions adopted the same collar badges as worn by the Regular Battalions The sealed pattern dated 15th November 1956 under Authority 54/Inf/8778 for the Loyal Regt (TA) (N Lancs) 5th Battalion show the Officers Sil/gilt/enamel collar badges and similar in anodised for soldiers.

Both the other ranks shield collar badge and those worn by Officers in bronze are known in blackened form.

Fig.1298

Fig.1299

Cyclist Coy, 1st V.B.
From 1882 to 1898, this Coy. wore a Glengarry badge of a circlet with the title and surmounted by a QVC. In the centre a cycle wheel, all in white-metal. During this period other ranks wore a similar cycle wheel, also in white-metal on their collars (Fig.1300). The one illustrated, and all the others examined, have a red cloth backing but there may well have been other colours used. They later wore the same collar badges as the rest of the 1st V.B., but in blackened form.

Fig.1300

WWI Service Battalions
The 2/4 Battalion was formed at Preston 14th September 1914 and are reputed to have worn on their collars, a badge in gilding-metal of a paschal lamb holding a fishtail flag and above the letters "PP" all on an horizontal lined background and with a scroll inscribed "PRESTON" (Fig.1301).

There are three other similar badges with different named scrolls, all with a two lug fitting. They are said to also have been arm badges or even shoulder badges. They are all oval shaped and are:-
(a) A continuous wreath of roses and leaves within which is a coronet with arrows in it's centre pointing upward all on a vertical lined background. Bottom scroll inscribed "BOLTON"
(b) Three diamonds under which a wavy line over what appears to be a section of water. Below a thick band with roses left and right with a deer in the middle, with another rose below the band. On a background of horizontal and vertical lines. Bottom scroll inscribed "HINDLEY" (Fig.1302).
(c) Top third has vertical lines with a coronet thereon. Across the centre a chevron proper on a mottled ground. on the chevron are three shields with motifs with a bottom scroll inscribed "CHORLEY".

Fig.1301

Fig.1302

General
The shield collar badges did not face.

On 25th march 1970, the Regiment amalgamated with The Lancashire Regiment (Prince of Wales's Vols) to form *The Queen's Lancashire Regiment*.

The Northamptonshire Regiment

Pre 1881
48th (Northamptonshire) Regiment of Foot.

Authorised on 16th July 1872, the official collar badge for wear by other ranks was the brass Imperial crown (Fig.333). They wore the same collar badge up to the 1881 amalgamation, and beyond. Confirmed by a Directive regarding the collar badge for the new combined Regiment, made in February 1882 including "48th previously wore the crown".

However, over the years it has been held that at some time pre 1881, the Regiment also wore another collar badge, never officially illustrated, but described as "The Talavera Laurel Wreath". There is no mystery regarding this, merely being a laurel wreath commemorating the distinguished service given by the 48th at the battle of Talavera, Portugal in 1809 and authorised 6th November 1816. Photographs of old collections in which such an item has appeared have been noted and such an item said to have been removed from the collar of a tunic worn by a soldier of the 48th is illustrated (Fig.1303).

Photographs have also shown that for a short time only, the numerals "48" were worn on the collar by some soldiers (Fig.1304)

Fig.1303

Fig.1304

58th (Rutlandshire) Regiment of Foot

The first other ranks collar badge was pattern 9514, sealed 6th October 1874. This was a small two tower castle with a turret rising from the top of the wall, between towers. A lookout in the top and bottom section of each tower together with one in the central turret. An open archway in the central wall has a partly opened portcullis. Below the castle is an horizontal key and flying from the central turret a flag facing to the right (Fig.1305). In brass, they did not face. Worn until 1882.

The Gibraltar honour, castle, key and motto "MONTIS INSIGNIA CALPE" was awarded to the 58th for taking part in the defence of the Rock 1779 -1783. Mons Calpe was the original name of Gibraltar.

Officers wore on their mess kit lapels, from c.1874, a castle with two scrolls in silver and gilt. The castle has three towers, the outside ones with two lookouts and the central tower with three. There is an archway from whence comes a chain running down to a vertical key below the castle. Over the castle a scroll inscribed "GIBRALTAR", the letters partly displaced by a flag flying to the left, from the central turret. Below the castle a scroll inscribed "MONTIS INSIGNIA CALPE". The castle in gilt, the scrolls in silver (Fig.1306). All the ones noted have the flag flying to the left.

Fig.1305

Fig.1306

Post 1881

On 1st July 1881, the 48th and 58th Regiments of Foot amalgamated to become the 1st and 2nd Battalions respectively, *The Northamptonshire Regiment*, each Battalion initially continuing to wear their old collar badges. By a verbal decision made by the AAG Horse Guards, it was instructed on 22nd October 1881 that "the new collar badge is to be the same as worn by it's Militia Battalion, but the number in the horseshoe, "Militia" and "Mediterranean" must be removed". However, on 16th November it was decreed that in order for the inscription on the collar badge to correspond to the title of the Regiment, as well as to assimilate the badge of Officers and men, the words "Northamptonshire Regiment" should be substituted for the words "Northamptonshire and Rutland". The next day, a

THE NORTHAMPTONSHIRE REGIMENT

further change was announced by Col. Blundel... the word "Northamptonshire" only to be used without the word "Regiment", the same as on the Helmet plate. The resulting collar badge, Pattern 10124 was sealed 22nd February 1882, "to replace Pattern 9514 of the 58th (48th wore the crown)."

All in gilding-metal, with the Cross of St. George within a circle inscribed "NORTHAMPTONSHIRE", the circle surmounted by a QVC and partly enclosed within a laurel wreath at the bottom of which was a horseshoe (Fig.1307). The Cross of St George and the horseshoe had Northamptonshire and Rutland Militia connections. (See under Militia for full details).

Whilst the 1st Battalion wore this collar badge up to the change in crown, it is believed that the 2nd Battalion wore until c.1884 a collar badge very similar to the one worn by Officers of the old 58th on their mess kit lapels pre-1881. The Officers badge had been in silver and gilt whereas the one worn by other ranks of the 2nd Battalion was in bi-metal, the castle in gilding-metal and the scrolls in white-metal (Fig.1308).

After c.1884, both Battalions wore the officially approved collar badge until 1899 when the standard pattern was renewed. Cut from new dies this was Pattern 10124a, sealed on 3rd August. Although there was no general change in design, there were minor modifications making it a more attractive badge (Fig.1309). Up to the introduction of a new field service cap in April 1898, the first pattern collar badge had also been worn on the field cap.

The other ranks pattern collar badge with Q.V.C. was, as stated, in gilding-metal with the single "NORTHAMPTONSHIRE" around the circle whereas the equivalent Officers pattern was in gilt with dark blue enamel and the two words "NORTHAMPTONSHIRE REGT". However, there is an hybrid, being the other ranks pattern in gilding-metal with the single title but with the background of the circle in dark blue enamel and the background to the cross in red enamel (Fig.1310).

Following on from the death of Queen Victoria, a new collar badge with K/C was required and the resulting Pattern 10123b was sealed 12th November 1901 under Authority. ACD/patts/434 (Fig.1311). In gilding-metal worn latterly with a single lug fitting until eventually replaced by similar with Q/C and worn up to amalgamation in 1960. The anodised version was not worn by the Line Battalions of the Regiment

Early Dress Regulations describe the Officers tunic collar badge as "in gilt metal, within a laurel wreath, a gilt circle pierced "Northamptonshire Regiment"; the ground of blue enamel. In relief, within the circle, on a raised ground of blue enamel, the Cross of St. George, in silver. Below the cross, and on the circle, a horseshoe in silver. The circle surmounted by a crown in gilt metal".

Overall, the design has remained the same throughout, initially on the tunic and later on the frock and mess dress although not on the scarlet serge patrol jacket taken into use in 1890, followed by Service Dress and No.1 Dress etc. Firstly, with a Q.V.C., of the flat topped variety (Fig.1312). Worn well into the 1900's and later replaced by similar but with a K/C (Fig.1313) and finally in 1953 by one with a Q/C (Fig.1314).

The 1950 Dress Regulations for the Northamptonshire Regiment, in "Details of Dress" in part II, instructed that this collar badge "will be worn with No.1 Dress and undress (patrol) uniforms. The inner edge of the badge will be 1¼ inches

Fig.1307

Fig.1308

Fig.1309

Fig.1310

Fig.1311

Fig.1313

Fig.1314

Fig.1312

HISTORY OF THE BRITISH ARMY INFANTRY COLLAR BADGE

Fig.1315

Fig.1316

Fig.1317

Fig.1318

Fig.1319

from the front centre of the collar". Later instructions were "for No.1 and No.3 Dress".

For the 1902 Officers Service Dress, Dress Regulations instructed the collar badge to be "as for forage cap", in bronze. This cap badge was described as "within a laurel wreath, the Castle and Key. Above the Castle a scroll inscribed "Gibraltar"; beneath, a scroll inscribed "Talavera". On the lower bend of the wreath, a scroll inscribed "Northamptonshire". Sealed 18th May 1903 (Fig.1315).

Although this collar badge was still being confirmed as such in the 1934 Dress Regulations, other collar badges in bronze were also being worn. The first, with Q.V.C., was similar in design to the ones in silver/gilt/enamel but in bronze, apart from the Cross and the horseshoe, which were in silver. Initially worn on the blue frock some had the usual voided cenre (Fig.1316) whilst other had a solid centre 9Fig 1317). There are also slight variations in the crowns but perhaps the most interesting pattern, and possibly a trial piece, has the usual bronze with Cross and horseshoe in silver but with a voided centre and blue enamel ground (Fig.1318).

The other ranks pattern, which has been bronzed is also known, possibly carried out when supplies of the correct badge were unobtainable. Similar to the Officers pattern but with K/C is thought to have been worn from c.1920 (Fig.1319). The final pattern with the Q/C was worn up to amalgamation (Fig.1320).

The Regimental "Details of Dress", 1950 records that these will be worn "on the Service Dress jacket, the lower edge of the badge will be ½ inch from the lower edge of the upper portion of the lapel; the outer edge of the badge will be ½ inch from the outer edge of the lapel. The upright of the Cross will be parallel to the outer edge of the lapel".

There are three other bronze collar badges that do not appear in Dress Regulations. The first is the three tower Gibraltar Castle with vertical key below, top scroll inscribed "GIBRALTAR" and bottom scroll inscribed "MONTIS INSIGNIA CALPE". (Fig.1321). This is known to have been worn c.1916. Photographs of Officers killed in the Great War show them being worn on Service Dress often with a separate bronze "T" below.

The second is a smaller version of the bronze cap/collar badge (Fig.1322).

The third is the cap/collar without the laurel leaves and title scroll and said to have been a WWI adaption. Worn with a separate "T" below. All have two lug fittings.

One other collar badge of which no official mention can be found, is the Gibraltar Castle with vertical key below in gilt and a top scroll inscribed "GIBRALTAR" and a bottom scroll inscribed "TALAVERA", both in silver. (Fig.1323). Thought to have been worn on the mess dress.

An embroidered collar badge is illustrated under Fig.1324, and it is believed that this was the pattern worn on the scarlet tunic c.1881.

Militia
Northampton and Rutland Militia

Collar badges in white-metal. for wear by other ranks on their tunic and frock collars, pattern 7581 were sealed 20th April 1876 under Authority

Fig.1320    *Fig.1321*    *Fig.1322*    *Fig.1323*    *Fig.1324*

51/Northamptonshire/396. This was the Cross of St. George within a circle inscribed "NORTHAMPTONSHIRE AND RUTLAND" and surmounted by a flat topped Q.V.C. Around the circle a laurel wreath and at the base of the circle a horseshoe with the numerals '48' within. This, above a scroll inscribed "MILITIA"; below another scroll inscribed "MEDITERRANEAN" (Line drawing Fig.1325).

The golden horseshoe is derived from the arms of the Royal and ancient Borough of Oakham which has a black horseshoe with silver nails on a gold ground. This is purported to commemorate Queen Elizabeth passing through the town when her horse cast a shoe, the town thereby acquiring the privilege of claiming a horseshoe from any Royal personage entering it's precincts. More likely, is that it is derived from the Arms of the ancient family of Ferrar, Earl of Derby. Wakeline de Farrars, who lived during the reign of King Stephen is said to have been Lord of the Castle of Oakham and for some grant to him, or to his ancestor, who was the Royal farrier, the Lordship of Oakham has retained the right of demanding from any nobleman who passed through the Barony for the first time, a shoe from the foot of one of his horses.

"Mediterranean" was the distinction awarded to the Regiment for their services during the Crimean War of 1854/5 when they volunteered to carry out garrison duties in order to free Line Regiments for active service. "48" was the Militia County precedence number.

The 1st Battalion became the 3rd Battalion, Northamptonshire Regiment 1st July 1881 and are believed, in order to emphasise their former Militia status, to have blackened their collar badges.

Fig.1325

Fig.1326

Rifle Volunteer Corps, Volunteer, Territorial Force & Territorial Army Battalions

The 1st Northamptonshire R.V.C. became a V.B. of the Northamptonshire Regiment 1st July 1881 and redesignated the 1st V.B. in December 1887. Their collar badges were similar to those worn by the Regular Battalions but were in white-metal for wear by other ranks, firstly with a Q.V.C. followed by similar but with K/C. Officers wore the same as their Regiular counterparts but in all silver on their tunic collars.

On 1st April 1908, they were reorganised to become the 4th Battalion (TF). They gradually adopted the collar badges as worn by the Regular Battalions but on Service Dress, Officers wore, in bronze, what was virtually the central part of their cap badge - castle and key with a bottom scroll inscribed "SOUTH AFRICA 1900 - 02" (Fig.1326). They also wore in bronze, similar to the cap/collar badge but with "4th BATTALION" in place of the "GIBRALTAR" scroll and with "SOUTH AFRICA 1900 - 01" on the scroll usually inscribed "TALAVERA" (Fig.1327). Both were sometimes worn with a separate 'T' below the collar badge.

A photograph of Officers of the 5th Battalion taken in September 1942 clearly shows them wearing a black/buff/blue Regimental flash on the extreme end of their battledress blouse collars. Although not a collar badge as generally accepted, it is worthy of note.

After amalgamation, the 4th and 5th Battalions expanded to form the 4/5 Battalion of the T/A, wearing the same collar badges previously worn before amalgamation.

When the *7th (Volunteer) Battalion, The Royal Anglian Regiment* was formed 1st April 1971, 'C' and 'D' Coys were formed from the Northamptons' and they wore their old collar badges, Officers in Sil/gilt/enamel with Q.C. and soldiers in gold anodised also with Q.C. sealed late 1973, this being Pattern 21010 (Fig.1328).

Fig.1327

Fig.1328

Cyclists
5th (Huntingdonshire) Battalion

Raised 27th February 1914 as *The Huntingdonshire Cyclist Battalion* and joining the Northamptonshire Regiment 7th February 1920 as the 5th (Huntingdonshire) Battalion, they wore as their collar badge a leaping stag on a ground above a scroll inscribed "HUNTINGDONSHIRE". The stag was taken from the Seal of

Fig.1329

Fig.1330

Fig.1331

Fig.1332

Huntingdonshire. Worn in facing pairs with the stag facing inwards towards the collar opening, in gilding-metal by other ranks and in bronze (Fig.1329) and in gilt (Fig.1330) by Officers. The Battalion was disembodied 14th April 1919.

V.T.C.
Northamptonshire V.T.C.
A photograph taken in 1915 shows an Officer wearing a grey uniform on which are bronze collar badges which are virtually the cap badge without the "Gibraltar" and "Talavera" scrolls. He is with the Daventry Company. Another item purporting to be connected with the V.T.C. is in silver plate with standing lions either side of a tower with scroll below inscribed "CASTELLO - PORTIOR - CONCORD" (Fig.1331). This, however, could well be of municipal background only.

WWI Service Battalions
5th (Service) Battalion
Raised 15th August 1914 and converted to Pioneers January 1915 in France. During their pioneer roll they wore the usual crossed rifle and pick collar badges (Fig.147).

6th (Service) Battalion
Photographs show other ranks of this Battalion wearing khaki Service Dress and the blue emergency isue both with their brass shoulder titles on the collars (Fig.1332).

General
On 1st June 1960, the Regiment amalgamated with The Royal Lincolnshire Regiment to form the *2nd East Anglian Regiment (Duchess of Gloucester's Own Royal Lincolnshire and Northamptonshire)*.

The Royal Berkshire Regiment (Princess Charlotte of Wales's)

Pre 1881
49th (Hertfordshire - Princess Charlotte of Wales's) Regiment of Foot

The "Dragon of China" was awarded to the 49th on 12th January 1843 to commemorate their service in China from 1841 - 1843 when it took part in the capture of Chusan, Canton, Anoy and Shanghai as well as in the ocupation of Ningpoo. So it was a natural choice for the China Dragon to be the first collar badge for other ranks to wear on their tunic collars.

Fig.1333

This particular dragon was quite a large one with a scaly body and fire emerging from it's mouth. Free standing, with one front leg raised it had two tails, one trailing out behind, the other rising up and across it's body ending above the centre of it's back. This was pattern 9537, in brass and sealed 26th April 1875 and worn in facing pairs with the dragon facing inwards towards the collar opening (Fig.1333). Two variations have been identified, the first fully die struck, the other struck from a thicker metal with, from the reverse of the badge, a deep narrow hollow extending from the head to the tail. The second type is also to be found in silver plate and with the brass pattern that has been silvered (Fig.1334). These were worn by WO's and senior NCO's, Officers wearing their badge of rank on their collar at this time.

Fig.1334

These were worn until 1879 at which time the Authorities became determined to standardise sphinx, tiger, bugle and dragon collar badges. On 30th July it was directed that there would be an asimilation of patterns, "49th Foot, pattern 9537 to be 55th Foot, Pattern 9325". Still freestanding, with one front foot raised, albeit at a different position, scaly body and two tails, it was a much smaller dragon. In brass, this was pattern 9325. Also worn in facing pairs (Fig.1335). Regiments often had a photograph taken just prior to, or almost immediately after, the 1881 amalgamations and such photographs, including one of the Band taken in Gibraltar in 1881, clearly show these later collar badges being worn. Worn until 1882.

Fig.1335

66th (Berkshire) Regiment of Foot

Authorised by a General Order 16th July 1872, the 66th Regiment of Foot adopted and wore from 1874, the brass Imperial crown on the collars of other ranks (Fig.333). A photograph taken in 1879 clearly shows these being worn, but it is interesting that some soldiers are wearing ordinary crowns on their collars whilst others are not wearing anything at all. These were worn up to the 1881 amalgamations and beyond with the new collar badge not being ready until February 1882.

It is recorded that in November 1880, Officers of the Regiment made application to wear a laurel wreath on their forage cap but this was refused. A thick laurel wreath formed part of the other ranks pre 1881 glengary badge and over the years it has been said that similar had been worn as a collar badge. Such an item, in brass, is illustrated (Fig.1336). There is no record in the Army Pattern Room records of any such item although, if worn unofficially, there is hardly likely to be. The very size of the badge makes it almost impossible to have been worn on the collar. WO's wore a smaller neater, gilt laurel wreath (Fig.1337). Worn for a short time only, and sometimes referred to as "the Douro Wreath", Douro being

Fig.1336

Fig.1337

HISTORY OF THE BRITISH ARMY INFANTRY COLLAR BADGE

Fig.1338

Fig.1339

Fig.1340

Fig.1341

Fig.1342

Fig.1343

a battle honour awarded to the Regiment, 14th August 1815, to commemorate Wellington's first victory after he had been entrusted with the supreme command in the Peninsula War.

Photographs have also shown some soldiers wearing the numerals '66' on their collars, date unknown (Fig.1338). Officers did not wear collar badges pre 1881.

Post 1881

On 1st July 1881, the 49th and 66th amalgamated to bcome the 1st and 2nd Battalions, respectively, of *The Princess Charlotte of Wales's (Berkshire Regiment)*, redesignated in 1885 as *The Royal Berkshire Regiment (Princess Charlotte of Wales's)*.

The "Dragon of China" again featured in the new collar badge with all the same features as the ones previously worn by the 49th, but smaller and of different format - with a rather startled look! The dragon now rested on a scroll inscribed "Princess Charlotte of Wales's", in gilding-metal this being Pattern 10126 sealed 22nd February 1882 (Fig.1339).

An entry in the Army Pattern Room journals under the date 30th July 1886 records "noted demand for collar badges can go forward" with the remark that "when a supply is wanted, contractors will be required to submit a pattern from drawings that will be given". Perhaps this relates to the Royal accolade of 1885 and possible new pattern.

A new field service cap was introduced in 1896 but after due consideration it was decided that the collar badge would remain as they were - this decision being taken on 28th July. However, it was decided on 7th December 1887 that the standard pattern of collar badge would be renewed and cut from new dies and the resulting Pattern, 10126a was sealed the same day under Authority ACD/Patts/9026. Although there was no general format alteration, the opportunity was taken to slightly modify the shape of the dragon and make it a smaller, neater creature (Fig.1340). Worn right up to 1959 amalgamation, latterly with a single lug fitting.

The 1883 Dress Regulations describe the Officers badge for the tunic collar as quite simply "The Dragon of China, in gold embroidery", but the 1891 Edition adds "on a blue cloth ground". These were also worn on the mess dress, one such being sealed by the War Office 18th May 1903, "for tunic and mess jacket" (Fig.1341). The same description is carried forward in subsequent Dress Regulations up to 1934 when "in pairs" is added. On the scarlet frock was worn a pattern similar to that of the other ranks but in gilt, these being sealed by the War office 4th January 1901 (Fig.1342).

The Gaunt pattern books show rubbings of both these embroidered and metal collar badges annotated "1st Battalion - embroidery, 2nd Battalion - metal". The gilt collar badge was also later worn on the blue frock coat and the blue tunic. Photographs c.1906 show a dragon on a thin ground, in gilt, being worn on the deep full dress and frock collars (Fig.1343). Believed to have been worn for a very short time only (See plate 18 for this collar badge being worn by Major A. G. Paske, c.1906).

For the 1902 Service Dress, the collar badge in bronze was to be "as for tunic collar, with scroll as for forage cap". This was the description in the 1902 Dress Regulations which also described the relative scroll as "Royal Berkshire". Repeated in the 1904 and 1911 Editions, slightly altered to read "as for tunic but smaller with scroll and for forage cap, in pairs". The 1934 Edition makes a further alteration being more specific regarding the scroll, "as for tunic, but smaller with scroll inscribed "Royal Berkshire" in pairs".

It is therefore difficult to understand how, during the years 1902 - 1934, the Regiment wore the incorrect collar badge on Service Dress!. The incorrect pattern was sealed 13th February 1903 under Authority 610002/Infy/587, this having a double scroll with the "PRINCESS CHARLOTTE OF WALES'S" above that of "ROYAL BERKSHIRE". Often worn with a red cloth backing in recognition of the service of the Light Company of the 49th at Brandywine in 1777 during the American War of Independence. The collar badges varied with different shaped

214

THE ROYAL BERKSHIRE REGIMENT

dragons and scrolls (Figs.1344, 1345 and 1346, worn with a red backing).

The correct pattern in bronze, was sealed 29th April 1934 under Authority 54/Officers/3079 (Fig.1347).

Both the incorrect and correct patterns are known in gilding-metal and were worn on the khaki drill uniforms.

The other ranks die struck pattern is also known, bronzed.

By 1951, the Regiment were wearing a gilt dragon on a torse on both No 1 Dress and on mess dress (Fig.1348). A similar badge had been worn for a short time on khaki drill in the early 1930's.

Militia
Royal Berkshire Militia

Collar badges, in white-metal for tunic and frock coat collars to be worn by other ranks were sealed 17th April 1879 under Authority PC/BM/162, this being Pattern 7192. The badge had a standing stag beneath a bent oak tree all within an oval wreath and at the base a three part scroll inscribed "ROYAL - BERKSHIRE - MILITIA". (1¾" x ⅞") (Line drawing Fig.1349). The stag under a tree forms part of the County Arms and as such an emblem of the "Merrie Greenwood" appropriate to the representatives of the famed English Archers. Officers wore similar but in silver.

On 1st July 1981, they became the 3rd Battalion The Princess Charlotte of Wales's (Berkshire Regiment).

Rifle Volunteer Corps, Volunteer, Territorial Force & Territorial Army Battalions

The 1st Berkshire R.V.C. became a VB of the Princess of Wales's (Berkshire Regiment) 1st July 1881, redesignated as the 1st VB 1st December 1882, other ranks wearing similar collar badges to those worn by the Regular Battalions, but in white-metal. Officers wore the same embroidered pattern as their Regular counterparts, but in silver embroidery. They later also wore the other ranks pattern but in silver plate. On their mess jackets they wore a small dragon on a torse, in silver, the earliest pattern being (Fig.1350), followed by (Fig.1351).

When they became part of the Territorial Force, they gradually adopted the same collar badges as worn by the Regular Battalions but Officers retained their individuality by wearing a separate "T" in bronze below the bronze collar badge on Service Dress. When the 4th and 6th Battalions amalgamated 1st January 1947 to become the 4/6th TA Battalion, they continued to wear the same collar badges and a sealed pattern 13th December 1961 annotated for 'C' Coy under Authority 54/Inf/8399 shows a small gilt dragon on a torse "for No 1 Dress" (Fig.1352). The usual dragon/torse/scroll collar badge in bronze is shown "for Service Dress". The collar badge shown for soldiers on a later pattern sealed 12th August 1964 is the gold anodised version of the former badge in gilding-metal

Fig.1344

Fig.1345

Fig.1346

Fig.1347

Fig.1349

Fig.1350    *Fig.1351*    *Fig.1352*    *Fig.1348*

Pattern 10126a being used as a guide. This was Pattern 19364 sealed under Authority 54/Inf/8871 (Fig.1353).

The 4/6th TA Battalion formed part of *The Royal Berkshire Territorials* becoming 'C' Coy on 1st April 1967 when they were to wear their former gilt collar badges on No 1 Dress and similar, but in bronze, on No.2 Dress (Figs.1354 and 1355). It is doubtful if these were ever worn. Soldiers were also to have worn similar in gold anodised but whether these were ever made is not known and thought to be doubtful. Became a Cadre 1st April 1969 and disbanded 1st April 1971.

Cadets

Bradfield College Rifle Corps. Attached to the 1st VB of The Princess Charlotte of Wales's (Berkshire Regiment), cadets wore a white-metal badge on both cap and collar. This was the Chinese dragon on a torse over a scroll inscribed "Bradfield College OTC". The same design of dragon as worn by the VB (Line drawing Fig.1356). Officers wore similar but in bronze.

Other badges

One collar badge sometimes thought to have been worn by the Regiment, in chrome, is, in fact, that worn by the Hong Kong Police (Fig.1357).

General

The Dragon of China has appeared in various designs from time to time during the Regiments existence, but standardised before the Regiments amalgamation with The Wiltshire Regiment (Duke of Edinburgh's) 9th June 1959 to form *The Duke of Edinburgh's Royal Regiment (Berkshire and Wiltshire)*.

All dragon collar badges were worn in facing pairs with the dragon facing inwards towards the collar opening.

Fig.1353

Fig.1354

Fig.1355

Fig.1356

Fig.1357

The Queen's Own Royal West Kent Regiment

Pre 1881
50th (The Queen's Own) Regiment of Foot
The Royal Crest was an old badge of the 50th so it was appropriate for this to be the first other ranks collar badge. The crowned lion stood on a large Imperial crown. In brass, this was Pattern 9326, sealed 18th May 1874 (Fig.1358). One variation is known with smaller lion and crown (Fig.1359). Worn until 1882 in facing pairs with the lion facing inwards towards the collar opening.

97th (The Earl of Ulster's) Regiment of Foot
From 1874, other ranks of the 97th wore as their collar badge the brass Imperial crown Authorised 16th July 1872 under Authority PC/Infy Gen/111 (Fig.333). Worn until 1882.

Post 1881
The 50th and 97th Regiments of Foot amalgamated 1st July 1881 to become the 1st and 2nd Battalions respectively, *The Queen's Own (Royal West Kent Regiment)*, redesignated 1st January 1921 as *The Royal West Kent (Queen's Own)*, and again redesignated 16th April 1921 as *The Queen's Own Royal West Kent Regiment*. A verbal decision was given on 22nd October by Colonel Blundell, AAG, Horse Guards, that "the present pattern for 50th foot, lion and crown - Pattern 9326 will continue to be worn".

However, this lasted for a short time only as on 20th January 1882 a new design in gilding-metal, Pattern 9968 was sealed "to replace 9326 of the 50th - (97th wore the Imperial crown)". Still with the Royal Crest, but this time with the crowned lion on the more conventional QVC (Fig.1360).

Renewal of the srtandard gilding metal pattern was "demanded" in 1899 and on 3rd August a new Pattern, 9968a was cut from new dies and sealed. The design remained the same with minor changes in the shape of the lion and crown (Fig.1361).

Following the death of Queen Victoria, a new Pattern 9968b was sealed 9th September 1902 under Authority ACD/patts/697. Again in gilding-metal but now with a K/C (Fig.1362). A larger pattern exists but where it was worn is not known (Fig.1363).

According to the Army Pattern Room journals the K/C Pattern 9968b was replaced by similar, but with Q/C but when recently a suppliers business ceased, a box (still unopened and sealed) was found from a manufacturer of badges. The box contained the K/C pattern but in gold anodised and one assumes these were made but never worn. These must be extremely scarce and illustrated are a facing pair (Figs.1364 and 1365). The Q/C version was Pattern 17103, in gilding-metal

Fig.1358

Fig.1359

Fig.1360

Fig.1361

Fig.1363    *Fig.1364*    *Fig.1365*    *Fig.1362*

HISTORY OF THE BRITISH ARMY INFANTRY COLLAR BADGE

and sealed 21st March 1956, later replaced by an anodised version, this being Pattern 19431 sealed 19th November 1964 under Authority A/54/Inf/8873 (Fig.1366). Worn up to amalgamation in 1961.

Early Dress Regulations describe the Officers collar badge for tunic collar as "The Royal Crest, in gold embroidery". This was repeated in all subsequent Editions up to and including 1934 and was still being worn when the Regiment amalgamated in 1961. On a crimson velvet cushion the first collar badge had the QVC followed by similar but with K/C (Fig.1367) and finally with QC (Fig.1368). Worn on tunic, mess jacket, No.1 and No.3 Dress. Similar in gilt metal was worn on the scarlet frock (Fig.1369).

For the 1902 Service Dress, Dress Regulations describe the collar badge, "As for tunic collar with scroll as for forage cap", in bronze and the resulting pattern was sealed 9th September 1902 under Authority 54/Officers/4025. Different manufacturers have produced slightly different designs and illustratd are four such patterns showing variations in the shape, size and position of the lion, crown and scrolls (Figs.1370, 1371, 1372 and 1373). These were also officially polished to gilding-metal by the Regiment and worn on the khaki drill. Officers of the 2nd Battalion also wore these polished collar badges on their Service Dress jackets during the first world war and for several years afterwards. For a short while some Officers wore, prior to WWI, bronze collar badges without a scroll, the lion and crown smaller than those on the official issue (Figs.1374 and 1375 for two variations). The bronze collar badge, with scroll, was eventually replaced by similar but with QC, sealed 18th October 1955 under Authority 55/Officers/4025 (Fig.1376).

A gilt K/C item is known, specially gilded by the Regiment for wear at the 1937 Coronation.

Fig.1366

Fig.1367

Fig.1368

Fig.1369

Fig.1370

Fig.1371

Fig.1372

Fig.1373

Fig.1374

Fig.1375

Fig.1376

THE QUEEN'S OWN ROYAL WEST KENT REGIMENT

Militia
West Kent Light Infantry Militia
White metal collar badges, Pattern 7487 for wear on other ranks tunic and frock collars were sealed 25th November 1875 under Authority PC/W Kent Militia/10. These were similar, but less ornate, than the centrepiece of the Regiment's shakoplate worn 1855-61 – a ribboned bugle with the White Horse of Kent above an "INVICTA" scroll within the strings (Line Drawing Fig.1377). Officers wore similar, but in silver and they were worn in facing pairs with the horse facing inwards towards the collar opening.

On 1st July 1881, they became the 3rd Battalion of The Queen's Own Royal West Regiment.

Fig.1377

Rifle Volunteer Corps, Volunteer, Territorial Force & Territorial Army Battalions
The 1st Kent R.V.C. became a VB of the Queen's Own (Royal West Kent Regiment) 1st July 1881, redesignated as the 1st VB 1st February 1883.

The 3rd Kent R.V.C. became a VB of the Regiment 1st July 1881, redesignated as the 2nd VB 1st February 1883.

Photographs clearly show both VB's initially wore the lion over QVC, similar to the Regular Battalions, but in white-metal. These were later replaced by similar but with KC. Officers wore similar collar badges to their Regular counterparts but in silver embroidery.

However, the 1st VB wore a quite different collar badge from c.1890 - 1899, clearly shown in the Gaunt pattern book. This was The Kent Horse over a scroll inscribed "INVICTA' (unconquered). This had been the badge of the West Kent Light Infantry Militia. The collar badge was worn in white-metal by other ranks (Fig.1378) and in blackened silver (Fig.1379) and in gilt, by Officers.

When the VB's became TF Battalions in 1908, they gradually adopted the collar badges worn by the Regular Battalions but Officers often wore a separate bronze 'T' below their collar badges on service dress.

Fig.1378

Fig.1379

Cyclists
6th (Cyclist) Battalion
Formed 1st April 1908 at Tonbridge and after various title changes became the *Kent Cyclist Battalion* in 1910. They too, wore their own distinctive collar badges, similar to those formerly worn by the 1st VB with the Horse of Kent over an "INVICTA" scroll but smaller and of a different design. Other ranks wore them in white-metal (Fig.1380) and they are also known in bi-metal believed to have been worn by Senior NCO's, whilst Officers wore them in silver (see Fig.1381), and bronze on Service Dress. (Fig.1382). WO's wore them in gilt. They were disembodied in February 1920.

Fig.1380

Fencibles
Kent Volunteer Fencibles 1914 - 18
Wore as their collar badge, similar to their cap badge but smaller. The White Horse of Kent on an oval beneath a scroll inscribed with the initials of their title, 'KVF' and above another scroll inscribed "INVICTA". In white-metal and worn in facing pairs with the horse facing inwards towards the collar opening. (Fig.99)

They later became the *Kent Volunteer Regiment* and in 1918 they formed the 1st - 4th VB's of The Queen's Own Royal West Kent Regiment

Fig.1381

General
Both the lion and the horse collar badges of the Regiment were worn in facing pairs with the animals facing inwards towards the collar opening.

The Regiment amalgamated with The Buffs (Royal East Kent Regiment) 1st March 1961 to form *The Queen's Own Buffs, Royal Kent Regiment*. After amalgamation the Regiment's collar badges continued to be worn by the 4/5th TA Battalions.

Fig.1382

The King's Own Yorkshire Light Infantry

Pre 1881
51st (2nd Yorkshire, West Riding) Regiment of Foot or The King's Own Light Infantry Regiment

Many suggestions have been made regarding the pre 1881 collar badges of the 51st. Of course, what a Regiment was officially supposed to wear and what they actually wore were not always the same, but according to Regimental histories, references are made to the year of 1874 which apparently describes the collar badges as "bugle horns with '51' in the curl - for NCO's and men to be worn on each end of the collar". Certainly these items exist in brass - I have seen seven such badges all facing to the left which perhaps stretches coincidence a little too far? These same items appear in the Gaunt pattern books annotated "For shell cases".

They also exist in embroidery appearing in various sizes, mostly with a pin back fitting (Fig.1383). Officers did not remove their rank badges until late 1880 and the largest of these items are cap badges.

It has also been suggested that the pre 1881 collar badge was a brass bugle horn inscribed "YORKSHIRE" (Fig.1384). These faced both ways and also appear in white-metal. (Fig.1385). However, these are not collar badges but formed part of the shoulder title and worn on tropical kit.

A small brass bugle horn with rose in the centre was also said to have been worn. Again, these items exist (Fig.1386), but it is most likely they are economy issue cap badges issued during WWI.

As yet no photographic or printed evidence of any collar badges being worn by the Regiment pre 1881 has come to light. They were in India in 1873 and, from 1874 until 1881, were engaged in the North West Frontier and in Afghanistan, so for the whole of the period when collar badges would have been worn they were on active service, mostly in columns of company strength and rarely as a Regiment, thus probably accounting for the lack of photographs etc.

The journals of the Army Clothing Dept pattern room record that a new collar badge for wear by other ranks of the newly formed King's Own Light Infantry (South Yorkshire Regiment) to be sealed on 2nd February 1882 "was to replace the previous brass universal pattern bugle as used by Light Infantry Regiment's as authorised on 16th July 1872 and sealed 15th February 1873". (Fig.1194).

So officially, it is known that the correct pre 1881 collar badge was the standard brass Light Infantry pattern bugle.

105th (Madras Light Infantry) Regiment of Foot

The first other ranks collar badge of the 105th Regiment of Foot was a French bugle horn surmounted by a QVC and with the figures '105' in a solid centre. In brass, this was Pattern 9553 sealed 13th March 1876. A similar item in white-metal was worn by the Band (Fig.1387).

This collar badge did not prominently display the '105', so it was quickly replaced by similar but with a voided centre and "with scarlet cloth in the centre". This was Pattern 9562, sealed 13th November 1876. Several slightly different shaped crowns have been noted (Figs.1388 and 1389 for two variations).

Post 1881

On 1st July 1881, the 51st and 105th Regiment's of Foot amalgamated to become the 1st and 2nd Battalions, respectively, *The King's Own Light Infantry (South*

Fig.1383

Fig.1384

Fig.1385

Fig.1386

Fig.1387

THE KING'S OWN YORKSHIRE LIGHT INFANTRY

Yorkshire Regiment), resulting in a new collar badge, Pattern 10014 being sealed 2nd February 1882.

Although both the 51st and the 105th had been Light Infantry Regiments with the bugle horn featuring prominently in their insignia, there was much discussion regarding the actual design of the new collar badge. A pattern submitted to Gaunt's in December 1881, albeit in gilt for Officers, shows an unusual design not worn before by either Regiment. (Line Drawing Fig.1390). This was not approved, Pattern 10014 in gilding-metal being adopted. This was a ribboned bugle above a scroll inscribed "KING'S OWN" (Fig.1391).

This was not a popular badge with the Regiment and described in The Regimental Journal as, "An ugly and unsatisfactory production", so when the title of the Regiment changed on 1st June 1887 to *The King's Own Yorkshire Light Infantry*, action was taken to have it replaced. The official letter of Submission was sent for the Queen's signature submitting that, because of the change in title, "it now becomes necessary to alter the badges of Officers, NCO's and men and a design is submitted for approval". This received the Royal approval 17th August1888 and on the 27th of the same month new standard pattern drawings "were demanded" under Order, Yorks LI/PC/IYork/73. These were sent, approved and the resulting pattern 1890 was sealed 2nd April 1889 "to replace Pattern 10014".

This was a bugle horn in gilding-metal, in the curl of which was the White Rose of Yorkshire, in white-metal (Fig.1392). The White Rose of York was an old badge of the 51st and it was the same Regiment that adopted the design of a French bugle horn in place of the more common one.

Renewal of the standard pattern was demanded 18th April 1898 and these were cut from new dies and sealed 26th January 1899. This new Pattern, 1890a was merely a renewal and there was no change in design. The sealed pattern is annotated "Also to be worn on Forage cap and Field Service Helmet but to be fitted with vertical shank".

The title of the Regiment was redesignated in 1902 as *The King's Own (Yorkshire Light Infantry)*.

In 1903, the Regiment requested "That the bugle collar badge to also be worn on the new Wolesley pith helmet now introduced (ie as a puggary badge but without the green cloth patch)". This was approved on 2nd December, with the Directive "When present stocks exhausted".

By Army Order 509, November 1920, the title of the Regiment was again altered, this time to *The King's Own Yorkshire Light Infantry*, as from 1st January 1921 with the authorised abbreviation K.O.Y.L.I. There was no change in the other ranks collar badge.

During WWI, bronze collar badges were issued to other ranks or were darkened under unit arrangements (Fig.1393).

In 1951, a new other ranks collar badge was introduced. Similar to the one it replaced this being pattern 14618 sealed on the 25th April and now all in white-metal and with a single lug fitting (Fig.1394). Similar, but in chrome, are said to have been worn by the Regimental Police in the mid 1950's but if so, unofficially. Pattern 14618 was used as the guide for a silver anodised version, pattern 19235 sealed 21st Jnauary 1964 under Authority 54/Inf/8550, "to replace Pattern 14618" (Fig.1395). There are also examples where the rose has been painted black but why this was done is not known. The anodised collar badges were only issued after existing stocks of those in white-metal had been exhausted and both were still being worn up to redesignation in 1968.

Fig.1388

Fig.1389

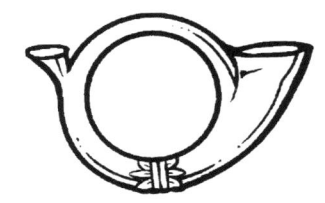

Fig.1390

Fig.1391

Fig.1392

Fig.1394

Fig.1395

Fig.1393

HISTORY OF THE BRITISH ARMY INFANTRY COLLAR BADGE

The Officers tunic collar badge is described in the 1883 Dress Regulations as "A French horn in gold embroidery, the white rose in silver embroidery in the centre of the horn". In 1890, there was a change as directed by the 1891 Edition stating "A French horn in gold embroidery; in the centre of the horn, on a raised ground of dark green cloth, the white rose, in silver metal" (Figs.1396, 1397 and 1398 for three variations, the larger ones were usually worn on the mess dress from 1897 onwards). Subsequent Dress Regulations carried the same description up to the 1934 Edition, which added, "In pairs". Worn until 1951 when replaced by similar, but smaller, and in metal. The French horn and rose were in silver plate, the rose being on a ground of black enamel. (Fig.1399).

Also worn, from 1882 - 1889 was the other ranks equivalent of bugle horn over "KING'S OWN" scroll, but in gilt (Fig.1400). Worn by WO's.

In 1902, Service Dress was introduced for Officers with Dress Regulations directing the bronze collar badge to be "As for forage cap but in pairs". (Fig.1401). Although these collar badges were described as such in each succeeding Dress Regulations up to an including the 1934 Edition, they were, in fact, worn for a very short time only. In 1904, the Regiment adopted similar collar badges for Service Dress but in black metal with a silver rose. (Fig.1402 for small rose and Fig.1403 for large rose). Some had a semi-gloss finish.

These were worn until 1951 including on battle dress from 1939. Officially, collar badges were not to be worn on battle dress but photographs clearly show them being worn. One such collar badge worn on both Service Dress and battle dress from c.1943, for a short time only, was in black plastic with the rose in silver. (Fig.1404).

Collar badges with the French horn in gilt and a silver rose on black enamel was worn on tropical kit and blue patrols 1902-51. (Figs.1405 and 1406 for two variations).

Yet another Officers variation has the bugle horn in chrome (Superior finish to that of the other ranks equivalent), with the rose in silver on the usual black enamel ground. (Fig.1407). These are believed to have been the Officers equivalent to that worn by other ranks and worn in the mid 1950's only.

Fig.1396

Fig.1397

Fig.1398

Fig.1399

Fig.1400

Fig.1401

Fig.1402

Fig.1403

Fig.1404

Fig.1405

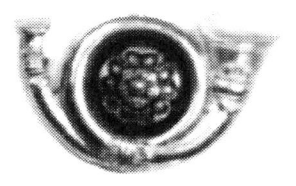

Fig.1406

Fig.1407

Militia
1st West York Rifles Militia

In 1875, on the introduction of an universal pattern button, bearing the Royal Arms, instead of the Regimental pattern button, authority was given for the badge of the White Rose to be worn on the collars by Officers and other ranks. Worn in white-metal by other ranks (Fig.1408) and in silver by Officers.

On 1st July 1881, they became the 3rd Battalion, The King's Own Light Infantry (South Yorkshire Regiment).

Similar to items already described in gilding-metal and gilt for the Regular Battalions and in white-metal for the VB's, is one in dark bronze. (Fig.1409) In mint condition only one has so far been noted and may have been a trial pattern for the 1902 Service Dress. However, it may well have been worn by the 3rd Battalion on their Service Dress, carrying on their Rifle tradition of darkening their badges.

Of interest there is a similar item, also in bronze, relating to the K.S.L.I. and illustrated under Fig.1430.

Fig.1408

Fig.1409

Rifle Volunteer Corps, Volunteer, Territorial Force & Territorial Army Battalions

The consolidated 3rd administrative Battalions *West York R.V.C.*, became a VB of The King's Own Light Infantry (South Yorkshire Regiment), 1st July 1881, redesignated the 1st VB 1st February 1883. A proposed collar badge was submitted by Hobson & Sons, London, and this was approvd 30th November 1883 under Authority V/5.W.York/345, "For rank and file". This was similar to the collar badge worn by the Regular Battalions, but in white-metal (Fig.1410). The Gaunt pattern books show similar for Officers but in silver. The one illustrated in the pattern book is dated 18th July 1888. It also illustrates the proposed rank and file collar badge which, from 1899, was again the Regulars design but in white-metal (Fig.1411). Unlike the ones worn much later by the Regular Battalions and which had a single lug fitting, these had the usual two lugs. They also wore the Regular Officers equivalent, still with silver rose centre but in silver embroidery. (Fig.1412). A smaller version is known but without the rose. (Fig.1413).

From 1889, the Officers collar badge also changed - again similar to their Regular Officers counterparts but in all silver apart from the black enamel as a ground for the rose.

On 1st April 1908, the 1st VB was reorganised as the 4th and 5th Battalions (TF) and gradually adopted the collar badges as worn by the Regular Battalions

Fig.1410

Fig.1411

WWI Service Battalions
12th (S) (Miners) Battalion (Pioneers)

Raised 5th September 1914 at Leeds by the West Yorkshire Coal Owners Association, they wore the usual crossed rifle and pick collar badges. (Fig.147). Disbanded at Ripon 24th May 1919.

General

All the bugle/horn collar badges worn by the Regiment were worn in facing pairs with the mouthpiece facing inwards (though there are many photographs showing them being worn the wrong way round). For a badge worn for such a long period there are bound to be many variations but they are of a minor nature only.

On 10th July 1968, the Regiment was redesignated as *2nd Battalion, The Light Infantry*.

Fig.1412

Fig.1413

The King's Shropshire Light Infantry

Fig.1414

Fig.1415

Fig.1416

Pre 1881
53rd (The Shropshire) Regiment of Foot

After the 53rd were amalgamatd in 1881, the Army Clothing Department pattern room journals, when recording detail for the new collar badge to be worn, notes, "53rd previously wore the crown". In all the other instances quoted in the journals, it has meant the flat topped Imperial crown. (Fig.333). However, the Regimental Museum have on display a quite different shaped crown of the Queen Victoria type, annotated as "O/r's collar badge 1874 - 1881. (Fig.1414).

It is well known that Regiments did not always adhere strictly to regulations so this may well be the case here, but so many other sources have listed "The brass Imperial crown" as the one worn by the 53rd, that one cannot but wonder if someone originally placed the wrong crown in the display and the error has been carried forward? Unfortunately, all the photographs I have seen are too indistinct to make any positive identification. Whichever one, was worn until 1882.

Officers removed their badges of rank from their collars in late 1880 but so far there is no evidence that they wore collar badges prior to the 1881 amalgamation.

85th (Bucks Volunteers)
(King's Light Infantry) Regiment of Foot

As with the 53rd, it is not entirely clear what the 85th wore on their collars pre 1881. Again, taking the official records, the pattern room journals record, after detailing the new collar badge after amalgamation, "To replace pattern 9299 of the 85th". As confirmed by other Light Infantry Regiments pre 1881 this was the universal brass bugle, ribboned and with tabs. (Fig.1194).

But again, the Regimental Museum illustrates a quite different bugle - corded and similar to the post 1881 universal bugle in gilding-metal. Certainly there is such an item in brass with brass lugs (Fig.1415), illustrated in Gaunt's pattern books alongside the brass numerals 85 annotated "Collar ornaments". There is nothing to say that this was adopted.

An official history of the Regiment records "In accordance with Army Order of 1874, the various units of the Army were ordered to adopt their own collar badge" In case of the 85th, it was to be brass, and to include the bugle and strings". The history then refers to, and illustrates, the Officers forage cap badge 1865 which has a bugle above the numerals 85 with the key to the insignia recording "as in Officers forage cap 1865 - bugle only". The bugle illustrated is corded but does, of course, relate to an Officer's item which often differs from those worn by the men.

Officers removed their rank badges to the shoulder cords in 1880 and then wore embroidered bugle collar badges. (Fig.1416 for an item said to have come from an Officer's uniform of the 85th).

It is recorded that in January 1842, other ranks wore a shell jacket with red collars "With a white bugle thereon".

Post 1881

When the 53rd and 85th Regiments of Foot amalgamated 1st July 1881 to become the 1st and 2nd Battalions, respectively, *The King's Light Infantry (Shropshire Regiment)* a new collar badge was required, the bugle being the obvious main theme choice. The resulting collar badge was Pattern 10015 sealed

THE KING'S SHROPSHIRE LIGHT INFANTRY

2nd February 1882, a ribboned bugle horn with tab ends extending both sides to the bugle ends and above a scroll inscribed "KINGS LIGHT INFANTRY" all in gilding-metal. (Fig.1417).

On 10th March 1882, the Regiment was redesignated as *The King's (Shropshire Light Infantry)*. The adopted collar badges proved unpopular with the Regiment and the Museum records they were only worn 1881 - 1882, although the collar badges that replaced them were not sealed until 1887. This is all well documented with the proposed collar badge approved on 22nd February 1887 "On condition that present stock is sufficient for 4/5 years is used up and the Regiment bear the cost of the die rendered useless, if the Contractors make a charge for it's value and which has been agreed to".

The Officer Commanding had been informed on the 2nd February that his proposal to issue the old pattern collar badges to the Militia Battalion had not been approved.

The new pattern collar badge, in gilding-metal, was Pattern 1149 sealed 12th July 1887 "In lieu of Pattern 10015". This was a large ribboned bugle with a knot in the centre of the bow and with two corded strings at the ends of which were tassels and below which were the initials "K.S.L.I.". Ornate designs on the bugle. (Figs.1418 and 1419 for early and later designs). The actual sealed pattern is annotated "To be worn with the mouthpiece to the front".

Although the Regimental Museum say this was worn from 1883, the pattern was not sealed until 1887 but, in view of the stocks estimated to be for 4/5 years in 1887 having first to be used up, when they were first actually worn can only be speculative. This probably accounts for the comparatively large numbers of the previous collar badges that have appeared over the years. The above sealed pattern also specifies that "WO's and 1st Class Sgts to wear similar but in Water Gilt".

No collar badges were worn during WWI but were reintroduced in 1919 but initially were only worn in review Order. When the 1st Battalion arrived in Aden in 1919, they disembarked wearing khaki drill, on which no collar badges were worn.

On 1st January 1921, a further redesignation occurred with the Regiment then becoming *The King's Shropshire Light Infantry*.

Pattern 1149 was worn until 1951. In that year a smaller collar badge was introduced, still with the same general design but with the "K.S.L.I." now on a straight line between a bar above and below. This was Pattern 14640 sealed 30th May 1951 and now in white-metal. Fig.1420). This pattern was used as the guide for the later version in silver anodised, this being pattern 18752 sealed 7th May 1962 under Authority 54/Inf/8551. (Fig.1421). Worn up to redesignation in 1968.

Early Dress Regulations describe the Officers tunic collar badge as "A bugle with strings, in gold embroidery, on a ground of dark blue cloth" (Figs.1442 and 1423 for a F.P.). This description was repeated in subsequent Editions up to and including 1934 when "In pairs" was added.

The Gaunt pattern books clearly show the early pattern of bugle with cords and not ribbons, annotated "23rd November 1881". However, evidence indicates that both ribboned and corded embroidered bugles were worn by the Regiment (Figs.1424 and 1425 for a F.P. of corded bugles as worn on the mess jacket).

From 1882, Officers also wore the equivalent of the other ranks collar badge,

Fig.1417

Fig.1418

Fig.1419

Fig.1420

Fig.1421

Fig.1423    *Fig.1424*    *Fig.1422*

HISTORY OF THE BRITISH ARMY INFANTRY COLLAR BADGE

Fig.1425

Fig.1426

Fig.1427

Fig.1428

Fig.1429

but in gilt (Fig.1426). From 1951, Officers wore the smaller collar badge as for the other ranks but in silver and gilt, the 'KSLI' in gilt, the remainder in silver.

For the 1902 Service Dress, the collar badge was to be the same as for the forage cap but in bronze and in pairs (Fig.1427). Considered too large for the collar these were only worn until 1914 when a small version, based on the other ranks type, was introduced. (Fig.1428). In 1951 this was replaced with the "K.S.L.I." on a straight line. (Fig.1429).

A bronze version of the bugle/KINGS LIGHT INFANTRY scroll is known and may have been a trial pattern. (Fig.1430). Of interest there was a similar item, also in bronze, relating to the K.O.Y.L.I. (Fig.1409).

Militia
Shropshire Militia

It has been suggested that white-metal ribboned bugles were worn by other ranks but no evidence has been found to support it. As they were not Light Infantry it seems doubtful.

On 1st July 1881, they became the 3rd Battalion, The King's Light Infantry (Shropshire Regiment) and from 1887 are reputed to have worn the same collar badges as the VB's.

Royal Herefordshire Militia

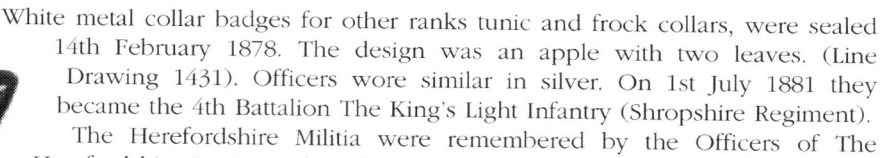

White metal collar badges for other ranks tunic and frock collars, were sealed 14th February 1878. The design was an apple with two leaves. (Line Drawing 1431). Officers wore similar in silver. On 1st July 1881 they became the 4th Battalion The King's Light Infantry (Shropshire Regiment).

The Herefordshire Militia were remembered by the Officers of The Herefordshire Regiment by adopting the badge of a sprig of apple on their buttons.

Rifle Volunteer Corps, Volunteer, Territorial Force & Territorial Army Battalions

The 1st Shropshire R.V.C. and the *2nd Shropshire R.V.C.* became VB's of the King's Light Infantry (Shropshire Regiment) 1st July 1881 and redesignated the 1st and 2nd VB's respectively 1st December 1887. It has been said that whilst a Rifle Volunteer Corps, Officers wore as a collar badge an embroidered corded bugle with the numerals "48" within the cords. (Fig.1432). No evidence can be found to support this, all the examples noted face the same way and the item is more likely to be a hat badge.

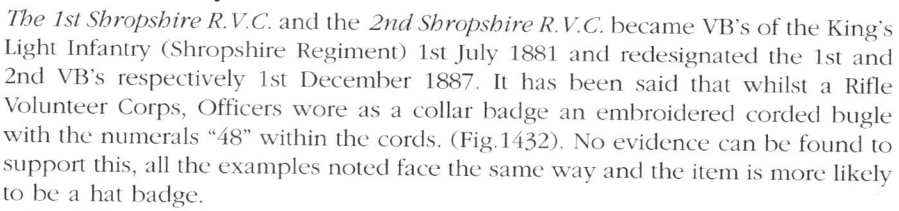

An Officers undress uniform of the 1st Shropshire R.V.C. c.1880 shows an embroidered strung bugle being worn on the collar. (Figs.1433 and 1434 for a F.P.).

From 1882 - 87, other ranks of the VB's wore similar collar badges to those worn by the Regular Battalions, but in white-metal. Volunteer Officers wore theirs in silverplate.

When the Regular Battalions adopted their new design collar badges in 1887, the Volunteer Battalions were quick to do the same. Gaunt's pattern books record a suggested pattern - shown as a F.P. - which has the bugle corded and with no

Fig.1430

Fig.1431

Fig.1432

THE KING'S SHROPSHIRE LIGHT INFANTRY

initials between the strings. Dated 28th January 1888. Obviously this design was not approved, with the Volunteer Battalions again wearing similar to the Regular Battalions, but in white-metal. These were worn until 1898 when it is recorded that the 1st Vol. Battalion then wore until 1908, ordinary white-metal corded bugles. (Fig.1435).

On 1st April 1908, the 1st and 2nd VB's amalgamated to form the 4th Battalion (TF), gradually adopting the collar badges as worn by the Regular Battalions However, some Officers wore a separate bronze 'T' below their bronze collar badges on their Service Dress.

Fig.1433

Cadets
Ellesmere College Cadet Corps
Affiliated to the 2nd VB, K.S.L.I. in 1899 they wore a smaller version of their cap badge as a collar badge, 1908 - 40. This was the K.S.L.I. badge with the initials replaced by "OTC Ellesmere". In gilding-metal.

General
The summing up of both the 53rd and 85th Regiments of Foot remain inconclusive, but details have been recorded concerning what they should have officially worn and that which the Regimental Museum say was actually worn.

Fig.1434

Post 1881, ribboned bugles were mainly worn but both ribboned and corded are known to have been worn in the embroidered form and corded are also said to have been worn by the 1st VB.

All bugle collar badges were worn in facing pairs with the bugle facing inwards towards the collar opening.

On 10th July 1968, the Regiment was redesignated as *3rd Battalion, The Light Infantry*.

Fig.1435

The Middlesex Regiment (Duke of Cambridge's Own)

Pre 1881
57th (West Middlesex) Regiment of Foot

A laurel wreath and the Honour, "Albuhera" was authorised to be worn by the 57th, 1st February 1816, to commemorate their heroic conduct and outstanding gallantry at the battle of the same name in May 1811. So, when the Regiment's first other ranks collar badge, Pattern 9546 was sealed 20th July 1875, having been authorised 16th July 1872, these Honours formed the chosen design. - A scroll inscribed "ALBUHERA" superimposed on a berried laurel wreath (Fig.1436). In brass, this was worn on the yellow collars of the tunic until 1882.

Fig.1436

77th (East Middlesex) Regiment of Foot (The Duke of Cambridge's Own)

The first other ranks' collar badge of the 77th was the Prince of Wales's coronet, plumes and motto, which had been granted to them on 20th February 1810. In white-metal, this was Pattern 9297 sealed 13th February 1873, a large item similar in design to the one worn on the glengarry from 1874 - 1881. (Fig.1437) This is the item as seen in several 'old' collections but one cannot but wonder whether it would have been physically possible for it to fit on the collar. In any case, it was felt to be too large so in 1875 a smaller version was introduced. Similar in design and still in white-metal, this was Pattern 9539 sealed on the 30th April. (Fig.1438) Worn until 1882.

Fig.1437

Post 1881

The 57th and 77th Regiments of Foot amalgamated 1st July 1881 to become the 1st and 2nd Battalions, respectively, *The Duke of Cambridge's Own (Middlesex Regiment)*, redesignated on 1st January 1921 as *The Middlesex Regiment (Duke of Cambridge's Own)*.

After amalgamation, both former Regiments continued to wear their own collar badges but on 22nd February 1882 the collar badge for the new Regiment, Pattern 10125 was sealed, "To replace 9546 of 57th and 9539 of 77th". This was the Prince of Wales's plumes, coronet and 'Ich Dien' motto over the coronet and cypher of HRH the Duke of Cambridge - a 'G' interlaced and reversed, all partly enclosed by a laurel wreath and with a scroll across the base of the badge inscribed "ALBUHERA". The plume, coronet and "Ich Dien" in white-metal the remainder in gilding metal. (Figs.1439 and 1440 for variations).

This was virtually the same as the cap badge but without the title scroll. This can lead to problems as far as collecting is concerned and illustrated (Fig.1441) is an item sometimes offered as "A rare other ranks pattern collar badge". On closer

Fig.1438

Fig.1439   *Fig.1440*   *Fig.1441*

THE MIDDLESEX REGIMENT (DUKE OF CAMBRIDGE'S OWN)

inspection one can detect where the scroll had once been attached. Other 'giveaway' features are the position and downward slope of the "Ich Dien" scroll, the shape and position of the title scroll and the coronet on the plumes being in gilding-metal on the cap badge. Caveat Emptor!

The standard pattern was renewed and cut from new dies in October 1888, this being pattern 1721 and again on 16th September 1899 the new Pattern No. being 1721a, sealed under Authority ACD/Patts/9798. These were worn right through to 1962, including the Home Counties Badge period, when Pattern 1721a was used as a guide for a gold and silver anodised version. This was Pattern 18659 sealed on the 23rd August (Fig.1442). Worn up to redesignation in 1966. For a variation in general shape and with thicker plumes and scroll see (Fig.1443).

One noted collar badge is the other ranks bi-metal pattern but all in white-metal (Fig.1444). It has been suggested that this was worn on "The walking out uniform" but, as they are also known in the "narrow wreath variety" (Fig.1445), which usually indicates an "early" item, this is unlikely. White metal cap badges were worn by WO's and Senior NCO's so it follows that they also could have worn white-metal collar badges. However, the cap badge was worn from c.1948 which again raises the question of the "early" pattern. It could well be that WO's and the Senior NCO's were wearing white-metal collar badges for some time before they adopted the white-metal cap badge, but again this is unlikely. It seems most likely that this item was worn by Vol Battalions before the use of battle Honours was discontinued for Volunteer units.

A smaller collar badge in white-metal was worn on the "blue patrols". Also known in silver and possibly worn by Senior NCO's (Fig.1446).

The ordinary bi-metal collar badge is also known in all gilding-metal, said to be the WWI economy issue. Doubtful, and more likely to be either a "one off" that has escaped the addition of the white metal or a gilt item, as worn by WO's and polished down to gilding-metal.

Early Dress Regulations describe the Officers tunic collar badge as "A laurel wreath in gilt metal; within the wreath, in silver, on a frosted gilt centre, the Prince of Wales's Plume; above the plume, a scroll inscribed "Albuhera"; below the plume, the Coronet and Cypher of HRH the Duke of Cambridge."

They vary in overall size, the shape and position of the "Albuhera" scroll and also the position, size and shape of the plumes and cypher. (Figs.1447, 1448 and 1449 for three variations).

This description was repeated in Dress Regulations up to and including the 1894 Edition but changed in the 1900 Dress Regulations. (The new Officers collar badge was sealed by the War Office 24th February 1897.) The description then, for tunic and scarlet frock, was "In silver, a laurel wreath; within the wreath the Prince of Wales's Plume; below the plume, the Coronet and Cypher of H.R.H. The Duke of Cambridge; on the lower bend of the wreath, "Albuhera". (Fig.1450). They are also found silvered and also silvered and burnished.

The above description is carried forward in subsequent Editions of Dress Regulations with the 1902 Edition adding "For mess jacket" and with the 1911 Edition making a small amendment by adding "The late George" after H.R.H. and before "Duke of Cambridge". The amended version also appears in the 1934 Dress Regulations.

During WWII, some Officers wore the other ranks pattern collar badge on their

Fig.1442

Fig.1443

Fig.1444

Fig.1445

Fig.1446

Fig.1448   *Fig.1449*   *Fig.1450*   *Fig.1447*

HISTORY OF THE BRITISH ARMY INFANTRY COLLAR BADGE

Fig.1451

Fig.1452

Fig.1453

Fig.1454

Fig.1455

Fig.1456

battle dress. This collar badge was worn in silver plate on No 1 Dress, together with the Home Counties Brigade cap badge during the time they formed part of the Brigade.

For the 1902 Service Dress, the collar badge was to be the same as worn on the forage cap but in bronze and in pairs. (Figs.1451 and 1452 for two different patterns). Sealed, War Office 18th May 1903. This pattern was officially polished to gilding-metal and worn on the K.D. uniform.

The cap/collar, in bronze, was considered to be too large for the collar and was replaced by one similar in design to the pattern in silver. (Fig.1453). This pattern was also worn on the forage cap. Officers also wore on their Service Dress, the other ranks pattern which they had bronzed.

An "hybrid" pattern which is known is the bronze cap/collar without the scroll. (Fig.1454). These appear genuine with no signs where they may once have been attached to a scroll.

The other ranks pattern is also known in gilt, possibly worn by WO's.

Militia
Royal Elthorne or 5th Middlesex Light Infantry Militia

White metal collar badges, Pattern 7481 for other ranks tunic and frock collars were sealed 14th October 1875 under Authority PC/5.M'sex Militia/195. These are said to have been bugles with the Royal Cypher "VR" in the centre, similar to the central device in the 1878/81 Helmet Plate. This is unconfirmed.

They became the 3rd Battalion, TheDuke of Cambridge's Own (Middlesex Regiment) 1st July 1881, renumbered the 5th in March 1900 and transferred to the Special Reserve 2nd August 1908.

Royal East Middlesex Militia

White metal collar badges, Pattern 7480 for other ranks tunic and frock collars were sealed 2nd September 1875 under Authority PC/1 East M'sex Militia/141. These were Saxon crowns of five points, said to represent their lineage going back as far as Alfred. (Fig.1455). Officers wore similar but in silver.

On 1st July 1881, they became the 4th Battalion, The Duke of Cambridge's Own (Middlesex Regiment), renumbered the 6th Battalion in March 1900 and transferred to the Special Reserve as the 6th Battalion 14th June 1908.

Militia Battalions

Wishing to retain their individuality, Militia Battalions of the Regiment wore their own distinctive collar badges. Other ranks wore similar to the bi-metal items worn by the Regular Battalions but with their "Albuhera" scroll, left blank. Officers, from 1881 until 1897, wore similar to their Regular Officers counterparts but in reverse metals and without the top "Albuhera" scroll (Fig.1456).

They are also known in the same metals as those worn by Regular Officers, again without the top scroll, and it may well be that one of the Militia Battalions wore these to distinguish itself from the other Militia Battalion

Officers of the 4th, later 6th, Militia Battalion wore the Saxon crown in gilt on their mess dress. They were the only Battalion in the Regiment to do so and wore them up to the outbreak of WWI.

After being transferred to the Special Reserve in 1908, both the 5th and 6th Battalions were redesignated Militia in 1921 receiving permission in 1922 to wear the same collar badges as those of the Line Battalions ie with battle honours. However, to be different and to emphasise their Militia designation, they wore similar to those worn by the Line Battalion Officers, but again in reverse metals.

Rifle Volunteer Corps, Volunteer, Territorial Force & Territorial Army Battalions

3rd Middlesex R.V.C. became the 1st VB 1st July 1881 and redesignated in December 1891 as *The Middlesex Volunteer Rifle Corps* and reorganised 1st April 1908 as 7th Battalion

THE MIDDLESEX REGIMENT (DUKE OF CAMBRIDGE'S OWN)

A proposed collar badge design was submitted by the 1st VB via contractors, Samuel Bros of London, and approved by the War office 19th April 1898 under Authority V/1/57/100. Annotated "for privates" this was a similar badge to that worn as a collar badge by the Regular Battalions but with a blank scroll in place of the Regulars' "Albuhera" and in all white-metal. (Fig.1457). Similar, but in silver, has been noted and is thought to have been worn before the Officers received their own collar badges.

The official Officers collar badge was of a quite different design but still retaining the blank scroll. (Fig.1458).

8th Middlesex R.V.C. became the 2nd VB 1st July 1881, redesignated in December 1891 as *The 8th Middlesex (South West Middlesex V.R.C.)* and reorganised as the 8th Battalion, 1st April 1908.

Determined to be different to the 1st VB, their other ranks collar badge was, in the main, similar to those of the 1st VB, again in all white-metal but with no scroll. (Fig.1459). Similar, but in silver, were worn by Officers. (Figs.1450 and 1461 for two variations).

Officially, Officers wore the same silver collar badges as the 1st VB as illustrated and described above.

7th, 8th and 9th Battalions (TF)

From 1908, other ranks wore similar collar badges to the ones they had worn when they were VB's but with a scroll inscribed "SOUTH AFRICA 1900 - 02". In white-metal (Fig.1462). Officers wore similar but in silver plate. The other ranks pattern is known in gilt, believed worn by WO's.

10th Battalion (TF)

From 1908, Officers wore a collar badge in silver with a blank scroll (as per Fig.1458). On Service Dress they wore similar to the Regular Bn's bronze cap/collar badges but with the scroll left blank. (Fig.1463). One variation has the blank scroll with vertical zig zag lines (Fig.1464).

The TF Battalions, gradually adopted the Regular Battalion collar badges and in 1922 were authorised to wear battle Honours as worn by the Line Battalions Some Officers wore a separate bronze "T" below their collar badges on Service Dress and some are also found blackened, possibly to emphasise their former Rifle connections.

In 1961, the Regiment was represented in the TA by the 5th Battalion with Officers wearing the same badge in silver plate as a beret badge and on No.1 Dress as a collar badge. Similarly, they wore their badge in bronze, on both the Service Dress cap and collar.

Middlesex Volunteer Regiment, 1914 - 18

Later forming the 1st - 7th VB's, The Middlesex Regiment, The Middlesex Volunteer Regiment wore as a collar badge a shield bearing a Saxon crown above three seaxes within an oval inscribed "MIDDLESEX VOLUNTEER REGIMENT". On the top of the oval, a crown. In gilding-metal for other ranks (Fig.1465) and in bronze for Officers.

Fig.1457

Fig.1458

Fig.1459

Fig.1460

Fig.1461

Fig.1462

Fig.1463

Fig.1464

HISTORY OF THE BRITISH ARMY INFANTRY COLLAR BADGE

Fig.1465

WWI Service Battalions

18th (1st Public Works Pioneer) (S) Battalion Raised 19th January 1915, disbanded 17th November 1919.
19th (2nd Public Works Pioneer) (S) Battalion Raised 15th April 1915, disbanded 9th March 1920.
26th (3rd Public works Pioneer) (S) Battalion Raised 9th August 1915, disbanded 14th November 1919.

Crossed rifle and pick collar badges were worn by all three of the above Battalions (Fig.147).

Cadets

Prior to 1919, Officers of the cadet units of The Middlesex Regiment wore the same bronze collar badge with blank scroll and zig zag lines as already described for the 10th Battalion (TF), but with a brass "C" affixed below. (Fig.1466). This is thought to have been worn unofficially as the official bronze collar badge with blank scroll had a small "C" between the bottom tie of the laurel wreath and the top of the title scroll. (Fig.1467). What the cadets wore, if anything, is not known but there is known to exist a badge with Cadets inscribed on the usual honour scroll and this may well have been the badge worn.

Harrow School Cadet Company

Recognised 12th December 1910, this unit was affiliated to the 9th Battalion The Middlesex Regiment, later becoming part of the 3rd Cadet Battalion byArmy Order 96/16.

In white-metal, the Cadets collar badge was a laurel wreath with two down pointing arrows crossing in the voided centre and piercing a length of ribbon. A top scroll was inscribed "HARROW RIFLES" and the bottom scroll inscribed "DECR 30 1859". (Fig.1468). This is the date of the foundation of the Corps.

Fig.1466

Middlesex Cadets

Middlesex Cadets, wore a collar badge in white-metal with the title on a circle, in the centre of which was a shield with Coronet above three seaxes. (Fig.1469).

Unidentified

1) A brass shield with the usual three seaxes, but in this case curving upwards (Fig.1470). A similar shield appears on a shoulder belt plate of the 57th Regiment of Foot.
2) A gilt POW's plume, coronet and motto scroll with very distinctive tops to the plumes. (Fig.1471). Similar is seen on the puggaree badge of the 77th Regiment of Foot.

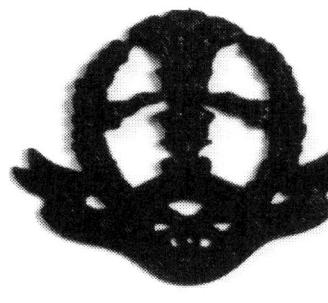

Fig.1467

General

To achieve uniformity, each Middlesex RVC has been entered under the Regiment it joined in July 1881 - see also under The Royal Fusiliers, K.R.R.C. and The Rifle Brigade.

On 31st December 1966, the Regiment (less Territorials) was redesignated as *4th Battalion, The Queen's Regiment (Middlesex)*, the sub title omitted 1st July 1968 and reduced to a "representative coy", 1st January 1971.

Fig.1468

Fig.1469

Fig.1470

Fig.1471

The King's Royal Rifle Corps

Pre 1881
60th (The King's Royal Rifle Corps) Regiment of Foot
By an Army Order dated 28th August 1874 it was directed that no collar badges would be worn by the 60th (K.R.R.C.) Regiment of Foot.

Fig.1472

Post 1881
On 1st July 1881, the 60th were redesignated *The King's Royal Rifle Corps*, again redesignated 1st January 1921 as *The King's Royal Rifles*, amended 10th February 1921 to *The King's Royal Rifle Corps*. On 7th November 1958 they became *The 2nd Green Jackets, The K.R.R.C.* and were further redesignated 1st January 1968 as *The 2nd Battalion, The Royal Green Jackets (The K.R.R.C.)* with the subtitle omitted 1st July 1968.

During that time no collar badges were worn except on mess dress. On display at The Royal Green Jackets Museum in Winchester is the mess jacket as worn by General Sir Evelyn Barker KCB, KBE, DSO, MC, Colonel Commandant of the 2nd Battalion K.R.R.C. 1902 - 39, which has a facing pair of small silver bugles on the lapels. (Fig.1472). These were authorised in the 1911 Dress Regulations which records "In Silver, a bugle as worn on the forage cap". Confirmed in the 1934 Edition.

Also on display is an uniform of the 1st Cadet Battalion, K.R.R.C. on the collar of which are black collar badges. On a dark red backing, a Maltese Cross and resting on the top limb, a tablet inscribed "CELER ET AUDAX' surmounted by a K/C. Inscribed on the four limbs starting at the top and going in a clockwise direction the following, 'SOUTH', '1902', 'AFRICA' and '1900'. In the centre of the cross, a circle inscribed "1st C.B. KING'S ROYAL RIFLES" and within the circle, a strung bugle. (Fig.1473). A variation has a slightly different design and is voided between the top limb of the cross and the tablet. (Fig.1474).

Fig.1473

The 1st Cadet Battalion was formed in 1894 and is the only Cadet unit to have been awarded a battle honour, "South Africa 1900 - 02". There is a QVC version of the above collar badge.

Church Lads Brigade
During WWI, many of the Cadet Coys affiliated to the K.R.R.C. were formed from Church Lads Brigades and for interest some of their collar badges are illustrated. (Figs.1475, 1476, 1477, 1478 and 1479) and the Scottish Cadet Battalion, Church Lads Brigade (Fig.1480).

Fig.1474

Fig.1479   *Fig.1478*    *Fig.1477*    *Fig.1476*    *Fig.1475*

HISTORY OF THE BRITISH ARMY INFANTRY COLLAR BADGE

Fig.1480

Militia

Huntingdonshire Rifles Militia became 5th Battalion K.R.R.C., 1st July 1881.
Royal Flint Rifles Militia became 6th Battalion, K.R.R.C., 1st July 1881.
2nd Royal Rifle Regiment of Middlesex Militia became 7th Battalion, K.R.R.C., 1st July 1881.
Carlow Rifles Militia became 8th Battalion K.R.R.C., 1st July 1881.
North Cork Rifles Militia became 9th Battalion K.R.R.C., 1st July 1881
   None of the above Militia wore collar badges.

Rifle Volunteer Corps, Volunteer, Territorial Force & Territorial Army Battalions
1st Middlesex RVC (Victoria Rifles)

Joined the K.R.R.C. as one of it's VB's 1st July 1881 and amalgamated with the 6th in 1892. Their collar badge was a smaller version of their Helmet Plate, a Maltese Cross with a tablet over the top limb inscribed "SOUTH AFRICA 1900 - 2" and with a KC above. In the centre, a circle inscribed "VICTORIA AND ST. GEORGE'S RIFLES" and within the circle the figures of St George and Dragon. In black metal, this was worn on the Officers Service Dress jacket but soon after WWI collar badges were discarded by the Regiment This item was also worn attached to the scarlet boss and green undress cap.

Fig.1481

After WWI, a silver St. George and Dragon was worn on the boss. It has been said that this device was also worn on the Officers mess dress.

Another collar badge worn by the Regiment was St. George and the Dragon in white-metal, worn in facing pairs with St. George facing inwards towards the collar opening. (Fig.1481). A similar larger item is known in both white-metal (Fig.1482) and in gilding-metal. It is unlikely that these larger items are collar badges.

(See also under 9th County of London Battalion, The London Regiment (Queen Victoria's).

Fig.1482

6th Middlesex RVC (St. George's)

Joined the K.R.R.C. 1st July 1881 as on of it's VB's and amalgamated with the 1st in 1892. A similar large white-metal item as described under the 1st is associated with the Regiment but whether these are collar badges is unconfirmed (Fig.1483). A smaller St. George and Dragon in gilt was worn by Officers on their mess jackets (Fig.1484).

(See also under the 9th county of London Battalion, The London Regiment (Queen Victoria"s).

2nd Middlesex RVC (South Middlesex)

Joined the K.R.R.C. 1st July 1881 as one of it's VB's. Their collar badges were the crest and motto of Viscount Ranelagh, who founded and commanded the Corps from it's inception until his death in Novermber 1885 - "A dexter arm, embowed in armour, the hand in a gauntlet, grasping a dart", over a scroll inscribed "C Æ LITUS MIHI VIRES" (My strength is from heaven), in facing pairs with the arm facing inwards towards the collar opening. In black metal (Fig.1485) and in silver (Fig.1486). Also known in bronze.

Fig.1483

Fig.1484

Fig.1485

Fig.1486

THE KING'S ROYAL RIFLE CORPS

4th Middlesex RVC (West London)
Joined the K.R.R.C. 1st July 1881 as one of it's VB's and wore as it's collar badge a small Maltese Cross, the outer edges of each limb being plain and with a ball at each point, the inner parts being lined. A QVC rested on the top limb, voided between the bottom of the crown and the top of the limb. In the centre, a circle inscribed with the motto 'SEMPER PARATUS' (Always ready), in the voided centre of which, a bugle horn. In white-metal for other ranks (Fig.1487) and in silver for Officers, they were later replaced by similar but with a KC. Also known in black metal.

Fig.1487

The 12th and 21st Middlesex RVC (Civil Service)
Various Government Departments were amalgamated to become the 21st Middlesex (Civil Service) RVC, renumbered 12th in September 1880 and on 1st July 1881 joined the K.R.R.C. as one of its VB's. Other ranks wore as their collar badges the POW's plume of feathers with distinctive 'ICH DIEN' scrolls, in white-metal. (Fig.1488). Officers wore similar in silver plate.

In 1908 they became the *15th (County of London Battalion.) The London Regiment (The POW's Civil Service Rifles).*

Fig.1488

13th, formerly the 22nd Middlesex RVC (Queen's Westminsters)
Originally formed as the *22nd (Queen's) Rifle Volunteers* and renumbered 13th Corps in 1880, joining the K.R.R.C. as a VB 1st July 1881, The Queen's Westminsters had as their badge, the portcullis, the principal charge in the coat of arms of the City of Westminster.

As a collar badge, it was worn surmounted by a QVC and worn with a red cloth backing. (Fig.1489), in black metal by other ranks and in silver by Officers. Also known in gilt (Fig.1490)

From 1902, the collar badge was changed, not only with a KC replacing the QVC but with the addition of a scroll between the top of the portcullis and the crown, inscribed "SOUTH AFRICA 1900 - 02". In both black metal and in white-metal (Fig.1491) and worn by other ranks and in silver as worn by Officers. One interesting item is a short-lived hybrid, the same design as the first collar badge with QVC but with KC and no honour scroll (Fig.1492). In silver plate, the only one noted is in mint condition and is possibly a trial pattern, not adopted.

One collar badge sometimes confused with those worn by the Regiment is similar with large KC which is actually the badge of HM Customs & Excise. (Fig.1493).

In 1908, the Regiment became the 16th (County of London) Battalion, The London Regiment (Queen's Westminster Rifles).

Fig.1489

Fig.1490

25th (formerly 50th) Middlesex (Bank of England) RVC
Originally raised from emplyees of The Bank of England, so it was fitting for the figure of Britannia to be chosen as their collar badge. Notable features of the Britannia, who is draped, and with a helmet, with the trident rising from her thigh, are the sailing ship in front of her and the lighthouse behind the shield. Both the ship and the lighthouse also appear on the old coinage, minted of course, by The Bank of England.

Fig.1492

Fig.1493

Fig.1491

HISTORY OF THE BRITISH ARMY INFANTRY COLLAR BADGE

Fig.1494

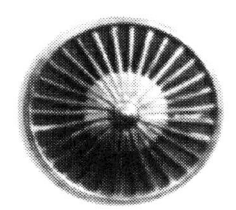

Fig.1495

Fig.1496

The collar badges are in both white-metal and brass each worn by other ranks and in silver and in gilt (Fig.1494), both worn by Officers.

The Regiment was disbanded in 1907, having joined the K.R.R.C. in 1881 as one of it's VB's.

26th Middlesex (Cyclist) RVC
Raised in 1888 as the 16th Middlesex (Cyclist) RVC and alloted to the K.R.R.C. as one of it's VB's, their collar badge was a plain cycle wheel of exactly the same size and design as in the centre of their cap badge. In white-metal (Fig.1495).

3rd London RVC
Formed 8th March 1861 becoming on 1st July 1881 a VB of the K.R.R.C.. They wore white-metal grenade collar badges, horizontally. (Fig.1496).

General
To achieve uniformity, each Middlesex RVC has been included under the Regiment they joined 1st July 1881. (See also under Royal Fusiliers, The Middlesex Regiment, and The Rifle Brigade).

Captain E. C. May, 87th Fusliers, c. 1875. Photograph shows collar badge being worn together with rank badge. Photo: Sraff College

236

The Wiltshire Regiment (Duke of Edinburgh's)

Pre 1881
62nd (The Wiltshire) Regiment of Foot

Officially, the collar badge as worn by other ranks of the 62nd pre 1881 was the usual brass Imperial crown (Fig.333). This is confirmed when the new collar badge was to be issued for the new Regiment, following the 1881 amalgamation, when it is recorded "The 62nd wore the crown" - this always refers to the brass Imperial crown. Furthermore, there is no pattern number for any collar badge for the 62nd in the pattern room journals.

It seems certain that, unofficially, they wore a Victoria crown within an oval wreath of laurel leaves interspersed with berries, in brass (Fig.1497).

Notes on the Regiment, record that from c.1873 to 1881, Bandsmen of the 62nd wore on their collars, a brass Maltese Cross on which was superimposed the Imperial crown, similar to ones worn by some Regiments in Malta (Fig.1498). The Maltese Cross was adopted by the 62nd as their badge, in Sicily in 1806, said to commemorate their services there.

Fig.1497

Fig.1498

99th (The Duke of Edinburgh's) Regiment of Foot

Authorised by General Order PC/Infy/111 dated 16th July 1872, for "Regiments with no special device", other ranks of the 99th wore as their first collar badge, the brass Imperial crown. (Fig.333). Photographs taken in 1873, clearly show them being worn by a group of Sergeants all of whom, as a matter of interest, were wearing the numerals "99" on their hats. For a short time only it is believed these numerals were also worn on the collar.

On the 23rd January 1875, the Officer Commanding the 99th Regiment submitted for approval a proposed badge for wearing on the Glengarry, together with a proposed new collar badge. This had the Duke of Edinburgh's cypher - the letter 'A' forward and reversed surmounted by his coronet and with the numerals '99' superimposed thereon (Line drawing Fig.1499). The Duke of Edinburgh's coronet and cypher were authorised to the 99th, with title, on 22nd April 1874.

Fig.1499

In his reply on the 1st February, Colonel Clifford, Adjutant General to the Forces, from his office in Horse Guards, Pall Mall, London, said he had been directed by the Field Marshall Commander in Chief to acquaint the C.O. that His Royal Highness would approve of the proposed badge for the Glengarry. He went on "His Royal Highness cannot sanction a collar badge for the 99th of Foot as the Regiment is not entitled to wear one and applications from other Corps have been refused, notwithstanding that they had, for years, borne special devices on their Regimental colours". The letter reference was PN/99/110/C8807.

There must have been a change of policy, however, as a letter from Horse Guards dated 22nd August 1877 under ref OC/1/2 Foot/107/C7846 to the O.C., 99th of Foot at Templemede, informed him "It having been proposed that the men of the Regiment under your command should be permitted to wear a badge on the collar of their tunic and frock, I am directed by The Field Marshall, C in C to request that you will acquaint me whether the measure meets with your concurrence and if so, that you will take steps for a drawing (in duplicate) of the badge being forwarded to this department for submission to His Royal Highness". The letter followed on with instructions, "The badge must not be more than ¾ inches in height and 1¼ inches in length and the cost not to exceed 4½d per pair as more than that sum will not be allowed by The Secretary of State for War.

HISTORY OF THE BRITISH ARMY INFANTRY COLLAR BADGE

Fig.1500

Fig.1501

Fig.1502

Fig.1503

Fig.1504

No badge, other than that already on the Colours (viz The Duke of Edinburgh's coronet and cypher)will be authorised".

All the requirements were observed and the resulting collar badge, Pattern 9608, was sealed 19th November 1877. In brass and worn until 1882 this was The Duke of Edinburgh's coronet between the double letter 'A' in decorated capitals (Fig.1500). These collar badges were worn by the Regiment during the Zulu War 1879 on the yellow collars of their scarlet undress frocks.

Post 1881

The Duke of Edinburgh's (Wiltshire Regiment) was formed 1st July 1881 by the amalgamation of the 62nd and 99th Regiments of Foot, who became the 1st and 2nd Battalions respectively. On 1st January 1921, the Regiment was redesignated *The Wiltshire Regiment (Duke of Edinburgh's)*, but there was no change in the collar badge.

The new Regiment's first collar badge for other ranks was Pattern 9975, sealed 20th January 1882. This was virtually the same as the centre-piece of the Helmet Plate centre. This was a cross patee, the ends of each limb plain, the remainder lined, in the centre of the cross, a circle within which was The Duke of Edinburgh's coronet over his cypher. In gilding-metal (Fig.1501).

A new field service cap badge was introduced in July 1896 but the current collar badge was confirmed. A renewal pattern was, however, demanded in 1897 and the resulting pattern 9975a, was cut from new dies and sealed on 7th December, authorised under CD/Patts/9026. The general design remained the same with minute alterations made to the size of the coronet and the shape of the cypher (Fig.1502). Still in gilding-metal with the later badges with a single lug fitting.

In 1874, Her Majesty The Queen approved the 99th Regiment of Foot being known as *The 99th Duke of Edinburgh's Regiment* with his coronet and cypher incorporated in the Regiment's devices. The Duke, the second son of Queen Victoria, had the christian names Alfred Ernest Albert and it is these three initials that appear in the centre of the collar badge below the coronet.

The present Duke of Edinburgh became Colonel in Chief of the Regiment in 1954 necessitating a new coronet and cypher, the letter "P" (Philip) reversed and interlaced. This appeared in the centre of the new collar badge, pattern 17152, in gilding-metal and sealed 4th May 1956. These lasted only a short time, being replaced by similar but in gold anodised, pattern 17152 being used as a guide (Fig.1503). Worn up to amalgamation in 1959.

Chrome caps, collar badges, buttons and shoulder titles are known and are believed to have been worn by Regimental Police in the mid/late 1950's.

The 1883 Dress Regulations describe the Officers tunic collar badge for Nos. 1 and 3 Battalions as "A Maltese Cross in lined silver, with burnished edges. On the cross, a round convex plate in burnished silver. On the plate in gilt metal the Coronet within the cypher" (Fig.1504). For the 2nd Battalion, "A Maltese Cross in silver embroidery, edged with gold. On the cross, a round convex circle in blue velvet edged with gold embroidery. On the circle in gilt metal the coronet within the cypher".

The descriptions were repeated in subsequent Dress Regulations up to the 1891 Edition which recorded the previous description for the No. 1 and 3 Battalions but now without specifying any particular Battalion The description was repeated up to the 1900 Edition which added "Frock Coat" and the 1902 Edition which added "Mess Jacket". A quite significant alteration was made to the description of the collar badge in the 1911 Dress Regulations, when "Maltese Cross" was replaced with "Cross Patee". A more minor alteration was " circular" replacing "round".

This followed much discussion regarding the Regiment's description "Maltese Cross". Certainly, it was not as described, a Maltese Cross being the one as used in the Order of St. John of Jerusalem or in Malta, but it is interesting that the Band collar badge as worn by the 62nd, and already described and illustrated, was a Maltese Cross.

THE WILTSHIRE REGIMENT (DUKE OF EDINBURGH'S)

In Burke's "General Armory", six families of the name "Wiltshire" were listed at the time, each including a cross in their arms or crests with four of them with the cross patee (or formee, which is the same). No "Wiltshire" appears to have served in the 62nd. The cross has no connections with the Arms of the City or See of Salisbury and the County of Wiltshire has no amorial bearings. It has been suggested that, at the time the badge originated, reference could have been made to a book related to heraldry and the name "Wiltshire" was taken to refer to the County.

The "cross patee" 'A' cypher collar badge was worn up to 1956 with no change apart from small differences in size and shape of the coronet and cypher, according to manufacturer.

From 1956 until amalgamation, Officers wore the "P" cypher equivalent to the collar badge as worn by soldiers but in silver and gilt, the coronet and cypher in gilt, the cross in silver. (Fig.1505). The pattern card, not sealed, is marked "Correct 3rd May 1956".

For the 1902 Service Dress, the collar badge was the same as worn on the forage cap but in bronze and in pairs. This was virtually the Regiment's collar badge with a coronet on the top limb of the cross and a scroll below inscribed "THE WILTSHIRE REGIMENT". Sealed 19th May 1903 (Fig.1506). They do vary slightly in size and design (Fig.1507 for a variation).

An other ranks pattern with "A" cypher in bronze is also known and thought to have been bronzed and worn when supplies of the correct collar badges were not available (Fig.1508).

Another other ranks "A" cypher pattern is also known in gilt, thought to have been worn by WO's.

Militia
Royal Wiltshire Militia

Under Authority PC/Wilts Militia/104 dated 28th October 1875 the Regiment was permitted to wear an approved collar badge Viz "Castle". Accordingly, these same collar badges in white-metal for wear on tunic and frock collars for other ranks were sealed on 31st December under Authority PC/Wilts Militia/112, this being pattern 7495. The only description regarding this item is that it was a "3 tower castle and flag" and it has been suggested that it may have been Devizes Castle.

Old journals record "In accordance with General Orders 41, 70 and 86 of 1881, The Royal Wiltshire Militia assumed the title of *The 3rd Battalion "The Duke of Edinburgh's (Wiltshire Regiment)"*. Further entries record "By 61002/2208 dated Horse Guards War Office 31st March 1882 from Adj. Gen. to G.O.C., Portsmouth:- The Col. Commandant was called upon to decide whether the badge (for forage cap and collar) of the1st and 2nd Battalions should be adopted by the Officers of the 3rd Battalion. The C.O. intimated that he preferred the metal badge as worn by the Officers of the 1st Battalion of The Territorial Regiment - dated Devizes 7th April 1882). The final entry relating to collar badges was as follows:- "On 1st April 1882 new collar badges (a brass Maltese cross with a coronet and cypher of The Duke of Edinburgh in the centre) were received for the Staff Sergeants and rank and file of the Battalion".

Rifle Volunteer Corps, Volunteer, Territorial Force & Territorial Army Battalions

Consolidated 16th March 1880, *The 1st Wiltshire V.R.C.* wore as their collar badge a smaller verion of their cap badge - crossed rakes on which is superimposed a barrel over a crescent moon, itself over a long scroll inscribed "1st WILTS V.R.C.". On the top of the barrel, a crown ("Fig.1509 illustrates this item with KC, worn c.1902 - 08). Although not noted, there seems no reason why similar, but with QVC, was not worn c.1898 - 1902. Recorded in both white-metal and gilding-metal for wear by soldiers and in both silver and bronze for wear by Officers.

Nominated a VB of The Duke of Edinburgh's (Wiltshire Regiment) 1st July 1881, but never adopting the title, redesignated the *1st Wiltshire V.R.C. (IVB)* in

Fig.1505

Fig.1506

Fig.1507

Fig.1508

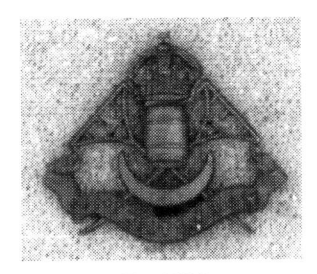

Fig.1509

HISTORY OF THE BRITISH ARMY INFANTRY COLLAR BADGE

December 1891 and reorganised as the 4th TF Battalion in 1908.

Little is recorded regarding collar badges of the 2nd VB. An item, similar to the pattern as worn by the Regular Battalions, but in white-metal may well have been worn by the 2nd VB (Fig.1510).

Collar badges for other ranks also appear with what at first appears to be a blank centre. The centre appears to have been hammered out into a dome but the cypher can still be seen from the back.

Other ranks collar badges are also known, blackened, said to have been worn by the 4th TF Battalion (Fig.1511). Officers also wore blackened badges on Service Dress (Fig.1512).

The TF Battalions, generally, wore the same collar badges as the Regular Battalions

Fig.1510

Fig.1511

Fig.1512

General

On 9th June 1959, the Regiment (less Territorials) amalgamated with The Royal Berkshire Regiment (Princess Charlotte of Wales's) (less Teritorials), to form *The Duke of Edinburgh's Royal Regiment (Berkshire & Wiltshire)*.

The Manchester Regiment

Pre 1881
63rd (West Suffolk) Regiment of Foot
Photographs of the Regiment show other ranks of the 63rd wearing their "pork pie" numerals "63" on their collars, from as early as 1873 and up to the end of 1875. Photographs taken in 1875 show these still being worn, others wearing similar but smaller figures (Fig.1513), whilst the majority were not wearing collar badges at all.

On 11th January 1876, a new collar badge, pattern 9551, was sealed for wear "by rank and file". In brass, this was a beaded, eight pointed star with seven rays in each section and with a plain raised domed centre (Fig.1514). Worn until 1882.

The "Brunswick Star", as it was called, had long been part of the insignia of the Regiment and, by tradition, was said to have been earned through their services in America from 1775 - 1781 when they frequently rode as mounted Infantry under Colonel Tarleton.

There is no evidence that Officers wore collar badges pre 1881.

96th Regiment of Foot
From 1873, other ranks of the 96th wore on their collars the joined numerals "96". These were worn up to 1875 when a sphinx collar badge was introduced. This was Pattern 9530, in brass, and sealed on the 10th February. Quite unlike any other sphinx collar badges worn at that time, this was a long bodied female sphinx with rounded head and with mantle extending to the shoulder and with tail rising from the back legs, over the body and with the tuft over the centre of the back. On a tablet inscribed "EGYPT" (Figs.1515 and 1516 for a different pattern FP). WO's wore similar but in gilt.

It has been said that for a short time both the numerals and the sphinx were worn as a double collar badge. This is unconfirmed.

After removing their rank badges from the collar in late 1880, Officers wore an embroidered sphinx collar badge (Figs.1517 and 1518 for a FP).

The sphinx and "Egypt" tablet was awarded to a previous 96th Regiment for service in 1801 and granted to the later 96th on 16th June 1874.

Post 1881
On 1st July 1881, the 63rd and 96th Regiment's of Foot amalgamated to become the 1st and 2nd Battalions respectively, *The Manchester Regiment* and on 21st October it was directed that the new collar badge would be Pattern 9530, as previously worn by the 96th. A new pattern, No 9970 was, however, sealed 20th January 1882, the same general design as the one worn by the 96th but in white-metal. This was "to replace pattern 9951 of the 63rd and Pattern 9530 of the 96th" (Fig.1519). This was the collar badge that was also worn on the field cap up to

Fig.1513

Fig.1514

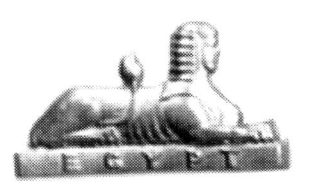

Fig.1515

Fig.1516

Fig.1517

Fig.1519

Fig.1518

HISTORY OF THE BRITISH ARMY INFANTRY COLLAR BADGE

Fig.1520

Fig.1521

Fig.1522

Fig.1523

Fig.1524

the introduction of a new field service cap in January 1898. On 27th November 1897, renewal of the standard pattern collar badge was "demanded", authorised on 14th December and sealed 6th April 1898. This was Pattern 9970a. Again in white-metal and same general design with slight variation in shape and size and design of mantle. (Fig.1520).

It is recorded that in 1901, Bandsmen wore scarlet tunics with white collars on which they wore their collar badges "an inch from each end".

Pattern 9970a was worn up to 1914, no collar badges being worn during WWI. There was no hurry to resume the wearing of collar badges after the War and it was not until 1924 that a new collar badge was introduced, this being an entirely different design. This was pattern 4039, sealed on 13th August under Authority 20/Inf/15708/601, a gilding-metal fleur-de-lys, a similar but larger item having been introduced as a cap badge on 9th April 1923. They vary in both size and shape the earlier issues being slightly smaller and with more voiding between the petals. (Fig.1521 for early pattern and Fig.1522 for later pattern). For a later smaller pattern (Fig.1523).

The fleur-de-lys, is associated with the old 63 Regiment of Foot and although documentation is said to have been lost, the Regiment is considered to have obtained authority to wear this item for their part in the action resulting in the capture of the Island of Guadaloupe in the West indies in 1759.

This collar badge was worn until 1948 at which time the 1st and 2nd Battalions amalgamated to form a single Battalion and badges were introduced in white-metal. This also applied to collar badges and on 10th February 1949, pattern 14054 was sealed under Authority 54/Officers/4025. The same differences occurred as with the gilding-metal collar badges both in size and voiding. There was also the later smaller equivalent as already described. Worn latterly with a single lug fitting.

These were replaced by similar but in silver anodised, introduced in 1957 together with an anodised cap badge. Sealed 19th October 1956 (Fig.1524).

Early Dress Regulations record the Officers tunic collar badge as "The sphinx over Egypt in gold embroidery'; the word "Egypt" embroidered in silver" (Fig.1525). The same description was later given for the mess jacket and repeated up to and including the 1934 Edition. The 1900 Dress Regulations records a similar collar badge for wear on the scarlet frock "but with metal substituted for embroidery" (Fig.1526).

It is recorded that in 1896, a scarlet serge patrol jacket with white collar was introduced but on which no collar badges were worn, and in 1901 "Mess jacket, collar badges as on tunic to be worn on the roll collar".

After the amalgamation of the 1st and 2nd Battalions in 1948, Officers adopted a similar pattern fleur-de-lys as worn by the other ranks, but in silver. Smaller ones were worn on the mess dress (Fig.1527). These were worn up to amalgamation in 1958.

In 1902, Service Dress was introduced for Officers, the collar badge to be "as worn in the centre of the Helmet Plate, with scroll as for forage cap", in bronze and in pairs. These were described as "the badge with motto of The City of Manchester" and "a scroll inscribed "Manchester". They vary, not only in size and shape, but also in design, some with the top "fringe" sat on top of the globe, some voided between the two and others with a bar resting on the heads of the animals. One variation has no bar crossing the globe, only stars, whilst even the number of sails on the sailing ship on the shield vary in number - some six others

Fig.1525

Fig.1526

Fig.1527

THE MANCHESTER REGIMENT

nine. (Figs.1528, 1529, 1530, 1531 and 1532 for five variations).

Officially polished to gilding-metal they were worn on khaki drill. The same pattern is also known in gilt believed to have been worn by WO's. Also in gilt, but without the title scroll. No information can be found regarding this item.

The Arms of The City of Manchester were adopted with title in 1881 and worn firstly as a helmet and Glengarry cap badge and later on Service Dress, as described, up to 1923.

It is recorded in the history of the Regiment that in 1904 certain alterations were made to the Officers service jacket and it is also recorded that the correct bronze collar badge was at that time being worn by the 2nd Battalion, whilst a bronze fleur-de-lys was worn by the 1st Battalion

On 2nd November 1922, Lt. Col. Dorling, C.O. of the 1st Battalion, at that time stationed in Ireland, made an application on behalf of the Regiment to the Army Council for the fleur-de-lys to be restored as the badge of the Regiment. Sanction was given by letter dated 31st January 1923 for wear as both a head-dress and a collar badge. Worn on Officers Service Dress in bronze (Fig.1533). Small variations have been noted in size and shape. Sealed 18th April 1923.

Also worn as collar badges by the Regiment, albeit unofficially, was the eight pointed rayed "Brunswick Star" with the top point displaced by a K/C. In the voided centre a sphinx over a tablet inscribed "EGYPT", within a circular strap inscribed either "THE MANCHESTER REGIMENT" (Figs.1534, 1535 for two variations) or "2nd BN MANCHESTER REGIMENT (Fig.1536). They are known in silver, bronze and gilt, the latter worn by WO's. These badges were also in silver and gilt (Star, sphinx and Egypt in silver, strap and crown in gilt) and worn on the forage and fatigue caps, as a puggaree brooch and on the lapels of Officers mess jackets and on the collar of the field Service Dress jacket. One of the bronze items noted is fitted with tangs. They vary in size and shape in both the star and the crown which is hardly surprising as some were made in India whilst others were made in Egypt. They were worn mainly on mess dress and blue patrols thought to be from c.1902 although they are also known in silver with "flat" QVC's so perhaps c.1900 would be more accurate.

Mention has already been made of the "Brunswick Star" and it's connection with the old 63rd and there is also a connection with the old 96th. They too, wore it as their badge which by tradition was the badge adopted by an Officer from The Coldstream Guards when he re-raised the Regiment in 1824.

Fig.1528

Fig.1529

Fig.1530

Fig.1531

Fig.1532

Fig.1533

Fig.1534

Fig.1535

Fig.1536

Militia
6th Royal Lancashire Militia

On 15th May 1877, white-metal collar badges were sealed for wear by other ranks on their tunic and frock collars. The description was "Lion and crown" but it has not been possible to confirm whether these were the same as worn by other Lancashire Militia.

On 1st July 1881, they became the 3rd and 4th Battalions, The Manchester Regiment

Rifle Volunteer Corps, Volunteer, Territorial Force & Territorial Army Battalions

The 1st, 3rd and 2nd Manchester R.V.C. became VB's, The Manchester Regiment 1st July 1881, redesignated the 2nd, 4th and 5th (Ardwick) VB's respectively 1st September 1888, becoming the 6th, 7th and 8th Battalions, TF 1st April 1908, the 8th becoming the 8th (Ardwick) Battalion in March 1909.

The 4th and 7th Lancashire R.V.C. also became VB's 1st July 1881 redesignated the 1st VB and 3rd VB respectively 1st September 1888 and the 5th and 9th Battalions TF 1st April 1908.

Blackened and white-metal rose collar badges were worn until 1888 after which the VB's wore similar to those worn by other ranks of the Regular Battalions but with the "EGYPT" tablet left blank. These are clearly shown in the Gaunt pattern books annotated "1st, 3rd and 5th VB's" (Figs.1537 and 1538 for two variations). See also Plate 19 showing these being worn by a private of the 1st VB. Worn as late as 1914 by the TF Battalions

Officers wore the same embroidered collar badges as their Regular counterparts but again with a blank tablet (Figs.1539 and 1540 for a FP).

The 2nd VB is said to have worn smaller versions of their cap badge, in bronze on their Service Dress collars.

Other ranks of the 4th VB wore as their cap badge a florenated fleur-de-lys in white-metal and similar, but slightly smaller were worn on the collar (Fig.1541). Officers wore them in bronze (Fig.1542). The later 7th Battalion also wore a florenated fleur-de-lys with Officers wearing them in bronze on Service Dress and in silver. They were worn by WO's in gilt. Also known blackened. Photographs of Officers of the 7th Battalion (TF) show some wearing a bronze "T" below their collar badges.

The TA Battalions gradually adopted the collar badges as worn by the Regular Battalions and a sealed pattern sealed 19th October 1956 under Authority 54/Officers/4025 has the silver fleur-de-lys annotated for "Manchester Regiment, T/A". On the same pattern card for "other ranks 'B' Coy" is similar but in silver anodised. The same collar badge is also annotated for *"Manchester Regiment T/A, (Ardwick & Ashton) (T)"*. Another silver anodised collar badge was sealed 26th June 1964 under Authority MOD 54/INF/8853. This was pattern 19270.

In 1959, both the 8th (Ardwick) Battalion and the 9th Battalion had their cap and collar badges chromed for the presentation of new Colours.

WWI Service Battalions
24th (Oldham) Service Battalion (Pioneers)

Raised 24th October 1914 at Oldham and disbanded 29th July 1919 at Ashton-under-Lyme, they wore the usual crossed rifle and pick collar badges (Fig.147).

General

All sphinx collar badges, including those on the unofficial "Brunswick Star" pattern face both ways with the sphinx facing inwards towards the collar opening.

The same long bodied sphinx was worn throughout and apart from the distinctive shape another feature is the deep pronounced ribs.

On 1st September 1958, the Regiment (less Territorials) amalgamated with The King's Regiment (Liverpool) (less Territorials) to form *The King's Regiment (Manchester & Liverpool)*, subtitle omitted 13th December 1968.

Fig.1537

Fig.1538

Fig.1539

Fig.1540

Fig.1541

Fig.1542

The North Staffordshire Regiment
(The Prince of Wales's)

Pre 1881
64th (2nd Staffordshire) Regiment of Foot

Officially, other ranks of the 64th Regiment of Foot wore the brass Imperial crown collar badge up to the 1881 amalgamation, authorised by Order PC/Infy. gen/111 dated 16th July 1872. (Fig.333). This is confirmed, both by the Official records of collar badges worn pre 1881, and by the Journals of the Army Clothing pattern room where no pattern number is recorded.

Unofficially, they also wore the "Stafford Knot" in brass and although there are examples of small badges, 33mm across (Fig.1543) and ranging up to 38mm (Fig.1544), they did generally wear the smaller badge, chiefly to distinguish themselves from the 38th (1st Staffordshire) and 80th (Staffordshire Vols) Regiments' of Foot. These same items appear after 1881 but were then in gilding-metal with copper lugs as against the pre 1881 badges which were in brass with brass lugs.

Officers of the 64th removed their badges of rank from the collar in late 1880 and then wore an embroidered "Stafford Knot" as a collar badge (Fig.1545). Smaller items were worn on their mess jacket lapels (Fig.1546).

The "Stafford Knot" had long been an old badge of the 64th.

98th (Prince of Wales's) Regiment of Foot

The first collar badge worn by other ranks of the 98th was the "Dragon of China", Pattern 9289 in brass, sealed 1st January 1873. This was a large, free-standing creature with body covered in scales and a "spiky" spine and tail with similar on it's under-belly. There are variations, some having one front foot almost horizontal (Fig.1547) whilst others, slightly smaller, have an inclined foot (Fig.1548). The position of the feet also vary as does

Fig.1543

Fig.1544

Fig.1545

Fig.1548

Fig.1546

Fig.1549

Fig.1547

245

HISTORY OF THE BRITISH ARMY INFANTRY COLLAR BADGE

Fig.1550

Fig.1551

Fig.1552

Fig.1553

Fig.1554

Fig.1555

the tail, sometimes reaching down and then curving upwards (as illustrated), whilst others have the tail almost touching the ground before it curves (Figs.1549 and 1550 for a FP). These are merely manufacturers quirks.

These were worn until 1878 when replaced by similar, also in brass, this being Pattern 9658, sealed on 22nd August. A larger, more frightening dragon, breathing fire. Also known in silver plate and worn by WO's and Senior NCO's (Fig.1551 for silver plate item).

At the time, the dragon collar badge of the 98th was the largest in the British Army. It commemorated the service of the Regiment in the China War of 1842. Authorised 12th January 1843.

Officers removed their badges of rank from their collars in late 1880 and wore up to amalgamation in 1881, embroidered dragons on their full dress tunics. On their frocks, the dragons were in gilt.

The dragon collar badges were worn facing both ways with the dragon facing inwards towards the collar opening.

Post 1881

On 1st July 1881, the 64th and 98th Regiments of Foot amalgamated to become the 1st and 2nd Battalions respectively, *The Prince of Wales's (North Staffordshire Regiment)*, later redesignated 1st January 1921 as *The North Staffordshire Regiment (The Prince of Wales's)*.

On 21st October 1881, it was announced that the collar badge for other ranks of the new Regiment would be "The Stafford Knot", Pattern 9523 (Fig.1047). As this was the collar badge that had been worn by the 80th (Staffordshire Vols) Regiment of Foot pre 1881 and for a while after they became the 2nd Battalion the South Staffordshire Regiment after the 1st July, this did not meet with the approval of the North Staffordshire Regiment

A new collar badge was therefore sealed 15th December 1881. In gilding-metal this was Pattern 9881 (Fig.1052) and it is perhaps ironic that this collar badge was also worn by the South Staffordshire Regiment

Prior to the 1st Battalion embarking for Malta in 1893, it was agreed with the 2nd Battalion that the collar badge should be the same as worn on the cap, The Prince of Wales's Plumes, coronet and "Ich Dien" scrolls on top of the knot. A submission was made and approval given on 22nd October 1894 and the resulting Pattern, 4277b was sealed 14th March 1895 for wear on the "undress" uniform.

It had been the intention of the Regiment that the plumes would be as in the case of the cap badge, above the knot but unfortunately, both the Authorities and the manufacturers took the direction "on top of the knot" too literally, and superimposed the plumes *on* the knot! (Fig.1552). Naturally the mistake was notified but even so, a similar incorrect design was sealed 13th February 1897, this being Pattern 4493.

Eventually the Authorities agreed to rectify the error "when existing stocks are exhausted" so it was not until 1901 that the correct pattern was finally introduced, this being pattern 4277c sealed on 18th January and described as "a new design, the knot is smaller and the plumes and coronet placed over instead of upon the knot". Authority ACD/N Staffs/568. Initially with a two lug fitting (Fig.1553) and latterly with a single fixing, they were worn up to amalgamation in 1959, the last ones being slightly different (Fig.1554). Also used as a beret badge in the 1940's.

An unusual collar badge, larger than the correct pattern, has been noted (Fig.1555). There is an equivalent in silver and gilt which may have been worn by WO's and Senior NCO's

The Prince of Wales's plume, coronet and motto was authorised for wear by the old 98th, 17th October 1876 when the title Prince of Wales's was conferred.

No collar badges were worn on the other ranks Service Dress until the 1920's,

THE NORTH STAFFORDSHIRE REGIMENT (THE PRINCE OF WALES'S)

nor officially on battle dress during WWII and up to the late 1940's, but photographs show these instructions were not always obeyed!

Early Dress Regulations describe the collar badge for the Officers tunic collar as "The Stafforshire knot, in gold embroidery" (Fig.1556). The 1902 Edition also includes mess jacket and these were similar but smaller (Fig.1557) repeated in the 1904 Dress Regulations.

The undress collar badge was worn until 1895 by which time it had been decided that the Regiment required a different collar badge to those also being worn by the South Staffordshire Regiment, this to be The Prince of Wales's plume over the "Stafford Knot". As already described under the other ranks section, the plume was mistakenly placed on the knot instead of over it. In silver and gilt, this was a smaller badge than those worn by the other ranks, with the plumes and motto scroll in silver and the coronet and knot in gilt (Fig.1558). These were worn until 1904.

Because of embroidery difficulties in respect of lack of precise detail for such a small badge, there was no embroidered version for wear on the mess jacket, so the plain gilt knot continued to be worn (Fig.1559).

In 1904, the "plumes on the knot" mistake was rectified and a new collar badge introduced. The new pattern was sealed by the War Office on the 19th April for "tunic, frockcoat and mess jacket". These were worn up to the 1959 amalgamation on all uniforms, firstly with the plumes separate, followed by similar but with the plumes together (Fig.1560). This pattern is also known with gilt motto scrolls.

It is recorded that in the late 1940's, Officers wore the other ranks collar badge on the beret, later changing to one of their own, this being the other ranks pattern but in silver/gilt. (Fig.1561). A larger pattern in silver/gilt is known, the equivalent to one as already described under other ranks possibly worn by WO's and Senior NCO's.

The 1904 pattern was confirmed in the 1911 Dress Regulations, "The Staffordshire Knot" surmounted by The Prince of Wales's Plume. The plume in silver, the remainder of the badge in gilt metal". Repeated in the 1934 Edition but with "The Staffordshire Knot" now correctly recorded as "The Stafford Knot".

For the 1902 Service Dress, Dress Regulations describe the new collar badge "as for forage cap, in bronze". The forage cap badge was "The Staffordshire Knot"

Fig.1556

Fig.1557

Fig.1558

Fig.1559

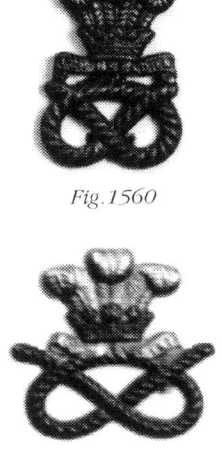

Fig.1560

Fig.1561

Fig.1562

Fig.1563

Fig.1564

Fig.1565

Fig.1566

Fig.1567

Fig.1568

Fig.1569

surmounted by The Prince of Wales's plume. Below the knot, a scroll inscribed "NORTH STAFFORD" (The actual description includes details of silver and gilt). These were sealed 19th April 1904 with the plumes separate, followed later by solid plumes (Figs.1562 and 1563).

In the intervening period between the introduction of Service Dress in 1902 and the introduction of the correct collar badge in 1904, Officers wore the other ranks pattern but in bronze, the first ones with separate plumes (Fig.1564). This pattern was officially confirmed in both the 1911 and 1934 Dress Regulations. As with the Officers collar badges in silver and gilt, there were the same bronze variations (Figs.1565 and 1566).

Militia
The King's Own (2nd Staffordshire) Light Infantry Militia
The first other ranks collar badge, in white-metal for tunic and frock, was pattern 7602 sealed 27th July 1876 these being worn for a short time only, as by a decision taken on 26th March 1878, it was decided to standardise the various bugle collar badges being worn at that time. Pattern 7602 was officially made obsolete and the pattern assimilated to Pattern 8935, as then worn by The Royal South Gloucester Militia (Fig.207). The Authority was PC/S Down Militia/195.

The King's Own (3rd Staffordshire) Rifles Militia
Like most "Rifles", no collar badges were worn.

Militia Battalions
On 1st July 1881, the 2nd and 3rd Staffordshire Militia became the 3rd and 4th Battalions respectively, The Prince of Wales's (North Staffordshire Regiment).

Wishing to be different from both the 1st and 2nd Battalions and the VB's, the Militia Battalions wore similar collar badges as their Regular counterparts, but in reverse metals. These were introduced in the mid 1890's, firstly the "error" pattern which had the plumes and motto in gilding-metal and the coronet in white-metal superimposed on a white-metal knot (Fig.1567). Similar were worn by Officers but in silver/gilt.

Rifle Volunteer Corps, Volunteer, Territorial Force & Territorial Army Battalions
The 2nd Staffordshire (Staffordshire Rangers) and 5th Staffordshire R.V.C.'S became on 1st July 1881, VB's of The Prince of Wales's (North Staffordshire Regiment). redesignated the 1st and 2nd VB's respectively, in February 1883 and reorganised as the 5th and 6th TF Battalions on 1st April 1908.

Similar patterns of collar badge to those worn by the Regular Battalions were worn, but in white-metal, by other ranks from 1883 until 1908. Firstly the Knot, followed by the "error" pattern (Fig.1569) and finally by the corrected pattern which is also known in silver plate.

Similarly, Officers wore the same as their Regular Officer counterparts, firstly in silver embroidery followed by the "error" pattern in silver and finally the plumes over the knot corrected version, also in silver (slightly smaller worn on the mess jacket).

Photographs of the 2nd VB taken at Camp show some soldiers wearing the correct "plumes over knot" collar badge whilst others are wearing the incorrect "error" pattern. This continued even after 1908.

The TA Battalions gradually adopted the collar badges as worn by the Regular Battalions but a questionnaire returned after WWI records that during the War "the TA Battalions wore polished instead of bronzed collar badges".

Photographs show Officers of the 5th Battalion (TF) wearing a bronze "T" below their collar badges.

A sealed pattern for the 5th/6th (Territorial) Battalion under Authority 54/Inf/8870 shows the usual silver/gilt collar badge for No.1 and No.3 Dress and

THE NORTH STAFFORDSHIRE REGIMENT (THE PRINCE OF WALES'S)

one in bronze for Service Dress. The collar badge for soldiers is the usual one in bi-metal. A photograph of the 5th/6th at annual Camp at Okehampton in the mid 1960's show Junior Officers wearing collar badges on the beret.

WWI Service Battalions
9th (Service) Battalion
Raised 20th September 1914 at Litchfield and converted to Pioneers by April 1915, when they wore the usual crossed rifle and pick collar badges (Fig.147). Disbanded at Catterick 24th April 1919.

Fig.1570

Home Guard
A sealed Pattern 16575 dated 23.6.54 under Authority 9/HG/363 shows the usual plumes/knot in silver/gilt (Fig.1570).

General
Although The Prince of Wales's plume, coronet and motto together with the Stafford Knot has featured throughout the Regiments history, the designs have changed with separate plumes and thinner ropes indicating the earlier issues, being replaced by ones with joined plumes and thicker ropes and scrolls.

It is perhaps as well to emphasise that the knot is the "Stafford Knot" and not the "Staffordshire Knot".

(See under South Staffordshire Regiment regarding facing pairs).

On 31st January 1959, the Regiment amalgamated with The South Staffordshire Regiment (both less Territorials) to form The Staffordshire Regiment (The Prince of Wales's).

Arthur Henderson, VC, MV

The York and Lancaster Regiment

Pre 1881
65th (2nd Yorkshire, North Riding) Regiment of Foot

Much has been written about the collar badges of the 65th Regiment of Foot indicating that they were worn from 1872, the Officers wearing a tiger in gilt and the same die being used for both the pre 1881 pattern and the later one worn by The York and Lancaster Regiment.

All, however, untrue. It is perhaps easy to see the error regarding the date as it was in 1872, on July 16th, that the Order was made authorising "Badges for Collars of Tunic Infy". But in the case of the 65th it was not until 1878 that the first collar badge was worn by other ranks on their tunic collars. This is confirmed, not only in the Official history of the Regiment, but also by the fact that the pattern was not sealed until 18th January.

This was Pattern 9625, a tiger, regarded by the Authorities as "the standard pattern tiger". At that time it was the intention to standardise the many different patterns and designs of tigers, bugles sphinx and dragons.

This was a Royal Tiger, "passant", one front paw raised and pointing upwards, the remaining three feet on a distinctly curved grassy ground and with tail reaching above the back and ending with a slight curve upwards. In brass, with brass lugs and worn until 1882 in FP's with the tiger facing inwards towards the collar opening (Figs.1571 and 1572 for a FP). Officers did not wear collar badges pre 1881.

By a Horse Guards Order dated 4th April 1823, the 65th were directed to "bear upon it's colours and appointments, the figure of the Royal Tiger with the word "India" superscribed and the word "Arabia" below the figure with the number of the Regiment". Conferred "in consideration of the distinguished conduct of the 65th Regiment during the period of it's service in India & Arabia".

Fig.1571

Fig.1572

Fig.1573

84th (York and Lancaster) Regiment of Foot

The collar badge adopted for wear by other ranks of the 84th Regiment of Foot was pattern 9302, "The Union Rose", sealed 1st March 1873. This was a double rose, each with five petals turned over at the edges and with a central vertical vein from which branched out horizontal veins. In between each petal, a sepal and the inner rose with a raised, dotted, centre. The inner rose in brass the outer in white-metal. (Fig.1573).

On 21st January 1809, it was directed that the 84th should assume and bear the name "York and Lancaster" in addition to it's numerical title, obviously suggested by the two Battalions having been raised respectively in Yorkshire and Lancashire. It seems probable that the badge of the Union (or Tudor) rose was adopted about the same time, although not officially recognised until 17th November 1820.

This collar badge was worn until 1882 and is the only one recorded in the official Pattern Room Journals. Another item is known, again the union rose but surmounted by a ducal coronet. In brass, they appear to have been broken off the pre 1881 other ranks glengarry badge. There is no evidence that these were ever worn as a collar badge.

The coronet was first seen on the shoulder belt plate, c.1811 and is thought to refer to the Regiments connection with the Duchy of Lancaster.

THE YORK AND LANCASTER REGIMENT

Post 1881

On 1st July 1881, the 65th and 84th Regiments of Foot amalgamated, becoming the 1st and 2nd Battalions respectively, *The York and Lancaster Regiment*, necessitating a new collar badge.

By a verbal decision taken by Colonel Blundell (A.A.G. Horse Guards) on 20th October 1881, "both The York and Lancaster Regiment and The Gordon Highlanders were to wear the Royal Tiger as a collar badge, always to be the same pattern". Following on from this the new collar badge, Pattern 9979 was sealed 20th January 1882. Well illustrated in the Gaunt pattern books, this was not as has been said, from the same die as used for the old 65th and although similar, differed both in the direction of the tail, which now had the end curving back towards the rear, and with a less pronounced curve to the ground. Also now in gilding-metal with copper lugs instead of brass for both as worn by the 65th (Fig.1574). These were worn on full dress and the scarlet frock tunic but not on khaki drill.

Although the 1st Battalion were happy to wear their tiger as formerly worn by the old 65th, the 2nd Battalion, formerly the old 84th, were most upset that their rose did not feature in the new collar badge.

It has been suggested that, to correct the situation, they had made and wore the Union rose in gilding-metal, larger in fact than their previous one - one suspects deliberately in order to emphasise the point they were making!. Such an item is illustrated (Fig.1575) although by it's very size it is difficult to see how it would have fitted on the collar. If it were worn, then certainly it was done so unofficially.

In 1884, there was much correspondence regarding the collar badge resulting in an Order dated 16th March 1885 under reference PC/1st Y & L/205 as follows "As the Regiment wish to revert to the pattern collar badge previously worn by the York and Lancaster Regiment, 1st Battalion, HRH approves of the change provided no expense to the Public is involved and that the present stock in store equal to the requirements of from two to three years must be used before the new badge can be introduced".

On 30th July 1886, it was officially noted "that demand for collar badges can go forward" with an accompanying remark that when a supply is wanted, the contractors will be required to submit a pattern from designs and descriptions that will be given". These were duly submitted, approved and the badge cut from new dies, the resulting Pattern 1514 being sealed 5th June 1888 "in lieu of Pattern 9979".

This was almost identical to the pattern worn by the old 65th but can easily be identified as the later pattern as it is in gilding-metal and with copper lugs whereas the former collar badge had a "brassy" look and had brass lugs. (For Pattern P1514 see Fig.1576 and for a variation Fig.1577). Worn until 1896. This pattern collar badge was also worn on the field cap up to the introduction of a new field service cap in October 1897.

As far back as 1881, Officers of the 2nd Battalion were unhappy that the Regimental collar badge was that formerly worn by the old 65th although the rose of the old 85th did appear on the Officers waist-belt clasp, helmet plate and the other ranks helmet plate. Over the years they continued to press for the rose to be included in the collar badge, their request being finally granted in 1895.

Several sketches were submitted by the CO, all turned down, and his letter dated 4th January 1895 asks if the latest one he had sketched "would be approved if reduced in size?". Agreement was finally reached and a sample supplied by manufacturers Bent & Parker on 18th June 1896. This sample was approved on 24th July and sealed on the 28th. This was Pattern 1514a "a new pattern of Rose and Tiger, replacing Pattern 1514". The relative authority was ACD/Patts 8205 and 8367.

The tiger was now a shorter, more upright animal, three feet standing on a straighter, shorter ground and the front raised paw, now pointing downwards. On it's back, a much smaller version of the old 84th's double rose.The inner rose in white-metal the remainder in gilding-metal (Figs.1578, 1579 and 1580 for three

Fig.1574

Fig.1575

Fig.1576

Fig.1577

Fig.1578

Fig.1579

Fig.1580

HISTORY OF THE BRITISH ARMY INFANTRY COLLAR BADGE

Fig.1581

Fig.1582

Fig.1583

Fig.1584

Fig.1585

Fig.1586

variations). An all gilding-metal (ie without the white rose) collar badge was made in India (Fig.1581).

These were worn on full dress and frock tunic from 1896 until 1914, the scarlet frock not being worn by other ranks after 1919 except for Bandsmen. Also worn on the khaki Service Dress from 1902 until 1939. Although there were exceptions, collar badges were not normally worn by other ranks during WWI. Also worn on khaki drill 1919 - 1939 and on Dress "blues" from 1937 until replaced by the anodised version. Collar badges were authorised for wear on battle dress from May 1952 and worn by soldiers who had them, others who did not, having to wait for the anodised badges.

Chrome cap badges, buttons, shoulder titles and collar badges are said to have been worn by Regimental Police during the mid 1950's and also by other ranks from 1961 until the anodised version was received by the Regiment

Although anodised cap badges were introduced c.1953, the anodised collar badge was not sealed until 1961. this was Pattern 18498 sealed on 17th March with the inner rose in silver anodised and the remainder in gold anodised (Fig.1582). Worn until disbandment in 1968.

Illustrated, to help collectors, (Fig.1583) is an item sometimes advertised as "scarce Y & L collar badge, without rose". They appear in many different metals and are the usual collar badge with the rose broken off. Caveat Emptor!

The early Dress Regulations describe the Officers tunic collar badge as "The Royal Tiger in dead gilt metal" repeated in the 1883, 1888, 1891 and 1894 Editions (Figs.1584 and 1585). Worn on full dress, mess dress and blue frock and later on the scarlet patrol jacket, but not on khaki drill,These were worn until 1896 when they were replaced by the tiger and rose pattern similar to those worn by the other ranks but with the inner rose in silver and the remainder in gilt. Described in the 1900 Dress Regulations as "The Royal Tiger, in dead gilt or gilding-metal, the rose above in gilt or gilding-metal and silver". Repeated in subsequent Editions with "in pairs" added in 1934.

Worn on full dress and by some Officers after 1918, the scarlet patrol jacket up to c.1902, blue frockcoat from circ. 1902, blue dress from c.1937 - 1968, blue patrol jacket and mess jacket (believed to have been the smaller of the two badges mentioned above). Although these continued to be worn after 1953 by those who already had them, new ones after that date were in gilt only.

In 1902, Service Dress was introduced for Officers and the then Dress Regulations describe the collar badge "as for tunic, in bronze" (Fig.1586). Worn on both the collar of the first tunic and the lapels of the 1913 pattern. Many variations are found, some with large tiger and large rose, others both small and some with a combination. Some are found blackened. There is no significance in any of the variations and they were worn by all Line Battalions and not by one to be distinguished from the others.

The Officers bronze pattern collar badges, but unbronzed and then polished, were worn by Officers on the khaki drill uniforms from 1919 until 1939. Some Officers also wore them on Service Dress and on battle dress from May 1952.

Officers wore the other ranks collar badge in gold/silver anodised on Service Dress, tropical tunic and battle dress from 1961 until 1968.

Although not mentioned in Dress Regulations, embroidered collar badges were worn on full dress as early as 1896. Embroidered collar badges in gold bullion wire were later worn on mess jackets, certainly pre 1939 and in the Regimental Magazine dated November 1956 it was stated "that Officers were wearing the new embroidered lapel badges on mess dress".

The very first ones are attractive badges with the tiger's face features picked out in black and red. Some, have a mother-of-pearl centre to the inner rose (Figs.1587 and 1588). They are also known with silver wire for the inner five petals and black beads for the eyes (Fig.1589). Some have a white cloth backing whilst others a parchment backing to the cloth and with a brass backing plate sewn on with cotton. Affixed, with a pin and two lug fitting. Later ones are far less ornate and have a "modern" look.

Militia
3rd West York Light Infantry Militia

The collar badge of this Militia was the "Union Rose", and Pattern 7582, in white-metal for other ranks tunic and frock, was sealed 28th April 1876 under Authority PC/3WYM/129. (see Fig.491) Officers wore an embroidered version (Fig.1590 for a collar badge attached to a section of collar).

On 1st July 1881, they became the 3rd Battalion York and Lancaster Regiment They wore the same collar badges as the 1st and 2nd Battalions but an interesting Order was made prior to the issue of the new 1896 pattern, "Militia to work off the existing Line stock and the issue to them of the new Line badge to be without a general free issue".

Although the 3rd Militia Battalion did adhere to the collar badge regulations, they did sometimes wear a metal "M" below the bronze Service Dress collar badge. For a short time only they wore the rose/tiger collar badge in all white-metal (Fig.1591). Officers wore similar but in silver plate.

During WWI, they became a Reserve Battalion and by 1920 had ceased to exist in all but name.

Rifle Volunteer Corps, Volunteer, Territorial Force & Territorial Army Battalions

2nd Yorkshire West Riding (Hallamshire) R.V.C. became a VB of the York and Lancaster Regiment 1st July 1881 and redesignated as the 1st (Hallamshire) VB in February 1883.

During that period and up to 1885, they wore a tiger collar badge similar in some ways to the pattern as worn by the Line Battalions but smaller and with one front paw pointing downwards. In silver for Officers and in white-metal for other ranks (Fig.1592).

From August 1885 until 1896, they wore similar to the Line Battalions but in white-metal for other ranks (Fig.1593). Worn in silver by Officers (Fig.1594). These are clearly shown in official Volunteer pattern books which record they were approved and sealed 4th August 1885 under Authority W/2 W Yorks/721. Officers wore similar, but smaller, on mess dress (Fig.1595).

In 1896, the Line Battalions adopted the rose/tiger collar badge and the 1st (H) VB, to be different to both the Line Battalions and the 2nd VB, adopted and wore on their scarlet uniform collars the same badge but in reverse metals, the rose in gilding-metal with the tiger and inner rose in white-metal. Officers wore similar but with the tiger and inner rose in silver and the outer rose in gilt on their scarlet full dress, patrol jacket and mess dress. These were worn until 1st April 1908 when, on the formation of the Territorial Force,

Fig.1587

Fig.1588

Fig.1589

Fig.1590

Fig.1592

Fig.1593

Fig.1591

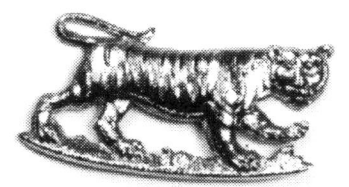

Fig.1594

Fig.1595

HISTORY OF THE BRITISH ARMY INFANTRY COLLAR BADGE

Fig.1596

Fig.1597

Fig.1598

Fig.1599

Fig.1600

they became the 4th TF Battalion and in March 1909 the 4th (Hallamshire) Battalion

From then on, the 4th were supposed to adopt the collar badges as worn by the Line Battalions but uniforms in the Regimental Museum show that this was not always the case. Certainly, up to at least 1925, Officers wore the bronze collar badge on Service Dress with a bronze "T" below. Their bronze collar badge was sometimes worn with the inner rose in silver (Fig.1596).

Post 1945, they also wore the polished unbronzed rose/tiger collar badge and from 1955 the jacket of a Lt. Col. of the Hallamshire Battalion (TA) has the collar badge with the tiger in gilt and the rose in silver and gilt with green and red enamel - a most attractive item (Fig.1597).

A reference is made regarding the Hallamshire Battalion in the Regimental Magazine for November 1956 when it was hoped that the Battalion "would continue to wear metal shoulder crowns and stars as well as metal lapel badges on mess kit".

Having been redesignated as The Hallamshire Battalion 30th January 1924 and going through many later changes, they finally became part of the 1st and 3rd Battalion, *The Yorkshire Volunteers*. They continued to wear their former Regiments collar badges and the tiger/rose in gold and silver anodised was sealed 21st June 1973 under Authority A/54/Inf/8789, this being pattern 18498a. The sealed pattern is annotated "'D' (Hallamshire) Coy 1st Battalion and 'D' (Hallamshire) Coy 3rd Battalion, Yorkshire Vols other ranks." Officers wore the gilt tiger with silver rose. These were worn with the Yorkshire Brigade cap badge.

Although this anodised collar badge was still the rose on the back of the tiger it did differ from the one worn by the York and Lancaster Regiment up to disbandment, being larger and with the rose also attached to the animal's back (Fig.1598). They are also known in all gold anodised, possibly a manufacturers error.

8th Yorkshire West Riding R.V.C. the consolidated 4th 'A' Battalion became a VB of the York and Lancaster Regiment 1st July 1881 and wore the tiger collar badge, in white-metal, for other ranks. This was the version with the front paw pointing downwards (Fig.1599). Officers wore similar but in silver.

In February 1883, they were redesignated the 2nd VB and adopted the same tiger collar badge as worn by the Line Battalions, but in white-metal instead of gilding-metal. Officers wore similar but in silver. Smaller versions in silver were worn on mess dress (Fig.1600).

A really beautiful collar badge, removed from the uniform of Capt. (later Major) Edward Robinson, the founder and CO of the 36th (Rotherham) A 4th Battalion R.V.C., was an embroidered tiger with one front paw raised and standing on a torse (Fig.1601). The uniform was the one he wore whilst serving with the 2nd VB and would be dated c.1883/85. Silver versions were also worn.

Before the rose and tiger collar badge was adopted by the Regiment in 1896, the 2nd VB submitted a design for approval. A specimen was sent by G&B Pearce & Co, Covent Gardens, London and approved 31st January 1885 under Authority V/8/W York/154. The authority was annotated "Union Rose collar badge must be similar to that worn by the Line Battalions viz gilt centre and white metal outer". By the metals, this obviously referred to the Officers collar badge which was worn

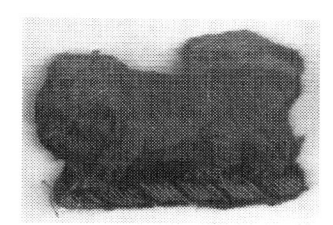

Fig.1601    *Fig.1602*    *Fig.1603*    *Fig.1604*

from 1896 on the scarlet full dress, patrol jacket and mess dress. It is interesting to note, that although the description was correct, the sketch in the official pattern book is coloured in the reverse colours, gilt outer and white-metal (silver) inner!

From 1896, other ranks wore similar collar badges to the Officers pattern but with tiger and outer rose in white-metal and the centre of the rose in gilding metal (Figs.1602 and 1603). Officers wore theirs in silver/gilt.

During 1904, there was an attempt by the 2nd VB to obtain a "red rose" effect on their collar badges. This they did by having the inner rose in copper (Fig.1604). This was not a success and was soon discontinued.

Worn by Officers on Service Dress from 1904 - 1908 was the bronze cap badge with "2nd VB" on the strap. The ones worn on the cap have lugs east and west whereas the ones worn on the collar have the lugs north and south. It seems likely that there were similar collar badges for the 1st VB but, although those for the cap exist there is no evidence that they were ever worn on the collar.

On 1st April 1908, the 2nd VB were redesignated the 5th Battalion (TF) and were ordered to wear the Line Battalion collar badges. However, this Order appears to have been largely ignored with Officers wearing the bronze cap badge on their Service Dress, with the tiger facing both ways (Fig.1605). They also wore them with a separate bronze 'T' below. Another version has the rose in bronze and white, green and red enamel. (Fig.1606).

In 1920, Lt. Col. Parkinson, entirely on his own inition and without any official authority introduced a special badge for wear by Officers of the 5th (TA) Battalion on their mess jackets. In gilt, they were about half the size of the cap badge and although worn in pairs the tiger always faces to the left as viewed. (Fig.1607). Worn until c.1924, they are extremely rare.

West Riding Volunteers

Part of the Volunteer Force 1914 - 19 consisting, amongst others, the 1st - 4th VB's the York and Lancaster Regiment Officers wore as their collar badge a silver rose, the same size as the one worn in the cap - in fact it was the same but without the three part title scroll. A single rose with large centre (Line drawing fig 1608).

Service Battalions, WWI

7th (Pioneer) Battalion. Raised 8th September 1914 at Pontefract as Infantry and converted to a Pioneer role in March 1915, wearing the usual crossed rifle and pick collar badges (Fig.147). Disbanded at Catterick 16th May 1919.

General

The Royal Tiger and Union Rose (affectionately dubbed the "cat and cabbage") has featured throughout in the collar badges of The York and Lancaster Regiment, the tiger facing inwards towards the collar opening (the exception is the unofficial mess dress collar badge as worn by the 5th (TA) Battalion).

The Regiment joined part of *The Yorkshire Badge* in 1958 but still wore their own collar badge. Disbanded at Sheffield 14th December 1968.

Fig.1605

Fig.1606

Fig.1607

Fig.1608

Durham Light Infantry

Fig.1609

Fig.1610

Pre 1881
68th (Durham Light Infantry) Regiment of Foot
A General Authority PC/Inf. Genrl/111 dated 16th July 1872 was issued to Light Infantry Regiments that "badges for collars of tunics should be bugles", and the relative item, Pattern 9299, was sealed 15th February 1873 (Fig.1194).

In brass, this was the bugle collar badge worn by other ranks of the 68th Regiment of Foot, confirmed after amalgamation in 1881 and worn until 1882.

106th (Bombay Light Infantry) Regiment of Foot
Records show that the other ranks collar badge as worn by the 106th Regiment of Foot was as described above for the 68th, i.e. Pattern 9299 by the same Authority. Again confirmed after 1881 and worn until 1882.

A photograph of the Sergeants' mess c.1880 shows these bugles being worn but with the bugles facing inwards towards the collar opening. This is incorrect and they should have been worn facing outwards.

It has been suggested that, in addition, a French horn was also worn. A most "un-British" looking item, possibly with an Indian influence and which featured in their pre 1881 glengarry badge and resembling those worn by some European Armies (Fig.1609). There is no evidence that this item was either authorised or worn.

Officers of both the 68th and 106th Regiments of Foot removed their badges of rank from their collars in late 1880 and then wore embroidered bugle collar badges.

Post 1881
On 1st July 1881, the 68th and the 106th Regiments of Foot amalgamated to become the 1st and 2nd Battalions respectively, The Durham Light Infantry. On 21st October 1881, the new collar badge was confirmed as Pattern 9299, "formerly worn by both 68th and 106th". However, on 2nd February 1882 a new pattern bugle collar badge was sealed, this being Pattern 10011 in gilding-metal. This was the standard pattern bugle and was worn until 1898. Corded instead of ribboned (Fig.1610 for an early item taken from an uniform c.1883)

On 27th November 1897, renewal of the standard Pattern 10011 was demanded and these were cut from new dies and Pattern 10011a was approved 14th December 1897 and sealed 6th April 1898. In gilding-metal there was no significant change in design.

The Authorities were always trying to "standardise" and on 9th January 1905 it was decreed that the D.L.I. collar badges were to be used "for the shoulder strap of jackets and greatcoats of the Channel Islands Light Infantry Militia".

There followed a further Order on 14th February, "all Light Infantry Regiments are to wear the D.L.I. bugle with the metal titles on the shoulder strap of drab jackets and greatcoats". Added was "plates for bugles, unnecessary".

On 7th September 1906, an Order was issued that "the right gilding-metal collar badge of the D.L.I., Pattern 10011a, to be used also for metal arm badges, Service Dress, buglers, Light Infantry".

On 9th June 1909, it was decided that an "additional shank be added to the top of collar badge 10011a". The resulting collar badge, in gilding-metal and now with a three lug fitting, was sealed 9th September 1910 under Authority

DURHAM LIGHT INFANTRY

ACD/Patts/2123 and 2113, this being Pattern 7232 (Fig.1611 for an early item worn on a dark green roundel). These were worn up to 1950 when an entirely new pattern was introduced. In white-metal, this was a very ornate bugle with "D.L.I." within the strings and a K/C at the top of the strings (Fig.1612). This was Pattern 14410 sealed on 21st September.

Similar, but with a Q/C, followed in 1955 when on 12th February Pattern 16641, again in white-metal, was sealed, this under Authority 54/Inf/8552 (Ord 17a). (Fig.1613). This pattern was used as a guide for the anodised version. This was Pattern 18554, in silver anodised, sealed 1st August 1961 (Fig.1614). Worn up to amalgamation in 1968.

The early Dress Regulations describe the Officers collar badge for tunic collar as "Bugle with strings, in gold embroidery". This was amended in the 1900 Edition with the additional "on a white cloth ground" and further amended in the 1902 Dress Regulations with "on a dark green cloth ground", this also for the mess jacket and frockcoat.

The 1911 Edition description was reduced to "Bugle with strings in gold embroidery", the original description. This was repeated until 1934 when "in pairs" was added. These ribboned collar badges are clearly shown in Gaunt's pattern books under the date 1898 (Fig.1615)

A studio photograph taken c.1897 of 2nd Lt. Walls shows him wearing a facing pair of bullion collar badges, as described, but with "D.L.I." between the strings. (See photograph 20 and for the actual collar badge Fig.1616).

From the late 1890's, Officers wore ribboned bugles in gilt on their scarlet frocks (Fig.1617). These are similar to, but slightly smaller than, those worn by the Sherwood Rangers.

Post WWII, Officers wore collar badges with a K/C similar to those worn by other ranks but in silver plate (see Fig.1612). These are very ornate and with a leaf motif. Worn on battle dress and No.1 Dress. Later replaced by similar but with Q/C.

In 1902, Service Dress was introduced for Officers, with Dress Regulations describing the collar badge "as for forage cap but in pairs, in bronze". The forage cap description was "a bugle ornamented with laurel leaves. Upon the strings, a crown. Within the strings 'D.L.I." (Fig.1618).

Fig.1611

Fig.1612

Fig.1613

Fig.1614

Fig.1615

Fig.1616

Fig.1618

Fig.1619

Fig.1620

Fig.1617

HISTORY OF THE BRITISH ARMY INFANTRY COLLAR BADGE

This was later replaced by a smaller version with a Q/C, the same size as the other ranks anodised collar badge. Worn on No.2 Dress until amalgamation (Fig.1619).

The K/C bronze collar badge was polished and worn on the khaki drill jacket (Fig.1620).

The other ranks pattern collar badge is known in a bronzed form (Fig.1621).

Fig.1621

Militia

1st South Durham Militia, who later became in 1874, *1st Durham Fusiliers Militia*, appropriately wore a grenade collar badge. In gilding-metal (or "German brass" as it is described in the pattern books under the date March 1876), the grenade has distinctive flames and in the centre of the ball, St. George's Cross within a strap inscribed "HONI SOIT QUI MAL Y PENSE" (Line drawing 1622).

On 1st July 1881, they became the 3rd Battalion, Durham Light Infantry.

2nd North Durham Militia wore a shield collar badge, this being in white-metal and sealed 12th August 1874 "for tunic and frock". Appropriately, the shield was from the Arms of the City of Durham, the cross of St. George and, in the four quarters, a rampant lion (Fig.1623).

On 1st July 1881, they became the 4th Battalion, Durham Light Infantry.

Fig.1622

Rifle Volunteer Corps, Volunteer, Territorial Force & Territorial Army Battalions

The 1st Durham (Durham and North Riding of York) RVC, the *2nd Durham, 3rd Durham (Sunderland)* and *4th and 5th Durham RVC's* became VB's of the Durham Light Infantry 1st July 1881 redesignated respectively, the 1st, 2nd, 3rd (Sunderland), 4th and 5th VB's 1st December 1887.

Other ranks of all the VB's wore the same pattern collar badge, the standard Light Infantry Bugle, corded and in white-metal, clearly shown in the official Volunteer pattern books for the 1st VB (Fig.1624). A group photograph of the Cyclist Coy of the 1st VB taken in August 1902 show these same collar bags being worn.

Fig.1623

The first collar badge worn by Officers of the VB's was a distinctive item, in silver with double strings and a knot in the centre of the three corded loops - an attractive badge (Fig.1625).

This was only worn for a short time, being replaced by a ribboned bugle with tab ends, all in silver plate (Fig.1626). Again, illustrated in the Volunteer pattern books.

On 1st April 1908, the 1st, 2nd, 3rd, 4th and 5th VB's became respectively, the 5th, 6th, 7th, 8th and 9th Battalions (TF) and gradually adopted the collar badges as worn by the Line Battalions

Perhaps, not surprisingly, there were exceptions, the 6th Battalion wearing their bugles, blackened. This was obviously acknowledged by the Authorities as it is recorded in the Official records under the date 20th September 1920 that "Bugles, gilding-metal bronzed were sealed for 6th Battalion, D.L.I., Pattern 3384". These same collar badges were also used as part of the 6th Battalion's shoulder titles.

Fig.1624

It is interesting that the same pattern number collar badge was also worn by *The Bermuda Volunteer Rifle Corps*.

On the introduction of the new pattern collar badge with D.L.I. within the strings in 1950, the practice of blackening continued. Officers of the Battalion also wore their collar badges, blackened (Fig.1627 for Service Dress collar badge).

The 10th (S) Battalion were raised 19th August 1914 at Newcastle and in an account of their arriving by train on home leave from France on 1st May 1916, they were wearing the usual insignia and were admonished and ordered that in future they were to wear a scarlet cloth bugle beneath the collar at the back. These were rather crudely made, probably by the soldiers themselves, but one must remember there was a War going on! (Fig.1628).

A further account written in November 1916 records one private soldier on home leave, wearing a bugle in gilding-metal on the back of his collar. The

Fig.1625

DURHAM LIGHT INFANTRY

Battalion was disbanded in France 9th March 1918.

As has been stated, the TF Battalions adopted the collar badges of the Line Battalions but a sealed pattern for the 6th Battalion D.L.I. (TA) dated 27th February 1961 show that no collar badges were being worn at that time.

Another sealed pattern annotated 'E' Coy and dated 15th November 1961 also records "no collar badges", this under Authority 54/Inf/8612. A later sealed pattern for the 8th Battalion (TA shows the usual collar badges in silver plate for No. I Dress and in bronze for Service Dress.

A sealed pattern for "6/8 (T) Battalion, D.L.I., E Coy" shows the silver anodised collar badge with Q/C, for soldiers (annotated "at Regimental expense") and again ones in silver plate for Officers No. I Dress and in bronze for No.2 Dress.

'E' Coy, the Northumbrian Volunteers was formed from 6/8 Battalion, D.L.I.

Fig.1626

Reserve Battalion

6th (Reserve) Battalion was formed 8th May 1915 at Bishop Auckland as the 3/6 Battalion and redesignated as the 6th (Reserve) Battalion 8th April 1916 only to be absorbed into the 5th (Reserve) Battalion on 1st September 1916.

During their short existence they designed their own collar badge and went as far as having a trial die made in lead, but due to lack of time this was as far as the venture went. The proposed design had the usual D.L.I. bugle surmounted by a K/C but with "VI" within the strings. A long scroll enclosing the bugle contained the words "6th RESERVE BATTALION D.L.I." (Fig.1629).

Fig.1627

WWI Service Battalions
11th (S) Battalion (Pioneers)

Raised 1st September 1914 at Newcastle, converted to Pioneers 6th January 19 and wore the usual crossed rifle and pick collar badges with the pick faci inwards towards the collar opening (Fig.147). Disbanded 16th June 1919.

22nd Battalion (3rd County Pioneers)

Raised 21st August 1915 at Durham and disbanded 12th July 1918, they too wo the usual crossed rifle and pick collar badges.

Fig.1628

General

Naturally for a Light Infantry Regiment, the bugle has featured prominently in the collar badges of the D.L.I. Some have been very ornate and they have used both corded and ribboned bugles.

Always worn in facing pairs the bugle is worn with the mouthpiece facing outwards from the collar opening.

It is quite easy to confuse the Regiments collar badge with "D.L.I." in the strings and surmounted by a K/C with those worn by *The Durban Light Infantry*, who wore similar.

On 10th July 1968, The D.L.I. became the *4th Battalion, The Light Infantry* and were disbanded at Colchester 31st March 1969.

Fig.1629

The Highland Light Infantry (City of Glasgow Regiment)

Pre 1881
71st (Highland Light Infantry) Regiment of Foot

There has probably been more conjecture regarding the pre 1881 collar badge of the 71st Regiment of Foot than any other Regiment of Foot. Various sources describe it as "French Horn in white-metal", "bugle horn in white-metal", "plain bugle horn", "universal Light Infantry bugle", "normal bugle with strings" etc, with dates mentioned from anywhere between 1872 and 1881. Not once has the description been accompanied by a photograph although attempts have been made with drawings.

A Museum did kindly forward a polaroid photograph of a Colour Sergeant's doublet annotated "71st Foot 1874 - 81" on which is affixed a corded strung bugle in gilding-metal. This must be disregarded as the particular pattern collar badge did not come into use until after 1881. (In any case the collar badge should have been in silver).

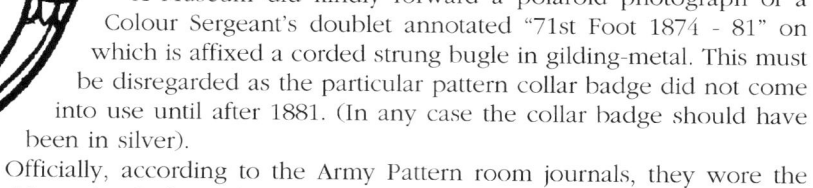

Fig.1630

Officially, according to the Army Pattern room journals, they wore the "standard brass bugle for Light Infantry Regiments", i.e. Pattern 9299 sealed 15th February 1873 (Fig.1194). No other collar badge is recorded against the 71st until a replacement Pattern 9700, was sealed 20th May 1880 annotated "bugles with pins brass (sic) deposited in lieu of Pattern 9299", No description is given but it was obviously not the standard pattern, not only because of the different pattern number from that of the "standard" collar badge, but a list compiled at the 1881 amalgamations lists the 71st's collar badge as "bugle special". In their jargon "special" indicated that it was not the standard pattern, this applying to both bugles and grenades.

"Dress Notes" of The H.L.I. record that during 1872/4, "the men of the 71st wore a cap badge, being the plain white-metal bugle horn enclosing the Number, the collar badge being a small plain bugle". No metal is mentioned.

An article in the H.L.I. Chronicle in 1905 records "1874 - Regimental badge to be worn on the mens' collars" and this would tie up with the official sealing date of the first collar badge. A further description records "1875 - silver bugle horn on collars of Colour Sergeants".

Photographs of The Regiment whilst in Malta show NCO's and men in 1874 and the Band in 1875 all wearing plain bugle horn collar badges.

The Gaunt pattern books clearly show the pre 1881 glengarry badge with "71" in the curl, alongside a bugle horn annotated "facing pair brass collar/bugle - solid". No date, but a reference, "227". Another firms pattern book also shows the same pattern annotated "brass collar - solid" (Line drawing Fig.1630). These collar badges are clearly seen on a photograph of a Piper Stobie of the 1st Battalion, H.L.I. taken at the time the 71st and 74th amalgamated and obviously still wearing the collar badge of the 71st.

Officers removed their rank badges from the collar in 1880 but as yet there is no evidence of any collar badges being worn up to amalgamation with the 74th, in 1881.

The French bugle horn was an old badge of the 71st, adopted c.1810.

74th (Highlanders) Regiment of Foot

Unlike the 71st, there is no confusion over the collar badge worn by other ranks of the 74th - an elephant with howdah cloth and chair howdah on its back and

THE HIGHLAND LIGHT INFANTRY (CITY OF GLASGOW REGIMENT)

standing on a grassy ground, partly enclosed by a wreath of palm fronds, tied at the bottom centre with a two looped ribbon bow.

In brass, this was pattern 9517 sealed 16th October 1874. Worn until 1882, there are the usual variations, not only in the shape and size of the elephant, but also in the designs on the chair and cloth and the shape and size of the bow at the base. Some are voided between the animals back and the wreath and also between its trunk and the top of its front feet whilst others are solid. The length of trunk also varies from short and curled up towards its mouth to reaching down to the ground (for variations see Figs.1631, 1632, 1633 and 1634). Senior NCO's wore similar collar badges but in silver.

As a reward for its distinguished service in India under Sir Arthur Wellesley, later The Duke of Wellington, and especially at the battle of Assaye on 12th September 1803 against the Mahrattas, the 74th were presented with an Honorary Colour in the centre of which was an elephant within a laurel wreath. Awarded 15th April 1817. On the Colour, the elephant was without howdah or trappings.

Post 1881

On 1st July 1881, the 71st and 74th Regiments of Foot amalgamated to become the 1st and 2nd Battalions respectively, *The Highland Light Infantry*, redesignated in 1923 as *The Highland Light Infantry (City of Glasgow Regiment)*.

The chosen collar badge for the new Regiment was a smaller version of the new Glengarry badge, itself a composite item consisting of the Thistle Star of the old 74th with the bugle horn of the old 71st superimposed in the centre. Above the bugle was a QVC, in the centre of the bugle the monogram "H.L.I." and below the bugle a scroll inscribed with the battle honour "ASSAYE" above an elephant, both from the 74th.

A Directive was issued 10th July 1882 that "the collar badge to be worn in white-metal - in pairs, the bell of the bugle and head of the elephant turned outwards in both cases" These were Pattern 10236 sealed 29th July 1882 with the crown being of the flat topped variety. There were many variations with large and small elephants, different shaped and sized crowns and long and short scrolls (Figs.1635 and 1636 for variations including difference in the letter "E" in "ASSAYE", some with "E" whilst others have "E"). Also known in a superior casting in gilding-metal, worn by Staff Sergeants (Fig.1637).

Photographs show that collar badges were not worn on the doublet collar until late 1882. Pipers of both the 1st and 2nd Battalions wore the Regimental collar badges on their doublets.

On 30th November 1896, a Directive ACD/Patts/8189 called for renewal of the standard pattern to be cut from new dies. This was carried out with Pattern 10236a being sealed on 14th December 1897. There was no significant change in design, merely being a renewal.

With the death of Queen Victoria in January 1901, a change of crown was necessary but it was not until 1905 that the new collar badge was sealed. This was Pattern 10236b sealed on 1st March "with Tudor crown to replace Pattern 10236a". These were not worn on Service Dress, introduced in 1902, and it was not until an ACI of 1924 permitted the wearing by "other ranks" of collar badges on the Service Dress jacket.

The standard pattern was renewed and cut from new dies, this being Pattern

Fig.1631

Fig.1632

Fig.1633

Fig.1634

Fig.1635

Fig.1637

Fig.1638

Fig.1639

Fig.1636

HISTORY OF THE BRITISH ARMY INFANTRY COLLAR BADGE

7279 sealed 2nd December 1910 but with no change in design (reference ACD/Contracts/6218). Worn until 1956, there were the same variations as already described for the QVC collar badge (Figs.1638 and 1639).

Of interest, the K/C collar badge also appears on a sealed Pattern 14361 dated 29th June 1950 annotated "badges - purses, H.L.I. R & F loops to be spaced ⅝ inch apart in the vertical position." The badge faces to the left.

Also, as with the QVC, in gilding-metal and cast brass Indian manufacture, (Fig.1640).

Fig.1640

The Q/C collar badge, in white-metal, was introduced in 1956 when Pattern 17263 was sealed on 6th November (Fig.1641). A similar item is shown as "a sporran badge", this being Pattern 17274 sealed 8th November 1956 under Authority 54/Gen/492. The badge faces to the left.

This pattern was used as a guide for the later version in silver anodised, not worn by the Regular Battalions, the white-metal collar badge being worn up to amalgamation in 1959.

Fig.1641

Whilst WO's wore the same collar badges in silver/gilt as Officers, Senior NCO's wore similar but in white metal/gilding metal, the crown, monogram, scroll and elephant in gilding-metal, the remainder in white-metal (Fig.1642). Only an item with K/C has been noted.

The 1881 Dress Regulations record that Highland Regiments "will be allowed metal collar badges for both tunic and frock when both garments are in use at Foreign Stations".

Fig.1642

Early Dress Regulations describe the Officers doublet collar as "in silver, the Star of the Order of the Thistle. On the star a silver horn. In the centre of the horn, the monogram H.L.I. in gilt metal. Above the horn, in gilt metal, the crown as represented in the collar of the Order of the Star of India; below the horn, a scroll, in gilt metal, inscribed "Assaye"; under the scroll, in gilt metal, the Elephant". The crown as represented in the collar of the Order of the Star of India commemorated the long and distinguished service of the old 74th in India.

These collar badges were of the same overall design as those worn by other ranks but usually slightly smaller and of course, better made and finished as one would expect with silver and gilt as against white-metal and gilding-metal. There were the same variations as for the other ranks badges and there was usually voiding with the elephant in the Officers items (Figs.1643, 1644 and 1645 for three variations and Fig.1646 for a most unusual version which has the bugle horn and the elephant facing in opposite directions).

Fig.1643

The description was repeated in all Dress Regulations up to the 1900 Edition which added "or gilding metal" after "gilt" was mentioned. An addition is made in the 1902 Edition, "mess jacket - no badge", and the 1911 Edition refers only to the collar of the doublet. The 1902 Edition and subsequent Editions up to and including those issued in 1934 omit "as represented in the collar of the Order of the Star of India", merely referring to "the crown". This is, of course, to cover the introduction of the Tudor crown in 1902 (Figs.1647, 1648 and 1649). Sealed by the War Office 11th March 1904 and again 28th November 1904.

These were worn until replaced by similar but with Q/C (Fig.1650).

Fig.1644

In 1902, Service Dress was introduced for wear by Officers with the corresponding Dress Regulations describing the collar badge "as for tunic, in bronze". There are two early sealed patterns relating to these bronze collar

Fig.1645   *Fig.1646*   *Fig.1647*   *Fig.1648*

THE HIGHLAND LIGHT INFANTRY (CITY OF GLASGOW REGIMENT)

badges, both sealed by the War Office, the first dated 11th March 1904, the second 28th November 1904. The later sealed pattern has the bronze collar badge with K/C, the earlier one has the item missing from the card. It is therefore not possible to describe the first item but illustrated is the second one together with variations. (Figs.1651, 1652 and 1653).

Also illustrated is an unusual collar badge, in bronze, but with a QVC (Fig.1654), in mint condition and possibly a trial pattern, not adopted. It is, however, possible that because of their right to wear the Imperial crown as represented in the collar of The Order of the Star of India, it was initially decided to continue wearing this crown whatever Monarch reigned in this Country. If this was the case and there are other examples, then perhaps this accounts for the missing item on the sealed pattern dated 11th March 1904?

Photographs confirm that the 1st Battalion wore the correct bronze collar badges on their Service Dress as soon as issued, whereas the 2nd Battalion, certainly in 1908 if not before, wore silver collar badges on their service dress.

The bronze collar badge with K/C was polished and worn on khaki drill.

On the change of Monarch, the same design bronze badge was worn but with Q/C (Fig.1655). Other known Officers collar badges are K/C in gilt and also in silver plate and Q/C in silver plate.

Militia

1st Royal Lanark Militia, who became the 3rd Battalion, H.L.I. 1st July 1881 wore a Thistle as a collar badge pre 1881. In white-metal for other ranks and in silver for Officers (Fig.1656).

After 1881, Officers wore their collar badges as for the Line Battalions but without any scroll. For an item in silver and gilt and with a QVC see (Fig.1657).

Rifle Volunteer Corps, Volunteer, Territorial Force & Territorial Army Battalions

5th Lanarkshire (Glasgow, 2nd Northern) RVC became a VB of The H.L.I. 1st July 1881, redesignated the 1st VB 1st December 1887 and reorganised as the 5th (TF) Battalion 1st April 1908.

Other ranks wore the H.L.I. collar badge but with the scroll left blank (Fig.1658). Some can be found where the wearer has obviously tried to erase "Assaye" from one as worn by the Line Battalions, and has not been too successful as traces of the battle honour can still be seen. The Officers equivalent was in silver.

In 1901, the 1st VB incorporated the initials 'IVB' in the previously blank scroll

Fig.1649

Fig.1650

Fig.1651

Fig.1652

Fig.1655

Fig.1656

Fig.1657

Fig.1653

Fig.1658

Fig.1659

Fig.1654

on their cap badges and this change was also incorporated in their collar badges.

Service dress was not adopted until 1905 when bronze collar badges were worn with a blank scroll (Fig.1659).

6th Lanarkshire RVC also became a VB of The H.L.I. 1st July 1881, redesignated 2nd VB 1st December 1887 and reorganised as the 6th (TF) Battalion 1st April 1908.

Other ranks wore the H.L.I. collar badge but with a scroll inscribed "SOUTH AFRICA 1900 - 2" (Fig.1660). Photographs show these were worn from 1903 whilst other taken in 1889 and the early 1900's show other ranks with no collar badges being worn.

Another other ranks collar badge in white-metal had an additional scroll inscribed "2nd VOLR BATT'N" (Fig.1661). Officers wore both the equivalent of the "SOUTH AFRICA 1900 - 2" scroll and the one with the extra scroll, but in bronze, from 1906 when Service Dress was first worn by the Battalion.

8th Lanarkshire (The Blythswood) RVC became a VB of The H.L.I. 1st July 1881, redesignated 1st December 1887 as 3rd (The Blythswood) VB and the 7th (TF) Battalion 1st April 1908.

Other ranks wore the usual white-metal collar badge but with blank scroll, initially with QVC (Fig.1662), followed by similar but with K/C (Fig.1663).

On Service Dress, Officers wore the equivalent to those worn by other ranks, but in bronze. As with the Regular Battalions there is one with a QVC (Fig.1664). There is also the more usual one, with K/C.

Officers also wore silver collar badges with blank scroll initially with QVC and later with K/C (Fig.1665). Also worn by Officers were blank scroll collar badges in silver/gilt. One, has the crown (QVC), monogram, scroll and elephant in gilt, the star and bugle in silver (Fig.1666). Another has the crown (QVC), monogram and elephant in gilt and the scroll, bugle horn and star in silver (Fig.1667) and yet another has the crown monogram and scroll in gilt and the bugle horn and elephant in silver.

9th Lanarkshire RVC became a VB of The H.L.I. 1st July 1881 and, although never officially designated as such, were in effect, the 4th VB. In December 1891 they were redesignated the 9th Lanarkshire VRC and reorganised 1st April 1908 as the 8th (TF) Battalion

They wore their own distinctive collar badges, similar to those worn by The H.L.I. but without either the scroll or the elephant and with the monogram LRV in the curl of the bugle. In both white-metal and also gilding-metal (Fig.1668). Officers wore similar but in gilt.

10th Lanarkshire (Glasgow Highland) RVC became a VB of The H.L.I. 1st July 1881, redesignated as the 5th (Glasgow Highland) VB 1st December 1887 and reorganised as 9th (TF) Battalion 1st April 1908.

From inception as an RVC, the 10th adopted, with minor differences, the uniforms as worn by The Black Watch. They continued to wear them even after becoming a VB of The H.L.I. and in consequence wore The Black Watch collar badges (Fig.1669 for other ranks collar badge in white-metal). Officers wore similar, but in bronze, for Service Dress (Fig.1670) and in silver (Fig.1671).

After 1908, the 5th, 7th and 8th Battalions continued wearing the blank scroll collar badges up to 1914 when, in general no collar badges were worn by other ranks. After the War, the TF Battalions gradually went over to wearing those worn by the Regular Battalions

Fig.1660

Fig.1661

Fig.1662

Fig.1663

Fig.1664

Fig.1665

Fig.1666

Fig.1667

Fig.1668

A report in 1915 records an Officer of the 8th Battalion wearing bronze collar badges on his Service Dress with a separate "T" below.

After amalgamation in 1959, the H.L.I. collar badges continued to be worn by the 5/6 TA Battalion silver/gilt Q/C collar badges were sealed for Officers 14th January 1957 and similar, but in white-metal for soldiers.

The 9th (TF) Battalion underwent several changes in title after 1908 eventually becoming *The Glasgow Highlanders*, The H.L.I., still wearing The Black Watch collar badges, the ones in white-metal for other ranks sealed 13th April 1953, Pattern 15715 and the silver anodised version sealed 16th January 1963 under Authority 54/Inf/8798. Officers collar badges in silver plate were sealed under Authority 54/Inf/8843.

On 1st April 1967, the *52nd Lowland Volunteers* were formed and "E" Coy The H.L.I. became part of the Force becoming part of the 1st Battalion when the 52nd were redesignated as such 1st April 1971.

Other ranks wore the H.L.I. collar badge in silver anodised with Q/C, this being Pattern 19908, sealed 2nd April 1968 and Fig.1672.

WWI Service Battalions

16th (2nd Glasgow) Service Battalion (Pioneers) raised as Infantry 21st September 1914 and converted to Pioneers 22nd February 1918 when they wore the usual crossed rifle and pick collar badges. (Fig.147) Disbanded 31st March 1920.

Other Badges

A word of warning to collectors. Sometimes offered as "a rare H.L.I. collar badge" is an item of an elephant over a tablet inscribed "Assaye" which would appear to be as described (Fig.1673). It has no connection with The H.L.I. but is an item as worn by the 1st Punjabi.

General

From 1881 until amalgamation in 1959, The H.L.I. wore the same design collar badge, albeit with different scrolls, some with "Assaye", some with "South Africa 1900 - 2", some blank and some without any scroll at all. As one would expect over some 78 years there were many variations. The star has varied in size from quite small to quite large. Apart from overall size the shape of the star has also varied from almost rounded to a squarish design. The rays of the star also vary, not only in thickness and length, but also the shape of the ends.

The shape and size of bugle, monogram and crown has also varied as has the position of the crown, usually just above the bugle but on occasions hiding the top central ray of the star. The length of the scroll has also varied as do the letters that appear thereon. There are many designs of elephant, some solid others partly voided. Some monograms and the curl of the bugle are also partly voided.

A mention here concerning the construction of the collar badge and fixing is relevant as there are so many of the Regiments collar badges that have a pin-back fitting as opposed to lugs, that a comment may be helpful. These are not only Officers items as one might expect but also appear in many cases on soldiers badges. There does not appear to be any valid reason, and one can only assume, that they were either at the whim of the manufacturer or preference of a particular Battalion at a particular time.

There are quite a number of separate pieces making up Senior NCO's and Officers collar badges, four, five and even six. Some are fitted together either in an easily dismantled form by removing one securing pin whilst others have bent over securing lugs in a semi-permanent form. Others are brazed together.

The collar badges were worn in facing pairs with the bugle horn and elephant facing outwards from the collar opening.

On 20th January 1959, The Regiment (less Territorials) amalgamated with The Royal Scots Fusiliers (less Territorials) to form *The Royal Highland Fusiliers*.

Fig.1669

Fig.1670

Fig.1671

Fig.1672

Fig.1673

Seaforth Highlanders
(Ross-Shire Buffs, The Duke of Albany's)

Pre 1881
72nd (Duke of Albany's Own Highlanders) Regiment of Foot

Authorised to wear collar badges 16th July 1872, other ranks of the 72nd Regiment of Foot initially wore the brass numerals 72 on their tunic collars (Fig.1674). This practice soon ceased and no collar badges were worn for several years and it was not until 1878 that a new collar badge was introduced.

In brass, pattern 9635 was sealed on 14th February, being a stag's head over a scroll inscribed "CABAR FEIDH" (The Antlers of the Deer). (Line drawing Fig.1675).

"Cabar Feidh" is the war-cry of the Seaforths'. The title, Duke of Albany's Own Highlanders was granted to The Regiment in 1823 by King George IV whose brother, Frederick Duke of York & Albany was C.I.C. of The Army.

78th (Highlanders) Regiment of Foot (The Ross-Shire Buffs)

A painting by R. Simkin within Vol I of "The History and Service of the 78th Highlanders" shows a Piper wearing a thistle device in white-metal on his dark green collar, the heading being "India - 1852". A similar painting in Vol II headed "1877", shows a private soldier wearing an elephant collar badge and this is generally acknowledged to have been the collar badge as worn by other ranks of the 78th. The elephant is painted being worn facing away from the collar opening - this is incorrect, the animal officially faced inwards.

The elephant collar badge, Pattern 9311, was sealed 15th July 1873. In brass, with brass lugs, it carried nothing on its back, its trunk down and standing with all four feet on a pebbled, grassy ground (Figs.1676 and 1677).

The Authorities tried, in the late 1870's, to standardise patterns of tigers, sphinx and elephants etc, so in 1879 it was decided to "assimilate the elephant collar badge of the 78th, Pattern 9311, to that of the 94th Foot, Pattern 9609". The Directive was dated 30th July.

Quite similar in design, the main difference being that the trunk extended right out to and rested on, the grassy ground (Fig.1678). It was also an altogether "flatter" pattern.

The Elephant, without howdah or trappings and the battle honour "Assaye" commemorates the part the 78th played in the battle of that name whilst serving in India, the battle taking place in September 1803. This was approved 16th April 1807.

The Regimental Museum of The Queen's Own Highlanders (Seaforth and Camerons) say they have no evidence from photographs that collar badges were worn pre 1881 by either the 72nd or the 78th. Perhaps this is hardly surprising because many of the photographs seen have soldiers with such large beards that one can hardly see the collar, leave alone any item being worn on it!

Post 1881

On 1st July 1881, the 72nd and 78th Regs of Foot amalgamated to become *Seaforth Highlanders (Ross-Shire Buffs)* but this was amended 22nd November 1881 to include the old title of the 72nd so that the new title was *Seaforth Highlanders (Ross-Shire Buffs, The Duke of Albany's)*. The prefix "The" was added to the title 1st January 1921.

The new Regiment went to a lot of trouble to accede to the requests from both

SEAFORTH HIGHLANDERS (ROSS-SHIRE BUFFS, THE DUKE OF ALBANY'S)

the old 72nd and 78th that their individual insignia would be included in any new badges. None more so than the new collar insignia with two items worn either side of the collar.

One was the "F" cypher of HRH, Frederick, the late Duke of York with a scroll below inscribed "CABER FEIDH" (Fig.1679). This, of course, delighted the old 72nd, and the 78th were equally pleased as the other collar badge was their old Elephant (Fig.1680). These were Pattern 10189, both in gilding-metal, and sealed 16th June 1882. The "F" cypher had an edge to it as did the scroll with a background of vertical lines to the motto and horizontal lines on the cypher. The elephant was almost identical to that worn by the 78th but now in gilding-metal and with copper lugs.

Regulations directed that the two collar badges should be worn with "the cypher of the late Duke of York being nearest the end of the collar". The cypher faced to the left only but the elephant, in facing pairs, was worn with the animal facing inwards towards the collar opening.

Although the two collar badges had placated both the former personnel of the old 72nd and 78th Regiments of Foot, it is obvious that "you cannot please all of the people all of the time" and the 2nd Battalion wore their collar badges with the elephant *in front* of the cypher! This practice ceased by the end of the 1880's.

On 9th February 1898, it was "demanded" that the collar badges were to be renewed and cut from new dies. The occasion was taken to slightly modify the badges although the designs remained much the same. This was Pattern 10189a, sealed 3th August 1999, "in lieu of Pattern 10189)" and with "the cypher next to the hook & eye". (Authority, Patts 9741 and 8991). Still in gilding-metal, the badges were very slightly smaller than the ones they replaced (Fig.1681 for cypher and Fig.1682 for elephant which has the elephant's trunk curving upwards similar to the one worn from 1873 by the old 78th). Worn until amalgamation in 1961.

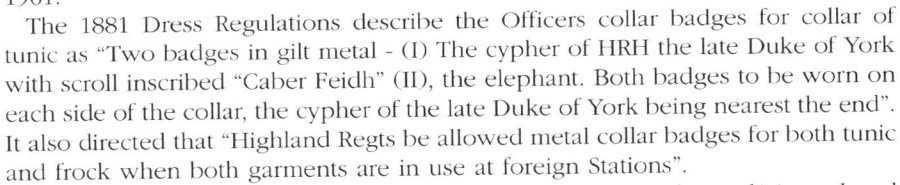

The 1881 Dress Regulations describe the Officers collar badges for collar of tunic as "Two badges in gilt metal - (I) The cypher of HRH the late Duke of York with scroll inscribed "Caber Feidh" (II), the elephant. Both badges to be worn on each side of the collar, the cypher of the late Duke of York being nearest the end". It also directed that "Highland Regts be allowed metal collar badges for both tunic and frock when both garments are in use at foreign Stations".

In the 1900 Edition of Dress Regulations "being nearest the end" is replaced with "Next the Hooks & Eye".

The Officers cypher collar badge was of the same design as those worn by other ranks with the same horizontal and vertical lines within the edges, but was smaller and neater. The "F" was raised from the scroll by a small plinth, plain with no lines and the middle cross piece was voided between the downstroke of the letter and the curl, which itself was voided. (Fig.1683 for cypher and Fig.1684 for elephant).

The description of the badges is repeated in the 1902 Dress Regulations with the addition "On mess jacket - no badge". Repeated in the 1904 Edition but omitted from the 1911 Dress Regulations.

Worn up to the 1961 amalgamation, latterly on No.1 and No.3 Dress, approved 1st August 1950, under Authority 54/Officers/4025.

Fig.1679

Fig.1680

Fig.1681

Fig.1682

Fig.1683

Fig.1684

Fig.1685

Fig.1686

HISTORY OF THE BRITISH ARMY INFANTRY COLLAR BADGE

Fig.1687

Fig.1688

Fig.1689

Fig.1690

Fig.1691

When Service Dress was introduced in 1902, Officers wore bronze collar badges described in Dress Regulations as "The stags head with a scroll below inscribed 'CUIDICH'N RIGH'". (Fig.1685 for "closed antlers" type and Fig.1686 for variation with "open antlers").

A stag's head cabossed and the gaelic motto "Cuidich'n Righ" (Help the King) belongs to the MacKenzie clan and tradition has it that in 1266, King Alexander II of Scotland was out hunting and was unhorsed by a wounded stag. He was saved only by the prompt action of Colin Fitzgerald, an ancestor of the MacKenzie's of Seaforth, who, with a cry of "Cuidich'n Righ" seized the stag by one of its antlers and severed the head immediately behind the antlers with a blow from his sword. In gratitude, the King granted Fitzgerald a stag's head and motto as a badge to his shield of Arms.

Fitzgerald's descendent's later became Earls of Seaforth and the family badge and motto were adopted by the Regiment. Incidentally, the Seaforth Highlanders were the only Regiment in the British Army to have a gaelic motto.

A more likely explanation is that the Arms and motto came from the annual feudal tribute of a stag which the MacKenzie's of Seaforth were required to hand to the Crown as Payment for their lands.

Sometimes mistaken as a collar badge is the stags head without a scroll and which is a sporran badge (Fig.1687).

Also worn on Service Dress with the double cypher and elephant collar badges in bronze. The cypher took the same form as the one in gilt and the elephant was similar to the other ranks pattern. (Figs.1688 for cypher and 1689 and 1690 for two different sized elephants). Pipe Majors wore their cypher and elephant collar badges in silver.

No collar badges were worn on No.2 Dress.

Militia
Ross, Caithness, Sutherland and Cromarty (Highland Rifle Militia)

Collar badges in white-metal, were sealed for other ranks 16th October 1879 "for tunic and frock", this being Pattern 7196. This was the outline of a heart surmounted by a crown and within which was a bugle horn over a chevron (Line drawing Fig.1691).

On 1st July 1881, they became the 3rd Battalion, Seaforth Highlanders (Ross-Shire Buffs).

Rifle Volunteer Corps, Volunteer, Territorial Force & Territorial Army Battalions

The 1st Ross-Shire (Ross Highland) RVC, 1St Sutherland (The Sutherland Highland) RVC and *The 1st Elgin RVC* became VB's of the Seaforth Highlanders (Ross-Shire Buffs) 1st July 1881, redesignated as 1st Ross Highland), 1st Sutherland (The Sutherland Highland VRC), (2nd VB) and 3rd (Morayshire) VB's respectively on 1st December 1887, December 1891 and 1st December 1887.

Their collar badges were of the same design as those worn by the Regular Battalions, but in white-metal for other rank's and in silver plate for Officers. They were submitted for approval by Hobsons, Little Windmill Street, London on behalf of the 1st VB in 1888 approval being received on 10th December under Authority V/I/Ross/285 and adopted by all Volunteer Battalions

In 1908, the VB's became TF Battalions continuing for a while with their own collar badges but gradually adopting those as worn by the Line Battalions

However, the 5th (The Sutherland and Caithness Highlanders) Battalion (TF) and later in 1921 the 4/5 (Ross, Sutherland and Caithness) Battalion TA wore their own distinctive collar badges.

This was a Cat-a-Mountain, Sejant, rampant, guardant with the motto "Sans Peur" (without fear). This was the crest of the Duke of Sutherland who raised the Regiment and, being a crest, they do not face. In white-metal for other ranks (Fig.1692) and in silver for Officers.

The 11th Battalion was formed 1st January 1947 to perpetuate the 5th (Caithness & Sutherland), 6th (Morayshire) and 7th (Morayshire) Battalions wearing the same collar badge as the Regular Battalions

The cypher and the elephant collar badges in gold anodised were introduced in 1956 under Authority 54/Offs/4025, being sealed on 17th October. A Further gold anodised collar badge was sealed 29th January 1964 this being Pattern 19239.

WWI Service Battalions
7th, 8th and 9th (Service) Battalions

Photographs show other ranks of these Battalions wearing the Seaforth shoulder title on both sides of their tunic collars (Fig.1693). There are also photographs of Prisoners of War wearing the same but which Battalion is not known.

All three Battalions were raised in 1914, the 7th and 8th disbanded in 1919.

Fig.1692

9th (Service) Battalion

Converted to Pioneers 10th May 1915 when they wore the usual crossed rifle and pick collar badges (Fig.147). Disbanded on the Rhine 12th June 1919.

Fig.1693

Other Badges

Often mistaken as a collar badge is a smaller version of an early cap badge with a stag's head below the coronet and cypher of HRH The Duke of Albany all above a scroll inscribed "CUIDICH'N RIGH". In a variety of metals and fixings. They are in fact sweetheart badges. (Fig.1694).

General

The general design of the elephant, cypher and stag collar badges have remained the same throughout The Seaforth Highlanders existence. There are naturally slight variations especially with the elephant both in shape and size, position of the trunk, voiding or non voiding between tail and body and shape and size of the animals ears.

Fig.1694

The Regiment was one of only two British Regiments to wear a double collar badge, the other being The Royal Irish Fusiliers.

On 7th February 1961, The Regiment (less Territorials) amalgamated with The Queen's Own Cameron Highlanders (less Territorials) to form *The Queen's Own Highlanders (Seaforth & Camerons)*.

The Gordon Highlanders

Fig.1695

Pre 1881
75th (Stirlingshire) Regiment of Foot

For a short time after the Authorisation of collar badges for the 75th Regiment of Foot on 16th July 1872, other ranks wore the brass numerals "75" on their collars. The collar badge eventually adopted for wear on the tunic and frock collars by other ranks of the Regiment was a long bodied "Royal Tiger", looking sideways, all four feet on a thin grassy ground and with tail dropping down between its back legs (Figs.1695 & 1696 for two slight variations). In brass, this was Pattern 9519, sealed 3rd November 1874.

The "Royal Tiger" was awarded to the Regiment 6th July 1807 and commemorates their nineteen years of eventful and arduous service in India from 1787 until 1806. The tigers tail between its legs is an illusion to the defeated of Tippoo Sahib, cowed after its defeat by the British in 1799.

Fig.1696

92nd (Gordon Highlanders) Regiment of Foot

In "Dress of the 92nd (Gordon Highlanders) Regiment of Foot" it states that in 1874 "A gilt Crown was ordered to be worn at each end of the collar by rank and file". Authorised 16th July 1872, this was the usual Imperial crown in brass (Fig.333).

The next Official reference to collar badges is found in The Army Clothing Dept pattern room journals where it is recorded that Pattern 9636 was sealed on 14th February 1878 - this being a sphinx over "EGYPT" tablet in white-metal. Also shown in the Gaunt pattern books, being rather a large item (Fig.1697).

No other collar badge is officially recorded until after the 1881 amalgamation but on display at the Scottish United Services Museum is a small brass collar badge with sphinx over Egypt tablet (Fig.1698). There is also another one, again in brass, (Fig.1699).

Fig.1697

The Regimental Museum of The Gordon Highlanders do not have a pre 1881 collar badge for the 92nd but do have details of the design. Again in brass this is a large full breasted female sphinx (Figs.1700 and 1701). Also in gilt worn by WO's.

After Officers removed their rank badge from the collar in late 1880, they wore similar, but embroidered (Fig.1702).

Post 1881

On 1st July 1881, the 75th and 92nd Regiments of Foot amalgamated to become *The Gordon Highlanders* and on 22nd October a verbal decision by Col. Blundell

Fig.1698

Fig.1699    *Fig.1700*    *Fig.1701*    *Fig.1702*

THE GORDON HIGHLANDERS

(AAG, Horse Guards) stated that "The York & Lancaster Regiment and The Gordon Highlanders are to wear the Royal Tiger as a collar badge. This Royal Tiger should always be the same pattern". (This was rescinded on 16th March 1885 when the York and Lancaster Regiment were allowed to revert to the pattern previously worn by the old 65th Regiment of Foot).

The General Register of Patterns records Pattern 9963 as being sealed 20th January 1882 under Authority ACD/Gen No/8479, in gilding-metal (Figs.1703 & 1704). Photographs and paintings show these gilding-metal collar badges being worn by Senior NCO's c.1900. However, the Army Clothing Dept pattern room Journals, under the same sealing date, records this as Pattern 9963 and in white-metal and annotated "white metal Tiger badge Pattern 9963 sealed in lieu of Pattern 9519 for 75th and 9636 for 92nd Regiments of Foot".

The same Journals record that renewal of the standard pattern was called for 30th November 1896 under Authority ACD/Patts/8189, these being sealed 14th December 1897, cut from new dies and being Pattern 9963a. Upon examination of the actual sealed pattern it is confirmed that Pattern 9963a is in white-metal (Figs.1705 & 1706). The last issue was made with a single lug fitting and worn immediately before the introduction of the anodised version. These were worn until 1960 when on 3rd August, Pattern 18341 was sealed under Authority 54/Inf/8799 "to supercede Pattern 9963a". This was the Tiger in silver anodised (Fig.1707).

This particular pattern was replaced in 1982 when Pattern 18341a was sealed on 13th September. Still the same general design but a sturdier animal (Fig.1708). This is a far different tiger to the one worn pre 1881 by the old 75th, now with one front paw raised and pointing downwards but most significantly, the cowed tail replaced by one rising up and over its back, the end pointing towards the rear.

Early Dress Regulations describe the Officers doublet collar badge as "The Royal Tiger, in gold embroidery". Similar to the metal collar badge worn by other ranks with one front paw raised and tail rising up over the back but standing on a torse instead of a grassy ground (Fig.1709). Repeated in subsequent Dress Regulations until 1902 which adds "On mess jacket - no badge". Repeated in the 1904 Edition but omitted from the 1911 Edition. These were worn on the appropriate uniforms, latterly on No.1 Dress when they were worn on a yellow cloth ground (Fig.1710).

A description in 1966 describes the Officers collar badge as "The Sphinx over "Egypt", in gilt, in pairs" (Fig.1711). The 1973 Dress Regulations records "The Sphinx on a plinth inscribed "Egypt" in silver plate, in pairs" (Fig.1712). Such an item in silver plate, Pattern 30153 was sealed 31st August 1978 and was also worn on No.3 Dress.

Fig.1703

Fig.1704

Fig.1705

Fig.1706

Fig.1709

Fig.1710

Fig.1711

Fig.1712

Fig.1707

Fig.1708

Fig.1713

Fig.1714

Fig.1715

Fig.1716

Fig.1717

Fig.1718

The Officers sphinx collar badge has an asp on the forehead, one of only two British Regiments to do so, the other being The Dorsetshire Regiment

These sphinx/Egypt collar badges in gilt, silver and bronze, although small items, do vary in their strikings. Always male, some have large heads and necks, others small and slimmer with even the front legs differing in size, some being quite thick whilst others are almost skeleton-like. The mantles also vary in shape, size and length.

The Sphinx superscribed "Egypt" commemorates the service of the 92nd in Egypt in 1801, being authorised 6th July 1802.

The 1986 Dress Regulations describes the Officers collar badge for No 1 Dress as "The Royal Tiger, in gold embroidery". The item examined has the eyes and mouth picked out in red and the teeth in white, the tiger being on a green backing.

In 1902, Service Dress was introduced for Officers and the relative Dress Regulations describes the collar badge to be worn in bronze as "Upon a dotted shield, the stags head and coronet, with scroll above, inscribed 'Bydand'". The 1911 Dress Regulations replaced "dotted" with "seeded". This item can easily be mistaken for similar used as a sporran top for NCO's and privates approved Horse Guards WO 29th October 1895 and a later Pattern 7704 in gilding-metal sealed 18th October 1912.

A similar item was worn as a sporran badge from 1902 by *The Cape Town Highlanders* (Fig.1713).

The stags head and motto "Bydand" variously translated as "Watchful" and "Steadfast" with coronet is the crest of the Marquis of Huntly, and an ivy wreath being the badge of the Gordon family, all confirmed to the 92nd Regiment of Foot in 1872.

When the 1934 Dress Regulations were issued, the Service Dress collar badge had changed to "A sphinx over 'Egypt'". (Figs.1714, 1715 and 1716). This was similar to the ones already described in silver. These continued to be worn, described in the 1973 Edition of Dress Regulations as "For No 2 Dress". Repeated in the 1986 Edition, one pattern, 30154 was sealed 13th November 1978. Similar was polished down to gilding-metal and worn on the khaki drill.

The other ranks tiger pattern collar badge, in silver, was worn by the R.S.M. and Pipe and Drum Majors. This pattern is also known in bronze.

Militia
Royal Aberdeenshire Highlanders Militia

Collar badges, in white-metal for tunic and frock were sealed 22nd December 1876. This was St. Andrew behind a cross and enclosed by a wreath of Ivy (Line drawing 1717).

On 1st July 1881, they became the 3rd Battalion, The Gordon Highlanders.

Rifle Volunteer Corps, Volunteer, Territorial Force & Territorial Army Battalions

1st Aberdeenshire R.V.C. changed their uniforms in 1879 to scarlet doublets with yellow facings and their collar badge was similar to the centre of their Glengarry badge, St. Andrew standing in front of the Cross. In white-metal for other ranks and in silver for Officers (Fig.1718).

By General Order 12, dated 1st February 1884, the *1st, 2nd, 3rd & 4th Aberdeenshire R.V.C.'s* became, respectively, the 1st, 2nd, 3rd (Buchan) and 4th VB's, The Gordon Highlanders.

By the same General Order the *1st Kincardineshire and Aberdeen or Deeside Highland R.V.C.* and the *1st Banffshire R.V.C.* became the 5th (Deeside Highland) and 6th VB's respectively.

On 19th December 1900, a 7th VB was raised in Shetland, receiving their Service Dress uniforms in 1902. Disbanded 1920.

On 30th October 1895, the full uniform of The Gordons was adopted by the 1st VB although the change was gradual and not completed until 1901. Drab Service Doublets were Authorised 9th July 1902.

The 3rd VB were authorised to wear the uniform and badges of The Gordon Highlanders from 1885, but with certain exceptions, and it was not until 1903 that they were Authorised to wear the full dress.

On 22nd April 1887, the 4th VB changed their uniforms to rifle green doublets.The 6th VB changed their uniforms to scarlet doublets 17th January 1891, adopting the Service Dress doublet in 1902.

Officers collar badges were submitted for approval in 1891 on behalf of the 6th VB and these were approved by Horse Guards on 17th March under Authority V/1 Banff/233. Similar were submitted and approved for the 3rd VB under Authority V/3 Aberdeen/488 on 27th March 1893 annotated "Collar ornament for tunic, white-metal for NCO's and men".

An Order was issued dated 30th October 1895 "That silver is to be used in place of gold" and uniforms c.1898 clearly show these collar badges with silver embroidery.

In 1908, the VB's became Battalions of the TF and whilst wearing the collar badges as worn by the Regular Battalions, photographs often show Officers wearing a separate bronze "T" below their sphinx collar badges, on Service Dress.

The 4/7 and 5/6 TF Battalions were amalgamated in 1961 to form the 3rd Battalion TA, the sphinx over Egypt in silver being worn by Officers on their No I Dress and in bronze on Service Dress. The sealed pattern is dated 27th November 1961. Soldiers wore the tiger collar badge in silver anodised.

In 1967, the *51st Highland Volunteers* were formed, The Gordon Highlanders being part of this group. The Catalogue of Clothing and Necessaries list the ordinary badges under 'D' (Gordon Highlanders) Coy, 2nd Battalion, HQ Coy and 3rd Battalion as "anodised silver - other ranks, The Royal Tiger handed design", "gilding-metal, bronze - Officers No.2 Dress, sphinx over 'Egypt', handed design and nickel silver, silver plated - Officers No.I Dress, the sphinx on a plinth inscribed 'Egypt' handed design".

London Scottish (Gordon Highlanders) TA

The London Scottish became part of the Gordon Highlanders in 1916 being redesignated by AO 168, 10th August 1937 as The London Scottish (Gordon Highlanders). They retained their own collar badges, the well known thistle within two sprays of leaves. Two such items were sealed in 1952. The first, issued by The Inspectorate of Clothing, Ministry of Supply was Pattern 15148, sealed on 23rd June and annotated "Working pattern - white-metal thistle collar - to be used to guide for anodised" (Fig.1719).

On the same date, another white-metal thistle collar badge was also sealed, this being Pattern 17377. This was a smaller, more fragile item, with single lug fitting (Fig.1720). The silver anodised version was introduced in 1961 under Authority 54/Inf/888, also with a single lug fitting (Fig.1721). A further pattern, 19545 was sealed 9th November 1965.

These other ranks collar badges, both in white-metal and silver anodised can easily be confused with those worn on the shoulder by soldiers of The Scots Guards. Although difficult to tell apart whilst being worn, those of The Guards differ from those of The London Scottish by having two square fittings on the reverse instead of round lug fixtures. Even the anodised badges of The Guards have the same and in addition those of The London Scottish have but the single fitting.

Officers wore similar, but in silver. One such was sealed 23rd November 1961 under Authority 54/Inf/8881. On Service Dress they wore the thistle in bronze.

They were all worn in facing pairs with the stem of the thistle pointing inwards towards the collar opening.

One item sometimes confused as a collar badge is the sporran badge in both white-metal and silver plate (Fig.1722).

(See also under Rifle Brigade).

Fig.1719

Fig.1720

Fig.1721

Fig.1722

WWI Service Battalions
9th (Service) Battalion, Pioneers
Raised 12th September 1914 at Aberdeen and converted to Pioneers 12th January 1915, then wearing the usual crossed rifle and pick collar badges (Fig.147). Disbanded 24th June 1919 at Dreghorn.

Other Badges
There are several items of insignia worn by The Gordon Highlanders which might appear to be collar badges. These include items worn on the sporran, headdress and cantles etc as well as sweetheart items. Illustrated are four such items, the first in bronze, the second in silver, and the third, with asp on forehead in silver anodised. The last item being Pattern 17061 sealed 30th January 1956 in white-metal "For sporran purse" (Figs.1723, 1724, 1725 and 1726).

General
Apart from Militia and Rifle Volunteers and with one exception, (The bronze shield collar badge worn on Service Dress) all collar badges of The Gordon Highlanders, including the 75th and 92nd Regiments of Foot, have been The Royal Tiger and the sphinx. In their several forms they have always been worn in facing pairs with the animals facing inwards towards the collar opening.

It was announced 23rd July 1991 that, under the defence cuts, The Gordon Highlanders were to be merged with The Queen's Own Highlanders (Seaforth & Camerons). Some proposed mergers were reversed 3rd February 1993 after which renewed efforts were made for The Gordons to retain their own individuality. Sadly, these efforts were to no avail and on 17th September 1993 the new Regiment was formed, *The Highlanders (Seaforths, Gordons, and Camerons)*.

Fig.1723

Fig.1724

Fig.1725

Fig.1726

The Queen's Own Cameron Highlanders

Pre 1881
79th (Queen's Own Cameron Highlanders) Regiment of Foot

Authorised by PC/Infy Gen/111 dated 16th July 1872, the 79th adopted as their first collar badge a simple but effective design of a thistle spray surmounted by a QVC.

This was a natural choice as "The thistle ensigned with the Imperial crown" was granted to the 79th, 12th May 1873 by Queen Victoria after she presented new Colours to The Regiment on 17th April and commanded, in July, they should in future be styled "The 79th (Queen's Own Cameron Highlanders)".

The design of the thistle surmounted by a crown is The Royal badge of Scotland given by Queen Anne in 1707 at the time of the passing of the Act of Union.

The other ranks collar badge, in white-metal, was Pattern 9513 and sealed 1st October 1874 "For tunic and frock collar". They vary slightly in size and design of crown, size of thistle and amount of voiding between thistle, leaves and crown (Figs.1727 and 1728).

After Officers removed their badges of rank from the collar in late 1880, they wore embroidered versions of the other ranks collar badge (Fig.1729).

Post 1881

Under the Army Reforms of 1881, the 79th were the only single Battalion to escape amalgamation and, as the old Regimental numbers were officially discontinued, the 79th became, on 1st July 1881, *The Queen's Own Cameron Highlanders*.

An interim statement issued by Horse Guards on 30th September confirmed "Collar badge as at present, Crown and Thistle". However, this was soon superceded when, on 29th December, a new collar badge for other ranks, Pattern 9911, was sealed. This was in gilding-metal "To replace Pattern 9513 in white-metal for the 79th" (Fig.1730).

An Order was made 10th August 1886 that "Collar badges are not to be worn on khaki drill frocks".

On 27th November 1897, renewal of the standard pattern was demanded to be cut from new dies and the resulting Pattern, 9911a was sealed 14th September 1899. No change in design.

Most Scottish Regiments seem to have favoured white-metal and silver collar badges for other ranks and Officers respectively and it is difficult to understand why, officially at least, the other ranks collar badge was in gilding-metal. From the many photographs noted where collar badges are being worn from the 1880's, they all appear to be in white-metal and this, together with the scarcity of QVC collar badges in gilding-metal, one cannot but wonder how much, or rather how little, they were actually worn, The Regiment continuing to wear those of the old 79th in white-metal.

The next change was brought about by the death of Queen Victoria in 1901 but it was not until 1904 that Pattern 9911b was introduced. In white-metal, this was sealed on 17th August "With Tudor Crown" under Authority ACD/Patts /1184. Still with the same general design but with the crown partly voided as against the ones with QVC, which were solid (Fig.1731). Also known in gilding-metal (Fig.1732).

Pattern 9911b was worn until 1959 when it was used as the guide for similar but in silver anodised, this being Pattern 18160 (Fig.1733).

Fig.1727

Fig.1728

Fig.1729

Fig.1730

Fig.1731

Fig.1732

HISTORY OF THE BRITISH ARMY INFANTRY COLLAR BADGE

Fig.1733

Fig.1734

Fig.1735

The Officers collar badge is described in the 1883 Dress Regulations quite simply as "The thistle surmounted by the Crown in silver embroidery". (See photograph 21, c.1890). This description was repeated in subsequent Editions until 1900 when it was altered to "The thistle surmounted by the Crown on a Crimson velvet cushion, in silver embroidery, on a blue cloth ground" (Fig.1734).

The 1902 Dress Regulations adds "On mess jacket - no badge". The next change comes in the 1911 Edition when for the collar badge for the doublet, "on a crimson velvet cushion" is no longer included in the description. Repeated up to and including the 1934 Edition.

After the death of Queen Victoria, a new collar badge with K/C was necessary and this item, on a crimson velvet cushion, was sealed 6th October 1903 (Fig.1735). For Service Dress, introduced in 1902, Dress Regulations direct the collar badge to be "As for Highland Head-dress, but smaller" and in bronze. The Head-dress badge was "A thistle wreath; within the wreath the figure of St. Andrew with Cross, but with a scroll on the lower bend of the wreath inscribed 'CAMERON'". (Fig.1736). Confirmed in the 1904 Edition.

Although there are photographs of these badges being worn by Officers in 1915, the 1911 Dress Regulations describe the Service Dress jacket collar badge "As for doublet", in bronze. This is the thistle surmounted by a K/C, the badge sealed by the War Office 6th October 1903 (Fig.1737). Repeated up to and including the 1934 Edition of Dess Regulations. The original sealed pattern has written on it in ink, and obviously added later, "Collar badge, No.I Dress, 54/Officers/4025, March 1949".

A similar, but smaller, item was later introduced in silver plate as a collar badge for No.3 Dress (Fig.1738). Known in white-metal, believed to have also been used as a sporran badge.

The other ranks pattern is known in silver with QVC (Fig.1739) and in silver plate with both K/C and Q/C. Also known in bronze (Figs.1740 and 1741).

Militia

Inverness, Banff, Elgin and Nairn Militia redesignated *Highland Light Infantry Militia* became the 2nd Battalion, The Queen's Own Camerons Highlanders, 1st July 1881.

By a decision PC/HLI Militia/268, dated 1st February 1879 the bugle collar badge worn by this Militia was to follow the Pattern 8935. In white-metal for other ranks (Fig.207) and in silver for Officers.

Rifle Volunteer Corps, Volunteer, Territorial Force & Territorial Army Battalions

1st Inverness-Shire (Inverness Highland) RVC under the Army Reforms of 1881 was attached to No.72 Regimental District but in 1883 when No.79

Fig.1736

Fig.1737

Fig.1738

Fig.1739

Fig.1740

Fig.1741

Regimental District was set up, the Battalion became an integral part of The Queen's Own Cameron Highlanders.

On 1st December 1887, they were redesignated the 1st (Inverness - Highland) VB and in 1893, with minor exceptions, adopted the uniforms of the parent Regiment They wore the same collar badges as the Regular Battalions and on 1st April 1908 became the 4th Battalion TF. There are photographs of Officers of the 4th Battalion TF wearing a separate bronze 'T' below the large thistle on their Service Dress jackets.

In 1947, the 4th and 5th Battalions amalgamated to become the 4/5 Battalion in The Territorial Army when they continued to wear the same collar badges. A sealed pattern dated 29th November 1961 shows the silver anodised collar badge with K/C for other ranks together with those for Officers, sealed 11th October 1955 - the K/C in silverplate "For No.3 Dress" and similar, but embroidered, "For No.1 Dress" - all these as already described and illustrated.

What is interesting is that the silver anodised collar badge, sealed in 1961, still has a K/C.

Fig.1742

Sporran/Purse Badges

These items can easily be mistaken for collar badges, especially the smaller ones. Illustrated are two such pieces (Figs.1742 & 1743).

Fig.1743

General

Although worn in pairs, the white-metal and gilding-metal collar badges of the other ranks did not face, neither did the same pattern in silver and in bronze. Some Officers collar badges, especially the embroidered items, do sometimes face and, when they do, they are worn with the thistle stalk facing inwards towards the collar opening.

On 7th February 1961, the amalgamation of the Regiment (less Territorials) took place at Redford Barracks Edinburgh with The Seaforth Highlanders (less Territorials), to form *The Queen's Own Highlanders*.

The Royal Ulster Rifles (formerly the Royal Irish Rifles)

Pre 1881
83rd (County of Dublin) Regiment of Foot

The first collar badge worn by other ranks of the 83rd Regiment of Foot was the brass Imperial crown (Fig.333). This was authorised 16th July 1872 under Order PC/Infy Gen/111 and worn until 1875, when their own special badge was introduced.

This was either Pattern 9533 or 9534, sealed on 3rd March. In brass, this was "The harp - maid" or, as it is popularly known as, "Angel harp", surmounted by a QVC. The strings of the harp are found both solid and voided (Figs.1744 and 1745 for the two variations). Worn in facing pairs with the angel facing inwards towards the collar opening.

The above information is recorded in the official journals of the Pattern Room of the Army Clothing Dept and confirmed by the Regimental HQ of The Royal Irish Rangers and specialist collectors.

However, one official source describes the pre 1881 collar badge of the 83rd as "Crown and Wreath", but it has not been possible to find out any information on such an item.

Another source, a Military Museum, illustrates an "Angel harp" within a wreath of shamrock, in brass (Fig.1746). A similar item, in white-metal, is more usually associated with Roscommon Militia. Again, this is unconfirmed.

The Regimental History records that in 1880, badges of rank were removed from the collar of the Officers tunic and displayed on the shoulder strap. There is no indication that Officers wore collar badges before the 1881 amalgamation.

86th (Royal County Down) Regiment of Foot

The Harp and Crown, together with the motto "Quis Separabit" (Who shall separate us?) was authorised for the 86th on 26th March 1832 so it was of no great surprise that this formed the basis for the Regiments first other ranks collar badge.

In brass, the design was of an "angel harp" surmounted by a QVC and with two downward facing scrolls at the base, inscribed "QUIS" and "SEPARABIT". Although the stings of the harp are solid, their is voiding between the strings and the angel figure (Fig.1747). This was Pattern 9500, authorised 30th June 1874 and sealed on 16th July.

In November, Officers were permitted to bear the same device on their forage caps and they also wore them in bronze on their tunic collars, after they removed their badges of rank in 1880. Similar to those worn by the other ranks but with no voiding (Fig.1748).

Both Officers and other ranks collar badges were worn in FP's with the angel facing inwards towards the collar opening.

Post 1881

By General Order 41 issued 1st July 1881, the 83rd and 86th Regiments of Foot were joined together to become 1st and 2nd Battalions respectively, *The Royal Irish Rifles*. Redesignated, 1st January 1921 as *The Royal Ulster Rifles*.

As both the 83rd and 86th had featured "the angel harp" and QVC in their former collar badges, it was logical that the new collar badge would follow with the same general design. This proved to be the case with the addition of a scroll at the base inscribed with the motto of the old 86th, "QUIS SEPARABIT". In

THE ROYAL ULSTER RIFLES

blackened gilding-metal (Fig.1749). This was also the cap badge.

Worn until 1902, when similar, but with K/C, was introduced (Fig.1750). These face both ways with the angel facing inwards towards the collar opening.

There is an interesting memorandum dated 1st April 1903 when the O.C. of the 83rd Regimental District reported that all the collar badges in wear had the scroll beneath and trusted that this would remain so.

In 1913, the collar badges changed to white-metal, also facing both ways (Fig.1751).

When the Brigade system was introduced in 1958, the Regiment joined *The North Irish Brigade*, adopting the Brigade cap badge but retaining their individual collar badge. This was the "angel harp" surmounted by a crown, now a Q/C. Below the harp, a ribboned bugle horn with scrolls either side of the bow inscribed with the motto "QUIS SEPARABIT". In black metal, this was Pattern 18856 sealed 3rd December 1962 (Fig.1752, worn with a red backing). Pipers wore similar but in chrome (Fig.1753). Again worn in FP's with the "angel harp" facing inwards towards the collar opening, up to reorganisation in 1968.

For the 83rd & 86th Regiments of Foot, both redcoat Regiments, it was an Honour granted by Royal favour to become, in 1881, a Rifle Regiment This meant a change of uniform more in keeping with Rifle tradition and no collar badges were worn. Confirmed in the 1881 Dress Regulations as "On collar of tunic - no badge".

The first mention of an Officers collar badge was in the 1902 Dress Regulations with "On mess jacket only, badge as on forage cap boss". this was described as "A Harp and Crown in silver across which is scroll inscribed 'Royal Irish Rifles'" (Fig.1754).

The change in Regimental title in 1921 necessitated a change of mess jacket collar badge but it was not until 1924 that the new pattern was introduced. Sealed by The War Office on 1st November, the scroll was now inscribed "ROYAL ULSTER RIFLES", this being confirmed in the 1934 Dress Regulations. This was eventually replaced by similar but, with Q/C, and worn until reorganisation in 1968.

When Service Dress for Officers was introduced in 1902, the relative Dress Regulations describe the collar badge, in bronze, as "The Harp and Crown with scroll beneath inscribed 'Quis Separabit'". Repeated in the 1904 Edition (Fig.1755). This was considered too large but worn until c.1910 when it gave way to a similar but smaller item (Fig.1756). Also known in silver plate.

Photographs show the smaller collar badge was still being worn in 1921 and a renewal pattern was cut from new dies and sealed 1st November 1924. During the WWI period an even smaller collar badge, in bronze, was worn on Service Dress (Fig.1757).

Later Dress Regulations including the 1934 Edition, direct black metal for Service Dress.

Fig.1749

Fig.1750

Fig.1751

Fig.1752

Fig.1754

Fig.1755

Fig.1756

Fig.1757

Fig.1753

Fig.1758

Fig.1759

Fig.1760

During the Brigade period, Officers wore similar Q/C collar badges as worn by their men, the pattern being sealed 3rd December 1962 under Authority 54/Inf/8796. A K/C item, over the usual "angel harp" and "QUIS SEPARABIT" scroll, 3.6mm high is known in gilt, usage unknown, possibly worn by WO's.

Militia
The Royal North Down Rifles Militia, The Royal Antrim Rifles Militia and *The Royal Louth Rifles Militia* became on 1st July 1881, the 3rd, 4th and 6th Battalions respectively, The Royal Irish Rifles.

No collar badges were worn.

Royal South Down Light Infantry Militia, who became the 5th Battalion, The Royal Irish Rifles on 1st July 1881, wore a bugle as their collar badge (Fig.1758). By a decision PC/S Down Militia/195 dated 26th March 1878, their collar badge was to be assimilated to Pattern 8935, sealed 1st August 1877 for the Royal South Gloucester Militia. in white-metal (Fig.207).

Territorial Army
With the introduction of The Territorial Army to Northern Ireland following WWII, the 6th Battalion was raised 1st January 1947, wearing the same collar badges as The Regular Battalions - the "angel harp" surmounted by a Q/C and with the "QUIS SEPARABIT" scroll below, in black metal for Officers and soldiers and in silver plate for Pipe Majors and Pipers. Their TAVR successor became the 6th (Territorial) Battalion, The Royal Ulster Rifles.

The 5th (Volunteer) Battalion, The Royal Irish Rangers were later partly formed from the 6th (T) Battalion and wore as their collar badge the same as worn during the Brigade period. Their black Q/C collar badges were sealed 3rd December 62 under Authority 54/Inf/8796 annotated "5th (Vol) Battalion, "B" Coy.

WWI Service Battalions
14th (Young Citizens) (Service) Battalion
The "Young Citizens" Volunteers of Ireland were raised 12th September 1912 for boys aged eighteen who were leaving The Boy Scouts, Boys Brigade and Church Lads Brigade. On the declaration of War, this organisation volunteered "en masse" and on 12th September 1914 became, at Belfast, The 14th (Young Citizens) (S) Battalion, The Royal Irish Rifles.

They continued to wear their own collar badge which was a veined shamrock leaf, in the middle of which was the Red hand of Ulster and surmounted by a K/C. In white-metal for other ranks (Fig.1759) and in silver plate for Officers worn on full dress. They did not face. No collar badges were worn on Service Dress. Disbanded 18th February 1918.

16th (2nd County Down) (Service) Battalion (Pioneers)
Raised 8th October 1914 at Belfast and converted to Pioneers 6th January 1915, when they wore the usual crossed rifle and pick collar badges (Fig.147). Disbanded 29th June 1919.

Royal Irish Reserve Regiment
Any unit attached to the Reserve Regiment wore as their collar badge, a harp surmounted by a flat topped QVC, in black. (Fig.1760).

General
Variations between The Regiments collar badges are minor, perhaps the main one being the strings of the harp, some being solid whilst others are voided.

On 1st July 1968, The Regiment joined the two surviving Irish Infantry Regiments to become the *2nd Battalion, The Royal Irish Rangers (27th (Inniskilling) 83rd and 87th)*.

(For London Irish Rifles, The Royal Ulster Regiment, see under 18th (County of London) Battalion, The London Regiment (London Irish Rifles).

The Royal Irish Fusiliers (Princess Victoria's)

Pre 1881
87th (Royal Irish Fusiliers) Regiment of Foot

Photographs, prints and drawings clearly show grenades being worn on the collars of soldiers of the 87th Regiment of Foot as early as 1844. They were certainly being worn at that time by both Bandsmen and by Pioneers on their undress uniforms, in worsted form. It is recorded that, when the 87th arrived in Gibraltar in 1865, their only badges were "87" and a grenade on the cap. The Master Tailor suggested that a white cloth grenade should be worn on the collar on the shell jacket and tunic. This was approved by the Colonel with the men agreeing to pay the additional cost themselves.

Officers also wore grenades on their collars together with their rank badges. These were embroidered/bullion with an eagle over a tablet on which was the figure "8", on the ball.

Unlike all other Fusilier Regiments, the grenade was worn behind the badge of rank. The earliest date so far noted for these being worn together, is 1855, this also being the date when the heavily laced and embroidered collars disappeared on the introduction of the tunic and rank badges transferred to the collars.

However, a watercolour dated 1847 shows an Officer with a silver grenade and eagle on his collar with the ball nearest the collar opening. Both the grenade and the eagle are horizontal (Fig.1761).

The Eagle with a wreath of laurel was authorised for wear by the 87th on 11th April 1811. This followed an incident during the Peninsula War when, under the command of Lord Gough and during the battle of Barossa on 5th March 1811, the 2nd Battalion captured The Eagle of the *8th French Light Infantry* - the first to be captured in the Peninsula War.

Illustrated, (Photograph 22) is an 87th's Officers 1857 pattern "Hot climate" shell jacket in superfine lightweight scarlet linen with a 2⅛ inch stand-up collar. Almost filling the collar space are two large (3 inches long and maximum width 1¾ inches), gilt/bullion grenades, on the ball of which are upright silver eagles (½ inch high and ⅜ of an inch wide), over the numerals "87". For an enlarged photograph of the actual collar badge (see Photograph 23).

An Order PC/Infy Gen/111 dated 16th July 1872 directed that Fusilier Regiments should wear grenades as collar badges on their tunic collars. The resulting brass grenade, Pattern 9281, was sealed on 2nd October and adopted and worn by other ranks of the 87th (Fig.122).

At the time of sealing, Arthur Herbert, Colonel AAG, Horse Guards, sent a memorandum to all Fusiliers Regiments advising them that "Several Regiments providing their own badges have been permitted to wear embroidered grenades providing no expense is incurred by the public".

The plain grenade in brass was worn up to 1879 when The Regiment introduced its own distinctive other ranks collar badge. This was similar in design to the one worn by the Officer in the 1847 watercolour as already described. Officially described as "brass grenade with eagle on ball", this was Pattern 9679, sealed 23rd April 1879 "to replace the discontinued universal grenade, Pattern 9281". The eagle was placed sideways on the ball so that it stood upright on the collar. As with all later "Eagle" collar badges, worn in FP's with the eagle facing inwards towards the collar opening. (Figs.1762 and 1763). Worn until 1882.

Fig.1761

Fig.1762

Fig.1763

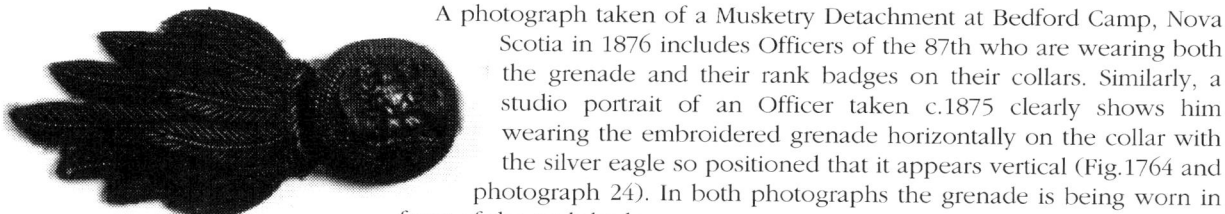

Fig.1764

A photograph taken of a Musketry Detachment at Bedford Camp, Nova Scotia in 1876 includes Officers of the 87th who are wearing both the grenade and their rank badges on their collars. Similarly, a studio portrait of an Officer taken c.1875 clearly shows him wearing the embroidered grenade horizontally on the collar with the silver eagle so positioned that it appears vertical (Fig.1764 and photograph 24). In both photographs the grenade is being worn in front of the rank badges.

89th (Princess Victoria's) Regiment of Foot

On 23rd April 1866, the 89th were granted the title of "Princess Victoria's Regiment" and Regimental Orders dated 4th February 1887 granted Officers permission to wear on their forage caps, above the numerals "89", the Princess's coronet.

Fig.1765

However, when on 16th July 1872 by Order PC/Gen Infy/111 "Badges for collar of tunic Infy", it was directed that "Corps with no special device" would wear crowns as their collar badge, it was this universal crown that the 89th decided to adopt. This was the brass item sealed 30th June 1874 (Fig.333).

The situation was remedied when by a Horse Guards letter C7846 dated 22nd August 1877, it was revealed that "Her Majesty is pleased to sanction the "Princess Victoria's Coronet", the Regimental badge, to be worn on the collars of the tunics, instead of the universal crown hitherto worn by men of The Regiment".

It was nearly a year later that the coronet, Pattern 9657 was sealed on 9th August 1878. In brass, the lower half of the coronet is decorated with five alternate shaped jewels, three square and the other two lozenge shaped and in between the jewels, five small circles in the shape of the five dots on a dice. Officers wore similar in silver when they removed their badges of rank from the collar in late 1880 (Fig.1765). Worn until 1882.

Post 1881

Army Order number 41 dated 11th April 1881 linked the 87th and 89th Regiments of Foot to become the 1st and 2nd Battalions respectively, *The Princess Victoria's (Royal Irish Fusiliers)*, the title changed by Army Order No 70 dated 30th June 1881. The Regiment were redesignated 1st 1st 1921 as *The Royal Irish Fusiliers (Princess Victoria's)*.

The Monogram of HRH The Princess Victoria was ordered to be worn as a collar badge by the 89th and on amalgamation both the grenade with eagle on the ball together with the Monogram and Coronet with sphinx above were to be adopted as the collar badges for the new Regiment and to be worn by both Battalions The sphinx superscribed "Egypt" commemorated the services of the 89th in Egypt 1801 and Authorised 6th July 1802.

By a decision PC/1 R Irish Fus/115 dated 17th April 1882, it was decided that "Grenades for collar badges are to be changed from the universal plain grenade to the special grenade formerly worn by The Regiment viz Pattern No 9679 which will be brought into charge again". A memorandum added to the label said they were to be in gilding-metal for other ranks instead of brass so that they would correspond with The Princess Victoria's Coronet which will be worn with them. The grenade collar badge referred to, with copper lugs as against those worn pre 1881 which had brass lugs, was Pattern 10110 sealed 16th February 1882.

The Gaunt pattern books clearly show the Monogram collar badge annotated 15th November 1881 and with the tablet below the sphinx inscribed "EGYPT". However, the finished article had the tablet, blank. For some reason some manufacturers seemed unable to inscribe such small lettering.

By a decision taken 10th June 1882, it was decided that "The P.V. with the coronet is to be worn in front nearest to the opening of the collar of the tunics and frocks" this being in answer to a question from the OC, 5th Battalion, asking which should be worn in front, the P.V. or the grenade which is also worn. (P.V. presumably stands for Princess Victoria).

THE ROYAL IRISH FUSILIERS (PRINCESS VICTORIA'S)

Fig.1766    *Fig.1767*    *Fig.1768*    *Fig.1769*

Both the monogram and the grenade face both ways and worn with the sphinx and the eagle facing inwards towards the collar opening (for an illustration of how all four items should be worn see Figs.1766, 1767, 1768 and 1769).

In 1888, a decision was taken for the Monogram and sphinx collar badge to be replaced by a large coronet but still to be worn with the grenade collar badge. On 27th May a request was made for a new pattern to be obtained "when supplies are requested after present stock exhausted". In September, under reference PC/6/5017, contractors were advised of the impending change and told they would be required to submit samples in due course. The resulting item was Pattern 1722 sealed in October (Fig.1770). These were worn until 1890 when, on 13th October, Pattern 2648 was sealed and the advantage taken to cut from new dies and slightly modify the design. (Figs.1771 and 1772 showing the correct position with the coronet nearest the collar opening).

Fig.1770

When a General Order, PC/Gen/1639 was issued 14th July 1893, that collar badges (left side) were to be worn upon the forage service cap by Infantry, The Royal Irish Fusiliers were exempted.

A renewal Pattern 4163 was cut from new dies and sealed in October 1894.

On 14th February 1905, all Fusilier Regiments were required to wear The Royal Artillery collar grenade (Pattern 9933a, sealed in 1897) with their metal titles on the shoulder straps of drab jackets and greatcoats.

On 9th June 1923, Pattern 3800 was sealed in white-metal "For Sergeant pipers and pipers" (Fig.1773 and Fig.1774 for smaller white-metal coronet). Eventually, c.1953, the gold anodised version was introduced with silver anodised coronet for wear on No.1 and No.3 Dress (Figs.1775 and 1776). Pipers wore similar but in silver anodised. Sealed Pattern 16145 sealed 12th February 1954 under Authority 1st 54/Officers/4025 shows a sideways grenade in gilding-metal with white-metal eagle on the ball with a separate white-metal coronet. This pattern was used as a guide for the later anodised version as worn by the 5th (Vol Battalion), Royal Irish Rangers, 'C' Coy).

Fig.1777

Besides the sideways or horizontal grenades, other ranks also wore the upright or vertical grenades. Pattern 10132 in bi-metal was sealed 15th October 1926 under Authority 54/Inf/5489, this having the grenade in gilding-metal and the

Fig.1771    *Fig.1772*

Fig.1773    *Fig.1774*    *Fig.1775* 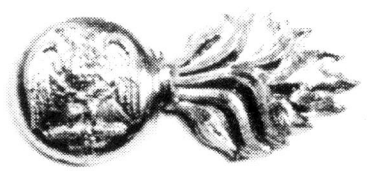   *Fig.1776*

283

HISTORY OF THE BRITISH ARMY INFANTRY COLLAR BADGE

eagle and coronet, which was attached to the grenade making it a one-piece item, in white-metal (Fig.1777). Later worn on No.1 and No.3 Dress. Also in all white-metal for wear by Sergeant Pipers and Pipers (Fig.1778). Later worn on No.2 Dress.

These were replaced by Pattern 19198 sealed 5th November 1963 in gold anodised. This also was a one-piece item with the grenade in gold anodised and the eagle and crown in silver anodised (Fig.1779). Pattern 19196, also sealed 5th November 1963, is in all silver anodised for wear by Pipe Majors and Pipers, this under Authority 54/Inf/8747. A renewal Pattern 19234 was sealed 17th January 1964. Illustrated is an "hybrid", with gold grenade and eagle and only the coronet in silver (Fig.1780). Almost certainly a manufacturing error.

Also illustrated is an all silver anodised small eagle with one central fixing (Fig.1781). Usage unknown, possibly worn on mess dress by Senior NCO's.

An unofficial collar badge is a chromed plumes/harp Officers item said to have been chromed and worn by The Regimental Police in the early 1950's.

The 1881 Dress Regulations describe the Officers tunic collar badge as "A grenade in gold embroidery, with badge on ball as for buttons, but in silver" (the description for the button was "An eagle with a wreath of laurel" below the eagle a small tablet inscribed with the figure 8") "Second badge - on a blue cloth backing the monogram in silver embroidery of HRH The Princess Victoria passing through a coronet in gold embroidery. Above the monogram, the sphinx over Egypt in silver embroidery. The word "Egypt" embroidered in black silk".

The grenade was of the nine flame variety with seven flames of varying length and a further two shorter flames in front of the others.

There is a one word alteration in the 1888 Dress Regulations with "Ground" replacing "backing".

The monogram collar badge, in silver, was worn on the frock coat (Fig.1782).

On 28th December 1888, a Letter of Submission was sent for the King's signature headed "New collar badges for Officers of The Royal Irish Fusiliers". The submission was "That the collar badge formerly worn in the 89th Regiment may be approved for the Officers of The Royal Irish Fusiliers, in place of the second badge adopted on the formation of the Territorial Regiment in 1881, The Officers of The Regiment having expressed a wish to wear the former badge of the 2nd Battalion The badge now asked for was granted to the late 89th Regiment in 1866 upon the occasion of the presentation of New Colours to the Regiment by Your Majesty in place of the colours presented by Your Majesty in 1833".

Submitted with the letter was the bullion grenade as already illustrated together

Fig.1778

Fig.1779

Fig.1780

Fig.1781

Fig.1782

Fig.1783

Fig.1784

THE ROYAL IRISH FUSILIERS (PRINCESS VICTORIA'S)

with the proposed new collar badge, the coronet of HRH Princess Victoria, in silver. (Also already illustrated). The Submission was successful as confirmed in the 1891 Dress Regulations with the second badge described as "Coronet of HRH, The Princess Victoria, in silver". Repeated in the 1894 Edition and the 1900 Dress Regulations with the addition of "Worn next the hooks and eyes", after the second badge.

Confirmed in the 1902 and 1904 Dress Regulations but reversed in the 1911 Edition with the coronet listed as "First badge" and "Worn nearer to the opening of the collar" replacing "Worn next the hooks and eyes" and the grenade as "Second Badge". Repeated in the 1934 Edition.

These grenade collar badges have been worn horizontally on the various uniforms throughout, varying little from the originals with resealing taking place over the years. One such took place in July 1949 under Authority 54/Officers/4025 and annotated "Approval of the WO sealed pattern 20th April 1904" The earlier pattern had been noted "For tunic, frock and mess jacket". A later one was dated December 1962 under Authority 54/Inf/8797 marked "No.1 Dress". Upright embroidered collar badges were also worn (Fig.1783 for a seven flamed grenade). The later mess jacket collar badges were smaller (Figs.1784 and 1785).

The sealed patterns have shown the coronets too, have varied very little in design over the years, but have differed in size (Figs.1786, 1787, 1788 and 1789).

As well as the embroidered collar badges, Officers of the Regiment have also worn collar badges in metal. With a silver eagle upon the ball of a gilt grenade, the horizontal collar badge was worn from the early 1880's. With distinctive flames, the early ones had large eagles (Fig.1790). The later ones were smaller and with a wider spread of flames. Such an item appears on a sealed pattern, December 1962, under Authority 54/Inf/8797 "For No.3 Dress (Fig.1791). all worn with a separate silver coronet. This pattern is also known in bi-metal believed to have been worn by Senior NCO's.

Silver/gilt collar badges were also worn vertically. The early ones had separate crowns (Fig.1792 and 1793). The later collar badges worn on No 2 Dress had the coronet attached to the grenade (Fig.1794).

In 1902, Service Dress was introduced for Officers and the relative Dress Regulations describe the collar badge to be worn "As for forage cap, second badge in bronze". This was described as "A grenade with the harp and plume on the ball" (Fig.1795). Later, worn in one piece (Fig.1796).

The description was slightly amended in the 1911 Dress Regulations by the addition "Of the Prince of Wales" after "Plume". (for an interesting collar badge in bronze with a different coronet see Fig.1797). Confirmed in the 1934 Edition and appearing on a sealed pattern dated July 1949 under Authority 54/Offrs/4025. Also on the same sealed pattern, similar but in silver plate annotated "No.1 Dress".

The Prince of Wales Coronet, plume and motto was adopted by the 87th

Fig.1785

Fig.1786

Fig.1787

Fig.1788

Fig.1789

Fig.1793    *Fig.1792*   *Fig.1791*    *Fig.1790*

HISTORY OF THE BRITISH ARMY INFANTRY COLLAR BADGE

Fig.1794

Fig.1795

Fig.1796

Regiment of Foot when raised in 1793 and the harp was also an old badge of the 87th.

One interesting item in bronze is the eagle by itself on a tablet with the numeral '8' (Fig.1798). The angular, all feathered wings, indicate an early design and is similar to those worn by Senior NCO's of the Essex Regiment from 1898 until 1902. This could be a trial pattern, either for the Officers Service Dress introduced in 1902, or possibly the mess jacket. It has the usual two lug fitting.

Militia

Armagh Light Infantry Militia who became the 3rd Battalion, Royal Irish Fusiliers, 1st July 1881, wore as their first collar badge a shamrock over a scroll inscribed "ARMAGH LIGHT INF^{Y}". In white metal this was Pattern 6945 sealed 13th April 1875 under Authority 51/Armagh/330 "For tunic and frock collar" (Line drawing Fig.1799). These were worn until 1878 when an Order, PC/S Down Militia/195 was made on 26th March that Pattern 6945 was to be made obsolete and in future they were to wear the white-metal Bugles Pattern 8935 as then being worn by The South Gloucestershire Militia (Fig.207).

On becoming the 3rd Battalion, Royal Irish Fusiliers they adopted the collar badges as worn by that Regiment but an Officers mess jacket worn c.1900 shows a silver coronet being worn as the only collar badge. (Fig.1800).

Cavan Militia wore as their collar badge, a white-metal item described as "Harp and crown", sealed 14th September 1878 (Fig.1801). Worn by Officers in silver.

Became the 4th Battalion, The Royal Irish Fusiliers, 1st July 1881.

Monaghan Militia. Their collar badge, in white-metal, for "tunic and frock collars" was Pattern 7593, sealed 26th May 1876 under Authority PC/Monaghan Militia/135. This was a Queen Victoria Crown (Fig.1802).

On 1st July 1881, they became the 5th Battalion, Royal Irish Fusiliers.

Territorial Force and Territorial Army Battalions

The 5th (TA) Battalion was formed 1st 1st 1947 wearing the same collar badges as worn by the Regular Battalions

The 7th Battalion was formed as a Cadre in 1969 and incorporated into the 5th (Volunteer) Battalion, *The Royal Irish Rangers*, in 1971. They formed 'C' Company wearing the collar badges of the former Royal Irish Fusiliers - Officers, the coronet in silver plate worn nearest the collar opening together with the embroidered grenade with silver eagle. This on No.1 Dress with a small grenade in silver/gilt on No.3 Dress and on Service Dress similar but worn below the coronet.

Pattern 16145 was used as the guide for the soldiers anodised collar badge. This was Pattern 18793, sealed 10th August 1962 under Authority 54/Inf/8797 in gold anodised with silver anodised coronets.

Fig.1797

Fig.1798

Fig.1799

THE ROYAL IRISH FUSILIERS (PRINCESS VICTORIA'S)

Reserve Battalions
Royal Irish Fusiliers Reserve Battalion (1899-1902)
This Reserve Battalion wore as their collar badge a grenade upon which was a shamrock on the ball. In gilding-metal for other ranks with the grenade in gilt and the shamrock leaf in silver, for Officers (Line drawing Fig.1803).

10th (Local Irish) (Reserve) Battalion
Raised at Armagh 23rd September 1915 and, although wearing the Royal Irish Fusiliers cap badge, wore as a collar badge, the Royal Coat of Arms. In gilding-metal by other ranks and in bronze by Officers (Fig.1804). Disbanded in Ireland 1st June 1918.

General
The Royal Irish Fusiliers were one of only two British Regiments to wear a double collar badge, the other being The Seaforth Highlanders.

Like most other Fusilier Regiments, they did not keep to one design of flames on their grenade collar badges and they varied, both in the number of flames, and the general shape.

The eagles on the grenade also varied both in design and size with the early ones with all feathered wings whilst the later ones were partly feathered and partly lined.

On 1st July 1968, The Regiment joined with two other Ulster Regiments, The Royal Inniskilling Fusiliers and The Royal Ulster Regiment to form *The Royal Irish Rangers (27th (Inniskilling), 83rd and 87th)*.

Fig.1800

Fig.1801

Fig.1802

Fig.1803

Fig.1804

The Connaught Rangers

Fig.1805

Fig.1806

Fig.1807

Fig.1808

Fig.1809

Pre 1881
88th (Connaught Rangers) Regiment of Foot

The first other ranks collar badge of the 88th Regiment of Foot was "A crowned harp", Pattern 9623 sealed 10th January 1878. In brass, this was a wide Erin harp of nine strings voided at the sides but not between the strings, the top decorated with shamrock and the sides with scrolls, all surmounted with a QVC. Worn in FP's with the harp facing inwards towards the collar opening (Figs.1805 and 1806 for a FP). Also known in blackened brass and in silver worn by Senior NCO's.

The "Harp and Crown" was the badge of The Regiment from formation, appearing on many of its badges including the two glengarry badges worn pre 1881. It was authorised to be retained 23rd December 1830 and to be used as a collar badge 16th July 1872 under reference PC/Infy Gen/111.

When Officers removed their badges of rank from the collar in late 1880, they wore an embroidered version of the other ranks collar badge on the collar.

94th Regiment of Foot

The many Army changes in 1872 included Regimental buttons being replaced by an universal pattern and, to compensate, special Regimental badges were to be worn on the mens collars. By the same Order as mentioned for the 88th, the 94th were authorised to wear a special badge, which in their case, was the Elephant.

This was an obvious choice as "The Elephant Caparisoned" was originally authorised in 1807 to the old 94th of 1802 - 18 for service in India. This honour was also given to the later 94th on 18th March 1874.

The actual Pattern, 9609, was sealed 23rd November 1877, in brass, of a very flat manufacture and the elephant, unlike most worn by other pre 1881 Regiments of Foot, had its trunk reaching down to, and resting on, the end of a grassy ground (Figs.1807 and 1808 for a FP).

Officers of the 94th wore an embroidered version of the other ranks collar badge after they removed their rank badges from the collar in late 1880. Illustrated is an interesting elephant collar badge purported to have been removed from an Officers tunic of the 94th that had so deteriorated that it had to be destroyed. (Fig.1809). Said to be c.1859 and worn on The North West Frontier, of very flat manufacture similar to the other ranks item already described, this badge is in gilt with a pin-back fitting, probably locally made in India. Of interest, is that the animal is free-standing. Certainly the 94th were in The North West Frontier at the time and although believed to be genuine, it has not been possible to further authenticate this badge.

Post 1881

On 1st July 1881, the 88th and 94th Regiments of Foot amalgamated to become the 1st and 2nd Battalions respectively, *The Connaught Rangers* and on 21st October the elephant Pattern 9609 of the old 94th was confirmed as the collar badge for the new Regiment

However, a new collar badge was cut from new dies and sealed 20th January 1882 "To replace brass 9623 of 88th and brass 9609 of 94th". This was Pattern 9965 and a different design to the pattern previously worn by the 94th, and now in gilding-metal with copper lugs. The most noticeable difference was in the elephant's trunk which now no longer reached down to the ground but curled up towards its mouth. (Fig.1810). Marked "Collar ornament" these are clearly shown in the Gaunt pattern books.

When a new field service cap was introduced 18th February 1896, it was decided to retain the collar badge. Renewal of the standard collar badge was demanded in 1897 and authorised on 14th December to be cut from new dies. This was Pattern 9965a, sealed 6th April 1898. Of the same general design the badge was a slightly smaller, neater, item. (Fig.1811).

Both Pattern 9965 and 9965a were being worn when The Regiment was disbanded in 1922, as was Pattern 9609 by those soldiers who were originally in the old 94th and who still had them. The sealed pattern card containing pattern 9965a is annotated "Rendered obsolete 4th August 1922".

Photographs of The Regiment taken in India clearly show NCO's and other ranks wearing the gilding-metal cap badge on both sides of their Service Dress collars (Fig.1812). This is confirmed by a questionnaire returned by the 2nd Battalion just after WWI when they wrote that this practice was not carried out "At Home", but only whilst in India.

The first Dress Regulations covering the Officers collar badge for tunic collar was described as "The elephant, in silver embroidery, on a ground of gold embroidery. Caparison in blue velvet edged with gold. Gold girths". A most attractive item. (Fig.1813). Worn until 1894.

These were then replaced by metal collar badges described quite simply in the 1900 Dress Regulations for tunic and scarlet frock as "The Elephant, in silver" (Fig.1814). Repeated in the 1902 Dress Regulations which adds "On mess jacket collar - the Harp and Crown in gold embroidery" (Fig.1815).

Also included, is the description for the newly introduced Service Dress, "The Harp and Crown; below the Harp a scroll inscribed 'Connaught Rangers', in bronze and in pairs" (Fig.1816). Repeated in the 1904 Edition and with the slight addition of "Strings in silver" after "Gold embroidery", in respect of the mess jacket collar, in the 1911 Edition.

The crowned harp and scroll collar badge was also worn on khaki drill, often in a polished form.

Dress Regulations give only "Elephant in silver" as a description for the collar badge worn after the one in bullion but illustrations show the animal without any trappings as shown in Fig.1814.

It might have been expected that the elephant would have had a caparison on its back as required for the badge in embroidery. Certainly such an item exists, the elephant, caparison, and girth straps all in silver (Fig.1817). There is also a version in white-metal, also said to have been worn by Officers (Fig.1818).

An elephant without trappings in white-metal is said to have been worn by Band/Pipers but there is no evidence to support this and it is more likely to have been worn by The Seaforth Highlanders who wore similar elephant collar badges. (Fig.1819).

Another collar badge said to have been at some time worn on Service Dress by Officers of the Connaught Rangers is an elephant in bronze, similar to Fig.1680. Although of the same design as worn by The Regiment, with trunk reaching down to the ground, this again, is more likely to have been a Seaforth's item.

Although not mentioned in Dress Regulations, Official sources record a metal crowned (K/C) harp to have been worn on "White mess jacket 1907 - 14".

Fig.1810

Fig.1811

Fig.1812

Fig.1813

Fig.1814

HISTORY OF THE BRITISH ARMY INFANTRY COLLAR BADGE

Militia
South Mayo Rifles Militia
It is possible that this Regiment wore as their collar badge, pre 1881, a white-metal ribboned bugle similar to the one that appears in their 1878 helmet plate and also in the centre of their Officers pouch belt badge (Fig.251).

On 1st July 1881, they became the 3rd Battalion, The Connaught Rangers.

Galway Militia
The collar badge for other ranks tunic and frock was sealed 22nd August 1878. In white-metal, this was "The Harp and Crown" (Fig.1820). Also worn by Officers, but in silver.

On 1st July 1881, they became the 4th Battalion, The Connaught Rangers.

Roscommon Militia
Other ranks collar badges "For tunic and frock" were sealed 9th February 1877 under Authority 51/RM/367. In white-metal, this was Pattern 8924. Described as "Harp and Wreath", this was an "Angel harp" within a wreath of shamrock (Figs.1821 and 1822 for a FP). Also known in gilding-metal and although unconfirmed, possibly worn after they became the 5th Battalion, The Connaught Rangers on 1st July 1881. Worn in FP's with the harp facing inwards towards the collar opening.

North Mayo Fusiliers Militia
This Regiment probably wore as their collar badge a crowned Irish "Angel harp" in white-metal (Fig.253).

On 1st July 1881, they became the 6th Battalion, The Connaught Rangers.

General
As the early Dress Regulations correctly describe The Regiments Indian Elephant "with caparison", it is surprising that so many of the collar badges are of elephants without anything on their backs.

All elephant collar badges face both ways with the animal facing inwards towards the collar opening. There are many variations, both in overall size, and size of both ears and trunk. Also voiding and non voiding between the tail and the body.

An Army Order dated 11th March 1922 contained the following extract - "HM The King has approved with great regret the disbandment, as soon as the exigencies of the Service permit, of the following Corps and Battalions of the Infantry of the Line - The Connaught Rangers, comprising 1st, 2nd, 3rd (Militia) and 4th (Militia) Battalions and Depot".

The Regiment was officially disbanded 31st July 1922.

Fig.1815

Fig.1816

Fig.1817

Fig.1818

Fig.1819

Fig.1820

Fig.1821

Fig.1822

290

The Argyll and Sutherland Highlanders (Princess Louise's)

Pre 1881
91st (Princess Louise's Argyllshire Highlanders) Regiment of Foot

Authorised under General Order PC/Infy Gen/111 dated 16th July 1872, the collar badge for other ranks of the 91st Regiment of Foot was Pattern 9508, sealed 19th September 1874, "For tunic and frock collar". In brass, this was a large boar's head, made to face both ways and worn with the head facing inwards towards the collar opening (Figs.1823 and 1824 for a FP).

There are many photographs of them being worn including soldiers taking part in the Zulu War in 1879 where they can be seen being worn on the pale yellow collars of the scarlet undress pattern tunic (see photograph 25 of a boy soldier at Belfast in 1877 wearing a FP of these boar's head collar badges on his tunic collar). WO's wore a smaller boar's head collar badge in gilt (Fig.1825).

Officers, after removing their badges of rank from their collars in late 1880, wore an embroidered version. All worn until 1883.

In 1871, the 91st provided the Guard of Honour at the marriage ceremony of the Marquis of Lorne, heir to the Duke of Argyll to Queen Victoria's daughter Princess Louise, who became the Regiment's Colonel in Chief. In honour of the occasion, The Regiment became Princess Louise's Argyllshire Highlanders and were authorised on 14th March 1872 to take the crest and motto of the Argyll family as their own badge, part of which was the boar's head.

93rd (Sutherland Highlanders) Regiment of Foot

By the same General Order as mentioned under the 91st Regiment of Foot, dated 16th July 1872, Regiments with no special devices were authorised to wear a crown as their collar badge. In brass, this was the Imperial crown, Pattern 9386, sealed 30th June 1874 (Fig.333). Worn until 1883.

When Officers removed their rank badges from the collar in late 1880, they are said to have then worn "A thistle device". Illustrated is such a pair in gilt (Figs.1826 and 1827). They do not face. Similar in embroidery is known to have been worn on the epaulette and a watercolour, now at the Scottish United Services Museum, shows a similar badge being worn on the sporran by a Bandsman of the 93rd, c.1854. A similar item on a sealed pattern card is headed "Lieutenant of Scottish Counties".

Post 1881

On 1st July 1881, the 91st and 93rd Regiments of Foot amalgamated to become the 1st and 2nd Battalions respectively, Princess Louise's (Sutherland and Argyll Highlanders) a title quickly changed to Princess Louise's (Argyll and Sutherland Highlanders) and redesignated 1st January 1921 as The Argyll and Sutherland Highlanders (Princess Louise's).

The former 91st and 93rd, continued to wear their own collar badges until 1883 when, on 28th February, a new collar badge was sealed in white-metal. This was Pattern 10287, "To replace brass 9508 of 91st (93rd wore the crown)".

The design was of a wreath of myrtle intertwined with a wreath of Butcher's Broom. Within the myrtle wreath, a boar's head on a scroll inscribed "NE OBLIVISCARIS" (Dinna forget) and within the broom wreath, a mountain cat on a scroll inscribed "SANS PEUR" (Without fear). Above the boar and the cat, a label

Fig.1823

Fig.1824

Fig.1825

Fig.1826

Fig.1827

Fig.1828

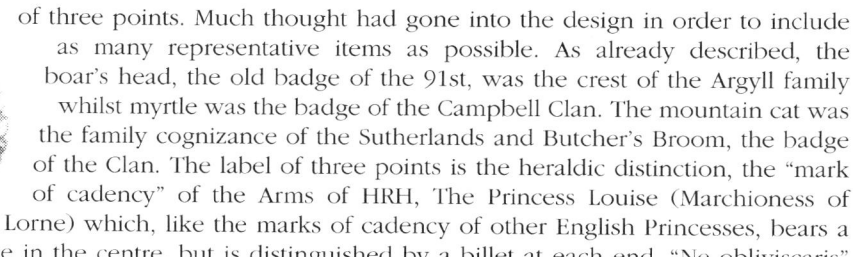

Fig.1829

Fig.1830

Fig.1831

Fig.1832

of three points. Much thought had gone into the design in order to include as many representative items as possible. As already described, the boar's head, the old badge of the 91st, was the crest of the Argyll family whilst myrtle was the badge of the Campbell Clan. The mountain cat was the family cognizance of the Sutherlands and Butcher's Broom, the badge of the Clan. The label of three points is the heraldic distinction, the "mark of cadency" of the Arms of HRH, The Princess Louise (Marchioness of Lorne) which, like the marks of cadency of other English Princesses, bears a rose in the centre, but is distinguished by a billet at each end. "Ne obliviscaris" is the motto of the Argyll family and "Sans Peur", the motto of the Sutherland family.

Between the formation of the new Regiment in July 1881 and the final finished article sealed in February 1883, there had been many proposed sketches and amended drawings sent to and from the principal clerk and the contractors, Bent & Parker. The latter, in 1882, pointed out that with the intended design at that time, the boar's head was likely to be broken if not carried up to the top. Yet another amended drawing was submitted by the manufacturers which was finally approved by Col Blundell, AAG Horse Guards, and returned to the manufacturers 19th December 1882.

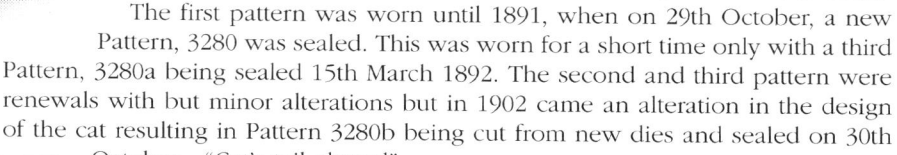

The first pattern was worn until 1891, when on 29th October, a new Pattern, 3280 was sealed. This was worn for a short time only with a third Pattern, 3280a being sealed 15th March 1892. The second and third pattern were renewals with but minor alterations but in 1902 came an alteration in the design of the cat resulting in Pattern 3280b being cut from new dies and sealed on 30th October - "Cat's tail altered".

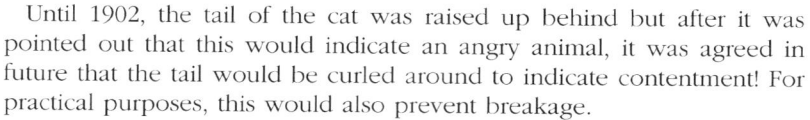

Until 1902, the tail of the cat was raised up behind but after it was pointed out that this would indicate an angry animal, it was agreed in future that the tail would be curled around to indicate contentment! For practical purposes, this would also prevent breakage.

This fourth pattern was worn until 1913, when on 20th December, an amended design, Pattern 7957, was sealed under Authority 20/Infy/416. Resealed 16th October 1956 and worn until 1963 when this pattern was used as the guide for the anodised version.

Over some eighty years of the same General design there are certain to be variations and one could almost make a separate study of all the many differences that are to be found. Quite apart from the differences in the overall badge there are numerous differences in the animals themselves, especially with the cat. There are fat and lean cats, some looking forward, others facing to the side, tails up (pre 1902), tails down (post 1902) some with short back legs whilst others reach out and touch the scroll. There is also both voiding and non voiding between the tail and the scroll and between the front paws. Some cats are attached to both ends of the scroll, others at one end only. There are fewer differences with the boar's head although both the size and the design vary. The mouth is sometimes solid, sometimes partly voided.

With both the cat and the boar there are many variations as to where their ears attach to the label itself or to the billet at the end. Sometimes the attachment is by one ear, in others by both ears and there is also both voiding and non voiding between the ears and the label/billet. (Figs.1828 and 1829 for different sized pre 1902 with cat's tail up, and for post 1902 with cat's tail down, Fig.1830 for fat cat looking sideways and Fig 1831 for fat cat looking forwards. Figs.1832 and 1833 both have the thin cat, the first being of a distinctive grey colour and the second being the last pattern with a single lug fitting.).

From these illustrations can also be seen the variations in attachment of the boar's head to the label, in Fig.1831 both ears attached to the middle, whereas in Fig.1830 one ear only attaches to the billet at the end.

The white-metal collar badges were worn until 1963 and beyond but on 19th February a silver anodised version, Pattern 18947, was sealed under Authority 54/Inf/8800 "To supercede Pattern 7957". As with that pattern used as

THE ARGYLL AND SUTHERLAND HIGHLANDERS (PRINCESS LOUISE'S)

a guide this version had a thin cat with tail down and the boar's mouth open (Fig.1834). A variation has the boar's mouth in solid form (Fig.1835).

The silver anodised collar badge was also worn by *277 Regiment, RA*.

The other ranks collar badge is also known in an attractive yellow gilding-metal said by some to have been a WWI economy issue (Fig.1836). By the position of the cat's tail it can be dated post 1902 so could be an economy issue but with the scarcity of these items, unlikely. Possibly worn by Senior NCO's. Also known in chrome believed to have been worn during the mid 1950's.

Early Dress Regulations describe the Officers tunic collar badge as "In frosted silver, a myrtle wreath interlaced with a wreath of butcher's broom. In gilt metal, within the myrtle wreath, the Boar's head on scroll inscribed Ne Obliviscaris' within the wreath of butcher's broom, the Cat on scroll inscribed Sans Peur. A label of three points in silver above the Boar's head and the Cat".

Later Editions added "or gilding metal" after "in gilt metal" and the 1902 and 1904 Dress Regulations also confirmed this collar badge for wear on the frockcoat adding "on the mess jacket - no badge". Repeated in 1911 and 1934 Dress Regulations "On collar of doublet" with no mention of mess dress. The 1973 and 1986 Dress Regulations have slightly different format with the description followed by "Boar's head and motto and Cat in gilt, remainder silver plate" and including "The boar's head nearest the opening of the collar".

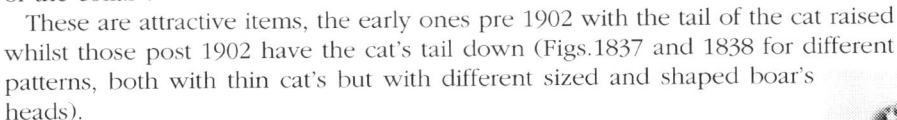

These are attractive items, the early ones pre 1902 with the tail of the cat raised whilst those post 1902 have the cat's tail down (Figs.1837 and 1838 for different patterns, both with thin cat's but with different sized and shaped boar's heads).

It is interesting that Pattern 30480, sealed 12th April 1983, whilst showing a FP of silver/gilt collar badges, has a different design of the boar's head on each item!

Luckily, there are many photographs of Officers wearing these collar badges over the years on the appropriate uniforms and in those taken at the turn of the Century, they can clearly be seen being worn on the yellow collars of the scarlet full dress doublet.

It is also interesting to note that, although only Commissioned Officers wore the full dress doublet, the privilege not extending to Sergeant Majors, the latter were still allowed to wear the silver and gilt collar badges as worn by their Officers.

When Service Dress was introduced in 1902, the relative Dress Regulations directed the collar badge to be "In bronze, as for doublet, with scroll and for waist-plate". This was a three part scroll inscribed "ARGYLL AND - SUTHERLAND - HIGHLANDERS". (Figs.1839 and 1840 which has the wreaths open at the top and Fig.1841 for three variations, all with the cat's tail up).

The description was repeated in the 1904, 1911 and 1934 Dress Regulations. However, unofficially, a bronze version of the other ranks collar badge was also being worn on the Service Dress. There appears to be no record of when this badge was first introduced, perhaps not surprising as

Fig.1833

Fig.1834

Fig.1835

Fig.1836

Fig.1838

Fig.1837

HISTORY OF THE BRITISH ARMY INFANTRY COLLAR BADGE

it was unofficial. The Regimental museum believe it was worn after WWI but photographs show they were certainly being worn before then. A photograph of Capt. Arthur Henderson VC, MC clearly shows him wearing the bronze version without scroll and he was killed 24th April 1917 in an action that resulted his being awarded a posthumous Victoria Cross (photograph 26).

The 1973 and 1986 Dress Regulations confirm the previous description and add "For No.2 Dress". All the variations already mentioned for the other ranks white-metal collar badges are found with the bronze collar badges with the addition of one with completely rounded wreaths ie no leaves protruding at all.

Even the sealed patterns differ as can be seen from Pattern 30161 sealed 9th June 1878. Although each of the FP has the cat with tail down, as one would expect for that date, one collar badge has a fat cat whilst the other one, a thin cat. The boars' heads differ in size and the places of attachment to the label are different. Even the number of leaves differ!

For variations see (Figs.1842, 1843 with rounded wreath with no protruding leaves, Fig.1844 for cat's tail up and 1845, 1846 and 1847 for cat's tail down.)

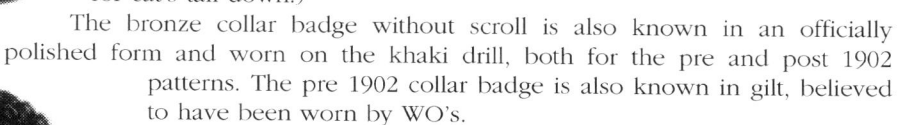

The bronze collar badge without scroll is also known in an officially polished form and worn on the khaki drill, both for the pre and post 1902 patterns. The pre 1902 collar badge is also known in gilt, believed to have been worn by WO's.

Militia

The Highland Borderers Light Infantry Militia and The Prince of Wales's Royal Regiment of Renfrew Militia became the 3rd and 4th Battalions respectively, Princess Louise's (Sutherland and Argyll Highlanders), 1st July 1881.

There is nothing recorded in the Army Clothing Department pattern room journals pre 1881 in respect of collar badges for The POW's Royal Regiment of Renfrew Militia and there is no evidence that any were worn.

However, The Highland Borderers Light Infantry Militia did wear collar badges, a bugle horn with the numerals "90" in the curl (Fig.1848). in white-metal by other ranks and in silver by Officers.

Fig.1839

Fig.1840

Fig.1841

Fig.1842

Fig.1843

Fig.1845

Fig.1846

Fig.1844

Fig.1847

Fig.1848

THE ARGYLL AND SUTHERLAND HIGHLANDERS (PRINCESS LOUISE'S)

Rifle Volunteer Corps, Volunteer, Territorial Force & Territorial Army Battalions

The 1st, 2nd and 3rd Renfrewshire RVC became VB's of Princess Louise's (Sutherland and Argyll Highlanders), 1st July 1881 redesignated as the 1st, 2nd and 3rd (Renfrewshire) VB's respectively, 1st December 1887, initially wearing their scarlet, yellow faced doublets and wearing on their collars, the same collar badges as worn by the Regular Battalions

Similarly, the *1st Stirlingshire RVC* and the *1st Argyllshire RVC* also eventually became the 4th (Stirlingshire) and 5th VB's, both wearing the same collar badges as the Line Battalions

The exception, regarding collar badges, was the *1st Dumbartonshire RVC* who became the 6th VB 1st July 1881 and redesignated as the *1st Dumbartonshire VRC* in December 1891.

They wore their own distinctive collar badge, a laurel wreath in the voided centre of which was an elephant with a decorated saddle cloth, girth strap and on its back a howdah in the shape of a castle and above which, a scroll inscribed "FORTITUDO ET FIDELITAS" (Strength and trust). The elephant stands with all four feet on a grassy ground. In white-metal as worn by other ranks (Fig.1849) and in silver, often with a pin-back fitting and in silver/gilt for Officers (Fig.1850). The wreath and grassy ground in silver and the elephant, castle and scroll in gilt with the castle and elephant of a different design than those in white-metal.

Mess waiters wore a small elephant with castle on its back and standing on a torse (Fig.1851). This was in gilding-metal. Officers wore similar, but in silver, on their mess jackets.

The collar badges for the other VB's were submitted for approval by Marshall & Sons, accoutrement makers to The Argyll and Sutherland Highlanders Regiment The pattern card shows the usual badges in white-metal marked "Right and left collar ornaments as shown" and approved by Horse Guards, War Office, 19th April 1888, under Authority V/3 Renfrew/173.

These are collar badges in all silver and are said to have been worn by some Volunteer Officers, both the early pattern with cat's tail up and the later pattern with the cat's tail down.

In the main though, the VB's did wear the same collar badges as the Line Battalions as they did when, in 1908, they became Battalions of the TF. However, there are photographs of Officers wearing a separate bronze "T" below the usual bronze collar badges on their Service Dress jackets. This particularly applied to the 7th Battalion (TA).

Pattern cards for the 7th and 8th Battalions (TA) show the usual collar badges in silver/gilt "For No.1 and No.3 Dress" and in bronze "for No.2 Dress", dated 21st December 1956 under Authority 54/Inf/8800 and in pencil "re-sealed 28th November 61".

Clackmannanshire and Kinross RVC, before becoming a VB, and by General Order 181, were redesignated as 7th (Clackmannan and Kinross) VB, 1st December 1887, wore as their collar badge an item very similar to their Pipers plaid brooch, in white-metal worn 1874 - 87.

In white-metal for other ranks this was St. Andrew standing in front of a cross, all within a wreath, one half of thistles the other of sugar cane (Fig.1852 for voided item with a scarlet cloth backing). There is also a silver version as worn by Officers.

Other Badges

One item sometimes thought to be a collar badge is the small white-metal sporran badge, one of which is Pattern 14073 sealed 26th April 1949. This has the boar's head and wild cat between the cypher of Princess Louise, reversed and interlaced and on to of which is her coronet (Fig.1853). Another item, similar, but with a K/C and often with a pin-back fitting and in silver is a Regimental Brooch (Fig.1854).

Fig.1849

Fig.1850

Fig.1851

Fig.1852

Fig.1853

Fig.1854

General

The boar's head and mountain cat collar badges of The Argyll and Sutherland Highlanders probably have more variations than any other in the British Army. Besides those variations already mentioned, the wreaths also vary. Whilst most are rounded some are oval and although the majority have their leaves protruding irregularly, a few have a smooth rounded shape. Some wreaths are circular whilst others are open at the top. Even the leaves vary in design, the number on each side and how they are placed.

All these, of course, have no real significance, merely being the manufacturers idea of how they should be. However, one item is a mistake - this collar badge has the "Sans Peur" scroll beneath the boar's head instead of the cat's

Some Officers collar badges have the animals standing out "Proud" from the remainder of the badge.

In all cases, the collar badges are worn in FP's with the animals facing inwards towards the collar opening.

During WWI, collar badges were also worn attached to a blue background and worn on the turned-up brim of the slouch hat.

No.1 Dress was first worn by all Regiments at the Coronation of the Queen on 2nd June 1953 but The Argyll and Sutherland Highlanders were the first Battalion to appear complete in No.1 Dress when the 1st Battalion were presented with new colours on 26th June.

The Prince of Wales's Leinster Regiment (Royal Canadians)

Pre 1881
100th (Prince of Wales's Royal Canadian) Regiment of Foot
The collar badge for other ranks of the 100th Regiment of Foot was Pattern 9313, sealed 11th August 1873 and worn on tunic and frock collars until 1882.

This was the Prince of Wales's plume of feathers, coronet and scrolls in white-metal over a wreath of maple leaves, in brass. The wreath is of quite a distinctive shape and the space between the wreath and the plumes is voided (Fig.1855).

The Prince of Wales's coronet, plumes and motto was the badge of the old 100th Regiment that had been disbanded in 1818 and awarded to the later 100th Regiment in 1860. The maple leaf is emblematic of Canada where the Regiment was raised and an expression of their loyalty at the time of the Indian Mutiny.

109th (Bombay Infantry) Regiment of Foot
The other ranks collar badge for the 109th Regiment of Foot was the brass universal pattern crown, Pattern 9386 and sealed 30th June 1874 (Fig.333). This had been authorised under Order PC/Infy Gen/111 dated 16th July 1872, when it was directed that Corps with no special device would wear a crown as their collar badge on their tunic collars. Worn until 1882.

Post 1881
On 1st July 1881, *The Prince of Wales's Leinster Regiment (Royal Canadians)* was formed from the amalgamation of the 100th and 109th Regiments of Foot who became the 1st and 2nd Battalions respectively.

The new collar badge for other ranks was the POW's plumes, coronet and scrolls of the old 100th but now without the maple leaf wreath. The design was different and chosen from a selection submitted by Smith & Wright and revised by Col. Blundell, AAG Horse Guards. His final selection was made on 22nd December 1881 when it was decided the new badge should be "In a combination of white-metal and gilding-metal".

The resulting pattern was 9981 sealed 20th January 1882 "To replace Pattern 9313 of 100th (109th wore a crown)". This was the same pattern as chosen for The Prince of Wales's own (West Yorkshire Regiment) (Fig.1856). Renewal of the standard pattern was demanded 9th February 1898 and these were duly cut from new dies and sealed 3rd August 1899, being Pattern 9981a "In lieu of patt 9891". there was no change in design. These were worn up to disbandment in 1922, the sealed pattern being marked "Obsolete AO/78/1922".

One different design of collar badge, actually taken from an old uniform, is larger than the ones on the sealed pattern (Fig.1857). Period and usage unknown.

Early Dress Regulations describe the Officers collar badge for tunic collars "The Prince of Wales's plume, in silver; the Coronet in gilt metal" (Fig.1858). Repeated in subsequent Editions with "Or gilding metal" being added after "Gilt metal" in the 1900 and 1902 Dress Regulations and the addition of "For mess jacket and frockcoat" in the 1904 and 1911 Editions. The design is similar to those worn by The West Yorkshire Regiment which is perhaps not surprising as other ranks of both Regiments wore the same collar badge.

In 1902, Service Dress for Officers was introduced with the collar badge being "As for forage cap", but in bronze. This was the usual POW's plume, coronet and motto above a scroll inscribed "THE LEINSTER". The shape of the motto scrolls

HISTORY OF THE BRITISH ARMY INFANTRY COLLAR BADGE

are unusual and distinctive (Fig.1859).

Some badges of The Regiment had the more usual shaped motto scrolls and those in bullion are more in keeping with those worn by The Welsh Regiment (Fig.1860). Such an item can clearly be seen on Officers full dress uniform collars c.1900. The plumes are separate and similar in design to those worn as a head-dress badge.

Fig.1859

Militia

The King's County Royal Rifles Militia who became the 3rd Battalion, The POW's Leinster Regiment (Royal Canadians), 1st July 1881 are said to have worn as their collar badge pre 1881, a FP of corded bugles with the numeral '98' in the curl, similar to their Glengarry badge. In brass for other ranks and possibly in silver for Officers. unconfirmed and, for a Rifle Regiment, doubtful.

The Royal Queen's County Rifles Militia and *The Royal Meath Militia* became the Regiments 4th and 5th Battalions respectively 1st July 1881 but there is no record in the Army Clothing Room pattern room journals that either wore collar badges.

General

The collar badges of the Regiment did not face. Like the other Irish Regiments recruited in the South, The Regiment was disbanded 31st July 1922.

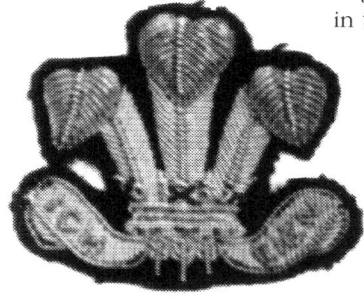

Fig.1860

The Royal Munster Fusiliers

Pre 1881
101st (Royal Bengal Fusiliers) Regiment of Foot

An extract from file PC/Infy Gen/111 dated 16th July 1872, "Badges for collars of tunics Infy" directed that Regiments with special badges should wear their special badges on their collars. Fusiliers in like manner - grenades".

As directed, the 101st adopted the grenade collar badge, this being Pattern 9281, in brass and sealed 2nd October 1872 (Fig.122). At the time of sealing, it was decreed that Fusilier Regiments were permitted to wear embroidered grenades (Pattern 9284, sealed 18th October 1872), "Provided no expense is incurred by the public". The Order was signed by Col. Arthur Herbert, AAG Horse Guards, War Office.

An extract from file PC/Indian Regiments/627 dated 17th March 1874 relating to Indian Regiments is recorded as "Regiments which have anything on the old button besides the Crown are to be considered as entitled to a collar badge (special)".

However, it was not until 1878, that the 101st introduced their own "special" collar badge. This was a brass grenade with plain ball and seven distinctive flames (Figs.1861 and 1862 for a FP). Sealed on 23rd May, the pattern number is not recorded in the pattern room journals but it is between 9637 and 9654. They were worn in FP's with the ball nearer the collar opening. Senior NCO's wore similar but in silver.

In 1874, Dress Regulations directed Fusilier Officers to wear a grenade emblem in gold at the end of the collar of their tunics, in front of their badges of rank (Figs.1863 and 1864 for nine flame embroidered grenade as seen on the collar of an Officer of the 101st c.1875).

104th (Bengal Fusiliers) Regiment of Foot

Under the same Order as mentioned for the 101st Regiment of Foot, the 104th wore as their other ranks collar badge the same brass grenade, Pattern 9281 (fig 122). There is nothing to indicate that any other collar badge was worn prior to the 1881 amalgamations.

Officers wore embroidered grenades in front of their rank badges, from 1874.

Post 1881

The Royal Munster Fusiliers were formed 1st July 1881 by the amalgamation of the 101st and 104th Regiments of Foot who became the 1st and 2nd Battalions respectively, of the new Regiment

The collar badge for the new Regiment was obviously going to feature the grenade but, to be different from other Fusilier Regiments, it was decided that on the ball of the grenade would be the Royal Tiger, this having been awarded the old 101st to commemorate their long service in India.

Drawings were prepared, submitted and approved and a trial pattern made (Fig.1865). All in gilding-metal, with a wide spread of flames and with the tiger facing sideways and with tail curving downwards between its back legs and with all four feet on a grassy ground.

However, on 12th December 1881, a Directive was issued which said "RMF - collar ornament - to be a plain grenade (ie Tiger ornament, which is incorrect, is to be removed)" The Regiment thereupon wore a similar plain grenade as

Fig.1861

Fig.1862

Fig.1863

Fig.1864

Fig.1865

HISTORY OF THE BRITISH ARMY INFANTRY COLLAR BADGE

previously worn by the old 104th but in gilding-metal instead of brass (Fig.1866). This was Pattern 9933, sealed 11th January 1882, "In lieu of previous Pattern 9281". This standard grenade pattern was renewed and cut from new dies in 1897 when on 7th December, Pattern 9933a was sealed. No.change in design, merely being a renewal and these were worn until disbandment in 1922.

On 14th February 1905, all Fusilier Regiments were directed to wear Pattern 9933a with their metal titles on the shoulder straps of drab jackets and greatcoats.

Early Dress Regulations describe the collar badge for Officers tunic collars as "A grenade in gold embroidery, with the Royal Tiger, in silver on the ball" (Fig.1867). The 1900 Dress Regulations mentions a metal collar badge for the scarlet frock and this was an upright grenade in gilt with the same design of tiger as described for the other ranks trial pattern, but in silver, on the ball of the grenade (Figs.1868 and 1869 for two variations).

A larger horizontal grenade in silver/gilt was also worn on the undress uniform (Fig.1870). A smaller version of the same design is also known. An upright embroidered grenade with silver tiger was worn on the mess jacket (Figs. 1871 and 1872 for two variations.)

In 1902, Service Dress was introduced for Officers with Dress Regulations describing the collar badge "As for forage cap, but in pairs, in bronze". This was "A grenade. On the ball, the Tiger and scroll inscribed 'Royal Munster'". (Fig 1873). Other bronze collar badges are known, smaller than the cap/collar and without the scroll (Fig.1874).

Militia

Clare Militia was designated to become the 3rd Battalion, The Royal Munster Fusiliers, 1st July 1881 but on 26th April 1882 was converted to the 7th Brigade, South Irish Division, RA.

Their collar badge was sealed 21st September 1876. In white-metal for other ranks tunic and frock collars this was an harp/maid surmounted by a crown and with a two part scroll either side of the central part of the item, inscribed "CLARE - MILITIA". (Line drawing Fig.1875).

The Regiment that did become the 3rd Battalion, R.M.F., 1st July 1881 was *The South Cork Light Infantry Militia*. There is no evidence that collar badges were worn.

The Kerry Militia became the 4th Battalion R.M.F. 1st July 1881. Their collar badge was Pattern 7577, sealed 6th April 1876, under Authority 51/Kerry/422. In white-metal for other ranks this was a harp/maid within a garter strap inscribed "KERRY REGIMENT", surmounted by a QVC, the whole upon a sprig of shamrock (Line drawing Fig.1876).

The 5th Battalion was provided from *The Royal Limerick County Militia (Fusiliers)* who joined The R.M.F. 1st July 1881. As a collar badge they are said to have worn what is virtually the centre of their Glengarry badge, a multi flamed grenade with a crowned harp/maid on the ball. In white-metal (Line drawing Fig.1877).

Fig.1866

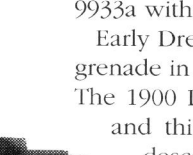

Fig.1867

Fig.1868

Fig.1869

Fig.1870

Fig.1871

Fig.1872

Fig.1873

Fig.1874

THE ROYAL MUNSTER FUSILIERS

General

The Royal Munster Fusiliers was one of many other Fusilier Regiments that appear to have been unable to agree on how many flames there should be on their grenade collar badges. Examples are known with seven, eight and nine flames and the difference did not stop there as the shape of the flames also varied from the standard Fusilier arrangement to one of a wide rounded design.

They were also unable to agree on the tiger. On some collar badges the animal appears with tail across its body (as in the OSD bronze cap/collar), but in most badges it appears as a cowed animal, with tail between its legs.

The Regiments collar badges were worn in FP's with the tiger facing inwards towards the collar opening.

The Royal Munster Fusiliers were disbanded 31st July 1922.

Fig.1875

Fig.1876

Fig.1877

The Royal Dublin Fusiliers

Fig.1878

Fig.1879

Fig.1880

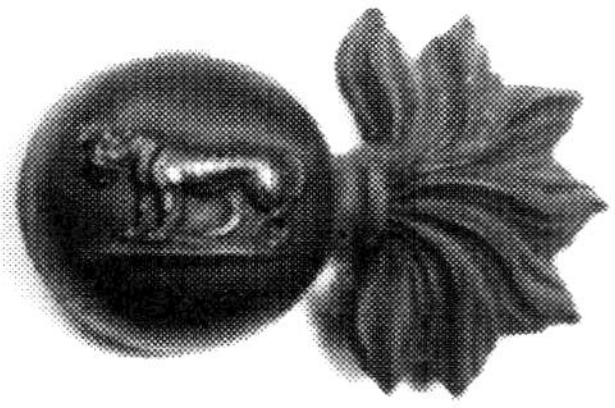

Fig.1881

Pre 1881
102nd (Royal Madras Fusiliers) Regiment of Foot

Fusilier Regiments were authorised to wear a brass grenade as a collar badge under an Order dated 16th July 1872 under reference PC/Infy Gen/111, this to be Pattern 9281, sealed 2nd October 1872. At the time of sealing it was decreed that Fusilier Regiments were permitted to wear embroidered grenades "Provided no expense is incurred by the public".

It is assumed that this universal brass grenade was adopted and worn by the Regiment, but there is no mention of them doing so in Official records. In fact, there is no mention at all of the 102nd wearing any collar badge pre 1881 in the journals of the Army Clothing Department pattern room. The first reference comes in March 1882 when, recording the collar badge for the new amalgamated Regiments, the entry under The Royal Dublin Fusiliers is recorded as "Deposited for brass grenade 9748 for the 103rd (102nd wore the crown)".

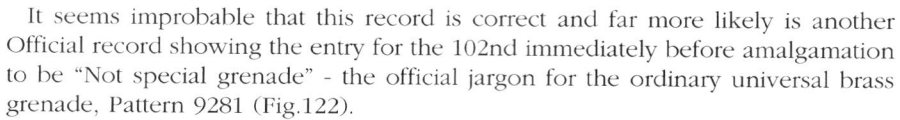

It seems improbable that this record is correct and far more likely is another Official record showing the entry for the 102nd immediately before amalgamation to be "Not special grenade" - the official jargon for the ordinary universal brass grenade, Pattern 9281 (Fig.122).

Over the years some collectors have catalogued two items said to have been worn pre 1881 by the 102nd. Both are illustrated, the first a long bodied tiger, in brass, similar to the one worn by the 75th Regiment of Foot, but on a grassy ground (Figs.1878 and 1879 for a FP). The second, said by some to have been worn after this badge and by others to have been worn before, is a brass grenade with a tiger on the ball. Two variations are known, the second having a different spread of flames with a central flame quite pointed (Figs.1880 and 1881).

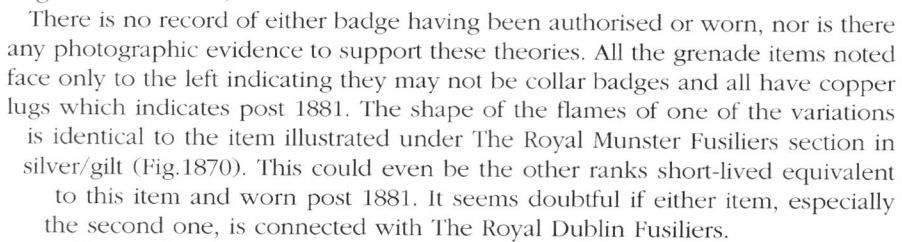

There is no record of either badge having been authorised or worn, nor is there any photographic evidence to support these theories. All the grenade items noted face only to the left indicating they may not be collar badges and all have copper lugs which indicates post 1881. The shape of the flames of one of the variations is identical to the item illustrated under The Royal Munster Fusiliers section in silver/gilt (Fig.1870). This could even be the other ranks short-lived equivalent to this item and worn post 1881. It seems doubtful if either item, especially the second one, is connected with The Royal Dublin Fusiliers.

Officers of the 102nd wore embroidered grenades at the end of their tunic collars in front of their badges of rank.

103rd (Royal Bombay Fusiliers) Regiment of Foot

Authorised to wear the grenade as a collar badge by the same Order 16th July 1872 as mentioned for the 102nd Regiment of Foot, the 103rd are recorded as wearing this brass grenade, Pattern 9281, sealed on 2nd October of the same year (Fig.122).

At the time of sealing, it was also directed that embroidered grenade collar badges, Pattern 9284, could also be worn providing no public expense was incurred. It is recorded that a white worsted grenade had been worn on the collar by other ranks of the 103rd from 1862 - 69. Officers wore their embroidered grenades at the end of their tunic collars in front of their badges of rank.

Other ranks wore their brass collar badge until 1880 when the Regiment introduced their own special collar badge. This was Pattern 9748 sealed on 26th November, "In lieu of Pattern 9281". In brass, this was a multi flame horizontal grenade with, on the ball, a tiger with tail between its back legs and standing on a grassy ground above a free standing elephant with a curved, partly lined, caparison on its back, all within a circle inscribed "ROYAL BOMBAY FUSILIERS" (Line drawing Fig.1882). The sealed pattern is annotated "1st Class Staff Sgts to be in gilt". These were worn until 1882 in FP's with the animals, which both face in the same direction, facing inwards towards the collar opening.

Fig.1882

Post 1881

The Royal Dublin Fusiliers were formed 1st July 1881 by the amalgamation of the 102nd and 103rd Regiments of Foot who became the 1st and 2nd Battalions respectively.

The Elephant was awarded to the 103rd, 6th November 1844, to commemorate their loyal service in India especially in Campaigns in the Carnatic and Mysore. The Royal Tiger commemorates the long and distinguished service of the 102nd in India, especially for its part in the capture of Nundy Droog in 1791. Conferred on the Regiment 6th November 1844.

With both former Regiments having been Fusiliers, it came as no surprise that the new Regiments first collar badge was a grenade with both animals featured on the ball of the grenade, one above the other. Perhaps the only surprise was that, unlike the Officers collar badges, the Royal Tiger of the 102nd featured below the Elephant of the 103rd.

In brass, this was Pattern 10136 sealed 8th March 1882 with a renewal of the standard pattern demanded 9th February 1898, these being cut from new dies with the resulting Pattern, 10136a sealed 3rd August 1899. No change in design and worn until disbandment in 1922, the sealed pattern marked "Obsolete 4th August 1922".

Fig.1883

Fig.1884

Both animals were standing on a grassy ground, the elephant with all its feet, the tiger with three and one front paw raised and pointing downwards. The elephant had its trunk raised upwards and faced to the front while the tiger faced sideways and with tail curving over its back with the tuft slightly curled towards the rear. There were minor variations both in the size and shape of the animals and in such details as the elephants tail, sometimes close to the body, other times trailing out behind (Figs.1883, 1884 and 1885 for variations). These were worn in FP's with the elephant facing inwards towards the collar opening which meant that the tiger, who in the other ranks collar badges always faced in the opposite way to the elephant, faced outwards.

Fig.1885

On 14th July 1893, an Order PC/Gen No./1639 decreed that collar badges (left side) were to be worn upon the field service cap by Infantry but an exception was made with The Royal Dublin Fusiliers, theirs to be "The R.A. grenade". On 14th February 1905 all Fusilier Regiments were directed to wear the R.A. collar grenade (Pattern 9933a sealed 7th December 1897) with their metal titles on the shoulder straps of drab jackets and greatcoats.

For a while, other ranks of the 1st Battalion unofficially wore plain grenade collar badges as a protest for their tiger being placed below the elephant (Fig.1886). The 2nd Battalion were happy to wear the official collar badge, with their elephant on top.

Fig.1886

Early Dress Regulations describe the Officers tunic collar badge as "A grenade in gold embroidery" in silver, on the ball, the Royal Tiger; below the tiger, the Elephant". Repeated in subsequent Editions, including for mess dress with a very slight addition in the 1911 Dress Regulations with the word "Mounted" after "Embroidery".

These vary quite considerably with both the shape and the number of flames. The same minor variations in size and shape of the animals occur as already described for other ranks collar badges. In addition to the usual "Cowed Tiger"

HISTORY OF THE BRITISH ARMY INFANTRY COLLAR BADGE

Fig.1887

Fig.1888

Fig.1889

Fig.1890

Fig.1891

Fig.1892

with tail dropping down to between its back legs, and with all four feet on the ground there is also one with the tiger's tail curving up over its back and with one front paw raised.

With the animals of the other ranks collar badge all in the one stamping and the animals of the Officers collar badge separately mounted in silver, much more detail can be expected from the latter. With the elephant, its tusks are shown in far greater detail. Although some have the same design of elephant as used for the other ranks with nothing on its back and with trunk curving upwards, some Officers badges have howdah cloths and girth straps (varying shapes and designs) and the trunk dropping down to the ground.

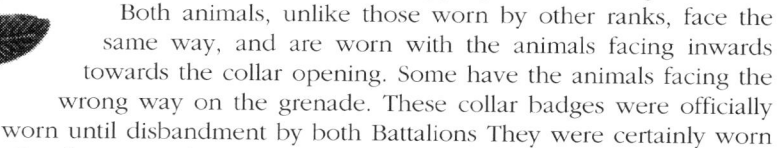

Both animals, unlike those worn by other ranks, face the same way, and are worn with the animals facing inwards towards the collar opening. Some have the animals facing the wrong way on the grenade. These collar badges were officially worn until disbandment by both Battalions They were certainly worn by the 1st Battalion, proud to have the tiger of the former 102nd above the elephant of the 103rd. However, unofficially, Officers of the 2nd Battalion wore their collar badges with the elephant above the tiger (Figs.1887, 1888 and 1889 for three variations of Officers embroidered collar badges. Fig.1889 has the more unusual tiger with tail over its back paw raised and both animals facing the wrong way).

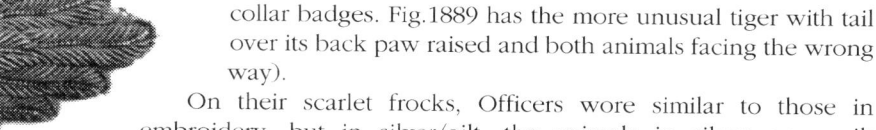

On their scarlet frocks, Officers wore similar to those in embroidery, but in silver/gilt, the animals in silver on a gilt grenade. The same differences are found as already described, including number of flames and the elephant above the tiger for the 2nd Battalion (Figs.1890 and 1891 for two variations of the nine flame grenade). There are also upright grenades in silver/gilt, again with the usual variations. On mess jackets, Officers wore vertical embroidered grenades with animals in silver.

When Service Dress was introduced in 1902, Officers collar badges were to be "As for forage cap, but in pairs" and in bronze instead of silver/gilt. This, described in Dress Regulations, as "A grenade. On the ball, the Tiger; below the Tiger, the Elephant. Below the grenade, a scroll inscribed "Royal Dublin Fusiliers" (Fig.1892). A multi-flame grenade with all the usual variations. This pattern was officially polished and worn on the khaki drill.

Introduced just prior to WWI, it was virtually the bronze Service Dress collar badge but without the scroll. Again, will all the variations as already described. (Figs.1893, 1894, 1895 and 1896 for variations including "sharp" flames). This pattern was also polished and worn on the khaki drill.

Militia

On 1st July 1881, *The Kildare Rifles Militia* became the 3rd Battalion, The Royal Dublin Fusiliers and in Rifle tradition did not wear collar badges.

On the same date *The Queen's Own Royal Dublin City Militia* became the 4th Battalion. Their collar badges were sealed 3rd August 1876 "For tunic and frock collar". In white-metal for other ranks these were a wreath of shamrock surmounted by a QVC and in the voided centre of which were three castles from the Arms of the City of Dublin (fig 1897). Officers wore similar, but in silver. They did not face.

The Dublin County Light Infantry Militia wore as their first collar badge, a bugle horn, this being Pattern 7586 sealed 28th April 1876 under Authority PC/DCM/93. In white-metal for other ranks and in silver for Officers..

A decision was made 26th March 1878 under Authority PC/S Down Militia/195 to assimilate all Militia bugles to an uniform pattern, the one chosen to be pattern 8935 as then being worn by the South Gloucester Militia

THE ROYAL DUBLIN FUSILIERS

(Figs.1898 and 1899 for a FP in white-metal for other ranks sealed 1st August 1877). Officers wore similar but in silver. All worn with the mouthpiece of the bugle nearest the collar opening.

On 1st July 1881, they became the 5th Battalion, Royal Dublin Fusiliers.

After 1st July 1881, the 3rd, 4th and 5th Militia Battalions adopted the same collar badges as the 1st and 2nd Battalions but some Officers wore an embroidered "M" at the end of the flames of their embroidered collar badges.

Other Items

One item sometimes thought to be a Regimental collar badge has the tiger over the elephant on the ball of a multi-flame grenade with a scroll below inscribed "THE DUBLIN FUSILIERS". The tiger being above the elephant indicates an Officers item as does the gilt finish and the tiger with tail over its back and with one front paw raised indicates an early item. All the ones noted are Regimental Brooches (Fig.1900) but it has been suggested that they were worn on the collar for a short time. To date, this is unconfirmed.

General

Like most other Fusilier Regiments, The Royal Dublin Fusiliers seem to have been unable to decide on the number of flames on their grenade collar badges.

Both the tiger and the elephant vary greatly as already described but in general it appears the tiger with its tail over the back was the first pattern with later patterns having the "Cowed" tiger.

The Regiment was disbanded 31st July 1922.

Fig.1893

Fig.1894

Fig.1895

Fig.1896

Fig.1897

Fig.1898

Fig.1899

Fig.1900

The Rifle Brigade (The Prince Consort's Own)

Badge articles relating to insignia of The Rifle Brigade invariably say that no collar badges were worn by the Regiment This is certainly correct as far as the early 1870's until the turn of the century, as confirmed by early Dress Regulations recording "No badge for Officers tunic collars".

An Order PC/Gen/1639 dated 14th July 1893 records "The collar badges (left side) to be worn upon the field service cap by Infantry, exceptions as under-Rifle Brigade, no badge".

The first mention of collar badges appears in the 1902 Dress Regulations relating to the recently introduced Service Dress for Officers. These are described "As for forage cap, but smaller" and in bronze. The description for the forage cap is given as "A wreath of laurel intertwined with a scroll bearing some of the battles of the Brigade. Within the wreath, a Maltese Cross, with a lion between each division. On each division, other battles of the Brigade. On the centre of the cross, a circle inscribed 'Rifle Brigade'; within the circle, a bugle with strings, surmounted by the crown. Above the Cross, a crown on a tablet inscribed 'Waterloo'; below the cross, a scroll inscribed 'Peninsula'". A long description, repeated in the 1904 Dress Regulations and again in the 1911 Edition with minor alterations. "Brigade" is replaced by "Regiment" and instead of "On each division" is now "On the divisions" and instead of "Surmounted by the Crown" becomes "Surmounted by a Crown" (Fig.1901).

These were worn until 1927 when, on 9th June, a new pattern was sealed by The War Office, the pattern card marked "Die 3600". This collar badge is first referred to in the 1934 Dress Regulations, again "As for forage cap, but smaller" and in bronze. The new description follows the one it supercedes but replaces "The Battles" with, more appropriately, "The Battle Honours" and adds the word "The" before Rifle Brigade for the inscription on the circle. The previous description is repeated down to the inscription "Waterloo". The new description continues with "Below the cross, two scrolls, inscribed "France and Flanders, 1914 - 18", "Macedonia 1915 - 18" on the lower part of the wreath a scroll inscribed "Prince Consort's Own (Fig.1902).

Although Dress Regulations do not specify the battle honours, they are as follows:-
- Top arm of the cross - Ciudad Rodrigo, Copenhagen, Peninsula, Corunna and Busaco
- East arm, as viewed - Fuentes D'onur, Badajos, Vimiera and Nivelle
- Bottom arm - Salamenca, Toulouse, Pyrenees, Vittoria and Nive
- West arm as viewed - Monte Video, Barosa, Roleia and Orthes.

There are another fourteen battle honours around the wreath.

Sealed at the same time as the bronze collar badge were other collar badges, one in silver (Fig.1903) and a FP of small ribboned bugle horns, also in silver, and annotated "Tropical mess dress" (Fig.1904).

Militia

The Queen's Own Royal Tower Hamlets Light Infantry Militia, formerly the *2nd Royal Tower Hamlets Militia* became, 1st July 1881, the 5th Battalion, The Rifle Brigade.

Their white-metal collar badges were sealed 3rd November 1875, "For tunic and frock collar". It has not been possible to find any written details for these badges but it has been suggested that it was the Tower of London, larger than the one

Fig.1901

Fig.1902

Fig.1903

Fig.1904

THE RIFLE BRIGADE (THE PRINCE CONSORT'S OWN)

worn by The Tower Hamlets RVC and similar in shape to the one in the centre of the glengarry badge worn by The Tower Hamlets Light Infantry Militia 1874 - 1881. It has also been said that the Regiments embroidered arm badge was also used as an Officers collar badge for a short time (Fig.1905 worn with a blue cloth backing). Again unconfirmed.

The Prince of Wales's Royal Regiment of Longford Light Infantry Militia became the 6th Battalion, The Rifle Brigade 1st July 1881. There is no evidence that collar badges were worn.

The King's Own Light Infantry Regiment of Militia (formerly the *1st Royal Tower Hamlets Militia*) became the 7th Battalion, The Rifle Brigade 1st July 1881. As with the 2nd Tower Hamlets Militia, there is no information regarding collar badges. If they did wear them, although unlikely, it could possibly have been a Light Infantry bugle horn.

Leitrim Rifles, formerly *Leitram Militia* and *Westmeath Rifles* formerly *Westmeath Militia* who 1st July 1881, became the 8th and 9th Battalions respectively, The Rifle Brigade, did not wear collar badges.

Rifle Volunteer Corps, Volunteer, Territorial Force & Territorial Army Battalions

The *15th Middlesex RVC* raised 2nd November 1859 were redesignated 3rd September 1880 as *7th Middlesex (London Scottish) RVC* wearing as their collar badge, the thistle.

A photograph of a Colour Sergeant taken in 1872 clearly shows the quite distinctive thistle being worn and illustrated as such an item removed from a pattern card dated 1874 (Fig.1906). Another photograph of a group of Sergeants, undated but probably taken about the same period, shows them wearing quite beautiful embroidered thistle collar badges, elongated and with the thistle heads picked out in green and red embroidery (Fig.1907).

On 1st July 1881, they became a Volunteer Battalion of The Rifle Brigade, redesignated 7th Middlesex (London Scottish) VRC in December 1891, transferring to the newly formed Territorial Force 1st April 1908 as *14th (County of London) Battalion, The London Regiment (London Scottish)*.

Whilst with The Rifle Brigade, they continued to wear a thistle collar badge in silver by Officers and in white-metal by other ranks (Fig.1908) worn in FP's with the stem facing inwards towards the collar opening.

See also under 14th (County of London) Battalion, The London Regiment (London Scottish).

14th (previously 23rd) (Inns of Court) RVC joined The Rifle Brigade in 1881 as one of its allotted VB's and, instead of becoming the intended 27th Battalion of The London Regiment in 1908, continued as The Inns of Court OTC, after which they adopted different collar badges.

During their time as a RVC, they wore their own distinctive collar badges. Within a laurel wreath, intertwined with four separate scrolls inscribed "SOUTH", "AFRICA", "1900" and "1901", four shields the bottom points of which met in the centre to form a cross. Each shield bore the arms of a different Inn. The top shield contained a number of mill-rinds (sometimes thirteen sometimes fourteen) with a lion rampant in the top left hand corner (canton), this representing Lincoln's Inn. Preceding clockwise, the next shield was the arms of The Inner Temple, a Pegasus or winged horse. Next came Gray's Inn, the shield containing a Griffin and finally the arms of Middle Temple with a pascal lamb in the centre of the Cross of St. George.

Illustrated are two different collar badges, both in blackened brass. The first a cap/collar (with thirteen mill-rinds) has a wavy scroll below the bottom shield inscribed "INNS OF COURT VRC" (Fig.1909). The second, a collar badge only, is smaller, has no scrolls intertwined in the Wreath, a curved scroll below the bottom shield inscribed "INNS OF COURT" and another scroll beneath inscribed on the

Fig.1905

Fig.1906

Fig.1907

Fig.1908

Fig.1909

HISTORY OF THE BRITISH ARMY INFANTRY COLLAR BADGE

Fig.1910

Fig.1911

Fig.1912

Fig.1913

Fig.1914

Fig.1915

Fig.1916

one side "R" and on the other "V". (Fig.1910).

The *15th Middlesex RVC* (formerly 26th) joined The Rifle Brigade as the 2nd VB in 1881 wearing as their collar badge a Maltese Cross surmounted by a Crown on a motto scroll. The Cross has lions between each limb and balls at each point, a motto scroll outside the East and West limbs as viewed, and an honours scroll below the South limb. Inscribed on the top scroll "LIBERTATE", West scroll, "PRO" East scroll, "PATRIAE" and bottom scroll, "S AFRICA 1900 - 1901". In the centre of the cross, a circle inscribed "15th MIDDLESEX RIFLE VOLS" and within which, a strung bugle facing to the left.

At one time the Corps was known as 15th Middlesex (The Customs and The Docks) RVC and wore as their collar badge an intertwined "VR" surmounted by a QVC. Officers wore their collar badges in gilt (Fig.1911) and, with a different shaped crown, in silver (Fig.1912). They did not face.

The 15th was amalgamated with the 2nd Tower Hamlets in 1908 becoming the 17th (County of London) Battalion of The London Regiment

The *16th (London Irish) Middlesex RVC (formerly 28th)* became the 3rd VB, The Rifle Brigade in 1881 and wore the shamrock as their collar badge. In blackened brass for other ranks (Fig.1913) and in silver for Officers (Fig.1914). They were worn in FP's with the stem of the shamrock facing inwards towards the collar opening.

In 1908, they transferred to the new Territorial Force becoming the 18th (County of London) Battalion, The London Regiment (London Irish Rifles) - see also under that title.

The *20th Middlesex (Artists) RVC (formerly 38th)* became the 6th VB, The Rifle Brigade in 1881 becoming in 1908 the 28th (County of London) Battalion, The London Regiment (Artists Rifles).

One of the original members of the old 38th was a private W.C. Wyon later to become one of the Countries most respected engravers, and it was he who designed the famous "Artists Rifles" badge by combining the heads of Mars, The God of War with Minerva, Goddess of the Arts. The design is clearly seen in the Gaunt pattern books, a FP annotated "20th Middlesex Rifles - Artists RV, January 2nd 1890".

The collar badge introduced c.1895 was worn by other ranks in brass (Fig.1915) and also in blackened brass and by Officers in silver (Figs.1916 and 1917 for two variations). Worn in FP's with the heads facing inwards towards the collar opening.

One item, with the heads above a scroll inscribed "ARTISTS RIFLES" is not a collar badge but is a "Sweetheart" badge (Fig.1918).

See also under 28th (County of London) Battalion, The London Regiment (Artists Rifles).

The *24th Middlesex (Post Office) RVC (formerly 49th)* became the 7th VB, The Rifle Brigade in 1881 and in 1908 the 8th (City of London) Battalion, The London Regiment (Post office Rifles).

The Regiment "Officially" adopted the dress of The Rifle Brigade in 1891, retaining their own badges. The collar badge had a solid centre with the numerals

THE RIFLE BRIGADE (THE PRINCE CONSORT'S OWN)

'24' in white-metal, within a strap inscribed "MIDDLESEX RIFLE VOLUNTEERS", itself within a wreath of oak leaves open at the top, the space being partly filled with a flat topped QVC. Apart from the numerals in white-metal, all in blackened brass. (Fig.1919). Also known in white-metal. Officers wore similar collar badges, but in silver.

See also under 8th (City of London) Battalion, The London Regiment (Post office Rifles).

2nd Tower Hamlets RVC (formerly the 3rd, 7th and 10th Tower Hamlets RVC's and later re-numbered the 3rd). Their collar badge appears in the Gaunt pattern books with an interesting annotation "Tower Hamlets - for collar - Hawkes 14th April 1880 @ 3/- each - silver castle, two wires". The collar badge was The Tower of London, in white-metal for other ranks (Fig.1920) and in silver for Officers (Fig.1921). They did not face, the flag always flying to the right.

In 1908, the 2nd Tower Hamlets and the 15th Middlesex were amalgamated to form the 17th (County of London) Battalion, The London Regiment (Poplar & Stepney Rifles), redesignated 17th London Regiment (Tower Hamlets Rifles) in 1926, later changed in 1937 to Tower Hamlets Rifles, The Rifle Brigade (Prince Consort's Own).

Officially, they wore no collar badges but an item of collar badge size is believed to have been worn for a short while. This was a laurel wreath within which was a Maltese Cross with lions between each limb, the top limb surmounted by a K/C over a blank tablet. On the top limb was inscribed "SOUTH" and on the bottom limb "AFRICA" with "19" on the West limb and "02" on the East limb. In the centre of the cross, a circle inscribed "RIFLE BRIGADE" and within which a crowned bugle facing to the left. On the bottom of the wreath a scroll inscribed "THE PRINCE CONSORT'S OWN". Found in blackened brass for other ranks (Fig.1922) and in silver for Officers. They did not face.

General

On 7th November 1958, The Regiment (less Territorials) were redesignated as *3rd Green Jackets, The Rifle Brigade* and again redesignated 1st January 1966, in accordance with the formation of the large Regiments, as *3rd Battalion, The Royal Green Jackets (The Rifle Brigade).* The subtitle was omitted from 1st July 1968.

(To achieve uniformity, The Middlesex RVC has been included under the Regiment they joined on 1st July 1881. See also under Royal Fusiliers, The Middlesex Regiment and The K.R.R.C.).

Fig.1917

Fig.1918

Fig.1919

Fig.1922

Fig.1920

Fig.1921

The Territorial Force, 1908

In 1907, the then Secretary of State for War, Richard Haldane, proposed many Army reforms amongst which was that the Yeomanry and Volunteer Forces at that time were to be amalgamated to form a new group to be known as The Territorial Force.

By-and-large, this meant that the Volunteer Battalions and Rifle Volunteers became Territorial Force Battalions of the Regiments to which they were already affiliated, with the Regiment having its Regular soldiers as the 1st and 2nd Line Battalions, the Militia, at that time known as Special Reserve, as the 3rd Battalion with the Territorials as the 4th and 5th Battalions with additional Battalions as required.

The Territorial Force was officially constituted on 1st April 1908 and at that time five new Regiments were formed - The Monmouthshire Regiment, The Cambridgeshire Regiment, The Hertfordshire Regiment, The Herefordshire Regiment and The London Regiment

London, having in 1908 only one Line Regiment to which TF Battalions could be attached, a decision was made to designate all London Volunteer Battalions to an entirely TF Corps, The London Regiment. Twenty eight Battalions were created but only 1- 26 were taken up, 26 and 27 being ignored by The Honourable Artillery Company and The Inns of Court Regiment respectively as they felt they deserved higher ranking in the new formation. Six further Battalions, 29 - 34 were raised during WWI.

On 7th July 1916, each Battalion became affiliated to other Line Regiments, usually to those they had been associated with prior to 1908. In 1922 each Battalion of The London Regiment was designated as a separate Regiment

By 1939, most of the connections by title with The London Regiment had gone, but some have reappeared since.

Army Order 298, issued 22nd September 1917, stated "In consideration of the services of The Territorial Force during the War, HM The King has been pleased to approve of units of The Territorial Force being permitted to wear on their badges, the mottoes and honours worn on the badges of the Corps, Regiments or Departments of which they form part.

The letter 'T' will still be worn below the collar badge by Officers of The Territorial Force, and no Officer will be called upon to change the badges he now has to wear. Badges in store, in wear and regimental charge will be used up before any new badges are issued".

Whether these instructions were put into effect by each unit is not known, but it is known that the 'T' was still being worn as late as 1931. It seems probable that most Infantry, if not all, did wear the 'T' but in this book, only those units where there is evidence of them actually being worn, are mentioned.

The Monmouthshire Regiment

In 1880, the 1st and 2nd Admin Battalions of *The Monmouthshire Rifle Volunteer Corps* became the *1st and 3rd Monmouthshire Rifle Volunteers* and in 1881 the 2nd and 4th VB's of The South Wales Borderers. On the formation of the Territorial Force in 1908, the two Battalions became the 1st and 3rd Battalions of the newly formed *The Monmouthshire Regiment*.

The 2nd Monmouthshire RVC were redesignated the 3rd VB, S.W.B. in 1885 becoming, in 1908, the *2nd Battalion, The Monmouthshire Regiment*.

Fig.1923

1st Battalion

The collar badge worn by the 1st Battalion is often referred to as "The Monmouthshire Dragon", in fact quite incorrectly, as the pattern was worn by other South Wales units as a collar badge before the formation of The Monmouthshire Regiment

A small dragon with swept-back wings and looped tail with three feet on a grassy ground and one foot pointing upwards. Worn on khaki Service Dress in gilding-metal by other ranks, 1908 - 1914 and from 1920 - 1937. War time photographs show they were rarely worn during the Great War of 1914 - 18 (Fig.1923). Also worn on Rifle green walking out dress, 1908 - 39, in blackened gilding-metal.

Fig.1924

Similar, but in silver plate, were worn by Officers on their full dress uniform collars 1908 - 20 and also on their Patrol/No.1 Dress from 1908 - 55. On Service Dress, Officers wore, from 1908 - 46, similar but in bronze. Photographs show a bronze "T" also being worn below the collar badge (Photograph 27).

The same pattern, but in white-metal, was certainly worn by VB's of the South Wales Borderers and it has been suggested that to differentiate from the 2nd Battalion, the 1st Battalion, The Monmouthshire Regiment did, for a while, wear these same collar badges in white-metal (Fig.1924).

In 1938, the 1st Battalion was converted into a Searchlight Regiment, RE (later RA) and in 1947 became *603 (M) Heavy A-A Regiment, RA* adopting the collar badges as worn by The Royal Artillery.

Fig.1925

2nd Battalion

Similar collar badges to those of the 1st Battalion were worn by the 2nd Battalion with other ranks wearing theirs in gilding-metal on khaki Service Dress 1908 - 37 and again from 1947 through to 1967. Officers wore similar, but in bronze, on their Service Dress 1908 - 46, often with a separate "T" below, post WWII until 1967 in either gilding-metal or gilt. The gilt collar badges were also worn on Officers full dress/No.1 Dress/Blue Patrols etc.

The above dates were kindly supplied by The Curator of The Welch Regiment Museum but a sealed Pattern 15927 shows a FP of dragons with upright wings - the type usually associated with the 2nd Battalion. In white-metal, this pattern was sealed 5th October 1953 under Authority 54/Officers/4051 (Fig.1925). Also recorded on a Gaunt sample card with the same white-metal dragons dated September 1952. The sealing card has been annotated "Obsolete pattern, Agency form NV/ACA5/02", with the date 30th December 1965. Although sealed, this does not of course mean, that they were either issued or worn. The pattern was used as a guide for the silver anodised versions, sealed 28th February 1964, being Pattern 19268 "for 2nd Monmouthshire Regiment".

3rd Battalion

The same pattern collar badges were worn as the 2nd Battalion 1908 - 37 by other ranks and 1908 - 47 by Officers.

The 3rd Battalion later became 637 (H) A-A Regiment, RA and a sealed Pattern 16487, sealed 22nd October 1954 shows similar dragons in gilding-metal to those of the "Swept-back wing" pattern worn by the old 3rd Battalion, Monmouthshire Regiment

The Monmouthshire (Territorial) Battalion, The South Wales Borderers

This TAVR III unit was formed 1st April 1967 from the 2nd Battalion The Monmouthshire Regiment (TA), wearing the "Upright wing" dragon collar badge as already described.

Worn by other ranks in gilding-metal (Fig.1926) and by Officers in bronze and later in gilt (Fig.1927) on Service Dress and in silver on No.1 Dress.

Prior to this, as the 2nd Battalion, The Monmouthshire Regiment (TA) they wore the same collar badges as worn by the South Wales Borderers, the Roman numerals "XXIV" within an unbroken wreath of immortelles. These appear on a sealed Pattern 18213, sealed 31st December 1959 in silver anodised under Authority 54/Infy/8792 for the South Wales Borderers with the card annotated "Also for 2nd Battalion, The Monmouthshire Regiment (TA) - Authority NV82/2154 and dated 23rd November 1964 (Fig.1928).

On 1st April 1969, they became a Cadre, The Monmouthshire Battalion, The South Wales Borderers, under the *Welsh Volunteers*, designated March 1971 as *The 3rd (Monmouthshire) Battalion, The Royal Regiment of Wales (24th/41st Foot)*.

On 1st April 1971, they disbanded to form *"B" Company, 3rd (V) Battalion, The Royal Regiment of Wales (24th/41st Foot)* and also formed a detachment of *211 (South Wales) Light AD Batty, RA (V) of 104 Light AD Regiment*.

Fig.1926

Fig.1927

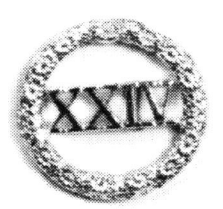

Fig.1928

Lt E. H. Hopkinson, MC, 1st Battalion The Cambridgeshire Regiment TF

The Cambridgeshire Regiment

In March 1908, the old Volunteer Force ceased to exist and the 3rd (Cambridgeshire) VB, The Suffolk Regiment, became, on the formation of the new Territorial Force, the 1st Battalion, The Cambridgeshire Regiment (see also under The Suffolk Regiment). The collar badge adopted by the new Regiment, was, appropriately, the Castle of Cambridge with the Arms of Ely superimposed on the central tower. There was an archway either side of the central tower. No flags flew from the turrets. Other ranks wore them in gilding-metal (Fig.1929) and in white-metal on their "Walking out" dress, whilst Officers wore similar in silver on their No.I Dress and in bronze on their Service Dress (Fig.1930). A gilt collar badge is also known and said to have been worn by WO's. Photographs taken during WWI show a separate "T" was usually worn below the bronze collar badge, to emphasise their Territorial status (photograph 28 as worn by Lt. E. H. Hopkinson, MC). After the War this practice gradually ceased and a photograph c.1933 of Lt. Col. C.V. Canning, MC the Officer Commanding the 1st Battalion, clearly shows the castle only, being worn.

During the Great War, the bronze cap badge was also worn as a collar badge by Officers on their Service Dress lapels. This badge was similar to the collar badge already described but with the addition of a scroll below the castle and inscribed "THE CAMBRIDGESHIRE REGIMENT" (Fig.1931). A version of this badge was made without the letter "E" in the title, said to have come from a new die made after the loss of the 1st Battalion in Malaya in 1942.

Also known is a bronze collar badge, similar but smaller, than the cap badge (Fig.1931) but with an additional bottom scroll inscribed "SOUTH AFRICA 1900 - 01".

When the Territorial Army was reformed in 1947, the Regiments role was transferred from Infantry to Light anti-aircraft and on 1st January became *629 (The Cambridgeshire Regiment) LAA Regiment, RA (TA)*. Although now forming part of the Royal Artillery, the Regiment was granted the right to retain its badges, including of course, the collar badge. A sealed pattern shows a white-metal collar badge for soldiers, similar to the first ones issued but in an inferior metal which did not have the old whiteness, was lighter and with a single lug fitting. This was Pattern 15363 sealed 24th October 1952, the card being annotated "To be used as a guide for a/a" (Fig.1932).

When Anti-Aircraft Command was disbanded in 1954, the Regiment became *629 (The Cambridgeshire Regiment), Parachute Light Regiment RA (TA)* but in 1956 was again restored to Infantry, once again becoming 1st Battalion, The Cambridgeshire Regiment TA. A sealed pattern shows the Officers collar badge in silver plate sealed 8th May 1957 under Authority 54/Officers/4051.

The Home Guard
Thirteen Home Guard units were raised in Cambridgeshire from 1940 wearing the Regimental badges. The post war units of the resuscitated Home Guard which were also raised in the County were also "Badged" to the Cambridgeshire Regiment

Schools
The Cambridgeshire Army Cadet Force was expanded in 1942 from one pre war school unit at Wisbech and affiliated to The Cambridgeshire Regiment.

General
On 1st April 1961, The Cambridgeshire Regiment amalgamated with The Suffolk Regiment to become *The Suffolk & Cambridgeshire Regiment TA* serving in an Infantry role until reduced to a Cadre in 1967 and finally disbanded.

Fig.1929

Fig.1930

Fig.1931

Fig.1932

… HISTORY OF THE BRITISH ARMY INFANTRY COLLAR BADGE

The London Regiment

1st - 4th (City of London Battalion) The London Regiment (Royal Fusiliers)

In 1908, the 1st, 2nd, 3rd and 4th VB's, The Royal Fusiliers became, respectively, the *1st, 2nd, 3rd and 4th (City of London) Battalions, The London Regiment (Royal Fusiliers)* and in 1922 the *1st, 2nd, 3rd and 4th Battalions City of London Regiment (The Royal Fusiliers), The London Regiment.*

In 1936, under Army Orders 209 and 216, the 4th Battalion was transferred to The Royal Artillery becoming the *60th (City of London) A-A Brigade, RA* and adopting The Royal Artillery collar badges. In 1937, the 1st 2nd and 3rd Battalions became, respectively, the 8th (1st City of London), 9th (2nd City of London) and 10th (3rd City of London) Battalions, The Royal Fusiliers (City of London Regiment).

In 1949, the 8th Battalion reverted to its title as in 1937 with the 9th and 10th Battalions becoming, respectively, the *624th and 625th LAA Regiment RA (Royal Fusiliers)* both adopting The Royal Artillery badges.

Whilst Volunteer Battalions of The Royal Fusiliers prior to 1908, the four Volunteer Battalions wore similar collar badges to the parent Line Battalions, but in white-metal - see under The Royal Fusiliers (City of London Regiment).

After 1908, they adopted the same collar badge in gilding-metal as worn by the Line Battalions of The Royal Fusiliers (City of London Regiment) - a flaming grenade with seven points to the flames, on the ball, the garter proper enclosing a double Tudor rose. Superimposed at the base of the flames and at the top centre of the garter, a K/C (Fig.190).

Similarly, Officers also wore the same K/C collar bags as worn by The Royal Fusiliers (City of London Regiment) in silver/gilt (Fig.200) and in bronze on their Service Dress (Fig.197). Photographs show a separate "T" often being worn below the bronze collar badges (see photograph 29 as being worn by Capt. F.O. Eiloart).

A gold embroidered grenade with silver rose was worn on mess dress (Fig.196).

5th (City of London) Battalion The London Regiment (London Rifle Brigade)

Originally raised 14th December 1859 as *1st London (City of London Volunteer Rifle Brigade) RVC* becoming the *9th VB, of the K.R.R.C.*, 1st July 1881 and redesignated as the *1st London VRC (City of London VRB)* in December 1891.

The Gaunt pattern books record an item annotated "Officers, NCO's and men of the 1st City of London Rifle Vol Bdge, badge for field service cap, approved Horse Guards WO 9th March 1893". The drawing is of a shield with wing on top and bearing the Arms of The City of London resting on top of the curved initials LRB. (Fig.1933). This is illustrated as it has often been mistakenly identified as a collar badge as has a similar item but with the additional initials "CC" below those of "LRB". (Fig.1934).

It is easy to understand why the confusion has occurred especially as the collar badge worn at that time was the shield only (see photograph 30). No metals are mentioned in the Gaunt pattern book but all the ones noted are blackened, which would be in keeping with Rifle units.

On 1st April 1908, the Corps were transferred to the newly formed Territorial Force as the *5th (City of London) Battalion The London Regiment (London Rifle Brigade)*. There were other title changes until 1922 when it became

Fig.1933

Fig.1934

Fig.1935

Fig.1936

Fig.1937

314

the *5th City of London Regiment (London Rifle Brigade), The London Regiment* and in 1937 *The London Rifle Brigade, The Rifle Brigade (Prince Consort's Own)* and then in 1950 amalgamated to become *The London Rifle Brigade/Rangers, The Rifle Brigade (Prince Consort's Own)*.

During this time, no collar badges were worn. However, one item, as worn on the field service cap is illustrated as it is sometimes mistaken for a collar badge. Within an oak wreath on which are various battle honours, a circle inscribed "LONDON RIFLE BRIGADE, SOUTH AFRICA 1900 - 02". In the centre of the circle, a shield bearing the Royal Arms. At the top of the circle, a scroll inscribed "FRANCE AND FLANDERS 1914 - 18" and surmounted by a K/C and at the bottom of the circle, two scrolls, the top inscribed "YPRES 1915 - 17" and below inscribed "PRIMUS IN URBE". Below this a small shield bearing the Arms of The City of London. Behind the circle, the crossed City mace and sword (Fig.1935 - this item has a partly voided centre and is in white-metal).

6th (City of London) Battalion The London Regiment (City of London Rifles)

Originally raised 16th May 1860 as the *2nd London RVC*, becoming the 10th VB, The King's Royal Rifle Corps, 1st July 1881 and transferred to the Territorial Force, 1st April 1908 as *The 6th (City of London) Battalion The London Regiment (City of London Rifles)*.

After several other changes they were reconstructed 7th February 1920 as the *6th Battalion The London Regiment (City of London Rifles)*, redesignated in 1922 as the *6th City of London Regiment (City of London Rifles)* before, on 15th December 1935, being converted to an Engineer role as *31 (City of London Rifles) A-A Battalion, RE*.

No collar badges were worn.

7th (City of London) Battalion The London Regiment

Originally raised on 8th March 1861 as *The 3rd London Rifle Volunteer Corps* eventually becoming the 11th VB, The King's Royal Rifle Corps in 1881 and transferring to the Territorial Force as the *7th (City of London) Battalion, The London Regiment* in 1908.

The 3rd London Rifle Volunteers were the first Corps of Volunteers to adopt a scarlet tunic similar to those worn by the Infantry of the Line and a coloured print shows a Lieutenant wearing horizontal embroidered, seven flame grenades, on his tunic collar (Figs.1936 and 1937 for a FP, worn as illustrated).

It is recorded that other ranks wore on their forage caps, a fused grenade with the numeral '3' on the ball, all in gilding-metal and it has been suggested that at some time they also wore similar but smaller as a collar badge. Certainly these items exist (Fig.1938) but there is no written or photographic evidence to confirm. They are also known in silver.

On becoming the 7th (City of London) Battalion in 1908, other ranks wore as their collar badge a gilding-metal metal grenade with distinctive flames (Fig.1939).

Again, it is known that the cap badge was a gilding-metal grenade with the numeral '7', in white-metal, on the ball. Similar, but smaller, items are known but whether, as has been suggested, they were collar badges remains unconfirmed. One such, in bronze has seven flames to the grenade with a floriated '7' on the ball (4 x 2.25cm). Another seven flame item is a gilt grenade and numeral with a red enamel surround (4.75 x 2.9cm). Both are vertical grenades, the latter with a brooch fitting. Again, unconfirmed and it is very unlikely that either was ever worn as a collar badge.

Yet another item, possibly a collar badge, is a seven flame horizontal grenade in gilt with a silver plated '7' on the plain ball (2.5 x 5.2cm). Again unconfirmed.

These three items are obviously for wear by Officers but there is also an unconfirmed item in gilding-metal which could have been worn by other ranks. This is a flamed grenade with the numeral '7' engraved on the ball (Fig.1940). Although collar badge size, the spread of flames is quite unlike the one illustrated

Fig.1938

Fig.1939

Fig.1940

Fig.1941

HISTORY OF THE BRITISH ARMY INFANTRY COLLAR BADGE

Fig.1942

Fig.1943

Fig.1944

Fig.1945

Fig.1946

Fig.1947

in Fig.1939. Perhaps this was unofficially engraved by a soldier in WWI?

There are many photographs of Officers of the 7th wearing bronze collar badges on their Service Dress with a separate bronze "T" below (Fig.1941).

In 1922, the Regiment amalgamated with the 8th Battalion to form the 7th City of London Battalion (Post Office Rifles). For a description of their collar badges, see under 8th (City of London) Battalion, The London Regiment (Post Office Rifles).

8th (City of London) Battalion The London Regiment (Post Office Rifles)

The 8th were raised in 1868 as the *49th Middlesex RVC* renumbered the *24th* in 1880, becoming a VB of The Rifle Brigade in 1881 and in 1908 transferring to The Territorial Force as the *8th (City of London) Battalion The LondonRegiment (Post Office Rifles)*.

For a description of collar badges worn by the 24th Middlesex RVC, see under The Rifle Brigade (The Prince Consort's Own).

In 1922, the Regiment amalgamated with the 7th Battalion to form the *7th City of London Battalion (Post Office Rifles)* and adopted as their new collar badge what was really a smaller version of the former cap badge of the old 8th Battalion This was a Maltese cross in the middle of which was a crowned bugle within a circle inscribed "THE POST OFFICE RIFLES". Above the top arm was a tablet inscribed "8th BATTALION" surmounted by the K/C. A laurel wreath, ending at either side of the tablet encircled the cross and on which were five scrolls, reading from top left to top right, "EGYPT", "1882", "CITY OF LONDON", "1899 - 02" and "S AFRICA".

Other ranks wore them in white-metal (Fig.1942), Officers wearing similar, but in silver. The bugle in the centre of the Maltese cross did not face but always faced to the left.

The two battle honours, "Egypt 1882" and "South Africa 1899 - 1902" are unique for Territorial Battalions with the latter usually dated 1900 - 02 for non-Regular units. "Egypt 1882" was awarded as a result of the Regiment finding personnel for the Army Post Office Corps during the suppression of the Arabi Pasha rebellion.

In 1935, the Regiment was converted to The Royal Engineers becoming the *32nd (7th City of London) A-A Battalion RE* later becoming the *567th (M) LAA/SL Regiment, RA (City of London)*. Since conversion to the RA in 1939, RA badges were worn.

9th (County of London) Battalion The London Regiment (Queen Victoria's) Rifles

Originally raised as the *Duke of Cumberland's Sharpshooters* in 1803, eventually becoming the *1st Middlesex (Victoria) VRC* and a VB of The King's Royal Rifle Corps in 1881.

The *11th Middlesex (St. George's) RVC* raised in 1860 and renumbered *6th* in 1880, also became a VB of The K.R.R.C. in 1881.

In 1892, the two amalgamated to become the *1st Middlesex (Victoria and St. George's Rifles) RVC.*

In 1860, the *37th Middlesex (St. Giles and St. George's Bloomsbury) RVC* was raised, renumbered *19th* in 1880 and becoming a VB of The Rifle Brigade in 1881.

On the creation of The Territorial Force in 1908, the 1st and 19th amalgamated to form the *9th (County of London) Battalion The London Regiment (Queen Victoria's) Rifles.*

Two different pattern collar badges are recorded. One is a smaller version of the cap badge, a Maltese cross in the centre of which, St. George and the dragon within a circle inscribed "QUEEN VICTORIA'S". On the top limb of the cross, a tablet inscribed "SOUTH AFRICA 1900 - 02" and surmounted by a K/C. Worn in blackened gilding-metal by other ranks (Fig.1943) and in black/silver by Officers, they do not face, with St. George facing to the right. The George and dragon commemorates the old St. George's RVC.

The second recorded collar badge is again of St. George and the dragon surmounted by a K/C. In silver, they do face both ways and were worn facing inwards on Officers mess dress (Figs.1944 and 1945 for a FP).

Photographs show Officers of the 9th Battalion (TF) wearing a separate "T" below their collar badges.

In 1937, under Army Order 168, the Regiment became the *Queen Victoria's Rifles, K.R.R.C.* and were finally amalgamated with The Queen's Westminster's, The K.R.R.C. in 1960 to form *The Queen's Royal Rifles*.

See under the King's Royal Rifle Corps for collar badges relating to the 1st Middlesex (Victoria) RVC and the 6th Middlesex (St. George's) RVC.

10th (County of London) Battalion The London Regiment (Paddington Rifles)

The 10th (County of London) Battalion traces its origin to 1860 when the *36th Middlesex RVC* was raised. Renumbered *18th* in 1880 they became a VB of The Rifle Brigade in 1881 and transferred to The Territorial Force in 1908 as the *10th (County of London) Battalion The London Regiment (Paddington Rifles)*.

Rifles green tunics were worn by the 18th and over the years followed the general pattern of Rifle Brigades, this uniform being retained for review Order only after the transfer to the new Territorial Force, khaki drill being introduced at that time.

Like most other Rifle Regiments, no collar badges were worn.

Because of falling numbers, the Regiment was disbanded in 1912 but reformed the same year as the *10th County of London Battalion The London Regiment (Hackney)*.

Like several other Battalions of The London Regiment, the collar badge chosen was a smaller version of the cap badge - an eight pointed rayed star the top point displaced by a K/C and within a laurel wreath. In the half voided centre, a tower standing on a ground, all within a circle inscribed "JUSTITIA TURRIS NOSTRA" (Justice is our tower). Below the star, a scroll inscribed "TENTH LONDON HACKNEY".

The tower is taken from the Seal of the Borough of Hackney and the height of the ground varies according to different manufacturers. Worn in blackened gilding-metal and in gilding-metal by other ranks (Fig.1946 for "Low" ground) and in gilt and in bronze by Officers (Fig.1947 for "High" ground). Also known in bi-metal, possibly worn by senior NCO's. They do not face.

In 1937, the Regiment became the 5th (Hackney) Battalion, The Royal Berkshire Regiment and in 1947 transferred to The Royal Artillery as 648 *HAA Regiment*.

11th (County of London) Battalion The London Regiment (Finsbury Rifles).

The 39th, Middlesex RVC were raised in 1860, renumbered *21st* in 1880, became a Volunteer Battalion of The King's Royal Rifle Corps in 1881 and, on the formation of The Territorial Force in 1908, took the title of *11th (County of London) Battalion, The London Regiment (Finsbury Rifles)*.

Like most Rifle units they did not wear collar badges but a photograph of an Officer c.1914/18 clearly shows the numerals "XI" in bronze being worn on the lapels of his Service Dress jacket (Fig.1948).

In 1936, under Army Orders 209 and 212 the Regiment was transferred to the Royal Artillery becoming *61st (Finsbury Rifles) A-A Brigade*, adopting the RA badges.

12th (County of London) Battalion The London Regiment (Rangers)

The 40th Middlesex RVC (Central London Rangers) raised 30th April 1860 were renumbered *22nd* in September 1880 becoming a VB of The King's Royal Rifle Corps in 1881 and the *12th (County of London) Battalion The London Regiment (Rangers)* on the formation of The Territorial Force in 1908.

Like several other Battalions of The London Regiment, the 12th adopted as their

Fig.1948

Fig.1949

Fig.1950

Fig.1951

Fig.1952

HISTORY OF THE BRITISH ARMY INFANTRY COLLAR BADGE

Fig.1953

Fig.1954

Fig.1955

Fig.1956

Fig.1957

Fig.1958

collar badge a smaller version of their cap badge. This was a Maltese cross in the centre of which was a bugle with strings within a circle inscribed "12th COUNTY OF LONDON". The top limb of the cross inscribed "SOUTH AFRICA 1900 - 02" with a tablet above the limb inscribed "EXCEL" and surmounted by a K/C. Below the cross, a scroll inscribed "THE RANGERS".

Variations include voided and non-voided crowns and voided and non-voided centres within the circle. The Bugles do not face, always facing to the left.

"Excel" is derived from the numerals "XL", from the old 40th Middlesex RVC.

Riflemen wore the collar badge in blackened gilding-metal with Officers wearing similar, but in gilt. (Fig.1949). Also known in silver. Gilding metal items do appear but are believed to be badges awaiting blackening.

In 1937, under Army Order 168, the Regiment became *The Rangers, The King's Royal Rifle Corps*.

13th (County of London) Battalion The London Regiment (Kensington)

The *4th Middlesex RVC* were raised in 1859 and in July 1864 gained the additional title (West London). In 1881, they became a VB of The King's Royal Rifle Corps becoming, on the formation of The Territorial Force in 1908, *The 13th (County of London) Battalion The London Regiment (Kensington)*.

They adopted as their collar badge the device that featured in the centre of their helmet plates - the Arms of The Royal Borough of Kensington - "Quarterly gules and or, a celestial crown in chief and a fleur-de-lys in base of the last, in the dexter canton a mullet argent in the first quarter: a cross flory between four martlets sable in the second: a cross botony gules between four roses of the last stalked and leaved proper in the third: a mitre of the second in the fourth: all within a bordure quarterly also or and sable". Below the Arms was a three part scroll inscribed with the motto "QUID-NOBIS-ARDUI" (Nothing too hard for us). In fact, because of the small space available, it was not practical to include the mullet in the first quarter.

These collar badges are known in two sizes, in die struck white-metal for wear by other ranks and in a superior white-metal with a solid back, which could quite easily be mistaken for silver, by Officers. (Fig.1950). An item in gilt has been noted, usage unknown, possibly worn by WO's. Also worn by Officers on their Service Dress, in bronze (Fig.1951). Often worn with a separate bronze 'T' below the collar badge (Photograph 31 as worn by Lt. T. E. Turner, c.1914 - 15). A smaller pattern, in the same superior white-metal with solid back, is said to have been worn by the Band who also wore their cap badges and shoulder titles in white-metal (Fig.1952).

In 1914, the title "Princess Louise's " was granted to the Regiment and on 10th August, 1937, the Regimental title was changed to become *Princess Louise's Kensington Regiment, The Middlesex Regiment*.

On 1st April 1947, the two Battalions amalgamated to form an Army Phantom Signal Regiment designated as *Signals Reporting Regiment (Princess Louise's Kensington Regiment), Royal Corps of Signals*. They later absorbed two independent signal squadrons and part of *565 Battery RA (TA)* to form *41 (Princess Louise's Kensington), Royal Corps of Signals* later becoming *41 (Princess Louise's Kensington) Signal Squadron (Vols) of the 31st (Greater London) Signal Regiment (Vols)*.

Fig.1959

318

THE LONDON REGIMENT

The collar badge they wore during this period was the cypher "L" of HRH The Princess Louise reversed and interlaced, surmounted by her coronet. Below the cypher, a scroll inscribed "PRINCESS LOUISE'S". A sealed Pattern 15651 dated 13th March 1953 shows this badge in white-metal, the card annotated "Signals Reporting Regiment, Princess Louise's Kensington Regiment" (Fig.1953). This was worn by other ranks as was the silver anodised version, Pattern 19372 sealed 24th September 1964, the card annotated "31 and 41 Signal Regiment, Princess Louise's Kensington Regiment - to supercede Pattern 15651". Worn by Officers in silver and in silver plate - some are marked sterling silver (Fig.1954) and in bronze on Service Dress.

There are many photographs, particularly of Officers, wearing their Regimental collar badges but one of a Captain Herbert Walker Barnett is interesting. A report says he was commissioned into the 4th Middlesex VRC in 1907, the Regiment being converted as the 13th (Kensington) Battalion, The London Regiment in 1908. The photograph of him in full dress uniform, undated but probably c.1908/9 shows him wearing The King's Crown helmet plate and K/C cross belt plate of the newly formed 13th Battalion, but with the QVC collar badges as previously worn by the 4th (West london) VB of The K.R.R.C. (Fig.1955). For full details see under K.R.R.C.

Fig.1960

14th (County of London) Battalion The London Regiment (London Scottish)

The 15th Middlesex RVC were raised in 1859, renumbered 7th in 1880 becoming a VB of The Rifle Brigade in 1881 and, on the formation of The Territorial Force in 1908, the 14th (County of London) Battalion The London Regiment (London Scottish).

Fig.1961

As a Rifle Volunteer Corps they wore thistle collar badges continuing to do so after 1908 albeit in a slightly different shape. The first pattern was quite small and worn in white-metal by other ranks (Fig.1720). Also worn by the Band. A similar pattern, but in gilding-metal, was worn on the soldiers best Service Dress c.1930 - 37 (Fig.1956).

Officers wore similar, but in bronze, on their Service Dress (Fig.1957), embroidered on their full dress uniforms and a larger size in silver, on their mess dress and undress jackets (Fig.1958).

Fig.1962

After 1908, Officers wore a larger pattern in bronze on their Service Dress (Fig.1959), often worn with a separate "T" below the collar badge. (Photograph 32 as worn by Capt. W. MacKennon). Other ranks also adopted the larger thistle collar badge in white-metal.

All collar badges were worn in FP's with the stem of the thistle towards the collar opening.

Fig.1963

By Army Order 168, the Regiment joined The Gordon Highlanders being redesignated 10th August 1937, *The London Scottish, The Gordon Highlanders.*

(See also under The Gordon Highlanders and The Rifle Brigade).

15th (County of London) Battalion The London Regiment (Prince of Wales's Own Civil Service Rifles)

The 21st Middlesex RVC were raised 2nd January 1860, renumbered 12th, 3rd September 1880 becoming a VB of The King's Royal Rifle Corps 1st July 1881.

Fig.1966   *Fig.1965*   *Fig.1964*

HISTORY OF THE BRITISH ARMY INFANTRY COLLAR BADGE

Fig.1967

Fig.1968

Fig.1969

Fig.1970

Fig.1971

Also becoming a VB of the K.R.R.C. in 1881 were the *25th Middlesex RVC* who were renumbered as such in 1880, originally being the *50th* raised in 1875.

The 12th and 25th amalgamated as the 12th in 1892 and, on the formation of The Territorial Force in 1908, became the *15th (County of London) Battalion, The London Regiment (Prince of Wales's Own Civil Service Rifles.*

With the Prince of Wales associated with the Regiment and included in the title, it was logical that his plumes and motto were adopted as the new collar badge, especially as they had figured as collar badges and worn when they were Rifle Volunteers (see under the K.R.R.C.).

A trial die (Fig.1960) shows the plumes under which was a scroll inscribed "CIVIL SERVICE RIFLES". This was not adopted and a quite distinctive pattern was approved and taken into use (The scrolls quite different from those on the trial die). Other ranks collar badges are known in both white-metal and blackened gilding-metal (Fig.1961) - in view of their "Rifle" connection, Officers wearing similar but in blackened silver (Fig.1962).

On 31st December 1921, The Regiment amalgamated with the 16th (County of London) Battalion, The London Regiment (Queen's Westminster Rifles) to form the *16th (County of London) Battalion, The London Regiment (Queen's Westminster and Civil Service Rifles).* This under Army Order dated 31st December 1921. (See also under that title).

In 1991, a quantity of anodised collar badges held by a Military tailor were "unearthed" amongst which were items for the 13th, 14th and 15th Battalions, The London Regiment. Successors of both the 13th and 14th Battalions did wear anodised collar badges (as described under their respective titles) but after the 15th were amalgamated in 1921, there is no trace of any unit bearing their title.

The sealed packets containing these items were marked "15th County of London (Prince of Wales's Own, Civil Service Rifles) and both the writing and the packet looked genuinely old, on the packet was marked "Book 167 (Earlier version) plate and pins catalogue No.9736".

With anodised collar badges only being introduced in the early 1950's, the matter remains unresolved and it is possible that at one time it was intended to raise a unit as for example, 491 (15th, County of London, Civil Service Rifles) LAA Regiment, RA and, although the badges were manufactured, the Regiment was never raised?

The item (Fig.1963) is similar to others in use at the present time and in no way follows the metal collar badges as worn by the old 15th Battalion

16th (County of London) Battalion The London Regiment (Queen's Westminster Rifles)

Raised at Pimlico on 25th February 1860, the *22nd (Queen's) RVC* were renumbered *13th* on 3rd September 1880, becoming a VB of The King's Royal Rifle Corps 1st July 1881 and the *16th (County of London) Battalion, The LondonRegiment (Queen's Westminster Rifles)* when The Territorial Force was created 1st April 1908.

The collar badge worn by the 16th was the portcullis from the Arms of The City of Westminster above which was a scroll inscribed with the battle honour, "SOUTH AFRICA 1900 - 02", surmounted by the K/C.

Worn in blackened gilding-metal (Fig.1964 with a red cloth backing) and in white-metal (Fig.1965) by other ranks and in silver by Officers (Fig.1966). A smaller version, also in silver, was worn by Officers on their Mess Dress jackets.

Fig.1972   *Fig.1973*   *Fig.1974*

THE LONDON REGIMENT

By Army Order dated 31st December 1921, The Regiment amalgamated with the 15th Battalion to form the *16th (County of London) Battalion, The London Regiment (Queen's Westminster and Civil Service Rifles)*.

A new collar badge was adopted which found favour with former soldiers of both the old 15th and 16th Battalions, incorporating the portcullis and coronet of the 15th and The POW's plumes and motto of the 16th - "Two oval escutcheons accollée, the dexter bearing the portcullis surmounted by a ducal coronet, the sinister, The Prince of Wales's plumes. A crown above". The escutcheon containing the plumes slightly overlaps the escutcheon containing the portcullis. They do not face.

Soldiers wore these collar badges in gilding-metal (Fig.1967 with ovals, non-voided). Officers collar badges, in silver were larger than the similar item worn on the red cord boss, and are voided in the ovals (Fig.1968). More delicate silver collar badges were worn on the Officers mess dress, again voided. (Figs.1969 and 1970 carrying 1931 and 1934 hallmarks respectively). A smaller other ranks pattern collar badge, in gilt, is believed to have been worn by WO's (Fig.1971).

In May 1938, The Regiment was, by Army Order No.98, redesignated *The Queen's Westminster's, The King's Royal Rifle Corps*.

17th (County of London) Battalion The London Regiment (Poplar and Stepney Rifles).

The 3rd, 7th and 10th Tower Hamlets RVC's were raised 4th May 1860 and grouped as the 1st Admin Battalion at Truman's Brewery, Spittlefields on 17th May 1861. Consolidated 25th May 1880 as the *3rd Tower Hamlets RVC*, renumbered *2nd* on 3rd September. They became a VB of The Rifle Brigade 1st July 1881.

The 26th Middlesex (The Customs and The Docks) RVC were raised 9th February 1860 and renumbered *15th* on 3rd September 1880, becoming VB of The Rifle Brigade, 1st July 1881.

On 1st April 1908, on the creation of the new Territorial Force, the 2nd Tower Hamlets and 15th Middlesex amalgamated to become *The 17th (County of London) Battalion The London Regiment (Poplar and Stepney Rifles)*.

No collar badges were worn.

In 1937, by Army Order No.168, The Regiment was redesignated *Tower Hamlets Rifles, The Rifle Brigade (Prince Consort's Own)*.

18th (County of London Battalion The London Regiment (London Irish Rifles)

The 28th Middlesex (London Irish) RVC were raised 21st March 1860, redesignated as the *16th*, 3rd September 1880 becoming a VB of The Rifle Brigade 1st July 1881 and transferring to the new Territorial Force 1st April 1908 as the *18th (County of London) Battalion The London Regiment (London Irish Rifles)*.

Another redesignation took place in 1922 when they became the *18th London Regiment (London Irish Rifles)* and yet another in 1937 when, on the 10th August, under Army Order 168, they were retitled *London Irish Rifles, The Royal Ulster Rifles*.

Not surprisingly, the shamrock was chosen as their collar badge with Officers wearing them in black metal on their Service Dress (Fig.1972) and often with a separate "T" below (photograph 33). Also worn by Officers, in silver, on other uniforms. Warrant Officers wore black metal collar badges whilst Pipers wore the same, but in silver.

A sealed pattern dated 27th May 1952 shows a white-metal shamrock, the card annotated "London Irish Rifles", this being Pattern 15042 (Fig.1973). The Army Pattern Room journals specify this "For Pipers". Another sealed pattern, also dated 27th May 1952, has what is described as gilding-metal but with a shiny black finish, this being Pattern 15041 annotated "For Warrant Officers (Fig.1974).

A later sealed pattern dated 14th January 1964 has the shamrock in silver anodised. This is Pattern 19231 sealed under Authority 54/Infy/8877 annotated "To supercede Pattern 15042" (Fig.1975). the card was marked "Declared obsolete

Fig.1975

Fig.1976

Fig.1977

Fig.1978

Fig.1979

321

HISTORY OF THE BRITISH ARMY INFANTRY COLLAR BADGE

Fig.1980

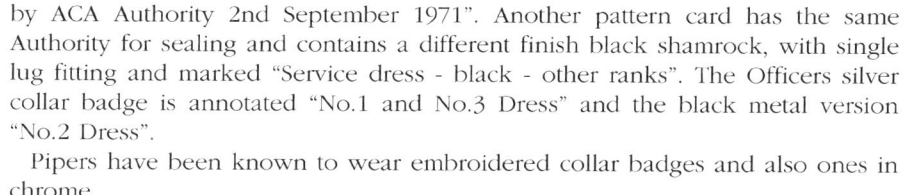

by ACA Authority 2nd September 1971". Another pattern card has the same Authority for sealing and contains a different finish black shamrock, with single lug fitting and marked "Service dress - black - other ranks". The Officers silver collar badge is annotated "No.1 and No.3 Dress" and the black metal version "No.2 Dress".

Pipers have been known to wear embroidered collar badges and also ones in chrome.

Worn with the stalk of the shamrock facing inwards towards the collar opening.

A similar shamrock collar badge was worn by the South Africa Irish Regiment, in black metal by other ranks 1940 - 45 and in white-metal by Officers during the same period and by all ranks from 1960.

19th (County of London) Battalion The London Regiment (St Pancras)

Raised as the *29th Middlesex (North Middlesex) RVC* 1st March 1860 and renumbered *17th*, 3rd September 1880 becoming a VB of The Middlesex Regiment 1st July 1881 and on 1st April 1908 the *19th (County of London) Battalion The London Regiment (St. Pancras)*.

Fig.1981

Forerunners of the old 29th Middlesex were the *St. Pancras Volunteers* raised in 1798 "For the Preservation of Public Tranquility, to assist the Civil Magistrate, and for the protection of Public Property, but not to march without their own consent beyond their own District".

Since those early days, The Regiment had enjoyed close and friendly relations with the Borough of St. Pancras, with their Regimental HQ always within the Borough, so it was natural for The Regiment to choose as its collar badge, an escutcheon with the helmet and crest used as Arms by The Borough of St. Pancras.

Worn by other ranks in gilding-metal (Fig.1976) and by Officers in bronze on their Service Dress (known in two sizes, Figs.1977 and 1978) and in gilt on their other uniforms. A much smaller version in gilt was worn on the Officers mess dress jackets (Fig.1979).

Fig.1982

On 15th December 1935, The Regiment took on an anti-aircraft role becoming the *33rd (St. Pancras) AA Battalion RE*, when it adopted Royal Engineer badges.

20th (County of London) Battalion The London Regiment (Blackheath and Woolwich)

Originally raised in February 1860 as the *26th Kent (Royal Arsenal) RVC* with the 4th Corps, raised, 21st December 1859 attached, redesignated the *4th Kent (Royal Arsenal) RVC*, 3rd September 1880 and becoming a VB of The Queen's Royal West Kent Regiment, 1st July 1881 and its 3rd VB, 1st February 83.

Raised in 7th November 1859 as the *3rd, 4th, 7th, 8th, 13th, 18th, 21st, 25th, 27th, 28th, 32nd, and 34th Kent RVC's* and grouped together to form the 1st Admin Battalion, of Kent RV's in 1860, consolidated 13th April 1880 to form the *3rd Kent (West Kent) RVC* becoming a VB of The Queen's Royal West Kent Regiment 1st July 1881 and its 2nd VB, 1st February 1883.

Fig.1983

The 2nd and 3rd VB's amalgamated 1st April 1908 to become the *20th (County*

Fig.1984  *Fig.1985*  *Fig.1986*

322

of London) Battalion, The London Regiment (Blackheath and Woolwich).

A natural choice of collar badge was the White Horse of Kent and this was placed on a scroll with the motto "INVICTA" (unconquered), inscribed in Old English lettering. Below, a three part scroll inscribed "20th - THE LONDON REGIMENT - BATN" - really, a smaller version of the cap badge.

Officers wore bronze collar badges on their Service Dress and there are numerous variations, not only large and small horses, some with front foot at the end of the scroll, others well before the end, tails that touch the scroll, others well above and different shapes to the scroll, but also some with "INVICTA" in the correct Old English letters whilst others are incorrect by having Roman lettering. A further minor variation is in the shortened "Battalion", sometimes inscribed "BAT$^\text{n}$", sometimes "BATN". (Figs.1980, 1981 and 1982 for three variations).

On other uniforms, Officers wore their collar badges in siler and gilt, the horse and top scroll in silver, the bottom scroll in gilt (Fig.1983). Similar variations exist as already listed.

There is no record of any equivalent collar badge for other rank's. However, it has been suggested that two items may have been worn. The first (Fig.1984), facing to the right, is certainly a collar badge and follows the Officers pattern but is rough cast and in black metal. The second (Fig.1985) has the horse over an "Invicta" scroll in Roman lettering. This is unlikely to have been worn by The Regiment and is more likely to be the collar badge as worn by The Buffs, post 1881.

All the Regiments collar badges were worn in FP's with the horse facing inwards towards the collar opening.

On 15th December 1925, under Army Orders 209 and 212, The Regiment was transferred to an anti-aircraft role becoming *34th (The Queen's Own Royal West Kent) A-A Battalion RE* adopting the collar badges of The Royal Engineers.

Fig.1987

21st (County of London) Battalion The London Regiment (1st Surrey Rifles)

Raised at Camberwell 14th June 1859 as the *1st Surrey RVC*, redesignated *1st Surrey (South London) RVC* and becoming a VB of The East Surrey Regiment 1st July 1881, again redesignated in December 1891 as *1st Surrey (South London) RVC* and on the formation of The Territorial Force 1st April 1908, reorganised to become the *21st (County of London) Battalion, The London Regiment (1st Surrey Rifles)*. Further redesignated in 1922 as *21st London Regiment (First Surrey Rifles)*, they were converted into a Searchlight unit 15th December 1935 as *35th (First Surrey Rifles) A-A Battalion RE* adopting Royal Engineer Uniform.

Officers wore as a collar badge a slightly smaller version of the other ranks cap badge - a Maltese cross with a lion passant guardant between the arms and in the centre of which was a strung bugle within a circle inscribed "FIRST SURREY RIFLES". Upon the upper arm of the cross was the honour "SOUTH AFRICA 1900 - 02" and on the lower arm the date "1803". Above the upper arm of the cross, a scroll inscribed with the Regimental motto "CONCORDIA VICTRIX" and surmounted by a K/C. Below the cross, a scroll inscribed "21st COUNTY OF LONDON".

The inhabitants of Camberwell, in the South East of London raised in May 1798, The Camberwell Military Association from whence came the *First Surrey Regiment of Volunteers*, formed in 1803 - hence the date on the collar badge. The Regimental motto, "Concordia Victrix" (Friendship conquers) appeared on The Regimental Colours of the Camberwell Military Association.

The collar badge, blackened, was worn on Officers Service Dress (Fig.1986) often with a separate black "T" below. The collar badges do not face.

Other ranks did not wear collar badges.

Whilst researching this particular unit one appreciates how easy it is to be mislead by a photograph (Photograph 34). This shows a Corporal Instructor explaining Searchlight techniques to an Officer and three Senior NCO's. The Corporal can be identified both by his metal T/21/London shoulder title on the

HISTORY OF THE BRITISH ARMY INFANTRY COLLAR BADGE

Fig.1988

Fig.1989

Fig.1990

Fig.1991

Fig.1992

shoulder strap, and by the cloth shoulder title on his upper arm above the stripes, "First Surrey Rifles" (although not in colour, this would have been red letters on dark green).

The photograph is undated but, as the Regiment converted to The Royal Engineers in 1935 when it is recorded they were equipped with searchlights and it is also recorded that even after transfer they continued to wear their "First Surrey Rifles" cloth titles and it it known that they wore them until 1939, it seems fairly safe to assume the date is between 1935 and 1939. Maltese cross collar badges can be identified on all of the three NCO's so it would *appear* that other ranks did wear collar badges after all.

However, closer examination, using a powerful glass, shows that the three metal shoulder titles are "Foresters" with one also having a "T" and a "6", indicating the 6th Battalion

In 1936, the 6th Foresters were converted to an anti-aircraft role and transferred as the 40th A-A Battalion, RE and of course they also wore Maltese cross collar badges. What this does show is that what photographs purport to show is not always correct.

Cadets

Alleyn's School Cadet Corps, London SE22 was recognised as such 14th July 1915 (County of London) under Army Order 343, 1915 and affiliated to the 21st (County of London) Battalion The London Regiment (1st Surrey Rifles).

Their collar badge was the School Arms - a shield with a chevron between three cinquefoils; on a chief ermine a cinquefoil. Below the shield, the motto "DETUR GLORIA SOLI DEO (Fig.1987).

22nd (County of London) Battalion The London Regiment (The Queen's)

The 10th Surrey RVC and the *23rd Surrey RVC* were raised at Bermondsey 7th February 1860 and Rotherhithe 1st February 1861 respectively, grouped on 10th October 1868 as the 4th Admin Battalion, consolidated 13th April 1880 to form the *10th Surrey RVC* renumbered the *6th Surrey RVC* 3rd September 1880 and becoming a VB of The Queen's (Royal West Surrey Regiment) and joining The Territorial Force 1st April 1908 as the *22nd (County of London) Battalion The London Regiment (The Queen's)*.

By Army Order 168, dated 1937, The Regiment, unlike most of the other London Battalions who were converted to either Artillery or Engineers, retained its Infantry role, rejoining the West Surreys as its 6th (Bermondsey) Battalion

The 22nd wore the same collar badges as worn by The Queen's (Royal West Surrey Regiment), often with a separate 'T' below the bronze collar badges. (See under The Queen's (Royal West Surrey Regiment) for full details).

23rd (County of London) Battalion The London Regiment

The 7th Surrey RVC raised 30th November 1859 at Southwark and the *26th Surrey RVC* raised at Clapham 28th April 1875 were amalgamated in 1880 to become a VB of The East Surrey Regiment 1st July 1881, redesignated as their 4th VB 1st December 1887 and reorganised as the *23rd (County of London) Battalion, The London Regiment* when The Territorial Force was established 1st April 1908. In October 1927, the subtitle, (The East Surrey Regiment) was added and the Regiment was redesignated as the *7th (23rd London) Battalion The East Surrey Regiment*, 10th August 1937 under Army Order 168.

The collar badge was virtually a smaller version of the cap badge and reflected their East Surrey ties by having The Arms of Guildford in a voided centre within a circle inscribed with the battle honour "SOUTH AFRICA 1900 - 2". This was placed on an eight pointed star, the top point displaced by a K/C, the whole above a scroll inscribed "23rd BATTALION THE LONDON REGT".

Other ranks collar badges were in bi-metal with the scroll, crown and the ground of the shield in gilding-metal and the remainder in white-metal. There are

THE LONDON REGIMENT

variations in the crown both in shape and voiding or non voiding and some patterns have the South Africa date as "1900 - 2" (Fig.1988), whilst others have "1900 - 02" (Fig.1989).

Officers wore similar collar badges, in bronze, on their Service Dress (Fig.1990). Variations also include voided and non voided centres. On other uniforms, Officers wore collar badges in silver/gilt and also in gilt, the latter also believed to have been worn by WO's. The collar badges do not face.

On 1st November 1938, The Regiment lost its Infantry role being transferred to The Royal Tank Corps, redesignated as *42nd (7th (23rd London) Battalion.), The East Surrey Regiment Battalion, RTC.*

24th (County of London) Battalion The London Regiment (The Queen's)

Raised at Lambeth 13th March 1860 as the *19th Surrey RVC*, redesignated 3rd September 1880 as the *7th Surrey RVC*, renumbered the *8th* on September 7th and becoming a VB of The Queen's (Royal West Surrey Regiment), 1st July 1881 and reorganised on the creation of The Territorial Force 1st April 1908 as the *24th (County of London) Battalion The London Regiment (The Queen's).*

By Army Order 168, the Regiment became, 10th August 1937 the 7th (Southwark) Battalion of The Queen's (Royal West Surrey Regiment).

The 24th wore the same collar badges as worn by The Queen's (Royal West Surrey Regiment) - see under that title for full details. Photographs show a separate 'T' was often worn below the bronze collar badge ({Photograph 35).

25th (County of London) (Cyclist) Battalion The London Regiment

Raised 1st April 1888 as the *26th Middlesex RVC* they were reorganised on the creation of The Territorial Force 1st April 1908 as the *25th (County of London) (Cyclist) Battalion, The London Regiment.* They were reconstituted 7th February 1920 and designated by 1923 as *47th (2nd London) Divisional Signals (later London, Corps Signals), Royal Corps of Signals.*

Not unnaturally, a cycle wheel figured prominently in their collar badge. In the centre of the spokes, the numerals "25", the wheel within a circle inscribed "COUNTY OF LONDON CYCLISTS", itself within a laurel wreath. Above the wheel a K/C and below the wheel a tablet inscribed with the motto "TENAX ET AUDAX" (Tenacious and bold).

Officers wore on their Service Dress the same bronze item as they wore on their cap (Fig.1991). A smaller version said to have been specifically for the collar is shown in Fig.1992.

A photograph of a large group of Officers of the 25th (R) Battalion The London Regiment taken at Richmond Park Camp on August 24th 1916 shows a number, wearing a separate bronze 'T' below the collar badge.

Other ranks wore similar collar badges in white-metal, smaller than the ones in bronze (Fig.1993). Also noted are similar in blackened gilding-metal, not unusual for Cyclist units. They do not face.

28th (County of London) Battalion The London Regiment (Artists Rifles)

Raised 28th February 1860 as the *38th Middlesex (Artists) RVC* and largely made up of artists and those with connections to the Arts (hence the title). Renumbered *20th*, 3rd September 1880 becoming a VB of The Rifle Brigade 1st July 1881, redesignated in December 1891 as *20th Middlesex (Artists) VRC* and transferred to The Territorial Force 1st April 1908 as the *28th (County of London) Battalion, The London Regiment (Artists Rifles).* For descriptions of the collar badges before joining The London Regiment in 1908, see under The Rifle Brigade.

Post 1908, they continued wearing the "Mars and Minerva" collar badges in gilding-metal. Black collar badges were worn by other ranks only, on their grey full dress (Fig.1994).

Fig.1993

Fig.1994

Fig.1995

Fig.1996

Fig.1997

Fig.1998

HISTORY OF THE BRITISH ARMY INFANTRY COLLAR BADGE

Fig.1999

Fig.2000

Fig.2001

White metal collar badges were worn by Officers and Sergeants with their mess dress and also on 'Patrols", c.1919 - 39. (Fig.1995).

On Service Dress, Officers wore collar badges in bronze (Fig.1996), retaining their silver collar badges for other uniforms.

In May 1937, The Regiment was redesignated as *The Artists Rifles, The Rifle Brigade (Prince Consort's Own)*.

The Inns of Court Officer Training Corps

Constituted in November 1859 and designated *The Inns of Court Volunteers* and re-formed at Lincoln's Inn 15th February 1860 as the *23rd Middlesex (Inns of Court) RVC*, The Regiment was made up from members of the Legal Profession. On 3rd September 1880, redesignated as the *14th Middlesex (Inns of Court) RVC* and in 1881 became a VB of The Rifle Brigade and on the creation of The Territorial Force 1st April 1908, were transferred as the *27th (County of London) Bn, The London Regiment (Inns of Court)*.

This was an unpopular title with The Regiment and the Order was ignored. They were then reorganised as *The Inns of Court Officers Training Corps* with the role of training Officers for both the TF and The Special Reserve. In April 1932, they were again reorganised to become *The Inns of Court Regiment* and in 1961 amalgamated with The City of London Yeomanry to become *The Inns of Court and City Yeomanry*.

The collar badge worn from 1908 was in the form of four shields all pointing in towards the centre forming a cross, within a laurel wreath and a title scroll below. Each shield bore the Arms of one of four Inns, the one uppermost, Lincoln's Inn (a number of mill rinds, either thirteen or fourteen with a lion rampant in the top left hand corner), followed in a clockwise direction by Inner Temple (a pegasus or winged horse), Gray's Inn (griffin) and Middle Temple (a pascal lamb in the centre of the cross of St. George). On the laurel wreath the South Africa battle honour on four separate scrolls, "SOUTH" and "AFRICA" on the left hand side as viewed and "1900" and "1901" on the right hand side, the one inscribed "1901" above the one inscribed "1900". The scroll inscribed "INNS OF COURT OTC". A K/C above the top shield.

Other ranks wore the collar badge in gilding-metal with Officers wearing similar but in gilt (Fig.1997). A larger pattern, but without the crown, was worn in bronze by Officers on their Service Dress, often with a separate 'T' below (Fig.1998). Also worn in silver on mess dress.

When the title of the Regiment changed in 1932, it was necessary to change the collar badges but the only change necessary was in the title so the new collar badges were inscribed "THE INNS OF COURT REGT".

Again worn in gilding-metal by other ranks and by Officers in gilt and also in silver plate (Fig.1999). Such a pattern in gilding-metal was sealed 13th November 1951 under Authority Enc/47/6 TO54/Officer/4051. This was Pattern 14752 with the sealed pattern annotated "To guide for anodised Spec UK/CIC/2124". The gold anodised version was sealed 13th November 1958 being Pattern 17965 but differing from the "Guide pattern by having a Q/C.

The Inns of Court Reserve Corps

Part of the Volunteer Force 1914 - 19 was *The Inns of Court Reserve Corps*. They wore as their collar badge a generally similar smaller version of the bronze collar badge already described, but without a crown and with a different title scroll. In place of the former title was "INNS OF COURT" on a different shaped scroll with an additional scroll below with the initials "R" and "C" (Reserve Corps).

Another quite significant difference was that this badge did not have the South Africa battle honour entwined upon the laurel wreath. Worn in gilding-metal by other ranks and in bronze on Service Dress by Officers (Fig.2000). Sometimes worn with a separate "T" below. Also worn in silver on other Officers uniforms (Fig.2001). They later became the 2nd Battalion.

The Hertfordshire Regiment

The 1st, 6th, 9th - 11th and 14th Hertfordshire RVC's were raised 22nd November 1859 and grouped 20th February 1861 as the 2nd Admin Battalion, with the Battalion consolidated 11th May 1880 to form the *1st Hertfordshire RVC*, becoming a Volunteer Battalion of the Bedfordshire Regiment 1st July 1881 and redesignated as the 1st (Hertfordshire) VB of that Regiment 1st December 1887.

The 1st (Sub Division), 3rd, 4th, 5th & 7th Hertfordshire RVC's raised 5th January 1860 were grouped 16th October 1860 as the 1st Admin Battalion, consolidated to form the *2nd Hertfordshire RVC* 11th May 1880, becoming a VB of The Bedfordhsire Regiment 1st July 1881 and redesignated as 2nd (Hertfordshire) VB of that Regiment, 1st December 1887.

On 1st April 1908, the 1st and 2nd (Hertfordshire) VB's amalgamated to form *The Hertfordshire Battalion, The Bedfordshire Regiment* and redesignated in March 1909 as the 1st Battalion The Hertfordshire Regiment whilst remaining part of the Corps of The Bedfordshire Regiment

In 1939, The Regiment was increased by the formation of a 2nd Battalion which was amalgamated with the 1st Battalion 1st January 1947 and further amalgamated 1st April 1961 to form part of *The Bedfordshire and Hertfordshire Regiment (TA)*.

Descriptions of collar badges worn in the early Rifle Volunteer days and up to 1908, together with the post 1961 period, have already been dealt with under The Bedfordshire Regiment, so this section will cover the period in between.

It was originally intended by The War Office that the newly formed Regiment would form part of The Bedfordshire Regiment, a suggestion that was not well received by the men of Hertfordshire and it was not until March 1909 that agreement was reached and Army Order 67 was issued confirming the arrangement.

There would appear to have been equal disagreement regarding the collar badge, the original suggestion being of a standing hart. Again, this was rejected by the men of Hertfordshire, the standing hart being associated with Bedfordshire.

The Gaunt pattern books record a kneeling hart annotated "Hertfordshire Regiment, gilding-metal - 2 shanks". Unfortunately, the illustration is not dated but other illustrations before and after, would indicate c.1908. This pattern was not adopted, however, illustrated is such an item so it would seem that a trial die was produced (Fig.2002).

Although this particular pattern was not approved, similar was, but with the addition of a title scroll "HERTFORDSHIRE". This was worn in gilding-metal by other ranks (Fig.2003) and by Officers in bronze and later in gilt (Fig.2004). The gilding-metal collar badge was also worn as a beret badge, sometimes fitted with a slider. Officers often wore a separate bronze "T" below their bronze collar badges, on their Service Dress collars.

A new pattern in gilding-metal was cut from new dies and sealed 25th February 1953, this being Pattern 15635. Following the same general design, the new pattern had a more delicate hart and the water depth was increased (Fig.2005). Similar patterns in bronze and in frosted gilt (Fig.2006).

Although no Official record has been located it is believed that, in 1911 only, some Officers wore on their Service Dress, the cap badge in bronze (Fig.2007). It is also said that this pattern is known with the hart facing to the right. This pattern is also known with the spelling 'Hartfordshire', the traditional spelling.

Records and photographs show that some other ranks wore their gilding-metal

Fig.2002

Fig.2003

Fig.2004

Fig.2005

Fig.2006

HISTORY OF THE BRITISH ARMY INFANTRY COLLAR BADGE

Fig.2007

T/Herts shoulder title on their collars (Fig.2008). This occurred in WWI but appears to have ceased by the end of the War in 1918.

Hertfordshire Volunteer Regiment

Formed in 1915 and finally disbanded in March 1920, The Hertfordshire Volunteer Regiment wore as their collar badge, similar to those worn by the Hertfordshire Regiment but with "HERTS V.R." on the scroll. Worn in bronze (Fig.2009) by Officers and in gilding-metal by other ranks.

Fig.2008

Fig.2009

The Herefordshire Light Infantry

Raised in April 1860 as the *1st - 8th Herefordshire RVC* and the *1st and 2nd Radnorshire RVC* and grouped 20th February 1861 as the *1st Admin Battalion, Herefordshire and Radnorshire RVC*, and consolidated 11th May 1880 as the *1st Herefordshire (Hereford and Radnor) RVC*. On 1st July 1881, they became a Volunteer Battalion of The King's (Shropshire Light Infantry), redesignated in December 1891 as *1st Herefordshire (Hereford and Radnor) VRC* and transferred to The Territorial Force 1st April 1908 as The Herefordshire Battalion, The King's (Shropshire Light Infantry) remaining with them until 1909 when in March they were again redesignated, this time as *1st Battalion, The Herefordshire Regiment*.

On 1st January 1947, they amalgamated with the 2nd Battalion and were reconstituted as the 1st Battalion and redesignated in February as *1st Battalion The Herefordshire Light Infantry*.

Pre 1880
No collar badges worn.

1880 - 1908
The Gaunt pattern books show an Officers collar badge, in silver, with the manufacturers name J & R Pearce & Co under the heading "Herefordshire 1 RV". Illustrated is a lion passant gaurdant, holding in one paw, a sword, the remaining three paws on a torse. (Fig.2010). On their Service Dress, Officers wore similar but in bronze (Figs.2011 and 2012 for two different patterns). Other ranks wore similar, but smaller and in white-metal (Fig.2013).

The close link between the Regiment and the City of Hereford is reflected in the choice of the collar badge, The City Arms containing "A lion passant guardant holding in the dexter paw, a sword".

1908 - 1947
On joining The Territorial Force in 1908, new badges were designed, the new collar badge being virtually the previous one but with a scroll below inscribed "HEREFORDSHIRE" Other ranks wore them initially in bi-metal, a white-metal lion and torse on a gilding-metal scroll (Fig.2014), later replaced by all white-metal.

As these collar badges were worn over such a long period there are minor variations according to manufacturer, mostly with the shape and size of the lion with the earlier patterns having a "Bar" from the animals back to the tuft on its tail (Figs.2015 and 2016).

Officers wore similar designed collar badges, but in bronze, on their Service Dress with variations as already described (Fig.2017 for early item with "Bar" and Fig.2018 for later pattern). They were often worn with a separate 'T' in bronze below the collar badge whilst some had the 'T' brazed onto the badge.

Full dress was not worn after WWI but was reintroduced for the Band in 1927 and worn until WWII. Full dress was, of course, worn in addition to Service Dress from 1908 and on their tunic collars, silver collar badges were worn (Fig.2019). This pattern is also known in gilt and in chrome, the latter said to have been worn by Cadets.

Fig.2010

Fig.2011

Fig.2012

Fig.2013

Fig.2014

HISTORY OF THE BRITISH ARMY INFANTRY COLLAR BADGE

Fig.2015

Fig.2016

Fig.2017

Post 1947

By Army Order 67, The Regiments title was changed to *The Herefordshire Light Infantry* but although the cap badge was changed, the old collar badges were retained.

A sealed Pattern 20th February 1952 shows Pattern 15137 with the usual collar badges in white-metal but with a single lug fitting (Fig.2020). This was replaced by similar but in silver anodised (made by Wm. Dowler & Sons). The pattern, 19386, was annotated Authority A/54/Inf/8553, sealed 5th October 1964.

In 1967, B Coy (Hereford Light Infantry), formerly 4th Battalion K.S.L.I. (TA) and "A" Coy K.S.L.I. amalgamated to become *The King's Shropshire and Herefordshire Light Infantry*. The former cap badge of The Herefordshire Light Infantry was then reduced in size and placed on the collars as collar badges. This was a strung bugle, in the middle of which was the old Herefordshire lion and sword on a tablet inscribed with the motto "MANU FORTI" (With a brave hand).

In silver plate for Officers and in white-metal and later in silver anodised for soldiers (Fig.2021). These are shown on a pattern card headed "King's Shropshire and Hereford LI" and annotated "Single lug anodised and Officers silver, Hereford LI (TA)". It is not a sealed pattern and is undated but in pencil is a date, 27th November 1961.

All lion collar badges as described were worn in FP's with the lion facing inwards towards the collar opening, the paw holding the sword depending on which way it faced.

When the bugle was adopted, they too were worn in FP's with the lion and bugle facing outwards from the collar opening.

Fig.2018

Fig.2019

Fig.2020

Fig.2021

Army Cyclists

Although there is a record of cyclists from Rifle Volunteer Corps being used as scouts during Easter manoeuvres held in 1885, it was not until 1888 that a unit was formed specifically to be used in a cyclist role - the *26th Middlesex (Cyclist) RVC*. (See under The King's Royal Rifle Corps).

Until The Territorial Force was created 1st April 1908, they remained the only Cyclist RVC although many other Rifle Volunteers formed their own Cyclist Coys. In 1908, the 26th now redesignated as the 25th (County of London) (Cyclist) Battalion, The London Regiment, were joined by nine other Battalions The nine were:-

10th (Cyclist) Battalion, *The Royal Scots* (from the 8th VB)
6th (Cyclist) Battalion, *The Norfolk Regiment*
7th (Cyclist) Battalion, *The Devonshire Regiment*
5th Cyclist) Battalion, *The East Yorkshire Regiment* (from the 2nd VB)
7th (Cyclist) Battalion, *The Welsh Regiment*
Highland Cyclist Battalion, (from 5th VB, The Black Watch).
Northern Cyclist Battalion
Kent Cyclist Battalion
Essex and Suffolk Cyclist Battalion

In 1911, The Essex and Suffolk Cyclist Battalion, was sub-divided to form the 6th Battalion, The Suffolk Regiment and the 8th Battalion, The Essex Regiment. At the same time two new Battalions were raised, 6th Battalion, *The Royal Sussex Regiment* and the 9th Battalion, *The Hampshire Regiment*. In 1914, the 14th Cyclist Battalion, was added, by the raising of the *Huntingdonshire Cyclist Battalion*.

After WWI their role diminished and they were finally disbanded in 1919, with only the 25th Battalion, The London Regiment remaining and by 1922 all trace of them had disappeared.

During their existence, khaki Service Dress was normally worn, usually with blackened collar badges and black tunic buttons of Rifle design. One assumes that this was done to emphasise their former Rifle connections but in two instances no direct lineage can be traced back to any Rifle connection. One wonders whether the blackening was for a more practical purpose - in their prime role as "Scouts" they would be close to the enemy and would wish to prevent being seen and their position being revealed by the sun glinting on polished badges?

There are many photographs of Cyclists and in many cases no collar badges were being worn.

The Northern Cyclist Battalion (TF)
For details of collar badges see under The Northumberland Fusiliers.

The Highland Cyclist Battalion (TF)
For details of collar badges see under The Black Watch.

The Kent Cyclist Battalion (TF)
For details of collar badges see under The Queen's Own Royal West Kent Regiment

HISTORY OF THE BRITISH ARMY INFANTRY COLLAR BADGE

The Huntingdonshire Cyclist BN
For details of collar badges see under The Northamptonshire Regiment.

Others
For other collar badge details relating to other Cyclist Battalions mentioned in this chapter, see under their respective Regiments.

The Volunteer Force 1914-1919

When WWI commenced in 1914, Volunteer units were formed throughout the Country, recognised officially by a War Office letter dated 19th November 1914.

Before standardisation, many different insignia were worn including lapel badges on civilian clothes. Although cap badges were many and varied, collar badges were few in number.

In July 1818, all County Volunteer Regiments were made VB's of Line Regiments and entered are details of such collar badges under each separate Regiment whenever applicable.

An exception to the attachment of Line Regiments were The City and County of London Regiments, who continued to keep their separate identities. They wore the following collar badges:-

(I)   The Arms of The City of London below which was a three part scroll inscribed "CORPS - OF - CITIZENS". In bronze (Fig.2022).
(II) Similar to (1) but smaller and the scroll inscribed "DOMINE - DIRIGE - NOS". Also in bronze (Fig.2023).
(III) Similar to (11) but a different design and in gilt (Fig.2024).

Another Unit without a special badge was *The South London Volunteer Training Corps*. Their collar badge, in bronze, had the shield from The Arms of The City of London below a K/C and above, a scroll inscribed "SOUTH LONDON VTC" (Fig.2025).

Fig.2022

Fig.2023

Fig.2024

Fig.2025

332